VAT ACTS

1996-97

Value Added Tax

VAT ACTS
1996-97

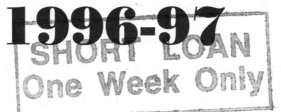

Value Added Tax

Editor
ALAN MOORE BA BComm MBA AITI

Editorial Board
TOM CORBETT BL AITI, Partner, BDO Simpson Xavier
FERGUS GANNON FCA AITI, Director, VAT Services, Deloitte Touche
TERRY O'NEILL ACA CPA AITI, Manager, Arthur Andersen
JAMES D SOMERS BComm, Partner in Charge, Tax, Ernst & Young

Butterworth Ireland Ltd
1996

Republic of Ireland   Butterworth (Ireland) Ltd, 26 Upper Ormond Quay, Dublin 7

United Kingdom   Butterworths, Halsbury House, 35 Chancery Lane, London
                       WC2A 1EL

Australia   Butterworth Ptd Ltd, Sydney, Melbourne, Brisbane, Adelaide,
                       Perth, Canberra and Hobart

Canada   Butterworths Canada, Toronto and Vancouver

Malaysia   Malayan Law Journal Sdn Bhd, Kuala Lumpur

New Zealand   Butterworths of New Zealand Ltd, Wellington and Auckland

Puerto Rico   Butterworths of Puerto Rico, Inc, San Juan

Singapore   Malayan Law Journal Pte Ltd, Singapore

USA   Butterworth Legal Publishers, Austin, Texas; Boston,
                       Massachusetts; Clearwater, Florida (D & S Publishers); Orford,
                       New Hampshire (Equity Publishing); St Paul, Minnesota; and
                       Seattle, Washington

© Butterworth Ireland Ltd

A CIP Catalogue record for this book is available from the British Library.

ISBN 1 85475 723 7

Printed in Ireland by Sciprint Ltd., Shannon

Colour Books, Dublin

CONTENTS

HOW TO USE THIS WORK

Tracing legislation

This book set out consolidated versions of the Value Added Tax Act 1972; together with the non-amending sections of the Finance Acts from 1973 to 1996 inclusive, and related regulations, orders and European law. Each section is annotated in respect of amendments, cross-references, definitions, construction, statutory instruments, statements of practice and former enactments.

The legislation is set out in the following manner:

(a) the full text of an amending provision is normally omitted, but effect is given to the amendment in the amended provision,

(b) the full text of a repealing provision is normally omitted, but effect is given to the repeal in the repealed provision.

Section and Schedule headings of repealed or amended legislation are retained for the purposes of clarity.

For ease of reference, section and Schedule numbers are conspicuously marked at the top of the page. If the section or Schedule is known, it can be found immediately because the legislation is printed in chronological order. Where only the subject matter is known, it may be traced through the index. The marginal notes in the Value Added Tax Act 1972 are direct cross-references to the Sixth Directive. The marginal notes in the Sixth Directive are direct cross-references to the Value Added Tax Act, 1972.

Standard abbreviations

The following are the standard abbreviations used in Butterworth Ireland Tax publications:

General

s, ss	section (or sections) of an Act
subs, subss	subsection (or subsections) of a section
Sch	Schedule to an Act
para, paras	paragraph (or paragraphs) of a Schedule
subpara, subparas	subparagraph (or subparagraphs) of a Schedule
Pt	Part (of an Act)
Ch	Chapter (or a Part of an Act)
r, reg	regulation (of a statutory instrument)

Statutes

CA	Companies Act
CATA 1976	Capital Acquisitions Act 1976
CGTA 1975	Capital Gains Tax Act 1975
CGTAA 1978	Capital Gains Tax (Amendment) Act 1978
CTA 1976	Corporation Tax Act 1976
FA	Finance Act
F(No 2)A	Finance (No 2) Act
F(MP)A	Finance (Miscellaneous Provisions) Act
IA 1937	Interpretation Act 1937
IRRA 1890	Inland Revenue Regulation Act 1890
ITA 1967	Income Tax Act 1967
PCTA 1927	Provisional Collection of Taxes Act 1927
TD(SC)A 1942	Taxes and Duties (Special Circumstances) Act 1942
VATA 1972	Value Added Tax 1972

Statutory Instruments

ITER	Income Tax (Employments) Regulations
SI 28/1960	Statutory Instrument Number 28 of 1960
IT(CC)R	Income Tax (Construction Contracts) Regulations

Practice

SP	Statement of Practice

Case law

ITR	Irish Tax Reports
IR	Irish Reports
STC	Simon's Tax Cases
TC	Tax Cases
TL	Tax Leaflet
ITC	Irish Tax Cases
ECJ	European Court of Justice

CURRENT VAT RATES

How to use this chart: With effect from 1 March 1996, there are four VAT rates: 0% (the zero rate), 2.8% (the flat rate), 12.5%, and 21%. Goods and services the supply of which is not exempt (VATA 1972 Sch 1) or liable at 0% (VATA 1972 Sch 2), 2.8% (VATA 1972 s 11), or 12.5% (VATA 1972 Sch 6) are, by default, liable at 21% (VATA 1972 s 11). This chart summarises goods and services that are exempt or liable at 0%, 2.5% or 12.5%. Therefore, if the supply is not shown on this chart it will most likely be liable at 21%.

Goods

Exempt (Sch 1)
Blood and organ banks (xviii)
Cultural bodies (viia)
Non deductible goods sold (xxiv)
Philanthropic societies (xxii)
Political parties (xxii)
Religious societies (xxii)
Trade unions (xxii)
Welfare services (non profit) (viii)

Goods *closely related* to
the body's activities)

0% (Sch 2)
Aircraft (international transport) (v)(b)
Aircraft (international transport) equipment (va)
Aircraft (international transport) fuel etc (vb)
Animal feed (not pet food)(vii)
Animal medicine (oral) (xiv)
Artificial body parts (xixa) (b)
Books (xva)
Candles (plain white) (xx)
Children's clothes (xvii)
Drink (coffee, tea etc) (xii)
Exports (i)
Exporters (supplies to) (via)
Fertiliser (farm) (vii)
Food (not confectionery, sweets) (xii)
Gold bullion (supplied to Central Bank) (x)
Imports (non EC, consigned to EC State) (iiib)
Medicine (oral) (xiii)
Seeds (food producing) (xv)
Ships (commercial seagoing, over 15 tons)(v)(a)
Tampons (xviii)
Wheelchairs (xixa)(a)

12.5% (Sch 6)
Antiques (xvia)
Art works (xvia)
Biscuits (not chocolate) (xxxi)(b)
Buildings (new) (xxviii)
Cakes (xxxi)(a)
Coal (fuel) ((i)(a)
Concrete ready to pour (xxxii)
Concrete blocks (xxxiii)
Electricity (i)(b)(
Newspapers (xii)
Oil (home heat) ((i)(d)
Peat (fuel) (i)(a)
Photographs etc (xxii)

2.8% (s 11(1))
Cattle
Deer
Goats
Greyhounds
Horses
Pigs
Sheep

Services

Exempt (Sch 1)
Banks (i)
Betting businesses (xv)
Blood and organ banks (xviii)
Circuses (no food or drink) (viii)
Creches (non profit making) (vi)

Cultural bodies (viiia)
Dental technicians (iiia)
Dentists (iiib)
Doctors (iii)
Financial service agents (ix)(d)
Funeral undertaking (xix)
Hospitals (v)
Hospital meals (xxv)
Insurance agents (ix)(b), (c)
Insurance businesses (xi)
Landlords (short leases) (iv)
Lottery businesses (xvi)
Opticians (iiib)
Musical shows (no food or drink)
 (viii)
Nursing home (v)
Nursing home meals (xxv)
Passenger transport (xiv)
Philanthropic societies (xxii)
Philosophical societies (xxii)
Political parties (xxii)
Postal services (An Post) (xia)
Radio broadcasts (RTE) (xiii)
Religious societies (xxii)
Schools (ii)
School meals (xxv)
Sporting events (xvii)
Sports facilities (non profit) (xxiii)
Stockbrokers (i)(a)
Television broadcasts (RTE) (xiii)
Trade unions (xxii)
Travel agents (ix)(a)
Theatres (no food or drink) (viii)
Universities (ii)
Welfare services (non profit) (vii)

0% (Sch 2)
Aircraft (int'nl transport) equipment repairs (va)
Aircraft repairs (v)(b)
Airport services (iv)
Contract work on non EU goods (xvi)
Export agent services (vi)
Haulage to/from EC (iii)

Import agent services (iv)
Lifeboat services (xi)
Lighthouse services (ix)
Port services (iv)
Ship repairs (v)(a)
Work on non EC goods (xvi)

12.5% (Sch 6)
Agricultural services (xi)
Boat hire (under five weeks) (xv)(b)
Building work (xxix)
Campsite facilities (xiii)
Caravan hire (under five weeks)
 (xv)(d)
Car hire (under five weeks) (xv)(a)
Cinemas (v)
Cleaning buildings etc (xxx)
Drink (vending machines) (ii)(a)
Driving lessons (xxvii)
Exhibitions (cultural etc) (ix)

Fairground entertainers (vii)
Food (vending machines) (ii)(a)
Gas (home heat) (i)(c)
Guesthouse accommodation (xiii)
Hairdressers (xix)
Health studios (xix)
Holiday home accommodation (xiii)

Hotel accommodation (xiii)
Jockeys (xx)
Meals (hot, takeaway etc) (iv)
Meals (restaurant etc) (ii)(b)-(c),(iii)
Musical shows (food, drink) (vi)
Photographers (xxiii)
Photographic services (xxv)
Repair services (xviii)
Sports facilities (commercial) (viia)
Theatres (food, drink) (vi)
Tour guides (xiv)
Veterinary surgeons (x)
Waste removal services (viii)

REVENUE ADDRESSES

How to use this chart: if the problem relates to rates of VAT, interpretation of legislation, see *VAT Administration*.

If the problem relates to setting up a client for VAT/PAYE etc, see Central Registration Information Office under *Inspector of Taxes*. This office deals with general queries for all taxes and provides basic information, booklets, forms etc for new and existing businesses.

If the problem relates to an established client's tax affairs (other than payment of tax) see the appropriate county in which the business is located under *Inspectors of taxes*. If the client's business is in an area formerly dealt with by Dublin VAT District, go to the appropriate audit office for the type of business.

If the problem relates to payment of tax, see *Collection of tax*.

VAT Administration

Address	Phone	Fax
Indirect Taxes Branch,Castle House, Sth Great Georges St, Dublin 2.	6792777	6718653

Inspectors of taxes

County	Address	Phone	Fax
All	Central Registration Information Office, Aras Brugha, Cathedral St, Dublin 2	8746821	6746078
	(registration, cancellation, change of address etc for all taxes, including VAT)		
Chief Inspr	Chief Inspector of Taxes, 1st Floor, Setanta Centre, Nassau St, Dublin 2	6716777	6716668
	Special Inquiry Branch, 3rd Floor, Setanta Centre, Nassau St, Dublin 2	6716777	6716668
	Taxes Investigation Branch, Setanta Centre, Nassau St, Dublin 2	6716777	6716668
Carlow	Kilkenny Tax District, Government Buildings, Hebron Road, Kilkenny	056 52222	056 51255
Cavan	Dundalk Tax District, Earl House, Earl House, Earl St, Dundalk, Co Louth	042 32251	042 34609
Clare	Limerick Tax District, River Hse, Charlotte Quay, Limerick	061 318711	061 417863
Cork	Cork Tax District, Government Buildings, Sullivan's Quay, Cork	021 966077	021 962141
Donegal	Letterkenny Tax District, Gov't Buildings, High Rd, Letterkenny, Co Donegal	074 21299	074 22357
Dublin	Agribusiness and Fisheries Audit District, Lansdowne Hse, Lansdowne Rd, Dublin 4	6689400	6686512
	Construction and Property Audit District, Findlater Hse, Cathal Brugha St, Dublin 2	8746821	8749277
	Financial Sector Audit District, Lansdowne Hse, Lansdowne Rd, Dublin 4	6689400	6686512
	Groups and PLCs Audit District, Lansdowne Hse, Lansdowne Rd, Dublin 4	6689400	6686512
	Investment/Rental Income Audit District, Lansdowne Hse, Lansdowne Rd, Dublin 4	6689400	6686512
	Professionals Audit District, Clanwilliam Court, Lr Mount St, Dublin 2	6616444	6609787
	Services Audit District (incl Hotels, Pubs etc), 4 Claremont Rd, Sandymount, Dublin 4	6607111	6606768
	Transport and Light Industry Audit District, 4 Claremont Rd, Sandymount, Dublin 4	6607111	6606768
	Wholesalers and Retailers Audit District, 4 Claremont Rd, Sandymount, Dublin 4	6607111	6606768
Galway	Galway Tax District, Hibernian Hse, Eyre Sq, Galway	091 63041	091 63987
Kerry	Tralee Tax District, Government Buildings, Spa Rd, Tralee, Co Kerry	066 21844	066 21895
Kildare	Agribusiness and Fisheries Audit District, Lansdowne Hse, Lansdowne Rd, Dublin 4	6689400	6686512
	Construction and Property Audit District, Findlater Hse, Cathal Brugha St, Dublin 2	8746821	8749277
	Financial Sector Audit District, Lansdowne Hse, Lansdowne Rd, Dublin 4	6689400	6686512
	Groups and PLCs Audit District, Lansdowne Hse, Lansdowne Rd, Dublin 4	6689400	6686512
	Investment/Rental Income Audit District, Lansdowne Hse, Lansdowne Rd, Dublin 4	6689400	6686512
	Professionals Audit District, Clanwilliam Court, Lr Mount St, Dublin 2	6616444	6609787
	Services Audit District (incl Hotels, Pubs etc), 4 Claremont Rd, Sandymount, Dublin 4	6607111	6606768
	Transport and Light Industry Audit District, 4 Claremont Rd, Sandymount, Dublin 4	6607111	6606768
	Wholesalers and Retailers Audit District, 4 Claremont Rd, Sandymount, Dublin 4	6607111	6606768
Kilkenny (N)	Kilkenny Tax District, Government Buildings, Hebron Road, Kilkenny	056 52222	056 51255
Kilkenny (S)	Waterford Tax District, Government Buildings, The Glen, Waterford	051 73565	051 77483
Laois	Kilkenny Tax District, Government Buildings, Hebron Road, Kilkenny	056 52222	056 51255
Leitrim	Sligo Tax District, Government Buildings, Cranmore Rd, Sligo	071 60322	071 43987
Limerick	Limerick Tax District, River Hse, Charlotte Quay, Limerick	061 318711	061 417863
Longford	Athlone Tax District, Government Buildings, Pearse St, Athlone, Co Westmeath	0902 92681	0902 92699
Louth (N)	Dundalk Tax District, Earl House, Earl House, Earl St, Dundalk, Co Louth	042 32251	042 34609
Louth (S)	Agribusiness and Fisheries Audit District, Lansdowne Hse, Lansdowne Rd, Dublin 4	6689400	6686512
	Construction and Property Audit District, Findlater Hse, Cathal Brugha St, Dublin 2	8746821	8749277
	Financial Sector Audit District, Lansdowne Hse, Lansdowne Rd, Dublin 4	6689400	6686512
	Groups and PLCs Audit District, Lansdowne Hse, Lansdowne Rd, Dublin 4	6689400	6686512
	Investment/Rental Income Audit District, Lansdowne Hse, Lansdowne Rd, Dublin 4	6689400	6686512
	Professionals Audit District, Clanwilliam Court, Lr Mount St, Dublin 2	6616444	6609787
	Services Audit District (incl Hotels, Pubs etc), 4 Claremont Rd, Sandymount, Dublin 4	6607111	6606768
	Transport and Light Industry Audit District, 4 Claremont Rd, Sandymount, Dublin 4	6607111	6606768
	Wholesalers and Retailers Audit District, 4 Claremont Rd, Sandymount, Dublin 4	6607111	6606768
Mayo	Castlebar Tax District, Michael Davitt Hse, Castlebar, Co Mayo	094 21344	094 24221
Meath	Agribusiness and Fisheries Audit District, Lansdowne Hse, Lansdowne Rd, Dublin 4	6689400	6686512
	Construction and Property Audit District, Findlater Hse, Cathal Brugha St, Dublin 2	8746821	8749277
	Financial Sector Audit District, Lansdowne Hse, Lansdowne Rd, Dublin 4	6689400	6686512
	Groups and PLCs Audit District, Lansdowne Hse, Lansdowne Rd, Dublin 4	6689400	6686512
	Investment/Rental Income Audit District, Lansdowne Hse, Lansdowne Rd, Dublin 4	6689400	6686512
	Professionals Audit District, Clanwilliam Court, Lr Mount St, Dublin 2	6616444	6609787
	Services Audit District (incl Hotels, Pubs etc), 4 Claremont Rd, Sandymount, Dublin 4	6607111	6606768
	Transport and Light Industry Audit District, 4 Claremont Rd, Sandymount, Dublin 4	6607111	6606768
	Wholesalers and Retailers Audit District, 4 Claremont Rd, Sandymount, Dublin 4	6607111	6606768
Monaghan	Dundalk Tax District, Earl House, Earl House, Earl St, Dundalk, Co Louth	042 32251	042 34609
Offaly (N)	Agribusiness and Fisheries Audit District, Lansdowne Hse, Lansdowne Rd, Dublin 4	6689400	6686512
	Construction and Property Audit District, Findlater Hse, Cathal Brugha St, Dublin 2	8746821	8749277
	Financial Sector Audit District, Lansdowne Hse, Lansdowne Rd, Dublin 4	6689400	6686512
	Groups and PLCs Audit District, Lansdowne Hse, Lansdowne Rd, Dublin 4	6689400	6686512
	Investment/Rental Income Audit District, Lansdowne Hse, Lansdowne Rd, Dublin 4	6689400	6686512
	Professionals Audit District, Clanwilliam Court, Lr Mount St, Dublin 2	6616444	6609787
	Services Audit District (incl Hotels, Pubs etc), 4 Claremont Rd, Sandymount, Dublin 4	6607111	6606768
	Transport and Light Industry Audit District, 4 Claremont Rd, Sandymount, Dublin 4	6607111	6606768

	Wholesalers and Retailers Audit District, 4 Claremont Rd, Sandymount, Dublin 4	6607111	6606768
Offaly (W)	Athlone Tax District, Government Buildings, Pearse St, Athlone, Co Westmeath	0902 92681	0902 92699
Roscommon	Athlone Tax District, Government Buildings, Pearse St, Athlone, Co Westmeath	0902 92681	0902 92699
Sligo	Sligo Tax District, Government Buildings, Cranmore Rd, Sligo	071 60322	071 43987
Tipperary	Thurles Tax District, Stradavoher, Thurles, Co Tipperary	0504 21544	0504 21475
Tipperary (SE)	Waterford Tax District, Government Buildings, The Glen, Waterford	051 73565	051 77483
Westmeath (E)	Athlone Tax District, Government Buildings, Pearse St, Athlone, Co Westmeath	0902 92681	0902 92699
Westmeath (W)	Agribusiness and Fisheries Audit District, Lansdowne Hse, Lansdowne Rd, Dublin 4	6689400	6686512
	Construction and Property Audit District, Findlater Hse, Cathal Brugha St, Dublin 2	8746821	8749277
	Financial Sector Audit District, Lansdowne Hse, Lansdowne Rd, Dublin 4	6689400	6686512
	Groups and PLCs Audit District, Lansdowne Hse, Lansdowne Rd, Dublin 4	6689400	6686512
	Investment/Rental Income Audit District, Lansdowne Hse, Lansdowne Rd, Dublin 4	6689400	6686512
	Professionals Audit District, Clanwilliam Court, Lr Mount St, Dublin 2	6616444	6609787
	Services Audit District (incl Hotels, Pubs etc), 4 Claremont Rd, Sandymount, Dublin 4	6607111	6606768
	Transport and Light Industry Audit District, 4 Claremont Rd, Sandymount, Dublin 4	6607111	6606768
	Wholesalers and Retailers Audit District, 4 Claremont Rd, Sandymount, Dublin 4	6607111	6606768
Wexford	Wexford Tax District, Distillery Rd, Wexford	053 22174	053 23287
Wicklow	Agribusiness and Fisheries Audit District, Lansdowne Hse, Lansdowne Rd, Dublin 4	6689400	6686512
	Construction and Property Audit District, Findlater Hse, Cathal Brugha St, Dublin 2	8746821	8749277
	Financial Sector Audit District, Lansdowne Hse, Lansdowne Rd, Dublin 4	6689400	6686512
	Groups and PLCs Audit District, Lansdowne Hse, Lansdowne Rd, Dublin 4	6689400	6686512
	Investment/Rental Income Audit District, Lansdowne Hse, Lansdowne Rd, Dublin 4	6689400	6686512
	Professionals Audit District, Clanwilliam Court, Lr Mount St, Dublin 2	6616444	6609787
	Services Audit District (incl Hotels, Pubs etc), 4 Claremont Rd, Sandymount, Dublin 4	6607111	6606768
	Transport and Light Industry Audit District, 4 Claremont Rd, Sandymount, Dublin 4	6607111	6606768
	Wholesalers and Retailers Audit District, 4 Claremont Rd, Sandymount, Dublin 4	6607111	6606768
Waterford	Waterford Tax District, Government Buildings, The Glen, Waterford	051 73565	051 77483

Collection of tax

Section	Address	Phone	Fax
Payments	Collector General, Sarsfield House, Limerick	061 310310	
Repayments	VAT Repayments (Registered Traders), Sarsfield House, Limerick	061 310310	
	For repayments to unregistered persons (farmers, fishermen, hospitals etc),		
	VAT Repayments (Unregistered) Section, Kilrush Road, Ennis, Co Clare	065 41200	065 40394
Tax clearance	Licensing: 5th Floor, Sarsfield House, Limerick	061 310310	061 410311
	Dublin callers	6774211	
VIMA	(VIES Intrastat Mutual Assistance), Newry Road, Dundalk	042 26262	

LEGISLATION

PROVISIONAL COLLECTION OF TAXES ACT 1927

(Number 7 of 1927)

ARRANGEMENT OF SECTIONS

An Act to give statutory effect for a limited period to resolutions of the committee on finance of Dáil Éireann imposing, renewing, varying, or abolishing taxation, and to make provision with respect to payments, deductions, assessments, charges, and other things made or done on account of any temporary tax in anticipation of the renewal of the tax by the Oireachtas. [19th March, 1927]

1 Definitions

In this Act —

the expression **"Committee on Finance"** means the Committee on Finance of Dáil Éireann when and so long as such Committee is a committee of the whole House;

the expression **"new tax"** means a tax which was not in force immediately before the end of the previous financial year;

the expression **"permanent tax"** means a tax which was last imposed without any limit of time being fixed for its duration;

the expression **"temporary tax"** means a tax which was last imposed or renewed for a limited period only;

the expression **"normal expiration"** when used in relation to a temporary tax means the end of the limited period for which the tax was last imposed or renewed;

the word **"tax"** includes duties of customs, duties of excise, income tax, ...[1] ...[2] [and value-added tax][3] [and capital gains tax][4] ...[5] [and corporation tax][6] [and gift tax and inheritance tax][7] [and residential property tax][8] [and stamp duties][9] but no other tax or duty.

Amendments
1 Words "and super-tax" repealed by FA 1974 s 86 and Sch 2 Pt I for 1974-75 and later tax years.
2 Words "and also turnover tax" repealed by VATA 1972 s 41.
3 Inserted by VATA 1972 s 38.
4 Inserted by CGTA 1975 s 50.
5 Words "and wealth tax" deleted by FA 1978 s 38.
6 Inserted by CTA 1976 s 6.
7 Inserted by CATA 1976 s 69.
8 Inserted by FA 1983 s 114(1).
9 Inserted by FA 1986 s 100.

---

2 Certain resolutions to have statutory effect

Whenever a resolution (in this Act referred to as a resolution under this Act) is passed by [Dáil Éireann][1] resolving —

(*a*)   that a new tax specified in the resolution be imposed, or

(*b*)   that a specified permanent tax in force immediately before the end of the previous financial year be increased, reduced, or otherwise varied, or be abolished, or

(*c*)   that a specified temporary tax in force immediately before the end of the previous financial year be renewed (whether at the same or a different rate and whether with or without modification) as from the date of its normal expiration or from an earlier date or be discontinued on a date prior to the date of its normal expiration,

and the resolution contains a declaration that it is expedient in the public interest that the resolution should have statutory effect under the provisions of this Act, the resolution shall, subject to the provisions of this Act, have statutory effect as if contained in an Act of the Oireachtas.

Amendments
1   Substituted by FA 1974 s 85(1)(*a*) with effect from 23 October 1974 (SI 312/1974); previously "the Committee on Finance".

---

3 Application of general taxing enactments

(1) Whenever a new tax is imposed by a resolution under this Act and such resolution describes the tax as a duty of customs or as a duty of excise or as an income tax ...[1], the enactments which immediately before the end of the previous financial year were in force in relation to customs duties generally, or excise duties generally, or income tax generally, ...[2] (as the case may require) shall, subject to the provisions of this Act, apply to and have full force and effect in respect of such new tax so long as the resolution continues to have statutory effect.

(2) Whenever a permanent tax is increased, reduced, or otherwise varied by a resolution under this Act, all enactments which were in force with respect to that tax immediately before the end of the previous financial year shall, so long as the resolution continues to have statutory effect and subject to the provisions of this Act, have full force and effect with respect to the tax as so increased, reduced, or otherwise varied.

(3) Whenever a temporary tax is renewed (whether at the same or a different rate and whether with or without modification) by a resolution under this Act, all enactments which were in force with respect to that tax immediately before the end of the previous financial year shall, so long as the resolution continues to have statutory effect and subject to the provisions of this Act, have full force and effect with respect to the tax as renewed by the resolution.

Amendments
1   Words "or as a super-tax" repealed by FA 1974 s 86 and Sch 2 Pt 1 for 1974-75 and later tax years.
2   Words "or super-tax generally" repealed by FA 1974 s 86 and Sch 2 Pt 1 for 1974-75 and later tax years.

---

4 Duration of statutory effect of resolution

[A resolution under this Act shall cease to have statutory effect upon the happening of whichever of the following events first occurs, that is to say:

[(*a*)   subject to section 4A of this Act, if a Bill containing provisions to the same effect (with or without modifications) as the resolution is not read a second time by Dáil Éireann—

(i)   where Dáil Éireann is in recess on any day between the eighty-second and the eighty-fourth day after the resolution is passed by Dáil Éireann, within the next five sitting days of the resumption of Dáil Éireann after that recess,

(ii)   in any other case, within the next eighty-four days after the resolution is passed by Dáil Éireann,][1]

(*b*)   if those provisions of the said bill are rejected by Dáil Éireann during the passage of the Bill through the Oireachtas;

(c) the coming into operation of an Act of the Oireachtas containing provisions to the same effect (with or without modification) as the resolution;

(d) [subject to section 4A of this Act][2] the expiration of a period of four months from that date on which the resolution is expressed to take effect or, where no such date is expressed, from the passing of the resolution by Dáil Éireann.][3]

Amendments
1 Para (a) substituted by Appropriation Act 1991 s 2(a)(i).
2 Inserted by Appropriation Act 1991 s 2(a)(ii).
3 Section 4 substituted by FA 1974 s 85(1)(b) with effect from 23 October 1974 (SI 312/1974).

4A Effect of dissolution of Dáil Éireann

[Where Dáil Éireann, having passed a resolution under this Act, has been dissolved on the date the resolution was so passed or within four months of that date, then the period of dissolution shall be disregarded for the purposes of calculating any period to which paragraph (a) or (d) of section 4 of this Act relates.][1]

Amendments
1 Section originally inserted by Appropriation Act 1991; substituted by FA 1992 s 250.
Definition
"Dáil Éireann": IA 1937 Sch.

5 Repayment of certain payments and deductions

(1) Whenever a resolution under this Act ceases to have statutory effect by reason of the happening of any event other than the coming into operation of an Act of the Oireachtas containing provisions to the same effect (with or without modification) as the resolution, all moneys paid in pursuance of the resolution shall be repaid or made good and every deduction made in pursuance of the resolution shall be deemed to be an unauthorised deduction.

(2) ...[1].

(3) Whenever an Act of the Oireachtas comes into operation containing provisions to the same effect with modifications as a resolution under this Act and such resolution ceases by virtue of such coming into operation to have statutory effect, all moneys paid in pursuance of such resolution which would not be payable under such Act shall be repaid or made good and every deduction made in pursuance of such resolution which would not be authorised by such Act shall be deemed to be an unauthorised deduction.

Amendments
1 Subs (2) repealed by FA 1974 s 85(1)(c) with effect from 23 October 1974 (SI 312/1974).

6 Certain payments and deductions deemed to be legal

(1) Any payment or deduction on account of a temporary tax to which this section applies made within two months after the expiration of such tax in respect of a period or event occurring after such expiration shall, if such payment or deduction would have been a legal payment or deduction if the tax had not expired, be deemed to be a legal payment or deduction subject to the conditions that —

(a) if a resolution under this Act renewing the tax (with or without modification) is not passed by [Dáil Éireann][1] within two months after the expiration of the tax, the amount of such payment or deduction shall be repaid or made good on the expiration of such two months, and

(b) if (such resolution having been so passed) an Act of the Oireachtas renewing the tax (with or without modification) does not come into operation when or before such resolution ceases to have statutory effect, the amount of such payment or deduction shall be repaid or made good on such cesser, and

(c) if (such Act having been so passed) the tax is renewed by such Act with such modifications that the whole or some portion of such payment or deduction is not a legal payment or deduction under such Act, the whole or such portion (as the case may be) of such payment or deduction shall be repaid or made good on the coming into operation of such Act.

(2) This section applies only to a temporary tax which was last imposed or renewed for a limited period not exceeding eighteen months and was in force immediately before the end of the financial year next preceding the financial year in which the payment or deduction under this section is made.

Amendments

1   Substituted by FA 1974 s 85(1)(*d*) with effect from 23 October 1974 (SI 312/1974); previously "the Committee on Finance".

---

7 Repeal

The Provisional Collection of Taxes Act, 1913, is hereby repealed.

8 Short title

This Act may be cited as the Provisional Collection of Taxes Act, 1927.

FINANCE ACT 1928

(Number 11 of 1928)

34 Care and management of taxes and duties

...

(2) Any information acquired, whether before or after the passing of this Act, by the Revenue Commissioners in connection with any tax or duty under their care and management may be used by them for any purpose connected with any other tax or duty under their care and management.

Cross-references
European Communities (Mutual Assistance in the Field of Value Added Tax) Regulations 1980 (SI407/1980).

INTERPRETATION ACT 1937

(Number 38 of 1937)

ARRANGEMENT OF SECTIONS

PART I
Preliminary and general

PART II
Form, citation, and operation of Acts of the Oireachtas

PART III
Meaning and construction of particular words and expressions

PART IV
Statutory powers and duties

PART V
Effect of repeals and revocations

SCHEDULE
Interpretation of particular expressions and words

An Act to make, for the purpose of the Constitution of Ireland lately enacted by the people, divers provisions in relation to the form, operation, and interpretation of Acts of the Oireachtas and of Instruments made under such Acts. [8th December, 1937]

PART I
Preliminary and general

1 Short title

This Act may be cited as the Interpretation Act, 1937.

2 Commencement

This Act shall come into operation immediately after the coming into operation of the Constitution of Ireland lately enacted by the People.

3 Definitions

In this Act —

the word **"statute"** includes (in addition to Acts of the Oireachtas) Acts of the Oireachtas of Saorstát Éireann, Acts of the Parliament of the former United Kingdom of Great Britain and Ireland, and Acts of a Parliament sitting in Ireland at any time before the coming into force of the Union with Ireland Act, 1800;

the word **"instrument"** means an order, regulation, rule, bye-law, warrant, licence, certificate, or other like document;

the expression **"statutory instrument"** means an instrument made, issued, or granted under a power or authority conferred by statute;

references to instruments made wholly or partly under an Act of the Oireachtas shall be construed as referring to instruments made, issued, or granted under a power or authority conferred by an Act of the Oireachtas or conferred by the joint operation of an Act of the Oireachtas and some other statute.

4 Application to certain Acts of the Oireachtas of Saorstát Éireann

Save as is otherwise expressly provided by this Act, every provision of this Act which relates to Acts of the Oireachtas shall apply and have effect in relation to this Act and every other Act of the Oireachtas of Saorstát Éireann (whether passed before or after this Act) which is expressed to come into operation immediately after the coming into operation of the Constitution, and accordingly this Act and every such other Act shall, for the purpose of such application but no further or otherwise, be deemed to be an Act of the Oireachtas and (save as is otherwise expressly provided by this Act) the expression **"Act of the Oireachtas"** shall in this Act be construed and have effect as including this Act and every such other Act of the Oireachtas of Saorstát Éireann.

5 Non-application of the Interpretation Act, 1923

(1) The Interpretation Act, 1923 (No 46 of 1923), shall not apply to any Act of the Oireachtas or to any instrument made wholly or partly under any such Act.

(2) The foregoing subsection of this section shall not preclude or prejudice the application to this Act and to other Acts of the Oireachtas of Saorstát Éireann which are expressed to come into operation immediately after the coming into operation of the Constitution of so much of the Interpretation Act, 1923 (No 46 of 1923), as concerns events happening or things to be done in relation to an Act before it comes into operation.

Definition
"instrument": s 3; "Act of the Oireachtas": s 4.

PART II
Form, citation, and operation of Acts of the Oireachtas

6 Form of Acts of the Oireachtas

(1) Every Act of the Oireachtas shall be a public document and shall be judicially noticed.

(2) Every Act of the Oireachtas shall be divided into sections numbered consecutively and any such section may be sub-divided in such manner and to such extent as is convenient.

(3) The sections of an Act of the Oireachtas may, where convenient, be grouped in Parts, Chapters, or other divisions numbered consecutively.

Definition
Act of the Oireachtas: s 4.

7 Citation of Acts of the Oireachtas

(1) Every Act of the Oireachtas may be cited in any other Act of the Oireachtas or in any instrument or other document either by the short title of the Act so cited or by the calendar year in which the Act so cited was passed and the consecutive number of such Act in such year.

(2) Any enactment contained in an Act of the Oireachtas may be cited in any other Act of the Oireachtas or in any instrument or other document by reference to the Part, section, subsection, or other sub-division of the first-mentioned Act which contains the enactment so cited.

Definition
"Act of the Oireachtas": s 4.

8 Date of passing of Acts of the Oireachtas

(1) The date of the passing of every Act of the Oireachtas shall be the date of the day on which the Bill for such Act is signed by the President.

(2) Immediately after the passing of every Act of the Oireachtas the Clerk of Dáil Éireann shall endorse on such Act, immediately after the title thereof, the date of the passing of such Act, and such date shall be taken to be part of such Act.

(3) Every enactment contained in an Act of the Oireachtas shall, unless the contrary intention is expressed in such Act, be deemed to be in operation as from the end of the day before the date of the passing of such Act.

(4) This section shall not apply to this Act or to any other Act of the Oireachtas of Saorstát Éireann which is expressed to come into operation immediately after the coming into operation of the Constitution, and accordingly the expression **"Act of the Oireachtas"** shall not in this section include any such Act of the Oireachtas of Saorstát Éireann.

Definition
"Act of the Oireachtas": s 4.

9 Commencement of Acts and instruments

(1) Where an Act of the Oireachtas, or a portion of any such Act, or an instrument made wholly or partly under any such Act, or a portion of any such instrument is expressed to come into operation on a particular day (whether such day is before or after the date of the passing of such Act or the making of such instrument and whether such day is named in such Act or instrument or is to be fixed or ascertained in any particular manner), such Act, portion of an Act, instrument, or portion of an instrument shall come into operation at the end of the day before such particular day.

(2) Every instrument made wholly or partly under an Act of the Oireachtas shall, unless the contrary intention is expressed in such instrument, be deemed to be in operation as from the end of the day before the day on which the instrument is made.

Definition
"instrument": s 3; "Act of the Oireachtas": s 4.

10 Exercise of statutory powers before commencement of the Act

(1) Where an Act of the Oireachtas or any particular enactment contained in any such Act is expressed to come into operation on a day subsequent to the date of the passing of such Act, the following provisions shall have effect, that is to say:—

(*a*) if the day on which such Act or such enactment (as the case may be) comes into operation is to be fixed or ascertained in any particular manner, the instrument, act, or thing whereby such day is fixed or ascertained may, subject to any restrictions imposed by such Act, be made or done at any time after the passing of such Act;

(*b*) if such Act confers a power to make or do, for the purposes of such Act or such enactment (as the case may be), any instrument, act, or thing the making or doing of which is necessary or expedient to enable such Act or enactment to have full force and effect immediately upon its coming into operation, such power may, subject to any restrictions imposed by such Act, be exercised at any time after the passing of such Act.

(2) In the application of this section to an Act of the Oireachtas of Saorstát Éireann which is expressed to come into operation immediately after the coming into operation of the Constitution, nothing in this section shall operate to enable any instrument, act, or thing to be made or done under or in relation to any such Act before the coming into operation of the Constitution.

Definition
"instrument": s 3; "Act of the Oireachtas": s 4.

PART III
Meaning and construction of particular words and expressions

11 Certain general rules of construction

The following provisions shall apply and have effect in relation to the construction of every Act of the Oireachtas and of every instrument made wholly or partly under any such Act, that is to say:—

(*a*) *Singular and plural.* Every word importing the singular shall, unless the contrary intention appears, be construed as if it also imported the plural, and every word importing the plural shall, unless the contrary intention appears, be construed as if it also imported the singular;

(*b*) *Masculine and feminine.* Every word importing the masculine gender shall, unless the contrary intention appears, be construed as if it also imported the feminine gender;

(*c*) *Person.* The word **"person"** shall, unless the contrary intention appears, be construed as importing a body corporate (whether a corporation aggregate or a corporation sole) and an unincorporated body of persons as well as an individual;

(*d*) *Time.* Every word or expression relating to time and every reference to a point of time shall, unless the contrary intention appears, be construed as relating or referring to Greenwich mean time, but subject to the provisions of any enactment whereunder the time in Ireland differs from Greenwich mean time during a specified period;

(*e*) *Distance.* Every word or expression relating to the distance between two points and every reference to the distance from or to a point shall, unless the contrary intention appears, be construed as relating or referring to such distance measured in a straight line on a horizontal plane;

(*f*) *Citations.* Every description of or citation from any statute, instrument, or other document shall, unless the contrary intention appears, be construed as including the word, subsection, section, or other portion mentioned or referred to as forming the beginning or as forming the end of the portion comprised in the description or citation or as being the point from which or to which such portion extends;

(g)   *Marginal notes.*   No marginal note placed at the side of any section or provision to indicate the subject, contents, or effect of such section or provision and no heading or cross-line placed at the head or beginning of a Part, section or provision or a group of sections or provisions to indicate the subject, contents, or effect of such Part, section, provision, or group shall be taken to be part of the Act or instrument or be considered or judicially noticed in relation to the construction or interpretation of the Act or instrument or any portion thereof;

(h)   *Periods of time.*   Where a period of time is expressed to begin on or be reckoned from a particular day, that day shall, unless the contrary intention appears, be deemed to be included in such period, and, where a period of time is expressed to end on or be reckoned to a particular day, that day shall, unless the contrary intention appears, be deemed to be included in such period;

(i)   *Offences by corporations.*   References to a person in relation to an offence (whether punishable on indictment or on summary conviction) shall, unless the contrary intention appears, be construed as including references to a body corporate.

Cross-references

Para (*b*): as regards legislation passed after 22 December 1993, every word importing the feminine gender, unless the contrary intention appears, also imports the masculine gender: Interpretation (Amendment) Act 1993.

Case law

Words in a charging provision, in the absence of a definition, to be interpreted according to normal usage: *De Brún v Kiernan* [1982] ITR Vol III, p 19.

Interpretation, misclassification of goods under customs tariff, negligence of Revenue Commissioners, legitimate expectation: *Carbury Milk Products Ltd v Minister for Agriculture,* HC, 23 April 1993, ITR Vol IV, p 492.

Definition

"person": s 11(*c*); "instrument": s 3; "Act of the Oireachtas": s 4.

---

12   Interpretation of the expressions and words in the Schedule

In every Act of the Oireachtas and every instrument made wholly or partly under any such Act, every word and every expression to which a particular meaning, construction, or effect is assigned in the Schedule to this Act shall, unless the contrary intention appears, have the meaning, construction, or effect so assigned to it.

Case law

Words in a charging provision, in the absence of a definition, to be interpreted according to normal usage: *De Brún v Kiernan* [1982] ITR Vol III, p 19.

Definition

"instrument": s 3; "Act of the Oireachtas": s 4.

---

13   Construction of certain statutory instruments

Every expression and every word used in an instrument made wholly or partly under an Act of the Oireachtas shall, unless the contrary intention appears, have in such instrument the same meaning as it has in the Act or Acts under which such instrument is made.

Definition

"instrument": s 3; "Act of the Oireachtas": s 4.

---

14   Offences under two or more laws

Where any act, whether of commission or omission, constitutes an offence under two or more statutes or under a statute and at common law, the offender shall, unless the contrary intention appears, be liable to be prosecuted and punished under either or any of those statutes or at common law, but shall not be liable to be punished twice for the same offence.

Definition
"statute": s 3.

PART IV
Statutory powers and duties

15 Construction and exercise of statutory powers

(1) Every power conferred by an Act of the Oireachtas or by an instrument made wholly or partly under any such Act may, unless the contrary intention appears in such Act or instrument, be exercised from time to time as occasion requires.

(2) Every power conferred by an Act of the Oireachtas or by an instrument made wholly or partly under any such Act on the holder of an office as such shall, unless the contrary intention appears in such Act or instrument, be deemed to be conferred on and may accordingly be exercised by the holder for the time being of such office.

(3) Every power conferred by an Act of the Oireachtas to make any regulations, rules, or bye-laws shall, unless the contrary intention appears in such Act, be construed as including a power, exercisable in the like manner and subject to the like consent and conditions (if any), to revoke or amend any regulations, rules, or bye-laws made under such power and (where requisite) to make other regulations, rules, or bye-laws in lieu of those so revoked.

Definition
"instrument": s 3; "Act of the Oireachtas": s 4.

16 Construction and performance of statutory duties

(1) Every duty imposed by an Act of the Oireachtas or by an instrument made wholly or partly under any such Act shall, unless the contrary intention appears in such Act or instrument, be performed from time to time as occasion requires.

(2) Every duty imposed by an Act of the Oireachtas or by an instrument made wholly or partly under any such Act on the holder of an office as such shall, unless the contrary intention appears in such Act or instrument, be deemed to be imposed on and shall accordingly be performed by the holder for the time being of such office.

Definition
"instrument": s 3; "Act of the Oireachtas": s 4.

17 Rules of Court

Whenever an Act of the Oireachtas confers any new jurisdiction on a court of justice or extends or varies an existing jurisdiction of a court of justice, the authority having for the time being power to make rules or orders regulating the practice and procedure of such court shall have, and may at any time exercise, power to make rules or orders for regulating the practice and procedure of such court in the exercise of the jurisdiction so conferred, extended, or varied.

Definition
"Act of the Oireachtas": s 4.

18 Service by post

Where an Act of the Oireachtas or an instrument made wholly or partly under any such Act authorises or requires a document to be served by post, whether the word "serve" or any of the words "give", "deliver", or "send", or any other word is used, then, unless the contrary intention appears, the service of such document may be effected by properly addressing, prepaying (where requisite), and posting a letter containing such document, and in such case the service of such document shall, unless the contrary is proved, be deemed to have been effected at the time at which such letter would be delivered in the ordinary course of post.

Definition
"instrument": s 3; "Act of the Oireachtas": s 4.

PART V
Effect of repeals and revocations

19 Date of operation of repeals and revocations

(1) Where an Act of the Oireachtas repeals the whole or a portion of a previous statute and substitutes other provisions for the statute or portion of a statute so repealed, the statute or portion of a statute so repealed shall, unless the contrary is expressly provided in the repealing Act, continue in force until the said substituted provisions come into operation.

(2) Where an instrument made wholly or partly under an Act of the Oireachtas revokes the whole or a portion of a previous statutory instrument (whether made wholly or partly under such Act or under another statute) and substitutes other provisions for the instrument or portion of an instrument so revoked, the instrument or portion of an instrument so revoked shall, unless the contrary is expressly provided in the revoking instrument, continue in force until the said substituted provisions come into operation.

Definition
"statute", "instrument", "statutory instrument": s 3; "Act of the Oireachtas": s 4.

20 Construction of references to repealed statutes and revoked instruments

(1) Whenever any statute or portion of a statute is repealed and re-enacted, with or without modification, by an Act of the Oireachtas, references in any other statute or in any statutory instrument to the statute or portion of a statute so repealed and re-enacted shall, unless the contrary intention appears, be construed as references to the portion of such Act of the Oireachtas containing such re-enactment.

(2) Whenever a statutory instrument or a portion of a statutory instrument is revoked and re-enacted, with or without modification, by an instrument made wholly or partly under an Act of the Oireachtas, references in any other statutory instrument to the statutory instrument or portion of a statutory instrument so revoked and re-enacted shall, unless the contrary intention appears, be construed as references to the said instrument containing such re-enactment.

Definition
"statute", "instrument", "statutory instrument": s 3; "Act of the Oireachtas": s 4.

21 Operation of repeals, cessers, and terminations of statutes

(1) Where an Act of the Oireachtas repeals the whole or a portion of a previous statute, then, unless the contrary intention appears, such repeal shall not —

(*a*) revive anything not in force or not existing immediately before such repeal takes effect, or

(*b*) affect the previous operation of the statute or portion of a statue so repealed or anything duly done or suffered thereunder, or

(*c*) affect any right, privilege, obligation, or liability acquired, accrued, or incurred under the statute or portion of a statue so repealed, or

(*d*) affect any penalty, forfeiture, or punishment incurred in respect of any offence against or contravention of the statute or portion of a statute so repealed which was committed before such repeal, or

(*e*) prejudice or affect any legal proceedings, civil or criminal, pending at the time of such repeal of any such right, privilege, obligation, liability, offence, or contravention as aforesaid.

(2) Where an Act of the Oireachtas repeals the whole or a portion of a previous statute, then, unless the contrary intention appears, any legal proceedings, civil or criminal, in respect of any right, privilege, obligation, or liability acquired, accrued, or incurred under

or any offence against or contravention of the statute or portion of a statute so repealed may be instituted, continued or enforced, and any penalty, forfeiture, or punishment in respect of any such offence or contravention may be imposed and carried out as if such statute or portion of a statute had not been repealed.

(3) Where an Act of the Oireachtas or a portion of any such Act ceases by any means or for any reason (other than repeal by a subsequent Act of the Oireachtas) to be in force, the preceding subsections of this section shall apply and have effect in relation to such Act or portion of an Act as if such cesser were caused by a repeal effected by an Act of the Oireachtas, and accordingly, for the purposes of such application, every reference in either of the said preceding subsections to a repeal shall be construed as a reference to a cesser by any means or for any reason (other than such repeal) to be in force.

Definition

"statute": s 3; "Act of the Oireachtas": s 4.

---

22 Operation of revocations, cessers and terminations of statutory instruments

(1) Where an instrument made wholly or partly under an Act of the Oireachtas revokes the whole or a portion of a previous statutory instrument, then, unless the contrary intention appears, such revocation shall not —

    (a)   revive anything not in force or not existing immediately before such revocation takes effect, or

    (b)   affect the previous operation of the statutory instrument or portion of a statutory instrument so revoked or anything duly done or suffered thereunder, or

    (c)   affect any right, privilege, obligation, or liability acquired, accrued, or incurred under the statutory instrument or portion of a statutory instrument so revoked, or

    (d)   affect any penalty, forfeiture, or punishment incurred in respect of any offence against or contravention of the statutory instrument or portion of a statutory instrument so revoked which was committed before such revocation, or

    (e)   prejudice or affect any legal proceedings, civil or criminal, pending at the time of such revocation in respect of any such right, privilege, obligation, liability, offence, or contravention as aforesaid.

(2) Where an instrument made wholly or partly under an Act of the Oireachtas revokes the whole or a portion of a previous statutory instrument, then, unless the contrary intention appears, any legal proceedings, civil or criminal, in respect of any right, privilege, obligation, or liability acquired, accrued, or incurred under or any offence against or contravention of the statutory instrument or portion of the statutory instrument so revoked may be instituted, continued, or enforced and any penalty, forfeiture, or punishment in respect of any such offence or contravention may be imposed and carried out as if such statutory instrument or portion of a statutory instrument had not been revoked.

(3) Where an instrument made wholly or partly under an Act of the Oireachtas or a portion of an instrument so made ceases by any means or for any reason (other than revocation by a subsequent such instrument) to be in force, the preceding subsections of this section shall apply and have effect in relation to such instrument or portion of an instrument as if such cesser were caused by a revocation effected by a subsequent such instrument, and accordingly, for the purposes of such application, every reference in either of the said preceding subsections to a revocation shall be construed as a reference to a cesser by any means or for any reason (other than such revocation) to be in force.

Definition

"instrument", "statutory instrument": s 3; "Act of the Oireachtas": s 4.

SCHEDULE
Interpretation of particular expressions and words

1. The word **"affidavit"**, in the case of persons for the time being allowed by law to declare instead of swearing, includes declaration.

2. The expression **"the Bank of Ireland"** means either, as the context requires, the Governor and Company of the Bank of Ireland or the bank of the said Governor and Company.

3. The expression **"British statute"** means an Act of the Parliament of the late United Kingdom of Great Britain and Ireland.

4. The expression **"the Circuit Court"**, means the Circuit Court of Justice as established and for the time being maintained by law.

5. The word **"commencement"**, when used in relation to a statute or a statutory instrument or a portion of a statute or statutory instrument, means the time at which such statute, statutory instrument, or portion of a statute or statutory instrument comes into operation.

6. The expression **"consular officer"** means a person in the Civil Service of Ireland who is a consul-general, a consul, or a vice-consul.

7. The expression **"the Constitution"** means the Constitution of Ireland enacted by the people on the 1st day of July, 1937.

8. The expression **"Dáil Éireann"** means the House of the Oireachtas to which that name is given by section 1 of Article 15 of the Constitution.

9. The expression **"the District Court"** means the District Court of Justice as established and for the time being maintained by law.

10. ...¹.

11. The expression **"the Government"** means the Government mentioned in Article 28 of the Constitution.

12. The expression **"Great Britain"** does not include the Channel Islands or the Isle of Man.

13. The expression **"the High Court"** means the High Court of Justice established and for the time being maintained by law in pursuance of Article 34 of the Constitution.

14. The word **"land"** includes messuages, tenements, and hereditaments, houses and buildings, of any tenure.

15. The expression **"the Lands Clauses Acts"** means the Lands Clauses Consolidation Act, 1845, the Lands Clauses Consolidation Acts Amendment Act, 1860, the Railways Act (Ireland), 1851, the Railways Act (Ireland), 1860, the Railways Act (Ireland), 1864, the Railways Traverse Act, the Acquisition of Land (Assessment of Compensation) Act, 1919, and every statute for the time being in force amending those Acts or any of them.

16. ...¹.

17. The word **"midnight"** means, in relation to any particular day, the point of time at which such day ends.

18. The expression [**"Minister of the Government"**]² means a member of the Government having charge of a Department of State.

19. The word **"month"** means a calendar month.

20. The word **"oath"**, in the case of persons for the time being allowed by law to affirm instead of swearing, includes affirmation.

21. The expression **"the Oireachtas"** means the National Parliament provided for by Article 15 of the Constitution.

22. The expression **"ordnance map"** means a map made under the powers conferred by the Survey (Ireland) Acts, 1825 to 1870, and the statutes for the time being in force amending those Acts or any of them.

23. The expression **"the President"** means the President of Ireland and includes any commission or other body or authority for the time being lawfully exercising the powers and performing the duties of the President.

24. The expression **"pre-union Irish statute"** means an Act passed by a Parliament sitting in Ireland at any time before the coming into force of the Union with Ireland Act, 1800.

25. The expression **"rateable valuation"** means the valuation under the Valuation Acts of the property in relation to which the expression is used.

26. The expression **"rules of court"** means rules made by the authority for the time being having power to make rules regulating the practice and procedure of the court in relation to which the expression is used.

27. The expression **"Saorstát Éireann statute"** means an Act of the Oireachtas of Saorstát Éireann.

28. The expression **"Seanad Éireann"** means the House of the Oireachtas to which that name is given by section 1 of Article 15 of the Constitution.

29. The expression **"statutory declaration"** means a declaration made by virtue of the Statutory Declarations Act, 1835.

30. The expression **"the Supreme Court"** means the Supreme Court of Justice as established and for the time being maintained by law in pursuance of Article 34 of the Constitution.

31. The word **"swear"**, in the case of persons for the time being allowed by law to affirm or declare instead of swearing, includes affirm and declare.

32. The word **"town"** means the area comprised in a town (not being an urban district) in which the Towns Improvement (Ireland) Act, 1854, is in operation.

33. The expression **"Valuation Acts"** means the Act for the time being in force relating to the valuation of rateable property.

34. The word **"week"**, when used without qualification, means the period between midnight on any Saturday and midnight on the next following Saturday.

35. The word **"week-day"** means a day which is not a Sunday.

36. The word **"writing"** includes printing, type-writing, lithography, photography, and other modes of representing or reproducing words in visible form, and cognate words shall be construed accordingly.

37. The word **"year"**, when used without qualification, means a period of twelve months beginning on the 1st day of the month of January in any year.

Amendments

1 Repealed by Exchequer and Local Financial Years Act 1974 s 2 except in relation to before 1 January 1975.

2 Substituted by the Ministers and Secretaries (Amendment) (No 2) Act 1977.

Definition

"person": s 11(*c*).

FINANCE ACT 1968

(Number 33 of 1968)

ARRANGEMENT OF SECTIONS

PART I
Income tax

An Act to charge and impose certain duties of customs and inland revenue (including excise), to amend the law relating to customs and inland revenue (including excise) and to make further provisions in connection with finance. [29th July, 1968]

PART I
Income tax

6 Obligation to keep certain records

[(1) In this section—

"linking documents" means documents that are drawn up in the making up of accounts and which show details of the calculations linking the records to the accounts;

"records" includes accounts, books of account, documents and any other data maintained manually or by any electronic, photographic or other process, relating to—

    (*a*)   all sums of money received and expended in the course of the carrying on or exercising of a trade, profession or other activity and the matters in respect of which the receipt and expenditure take place,

    (*b*)   all sales and purchases of goods and services where the carrying on or exercising of a trade, profession or other activity involves the purchase or sale of goods or services,

    (*c*)   the assets and liabilities of the trade, profession or other activity referred to in paragraph (*a*) or (*b*), and

    (*d*)   all transactions which constitute an acquisition or disposal of an asset for capital gains tax purposes.

(2)   (*a*)   Every person who, on his own behalf or on behalf of any other person, carries on or exercises any trade, profession or other activity the profits or gains of which are chargeable under Schedule D, or who is chargeable to tax under Schedule D or Schedule F in respect of any other source of income, or who is chargeable to capital gains tax in respect of chargeable gains, shall keep, or cause to be kept on his behalf, such records as will enable true returns to be made, for the purposes of income tax and capital gains tax, of such profits or gains or chargeable gains.

    (*b*)   The records shall be kept on a continuous and consistent basis, that is to say the entries therein shall be made in a timely manner and be consistent from one year to the next.

(c)   Where accounts are made up to show the profits or gains from any such trade, profession or activity or in relation to a source of income, of any person, that person shall retain, or cause to be retained on his behalf, linking documents.

(d)   Where any such trade, profession or other activity is carried on in partnership, the precedent partner, within the meaning of section 69 of the Income Tax Act, 1967, shall, for the purposes of this section, be deemed to be the person carrying on that trade, profession or other activity.

(3) Records required to be kept or retained by virtue of this section, shall be kept—

(a)   in written form in an official language of the State, or

(b)   subject to section 113(2) of the Finance Act, 1986, by means of any electronic, photographic or other process.

(4) Linking documents and records kept pursuant to the preceding provisions of this section shall be retained by the person required to keep the records for a period of 6 years after the completion of the transactions, acts or operations to which they relate or, in the case of a person who fails to comply with section 10 (1) of the Finance Act, 1988, requiring the preparation and delivery of a return on or before the specified return date for a year of assessment, until the expiry of a period of 6 years from the end of the year of assessment in which a return has been delivered showing the profits or gains or chargeable gains derived from the said transactions, acts or operations:

Provided that, this subsection shall not—

(a)   require the retention of linking documents and records in respect of which the inspector notifies in writing the person who is required to retain them that retention is not required, or

(b)   apply to the books and papers of a company which have been disposed of in accordance with section 305(1) of the Companies Act, 1963.

(5) Any person who fails to comply with the provisions of subsection (2), (3) or (4) in respect of any records or linking documents in relation to a return for any year of assessment shall be liable to a penalty of £1,200:

Provided that a penalty shall not be imposed under this subsection if it is proved that no person is chargeable to tax in respect of the profits or gains for that year of assessment.][1]

Amendments
1   Section substituted by FA 1992 s 231.
Cross-references
Corporation tax, this section applied by CTA 1976 s 147(2).
Subs (5): tax defaulters, publication of names: FA 1983 s 23; Revenue offences, penalties: FA 1983 s 94.
PAYE, equivalent obligations: ITER 1960 r 9.
Value added tax, equivalent obligations: VATA 1972 s 16.
Definition
"person": IA 1937 s 11(c); "profession": ITA 1967 s 1(1); "trade": ITA 1967 s 1(1); "year of assessment": ITA 1967 s 1(1).

PART VII
Miscellaneous

47 Care and management of taxes and duties

All taxes and duties imposed by this Act are hereby placed under the care and management of the Revenue Commissioners.

48 Short title, construction and commencement

(1) This Act may be cited as the Finance Act, 1968.

(2) Part I and (so far as relating to income tax, ...[1]) sections 34 to 39 and section 41 of this Act shall be construed together with the Income Tax Acts.

...

(4) ...[2].

(5) Part I and sections 34 to 39 of this Act shall, save as is otherwise expressly provided therein, be deemed to have come into force and shall take effect as on and from the 6th day of April, 1968.

(6) Any reference in this Act to any other enactment shall, except so far as the context otherwise requires, be construed as a reference to that enactment as amended by or under any other enactment, including this Act.

Amendments
1   Words "including sur-tax" deleted by FA 1974 s 86 and Sch 2 Pt I for 1974-75 and later tax years.
2   Subs (4) repealed by CTA 1976 s 164 and Sch 3 Pt II.
Definition
"commencement": IA 1937 Sch; "Income Tax Acts": ITA 1967 s 3.

VALUE ADDED TAX ACT 1972

(Number 22 of 1972)

ARRANGEMENT OF SECTIONS

FIRST SCHEDULE
Exempted Activities

SECOND SCHEDULE
Goods and services chargeable at the rate of zero per cent

THIRD SCHEDULE
Goods and services chargeable at the rate specified in section 11(1)(c)*[10%]*

FOURTH SCHEDULE
Services that, where taxable are taxed where received

FIFTH SCHEDULE
PART I: Annex A of Council Directive No 77/388/EEC of 17 May, 1977

LIST OF AGRICULTURAL PRODUCTION ACTIVITIES

PART II
Annex B of Council Directive No.77/388/EEC of 17 May, 1977: List of agricultural services

SIXTH SCHEDULE
Goods and services chargeable at the rate specified in section 11(1)(d)*[12.5%]*

SEVENTH SCHEDULE

An Act to charge and impose certain duties of inland revenue (including excise), to amend the law relating to inland revenue (including excise) and to make further provisions in connection with finance.[26th July, 1972]

1 Interpretation

(1) In this Act, save where the context otherwise requires—

...[1]

["**agricultural produce**" has the meaning assigned to it by section 8;][2]

Annex A

["**agricultural service**" has the meaning assigned to it by section 8;][3]

Annex B

["**antiques**" has the meaning assigned to it by section 10A;][4]

"**Appeal Commissioners**" means persons appointed in accordance with section 156 of the Income Tax Act, 1967, to be Appeal Commissioners for the purpose of the Income Tax Acts;

"**body of persons**" means any body politic, corporate, or collegiate, and any company, partnership, fraternity, fellowship and society of persons, whether corporate or not corporate;

"**business**" includes farming, the promotion of dances and any trade, commerce, manufacture, or any venture or concern in the nature of trade, commerce or manufacture, and any profession or vocation, whether for profit or otherwise;

["**clothing**" does not include footwear;][5]

"**Collector-General**" means the Collector-General appointed under section 162 of the Income Tax Act 1967;

["**collectors' items**" has the meaning assigned to it by section 10A;][6]

["**Community**", except where the context otherwise requires, has the same meaning as it has in Article 3 of Council Directive No 77/388/EEC of 17 May 1977 (as last amended by Council Directive No 92/111/EEC of 14 December 1992), and cognate references shall be construed accordingly,][7]

["**contractor**", in relation to contract work, means a person who makes or assembles movable goods;

"**contract work**" means the service of handing over by a contractor to another person of movable goods made or assembled by the contractor from goods entrusted to the contractor by that other person, whether or not the contractor has provided any part of the goods used;][8]

"**the customs-free airport**" means the land which under the Customs-Free Airport Act 1947, for the time being constitutes the Customs-free airport;

"**development**", in relation to any land, means —

    (*a*)   the construction, demolition, extension, alteration or reconstruction of any building on the land, or

    (*b*)   the carrying out of any engineering or other operation in, on, over, or under the land to adapt it for materially altered use,

and "**developed**" shall be construed correspondingly [, and in this definition, "**building**" includes, in relation to a transaction, any prefabricated or like structure in respect of which the following conditions are satisfied:

a 4(3)(*a*)
a 4(3)(*b*)

    (*a*)   the structure—

        (i)   has a rigid roof and one or more rigid walls, and except in the case of a structure used for the cultivation of plants, a floor,

        (ii)   is designed so as to provide for human access to, and free movement in, its interior,

        (iii)   is for a purpose that does not require that it be mobile or portable, and

        (iv)   does not have or contain any aids to mobility or portability,

        and

    (*b*)   (i)   neither the agreement in respect of the transaction nor any other agreement between the parties to that agreement contains a provision relating to the rendering of the structure mobile or portable or the movement or re-location of the structure after its erection, and

(ii) the person for whom the structure is constructed, extended, altered or reconstructed signs and delivers, at the time of the transaction, to the person who constructed, altered or reconstructed the structure a declaration of his intention to retain it in the site on which it is at that time located;][9]

...[10];

["**establishment**"][11] means any fixed place of business, but does not include a place of business of an agent of a person unless the agent has and habitually exercises general authority to negotiate the terms of and makes agreements on behalf of the person or has a stock of goods with which he regularly fulfils on behalf of the person agreements for the supply of goods;

["**excisable products**" means the products referred to in section 104 of the Finance Act, 1992;][12]

"**exempted activity**" means -

(a) a [supply][13] of immovable goods in respect of which pursuant to section 4(6) tax is not chargeable, and

(b) a [supply of any goods or services][14] of a kind specified in the First Schedule or declared by the Minister by order for the time being in force under section 6 to be an exempted activity;

["**exportation of goods**" means the exportation of goods to a destination outside the Community and, where the context so admits, cognate words shall be construed accordingly;][15]

a 25   ["**farmer**" has the meaning assigned to it by section 8;][16]

a 25   ["**flat-rate addition**" has the meaning assigned to it by section 12A;][17]

a 25   ["**flat-rate farmer**" has the meaning assigned to it by section 12A;][18]

["**footwear**" includes shoes, boots, slippers and the like but does not include stockings, under-stockings, socks, ankle-socks or similar articles or footwear without soles or footwear which is or incorporates skating or swimming equipment;][19]

["**free port**" means the land declared to be a free port for the purposes of the Free Port Act, 1986 (No 6 of 1986), by order made under section 2 of that Act;][20]

["**fur skin**" means any skin with the fur, hair or wool attached except skin of woolled sheep or lamb;][21]

"**goods**" means all movable and immovable objects, but does not include things in action or money and references to goods include references to both new and [used][22] goods;

...[23]

"**hire**", in relation to movable goods, includes a letting on any terms including a leasing;

...[24];

"**immovable goods**" means land;

a 7   ["**importation of goods**" means the importation of goods from outside the Community into [the State][25] either —

(a) directly, or

(b) through one or more than one other Member State where value added tax referred to in Council Directive No.77/388/EEC of 17 May 1977 has not been chargeable on the goods in such other Member State or Member States in respect of the transaction concerned, and, where the context so admits, cognate words shall be construed accordingly;][26]

"inspector of taxes" means an inspector of taxes appointed under section 161 of the Income Tax Act, 1967;

[**"intra-Community acquisition of goods"** has the meaning assigned to it by section 3A;][27] a 28a(3)

"livestock" means live cattle, [horses,][28] sheep, [goats, pigs and deer][29];

"local authority" has the meaning assigned to it by section 2(2) of the Local Government Act 1941, and includes a health board established under the Health Act, 1970;

[**"margin scheme"** has the meaning assigned to it by section 10A;][30]

...[31];

"the Minister" means the Minister for Finance;

[**"monthly control statement"** has the meaning assigned to it by section 17;][32]

"movable goods" means goods other than immovable goods;

[**"new means of transport"** means motorised land vehicles with an engine a 28a(2) cylinder capacity exceeding 48 cubic centimetres or a power exceeding 7.2 kilowatts, vessels exceeding 7.5 metres in length and aircraft with a take-off weight exceeding 1,550 kilogrammes—

(*a*) which are intended for the transport of persons or goods, and

(*b*) [(i) which in the case of vessels and aircraft were supplied three months or less after the date of first entry into service and in the case of land vehicles were supplied six months or less after the date of first entry into service, or][33]

(ii) which have travelled [6,000 kilometres][34] or less in the case of land vehicles, sailed for 100 hours or less in the case of vessels or flown for 40 hours or less in the case of aircraft,

other than vessels and aircraft of the kind referred to in paragraph (v) of the Second Schedule;][35]

[**"a person registered for value added tax"** means, in relation to another Member State, a person currently issued with an identification number in that State for the purposes of accounting for value added tax referred to in Council Directive No. 77/388/EEC of 17 May 1977 and, in relation to the State, means a registered person;][36]

"registered person" means a person who is registered in the register maintained under section 9;

"regulations" means regulations under section 32;

...[37];

...[38];

[**"second-hand goods"** has the meaning assigned to it by section 10A;][39]

"secretary" includes such persons as are mentioned in section 207(2) of the Income Tax Act 1967, and section 55(1) of the Finance Act 1920;

"the specified day" means the day appointed by the Minister by order to be the specified day for the purpose of this Act;

[**"supply"**, in relation to goods, has the meaning assigned to it by section 3 and, in a 5,6 relation to services, has the meaning assigned to it by section 5, and cognate words shall be construed accordingly;][40]

"tax" means value added tax chargeable by virtue of this Act;

[**"taxable dealer"**, in relation to supplies of movable goods other than means of transport, has the meaning assigned to it by section 10A and, in relation to supplies of means of transport, has the meaning assigned to it by section 12B;][41]

"taxable goods", in relation to any [supply, intra-Community acquisition or importation][42], means goods the [supply][13] of which is not an exempted activity;

"taxable period" means a period of two months beginning on the first day of January, March, May, July, September or November [provided that the taxable period immediately following that commencing on the 1st day of May, 1973, shall be the period commencing on the 1st day of July, 1973, and ending on the 2nd day of September, 1973, and the next succeeding taxable period shall be the period commencing on the 3rd day of September, 1973, and ending on the 31st day of October, 1973][43];

a 4(3)   [**"taxable person"** has the meaning assigned to it by section 8;][44]

"taxable services" means services the [supply][13] of which is not an exempted [activity;][45]

[**"vessel"**, in relation to transport, means a waterborne craft of any type, whether self-propelled or not, and includes a hovercraft.][46]

[**"works of art"** has the meaning assigned to it by section 10A.][47]

(2) In this Act references to moneys received by a person include references to—

(*a*)   money lodged or credited to the account of the person in any bank, savings bank, building society, hire purchase finance concern or similar financial concern, and

(*b*)   money, other than money referred to in paragraph (*a*), which, under an agreement, other than an agreement providing for discount or a price adjustment made in the ordinary course of business or an arrangement with creditors, has ceased to be due to the person, and

[(*bb*)   money due to the person which, in accordance with the provisions of section 73 of the Finance Act, 1988, is paid to the Revenue Commissioners by another person and has thereby ceased to be due to the person by that other person, and][48]

[(*c*)   money, which, in relation to money received by a person from another person has been deducted in accordance with the provisions of—

(i)   Chapter III of Part I of the Finance Act, 1987, or

(ii)   section 17 of the Finance Act, 1970,

and has thereby ceased to be due to the first-mentioned person by the other person,][49]

and money lodged or credited to the account of a person as aforesaid shall be deemed to have been received by the person on the date of the making of the lodgment or credit and money which has ceased to be due to a person as aforesaid shall be deemed to have been received by the person on the date of the cesser.

a 3   [(2A) In this Act, save where the context otherwise requires, a reference to the territory of a Member State has the same meaning as it has in Article 3 (inserted by Council Directive No. 91/680/EEC of 16 December 1991 of Council Directive No. 77/388/EEC of 17 May 1977, and references to Member States and cognate references shall be construed accordingly.][50]

(3) Any reference in this Act to any other enactment shall, except so far as the context otherwise requires, be construed as a reference to that enactment as amended or extended by any subsequent enactment.

(4) In this Act—

(*a*)   a reference to a section or Schedule is to a section or Schedule of this Act, unless it is indicated that reference to some other enactment is intended, and

(*b*)   a reference to a subsection, paragraph or subparagraph is to the subsection, paragraph or subparagraph of the provision (including a Schedule) in which the reference occurs, unless it is indicated that reference to some other provision is intended.

Amendments

1. Definition of "accountable person" deleted by VATAA 1978 s 2(*a*) with effect from 1 March 1979; prior to its deletion it read: "accountable person" means a person who is accountable in accordance with section 8.
2. Definition of "agricultural produce" inserted by VATAA 1978 s 2(*c*) with effect from 1 March 1979.
3. Definition of "agricultural service" inserted by VATAA 1978 s 2(*c*) with effect from 1 March 1979.
4. Definition of "antiques" inserted by FA 1995 s 119(*a*) with effect from 1 July 1995.
5. Definition of "clothing" inserted by FA 1984 s 85(*a*) with effect from 1 May 1985.
6. Definition of "collectors' items" inserted by FA 1995 s 119(*b*) with effect from 1 July 1995.
7. Definition of "Community" substituted by EC(VAT)R 1992 r 4(*a*) with effect from 1 January 1993; previously: "Community" means European Economic Community (VATAA 1978 s 2(*c*)).
8. Definitions of "contractor" and "contract work" inserted by FA 1996 s 88(*a*) with effect from 1 January 1996.
9. Definition of "development" extended by FA 1981 s 43 with effect from 1 November 1972.
10. Definition of "established" deleted by VATAA 1978 s 2(*a*) with effect from 1 March 1979; prior to its deletion it read: "Established" means having a permanent establishment.
11. Substituted by VATAA 1978 s 2(*b*) with effect from 1 March 1979; previously "permanent establishment".
12. Definition of "excisable products" inserted by EC(VAT)R 1992 r 4(*b*).
13. Substituted by VATAA 1978 s 30(2) and Sch 2 with effect from 1 March 1979; previously "delivery".
14. Substituted by VATAA 1978 s 30(2) and Sch 2 with effect from 1 March 1979; previously "delivery of any goods or a rendering of any services".
15. Definition of "exportation of goods" inserted by FA 1992 s 165(*a*)(i) with effect from 1 January 1993.
16. Definition of "farmer" inserted by VATAA 1978 s 2(*c*) with effect from 1 March 1979.
17. Definition of "flat-rate addition" inserted by VATAA 1978 s 2(*c*) with effect from 1 March 1979.
18. Definition of "flat-rate farmer" inserted by VATAA 1978 s 2(*c*) with effect from 1 March 1979.
19. Definition of "footwear" inserted by FA 1984 s 85(*b*) with effect from 1 May 1984.
20. Definition of "free port" inserted by FA 1986 s 80 with effect from 27 May 1986.
21. Definition of "fur skin" inserted by FA 1976 s 61 and Sch 1 Pt II with effect from 1 March 1976.
22. Substituted by FA 1996 s 88(*b*) with effect from 15 May 1996; previously "second-hand".
23. Definition of "hotel" deleted by FA 1991 s 77 with effect from 1 January 1992; previously it read: "hotel" includes any guest house, holiday hostel, holiday camp, motor hotel, motel, coach hotel, motor inn, motor court, tourist court, caravan park or camping site.
24. Definition of "harbour authority" deleted by FA 1992 s 165(*a*)(ii) with effect from 28 May 1992; previously it read "harbour authority" has the meaning assigned to it by section 2 of the Harbours Act, 1946.
25. Substituted by FA 1996 s 88(*c*) with effect from 15 May 1996; previously " a Member State".
26. Definition of "importation of goods" inserted by FA 1992 s 165(*a*)(iii) with effect from 1 January 1993.
27. Definition of "intra-Community acquisition of goods" inserted by FA 1992 s 165(*a*)(iv) with effect from 1 January 1993.
28. Inserted by FA 1990 s 98 with effect from 30 May 1990.
29. Substituted by FA 1987 s 39(*a*)(i) with effect from 9 July 1987; previously "and pigs" (FA 1973 s 90 and Sch 10 with effect from 3 September 1973); previously "pigs and horses".
30. Definition of "margin scheme" inserted by FA 1995 s 119(*c*) with effect from 1 July 1995.
31. Definition of "manufacturer" deleted by VATAA 1978 s 2(*a*) with effect from 1 March 1979.
32. Definition of "monthly control statement" inserted by FA 1992 s 165(*a*)(v) with effect from 1 November 1992.
33. Subs (*b*)(i) in the definition of "new means of transport" substituted by FA 1994 s 91(*a*) with effect from 1 January 1995.
34. Substituted by FA 1994 s 91(*b*) with effect from 1 January 1995; previously "3,000 kilometres".
35. Definition of "new means of transport" inserted by FA 1992 s 165(*a*)(vi) with effect from 1 January 1993.
36. Definition of "a person registered for value added tax" inserted by FA 1992 s 165(*a*)(vii) with effect from 1 January 1993.
37. Definition of "rendering" deleted by VATAA 1978 s 2(*a*) with effect from 1 March 1979; previously: "rendering", in relation to a service has the meaning assigned to it by section 5.
38. Definition of "residing" deleted by VATAA 1978 s 2(*a*) with effect from 1 March 1979; previously: "residing", in relation to an individual, means resident for the purposes of the Income Tax Acts.
39. Definition of "second-hand goods" substituted by FA 1995 s 119(*d*) with effect from 1 July 1995.
40. Definition of "supply" inserted by VATAA 1978 s 2(*c*) with effect from 1 March 1979.
41. Definition of "taxable dealer" inserted by FA 1995 s 119(*e*) with effect from 1 July 1995.
42. Words "supply, intra-Community acquisition or importation" substituted by FA 1992 s 165(*a*)(viii) with effect from 1 January 1993.
43. Inserted by FA 1973 s 90 and Sch 10 with effect from 3 September 1973.
44. Definition of "taxable person" inserted by VATAA 1978 s 2(*c*) with effect from 1 March 1979.
45. Substituted by FA 1992 s 165(*a*)(ix) with effect from 1 January 1993.
46. Definition of "vessel" inserted by FA 1992 s 165(*a*)(x) with effect from 1 January 1993.
47. Definition of "works of art" inserted by FA 1995 s 119(*f*) with effect from 1 July 1995.
48. Subs (2)(*bb*) inserted by FA 1988 s 60 with effect from 1 October 1988.
49. Subs (2)(*c*) inserted by FA 1987 s 39(*a*) with effect from 6 June 1987.
50. Subs (2A) inserted by FA 1992 s 165(*b*) with effect from 1 January 1993.

Orders

Specified day: 1 November 1972, Value Added Tax (Specified Day) Order 1972 (SI 180/1972).

Definition

"land": IA 1937 Sch; "person": IA 1937 s 11(*c*).

Notes

Subs (2A): OJ L367, 31 December 1991, page 1.

2 Charge of value added tax

a 2
(1) With effect on and from the specified day a tax, to be called value added tax, shall, subject to this Act and regulations, be charged, levied and paid—

a 3
    [(*a*) on the supply of goods and services effected within the State for consideration by a taxable person in the course or furtherance of any business carried on by him, and]¹

    (*b*) on goods imported into the State.

[(1A) Without prejudice to subsection (1), with effect on and from the 1st day of January, 1993, value added tax shall, subject to this Act and regulations, be charged, levied and paid—

a 28a(3)
    (*a*) on the intra-Community acquisition of goods, other than new means of transport, effected within the State for consideration by a taxable person, and

a 28a(2)
    (*b*) on the intra-Community acquisition of new means of transport effected within the State for consideration.]²

(2) ...³

Amendments
1 Subs (1)(*a*) substituted by VATAA 1978 s 3 with effect from 1 March 1979.
2 Subs (1A) inserted by FA 1992 s 166 with effect from 1 January 1993.
3 Subs (2) deleted by VATAA 1978 s 30(1) with effect from 1 March 1979.

Cross-references
Goods in transit, new Member States after 1 January 1994 (subs (1)(*b*)): s 15B(1)(*b*), (5).
Intra-Community acquisition of goods: s 3A.
Margin scheme goods (subs (1)(*a*)): s 10A(3).
Special scheme for auctioneers (subs (1)(*a*)): s 10B(3).
Supply of goods: s 3; supply of services: s 5; imports: s 15.

Orders
Specified day: 1 November 1972: Value Added Tax (Specified Day) Order 1972 (SI 180/1972).

Narrative
Irish Value Added Tax: Chapter 3; *Guide to Value Added Tax (Revenue Commissioners)*: Chapter 1.

Definition
"business": s 1(1); "Community": s 1(1); "goods": s 1(1); "intra-Community acquisition of goods": ss 1(1), 3A; "new means of transport": s 1(1);"person": IA 1937 s 11(*c*); "regulations": s 1(1), 32; "the specified day": s 1(1); "supply": s 1(1); "tax": s 1(1); "taxable person": s 1(1), 8.

Personal notes

3 [Supply] of goods

(1) [In this Act **"supply"**, in relation to goods, means—][1]   a 5

 (*a*) the transfer of ownership of the goods by agreement [other than the   a 5(1)
transfer of ownership of the goods to a person supplying financial
services of the kind specified in subparagraph (i)(*e*) of the First
Schedule, where those services are supplied as part of an agreement of
the kind referred to in paragraph (*b*) in respect of those goods][2],

 [(*aa*) the sale of movable goods pursuant to a contract under which
commission is payable on purchase or sale by an agent or auctioneer
who concludes agreements in such agent's or auctioneer's own name
but on the instructions of, and for the account of, another person,][3]

 (*b*) the handing over of the goods to a person pursuant to an agreement   a 5(4)(*b*)
which provides for the renting of the goods for a certain period subject
to a condition that ownership of the goods shall be transferred to the
person on a date not later than the date of payment of the final sum
under the agreement,

 [(*c*) the handing over by a person (in this paragraph referred to as the
developer) to another person of immovable goods which have been
developed from goods entrusted to the developer by that other person
for the purpose of such development, whether or not the developer has
supplied any part of the goods used,][4]

 (*d*) the transfer of ownership of the goods pursuant to—   a 5(4)(*a*)

  (i) their acquisition, otherwise than by agreement, by or on behalf
of the State or a local authority, or

  (ii) their seizure by any person acting under statutory authority,

 [(*e*) the application (otherwise than by way of disposal to another person)   a 5(7)
by a person for the purposes of any business carried on by him of the
goods, being goods which were developed, constructed, assembled,
manufactured, produced, extracted, purchased[, imported or otherwise
acquired][5] by him or by another person on his behalf, except where tax
chargeable in relation to the application would, if it were charged, be
wholly deductible under section 12 ...,[6]

 (*f*) the appropriation by a taxable person for any purpose other than the   a 5(6)
purpose of his business or the disposal free of charge of the goods
where tax chargeable in relation to the goods—

  [(i) upon their purchase, intra-Community acquisition or
importation by the taxable person, or][7]

  (ii) upon their development, construction, assembly, manufacture,
production, extraction ...[8] or application under paragraph (*e*),

 as the case may be, was wholly or partly deductible under section 12,][9]
[and][10]

 [(*g*) the transfer by a person of goods from his business in the State to the   a 28a(5)(*b*)
territory of another Member State for the purposes of his business, [or
a transfer of a new means of transport by a person in the State to the
territory of another Member State,][11] other than for the purposes of any
of the following:

  (i) the transfer of the goods in question under the circumstances
specified in paragraph (*b*)[, (*cc*)][12] or (*d*) of subsection (6),

  (ii) the transfer of the goods referred to in paragraphs (i), (v), (*va*) [,
(*vb*))][13] and (x) of the Second Schedule,

  ...[14]

       [(iii*a*)   the transfer of goods for the purpose of having a service carried out on them:

               Provided that the goods which were so transferred by the person are, after being worked upon, returned to that person in the State,][15]

     (iv)   the temporary use of the goods in question in the supply of a service by him in that other Member State,

     (v)   the temporary use of the goods in question, for a period not exceeding 24 months, in that other Member State, where the importation into that other Member State of the same goods with a view to their temporary use would be eligible for full exemption from import duties.][16]

a 5(7)   [1A) Anything which is a supply of goods by virtue of paragraph [(*e*), (*f*) or (*g*)][17] of subsection (1) shall be deemed, for the purposes of this Act, to have been effected for consideration in the course or furtherance of the business concerned:

Provided however, that the following shall not be deemed to have been effected for consideration, that is to say:

a 5(6)   (*a*)   a gift of goods made in the course or furtherance of the business (otherwise than as one forming part of a series or succession of gifts made to the same person) the cost of which to the donor does not exceed a sum specified for that purpose in regulations,

     (*b*)   the gift, in reasonable quantity, to the actual or potential customer, of industrial samples in a form not ordinarily available for sale to the public.][18]

a 5(2)   [(1B) The provision of electricity, gas and any form of power, heat, refrigeration or ventilation shall be deemed, for the purposes of this Act, to be a supply of goods and not a supply of services.][19]

(2) If three or more persons enter into agreements concerning the same goods and fulfil those agreements by a direct [supply][20] of the goods by the first person in the chain of sellers and buyers to the last buyer, then the [supply][20] to such last buyer shall be deemed, for the purposes of this Act, to constitute a simultaneous [supply][20] by each seller in the chain.

    ...[21]

a 5(4)(*c*)   [(4) Where an agent or auctioneer makes a sale of goods in accordance with paragraph (*aa*) of subsection (1) the transfer of those goods to that agent or auctioneer shall be deemed to be a supply of goods to the agent or auctioneer at the time that that agent or auctioneer makes that sale.][22]

    (5)   (*a*)   The transfer of ownership of goods pursuant to a contract of the kind referred to in subsection (1)(*b*) shall be deemed, for the purposes of this Act, not to be a [supply][20] of the goods.

     (*b*)   The transfer of ownership of goods—

       (i)   as security for a loan or debt, or

       (ii)   where the goods are held as security for a loan or debt, upon repayment of the loan or debt, or

a 5(8)   (iii)   in connection with the transfer of a business or part thereof to another [taxable][23] person,

        shall be deemed, for purposes of this Act, not to be a [supply][18] of the goods ...[24].

[(6) The place where goods are supplied shall be deemed, for the purposes of this Act, to be—

    (*a*)   in the case of goods dispatched or transported and to which paragraph (*d*) does not apply, the place where the dispatch or transportation to the person to whom they are supplied begins,   a 8(1), a 28bB(*a*)

        [Provided that where the goods are dispatched or transported from a place outside the Community, the place of supply by the person who imports the goods and the place of any subsequent supplies shall be deemed to be where the goods are imported,][25]

    (*b*)   in the case of goods which are installed or assembled, with or without a trial run, by or on behalf of the supplier, the place where the goods are installed or assembled,

    (*c*)   in the case of goods not dispatched or transported, the place where the goods are located at the time of supply,

  [(*cc*)   in the case of goods supplied on board vessels, aircraft or trains during transport, the places of departure and destination of which are within the Community, the place where the transport began,][26]   a 8

    (*d*)   notwithstanding paragraph (*a*) or (*b*), in the case of goods, other than new means of transport, dispatched or transported by or on behalf of the supplier-

        (i)   (I)   from the territory of another Member State, or

              (II)   from outside the Community through the territory of another Member State into which the said goods have been imported,

             to a person who is not a taxable person in the State, or

        (ii)   from ...[27] the State to a person in another Member State who is not registered for value added tax,

        the place where the goods are when the dispatch or transportation ends: a 28bB(1)

        [Provided that this paragraph shall not apply to the supply of goods, other than goods subject to a duty of excise, where the total consideration for such supplies does not exceed or is not likely to exceed—

        (A)   in the case of goods to which subparagraph (i) relates, £27,000 in a calendar year, unless the supplier, in accordance with regulations elects that it shall apply, and

        (B)   in the case of goods to which subparagraph (ii) relates, the amount specified in the Member State in question in accordance with Article 28b.B(2) (inserted by Council Directive No 91/680/EEC of 16 December 1991) of Council Directive No 77/388/EEC of 17 May 1977 unless the supplier elects that it shall apply and registers and accounts for value added tax in that Member State in respect of such supplies.][28]][29]   a 28bB(2)

[(7)   (i)   Where, in the case of a business carried on, or that has ceased to be carried on, by a taxable person, goods forming part of the assets of the business are, under any power exercisable by another person, including a liquidator and a receiver, disposed of by the other person in or towards the satisfaction of a debt owed by the taxable person, or in the course of the winding up of a company, they shall be deemed to be supplied by the taxable person in the course or furtherance of his business.   a 5(7)(c)

> (ii)   A disposal of goods under this subsection shall include any disposal which is deemed to be a supply of immovable goods under section 4(2).][30]

a 28bA(2)   [(8) Where a taxable person who is not established in the State makes an intra-Community acquisition of goods in the State and makes a subsequent supply of those goods to a taxable person in the State, the person to whom the supply is made shall be deemed for the purposes of this Act to have made that supply and the intra-Community acquisition shall be disregarded:

Provided that this provision shall only apply where—

> (a)   the taxable person who is not established in the State has not exercised his option to register in accordance with section 9 by virtue of section 8(3D), and

> (b)   the person to whom the supply is made is registered in accordance with section 9.][29]

Amendment

1   Substituted by VATAA 1978 s 4(a) with effect from 1 March 1979; previously "In this Act, "delivery", in relation to goods, shall, subject to subsection (1A) include—".
2   Inserted by FA 1995 s 120(a) with effect from 2 June 1995.
3   Subs (1)(aa) substituted by FA 1996 s 89(a)(i) with effect from 15 May 1996.
4   Subs (1)(c) substituted by FA 1996 s 89(a)(ii) with effect from 1 January 1996.
5   Substituted by FA 1992 s 167 previously "or imported".
6   Deleted by FA 1992 s 167(a)(i)(II) with effect from 1 January 1993; previously "and".
7   Subs (1)(f)(i) substituted by FA 1992 s 167(a)(ii)(I) with effect from 1 January 1993.
8   Deleted by FA 1992 s 167(a)(ii)(II); previously ", importation".
9   Subs (1)(e)-(f) substituted by VATAA 1978 s 4(a) with effect from 1 March 1979; subs (1)(e) previously substituted by FA 1976 s 51.
10   Inserted by FA 1992 s 167(a)(ii)(III) with effect from 1 January 1993.
11   Inserted by FA 1993 s 82.
12   Inserted by EC(VAT)R 1992 r 5(a)(i) with effect from 1 January 1993 (SI 413 of 1992).
13   Inserted by FA 1994 s 92 with effect from 23 May 1994.
14   Subs (1)(g)(iii) deleted by FA 1996 s 89(a)(iii)(I) with effect from 1 January 1996.
15   Subs (1)(g)(iiia) substituted by FA 1996 s 89(a)(iii)(II) with effect from 1 January 1996.
16   Subs (1)(g) inserted by FA 1992 s 167(a)(iii).
17   Substituted by FA 1992 s 167(b) with effect from 1 January 1993; previously "(e) or (f)".
18   Subs (1A) inserted by FA 1973 s 78 with effect from 3 September 1973.
19   Subs (1B) inserted by VATAA 1978 s 4 with effect from March 1 1979.
20   Substituted by VATAA 1978 s 30(2); previously "delivery".
21   Subs (3) deleted by FA 1996 s 89(b) with effect from 15 May 1996.
22   Subs (4) substituted by FA 1996 s 89(c) with effect from 15 May 1996.
23   Substituted by VATAA 1978 s 30(2); previously "accountable".
24   Words " unless the goods are goods of a kind specified in the Fourth Schedule and the supply of the goods is one in relation to which tax at either of the rates for the time being specified in section 11(1)(c) is chargeable" deleted by VATAA 1978 s 30(1) and Sch 1 with effect from 1 March 1979.
25   Subs (6)(a)(proviso) inserted by EC(VAT)R 1992 r 5(b)(i) with effect from 1 January 1993.
26   Subs (6)(cc) inserted by EC(VAT)R 1992 r 5(b)(ii) with effect from 1 January 1993.
27   Deleted by EC(VAT)R 1992 r 5(b)(iii)(I) with effect from 1 January 1993; previously "a taxable person".
28   Subs (6)(d)(proviso) substituted by EC(VAT)R 1992 r 5(b)(iii)(II) with effect from 1 January 1993.
29   Subs (6) substituted by FA 1992 s 167(c) with effect from 1 January 1993.
30   Subs (7) inserted by FA 1983 s 78.
31   Subs (8) inserted by EC(VAT)R 1992 r 5(c) with effect from 1 January 1993.

Cross-references

Auctioneers, special scheme (subs (6)(d)): s 10B(8).
Boats, caravans, vehicles etc, short term hire of (subs (1)(b)): Sch 6 para (xv).
Business gifts under £15 exempt: VATR 1979 r 31.
Hire purchase transactions (subs (1)(b)), obligation of supplier to issue invoice to finance provider: s 17(1)(proviso).
Exporters, zero rating of supplies to (subs (3)(1)(e), (f)): Sch 2 para (via).
Margin scheme goods (subs (6)(d)): s 10A(11).
Option not to apply (subs (6)(d)(proviso)), Revenue may prescribe circumstances: s 32(1)(ii).
Supplier of goods also supplying financial services (subs (1)(b); Sch 1 para (i)(e)), taxable amount: s 10(4C).
Taxable dealers supplying means of transport, special scheme (subs (6)(d)): s 12B(6).

Statement of practice

Business gifts: SP VAT 3/94.

Narrative

Irish Value Added Tax, Chapters 3, 4; *Guide to Value Added Tax (Revenue Commissioners)*: Chapter 3.

Definition

"business": s 1(1); "Community"; s 1(1); "development": s 1(1); "developed": s 1(1); "goods": s 1(1); "livestock": s 1(1); "local authority": s 1(1); "intra-Community acquisition of goods": s 1(1), 3A; "new means of transport": s 1(1);"person": IA 1937 s 11(c); "regulations": s 1(1), 32; "supply": s 1(1); "tax": s 1(1);"taxable person": s 1(1), 8.

3A Intra-Community acquisition of goods

[(1) In this Act **"intra-Community acquisition of goods"** means the acquisition   a 28a(3)
of—

  (*a*)   movable goods, other than new means of transport, supplied by a   a 28cA
          person registered for value added tax in a Member State [, or by a
          person who carries on an exempted activity in a Member State,]¹ [or
          by a flat-rate farmer in a Member State,]² to a person in another
          Member State (other than an individual who is not a taxable person or
          who is not entitled to elect to be a taxable person[, unless the said
          individual carries on an exempted activity]³⁾ and which have been
          dispatched or transported from the territory of a Member State to the
          territory of another Member State as a result of such supply, or

  [(*b*) new means of transport supplied by a person in a Member State to a   a 28b(2)
          person in another Member State and which has been dispatched or
          transported from the territory of a Member State to the territory of
          another Member State as a result of being so supplied.]⁴

[(1A) An intra-Community acquisition of goods shall be deemed not to occur
where the supply of those goods is subject to value-added tax referred to in
Council Directive No. 77/388/EEC of 17 May 1977 in the Member State of
dispatch under the provisions implementing Article 26a or 28o (inserted by
Council Directive No. 94/5/EC of 14 February 1994) of that Directive in that
Member State.]⁵

(2) (*a*)   The place where an intra-Community acquisition of goods occurs shall   a 28a(1)
             be deemed to be the place where the goods are when the dispatch or
             transportation ends.

     (*b*)   Without prejudice to paragraph (*a*), when the person acquiring the   a 28b(2)
             goods quotes his value added tax registration number for the purpose
             of the acquisition, the place where an intra-Community acquisition of
             goods occurs shall be deemed to be within the territory of the Member
             State which issued that registration number [, unless the person
             acquiring the goods can establish that that acquisition has been subject
             to value added tax referred to in Council Directive No 77/388/EEC of
             17 May 1977 in accordance with paragraph (*a*)]⁶·

(3) For the purposes of this section—

  (*a*)   a supply in the territory of another Member State shall be deemed to   a 28a(7)
          have arisen where, under similar circumstances, a supply would have
          arisen in the State under section 3, and

  [(*aa*) an activity in another Member State shall be deemed to be an
          exempted activity where the same activity, if carried out in the State,
          would be an exempted activity, and

  (*ab*) a person shall be deemed to be a flat-rate farmer in another Member
          State where, under similar circumstances, the person would be a flat-
          rate farmer in the State in accordance with section 12A, and]⁷

  (*b*)   a person shall be deemed to be a taxable person or a person who is
          entitled to elect to be a taxable person in another Member State where,
          under similar circumstances, the person would be a taxable person or
          entitled to elect to be a taxable person in the State in accordance with
          section 8.

(4) Where goods are dispatched or transported from outside the Community to a   a 28a(3)
person in the State who is not registered for tax and who is not an individual, and
value added tax referred to in Council Directive No. 77/388/EEC of 17 May 1977
is chargeable on the importation of the said goods into another Member State then,
for the purposes of subsection (1), the person shall be deemed to be registered for

value added tax in that other Member State and the goods shall be deemed to have been dispatched or transported from that other Member State.][8]

[(5) Paragraph (*b*) of subsection (2) shall not apply where —

  (i) a person quotes the registration number assigned to him in accordance with section 9 for the purpose of making an intra-Community acquisition and the goods are dispatched or transported from the territory of a Member State directly to the territory of another Member State, neither of which are the State,

  (ii) the person makes a subsequent supply of the goods to a person registered for value added tax in the Member State where the dispatch or transportation ends,

  (iii) the person issues an invoice in relation to that supply in such form and containing such particulars as would be required in accordance with section 17(1) if he made the supply of the goods in the State to a person registered for value added tax in another Member State, and containing an explicit reference to the EC simplified triangulation arrangements and indicating that the person in receipt of that supply is liable to account for the value added tax due in that Member State, and

  (iv) in accordance with regulations, the person includes a reference to the supply in the statement referred to in section 19A as if it were an intra-Community supply for the purposes of that section.][9]

Amendments

1 Inserted by FA 1993 s 83(*a*).
2 Inserted by EC(VAT)R 1992 r 6(*a*)(i) with effect from 1 January 1993.
3 Inserted by EC(VAT)R 1992 r 6(*a*)(ii) with effect from 1 January 1993.
4 Subs (1)(*b*) substituted by FA 1993 s 83(*b*).
5 Subs (1A) inserted by FA 1995 s 121 with effect from 1 July 1995.
6 Inserted by EC(VAT)R 1992 r 6(*b*) with effect from 1 January 1993.
7 Subs (3)(*aa*)-(*ab*) inserted by EC(VAT)R 1992 r 6(*c*) with effect from 1 January 1993.
8 Section 3A inserted by FA 1992 s 168 with effect from 1 January 1993.
9 Subs (5) inserted by EC(VAT)R 1992 r 6(*d*) with effect from 1 January 1993.

Narrative

Guide to Value Added Tax (Revenue Commissioners): Chapter 11.

Statement of practice

EU imports by Government departments, local authorities, etc: SP VAT 11/92.

Definition

"Community": s 1(1); "exempted activity": s 1(1); "flat rate farmer": s 1(1), 12A; "goods": s 1(1); "new means of transport": s 1(1); "person": IA 1937 s 11(*c*); "a person registered for value added tax": s 1(1); "taxable person": s 1(1), 8.

Personal notes

3B Alcohol products

[(1) Where alcohol products are supplied while being held under a duty-suspension arrangement then any such supply effected while the products are held under that arrangement, other than the last such supply in the State, shall be deemed not to be a supply for the purposes of this Act other than for the purposes of section 12 and any previous—

    (*a*)   intra-Community acquisition, or

    (*b*)   importation,

of such products shall be disregarded for the purposes of this Act.

(2) Where tax is chargeable on a supply referred to in subsection (1) then, notwithstanding section 19(1), the tax on that supply shall be due at the same time as the duty of excise on the products is due:

Provided that this subsection shall not apply to a supply of the kind referred to in subparagraph (*a*)(I), (*b*) or (*cc*) of paragraph (i) or in paragraph (i*a*) of the Second Schedule.

(3) Where, other than in the circumstances set out in section 8(2B)(*b*), a taxable person makes an intra-Community acquisition of alcohol products and by virtue of such acquisition, and in accordance with Chapter II of Part II of the Finance Act, 1992, and any other enactment which is to be construed together with that Chapter, the duty of excise on those products is payable in the State, then, notwithstanding section 19(1A), the tax on the said intra-Community acquisition shall be due at the same time as the duty of excise on the products is due.

(4) Where tax is chargeable on the importation of alcohol products, which are then placed under a duty-suspension arrangement then, notwithstanding section 15(6), the tax on that importation shall be due at the same time as the duty of excise on the products is due.

(5) Notwithstanding subsections (1) and (1A) of section 10 and section 15(3), where the provisions of subsection (2), (3) or (4) apply, the amount on which tax is chargeable shall include the amount of the duty of excise chargeable on the products on their release for consumption in the State.

(6) Notwithstanding any other provision to the contrary contained in this Act, where the provisions of subsection (2), (3) or (4) apply then—

    (*a*)   the tax shall be payable at the same time as the duty of excise is payable on the products,

    (*b*)   the provisions of the statutes which relate to the duties of excise and the management thereof and of any instrument relating to duties of excise made under statute, shall, with any necessary modifications and exceptions as may be specified in regulations, apply to such tax as if it were a duty of excise, and

    (*c*)   the person by whom the tax is payable shall complete such form as is provided for the purposes of this subsection by the Revenue Commissioners.

(7) In this section—

"alcohol products" means the excisable products referred to at subsections (*a*), (*b*), (*c*), (*d*) and (*e*) of section 104 of the Finance Act, 1992;

"duty-suspension arrangement" has the meaning assigned to it by section 103 of the Finance Act, 1992.][1]

Amendment
1   Section 3B inserted by FA 1993 s 84 with effect from 1 August 1993.
Cross-references
Deductible tax: s 12(1)(*a*)(iic).
Narrative
Guide to Value Added Tax (Revenue Commissioners): Chapter 6.3.

Statement of practice
Payment of VAT on alcohol products at time of payment of excise duty: SP VAT 3/93
Definitions
"excisable products": s 1(1); "intra-Community acquisition of goods": s 1(1), 3A; "person": IA 1937 s 11(*c*); "regulations": s 1(1), 32; "statute": IA 1937 s 3; "supply": s 1(1); "tax": s 1(1); "taxable person": s 1(1).

Personal notes

4 Special provisions in relation to the [supply] of immovable goods

(1) (*a*) This section applies to immovable goods—

> (i) which have been developed by or on behalf of the person [supplying]¹ them, or a 4, 5(3)

> (ii) in respect of which the person [supplying]¹ them was, or would, but for the operation of section 3(5)(*b*)(iii), have been at any time entitled to claim a deduction under section 12 for any tax borne or paid in relation to a [supply]² or development of them. a 5(5)(*b*)

(*b*) In this section **"interest"**, in relation to immovable goods, means an estate or interest therein which, when it was created, was for a period of at least ten years but does not include a mortgage, and a reference to the disposal of an interest includes a reference to the creation of an interest.

(2) Subject to ...³· paragraphs (*c*), (*d*), (*e*) and (*f*) of section 3(1), section 19(2) and subsections (3), (4) and (5), a [supply]² of immovable goods shall be deemed, for the purposes of this Act, to take place if, but only if, a person having an interest in immovable goods to which this section applies disposes, as regards the whole or any part of those goods, of that interest or of an interest which derives therefrom.

(3) (*a*) Subject to paragraph (*b*), where a person having an interest in immovable goods to which this section applies surrenders possession of those goods or of any part thereof in such circumstances that the surrender does not constitute a [supply]² of the goods for the purposes of subsection (2), the surrender shall be deemed, for the purposes of section 3(1)(*f*), to be an appropriation of the goods or of the part thereof, as the case may be, for a purpose other than the purpose of his business.

(*b*) This subsection shall not apply to—

> (i) any such surrender of possession made in accordance with an agreement for the leasing or letting of the goods if the person surrendering possession is chargeable to tax in respect of the rent or other payment under the agreement, or

> (ii) a surrender in connection with a transfer which, in accordance with section 3(5), is declared, for the purposes of this Act, not to be a [supply]²·

(4) Where a person having an interest in immovable goods to which this section applies disposes, as regards the whole or any part of those goods, of an interest which derives from that interest in such circumstances that he retains the reversion on the interest disposed of, he shall, in relation to the reversion so retained, be deemed, for the purposes of section 3(1)(*f*), to have made an appropriation of the goods or of the part thereof, as the case may be, for a purpose other than the purpose of his business.

[(5) Where a person disposes of an interest in immovable goods to another person and in connection with that disposal a taxable person enters into an agreement with that other person or person connected with that other person to carry out a development in relation to those immovable goods, then—

(*a*) the person who disposes of the interest in the said immovable goods shall, in relation to that disposal, be deemed to be a taxable person,

(*b*) the disposal of the interest in the said immovable goods shall be deemed to be a supply of those goods made in the course or furtherance of business, and

(*c*) the disposal of the interest in the said immovable goods shall, notwithstanding subsection (1), be deemed to be a disposal of an interest in immovable goods to which this section applies.]⁴

(6) Notwithstanding anything in this section or in section 2 tax shall not be charged on the [supply]² of immovable goods—

    (*a*) in relation to which a right in favour of the person making the [supply]² to a deduction under section 12 in respect of any tax borne or paid on the [supply]² or development of the goods did not arise and would not, apart from section 3(5)(*b*)(iii), have arisen, or

    (*b*) which had been occupied before the specified day and had not been developed between that date and the date of the [supply]²·[other than a supply of immovable goods to which the provisions of subsection (5) apply]⁵.

(7) The provisions of section 8(3) shall not apply in relation to a person who makes a [supply]² of goods to which this section applies.

Amendments

1 Substituted by VATAA 1978 s 30(2) with effect from 1 March 1979; previously "delivering".
2 Substituted by VATAA 1978 s 30(2) with effect from 1 March 1979; previously "delivery".
3 Deleted by VATAA 1978 s 30(1) with effect from 1 March 1979; previously "section 2(2)".
4 Subs (5) substituted by FA 1995 s 122(*a*) with effect from 1 July 1995.
5 Inserted by FA 1995 s 122(*b*) with effect from 2 June 1995.

Cross-references

Tax (subss (1)(*a*)(ii) and (6)(*a*)) charged at 0% (s 11(1)(*b*)) by virtue of Sch 2 para (v*i*a) is deemed to be deductible under s 12: s 13A(7).

Valuation of interests in immovable goods, Revenue may make regulations: s 32(1)(*t*); regulations: VATR 1979 r 19.

Case law

Property unit trust, deductibility of pre and post lease expenditure: *Erin Executor and Trustee Company Ltd v Revenue Commissioners*, [1994] ITR 179.

Narrative

Irish Value Added Tax, Chapters 3, 4, 6.

Definition

"business": s 1(1); "development": s 1(1); "developed": s 1(1); "goods": s 1(1); "immovable goods": s 1(1); "person": IA 1937 s 11(*c*); "a person registered for value added tax": s 1(1); "regulations": s 1(1), 32; "the specified day": s 1(1); "supply": s 1(1); "tax": s 1(1); "taxable person": s 1(1), 8.

Personal notes

4A Person liable to pay tax in relation to certain supplies of immovable goods

[(1) Subject to the provisions of subsection (3), where tax is chargeable in respect of the letting of immovable goods which is deemed to be a supply of goods in accordance with section 4 and the lessee would, but for the operation of this section, have been entitled to claim a deduction under section 12(1)(*a*)(i) for all the said tax borne in relation to that supply, the lessor shall not be liable to pay the said tax and, in that case, the lessee shall be liable to pay the said tax as if the lessee had supplied the goods in the course or furtherance of business.

(2) Where, in relation to a supply, the lessor and the lessee wish the provisions of subsection (1) to apply they shall–

(*a*) complete such application form as may be provided by the Revenue Commissioners for that purpose,

(*b*) certify the particulars shown on such form to be correct, and

(*c*) submit to the Revenue Commissioners the completed and certified application form, together with such further information in support of the application as may be requested by the said Commissioners.

(3) Where, in relation to a supply of goods referred to in subsection (1), the lessor and lessee have furnished the particulars referred to in subsection (2), the Revenue Commissioners shall, where they are satisfied that it is in order to apply the provisions in subsection (1) in relation to that supply, notify the lessor and the lessee by notice in writing that the provisions of subsection (1) are to be applied in relation to that supply.

(4) Where the provisions of subsection (1) apply in relation to a supply, the invoice issued by the lessor in accordance with section 17 shall show the following endorsement in lieu of the amount of tax chargeable:

"In accordance with section 4A of the Value-Added Tax Act, 1972, the lessee is liable for the value-added tax of £X.',

and, in that endorsement, the lessor shall substitute the amount of tax chargeable in respect of that supply of goods for '£X'.

(5) Every notification received by a taxable person, which has been issued to that person by the Revenue Commissioners in accordance with subsection (3), shall be part of the records which that person is required to keep in accordance with section 16.

(6) For the purposes of this section, and subject to the direction and control of the Revenue Commissioners, any power, function or duty conferred or imposed on them may be exercised or performed on their behalf by an officer of the Revenue Commissioners.

(7) In this section–

"lessee" means the person who receives the goods referred to in subsection (1);

"lessor" means the person who supplies the goods referred to in subsection (1).][1]

Amendments

1 Section 4A inserted by FA 1994 s 93 with effect from 7 July 1995 (the date appointed by the Minister for Finance - Finance Act, 1994 (Commencement of Sections 93 and 96(*a*)) Order 1995, SI 184/1995).

Definitions

"business": s 1(1); "immovable goods": s 1(1); "supply": s 1(1); "tax": s 1(1); "taxable person": s 1(1).

Personal notes

---

a 6

5 [Supply] of services

a 6(1)

[(1) In this Act **"supply"**, in relation to a service, means the performance or omission of any act or the toleration of any situation other than the supply of goods and other than a transaction specified in section 3(5).

(2) The provision of food and drink, of a kind specified in paragraph (xii) of the Second Schedule, in a form suitable for human consumption without further preparation—

     (*a*)   by means of a vending machine,

     (*b*)   in the course of operating a hotel, restaurant, cafe, refreshment house, canteen, establishment licensed for the sale for consumption on the premises of intoxicating liquor, catering business or similar business, or

     (*c*)   in the course of operating any other business in connection with the carrying on of which facilities are provided for the consumption of the food or drink supplied,

shall be deemed, for the purposes of this Act, to be a supply of services and not a supply of goods.

(3) Any of the following shall, if so provided by regulations, and in accordance therewith, be deemed, for the purposes of this Act, to be a supply of services by a person for consideration in the course or furtherance of his business—

a 6(2)

     (*a*)   the use of goods forming part of the assets of his business for purposes other than those of his business,

     (*b*)   the supply by him of services for his own private or personal use and the supply by him of services free of charge for the private or personal use of his staff or for any purposes other than those of his business,

     (*c*)   the supply of services for his own private or personal use or that of his staff, for the supply of which he provides materials or facilities or towards the cost of which he contributes in whole or in part,

a 6(3)

     (*d*)   the supply by him of services, other than those referred to in preceding paragraphs of this subsection, for the purposes of his business except where tax on such services, if it were chargeable, would be wholly deductible under section 12.

[(3A) Where a person is in receipt of a service, other than a service [specified in paragraphs (*f*) and (*g*) of subsection (6) or in the Fourth Schedule][1,] for the purposes of his business and the circumstances are such that value added tax referred to in Community Council Directive No.77/388/EEC is not payable on the supply or, if it is payable, is, in accordance with the laws of the country in which the supplier has his establishment, repayable to or deductible by the person, that person shall be deemed, for the purposes of this Act, to have himself supplied the service for consideration in the course or furtherance of his business and shall be liable for tax on the supply except where such tax, if it were chargeable, would be wholly deductible under section 12.][2]

a 6(4)

(4) The supply of services through a person (in this subsection referred to as the agent) who, while purporting to act on his own behalf, concludes agreements in his own name but on the instructions of and for the account of another person, shall be deemed for the purposes of this Act, to constitute a supply of the services to and simultaneously by the agent.

[(4A) Where services are supplied by a person and the person is not legally entitled to recover consideration in respect of or in relation to such supply but moneys are received in respect of or in relation to such supply, the services in question shall be deemed, for the purposes of this Act, to have been supplied for consideration and the moneys received shall be deemed to be consideration that the person who supplied the services in question became entitled to receive in respect of or in relation to the supply of those services.][3]

[(4B) Where a person is indemnified under a policy of insurance in respect of any amount payable in respect of services of a barrister or solicitor, those services shall be deemed, for the purposes of this Act, to be supplied to, and received by, the said person.]⁴

(5) Subject to subsection (6) and (7), the place where a service is supplied shall be deemed, for the purposes of this Act, to be the place where the person supplying the service [has established his business or]⁵ has his establishment or (if more than one) the establishment of his which is most concerned with the supply or (if he has no establishment) his usual place of residence.

a 9,
28b,c-e

(6) (*a*) The place of supply of services connected with immovable goods, including the services of estate agents, architects and firms providing on-site supervision in relation to such goods, shall be deemed, for the purposes of this Act, to be the place where the goods are situated. — a 9(2)(*a*)

[(*b*) Transport services, with the exception of intra-Community transport of goods, shall be deemed, for the purposes of this Act, to be supplied where the transport takes place.]⁶ — a 9(2)(*b*)

(*c*) The following services shall be deemed, for the purposes of this Act, to be supplied where they are physically performed: — a 9(2)(*c*)

   (i) cultural, artistic, sporting, scientific, educational, entertainment or similar services,

   [(ii) ancillary transport activities such as loading, unloading and handling, with the exception of activities ancillary to the intra-Community transport of goods received by a person registered for value added tax in any Member State,]⁷ — a 28bD

   (iii) valuation of movable goods, [except where the provisions of subparagraph (iv) of paragraph (*f*), apply]⁸ ,

   (iv) work on movable goods [including contract work, except where the provisions of subparagraph (iv) of paragraph (*f*) apply]⁹.

[(*d*) In confirmation of the provisions contained in the Value Added Tax (Place of Supply of Certain Services) Regulations, 1985 (SI No 343 of 1985), which regulations are hereby revoked, the place of supply of services consisting of the hiring out of movable goods by a person established outside the Community shall be deemed to be the place where the movable goods are, or are to be, effectively used.]¹⁰

[(*e*) The place of supply of services of any of the descriptions specified in the Fourth Schedule, (with the exception of services of the description specified in paragraph (*ia*) of the said Schedule supplied by a person who has his establishment outside the Community,) shall be deemed, for the purposes of this Act to be— — a 9(2)(*e*)

   (i) in case they are received, otherwise than for a business purpose, by a person whose usual place of residence is situated outside the Community, the place where he usually resides,

   (ii) in case they are received, for the purposes of any business carried on by him, by a person—

      (I) who has his establishment outside the Community and has not also an establishment in the Community, or

      (II) who has his establishment in the Community but does not have his establishment or, if he has more than one establishment, his principal establishment in the country in which, but for this subparagraph, the services would be deemed to be supplied, [or]¹¹

      [(III) who has an establishment in the State and his principal establishment in the country in which, but for this subparagraph, the services would be deemed to be supplied,]¹² the place where he has his establishment or, if he has more than one establishment, the establishment of his at which or for the purposes of which the services are most directly used or to be used, as the case may be,

(iii)   in case they are received, for the purposes of any business carried on by him, by a person resident in the Community who has no establishment anywhere, the place where he usually resides,

(iv)   in case they are received by a department of State, by a local authority or by a body established by statute, and are supplied—

   (I)   by a person who has his establishment outside the Community and has not also an establishment in the Community, or

   (II)   by a person who has his establishment in another Member State of the Community, in circumstances in which value added tax referred to in Community Council Directive No.77/388/EEC is not payable in that Member State in respect of the supply,

   the State,

(v)   in any other case, the place specified in subsection (5) that is appropriate to the circumstances.][13]

[(*f*)   The place of supply of the following services received by a person registered for value added tax in a Member State shall be deemed, for the purposes of this Act, to be within the territory of the Member State that so registered the person for value added tax, that is to say:

a 28bC(3)   (i)   the intra-Community transport of goods,

a 28bD   (ii)   activities ancillary to the intra-Community transport of goods such as loading, unloading and handling,

a 28bE(1)   (iii)   services of an agent acting in the name and on behalf of another person in the arrangement of services other than those specified in paragraph (vii) of the Fourth Schedule.

[(iv)   valuation of or work on movable goods, including contract work, in cases where the goods are dispatched or transported out of the Member State where the valuation or work was physically carried out.][14]

(*g*)   The place of supply of the following services supplied to persons other than those specified in paragraph (*f*) shall be deemed for the purposes of this Act to be—

(i)   the place of departure in the case of—

a 28bC(2)   (I)   the intra-Community transport of goods,

a 28bE(1)   (II)   services of an agent acting in the name and on behalf of another person in the arrangement of intra-Community transport of goods, and

a 28bE(2)   (ii)   the place where they are physically performed in the case of services of an agent acting in the name and on behalf of another person in the arrangement of services other than those specified in subparagraph (i)(II) of this paragraph and paragraph (vii) of the Fourth Schedule.

a 28bC   (*h*)   In this subsection—

"**intra-Community transport of goods**" means transport where the place of departure and the place of arrival are situated within the territories of two different Member States;

> **"the place of departure"** means the place where the transport of goods actually starts, leaving aside distance actually travelled to the place where the goods are;
>
> **"the place of arrival"** means the place where the transport of goods actually ends.][15]

(7) Provision may be made by regulations for varying, in relation to services generally or of a description specified therein, the rules for determining their place of supply, and for that purpose the Fourth Schedule may be added to or varied.

(8) The transfer of the goodwill or other intangible assets of a business, in connection with the transfer of the business or part thereof, to another taxable person shall be deemed, for the purposes of this Act, not to be a supply of services.][16]

a 6(5)

Amendments

1 Substituted by FA 1992 s 169(*a*) with effect from 1 January 1993; previously "specified in the Fourth Schedule".
2 Subs (3A) inserted by FA 1986 s 81 with effect from 27 May 1986.
3 Subs (4A) inserted FA 1982 s 76 with effect from 1 September 1982.
4 Subs (4B) inserted by FA 1989 s 54 with effect from 1 March 1989.
5 Inserted by FA 1995 s 123 with effect from 2 June 1995.
6 Subs (6)(*b*) substituted by FA 1992 s 169(*b*)(i) with effect from 1 January 1993.
7 Subs (6)(*c*)(ii) substituted by FA 1992 s 169(*b*)(ii) with effect from 1 January 1993.
8 Inserted by FA 1996 s 90(*a*)(i) with effect from 1 January 1996.
9 Inserted by FA 1996 s 90(*a*)(ii) with effect from 1 January 1996
10 Subs (6)(*d*) inserted by FA 1986 s 81 with effect from 27 May 1986.
11 Inserted by FA 1990 s 100 with effect from 30 May 1990.
12 Subs (6)(*e*)(ii)(III) inserted by FA 1990 s 100 with effect from 30 May 1990.
13 Subs (6)(*e*) substituted by FA 1986 s 81 with effect from 27 May 1986.
14 Subs (6)(*f*)(iv) inserted by FA 1996 s 90(*b*) with effect from 1 January 1996.
15 Subs (6)(*f*)-(*h*) inserted by FA 1992 s 169(*b*)(iii) with effect from 1 January 1993.
16 Section 5 substituted by VATAA 1978 s 5 with effect from 1 March 1979.

Cross-references
Self-supplied services (subs (3)), Revenue may make regulations: s 32(1)(*b*); Regulations (staff meals): VATR 1979 r 24.
Regulations (subs (7)) require consent of Minister for Finance: s 32(2A).

Case law
Insurance legal services held to be supplied to the insurer not the insured: *Bourke v Bradley and Sons*, IV ITR 117; subs (4B) inserted to reverse the effect of this decision.
Administration of copyright in sound recordings, a service: *Phonographic Performance (Ireland) Ltd v Somers*, IV ITR 314.

Statement of practice
Food and drink supplied through catering business, hotel, restaurant, pub, take-away etc, rates of VAT: VAT SP 10/92.
Services received from abroad: SP VAT 1/90.
Transport of goods between EC Countries after 1 January 1993: SP VAT 12/92.

Narrative
Irish Value Added Tax, Chapters 3, 4, 6; *Guide to Value Added Tax (Revenue Commissioners)*: Chapter 4.

Definition
"business": s 1(1); "Community": s 1(1); "goods": s 1(1); "immovable goods": s 1(1); "local authority": s 1(1); "movable goods": s 1(1); "establishment": s 1(1); "person": IA 1937 s 11(*c*); "a person registered for value added tax": s 1(1); "regulations": s 1(1), 32; "statute": IA 1937 s 3; s 1(1); "supply": s 1(1); "tax": s 1(1); "taxable person": s 1(1), 8.

Notes
Subs (3A): OJ .L145/1 (13.6.1977).

Personal notes

_____

_____

_____

_____

_____

_____

_____

6 Exemptions

a 13

(1) Tax shall not be chargeable in respect of any exempted activity.

(2)   (*a*)   The Minister may by order declare the [supply of goods or services][1] of any kind to be an exempted activity.

      (*b*)   The Minister may by order amend or revoke an order under this subsection, including an order under this paragraph.

a 28cA, B   (*c*)   An order under this subsection shall be laid before Dáil Éireann as soon as may be after it is made and, if a resolution annulling the order is passed by Dáil Éireann within the next twenty-one days on which Dáil Éireann has sat after the order is laid before it, the order shall be annulled accordingly, but without prejudice to the validity of anything previously done thereunder.

Amendments

1 Substituted by VATAA 1978 s 30(2) with effect from 1 March 1979; previously "delivery of goods of any kind or the rendering of a service".

Cross-references

Exempted activities: Sch 1.

European Communities (Exemption from Value Added Tax on the Permanent Importation of Certain Goods) Regulations 1985 (SI 183/1985).

Definition

"Dáil Éireann": IA 1937 Sch; "exempted activity": s 1(1); "goods": s 1(1); "the Minister": s 1(1); "supply": s 1(1); "tax": s 1(1).

Personal notes

7 Waiver of exemption

(1) Where, but for the provisions of section 6, tax would be chargeable in respect of the [supply]¹ of any of the services [to which paragraph (iv) of the First Schedule relates]² a person [supplying]³ any such services may, in accordance with regulations, waive his right to exemption from tax in respect thereof. Any such waiver shall extend to all the [services to which the said paragraph (iv) relates]⁴ that the person [supplies]⁵

(2) A waiver of exemption under subsection (1) shall have effect from the commencement of such taxable period as may be agreed between the person making the waiver and the Revenue Commissioners and shall cease to have effect at the end of the taxable period during which it is cancelled in accordance with subsection (3).

(3) Provision may be made by regulations for the cancellation, at the request of a person, of a waiver made by him under subsection (1) and for the payment by him to the Revenue Commissioners as a condition of cancellation of such sum (if any) as when added to the net total amount of tax (if any) paid by him in accordance with section 19 in relation to the [supply]¹ of services by him in the period for which the waiver had effect is equal to the amount of tax repaid to him during such period in respect of tax borne or paid in relation to the [supply]¹ of such services.

(4) Where exemption has been waived under subsection (1) in respect of the [supply]¹ of any such service, tax shall be charged in relation to the person making such waiver during the period for which such waiver has effect as if the service to which the waiver applies was not specified in the First Schedule.

Amendments
1 Substituted by VATAA 1978 s 30(2) with effect from 1 March 1979; previously "rendering".
2 Substituted by FA 1991 s 78 with effect from 1 January 1992; previously "specified in paragraphs (iv) and (x) of the First Schedule".
3 Substituted by VATAA 1979 s 30(2) with effect from 1 March 1979; previously "rendering".
4 Substituted by FA 1991 s 78 with effect from 1 January 1992; previously "services specified in the paragraph or paragraphs".
5 Substituted by VATAA 1979 s 30(2) with effect from 1 March 1979; previously "renders".

Cross-references
Revenue may make regulations: s 32(1)(*a*); waiver of exemption procedure: VATR 1979 r 4.
Supply of services: s 5.

Definition
"person": IA 1937 s 11(*c*); "regulations": ss 1(1), 32; "supply": s 1(1); "tax": s 1(1); "taxable period": s 1(1).

Personal notes

---

8 Taxable persons

a 4   [(1) A person who, otherwise than as an employee of another person, engages in the supply, within the State, of taxable goods or services in the course [or furtherance][1] of business shall, in addition to the persons referred to in section 4(5) and [subsections [1A],][2] (2), (2A) and (8)][3] be a taxable person and shall be accountable for and liable to pay the tax charged in respect of such supply.][4]

[(1A) (*a*)   Where a person engages in the intra-Community acquisition of goods in the State in the course or furtherance of business he shall be a taxable person and shall be accountable for and liable to pay the tax chargeable.

(*b*)   Subject to subsection (2), and notwithstanding paragraph (*a*), a person for whose intra-Community acquisitions of goods (being goods other than new means of transport or goods subject to a duty of excise) the total consideration for which has not exceeded and is not likely to exceed £32,000 in any continuous period of 12 months shall not, unless he otherwise elects and then only during the period for which such election has effect, be a taxable person:

Provided that where the provisions of subsection (1) apply to that person, this paragraph shall not apply unless the provisions of subsection (3) also apply to him

(*c*)   A person who is a taxable person by virtue of this subsection and who is a person referred to in paragraph (*a*) or (*b*) of subsection (3) shall be deemed to be a taxable person only in respect of—

(i)   intra-Community acquisitions of goods which are made by him, and

(ii)   any services of the kind referred to in subsection (2) which are received by him:

Provided that a person may elect that this paragraph shall not apply to him.

(*d*)   A person who is a taxable person by virtue of this subsection and who is a person referred to in subsection (3A) shall be deemed to be a taxable person only in respect of—

(i)   intra-Community acquisitions of goods which are made by him,

(ii)   racehorse training services which are supplied by him, and

(iii)   any services of the kind referred to in subsection (2) which are received by him:

Provided that a person may elect that this paragraph shall not apply to him.

(*e*)   For the purposes of this subsection, where an intra-Community acquisition is effected in the State by—

(i)   a Department of State or local authority,

(ii)   a body established by statute, or

(iii)   a person for the purpose of any activity [specified in the First Schedule][5]

the acquisition shall be deemed to have been effected in the course or furtherance of business.][6]

a 9(3),28a   [(2)   (*a*)   Where by virtue of [subparagraph (ii), (iii) or (iv) of paragraph (*e*), or paragraph (*f*), of subsection (6) of section 5][7] a taxable service that, apart from that provision, would be treated as supplied abroad, is deemed to be supplied in the State, the person who receives the service shall, in relation thereto, be a taxable person and be liable to pay the tax charged as if he had himself supplied the service for consideration in the course or furtherance of his business.]⁸

[(*b*) A person who is a taxable person by virtue of this subsection and who is a person referred to in paragraph (*a*) or (*b*) of subsection (3) shall be deemed to be a taxable person only in respect of—

    (i) any intra-Community acquisitions of goods which are made by him, and

    (ii) services of the kind referred to in this subsection which are received by him:

Provided that a person may elect that this paragraph shall not apply to him.

(*c*) A person who is a taxable person by virtue of this subsection and who is a person referred to in subsection (3A) shall be deemed to be a taxable person only in respect of—

    (i) any intra-Community acquisitions of goods which are made by him,

    (ii) racehorse training services which are supplied by him, and

    (iii) services of the kind referred to in this subsection which are received by him:

Provided that a person may elect that this paragraph shall not apply to him.]⁹

(2A) (*a*) The Minister may, following such consultations as he may deem appropriate, by order provide that the State and every local authority shall be taxable persons with respect to specified categories of supplies made by them of goods or services and accordingly, during the continuance in force of any such order, but not otherwise, the State and every local authority shall be accountable for and liable to pay tax in respect of any such supplies made by them as if the supplies had been made in the course of business.   a 4(5)

[Provided that, where supplies of the kind referred to in, subject to subsection (3E), paragraph (xxiii) of the First Schedule or in paragraph (viic) of the Sixth Schedule are provided by the State or by a local authority, an order under this subsection shall be deemed to have been made in respect of such supplies by the State or by the local authority.]¹⁰

(*b*) The Minister may by order amend or revoke an order under this subsection, including an order under this paragraph.

(*c*) An order under this subsection shall be laid before Dáil Éireann as soon as may be after it is made and, if a resolution annulling the order is passed by Dáil Éireann within the next twenty-one days on which Dáil Éireann has sat after the order is laid before it, the order shall be annulled accordingly, but without prejudice to the validity of anything previously done thereunder.

[(2B) (*a*) Where a person is a taxable person only because of an intra-Community acquisition of a new means of transport, then the person shall not, unless he so elects, be a taxable person for any purposes of this Act with the exception of subsection (4) of section 19.   a 28a(4)

(*b*) Where

    (i) a person is a taxable person only because of an intra-Community acquisition of excisable products, and

    (ii) by virtue of this acquisition, and in accordance with Chapter II of Part II of the Finance Act, 1992, and any other enactment which is to be construed together with that Chapter, the duty of excise on those products is payable in the State,

the person shall not, unless he so elects, be a taxable person for any purposes of the Act with the exception of subsection (5) of section 19.]¹¹

a 24,25 [(3) [Subject to subsections (1A) and (2), and notwithstanding the provisions of subsections (1)]¹², the following persons shall not, unless they otherwise elect and then only during the period for which such election has effect, be taxable persons—

(*a*)   a farmer, for whose supply of agricultural services, other than insemination services, stock-minding or stock-rearing, the total consideration has not exceeded and is not likely to exceed [£20,000]¹³ in any continuous period of twelve months,

(*b*)   a person whose supplies of taxable goods or services consist exclusively of—

(i)   supplies to taxable persons and persons to whom section 13(3) applies of fish (not being at a stage of processing further than that of being gutted, salted and frozen) which he has caught in the course of a seafishing business, or

(ii)   supplies of the kind specified in subparagraph (i) and of either or both of the following, that is to say:

(I)   supplies of machinery, plant or equipment which have been used by him in the course of a sea-fishing business, and

[(II)   supplies of other goods and services the total consideration for which is such that such person would not, because of the provisions of paragraph (*c*) or (*e*), be a taxable person if such supplies were the only supplies made by such person,]¹⁴

(*c*)   (i)   subject to subparagraph (ii), a person for whose supply of taxable goods (other than supplies of the kind specified in section 3(6)(*d*)(i)) and services the total consideration has not exceeded and is not likely to exceed [£40,000]¹⁵ in any continuous period of 12 months,

(ii)   subparagraph (i) shall apply if, but only if, not less than **90 per cent**, of the total consideration referred to therein is derived from the supply of taxable goods (not being goods chargeable at any of the rates specified in [paragraphs (*a*), (*c*), and (*d*)]¹⁶ of subsection (1) of section 11 which were produced or manufactured by him wholly or mainly from materials chargeable at the rate specified in paragraph (*b*) of that subsection),

(*d*)   ...¹⁷

(*e*)   a person, other than a person to whom paragraph (*a*), (*b*) or (*c*) applies, for whose supply of taxable goods and services the total consideration has not exceeded and is not likely to exceed [£20,000]¹⁸ in any continuous period of twelve months:

Provided that—

(i)   where in the case of two or more persons one of whom exercises control over one or more of the other persons, supplies of goods of the same class or of services of the same nature are made by two or more of those persons, the total of the consideration relating to the said supplies shall, for the purposes of the application of paragraphs (*c*) and (*e*) in relation to each of the persons aforesaid who made the said supplies be treated as if all of the supplies in question had been made by each of the last-mentioned persons;

[(ii) the provisions of this subsection shall not apply to a supply of the kind referred to in subsection (2).][18]][20]

[(3A) Where a person who supplies services consisting of the training of horses for racing, the consideration for which has exceeded [£20,000][21] in any continuous period of 12 months, would, but for the supply of such services be a farmer, he shall be deemed to be a taxable person only in respect of the supply of those services [and any intra-Community acquisitions of goods made by him and any services of the kind referred to in subsection (2) received by him][22] and, in the absence of an election, shall, in relation to the supply of any of the goods and services specified in paragraph (*a*) and subparagraphs (i) and (iii) of paragraph (*b*) of the definition of **"farmer"** in subsection (9), be deemed not to be a taxable person][23]

[(3B) In this section **"control"**, in relation to a body corporate, means the power of a person to secure, by means of the holding of shares or the possession of voting power in or in relation to that or any other body corporate, or by virtue of any powers conferred by the articles of association or other document regulating that or any other body corporate, that the affairs of the first-mentioned body corporate are conducted in accordance with the wishes of that person, and, in relation to a partnership, means the right to a share of more than one-half of the assets, or of more than one-half of the income, of the partnership.][24]

[(3C) (*a*) The licensee of any premises (being premises in respect of which a licence for the sale of intoxicating liquor either on or off those premises was granted) shall be deemed to be the promoter of any dance held, during the subsistence of that licence, on those premises and shall be deemed to have received the total money, excluding tax, paid by those admitted to the dance together with any other consideration received or receivable in connection with the dance.

    (*b*) For the purposes of this subsection **"licensee"** means—

        (i) where the licence is held by the nominee of a body corporate, the body corporate, and

        (ii) in any other case, the holder of the licence.][25]

[(3D) (*a*) The provisions of paragraphs (*b*), (*c*) and (*e*) of subsection (3) shall not apply to a person who is not established in the State.

    (*b*) A person who is not established in the State shall, unless he opts to register in accordance with section 9, be deemed not to have made an intra-Community acquisition or a supply of those goods in the State where the only supplies by him in the State are in the circumstances set out in section 3(8).][26]

[(3E) (*a*) Notwithstanding the provisions of section 6(1) and of subsection (1), and subject to the provisions of subsection (3), where—

        (i) a person supplies services which are exempt in accordance with section 6 and paragraph (xxiii) of the First Schedule, or

        (ii) the State or a local authority supplies services of the kind referred to in paragraph (xxiii) of the First Schedule,

    then an authorised officer of the Revenue Commissioners shall—

        (I) where such officer is satisfied that such supply of such services has created or is likely to create a distortion of competition such as to place at a disadvantage a commercial enterprise which is a taxable person supplying similar-type services, or

(II) where such officer is satisfied that such supply of such services is managed or administered by or on behalf of another person who has a direct or indirect beneficial interest, either directly or through an intermediary, in the supply of such services,

make a determination in relation to some or all of such supplies as specified in that determination deeming—

(A) such person, the State or such local authority to be supplying such supplies as specified in that determination in the course or furtherance of business,

(B) such person, the State or such local authority to be a taxable person in relation to the provision of such supplies as specified in that determination, and

(C) such supplies as specified in that determination to be taxable supplies to which the rate specified in section 11(1)(*d*) refers.

(*b*) Where a determination is made under paragraph (*a*), the Revenue Commissioners shall, as soon as may be after the making thereof, issue a notice in writing of that determination to the party concerned, and such determination shall have effect from such date as may be specified in the notice of that determination:

Provided that such determination shall have effect no sooner than the start of the next taxable period following that in which the notice issued.

(*c*) Where an authorised officer is satisfied that the conditions that gave rise to the making of a determination under paragraph (*a*) no longer apply, that officer shall cancel that determination by notice in writing to the party concerned and that cancellation shall have effect from the start of the next taxable period following that in which the notice issued.

(*d*) In this subsection **"authorised officer"** means an officer of the Revenue Commissioners authorised by them in writing for the purposes of this subsection.][27]

[(4) Where, by virtue of subsection (3) or (6), a person has not been a taxable person and a change of circumstances occurs from which it becomes clear that he is likely to become a taxable person, he shall be deemed, for the purposes of this Act, to be a taxable person from the beginning of the taxable period commencing next after such change][28]

(5) Provision may be made by regulation for the cancellation, by the request of a person, of an election made by him under this section and for the payment by him to the Revenue Commissioners of such a sum as a condition of cancellation as when added to the net total amount of tax (if any) paid by him in accordance with section 19 in relation to the [supply of such goods or services][29] [and the tax deductible under section 12 in respect of intra-Community acquisitions made by him during such period][30] by him in the period for which the election had effect is equal to [the sum of][31] the amount of tax repaid to him during such period in respect of tax borne or paid in relation to the [supply of goods or services][32]

[(6) A taxable person, other than a person to whom subsection (5) applies, may, in accordance with regulations, be treated, for the purposes of this Act, as a person who is not a taxable person if the Revenue Commissioners are satisfied that, in the absence of an election under subsection (3), he would not be a taxable person.][33]

[(7) Where any goods or services are provided by a club or other similar organisation in respect of a payment of money by any of its members, then, for the purposes of this Act, the provision of the goods or services shall be deemed to be a supply by the club or other organisation of the goods or services (as the case may be) in the course or furtherance of a business carried on by it and the money shall be deemed to be consideration for the supply.]³⁴

[(8) (*a*) Where the Revenue Commissioners are satisfied that two or more a 4(4) persons established in the State are closely bound by financial, economic and organisational links and that it would be expedient in the interest of efficient administration of the tax to do so then, subject to such conditions as they may impose by regulations, the said Commissioners, for the purpose of this Act, may —

  (i) by notice in writing to each of the persons concerned, deem the activities relating to those links to be carried on by any one of the persons, and all transactions by or between such persons shall be deemed, for that purpose, to be transactions by that one person and all rights and obligations under this Act shall be determined accordingly, and

  (ii) make each such person jointly and severally liable to comply with all the provisions of this Act and regulations (including the provisions requiring the payment of tax) that apply to each of those persons and subject to the penalties under this Act to which they would be subject if each such person was liable to pay to the Revenue Commissioners the whole of the tax chargeable, apart from regulations under this subsection, in respect of each such person:

  Provided that this subsection shall not apply in the case of:

  (I) the supply of immovable goods by any such person to any other such person, or

  [(IA) the requirement to issue an invoice or other document, in accordance with section 17, in respect of supplies to persons other than supplies between persons who are jointly and severally liable to comply with the provisions of this Act in accordance with subparagraph (ii), or

  (IB) the requirement to furnish a statement in accordance with section 19A, or]³⁵

  (II) the transfer of ownership of goods specified in section 3(5)(*b*)(iii) from any such person to any other such person, except where, apart from the provisions of this subsection, each of the persons whose activities are deemed to be carried on by that one person is a taxable person.

(*b*) The Revenue Commissioners may by notice in writing to each of the persons whose activities are, by virtue of a notification issued in accordance with paragraph (*a*)(i), deemed to be carried on by one of those persons, and as on and from the date specified in the notice (which date shall not be earlier than the date of issue of the notice) cancel the notification under the said paragraph; and as on and from the date specified in the said notice the provisions of the Act and regulations shall apply to all the persons as aforesaid as if a notification under the said paragraph had not been issued, but without prejudice to the liability of any of the persons for tax or penalties in respect of anything done or not done during the period for which the said notification was in force.

(*c*) The Revenue Commissioners may, for the purpose of this subsection, deem a person engaged in the supply of non-taxable goods or services in the course or furtherance of business to be a taxable person.]³⁶

9 Registration

a 22(1)

[(1) The Revenue Commissioners shall set up and maintain a register of persons who may become or who are taxable persons [or who are persons who dispose of goods which pursuant to section 3(7) are deemed to be supplied by a taxable person in the course or furtherance of his business][1]][2]

[(1A) The Revenue Commissioners shall assign to each person registered in accordance with subsection (1) a registration number.][3]

(2) Every person who on the appointed day or on any day thereafter would be [a taxable person][4] if tax were chargeable with effect as on and from the appointed day shall, within the period of thirty days beginning on the appointed day or on the day thereafter on which the person first becomes [a taxable person][4] or would become such a person if tax were chargeable as aforesaid, furnish in writing to the Revenue Commissioners the particulars specified in regulations as being required for the purpose of registering such person for tax.

[(2A) Every person who disposes of goods which pursuant to section 3(7) are deemed to be supplied by a taxable person in the course or furtherance of his business shall, within fourteen days of such disposal, furnish in writing to the Revenue Commissioners the particulars specified in regulations as being required for the purpose of registering such person for tax][5]

(3) Any person who on the appointed day was registered for the purposes of turnover tax on the basis of particulars furnished in accordance with section 49(2) of the Finance Act, 1963, shall be deemed, unless he notifies the Revenue Commissioners in writing that he does not wish to be so deemed, to have furnished the particulars required by subsection (2).

(4) In this section **"the appointed day"** means the day appointed by the Minister by order to be the appointed day for the purposes of this section.

Amendments

1   Inserted by FA 1983 s 80 with effect from 1 September 1983.
2   Subs (1) substituted by VATAA 1978 s 7 with effect from 1 March 1979.
3   Subs (1A) inserted by FA 1992 s 171 with effect from 28 May 1992.
4   Words substituted by VATAA 1978 s 30(2) with effect from 1 March 1979; previously "an accountable person".
5   Subs (2A) inserted by FA 1983 s 80 with effect from 1 September 1983.

Cross-references

Failure to register (Subs (2)), penalty: s 26(1).
Fraud, negligence (subs (1A)): penalties: s 27(1).
Registration particulars, Revenue may prescribe: s 32(1)(c); registration details: Value Added Tax (Registration) Regulations 1993 (SI 30/1993).

Orders

"appointed day": 1 September 1972: Value Added Tax (Appointed Day) Order 1972 (SI 192/1972).

Case law

A non-resident company engaging in a single trading transaction within the State was held entitled to be registered: *WLD Worldwide Leather Diffusion Ltd v Revenue Commissioners*, [1994] ITR 165.

Narrative

Irish Value Added Tax, Chapter 2; *Guide to Value Added Tax (Revenue Commissioners)*: Chapter 2.

Definition

"business": s 1(1); "farmer": s 1(1); "goods": s 1(1); "the Minister": s 1(1); "person": IA 1937 s 11(c); "regulations": ss 1(1), 32; "tax": s 1(1); "taxable person": ss 1(1), 8; "writing": IA 1937 Sch.

Personal notes

10 Amount on which tax is chargeable

[(1) The amount on which tax is chargeable by virtue of section 2(1)(*a*) shall, subject to this section, be the total consideration which the person supplying goods or services becomes entitled to receive in respect of or in relation to such supply of goods or services, including all taxes, commissions, costs and charges whatsoever, but not including value added tax chargeable in respect of the supply. a 11

[(1A) The amount on which tax is chargeable on the intra-Community acquisition of goods by virtue of section 2(1A) shall, subject to this section, be the total consideration, including all taxes, commissions, costs and charges whatsoever, but not including value added tax chargeable, in respect of that acquisition.][1] a 28c1

(2) If the consideration referred to in [subsections (1) or (1A)][2] does not consist of or does not consist wholly of an amount of money, the amount on which tax is chargeable shall be the total amount of money which might reasonably be expected to be charged if the consideration consisted entirely of an amount of money equal to the open market price:

...[3]

(3)   [(*a*)   If for any non-business reason the actual consideration in relation to— a 11A1

       (i)   the supply of any goods or services, or

       (ii)   the intra-Community acquisition of goods,

    is less than the open market price or there is no consideration, the amount on which tax is chargeable shall be the open market price.][4]

    (*b*)   If the consideration actually received in relation to the supply of any goods or services exceeds the amount which the person supplying the goods or services was entitled to receive, the amount on which tax is chargeable shall be the amount actually received, excluding tax chargeable in respect of the supply.

    (*c*)   If, in a case not coming within paragraph (*a*), the consideration actually received in relation to the supply of any goods or services is less than the amount on which tax is chargeable or no consideration is actually received, such relief may be given by repayment or otherwise in respect of the deficiency as may be provided by regulations. a 11C

    [Provided that in any event this paragraph shall not apply in the case of the letting of immovable goods which is a taxable supply of goods in accordance with section 4.][5]

(4) The amount on which tax is chargeable in relation to a supply of goods referred to in paragraph (*d*)(ii), (*e*) or (*f*) of section 3(1) or a supply of services by virtue of regulations made for the purposes of section 5(3) shall be the cost, excluding tax, of the goods to [the person supplying or acquiring the goods][6] or the cost, excluding tax, of supplying the services, as the case may be. a 11A(*b*)

[(4A) Where goods chargeable with a duty of excise [, other than alcohol products within the meaning of section 3B,][7] are supplied while warehoused, and before payment of the duty, to an unregistered person, the amount on which tax is chargeable in respect of the supply shall be increased by an amount equal to the amount of duty that would be payable in relation to the goods if the duty had become due at the time of the supply.][8]

[(4B) The amount on which tax is chargeable in relation to the supply of goods referred to in section 3(1) (*g*) shall be the open market price.][9]

[(4C) In the case of a supply of goods of the type referred to in section 3(1)(*b*), where, as part of an agreement of the kind referred to in that provision, the supplier of the goods is also supplying financial services of the kind specified in subparagraph (i)(*e*) of the First Schedule in respect of those goods, the amount on which tax is chargeable in respect of the supply of the goods in question shall be either—

(*a*)   the open market price of the goods, or

(*b*)   the amount of the total consideration as specified in subsection (1) which the person supplying the goods becomes entitled to receive in respect of or in relation to such supply,

whichever is the greater.][10]

(5) The amount on which tax is chargeable in relation to services for the tax chargeable on which the recipient is, by virtue of section 8(2), liable shall be the consideration for which the services were in fact supplied to him.

[(5A) Where,

(*a*)   an intra-Community acquisition is deemed to have taken place in the territory of another Member State in accordance with section 3A(2)(*a*),

(*b*)   the intra-Community acquisition has been subject to value added tax, referred to in Council Directive No. 77/388/EEC of 17 May 1977, in that other Member State, and

(*c*)   the intra-Community acquisition is also deemed to have taken place in the State, in accordance with section 3A(2)(*b*),

then the consideration for the intra-Community acquisition to which paragraph (*c*) relates shall be reduced to nil.][11]

(6) Where a right to receive goods or services for an amount stated on any token, stamp, coupon or voucher is granted for a consideration, the consideration shall be disregarded for the purposes of this Act except to the extent (if any) that it exceeds that amount.

(7) Provision may be made by regulations for the purpose of determining the amount on which tax is chargeable in relation to one or more of the following:

(*a*)   supplies of goods and services to which an order under section 8 (2A) applies,

(*b*)   supplies of stamps, coupons, tokens or vouchers when supplied as things in action (not being stamps, coupons, tokens or vouchers specified in subsection (6)),

(*c*)   supplies of goods or services wholly or partly in exchange for stamps, coupons, tokens or vouchers of a kind specified in subsection (6) or paragraph (*b*),

(*d*)   supplies deemed, pursuant to subsection (3) or (4) of section 3, to be made to and by the persons therein mentioned,

and such regulations may, in the case of supplies referred to in paragraph (*b*), provide that the amount on which tax is chargeable shall be nil.

(8)   (*a*)   Where the value of movable goods (not being goods of a kind specified in paragraph (xii) of the Second Schedule) provided under an agreement for the supply of services exceeds two-thirds of the total consideration under the agreement for the provision of those goods and the supply of the services, other than transport services in relation to them, the consideration shall be deemed to be referable solely to the supply of the goods and tax shall be charged at the appropriate rate or rates specified in section 11 on the basis of any apportionment of the total consideration made in accordance with paragraph (*b*).

(*b*)   Where goods of different kinds are provided under an agreement of the kind referred to in paragraph (*a*), the amount of the consideration referable to the supply of goods of each kind shall be ascertained for the purposes of that paragraph by apportioning the total consideration in proportion to the value of the goods of each kind provided.

(*c*)   This subsection shall also apply to an agreement for the supply of immovable goods and, accordingly, the references in paragraphs (*a*) and (*b*) to an agreement for the supply of services shall be deemed to include a reference to such an agreement.

(9) (*a*) On the supply of immovable goods and on the supply of services consisting of the development of immovable goods, the value of any interest in the goods disposed of in connection with the supply shall be included in the consideration.

a 11A(1)(*a*)

(*b*) The value of any interest in immovable goods shall be the open market price of such interest.

[(9A) In relation to the tax chargeable by virtue of section 2(1)(*a*) or 2(1A), where an amount is expressed in a currency other than the currency of the State the exchange rate to be used shall be —

a 11C(2)

(*a*) unless paragraph (*b*) applies, the latest selling rate recorded by the Central Bank of Ireland for the currency in question at the time the tax becomes due,

(*b*) where there is an agreement with the Revenue Commissioners for a method to be used in determining the exchange rate, the exchange rate obtained using the said method:

Provided that where paragraph (*b*) applies the method agreed in accordance with that paragraph shall be applied for all transactions where an amount is expressed in a currency other than that of the State until the agreement to use such method is withdrawn by the Revenue Commissioners.][12]

(10) In this section—

a 11A(1)(*d*)

"interest", in relation to immovable goods, and **"disposal"**, in relation to any such interest, shall be construed in accordance with section 4(1);

"the open market price", in relation to the supply of any goods or services, [or the intra-Community acquisition of goods][13] means the price, excluding tax, which the goods might reasonably be expected to fetch or which might reasonably be expected to be charged for the services if sold in the open market at the time of the event in question.][14]

Amendments

1   Subs (1A) inserted by FA 1992 s 172(*a*) with effect from 1 January 1993.
2   Substituted by FA 1992 s 172 with effect from 1 January 1993; previously "subsection (1)" .
3   Subs (2)(proviso) deleted by FA 1995 s 125(*a*) with effect from 1 July 1995.
4   Subs (3)(*a*) substituted by FA 1992 s 172(*d*) with effect from 1 January 1993.
5   Subs (3)(*c*)(proviso) inserted by FA 1994 s 95 with effect from 23 May 1994.
6   Substituted by FA 1992 s 172(*e*) with effect from 1 January 1992; previously "the person supplying the goods" .
7   Inserted by FA 1993 s 86.
8   Subs (4A) inserted by FA 1982 s 78 with effect from 1 September 1982.
9   Subs (4B) inserted by FA 1992 s 172(*f*) with effect from 1 January 1993.
10 Subs (4C) inserted by FA 1995 s 125(*b*) with effect from 2 June 1995.
11 Subs (5A) inserted by FA 1992 s 172(*g*) with effect from 1 January 1993.
12 Subs (9A) inserted by EC(VAT)R 1992 r 8 with effect from 1 January 1993.
13 Inserted by FA 1992 s 172(*h*) with effect from 1 January 1993.
14 Section 10 substituted by VATAA 1978 s 8 with effect from 1 March 1979.

Cross-references
Alcohol products (subss (1), (1A)): s 3B(5).
Bad debts, discounts etc: VATR 1979 r 8.
Immovable goods, valuation of interests in: VATR 1979 r 19.
Margin scheme goods: s 10A(3); special scheme for auctioneers: s 10B(3).
Staff canteens: VATR 1979 r 24.
Stamps, coupons etc supplies of: VATR 1979 r 32; supplies in exchange for: VATR 1979 r 33.

Narrative
Irish Value Added Tax, Chapter 6; *Guide to Value Added Tax (Revenue Commissioners)*: Chapter 5.

Definition
"business": s 1(1); "Community": s 1(1); "development" s 1(1); "goods": s 1(1); "immovable goods": s 1(1); "intra-Community acquisition of goods": ss 1(1), 3A; "movable goods": s 1(1); "person": IA 1937 s 11(*c*); "regulations": ss 1(1), 32; "second-hand": s 1(1); "supply": s 1(1); "tax": s 1(1).

10A Margin scheme goods

[(1) In this section—

"antiques" means any of the goods specified in paragraph (xvia) of the Sixth Schedule or in paragraph (iii) of the Eighth Schedule;

"collectors' items" means any of the goods specified in paragraph (ii) of the Eighth Schedule;

"margin scheme" means the special arrangements for the taxation of supplies of margin scheme goods;

"margin scheme goods" means any works of art, collectors' items, antiques or second-hand goods supplied within the Community to a taxable dealer--

    (*a*)   by a person, other than a person referred to in paragraph (*c*), who was not entitled to deduct, under section 12, any tax in respect of that person's purchase, intra-Community acquisition or importation of those goods:

         Provided that person is not a taxable person who acquired those goods from—

        (i)   a taxable dealer who applied the margin scheme to the supply of those goods to that taxable person, or

        (ii) an auctioneer within the meaning of section 10B who applied the auction scheme within the meaning of section 10B to the supply of those goods to that taxable person,

    or

    (*b*)   by a person in another Member State who was not entitled to deduct, under the provisions implementing Article 17 of Council Directive No. 77/388/EEC of 17 May 1977, in that Member State, any value-added tax referred to in that Directive in respect of that person's purchase, intra-Community acquisition or importation of those goods, or

    (*c*)   by another taxable dealer who has applied the margin scheme to the supply of those goods or applied the provisions implementing Article 26a (inserted by Council Directive No. 94/5/EC of 14 February 1994) of Council Directive No. 77/388/EEC of 17 May 1977, in another Member State to the supply of those goods;

"precious metals" means silver (including silver plated with gold or platinum), gold (including gold plated with platinum), and platinum, and all items which contain any of these metals when the consideration for the supply does not exceed the open market price, as defined in section 10, of the metal concerned;

"precious stones" means diamonds, rubies, sapphires and emeralds, whether cut or uncut, when they are not mounted, set or strung;

"profit margin" means the profit margin in respect of a supply by a taxable dealer of margin scheme goods and shall be deemed to be inclusive of tax and shall be an amount which is equal to the difference between the taxable dealer's selling price for those goods and the taxable dealer's purchase price for those goods:

Provided that, in respect of that supply, where the purchase price is greater than the selling price, the profit margin shall be deemed to be nil;

"purchase price", in relation to an acquisition of margin scheme goods, means the total consideration including all taxes, commissions, costs and charges whatsoever, payable by a taxable dealer to the person from whom that taxable dealer acquired those goods;

"second-hand goods" means any tangible movable goods which are suitable for further use either as they are or after repair, other than means of transport, works of art, collectors' items, antiques, precious metals and precious stones;

"selling price" means the total consideration which a taxable dealer becomes entitled to receive in respect of or in relation to a supply of margin scheme goods including all taxes, commissions, costs and charges whatsoever and value-added tax, if any, payable in respect of the supply;

"taxable dealer" means a taxable person who in the course or furtherance of business, whether acting on that person's own behalf, or on behalf of another person pursuant to a contract under which commission is payable on purchase or sale, purchases or acquires margin scheme goods or the goods referred to in paragraphs (b) and (c) of subsection (4), with a view to resale, or imports the goods referred to in paragraph (a) of subsection (4), with a view to resale, and a person in another Member State shall be deemed to be a taxable dealer where, in similar circumstances, that person would be a taxable dealer in the State under this section;

"works of art" means any of the goods specified in paragraph (xvi), or subparagraph (a) of paragraph (xxii), of the Sixth Schedule or in paragraph (i) of the Eighth Schedule.

(2) Subject to and in accordance with the provisions of this section, a taxable dealer may apply the margin scheme to a supply of margin scheme goods.

(3) Where the margin scheme is applied to a supply of goods, then notwithstanding section 10, the amount on which tax is chargeable by virtue of section 2(1)(a) on that supply shall be the profit margin less the amount of tax included in the profit margin.

(4) Subject to such conditions (if any) as may be specified in regulations, a taxable dealer may, notwithstanding subsection (2), opt to apply the margin scheme to all that dealer's supplies of any of the following as if they were margin scheme goods—

    (a)   a work of art, collector's item or antique which the taxable dealer imported, or

    (b)   a work of art which has been supplied to the taxable dealer by its creator or the creator's successors in title, or

    (c)   a work of art which has been supplied to the taxable dealer by a taxable person other than a taxable dealer, where the supply to that dealer is of the type referred to in section 11(1AA)(b)(ii):

        Provided that where a taxable dealer so opts in accordance with this subsection, such option shall be for a period of not less than two years from the date when such option was exercised.

(5) Where a taxable dealer exercises the option in accordance with subsection (4), in respect of the goods specified at paragraph (a) thereto, then notwithstanding the definition of purchase price in subsection (1), the purchase price for the purposes of determining the profit margin in relation to a supply of those goods shall be an amount equal to the value of those goods for the purposes of importation determined in accordance with section 15 increased by the amount of any tax payable in respect of the importation of those goods.

(6) Subject to subsection (7) and notwithstanding section 12, a taxable dealer who exercises the option in respect of the supply of the goods specified in subsection (4) shall not be entitled to deduct any tax in respect of the purchase or importation of those goods.

(7) Where a taxable dealer exercises the option in accordance with subsection (4), that dealer may, notwithstanding the proviso to subsection (4), in respect of any individual supply of the goods specified in subsection (4), opt not to apply the margin scheme to that supply, and in such case the right to deduction of the tax charged on the purchase, intra-Community acquisition or importation of those goods shall, notwithstanding section 12, arise only in the taxable period in which the dealer supplies those goods.

(8)   (*a*)   Notwithstanding subsection (3), and subject to and in accordance with regulations (if any)—

      (i)   where a taxable dealer acquires low value margin scheme goods in job lots or otherwise, the amount of tax due and payable in respect of that dealer's supplies of low value margin scheme goods shall, in respect of a taxable period, be the amount of tax included in that dealer's aggregate margin, or margins, for that period and the amount of tax in each aggregate margin shall be determined by the formula:

$$A \times \frac{B}{B+100}$$

where—

A is the aggregate margin for the taxable period in question, and

B is the percentage rate of tax chargeable in relation to the supply of those goods, and

      (ii)   where the taxable dealer referred to in paragraph (i) in any taxable period makes supplies which are subject to different rates of tax, that taxable dealer shall calculate separate aggregate margins for that taxable period in respect of the supplies at each of the relevant rates.

   (*b*)   Subject to, and in accordance with regulations (if any), where a taxable dealer supplies a low value margin scheme good for an amount in excess of £500 then—

      (i)   notwithstanding the definition of low value margin scheme goods in paragraph (*c*), the supply of that good shall be deemed not to be a supply of a low value margin scheme good,

      (ii)   in determining the aggregate margin for the taxable period in which the supply occurs, the taxable dealer shall deduct the purchase price of that good from the sum of the taxable dealer's purchase prices of low value margin scheme goods for that period, and

      (iii)   the purchase price of that good shall be used in determining the profit margin in relation to the supply of that good.

   (*c*)   In this subsection—

"aggregate margin", in respect of a taxable period, means an amount which is equal to the difference between the taxable dealer's total turnover in that period from supplies of low value margin scheme goods, to which the same rate of tax applies, less the sum of that taxable dealer's purchase prices of low value margin scheme goods to which that rate of tax applies to the supply thereof, in that taxable period:

Provided that where the sum of that dealer's said purchase prices is in excess of the said total turnover, the appropriate aggregate margin shall be deemed to be nil and subject to, and in accordance with, regulations (if any), the amount of the excess shall be carried forward and added to the sum of that dealer's purchase prices for low value margin scheme goods for the purposes of calculating that dealer's appropriate aggregate margin for the immediately following taxable period;

"low value margin scheme goods" means margin scheme goods where the purchase price payable by the dealer for each individual item is less than £500.

(9) Notwithstanding section 17, a taxable dealer shall not, in relation to any supply to which the margin scheme has been applied, indicate separately the amount of tax chargeable in respect of the supply on any invoice or other document in lieu thereof issued in accordance with that section.

(10) Where the margin scheme is applied to a supply of goods dispatched or transported from the State to a person registered for value-added tax in another Member State, then notwithstanding paragraph (i)(*b*) of the Second Schedule, the provisions of section 11(1)(*b*) shall not apply, unless such goods are of a kind specified elsewhere in the Second Schedule.

(11) Notwithstanding section 3(6)(*d*), where the margin scheme is applied to a supply of goods dispatched or transported, the place of supply of those goods shall be deemed to be the place where the dispatch or transportation begins.

(12) Where a taxable dealer applies the margin scheme to a supply of goods on behalf of another person pursuant to a contract under which commission is payable on purchase or sale, the goods shall be deemed to have been supplied by that other person to the taxable dealer when the said taxable dealer supplies those goods.

(13) Notwithstanding paragraph (xxiv) of the First Schedule, where a taxable person acquires goods to which the margin scheme has been applied and that person subsequently supplies those goods, the provisions of that paragraph shall not apply to that supply.][1]

Amendments
1 Section 10A inserted by FA 1995 s 126 with effect from 1 July 1995.

Cross-references
Antiques supplied by taxable dealer, other than in accordance with subss (3), (8): Sch 6 para (xvi*a*).
Concrete blocks supplied by taxable dealer, other than in accordance with subss (3), (8): Sch 6 para (xxxiii).
Concrete ready to pour supplied by taxable dealer, other than in accordance with subss (3), (8): Sch 6 para (xxxii).
Works of art supplied by taxable dealer, other than in accordance with subss (3), (8): Sch 6 para (xvi).
Regulations, Revenue power to make in order to determine conditions for taxable dealer to opt to apply the margin scheme (subs (4)): s 32(1)(*da*); in order to determine aggregate margin (subs (8)): s 32(1)(*db*).
Restriction of deduction (subss (3), (8)): s 12(3A)(*a*).

Definitions
"Community": s 1(1); "goods": s 1(1); "importation of goods": s 1(1); "intra-Community acquisition of goods": s 1(1); "second-hand goods": s 1(1); "supply": s 1(1); "taxable person": s 1(1).

Personal notes

10B Special scheme for auctioneers

[(1) In this section—

"auctioneer" means a taxable person who, in the course or furtherance of business, acting on behalf of another person pursuant to a contract under which commission is payable on purchase or sale, offers tangible movable goods for sale by public auction with a view to handing them over to the highest bidder;

"auctioneer's margin" means an amount which is equal to the difference between the total amount, including any taxes, commissions, costs and charges whatsoever, payable by the purchaser to the auctioneer in respect of the auction of auction scheme goods and the amount payable by the auctioneer to the principal in respect of the supply of those goods and shall be deemed to be inclusive of tax;

"auction scheme" means the special arrangements for the taxation of supplies of auction scheme goods;

"auction scheme goods" means any works of art, collectors' items, antiques or second-hand goods sold by an auctioneer at a public auction while acting on behalf of a principal who is—

    (*a*) a person, other than a person referred to in paragraph (*c*), who was not entitled to deduct, under section 12, any tax in respect of that person's purchase, intra-Community acquisition or importation of those goods:

        Provided that person is not a taxable person who acquired those goods from--

        (i) an auctioneer who applied the auction scheme to the supply of those goods to that taxable person, or

        (ii) a taxable dealer who applied the margin scheme to the supply of those goods to that taxable person,

      or

    (*b*) a person in another Member State who was not entitled to deduct, under the provisions implementing Article 17 of Council Directive No. 77/388/EEC of 17 May 1977, in that Member State, any value-added tax referred to in that Directive in respect of that person's purchase, intra-Community acquisition or importation of those goods, or

    (*c*) a taxable dealer who applied the margin scheme to the supply of those goods or applied the provisions implementing Article 26a (inserted by Council Directive No. 94/5/EC of 14 February 1994) of Council Directive No. 77/388/EEC of 17 May 1977, in another Member State to the supply of those goods;

"principal" means the person on whose behalf an auctioneer auctions goods;

"purchaser" means the person to whom an auctioneer supplies auction scheme goods.

(2) Subject to and in accordance with the provisions of this section, an auctioneer shall apply the auction scheme to any supply of auction scheme goods.

(3) Notwithstanding section 10, the amount on which tax is chargeable, by virtue of section 2(1)(*a*), on a supply by an auctioneer of auction scheme goods shall be the auctioneer's margin less the amount of tax included in that auctioneer's margin.

(4) Where auction scheme goods are auctioned, the auctioneer shall issue, subject to such conditions (if any) as may be specified in regulations, to both the principal and the purchaser, invoices or documents in lieu thereof setting out the relevant details in respect of the supply of the auction scheme goods.

(5) Notwithstanding section 17, an auctioneer shall not, in relation to any supply to which the auction scheme has been applied, indicate separately the amount of tax

chargeable in respect of the supply on any invoice or other document in lieu thereof issued in accordance with that section.

(6) Where auction scheme goods are auctioned by an auctioneer on behalf of a principal who is a taxable person, the invoice or document in lieu thereof issued to the principal in accordance with subsection (4) shall be deemed to be an invoice for the purposes of section 17, and the said principal shall be deemed to have issued same.

(7) Where the auction scheme is applied to a supply of goods dispatched or transported from the State to a person registered for value-added tax in another Member State then, notwithstanding paragraph (i)(*b*) of the Second Schedule, the provisions of section 11(1)(*b*) shall not apply, unless such goods are of a kind specified elsewhere in the Second Schedule.

(8) Notwithstanding section 3(6)(*d*), where the auction scheme is applied to a supply of goods dispatched or transported, the place of supply of those goods shall be deemed to be the place where the dispatch or transportation begins.

(9) Where an auctioneer supplies [auction scheme goods][1] by public auction, the principal shall be deemed to have made a supply of the auction scheme goods in question to the auctioneer when the said auctioneer sells those goods at a public auction.

(10) Notwithstanding paragraph (xxiv) of the First Schedule, where a taxable person acquires goods to which the auction scheme has been applied and that person subsequently supplies those goods, the provisions of that paragraph shall not apply to that supply.][2]

Amendments
1   Substituted by FA 1996 s 91 with effect from 15 May 1996.
2   Section 10B inserted by FA 1995 s 127 with effect from 1 July 1995.

Cross-references
Antiques supplied by taxable dealer, other than in accordance with subs (3): Sch 6 para (xvi*a*).
Concrete blocks supplied by taxable dealer, other than in accordance with subs (3): Sch 6 para (xxxiii).
Concrete ready to pour supplied by taxable dealer, other than in accordance with subs (3): Sch 6 para (xxxii).
Regulations, Revenue power to make in order to determine form of invoice (subs (4)): s 32(1)(*dc*).
Restriction of deduction (subs (3)): s 12(3A)(*a*).
Works of art supplied by taxable dealer, other than in accordance with subs (3): Sch 6 para (xvi).

Definitions
"antiques": s 1(1); "business": s 1(1); "collectors' items": s 1(1); "Community": s 1(1); "goods": s 1(1); "importation of goods": s 1(1); "intra-Community acquisition of goods": s 1(1); "second-hand goods": s 1(1); "supply": s 1(1); "taxable dealer": s 1(1); "taxable person": s 1(1); "works of art": s 1(1).

Personal notes

_____

_____

_____

_____

_____

_____

_____

_____

_____

_____

^{a 12}   **11 Rates of tax**

[(1) Tax shall be charged, in relation to the supply of taxable goods or services [, the intra-Community acquisition of goods][1] and the importation of goods, at whichever of the following rates is appropriate in any particular case—

    (*a*)   **21 per cent** of the amount on which tax is chargeable other than in relation to goods or services on which tax is chargeable at any of the rates specified in paragraphs (*b*), (*c*), (*d*) ...[2] and (*f*),

^{a 28c(3)-(4)}   (*b*)   **zero per cent** of the amount on which tax is chargeable in relation to goods in the circumstances specified in paragraph (i) [or (i*a*)][3] of the Second Schedule or of goods or services of a kind specified in paragraphs (iii) to (xx) of that Schedule,

    (*c*)   **10 per cent** of the amount on which tax is chargeable in relation to goods or services of a kind specified in the Third Schedule,

    (*d*)   **12.5 per cent** of the amount on which tax is chargeable in relation to goods or services of a kind specified in the Sixth Schedule, [and][4]

    ...[5]

    (*f*)   [**2.8 per cent**][6] of the amount on which tax is chargeable in relation to the supply of livestock and live greyhounds and to the hire of horses.][7]

[(1A) (*a*)   The rate at which tax shall be chargeable shall, in relation to tax chargeable under [subsection (1)(*a*) or (1A) of section 2],[8] be the rate for the time being in force at the time at which the tax becomes due in accordance with [subsection (1), (1A) or (2)],[9] as may be appropriate, of section 19.

    (*b*)   Goods or services which are specifically excluded from any paragraph of a Schedule shall, unless the contrary intention is expressed, be regarded as excluded from every other paragraph of that Schedule, and shall not be regarded as specified in that Schedule.

[(1AA) Notwithstanding subsection (1), tax shall be charged at the rate specified in section 11(1)(*d*) of the amount on which tax is chargeable in relation to—

    (*a*)   the importation into the State of goods specified in the Eighth Schedule,

    (*b*)   the supply of a work of art of the kind specified in paragraph (i) of the Eighth Schedule, effected—

        (i)   by its creator or the creator's successors in title, or

        (ii)   on an occasional basis by a taxable person other than a taxable dealer where--

            (I)   that work of art has been imported by the taxable person, or

            (II)   that work of art has been supplied to the taxable person by its creator or the creator's successors in title, or

            (III)   the tax chargeable in relation to the purchase, intra-Community acquisition or importation of that work of art by the taxable person was wholly deductible under section 12,

        and

    (*c*)   the intra-Community acquisition in the State by a taxable person of a work of art of the kind specified in paragraph (i) of the Eighth Schedule where the supply of that work of art to that taxable person which resulted in that intra-Community acquisition is a supply of the type that would be charged at the rate specified in section 11(1)(*d*) in accordance with paragraph (*b*), if that supply had occurred within the State.][10]

[(1AB) Notwithstanding subsection (1), the rate at which tax is chargeable on a supply of contract work shall be the rate that would be chargeable if that supply of services were a supply of the goods being handed over by the contractor to the person to whom that supply is made:

Provided that this subsection shall not apply to a supply of contract work in the circumstances specified in paragraph (xvi) of the Second Schedule.]¹¹

[(1B) (*a*)   On receipt of an application in writing from [a taxable person]¹² the Revenue Commissioners shall, in accordance with regulations and after such consultation (if any) as may seem to them to be necessary with such person or body of persons as in their opinion may be of assistance to them, make a determination concerning—

     (i)   whether an activity of any particular kind carried on by the person is an exempted activity, or

     [(ii)   the rate at which tax is chargeable in relation to the supply or intra-Community acquisition by the person of goods of any kind, the supply or intra-Community acquisition of goods in any particular circumstances or the supply by the person of services of any kind.]¹³

    (*b*)   The Revenue Commissioners may, whenever they consider it expedient to do so, in accordance with regulations and after such consultation (if any) as may seem to them to be necessary with such person or body of persons as in their opinion may be of assistance to them, make a determination concerning—

     (i)   whether an activity of any particular kind is an exempted activity, or

     [(ii)   the rate at which tax is chargeable in relation to the supply or intra-Community acquisition of goods of any kind, the supply or intra-Community acquisition of goods in any particular circumstances or the supply of services of any kind.]¹⁴

    (*c*)   A determination under this subsection shall have effect for all the purposes of this Act, in relation to [a taxable person]¹² who makes an application therefor, as on and from the date upon which particulars of the determination are communicated to him in accordance with paragraph (*e*)(i) and, in relation to any other person, as on and from the date of publication of the determination in the *Iris Oifigiúil*.

    (*d*)   The Revenue Commissioners shall not make a determination under this section concerning any matter which has been determined on appeal under this Act or which is for the time being governed by an order under section 6(2) or 11(8), and shall not be required to make such a determination in relation to any of the matters referred to in an application under paragraph (*a*) if—

     (i)   a previous determination has been published in regard to the matter, or

     (ii)   in their opinion the subject matter of the application is sufficiently free from doubt as not to warrant the making and publication of a determination.

    (*e*)   (i)   A determination under paragraph (*a*) shall, as soon as may be after the making thereof, be communicated to the person who made the application therefor by the service on him by the Revenue Commissioners of a notice containing particulars of the determination.

     (ii)   A determination under paragraph (*a*) may and a determination under paragraph (*b*) shall be published in the *Iris Oifigiúil* and, in that event, it shall also be published in at least one daily newspaper published in the State.

(f) A person, aggrieved by determination under paragraph (a) made pursuant to an application by him, may, on giving notice in writing to the Revenue Commissioners within the period of twenty-one days beginning on the date of service on him of notice of the determination in accordance with paragraph (e)(i), appeal to the Appeal Commissioners.

(g) Any [taxable person][15] who, in the course of business, [supplies goods or makes an intra-Community acquisition of goods, or supplies services][16] of a kind or in circumstances specified in a determination under paragraph (a) or (b) may, on giving notice in writing to the Revenue Commissioners within the period of twenty-one days beginning on the date of the publication of the determination in the *Iris Oifigiúil*, appeal to the Appeal Commissioners.][17]

(2) ...[18].

[(3) Subject to section 10(8) [in relation to supplies of goods and services][19] where—

(a) supplies of different kinds are made for a consideration in money which is referable to all the supplies [or intra-Community acquisitions][20] and not separately to the different kinds of supplies [or intra-Community acquisitions][20] and

(b) one or both of the following subparagraphs applies or apply, that is to say—

(i) but for this subsection, tax would not be chargeable in respect of one or more (but not all) of the supplies,

(ii) but for this subsection, tax would ...[21] fall to be charged at two or more of the rates specified in subsection (1) in respect of the supplies [or intra-Community acquisitions][20]

then, unless regulations provide for apportionment of the consideration—

(c) where subparagraph (i) (but not subparagraph (ii)) of paragraph (b) applies, tax shall be chargeable in respect of all the supplies [or intra-Community acquisitions][20] at the rate specified in subsection (1) appropriate to the supply of taxable goods or services [, or intra-Community acquisition of goods][21] included in the supplies [or intra-Community acquisitions].[20]

(d) where subparagraph (ii) of paragraph (b) applies (whether alone or with subparagraph (i) of that paragraph), tax shall be chargeable in respect of all the supplies [or intra-Community acquisitions][20] at the higher or highest rate (as the case may be) specified in subsection (1) appropriate to the supply of any taxable goods or services [, or any intra-Community acquisition of goods][23] included in the supplies [or intra-Community acquisitions][20]:

Provided that, where goods—

(I) are chargeable with tax at different rates,

(II) are packaged for sale as a unit, and

(III) are offered for sale for a consideration in money which is referable to the package as a whole and not to the different kinds of goods included therein,

the inclusion in the package of goods chargeable at a particular rate shall not be taken into account for the purpose of the preceding provisions of this subsection where the total tax-exclusive value of such goods does not exceed **50 per cent** of the total tax-exclusive consideration for the package or 5 pence, whichever is the lesser, and, in any such case, the rate of tax chargeable in relation to the package shall be determined by reference to the other goods included therein.][24]

[(4) Where goods for the manufacture of which materials have been supplied by or on behalf of any person are [supplied]²⁵ by the manufacturer to that person and the rate of tax chargeable in relation to the [supply]²⁶ of the goods exceeds that which would be chargeable in relation to a [supply]²⁶ within the State of the materials, the person who [supplies]²⁷ the goods shall, in respect of the [supply]²⁶ of such goods, be liable, in addition to any other liability imposed on him by this Act, to pay tax on the value of the materials [provided]²⁸ to him at a rate equivalent to the difference between the two aforementioned rates.]²⁹

[(4A) Where—

> (*a*) goods of a kind specified in paragraph (xii) of the Second Schedule are used by a person in the course of the supply by him of taxable services, and

> (*b*) the goods are provided by or on behalf of the person to whom the services are supplied,

the person who supplies the taxable services shall be liable in respect thereof, in addition to any other liability imposed on him under this Act, to pay tax on the value of the goods so used at the rate specified in [section 11(1)(*d*)]³⁰.]³¹

...³²

(6) Where immovable goods consisting of machinery or business installations are let separately from other immovable goods of which they form part, tax shall be chargeable in respect of the transaction at the rate which would be chargeable if it were a hiring of movable goods of the same kind.

...³³.

(8) [(*a*) The Minister may by order vary the [Second, Third, or Sixth Schedule]³⁴ by adding to or deleting therefrom descriptions of goods or services of any kind or by varying any description of goods or services for the time being specified therein, ...³⁵ but no order shall be made under this section for the purpose of increasing any of the rates of tax or extending the classes of activities or goods in respect of which tax is for the time being chargeable.]³⁶

> (*b*) The Minister may by order amend or revoke an order under this subsection, including an order under this paragraph.

> (*c*) An order under this subsection shall be laid before Dáil Éireann as soon as may be after it has been made and, if a resolution annulling the order is passed by Dáil Éireann within the next twenty-one days on which Dáil Éireann has sat after the order is laid before it, the order shall be annulled accordingly, but without prejudice to the validity of anything previously done thereunder.

(9) ...³⁷.

Amendments

1   Inserted by FA 1992 s 173(3)(*a*) with effect from 1 January 1993.
2   Deleted by FA 1993 s 87(*a*)(i) with effect from 1 March 1993; previously ", (*e*)".
3   Inserted by EC(VAT)R 1992 r 9 with effect from 1 January 1993.
4   Inserted by FA 1993 s 87(*a*)(ii)with effect from 1 March 1993.
5   Subs (1)(*e*) deleted by FA 1993 s 87 with effect from 1 March 1993.
6   Substituted by FA 1996 s 92(*a*) with effect from 1 March 1996; previously "2.5 per cent" (FA 1993 s 87(*a*)(iv)); previously "2.7 per cent".
7   Subs (1) substituted by FA 1992 s 173(2) with effect from 28 May 1992.
8   Substituted by FA 1992 s 173(3)(*b*) with effect from 1 January 1993; previously: "section 2(1)(*a*)" .
9   Substituted by FA 1992 s 173(3)(*b*) with effect from 1 January 1993; previously: "subsection (1) or (2)".
10   Subs (1AA) inserted by FA 1995 s 128(*a*) with effect from 1 July 1995.
11   Subs (1AB) inserted by FA 1996 s 92(*b*) with effect from 1 March 1996.
12   Substituted by VATAA 1978 s 30(2) with effect from 1 March 1979; previously "an accountable person".
13   Subs (1B)(*a*)(ii) substituted by FA 1992 s 173(3)(*c*)(i) with effect from 1 January 1993.
14   Subs (1B)(*b*)(ii) substituted by FA 1992 s 173(3)(*c*)(ii) with effect from 1 January 1993.
15   Substituted by VATAA 1978 s 30(2) with effect from 1 March 1979; previously "accountable person".
16   Substituted by FA 1992 s 173(3)(*c*)(iii) with effect from 1 January 1993; previously: "supplies goods or services".

17   Subss (1A)-(1B) inserted by FA 1973 s 80 with effect from 3 September 1973.
18   Subs (2) deleted by FA 1985 s 43 with effect from 1 March 1985.
19   Inserted by FA 1992 s 173(3)(*d*)(i) with effect from 1 January 1993.
20   Inserted by FA 1992 s 173(3)(*d*)(ii) with effect from 1 January 1993.
21   Words "(apart from subsection (2))" deleted by FA 1985 s 43 with effect from 1 March 1985.
22   Inserted by FA 1992 s 173(3)(*d*)(iii) with effect from 1 January 1993.
23   Inserted by FA 1992 s 173(3)(*d*)(iv) with effect from 1 January 1993.
24   Subs (3) substituted by VATAA 1978 s 9 with effect from 1 March 1979.
25   Substituted by VATAA 1978 s 30(2) with effect from 1 March 1979; previously "delivered".
26   Substituted by VATAA 1978 s 30(2) with effect from 1 March 1979; previously "delivery".
27   Substituted by VATAA 1978 s 30(2) with effect from 1 March 1979; previously "delivers goods or services".
28   Substituted by VATAA 1978 s 30(2) with effect from 1 March 1979; previously "rendered".
29   Subs (4) substituted by FA 1975 s 51 with effect from 16 January 1975.
30   Substituted by FA 1993 s 87(*b*); previously "section 11(1)(*c*)".
31   Subs (4A) substituted by VATAA 1978 s 9 with effect from 1 March 1979.
32   Subs (5) deleted by FA 1995 s 128(*b*) with effect from 2 June 1995.
33   Subs (7) deleted by FA 1992 s 173(2)(*b*) with effect from 28 May 1992.
34   Substituted by FA 1993 s 87(*c*); previously "Second, Third, Sixth or Seventh Schedule".
35   Words "and may, in like manner, vary the Fourth Schedule by deleting therefrom descriptions of goods of any kind or by varying any description of goods for the time being specified therein" deleted by VATAA 1978 s 30(1) with effect from 1 March 1979.
36   Subs (8)(*a*) substituted by FA 1973 s 80 with effect from 3 September 1973.
37   Subs (9) repealed by VATAA 1978 s 30(1) with effect from 1 March 1979.

Cross-references
Apportionment of taxable consideration (subs (3)), Revenue may prescribe manner: s 32(1)(*e*); apportionment: VATR 1979 r 34.
Distortion of competition, Revenue may determine a person to be a taxable person (subs (1)(*d*)): s 8(3E)(*a*).
Income tax appeal procedures (subs (1B)) applied by s 25(2)(*k*); determination of rate, Revenue may prescribe manner: s 32(1)(xxx); Value Added Tax (Determination in Regard to Tax) Regulations 1992 (SI 278/1992).
Margin scheme goods, subs (1)(*b*) does not apply unless goods are otherwise zero-rated: s 10A(10); option to apply margin scheme (subs (1AA)(*b*)(ii)): s 10A(4)(*c*).
Residual tax deductible by taxable dealer when acquiring means of transport: s 12B(4)(*a*), (7), (8).
Special scheme for auctioneers, subs (1)(*b*) does not apply unless goods are otherwise zero-rated: s 10B(7).

Statements of practice
Farmers agricultural services: SP VAT 5/92.
Food and drink supplied through catering business, hotel, restaurant, pub etc: SP VAT 10/92.
Live horses: SP VAT 3/90.
Services rates of VAT: SP VAT 1/92.
Zero rating of sales of goods to other EC States after 1 January 1993: SP VAT 8/92.

Narrative
Irish Value Added Tax, Chapter 8; *Guide to Value Added Tax (Revenue Commissioners)*: Chapters 15, 16.

Definition
"Appeal Commissioners": s 1(1); "body of persons": s 1(1); "business": s 1(1); "Dáil Éireann": IA 1937 Sch; "exempted activity": s 1(1); "goods": s 1(1); "hire": s 1(1); "immovable goods": s 1(1); "intra-Community acquisition of goods": ss 1(1), 3A; "livestock": s 1(1); "the Minister": s 1(1); "movable goods": s 1(1); "person": IA 1937 s 11(*c*); "regulations": ss 1(1), 32; "supply": s 1(1); "tax": s 1(1); "taxable goods": s 1(1); "taxable person": s 1(1), 8; "writing": IA 1937 Sch.

___

Personal notes

___

___

___

___

___

___

___

___

___

___

___

12 Deduction for tax borne or paid

[(1)   (a)   In computing the amount of tax payable by him in respect of a taxable period, a taxable person may, insofar as the goods and services are used by him for the purposes of his taxable supplies or of any of the qualifying activities, deduct—   a 17, 18, 19

     (i)   the tax charged to him during the period by other taxable persons by means of invoices, prepared in the manner prescribed by regulations, in respect of supplies of goods or services to him,   a 20

     (ii)   in respect of goods imported by him in the period, the tax paid by him or deferred as established from the relevant customs documents kept by him in accordance with section 16(3),   a 17(2)(b)

     [(ia)   the amount in respect of tax indicated separately on a document issued during the period in accordance with section 17(1AA) in respect of a supply of goods to him.][1]

     [(iia)   subject to such conditions (if any) as may be specified in regulations, the tax chargeable during the period, being tax for which he is liable in respect of intra-Community acquisitions of goods,

     (iib)   subject to and in accordance with regulations, in respect of goods supplied under section 3(1)(g) an amount equal to any residual tax included in the consideration for the supply,][2]

     [(iic)   subject to such conditions (if any) as may be specified in regulations, in respect of goods referred to in section 3B, the tax due in the period in accordance with that section,][3]

     (iii)   the tax chargeable during the period in respect of goods [other than supplies of goods referred to in section 3(6)(d))][4] treated as supplied by him in accordance with section 3(1)(e),

     [(iiia)   the tax charged to him during the period by other taxable persons in respect of services directly related to the transfer of ownership of goods specified in section 3(5)(b)(iii),][5]

     [(iiib)   the tax chargeable during the period, being tax for which he is liable by virtue of section 4A (1), in respect of goods received by him.][6]

     (iv)   the tax chargeable during the period in respect of services treated as supplied by him for consideration in the course or furtherance of his business in accordance with section 5(3)(d),

     (v)   the tax chargeable during the period, being tax for which he is liable by virtue of section 5(3A), in respect of services received by him,

     [(vi)   subject to and in accordance with regulations (if any), residual tax referred to in section 12B,][7]

     (vii)   the tax chargeable during the period, being tax for which he is liable by virtue of section 8(2), in respect of services received by him, and

     (viii)   [flat-rate addition, which shall be deemed to be tax,][8] charged to him during the period by means of invoices prepared in the manner prescribed by regulations and issued to him in accordance with section 12A.   a 25(6)(a)

   [Provided that this paragraph shall not apply to—

     (I)   a taxable person referred to in subsection (1A)(c) or (2)(b) of section 8, or

(II) a taxable person referred to in subsection (1A)(*d*) or (2)(*c*) of section 8 unless the tax relates to racehorse training services supplied by him.]⁹

a 17(3)(c)

(*b*) In paragraph (*a*) **"qualifying activities"** means—

(i) transport outside the State of passengers and their accompanying baggage,

[(*ia*) supplies of goods which, by virtue of section 3(6)(*d*), are deemed to have taken place in the territory of another Member State:

Provided that the supplier is registered for value added tax in that other Member State,]¹⁰

a 17(3)(b)

(ii) services specified in paragraph (i), (ix)(*b*), (*c*) or (*d*), or (xi), of the First Schedule, supplied—

(I) outside the Community, or

(II) directly in connection with the export of goods to a place outside the Community, and

a 17(3)(a)

(iii) supplies of goods or services outside the State which would be taxable supplies if made in the State.]¹¹

[(1A) (*a*) A person who, by election or in accordance with the provisions of sections 8(4) is deemed to become [a taxable person],¹² shall, in accordance with regulations, be entitled, in computing the amount of tax payable by him in respect of the first taxable period for which he is so deemed to be [a taxable person]¹² to treat as tax deductible under subsection (1) such part of the value of the stock-in-trade (within the meaning of section 34) held by him immediately before the commencement of that taxable period as could reasonably be regarded as the amount which he would be entitled to claim under the said subsection (1) if he had been [a taxable person]¹² at the time of the delivery to him of such stock-in-trade.

(*b*) No claim shall lie under this subsection for a deduction for the tax relating to any stock-in-trade (within the meaning of section 34) if, and to the extent that, a deduction under subsection (1) could be claimed apart from this subsection.

(*c*) This subsection shall have effect in relation to taxable periods commencing on or after the 3rd day of September, 1973.]¹³

a 18(4)

(2) If, in relation to any taxable period, the total amount deductible under this section exceeds the amount which, but for this section, would be payable in respect of such period, the excess shall be [refunded to the taxable person in accordance with section 20(1)]¹⁴ [, but subject to section 20(1A).]¹⁵

a 17(6)

[(3) (*a*) Notwithstanding anything [in this section, a deduction of tax under this section]¹⁶ shall not be made if, and to the extent that, the tax relates to —

(i) the provision of food or drink, or accommodation or other personal services, for the taxable person, his agents or his employees, except to the extent, if any, that such provision constitutes a supply of services in respect of which he is accountable for tax,

[(*ia*) expenditure incurred by the taxable person on food or drink, or accommodation or other entertainment services, where such expenditure forms all or part of the cost of providing an advertising service in respect of which tax is due and payable by the taxable person,]¹⁷

(ii) entertainment expenses incurred by the taxable person, his agents or his employees,

(iii) the [purchase, hiring, intra-Community acquisition or importation]¹⁸ of motor vehicles otherwise than as stock-in-trade or for the purposes of a business which consists in whole or part of the hiring of motor vehicles or for use, in a driving school business, for giving driving instruction, [or]¹⁹

(iv) the purchase [intra-Community acquisition or importation]²⁰ of petrol otherwise than as stock-in-trade, ...²¹

[(iv*a*) the procurement of a supply of contract work where such supply consists of the handing over of goods to which this paragraph applies.]²¹

(v) ...²².

(*b*) In paragraph (*a*) of this subsection **"motor vehicles"** means motor vehicles designed and constructed for the conveyance of persons by road and sports motor vehicles, estate cars, station wagons, motor cycles, motor scooters, mopeds and auto cycles, whether or not designed and constructed for the purpose aforesaid, excluding vehicles designed and constructed for the carriage of more than 16 persons (inclusive of the driver), invalid carriages and other vehicles of a type designed for use by invalids or infirm persons.]²³

[(*c*) In subparagraph (i) of paragraph (*a*), reference to the provision of accommodation includes expenditure by the taxable person on a building, including the fitting out of such building, to provide such accommodation.

(*d*) In subparagraph (ii) of paragraph (*a*), "entertainment expenses" includes expenditure on a building or facility, including the fitting out of such building or facility, to provide such entertainment.]²⁴

[(3A) Notwithstanding anything in this section, where—

(*a*) the provisions of subsection (3) or (8) of section 10A or subsection (3) of section 10B have been applied to a supply of goods to a taxable person, or

(*b*) a taxable dealer deducts residual tax, in accordance with subsection (1)(*a*)(vi), in respect of a supply of a means of transport to a taxable person,

that taxable person shall not deduct, in accordance with subsection (1), any tax in relation to the supply to that person.]²⁵

[(4) Where goods or services (not being goods or services on the acquisition of which a deduction of tax shall not, in accordance with subsection (3), be made) are used by a taxable person for the purposes of supplies or activities in relation to which tax is deductible in accordance with this section and also for the purposes of other supplies or activities, such proportion only of tax shall be deductible as is attributable to those first-mentioned supplies or activities and the said proportion shall be determined in accordance with regulations.]²⁶

a 16,
a 17(5), 19

Amendments

1 Subs (1)(i*a*) inserted by FA 1996 s 93(*a*) with effect from 1 July 1996.
2 Subs (1)(*a*)(ii*a*)-(ii*b*) inserted by FA 1992 s 174(*a*) with effect from 1 January 1993.
3 Subs (1)(*a*)(ii*c*) inserted by FA 1993 s 88(*a*) with effect from 1 August 1993.
4 Inserted b y EC(VAT)R 1992 r 10(*b*) with effect from 1 January 1993.
5 Subs (1)(*a*)(iii*a*) inserted by FA 1991 s 81 with effect from 29 May 1991.
6 Subs (1)(*a*)(iii*b*) inserted by FA 1994 s 96(*a*) with effect from such date as the Minister for Finance may appoint.
7 Subs (1)(*a*)(vi) substituted by FA 1995 s 129(*a*) with effect from 1 July 1995.
8 Substituted by FA 1993 s 88(*b*) with effect from 17 June 1993; previously "tax".
9 Subs (1)(*a*)(proviso) inserted by FA 1993 s 88(*c*) with effect from 17 June 1993.
10 Subs (1)(*b*)(i*a*) inserted by EC(VAT)R 1992 r 10(*a*) with effect from 1 January 1993.
11 Subs (1) substituted by FA 1987 s 41 with effect from 1 November 1987.
12 Substituted by VATAA 1978 s 30(2) with effect from 1 March 1979; previously "an accountable person".

13   Subs (1A) inserted by FA 1973 s 81 with effect from 3 September 1973.

14   Substituted by FA 1981 s 44 with effect from 28 May 1981; previously "repaid to the taxable person".

15   Inserted by FA 1986 s 84 with effect from 27 May 1986.

16   Substituted by FA 1987 s 41 with effect from 1 November 1987; previously "in subsection (1), a deduction of tax under that subsection".

17   Subs (3)(*a*)(i*a*) inserted by FA 1994 s 96(*b*)(i) with effect from 23 May 1994.

18   Substituted by FA 1992 s 174(*b*)(i) with effect from 1 January 1993; previously "acquisition (including hiring)".

19   Inserted by FA 1987 s 41 with effect from 1 November 1987.

20   Inserted by FA 1992 s 174(*b*)(ii) with effect from 1 January 1993.

21   Word "or" deleted and subs (3)(*a*)(iv*a*) inserted by FA 1996 s 93(*b*) with effect from 15 May 1996.

22   Subs (3)(*a*)(v) deleted by FA 1987 s 41 with effect from 1 November 1987.

23   Subs (3) substituted by VATAA 1978 s 10 with effect from 1 March 1979.

24   Subs (3)(*c*)-(*d*) inserted by FA 1994 s 96(*b*)(ii) with effect from 23 May 1994.

25   Subs (3A) inserted by FA 1995 s 129(*b*) with effect from 1 July 1995.

26   Subs (4) substituted by FA 1987 s 41 with effect from 1 November 1987.

Cross-references

Apportionment between deductible and non-deductible tax (subs (4)), Revenue may determine method: s 32(1)(x); method: VATR 1979 r 16.

Art works, rate of tax: s 11(1AA)(*b*).

Auction scheme goods, defined: s 10B(1).

Exporter (subs (3)(*b*)), charge of tax at 0% to, "qualifying goods" means all taxable goods excluding motor vehicles within the meaning of this subsection (and petrol): s 13A(1).

Intra-EU acquisitions (subs (1)(*a*)(ii*a*)), Revenue may prescribe manner of deduction of tax: s 32(1)(*aa*).

Motor vehicles (subs (3)(*b*)), taxable dealers supplying means of transport, special scheme: s 12B(10).

Person not entitled to deduction under this section, intra-Community acquisitions of new vehicle, boat or plane: s 19(4)(*a*).

Regulations (subs (1)(*a*)(vi)) require Minister for Finance's consent: s 32(2A).

Residual tax (subs (1)(*a*)(ii*b*)), Revenue may prescribe manner of calculation: s 32(1).

Second-hand motor vehicles bought from non taxable persons: Value Added Tax (Second-hand Motor Vehicles) Regulations 1988 (SI 121/1988).

Stock relief on registering (subs (1A)), Revenue may prescribe amount to be given: s 32(1)(xx); relief: VATR 1979 r 22.

Taxable dealers supplying means of transport (subs (1)(*a*))(vi)), special scheme: s 12B(1), (2), (4); Revenue may prescribe manner of deduction of tax: s 32(1)(*dd*).

Tax (subs (1)(*b*)), charged at 0% (for the purposes of s 4(1)(*a*) or 4(6)(*a*)) by virtue of Sch 2 para (vi*a*) is deemed to be deductible: s 13A(7).

Narrative

Irish Value Added Tax, Chapter 7; *Guide to Value Added Tax (Revenue Commissioners)*: Chapter 6.

Case law

Property unit trust, deductibility of pre and post lease expenditure: *Erin Executor and Trustee Company Ltd v Revenue Commissioners*, [1994] ITR 179.

Television aerial regarded as a fixture when installed *Maye v Revenue Commissioners*, III ITR 332.

Definition

"business": s 1(1); "Community" s 1(1); "goods": s 1(1); "intra-Community acquisition of goods": s 1(1), 3A; "person": IA 1937 s 11(*c*); "regulations": ss 1(1), 32; "second-hand": s 1(1); "supply": s 1(1); "tax": s 1(1); "taxable period": s 1(1); "taxable person": s 1(1), 8.

Statement of practice

Shares, VAT not deductible: SP VAT 2/90.

Personal notes

12A Special provisions for tax invoiced by flat-rate farmers

[(1) Where a flat-rate farmer supplies agricultural produce or an agricultural service to a person, the farmer shall, subject to section 17(2), issue to the person an invoice indicating the consideration (exclusive of the flat-rate addition) in respect of the supply and an amount (in this Act referred to as **"a flat-rate addition"**) equal to [**2.8 per cent**]¹ of the said consideration (exclusive of the said addition) ...².   a 25(5)

[(2) In this Act **"flat-rate farmer"** means—

     (*a*)   a farmer who is not a taxable person,

     (*b*)   a farmer who is a taxable person referred to in subsection (1A)(*c*) or (2)(*b*) of section 8, or

     (*c*)   a person who, in accordance with section 8(3A), is deemed not to be a taxable person in relation to the supplies specified in the definition of 'farmer' in section 8(9).]³

Amendments

1   Substituted by FA 1996 s 94 with effect from 1 March 1996; previously "2.5 per cent" (FA 1993 s 89(*a*) with effect from 1 March 1993); previously "2.7 per cent" (FA 1992 s 175(1) with effect from 1 March 1992); previously "2.3 per cent" (FA 1990 s 103, with effect from 1 January 1991); previously "2 per cent".

2   Words "and the person shall, if he is a taxable person, be entitled to treat the flat-rate addition as tax deductible under section 12 subject, however, to any restrictions imposed by or under subsection (3) or (4) of that section" deleted by FA 1992 s 175(2) with effect from 1 January 1993.

3   Subs (2) substituted by FA 1993 s 89(*b*).

Cross-references

Non compliance, penalties: s 26(1), (2A).

Narrative

Irish Value Added Tax, Chapter 7.

Statement of practice

Flat-rate farmers and the Single Market: SP VAT 2/93.

Definition

"agricultural produce": s 1(1); "agricultural service": s 1(1); "farmer": ss 1(1), 8; "person": IA 1937 s 11(*c*); "supply": s 1(1); "tax": s 1(1); "taxable person": ss 1(1), 8.

Personal notes

12B Special scheme for means of transport supplied by taxable dealers

[(1) Where a taxable dealer supplies a means of transport, the residual tax which is deductible in accordance with section 12(1)(*a*)(vi) shall be deemed to be tax and shall be the amount referred to in subsection (4).

(2) The entitlement to deduct residual tax referred to in subsection (1) shall arise only where a taxable dealer purchases or acquires--

> (*a*) a means of transport from a person, other than a person referred to in subsection (10), who was not entitled to deduct, under section 12, any tax in respect of that person's purchase, intra-Community acquisition or importation of that means of transport, or

> (*b*) a means of transport other than a new means of transport from a person in another Member State who was not entitled to deduct, under the provisions implementing Article 17 of Council Directive No. 77/388/ EEC of 17 May 1977 in that Member State, any value-added tax referred to in that Directive in respect of that person's purchase, intra-Community acquisition or importation of that means of transport, or

> (*c*) a means of transport from a taxable person who has exercised the entitlement under section 12(1)(*a*)(vi) to deduct the residual tax in respect of that person's supply of that means of transport to the said dealer, or

> (*d*) a means of transport other than a new means of transport from a taxable dealer in another Member State who has applied the provisions implementing Article 26a or 28o (inserted by Council Directive No. 94/5/EC of 14 February 1994) of Council Directive No. 77/388/EEC of 17 May 1977 to the supply of that means of transport, in that other Member State.

(3) In this section—

"taxable dealer" means a taxable person who in the course or furtherance of business, whether acting on that person's own behalf, or on behalf of another person pursuant to a contract under which commission is payable on purchase or sale, purchases or acquires means of transport as stock-in-trade with a view to resale, and a person in another Member State shall be deemed to be a taxable dealer where, in similar circumstances, that person would be a taxable dealer in the State under this section;

"means of transport" means motorised land vehicles with an engine cylinder capacity exceeding 48 cubic centimetres or a power exceeding 7.2 kilowatts, vessels exceeding 7.5 metres in length and aircraft with a take-off weight exceeding 1,550 kilogrammes, which are intended for the transport of persons or goods, other than vessels and aircraft of the kind referred to in paragraph (v) of the Second Schedule.

(4) The residual tax which may be deducted by a taxable dealer in accordance with section 12(1)(*a*)(vi) shall be the residual tax deemed to be included in the purchase price payable by such dealer when acquiring a means of transport and shall be determined by the formula—

$$A \times \frac{B}{B+100}$$

where—

A is the purchase price of the means of transport, and

B is the percentage rate of tax specified—

> (*a*) in section 11(1)(*a*) where the means of transport is deemed to be supplied within the State to the taxable dealer, or

(*b*)   in provisions implementing Article 12(1) of Council Directive No. 77/ 388/EEC of 17 May 1977 in another Member State where the means of transport is deemed to be supplied within that Member State to the taxable dealer:

Provided that, subject to subsection (8), where the amount so calculated is in excess of the tax chargeable on the supply by the taxable dealer of the means of transport, the residual tax shall be an amount equal to the amount of tax chargeable on that supply.

(5) Notwithstanding section 17, where a taxable dealer deducts residual tax referred to in subsection (1) in respect of a supply of a means of transport, that dealer shall not indicate separately the amount of tax chargeable in respect of that supply on any invoice or other document issued in lieu thereof in accordance with that section.

(6) Notwithstanding section 3(6)(*d*), in the case of a supply of a means of transport which is dispatched or transported and where--

(*a*)   a taxable dealer deducts residual tax referred to in subsection (1) in respect of the supply of that means of transport, or

(*b*)   a taxable dealer in another Member State has applied the provisions implementing Article 26a or 28o of Council Directive No. 77/388/ EEC of 17 May 1977 in that other Member State, to the supply of that means of transport,

the place of supply shall be deemed to be the place where the dispatch or transportation begins.

(7) Where a taxable dealer deducts residual tax referred to in subsection (1) in respect of a supply of a means of transport, then, subject to subsection (8), the provisions of section 11(1)(*b*) shall not apply in respect of that supply.

(8) Notwithstanding subsection (7), where a taxable dealer deducts residual tax referred to in subsection (1) in respect of the supply of a new means of transport dispatched or transported by the supplier to a person in another Member State, the provisions of section 11(1)(*b*) shall apply, and in determining the amount of the residual tax in accordance with subsection (4) the proviso to that subsection shall not apply.

(9) Where a taxable dealer supplies a means of transport on behalf of another person pursuant to a contract under which commission is payable on purchase or sale, the means of transport shall be deemed to have been supplied by that other person to the taxable dealer when the said taxable dealer supplies that means of transport.

(10) Notwithstanding paragraph (xxiv) of the First Schedule, the provisions of that paragraph shall not apply to--

(*a*)   a supply by a taxable person of a means of transport, other than a motor vehicle as defined in section 12(3)(*b*), which that person acquired from a taxable dealer who deducted residual tax in respect of the supply of that means of transport to that person, and

(*b*)   a supply by a taxable person other than a taxable dealer of a motor vehicle, as defined in section 12(3)(*b*), which that person acquired as stock-in-trade or for the purposes of a business which consists in whole or part of the hiring of motor vehicles or for use, in a driving school business, for giving driving instruction, from a taxable dealer who deducted residual tax in respect of the supply of that motor vehicle to that person.][1]

Amendments
1 Section 12B inserted by FA 1995 s 130 with effect from 1 July 1995.
Cross-references
Deductible tax: s 12(1)(*a*)(vi).
Definitions
"business": s 1(1); "Community": s 1(1); "person": IA 1937 s 11(*c*); "supply": s 1(1); "tax": s 1(1); "taxable person": s 1(1).

Personal notes

13 Remission of tax on goods exported, etc

a 15, 16, 17

[(1) Regulations may make provision for remitting or repaying, subject to such conditions (if any) as may be specified in the regulations or as the Revenue Commissioners may impose, the tax chargeable in respect of the supply of goods, or of such goods as may be specified in the regulations, in cases where the Revenue Commissioners are satisfied—

    (*a*)   that the goods have been or are to be exported,

    (*b*)   that the goods have been shipped on board an aircraft or ship proceeding to a place outside the State,

    (*c*)   that the goods are, or are to be used in, a fishing vessel used or to be used for the purposes of commercial sea fishing.

(2) Regulations may make provision for remitting or repaying, subject to such conditions (if any) as may be specified in the regulations or as the Revenue Commissioners may impose, the tax chargeable in respect of the supply of all or any one or more (as may be specified in the regulations) of the following services:

a 17(4)

    (*a*)   services directly linked to the export of goods or the transit of goods from a place outside the State to another place outside the State,

    (*b*)   the repair, maintenance and hiring of plant or equipment used in a vessel or an aircraft specified in paragraph (v) of the Second Schedule,

    (*c*)   the repair, maintenance and hiring of a vessel used, or of plant or equipment used in a vessel used, for the purposes of commercial sea fishing.

(3)   (*a*)   The Revenue Commissioners shall, in accordance with regulations, repay to a person to whom this subsection applies, deductible tax chargeable in respect of supplies of goods or services to him or in respect of goods imported by him.

a 17(4)

    (*b*)   This subsection applies to a person who shows to the satisfaction of the Revenue Commissioners that he carries on a business outside the State and that he supplies no goods or services in the State.

    (*c*)   In this subsection **"deductible tax"**, in relation to a person to whom this subsection applies, means tax chargeable [(including any flat-rate addition)][1] in respect of goods or services used by him for the purposes of any business carried on by him to the extent that such tax would be deductible by him under section 12 if the business were carried on by him within the State but does not include tax chargeable in respect of goods for supply within the State [or in respect of means of transport for hiring out for utilisation within the State][2] ...[3]

[(3A) (*a*)   The Revenue Commissioners shall, in accordance with regulations, repay to a person to whom this subsection applies the residual tax included in the consideration for supply of a new means of transport, where such new means of transport is subsequently dispatched or transported to another Member State.

    (*b*)   This subsection applies to a person not entitled to a deduction under section 12 of the tax borne or paid by him on the purchase, intra-Community acquisition or importation of the goods in question.][4]

(4) ...[5]

(5) ...[5.][6]

Amendments

1 Inserted by FA 1992 s 176(*a*) with effect from 1 January 1993.

2 Inserted by FA 1987 s 43 with effect from 9 July 1987.

3 Words "or for hiring out for utilisation within the State" deleted by FA 1985 s 45 with effect from 30 May 1985.

4 Subs (3A) inserted by FA 1992 s 176(*b*) with effect from 1 January 1993.

5 Subss (4)-(5) deleted by FA 1982 s 82 with effect from 1 September 1982.

6 Section 13 inserted by VATAA 1978 s 12; previously repealed by FA 1976 s 81.

Cross-references

Fishing boats, etc, tax refund procedures: VATR 1979 r 29.

Foreign traders (unregistered), refund procedures: VATR 1979 r 30.

Goods allegedly exported liable to forfeiture: ss 27(9), (9A).

Residual tax (subs (3A)), Revenue may prescribe manner of calculation and repayment: s 32(1)(*ac*).

Regulations (subss (1)-(2)) require consent of Minister for Finance: s 32(2A).

Retail exporters (goods sold to tourists etc): Value Added Tax (Exported Goods) Regulations 1992 (SI 438/92)

Narrative

Irish Value Added Tax, Chapter 7; *Guide to Value Added Tax (Revenue Commissioners)*: Chapter 14.

Definition

"business": s 1(1); "flat-rate addition": ss 1(1), 12A; "goods": s 1(1); "intra-Community acquisition of goods": ss 1(1), 3A; "new means of transport": s 1(1); "person": IA 1937 s 11(*c*); "regulations": ss 1(1), 32; "supply": s 1(1); "tax": s 1(1); "vessel": s 1(1).

Personal notes

13A Supplies to, and intra-Community acquisitions and imports by, certain   s 16
taxable persons

[(1) For the purposes of this section and paragraph (vi*a*) of the Second Schedule—

"authorised person" means a qualifying person who has been authorised in accordance with subsection (3);

"qualifying person" means a taxable person whose turnover from his supplies of goods made in accordance with subparagraph (*a*)(I) or (*b*) of paragraph (i) of the Second Schedule [, supplies of contract work where the place of supply is deemed to be a Member State other than the State and supplies of contract work made in accordance with paragraph (xvi) of the Second Schedule][1] amounts to, or is likely to amount to, **75 per cent** of his total annual turnover from his supplies of goods and services:

Provided that the turnover from a supply of goods to a taxable person which are subsequently leased back from that person is excluded from the total annual turnover for the purposes of establishing whether the person is a qualifying person;

"qualifying goods" means all taxable goods excluding motor vehicles within the meaning of section 12(3)(*b*) and petrol;

"qualifying services" means all taxable services excluding the provision of food or drink, accommodation, other personal services, entertainment services or the hire of motor vehicles within the meaning of section 12(3)(*b*).

(2) A person who wishes to become an authorised person shall—

> (*a*)   complete such application form as may be provided by the Revenue Commissioners for that purpose,

> (*b*)   certify the particulars shown on such form to be correct, and

> (*c*)   submit to the Revenue Commissioners the completed and certified application form, together with such further information in support of the application as may be requested by them.

(3)   (*a*)   Where a person has furnished the particulars required under subsection (2), the Revenue Commissioners shall, where they are satisfied that he is a qualifying person, issue to that person in writing an authorisation certifying him to be an authorised person.

> (*b*)   An authorisation issued in accordance with paragraph (*a*) shall be valid for such period as may be determined by the Revenue Commissioners.

> (*c*)   Where a person who has been authorised in accordance with paragraph (*a*) ceases to be a qualifying person, he shall, by notice in writing, advise the Revenue Commissioners accordingly not later than the end of the taxable period during which he ceased to be a qualifying person.

> (*d*)   The Revenue Commissioners shall, by notice in writing, cancel an authorisation issued to a person in accordance with paragraph (*a*) where they are satisfied that he is no longer a qualifying person and such cancellation shall have effect from the date specified in the notice.

(4) An authorised person shall furnish a copy of the authorisation referred to in subsection (3) to each taxable person in the State who supplies taxable goods or taxable services to him.

(5) A taxable person who supplies goods or services in circumstances where the provisions of paragraph (vi*a*) of the Second Schedule apply, shall, in addition to the details to be included on each invoice, credit note or other document required to be issued in accordance with section 17, include on such invoice, credit note or other document a reference to the number of the authorisation issued to the authorised person in accordance with subsection (3).

(6) In relation to each consignment of goods to be imported by an authorised person at the rate specified in section 11(1)(*b*) by virtue of paragraph (v*ia*) of the Second Schedule the following conditions shall be complied with:

(*a*)   a copy of the authorisation referred to at subsection (3) shall be produced with the relevant customs entry; and

(*b*)   the relevant customs entry shall incorporate—

(i)   a declaration by the authorised person, or by his representative duly authorised in writing for that purpose, that he is an authorised person in accordance with this section for the purposes of paragraph (v*ia*) of the Second Schedule, and

(ii)   a claim for importation at the rate specified in section 11(1)(*b*).

(7) For the purposes of subsections (1)(*a*)(ii) and (6)(*a*) of section 4, the tax charged at the rate specified in section 11(1)(*b*) by virtue of paragraph (v*ia*) of the Second Schedule shall be deemed to be tax which is deductible under section 12.

(8) Where an authorised person is in receipt of a service in respect of which, had the provisions of paragraph (v*ia*) of the Second Schedule not applied, tax would have been chargeable at a rate other than the rate specified in section 11(1)(*b*) and all or part of such tax would not have been deductible by him under section 12, then the authorised person shall, in relation to such service, be liable to pay tax as if he himself had supplied the service for consideration in the course or furtherance of his business to a person who is not an authorised person.

(9) For the purposes of this section, and subject to the direction and control of the Revenue Commissioners, any power, function or duty conferred or imposed on them may be exercised or performed on their behalf by an officer of the Revenue Commissioners.][2]

Amendments
1   Inserted by FA 1996 s 95 with effect from 1 January 1996.
2   Section 13A inserted by FA 1993 s 90 with effect from 1 August 1993.
Cross-references
Charge of tax at 0% to authorised persons: Sch 2 para (v*ia*).
Narrative
Guide to Value Added Tax (Revenue Commissioners): Chapter 13.
Statement of practice
Zero-rating of goods in accordance with section 13A of the VAT Act: SP VAT 1/93.
Definitions
"excisable products": s 1(1); "intra-Community acquisition of goods": s 1(1), 3A; "person": IA 1937 s 11(*c*); "regulations": s 1(1), 32; "statute": IA 1937 s 3; "supply": s 1(1); "tax": s 1(1); "taxable person": s 1(1).

Personal notes

_____

_____

_____

_____

_____

_____

_____

_____

_____

_____

14 Payment based on cash receipts

[(1) A person who satisfies the Revenue Commissioners that–

    (*a*)   taking one period with another, not less than 90 per cent. of such person's turnover is derived from taxable supplies to persons who are not registered persons, or

    (*b*)   the total consideration which such person is entitled to receive in respect of such person's taxable supplies has not exceeded and is not likely to exceed £250,000 in any continuous period of twelve months,

may, in accordance with regulations, be authorised to determine the amount of tax which becomes due by such person during any taxable period (or part thereof) during which the authorisation has effect by reference to the amount of the moneys which such person receives during such taxable period (or part thereof) in respect of taxable supplies.]¹

[(1A) Where an authorisation to which subsection (1) relates has not been cancelled under subsection (2), then—

    (*a*)   the rate of tax due by the person concerned in respect of a supply shall be the rate of tax chargeable at the time the goods or services are supplied,

    (*b*)   if tax on a supply has already been due and payable under any other provisions of this Act prior to the issue of such authorisation, tax shall not be due again in respect of any such supply as a result of the application of subsection (1), and

    (*c*)   if no tax is due or payable on a supply made prior to the issue of such authorisation, tax shall not be due in respect of any such supply as a result of the application of subsection (1).]²

[(1B) (*a*)   The Minister may, by order—

        (i)   increase the amount specified in subsection (1)(*b*), or

        (ii)   where an amount stands specified by virtue of an order under this paragraph, including an order relating to this subparagraph, further increase the amount so specified.

    (*b*)   An order under paragraph (*a*) shall be laid before Dáil Éireann as soon as may be after it is made and, if a resolution annulling the order is passed by Dáil Éireann within the next twenty-one sitting days on which Dáil Éireann has sat after the order is laid before it, the order shall be annulled accordingly, but without prejudice to the validity of anything previously done thereunder.]³

(2) The Revenue Commissioners may, in accordance with regulations, cancel an authorisation under ...⁴ subsection (1), and may, by regulations exclude from the application of [that subsection]⁵...⁶ any tax due in respect of specified descriptions of supplies of goods or services and any moneys received in respect of such supplies.

[(3) This section shall not apply to tax provided for by subsection (1)(*b*) [or (1A)]⁷ of section 2.]⁸]⁹

Amendments
1 Subs (1) substituted by FA 1994 s 97(*a*) with effect from 23 May 1994.
2 Subs (1A) inserted by FA 1992 s 177(1)(*b*) with effect from 28 May 1992.
3 Subs (1B) inserted by FA 1995 s 131 with effect from 2 June 1995.
4 Deleted by FA 1994 s 97(*b*)(i) with effect from 23 May 1994; previously "paragraph (*a*) of".
5 Substituted by FA 1994 s 97(*b*)(ii) with effect from 23 May 1994; previously "the said paragraphs (*a*)".
6 Words "and (*b*)" deleted by FA 1992 s 177(1)(*c*) with effect from 1 January 1993.
7 Words "or (1A)" inserted by FA 1992 s 177(2) with effect from 1 January 1993.
8 Subs (3) inserted by FA 1992 s 177(1)(*d*) with effect from 28 May 1992.
9 Section 14 substituted by VATAA 1978 s 13 with effect from 1 March 1979.
Cross-references
Cash basis, Revenue may prescribe how determined, and adjustments required: s 32(1)(*g*); regulations: Value Added Tax (Determination of Tax Due by Reference to Moneys Received) Regulations 1992 (SI 306/1992).

Narrative

Irish Value Added Tax, Chapter 6; *Guide to Value Added Tax (Revenue Commissioners)*: Chapter 8.

Definition

"Dáil Éireann": IA 1937 Sch; "goods": s 1(1); "the Minister": s 1(1); "moneys received": s 1(2); "person": IA 1937 s 11(c); "regulations": ss 1(1), 32; "the specified day": s 1(1); "supply": s 1(1); "tax": s 1(1); "taxable goods": s 1(1); "taxable period": s 1(1).

Statement of practice

Cash receipts basis; eligibility, change in operation with effect from 1 January 1993: SP VAT 16/92.

Personal notes

15 Charge of tax on imported goods

[(1) Tax shall be charged on the importation of goods at whichever of the rates   a 12(5) specified in section 11(1) is the appropriate rate in respect of such goods.]¹

(2) ...²

(3) The value of imported goods for the purposes of this section shall be their   a 11B value determined in accordance with the acts for the time being in force adopted by the institutions of the Community relating to the valuation of goods for customs purposes, modified by the substitution of references to the territory of the State for references to the customs territory of the Community, together with any taxes, duties [, expenses resulting from the transport of the goods to another place of destination within the Community, if that destination is known at the time of the importation,]³ and other charges levied either outside or, by reason of importation, within the State (except value added tax) on the goods and not included in the determination.

(4) ...⁴

(5) The Revenue Commissioners may, in accordance with regulations, remit or repay, if they think fit, the whole or part of the tax chargeable—

    (*a*)   on the importation of any goods which are shown to their satisfaction to have been previously exported,

    (*b*)   on the importation of any goods if they are satisfied that the goods have been or are to be re-exported,

    (*c*)   on the importation of any goods from the customs-free airport by an unregistered person who shows to the satisfaction of the Revenue Commissioners that he has already borne tax on the goods,

[(5A) The Revenue Commissioners shall, in accordance with regulations, repay   a 28a(3) the tax chargeable on the importation of goods where the goods have been dispatched or transported:

    (*a*)   to another Member State from outside the Community, and

    (*b*)   to a person, other than an individual, who is not registered for value added tax in that other Member State:

Provided that this subsection shall only apply where it is shown to the satisfaction of the Revenue Commissioners that the goods in question have been subject to value added tax referred to in Council Directive No. 77/388/EEC of 17 May 1977 in that other Member State.]⁵

(6) Subject to the foregoing provisions of this section, the provisions of the Customs Consolidation Act, 1876, and of other law in force in the State relating to customs shall apply with such exceptions and modifications (if any) as may be specified in regulations, to tax referred to in this section as if it were a duty of customs.

[(6A) Regulation 26 of the Value Added Tax Regulations, 1979 (S.I. No.63 of 1979), is hereby revoked and tax charged under section 2(1)(*b*) shall, in accordance with the provisions of the Customs Consolidation Act, 1876, and of other law in force in the State relating to customs, as applied to tax by subsection (6) and regulations thereunder, be paid in the manner and at the time that it would have been payable if that regulation had not been made]⁶.

(7) Regulations may—

    (*a*)   make provision for enabling goods imported by registered persons or by such classes of registered persons as may be specified in the regulations for the purposes of a business carried on by them to be delivered or removed, subject to such conditions or restrictions as may be specified in the regulations or as the Revenue Commissioners may impose, without payment of the tax chargeable on the importation, and (*b*)   provide that the tax be accounted for by the persons or classes of persons aforesaid in the return, made by them under section 19(3), in respect of the taxable period during which the goods are so delivered or removed.][7]

Amendments

1   Subs (1) substituted by FA 1992 s 178(*a*) with effect from 28 May 1992.
2   Subs (2) deleted by FA 1992 s 178(*b*) with effect from 28 May 1992.
3   Inserted by FA 1996 s 96 with effect from 1 January 1996.
4   Subs (4) deleted by FA 1985 s 46 with effect from 1 March 1985.
5   Subs (5A) inserted by FA 1992 s 178(*c*) with effect from 1 January 1993.
6   Subs (6A) inserted by FA 1982 s 84 with effect from 1 September 1982.
7   Section 15 substituted by VATAA 1978 s 14 with effect from 1 March 1979.

Cross-references

Alcohol products (subss (3) and (6)): s 3B(5) and (4).
Imports (subs (7)): Value Added Tax (Imported Goods) Regulations 1992 (SI 439/1992).
Repayment of tax charged at import (subs (5A)), Revenue may make regulations: s 32(1)(*ad*).
Regulations (subss (6)-(7)) require consent of Minister for Finance: s 32(2A).
Transport services relating to importation of goods, where value of service is included in taxable amount (subs (3)): Sch 2 para (xvi*a*).

Sixth Directive

Imports: a 7; chargeable event: a 10; within the territory of the country: a 11; exemptions on importation: a 14; persons liable to pay tax to the authorities: a 21; obligations under the internal system: a 22; obligations in respect of imports: a 23.

Narrative

Irish Value Added Tax, Chapter 9; *Guide to Value Added Tax (Revenue Commissioners)*: Chapter 13.

Definition

"business": s 1(1); "Community": s 1(1); "the customs-free airport": s 1(1); "goods": s 1(1); "importation of goods": s 1(1); "livestock": s 1(1); "person": IA 1937 s 11(*c*); "regulations": ss 1(1), 32; "tax": s 1(1); "taxable period": s 1(1).

Personal notes

_____

_____

_____

_____

_____

_____

_____

_____

_____

_____

_____

_____

_____

_____

_____

_____

_____

_____

15A Goods in transit

(1) Where —

    (*a*)   goods from another member State were imported into the State on or   a 28n
before the 31st day of December, 1992, and

    (*b*)   the tax referred to in section 2(1)(*b*) was not chargeable because the goods were, at the time of such importation, placed under one of the arrangements referred to in subparagraph (*b*) or (*c*) of paragraph 1 of Article 14, or subparagraph A of paragraph 1 of Article 16, of Council Directive No 77/388/EEC of 17 May 1977, and

    (*c*)   the goods are still subject to such an arrangement on the 1st day of January, 1993,

then, the provisions in force at the time the goods were placed under the arrangement shall continue to apply in relation to those goods until such time as, in accordance with those provisions, the goods cease to be covered by those arrangements.

(2)   (*a*)   Notwithstanding the definition of "importation of goods" in section 1, an importation within the meaning of that definition shall be deemed to occur in the following cases:

        (i)   where goods have been placed under an internal Community transit operation in another Member State before the 1st day of January, 1993, and the operation terminates in the State on or after that date;

        (ii)   where goods referred to in subsection (1) cease to be covered by the arrangements referred to in that subsection;

        (iii)   where goods are returned to the State after the 1st day of January, 1993, being goods which were exported from the State before that date and imported into another member State in accordance with any of the arrangements referred to in subsection (1)(*b*).

    (*b*)   In this subsection **"internal Community transit operation"** means the dispatch or transport of goods under cover of the internal Community transit arrangement referred to in paragraph 3 of Article 1 of Council Regulation (EEC) No 222/77 of 13 December 1976, or under the cover of a T2L or equivalent document provided for in that Regulation and includes the sending of goods by post.

(3) The tax referred to in section 2(1)(*b*) shall not be chargeable in the cases referred to in subsection (2) where —

    (*a*)   the goods are dispatched or transported outside the Community,

    (*b*)   the goods are other than a means of transport and are being returned to the State and to the person who exported them from the State, or

    (*c*)   the goods are a means of transport which was acquired or imported before the 1st day of January, 1993, and in respect of which value added tax referred to in Council Directive No 77/388/EEC of 17 May 1977 has been paid in a Member State and that value added tax has not subsequently been refunded because of exportation from that Member State of the means of transport:

    Provided that this paragraph shall be deemed to be complied with where it is shown to the satisfaction of the Revenue Commissioners that the first use of the means of transport was prior to the 1st day of January, 1985, or that the tax due does not exceed £100.

(4) In this section, references to subparagraph (*b*) or (*c*) of paragraph 1 of Article 14, and to subparagraph A of paragraph 1 of Article 16, of Council Directive No 77/388/EEC of 17 May 1977 shall be deemed to be references to those provisions of the Directive immediately prior to their amendment by Council Directive 91/680/EEC of 16 December 1991.]¹

Amendments
1   Section 15A inserted by EC(VAT)R 1992 r 11 with effect from 1 January 1993.
Definition
"Community": s 1(1); "goods": s 1(1); "importation of goods": s 1(1).
Notes
Subs (2)(*b*): OJ No L38, 9 February 1977.

Personal notes

15B Goods in transit (additional provisions)

[(1) Where —

    (*a*)   goods from a new Member State were imported into the State on or before the 31st day of December, 1994, and

    (*b*)   the tax referred to in section 2(1)(*b*) was not chargeable because the goods were, at the time of such importation, placed —

        (i)   under an arrangement for temporary importation with total exemption from customs duty, or

        (ii)   under one of the arrangements referred to in clauses (*a*), (*b*), (*c*) and (*d*) of subparagraph B of paragraph 1 of Article 16, of Council Directive No 77/388/EEC of 17 May 1977, and

    (*c*)   the goods are still subject to such an arrangement on the 1st day of January, 1995,

then, the provisions in force at the time the goods were placed under that arrangement shall continue to apply until the goods leave that arrangement on or after the 1st day of January, 1995.

(2)   (*a*)   Where —

        (i)   goods were placed under the common transit procedure or under another customs transit procedure in a new Member State on or before the 31st day of December, 1994, and

        (ii)   those goods have not left the procedure concerned before the 1st day of January, 1995,

        then the provisions in force at the time the goods were placed under that procedure shall continue to apply until the goods leave that procedure on or after the 1st day of January, 1995.

    (*b*)   In this subsection **"common transit procedure"** means the procedure approved by the Council of the European Communities by Council Decision No 87/415/EEC of 15 June 1987, approving the Convention done at Interlaken on the 20th day of May, 1987, between the European Community, the Republic of Austria, the Republic of Finland, the Republic of Iceland, the Kingdom of Norway, the Kingdom of Sweden, and the Swiss Confederation on a common transit procedure, the text of which is attached to that Council Decision.

(3) Where goods were in free circulation in a new Member State prior to entry into the State, an importation into the State shall be deemed to occur in the following cases:

    (*a*)   the removal, including irregular removal, within the State of the goods referred to in subsection (1) from the arrangement referred to in subparagraph (i) of paragraph (*b*) of that subsection;

    (*b*)   the removal, including irregular removal, within the State of the goods referred to in subsection (1) from the arrangement referred to in subparagraph (ii) of paragraph (*b*) of that subsection;

    (*c*)   the termination within the State of any of the procedures referred to in subsection (2).

(4) An importation into the State shall be deemed to occur when goods, which were supplied within a new Member State on or before the 31st day of December, 1994, and which were not chargeable to a value added tax in that new Member State, because of their exportation from that new Member State, are used in the State on or after the 1st day of January, 1995, and have not been imported before that date.

(5) The tax referred to in section 2(1)(*b*) shall not be chargeable where —

    (*a*)   the imported goods referred to in subsections (3) and (4) are dispatched or transported outside the enlarged Community,

    (*b*)   the imported goods referred to in paragraph (*a*) of subsection (3) are other than means of transport and are being returned to the new Member State from which they were exported and to the person who exported them, or

    (*c*)   the imported goods referred to in paragraph (*a*) of subsection (3) are means of transport which were acquired in or imported into a new Member State before the 1st day of January, 1995 in accordance with the general conditions of taxation in force on the domestic market of that new Member State and which have not been subject by reason of their exportation to any exemption from or refund of a value added tax in that new Member State:

          Provided that this paragraph shall be deemed to be complied with where it is shown to the satisfaction of the Revenue Commissioners that the first use of the means of transport was prior to the 1st day of January, 1987, or that the tax due does not exceed £100.

(6) The provisions of section 15A shall not apply to goods imported or deemed to be imported from a new Member State.

(7)   (*a*)   In this section —

          "the enlarged Community" means the Community after the accession of the new Member States;

          "new Member State" means the Republic of Austria, the Republic of Finland (excluding the Aland Islands) or the Kingdom of Sweden.

    (*b*)   A word or expression that is used in this section and is also used in Council Directive No 94/76/EC of 22 December 1994, has, unless the contrary intention appears, the meaning in this section that it has in that Council Directive.][1]

Amendments
1   Section 15B inserted by EC(VAT)R 1994 r 4 with effect from 1 January 1995.
Definition
"Community": s 1(1); "goods": s 1(1); "importation of goods": s 1(1); "new means of transport": s 1(1).
Notes
Subs (2)(*b*): OJ No L26, 13 August 1977.

Personal notes

---

16 Duty to keep records

(1) Every [taxable person][1] shall, in accordance with regulations, keep full and true records of all transactions which affect or may affect his liability to tax. a 22

(2) Every person, other than [a taxable person][2,] who [supplies goods or services in the course or furtherance of any business][3] shall keep all invoices issued to him in connection with the [supply of goods or services][4] to him for the purpose of such business ...[5]

(3) Records ...[6] kept by a person pursuant to this section and any books [invoices, [monthly control statements,][7] copies ...[8] of customs entries][9,] credit notes, debit notes, receipts, accounts, vouchers, bank statements or other documents whatsoever which relate to the [supply of goods or services,][10] [the intra-Community acquisition of goods][11] [, or the importation of goods][12] by the person and are in the power, possession or procurement of the person and, in the case of any such book, invoice, [monthly control statement,][13] credit note, debit note, receipt, account, voucher, or other document which has been issued by the person to another person, any copy thereof which is in the power, possession or procurement of the person shall be retained in his power, possession or procurement for a period of six years from the date of the latest transaction to which the [records, invoices, monthly control statements][14] or any of the other documents relate:

Provided that this section shall not require the retention of records or invoices or any of the other documents in respect of which the Revenue Commissioners notify the person concerned that retention is not required, nor shall it apply to the books and papers of a company which have been disposed of in accordance with section 305(1) of the Companies Act, 1963.

Amendments
1 Substituted by VATAA 1978 s 30(2) with effect from 1 March 1979; previously "accountable person".
2 Substituted by VATAA 1978 s 30(2) with effect from 1 March 1979; previously "an accountable person".
3 Substituted by VATAA 1978 s 30(2) with effect from 1 March 1979; previously "delivers goods in the course of business or renders services in the course of business".
4 Substituted by VATAA 1978 s 30(2) with effect from 1 March 1979; previously "delivery of goods or the rendering of services".
5 Words "and, in respect of goods imported by him, copies, stamped on behalf of the Revenue Commissioners, of the relevant customs entries" deleted by FA 1992 s 179(*a*) with effect from 1 January 1993.
6 Words "and invoices" deleted by FA 1982 s 85 with effect from 1 September 1982.
7 Inserted by FA 1992 s 179(*b*)(iii) with effect from 1 November 1992.
8 Words ", stamped on behalf of the Revenue Commissioners, " deleted by FA 1992 s 179(*b*)(i) with effect from 28 May 1992.
9 Inserted by FA 1982 s 85 with effect from 1 September 1982.
10 Substituted by VATAA 1978 s 30(2) with effect from 1 March 1979; previously "delivery of goods by the person or the rendering of services".
11 Inserted by FA 1992 s 179(*b*)(ii) with effect from 1 January 1993.
12 Words inserted by FA 1982 s 85 with effect from 1 September 1982.
13 Inserted by FA 1992 s 179(*b*)(v) with effect from 1 November 1992.
14 Substituted by FA 1992 s 179(*b*)(iv) with effect from 1 November 1992: previously "records or invoices".

Cross-references
Fraud, negligence: penalties: s 27(1).
Hire purchase transactions, supplier (who is obliged to issue invoice to financial service provider) is a taxable person for the purposes of this section: s 17(1AB)
Non compliance, penalty: s 26(1); obligation to keep records: FA 1968 s 6.
Records to be kept, Revenue may prescribe details and retention period: s 32(1)(*h*); regulations: VATR 1979 r 9.

Statement of practice
Revenue powers: SP GEN/1/94, May 1994.

Narrative
Irish Value Added Tax, Chapter 11; *Guide to Value Added Tax (Revenue Commissioners)*: Chapter 10.

Definition
"business": s 1(1); "goods": s 1(1); "intra-Community acquisition of goods": ss 1(1), 3A; "monthly control statement": ss 1(1), 17; "person": IA 1937 s 11(*c*); "regulations": ss 1(1), 32; "supply": s 1(1); "tax": s 1(1); "taxable person": ss 1(1), 8.

Personal notes

---

17 Invoices

(1) [A taxable person]¹ who [supplies goods or services]² to another [taxable person]³ [or ...⁴ to a person, other than an individual, in another Member State of the Community]⁵ in such circumstances that tax is chargeable [at any of the rates specified in section 11(1), [or who supplies goods to a person in another Member State of the Community in the circumstances referred to in section 3(6)(*d*)(ii),]⁶ ...⁷]⁸ shall issue to that [person]⁹ in respect of each such [supply of goods or services]¹⁰ an invoice in such form and containing such particulars as may be specified by regulations.

[Provided that, where goods are supplied in accordance with the terms of paragraph (*b*) of subsection (1) of section 3, and the ownership of those goods is transferred to a person supplying, in respect of those goods, financial services of the kind specified in subparagraph (*e*) of paragraph (i) of the First Schedule, the taxable person making the supply of the goods in question shall issue the invoice to the person supplying the said financial services in lieu of the taxable person to whom the supply of the goods is made and that invoice shall include the name and address of the person supplying those financial services.]¹¹

[(1A) (*a*)   An invoice or other document required to be issued under this section shall, subject to paragraph (*b*), be deemed to be so issued if the particulars which are required by regulations to be contained in such invoice or other document, as the case may be, are recorded and retained in an electronic data processing system and are transmitted by electronic means without the issue of any invoice or other document.

[(*b*)   An invoice or other document required to be issued under this section shall not be deemed by paragraph (*a*) to be issued unless the person, who is required to issue such invoice or other document, as the case may be, has been authorised by the Revenue Commissioners to issue such invoice or other document to a recipient who has been authorised by the Revenue Commissioners in accordance with paragraph (*c*), and he complies with such conditions as may be specified by regulations.

(*c*)   A person who receives the transmissions referred to in paragraphs (*a*) and (*b*) shall not be deemed to be issued with an invoice or other document, as the case maybe, required to be issued under this section unless he has been authorised in that respect by the Revenue Commissioners and he complies with such conditions as may be specified by regulations.

(*d*)   The Revenue Commissioners may, in accordance with regulations, cancel an authorisation under paragraph (*b*) or (*c*)]¹²]¹³

[(1AA) Where the proviso to subsection (1) applies, the person supplying the financial services in question shall issue a document to the person to whom the supply of goods is made and shall indicate thereon—

(*a*)   the amount which is set out in respect of tax on the invoice issued to the person supplying the financial services in accordance with the said proviso in respect of that supply of goods, and

(*b*)   such other particulars as are specified by regulations in respect of an invoice issued in accordance with subsection (1).

(1AB) Where any person issues a document for the purposes of subsection (1AA) that person shall, in respect of the document, be treated as a taxable person for the purposes of sections 16 and 18.]¹⁴

[(1B) A taxable person who supplies goods to another taxable person in such circumstances that tax is chargeable at any of the rates specified in section 11(1) shall issue to that other taxable person a single document in this Act referred to as a monthly control statement in respect of all such supplies to that other taxable person during each calendar month, and every such statement shall be in such form, contain such particulars, and be issued within such time as may be specified by regulations:

[Provided that this provision shall not apply—

    (*a*)   to taxable persons whose taxable turnover in respect of supplies of goods to other taxable persons has not exceeded £2,000,000 in the previous period of 12 months, and

    (*b*)   in any event, in respect of all such supplies made in the taxable periods commencing on or after the 1st day of May, 1995.][15][16]

a 22(2)-(3), 25(6)

[(2) A flat-rate farmer who, in accordance with section 12A, is required to issue an invoice in respect of the supply of agricultural produce or an agricultural service shall, in respect of each such supply, issue an invoice in the form and containing such particulars (in addition to those specified in the said section 12A) as may be specified by regulations if the following conditions are fulfilled:

    (*a*)   the issue of an invoice is requested by a [purchaser],[17]

    (*b*)   the [purchaser][15] provides the form for the purpose of the invoice and enters the appropriate particulars thereon, and

    (*c*)   the [purchaser][15] gives to the flat-rate farmer a copy of the invoice,

but may issue the invoice if those conditions or any of them are not fulfilled.][18]

a 22(3)

(3) Where, subsequent to the issue of an invoice by a person [to another person][19] in accordance with subsection (1), the consideration as stated in the invoice is increased or reduced, or a discount is allowed, whichever of the following provisions is appropriate shall have effect:

    (*a*)   if the consideration is increased, the person shall issue [to that other person][20] another invoice in such form and containing such particulars as may be specified by regulations in respect of such increase,

    (*b*)   if the consideration is reduced or a discount is allowed, the person shall issue [to that other person][21] a document (in this Act referred to as a credit note) containing particulars of the reduction or discount in such form and containing such other particulars as may be specified by regulations, [and, if that other person is a taxable person, the amount][22] which the [taxable person][3] may deduct under section 12 shall, in accordance with regulations, be reduced by the amount of tax shown on the credit note.

[(3A) Notwithstanding subsections (5) and (9), where a person issues an invoice in accordance with subsection (1) which indicates a rate of tax and subsequent to the issue of that invoice it is established that a lower rate of tax applied, then—

    (*a*)   the amount of consideration stated on that invoice shall be deemed to have been reduced to nil,

    (*b*)   the provisions of subsection (3)(*b*) shall have effect, and

    (*c*)   following the issue of a credit note in accordance with the provisions of subsection (3)(*b*), the person shall issue another invoice in accordance with this Act and regulations made thereunder.][23]

[(3AB) Where any person supplying financial services receives a credit note issued under the terms of paragraph (*b*) of subsection (3) in respect of a supply of goods to which the proviso to subsection (1) applies, that person shall, within seven days of receipt of such credit note, issue to the person to whom the goods in question were supplied, a document corresponding to that credit note indicating such particulars as are specified by regulations in respect of the issue of such credit notes, and the amount which the taxable person to whom the goods were supplied may deduct under section 12 in respect of that supply shall be reduced by the amount in respect of tax shown in the document.][24]

a 22(3)

[(4) Where subsequent to the issue by a flat-rate farmer of an invoice in accordance with subsection (2), the consideration as stated on the invoice is increased or reduced, or a discount is allowed, whichever of the following provisions is appropriate shall have effect:

    (*a*)   in case the consideration is increased, the flat-rate farmer shall issue another invoice (if the conditions referred to in subsection (2) are fulfilled in relation to it) containing particulars of the increase and of the flat-rate addition appropriate thereto and in such form and containing such other particulars as may be specified by regulations and such other invoice shall be deemed, for the purposes of section 12, to be issued in accordance with section 12A, but the said farmer may not issue the invoice if the said conditions or any of them are not fulfilled,

(b) in case the consideration is reduced or a discount is allowed, the flat-rate farmer shall, ...[25] issue a document (in this section referred to as "**a farmer credit note**") containing particulars of the reduction or discount and in such form and containing such other particulars as may be specified by regulations, [and the amount which the person may deduct under section 12 or is entitled to be repaid under section 13 shall,][26] in accordance with regulations, be reduced by an amount equal to the amount of the flat-rate addition appropriate to the amount of the reduction or discount][27].

(5) If [a taxable person][1] issues an invoice stating a greater amount of tax than that properly attributable to the consideration stated therein, or issues a credit note stating a lesser amount of tax than that properly attributable to the reduction in consideration or the discount therein, he shall be liable to pay to the Revenue Commissioners the excess amount of tax stated in the invoice or the amount of the deficiency of tax stated in the credit note.

[(5A) If any person issues a document for the purposes of subsection (1AA) in relation to a supply of goods indicating a greater amount in respect of tax than the amount of tax invoiced in accordance with the proviso to subsection (1) in relation to that supply, that person shall, in relation to that excess, be deemed for the purposes of this Act to be a taxable person and a person to whom subsection (5) applies, and that excess shall be deemed to be tax.][28]

(6) A person who is not a registered person and who, ...,[29] issues an invoice stating an amount of tax shall, in relation to the amount of tax stated, be deemed, for the purposes of this Act, to be [a taxable person][1] and shall be liable to pay the amount to the Revenue Commissioners.

[(6A) (a) If a person, other than a flat-rate farmer, issues an invoice stating an amount of flat-rate addition, he shall be liable to pay to the Revenue Commissioners as tax the amount of flat-rate addition stated and shall, in relation to such amount, be deemed, for the purpose of this Act, to be a taxable person.

(b) If a flat-rate farmer issues an invoice stating an amount of flat-rate addition otherwise than in respect of an actual supply of agricultural produce or an agricultural service or in respect of such a supply but stating a greater amount of flat-rate addition than is appropriate to the supply, he shall be liable to pay to the Revenue Commissioners as tax the amount or the excess amount, as the case may be, of the flat-rate addition stated and shall, in relation to such amount or such excess amount, be deemed, for the purposes of this Act, to be a taxable person.

(c) If a flat-rate farmer, in a case in which he is required to issue a farmer credit note under subsection (4)(b), fails to issue the credit note within the time allowed by regulations or issues a credit note stating a lesser amount of flat-rate addition than is appropriate to the reduction in consideration or the discount, he shall be liable to pay to the Revenue Commissioners as tax the amount of flat-rate addition which should have been stated on the credit note or the amount of the deficiency of flat-rate addition, as the case may be, and shall, in relation to such amount or such deficiency, be deemed, for the purposes of this Act, to be a taxable person.][30]

(7) An invoice or credit note shall be issued within such time after the date of [supplying goods or services][31] as may be specified by regulations and an

amendment of an invoice pursuant to subsection (4)(*b*) shall be affected within such time as may be specified by regulations.

[(7A) A document required to be issued in accordance with subsection (1AA) shall be issued within twenty-two days next following the month of supply of the goods.]³²   a 22(3)

(8) Notwithstanding anything in subsection (7), where payment for the [supply of goods or services]³³[, other than supplies of the kind specified in subparagraph (*b*) or (*c*) of paragraph (i) of the Second Schedule]³⁴ is made to a person, either in full or by instalments, before the [supply]³⁵ is completed, the person shall issue an invoice in accordance with subsection (1) [or subsection (2), as may be appropriate,]³⁶ within such time after the date of actual receipt of the full payment   a 22(9) or the instalment as may be specified by regulations.

(9) (*a*)   Notwithstanding anything in subsection (3), where, subsequent to the issue to a registered person of an invoice in accordance with subsection (1), the consideration stated in the invoice is reduced or a discount is allowed in such circumstances that, by agreement between the persons concerned, the amount of tax stated in the invoice is unaltered, paragraph (*b*) of the said subsection (3) shall not apply in relation to the person by whom the invoice was issued.

[(*aa*)   Paragraph (*a*) shall not apply where the person who issued the invoice referred to therein was, at the time of its issue, a person authorised, in accordance with section 14(1), to determine his tax liability in respect of supplies of the kind in question by reference to the amount of moneys received.]³⁷

(*b*)   In a case to which paragraph (*a*) applies—

(i)   the reduction or discount concerned shall not be taken into account in computing the liability to tax of the person making the reduction or allowing the discount,

(ii)   subsection (5) shall not apply, and

(iii)   the amount which the person in whose favour the reduction or discount is made or allowed may deduct in respect of the relevant transaction under section 12 shall not be reduced.   a 22(10)

(10) Where—

(*a*)   [goods or services are supplied]³⁸ to a registered person by another registered person [or agricultural produce or agricultural services are supplied to a registered person by a flat-rate farmer]³⁹ ...⁴⁰ and

(*b*)   the person to whom the [goods or services are supplied]⁴¹ issues to the other person, before the date on which an invoice is issued by that other person, a document (in this Act referred to as a settlement voucher) in such form and containing such particulars as may be specified by regulations, then, for the purposes of this Act—

(i)   the person who issues the settlement voucher shall, if the person to whom it is issued accepts it, be deemed to have received from the person by whom the voucher was accepted an invoice containing the particulars set out in the voucher, and

(ii)   the person to whom the settlement voucher is issued shall, if he accepts it, be deemed to have issued to the person from whom the voucher was received an invoice containing the particulars set out in the voucher.

(11) Where a person who is entitled to receive a credit note under subsection (3)(*b*) from another person issues to that other person, before the date on which a credit note is issued by that other person, a document (in this subsection referred to as a "debit note") in such form and containing such particulars as may be specified by regulations, then, for the purposes of this Act—

(*a*)   the person who issues the debit note shall, if the person to whom it is issued accepts it, be deemed to have received from the person by whom the note was accepted a credit note containing the particulars set out in such debit note, and

(b)   the person to whom such debit note is issued shall, if he accepts it, be deemed to have issued to the person from whom the debit note was received a credit note containing the particulars set out in such debit note.

[(11A) Where a person who is entitled to receive a farmer credit note under subsection (4)(b) from another person issues to that other person, before the date on which a farmer credit note is issued by that other person, a document (in this section referred to as **"a farmer debit note"**) in such form and containing such particulars as may be specified by regulations, then, for the purposes of this Act—

(a)   the person who issues the debit note shall, if the person to whom it is issued accepts it, be deemed to have received from the person by whom the debit note was accepted a farmer credit note containing the particulars set out in such debit note, and

(b)   the person to whom such debit note is issued shall, if he accepts it, be deemed to have issued to the person from whom the debit note was received a farmer credit note containing the particulars set out in such debit note.]⁴²

(12) (a)   [A taxable person]¹ shall—

(i)   if requested in writing by another person and if the request states that the other person is entitled to repayment of tax under section 20(3), give to that other person in writing the particulars of the amount of tax chargeable to the [taxable person]³ in respect of the [supply]⁴³ by him of the goods specified in the request or of the [supply]⁴⁴ by him of the services so specified,

(ii)   if requested in writing by another person and if the request states that the other person is entitled to repayment of tax under [section 13],⁴⁵ give to that other person in writing the particulars specified in regulations for the purposes of subsection (1) in respect of the [goods or]⁴⁶ services [supplied]⁴⁷ by the [taxable person]³ to that other person that are specified in the request, and

(iii) if requested in writing by another person and if the request states that that other person is entitled to repayment of tax under section 20(2), give to that other person in writing the particulars of the amount of tax chargeable to the [taxable person]³ in respect of the [supply]² by him of the radio broadcasting reception apparatus and parts thereof that are specified in the request.

[(ai) A flat-rate farmer shall, if requested in writing by another person and if the request states that the other person is entitled to repayment of the flat-rate addition under section 13, give to that other person in writing the particulars specified in regulations for the purpose of subsection (2) in respect of the goods or services supplied by the flat-rate farmer to that other person that are specified in the request.]⁴⁸

(b)   A request under paragraph (a) shall be complied with by the person to whom it is given within thirty days after the date on which the request is received by him.

[(13) The provisions of this Act (other than this section) relating to credit notes and debit notes issued under subsection (3) and (11), respectively, of this section shall apply in relation to farmer credit notes and farmer debit notes as they apply in relation to the credit notes and debit notes aforesaid.]⁴⁹

Amendments

1   Substituted by VATAA 1978 s 30(2) with effect from 1 March 1979; previously "an accountable person".
2   Substituted by VATAA 1978 s 30(2) with effect from 1 March 1979; previously "delivers goods or services".
3   Substituted by VATAA 1978 s 30(2) with effect from 1 March 1979; previously "accountable person".
4   Word "goods" deleted with effect from 1 January 1993 by EC(VAT)R 1992 r 12.
5   Inserted by FA 1992 s 180(a)(i) with effect from 1 January 1993.

6   Inserted by FA 1993 s 91(*a*).
7   Words ", including the rate of zero per cent," deleted by FA 1992 s 180(*a*)(ii) with effect from 1 January 1993.
8   Inserted by FA 1973 s 90 with effect from 3 September 1973.
9   Substituted by FA 1992 s 180(*a*)(iii) with effect from 1 January 1993; previously "other taxable person" .
10   Substituted by VATAA 1978 s 30(2) with effect from 1 March 1979; previously "delivery of goods or rendering of services".
11   Subs (1)(proviso) inserted by FA 1996 s 97(*a*) with effect from 1 July 1996.
12   Subs (1A)(*b*)-(*d*) substituted by FA 1992 s 180(b) with effect from 28 May 1992.
13   Subs (1A) inserted by FA 1986 s 86 with effect from 27 May 1986.
14   Subss (1AA)-(1AB) inserted by FA 1996 s 97(*b*) with effect from 1 July 1996.
15   Subs (1B(proviso) substituted by FA 1995 s 132 with effect from 2 June 1995.
16   Subs (1B) inserted by FA 1992 s 180(*c*) with effect from 1 November 1992.
17   Substituted by FA 1992 s 180(*d*) with effect from 1 January 1993; previously "taxable person" .
18   Subs (2) inserted by VATAA 1978 s 15 with effect from 1 March 1979; previously repealed by FA 1976 s 81 with effect from 1 March 1976.
19   Substituted by FA 1992 s 180(*e*)(i) with effect from 1 January 1993; previously "to a taxable person" .
20   Substituted by FA 1992 s 180(*e*)(ii) with effect from 1 January 1993; previously "to the taxable person".
21   Substituted by FA 1992 s 180(*e*)(iii)(I) with effect from 1 January 1993; previously "to the taxable person".
22   Substituted by FA 1992 s 180(*e*)(iii)(xx) with effect from 1 January 1993; previously "the amount" .
23   Subs (3A) inserted by FA 1993 s 91(*b*).
24   Subs (3AB) inserted by FA 1996 s 97(*c*) with effect from 1 July 1996.
25   Words ", if the person to whom the supply was made is a taxable person," deleted y FA 1992 s 180(*f*)(i) with effect from 1 January 1993.
26   Substituted by FA 1992 s 180(*f*)(ii) with effect from 1 January 1993; previously "and the amount which the taxable person may deduct under section 12 shall," by .
27   Subs (4) inserted by VATAA 1978 s 15 with effect from 1 March 1979; previously repealed by FA 1976 s 81 with effect from 1 March 1976.
28   Subs (5A) inserted by FA 1996 s 97(*d*) with effect from 1 July 1996.
29   Words "otherwise than as required by section 13," deleted by FA 1976 s 81 with effect from 1 March 1976.
30   Subs (6A) inserted by VATAA 1978 s 15 with effect from 1 March 1979.
31   Substituted by VATAA 1978 s 30(2) effect from 1 March 1979; previously "delivering goods or rendering services".
32   Subs (7A) inserted by FA 1996 s 97(*e*) with effect from 1 July 1996.
33   Substituted by VATAA 1978 s 30(2) with effect from 1 March 1979; previously "delivery of goods or the rendering of services".
34   Inserted by FA 1992 s 180(*g*) with effect from 1 January 1993.
35   Substituted by FA 1978 s 30(2) with effect from 1 March 1979; previously "delivery or rendering".
36   Inserted by VATAA 1978 s 15 with effect from 1 March 1979.
37   Subs (9)(*aa*) inserted by VATAA 1978 s 15 with effect from 1 March 1979.
38   Substituted by VATAA 1978 s 30(2) with effect from 1 March 1979; previously "goods are delivered or services are rendered".
39   Inserted by VATAA 1978 s 15 with effect from 1 March 1979.
40   Words "but who is required under section 13(1) to issue an invoice to a registered person" deleted by FA 1976 s 81 with effect from 1 March 1976.
41   Substituted by VATAA 1978 s 30(2) with effect from 1 March 1979; previously "goods are delivered or the services are rendered".
42   Subs (11A) inserted by VATAA 1978 s 15 with effect from 1 March 1979.
43   Substituted by VATAA 1978 s 30(2) with effect from 1 March 1979; previously "delivery".
44   Substituted by VATAA 1978 s 30(2) with effect from 1 March 1979; previously "rendering".
45   Substituted by VATAA 1978 s 30(2) with effect from 1 March 1979; previously "section 5(4)".
46   Inserted by VATAA 1978 s 15 with effect from 1 March 1979.
47   Substituted by VATAA 1978 s 30(2) with effect from 1 March 1979; previously "rendered".
48   Subs (12)(*ai*) inserted by FA 1992 s 180(*h*) with effect from 1 January 1993.
49   Subs (13) inserted by VATAA 1978 s 15 with effect from 1 March 1979.

Cross-references
Appeal (subss (5)-(6)): s 25(1)(*a*).
Auctioneer, special scheme, tax not to be shown separately: s 10B(5); invoice deemed to be issued (subs (4)) by principal where goods auctioned on his behalf: s 10B(6).
Authorised persons (exporters, charge of tax at 0% to), authorisation number to be shown on invoice: s 13A(5).
Bad debts, discounts, goods returned: Revenue may prescribe manner of adjustment: s 32(1)(*s*); adjustments: VATR 1979 r 8.
Computer and microfirm based records: FA 1986 s 113.
Hire purchase transactions, deductible tax where supplier invoices financial service provider (subs (1AA)): s 12(1)(*a*)(i*a*).
Fraud, negligence; penalties: s 27(1).
Invoices etc, Revenue may prescribe particulars to be shown: s 32(1)(*i*); details: Value Added Tax (Invoices and Other Documents) Regulations 1992 (SI 275/1992); time limits: Value Added Tax (Time Limits for Issuing Certain Documents) Regulations (SI 276/1992); electronic transmission: Value Added Tax (Electronic Data Exchange and Storage) Regulations 1992 (SI 269/1992).
Monthly control statement, Revenue may prescribe particulars to be shown: VATA 1972 s 32(1)(*i*); details: Value Added Tax (Monthly Control Statement) Regulations 1992 (SI 230/1992).
Non compliance, penalty: s 26(1); (subs (4)(*a*)), penalty: s 26(2A).
Taxable dealers supplying means of transport, tax not to be shown separately: s 12B(5).

Narrative
Irish Value Added Tax, Chapter 11; *Guide to Value Added Tax (Revenue Commissioners)*: Chapter 9.

Definition
"agricultural produce": s 1(1); "agricultural service": s 1(1); "farmer": s 1(1); "flat-rate addition": ss 1(1), 12A; "flat-rate farmer": ss 1(1), 12A; "goods": s 1(1); "monthly control statement": ss 1(1), 17; "person": IA 1937 s 11(*c*); "registered person": s 1(1); "regulations": ss 1(1), 32; "supply": s 1(1); "tax": s 1(1); "taxable person": ss 1(1), 8; "writing": IA 1937 Sch.

Statement of practice
Electronic invoicing: authorisation procedure, system capacity, keeping of records, etc: SP VAT 9/92.
Monthly control statement: details to be included, use of commercial statement, etc: SP VAT 7/92.

18 Inspection and removal of records

a 22   [(1)   (*a*)   For the purposes of this Act and regulations, an authorised officer may at all reasonable times enter any premises or place where he has reason to believe that business is carried on or anything is done in connection with business and—

        (i)   may require that person carrying on the business, or any person on those premises or in that place who is employed by the person carrying on the business or who is associated with him in the carrying on of the business, to produce any books, records, accounts or other documents relating to the business or to any other business which he has reason to believe may be, or have been, connected with the said business or have, or have had, trading relations with the said business,

        (ii)   may, if he has reason to believe that any of the books, records, accounts or other documents, which he has required to be produced to him under the provisions of this subsection have not been so produced, search in those premises or that place for those books, records, accounts or other documents,

a 22   [(ii*a*)   may, if he has reason to believe that a person is carrying or has in his possession any records which may be required as evidence in criminal proceedings in accordance with section 94 (as amended by section 243 of the Finance Act, 1992) of the Finance Act, 1983, in relation to the tax, request the person to produce any such records, and if that person should fail to do so, the authorised officer or a member of the Garda Síochána may search that person:

            Provided that—

        (A)   the officer or the member of the Garda Síochána conducting the search shall ensure, as far as practicable, that the person understands the reason for the search,

        (B)   the search is conducted with due regard to the privacy of that person,

        (C)   the person being searched shall not be searched by an officer or member of the Garda Síochána of the opposite sex, and

        (D)   the person being searched shall not be requested to remove any clothing other than headgear or a coat, jacket, glove or a similar article of clothing.][1]

        (iii)   may, in the case of any such books, records, accounts or other documents produced to or found by him, take copies of or extracts from them and remove and retain them for such period as may be reasonable for their further examination or for the purposes of any proceedings ...[2] in relation to tax,

        (iv)   may, if he has reason to believe that goods connected with taxable supplies [, intra-Community acquisitions][3] or importations are held on those premises or in that place and that particulars of such goods have not been kept and retained, as required by this Act or by regulations, in the books, records, accounts or other documents of the business or of any other business similarly required to keep and retain particulars of those goods, search those premises or that place for the said goods and, on their discovery, examine and take particulars of them,

        (v)   may require the person carrying on the business, or any person on those premises or in that place, who is employed by the person carrying on the business or who is associated with him in the carrying on of the business, to give the authorised officer all reasonable assistance [, including providing information and explanations and furnishing documents in connection with the business, as required by the authorised officer]⁴.

(*b*) Nothing in this subsection shall be construed as requiring any person carrying on a profession, or any person employed by any person carrying on a profession, to produce to an authorised officer any documents relating to a client, other than such documents as are material to the tax affairs of the person carrying on the profession, and, in particular, he shall not be required to disclose any information or professional advice of a confidential nature given to a client]⁵.

[(1A) A taxable person shall, on request from an authorised officer, furnish to that officer, in respect of a specified period, the following information:

(*a*) the name and address of each of his customers and the total consideration payable in respect of supplies of goods and services made by him to each customer and the tax thereon [and the value and description of any gifts or promotional items given by him to any person in connection with such supplies or any other payments made by him to any person in connection with such supplies]⁶, and

(*b*) the name, address and registration number of each of his suppliers and the total consideration payable in respect of goods and services supplied to him from each supplier and the tax thereon.

(1B) In this section "records" means any document, or any other written or printed material in any form, including any information stored, maintained or preserved by means of any mechanical or electronic device, whether or not stored, maintained or preserved in a legible form, which a person is required to keep, retain, issue or produce for inspection or which may be inspected under any provision relating to tax.]⁷

(2) ...⁸.

(3) A person shall not wilfully obstruct or delay an authorised officer in the exercise of his powers under this section.

(4) Where, in pursuance of this section, an authorised officer enters any premises, carries out any search or requests production of any documents, he shall, on request, show his authorisation for the purpose of this section to the person concerned.

(5) In this section **"authorised officer"** means an officer of the Revenue Commissioners authorised by them in writing for the purposes of this section.

Amendments
1 Subs (1)(ii*a*) inserted by FA 1992 s 181(*a*)(i) with effect from 1 January 1993.
2 Words "for the recovery of a penalty" deleted by FA 1992 s 181(*a*)(ii) with effect from 28 May 1992.
3 Inserted by FA 1992 s 181(*a*)(iii) with effect from 1 January 1993.
4 Inserted by FA 1992 s 181(*a*)(iv) with effect from 28 May 1992.
5 Subs (1) substituted by FA 1984 s 89 with effect from 23 May 1984.
6 Inserted by FA 1995 s 133 with effect from 2 June 1995.
7 Subss (1A-(1B) inserted by FA 1992 s 181(*b*) with effect from 28 May 1992.
8 Subs (2) deleted by FA 1984 s 89 with effect from 23 May 1984.

Cross-references
Books etc to be kept: VATR 1979 r 9.
Fraud, negligence: penalties: s 27(1).
Hire purchase transactions (supplier who is obliged to issue invoice to financial service provider) is a taxable person for the purposes of this section: s 17(1AB).
Information, disclosure regarding supplies made, Revenue may make regulations: s 32(1)(*n*); regulations: VATR 1979 r 35.
Intra-Community acquisition of goods: s 3A.
Revenue may make regulations regarding nomination of officers to perform functions: s 32(1)(*k*).
non compliance (subs (3)), penalty: s 26(3A).

Statement of practice
Revenue powers: SP GEN/1/94, May 1994.

Narrative
Irish Value Added Tax, Chapter 12; *Guide to Value Added Tax (Revenue Commissioners)*: Chapter 10.10.

Definition
"business": s 1(1); "goods": s 1(1); "person": IA 1937 s 11(*c*); "regulations": ss 1(1), 32; "tax": s 1(1); "taxable person": ss 1(1), 8; "writing": IA 1937 Sch.

19 Tax due and payable

a 10   (1) Tax chargeable under section 2(1)(*a*) shall be due—

       (*a*)   in case an invoice is required under section 17 to be issued, at the time of issue of the invoice, or if the invoice is not issued in due time, upon the expiration of the period within which the invoice should have been issued;

       (*b*)   in case a person is liable under subsection (5) or (6) of section 17 to pay an amount of tax by reference to an invoice or credit note issued by him, at the time of issue of such invoice or credit note, and

       (*c*)   in any other case, at the time the [goods or services are supplied][1]:

    ...[2].

    [(1A) Tax chargeable under section 2(1A) shall be due—

a 10(2)   (*a*)   on the fifteenth day of the month following that during which the intra-Community acquisition occurs;

       (*b*)   in case an invoice is issued before the date specified in paragraph (*a*) by the supplier in another Member State to the person acquiring the goods, when that invoice is issued.][3]

    (2) Notwithstanding anything in this Act, the tax chargeable under section 2(1)(*a*) [, other than tax chargeable in respect of supplies of the kind specified in subparagraph (*b*) or (*c*) of paragraph (i) of the Second Schedule,][4] or the relevant part thereof, shall fall due not later than the time when the amount in respect of which it is payable has been received either in full or in part and where the amount is received in full or in part before the [supply of the goods or services][5] to which it relates, a [supply][6] for a consideration equal to the amount received of such part of the goods or services as is equal in value to the amount received, shall be deemed, for the purposes of this Act, to have taken place at the time of such receipt.

a 22(4)   [(3) (*a*)   Subject to paragraph (*b*), a taxable person shall, within 9 days immediately after the tenth day of the month immediately following a taxable period, furnish to the Collector-General a true and correct return prepared in accordance with regulations of the amount of tax which became due by him during the taxable period, not being tax already paid by him in relation to goods imported by him, and the amount, if any, which may be deducted in accordance with section 12 in computing the amount of tax payable by him in respect of such taxable period and such other particulars as may be specified in regulations, and shall at the same time remit to the Collector-General the amount of tax, if any, payable by him in respect of such taxable period.

         [Provided that—

       (*a*)   where the taxable period is the period ending on the 31st day of December, the amount of tax payable for such period shall be reduced by the amount paid, if any, in accordance with subsection (6)(*a*) where that amount was due during that taxable period;

       (*b*)   the Revenue Commissioners shall refund the amount of the excess where—

          (i)   the taxable period is the period ending on the 31st day of December, and

          (ii)   the amount paid in accordance with subsection (6)(*a*) and which was due during that taxable period exceeds the amount of tax which would be so payable before such reduction.][7]

[(*aa*)   (i)   In this paragraph:

["**accounting period**" means a period, as determined by the Collector-General from time to time in any particular case, consisting of a number of consecutive taxable periods not exceeding six or such other period not exceeding a continuous period of twelve months as may be specified by the Collector-General:

Provided that—

(I)   where an accounting period begins before the end of a taxable period, the period of time from the beginning of the accounting period to the end of the taxable period during which the accounting period begins shall, for the purposes of this paragraph, be treated as if such period of time were a taxable period, and

(II)   where an accounting period ends after the beginning of a taxable period, the period of time from the beginning of the taxable period during which the accounting period ends to the end of the accounting period shall, for the purposes of this paragraph, be treated as if such period of time were a taxable period,

and any references in this paragraph to a taxable period shall be construed accordingly;][8]

"**authorised person**" means a taxable person who has been authorised in writing by the Collector-General for the purposes of this paragraph and "**authorise**" and "**authorisation**" shall be construed accordingly.

(ii)   Notwithstanding the provisions of paragraph (*a*)—

(I)   the Collector-General may, from time to time, authorise in writing a taxable person for the purposes of this paragraph, unless the taxable person objects in writing to the authorisation,

and

(II)   an authorised person may, within nine days immediately after the tenth day of the month immediately following an accounting period furnish to the Collector-General a true and correct return prepared in accordance with regulations of the amount of tax which became due by him during the taxable periods which comprise the accounting period not being tax already paid by him in relation to goods imported by him, and, the amount, if any, which may be deducted in accordance with section 12 in computing the amount of tax payable by him in respect of such taxable periods and such other particulars as may be specified in regulations, and at the same time remit to the Collector-General any amount of tax payable by him in respect of such taxable periods, and, where the authorised person concerned so furnishes and remits, he shall be deemed to have complied with the provisions of paragraph (*a*) in relation to the said taxable periods.

(iii)   For the purposes of issuing an authorisation to a taxable person, the Collector-General shall, where he considers it appropriate, have regard to the following matter—

(I)   he has reasonable grounds to believe that—

(A)   the authorisation will not result in a loss of tax, and

(B) the taxable person will meet all his obligations under the authorisation,

and

(II) the taxable person has—

(A) been a registered person during all of the period consisting of the six taxable periods immediately preceding the period in which an authorisation would, if it were issued, have effect, and

(B) complied with the provisions of paragraph (*a*).

(iv) An authorisation may—

(I) be issued either without conditions or subject to such conditions as the Collector-General, having regard in particular to the considerations mentioned in subparagraph (iii), considers proper and specified in writing to the taxable person concerned when issuing the authorisation,

(II) without prejudice to the generality of the foregoing, require an authorised person to remit to the Collector-General, within nine days immediately after the tenth day of the month immediately following each taxable period (other than the final taxable period) which is comprised in an accounting period, such an amount as may be specified by the Collector-General.

(v) The Collector-General may, by notice in writing, terminate an authorisation and, where a taxable person requests him to do so, he shall terminate the authorisation.

(vi) For the purposes of terminating an authorisation the Collector-General shall, where he considers it appropriate, have regard to the following matters:

(I) he has reasonable grounds to believe that the authorisation has resulted or could result in a loss of tax, or

(II) the taxable person—

(A) has furnished, or there is furnished on his behalf, any incorrect information for the purposes of the issue to him of an authorisation, or

(B) has not complied with the provisions of paragraph (*a*) or of this paragraph, including the conditions, if any, specified by the Collector-General under subparagraph (iv) in relation to the issue to him of an authorisation.

(vii) In relation to any taxable period in respect of which he has not complied with the provisions of paragraph (*a*), a person whose authorisation is terminated shall be deemed to have complied with paragraph (*a*) if, within twenty-one days of issue to him of a notice of termination, he furnishes to the Collector-General the return specified in paragraph (*a*) and at the same time remits to the said Collector-General the amount of tax payable by him in accordance with that paragraph.

(viii) (I)An authorisation shall be deemed to have been terminated by the Collector-General on the date that an authorised person—

(A) ceases to trade (except for the purposes of disposing of the stocks and assets of his business), whether for reasons of insolvency or any other reason,

(B) being a body corporate, goes into liquidation, whether voluntarily or not, or

(C) ceases to be a taxable person or a registered person, dies or becomes bankrupt.

(II) A taxable person to whom this subparagraph relates shall, in relation to any taxable period (or part of a taxable period) comprised in the accounting period which was in operation in his case on the date to which clause (I) of this subparagraph relates, be deemed to have complied with paragraph (*a*) if he furnishes to the Collector-General the return specified in subparagraph (ii)(II) and at the same time remits to the said Collector-General the amount of tax payable by him for the purposes of that subparagraph as if he were an authorised person whose accounting period ended on the last day of the taxable period during which the termination occurred:

Provided that the personal representative of a person who was an authorised person shall be deemed to be the taxable person concerned.]⁹

(*b*) A person who disposes of goods which pursuant to section 3(7) are deemed to be supplied by a taxable person in the course or furtherance of his business—

(i) shall within 9 days immediately after the tenth day of the month immediately following a taxable period furnish to the Collector-General a true and correct return, prepared in accordance with regulations, of the amount of tax which became due by such taxable person in relation to the disposal, and such other particulars as may be specified in regulations, and shall at the same time remit to the Collector-General the amount of tax payable in respect of the taxable period in question,

(ii) shall send to the person whose goods were disposed of a statement containing such particulars as may be specified in regulations, and

(iii) shall treat the said amount of tax as a necessary disbursement out of the proceeds of the disposal.

(*c*) The owner of goods which pursuant to section 3(7) are deemed to be supplied by a taxable person in the course or furtherance of his business shall exclude from any return, which he is or, but for this subparagraph, would be, required to furnish under this Act, the tax payable in accordance with paragraph (*b*)].¹⁰

[(4) (*a*) Notwithstanding subsection (3), where—

(i) a person makes an intra-Community acquisition of a new means of transport, other than a vessel or aircraft, in respect of which he is not entitled to a deduction under section 12, then—

(I) the tax shall be payable at the time of payment of vehicle registration tax or, if no vehicle registration tax is payable, at the time of registration of the vehicle,

(II) the person shall complete such form as may be provided by the Revenue Commissioners for the purpose of this subsection, and

        (III)   the provisions relating to recovery and collection of vehicle registration tax shall apply, with such exceptions and modifications (if any) as may be specified in regulations, to tax referred to in this subparagraph as if it were vehicle registration tax,

    and

  (ii) a person makes an intra-Community acquisition of a new means of transport which is a vessel or aircraft, in respect of which he is not entitled to a deduction under section 12, then—

        (I)   the tax shall be payable at a time and in a manner to be determined by regulations, and

        (II) the provisions relating to the recovery and collection of a duty of customs shall apply, with such exceptions and modifications (if any) as may be specified in regulations, to tax referred to in this subparagraph as if it were a duty of customs.

  (*b*) In this subsection—

"registration of the vehicle" means the registration of the vehicle in accordance with section 131 of the Finance Act, 1992;

"vehicle registration tax" means the tax referred to in section 132 of the Finance Act, 1992.][11]

[(5) Notwithstanding the provisions of subsection (3), where the provisions of section 8(2B)(*b*) apply, the tax shall be payable at the time of payment of the duty of excise on the goods and the provisions relating to recovery and collection of that duty of excise shall apply, with such exceptions and modifications (if any) as may be specified in regulations, to tax referred to in this subsection as if it were that duty of excise.

(6) (*a*) Notwithstanding the provisions of subsection (3), a taxable person shall on the 1st day of December, 1993, and on each 1st day of December thereafter pay to the Collector-General an amount (hereafter referred to in this subsection as the **"advance payment"**) equal to one-twelfth of the total net tax due by the taxable person for the relevant period:

Provided that as respects any such 1st day of December, this paragraph shall not apply so as to require an advance payment from a taxable person if the total net tax due by the taxable person for the relevant period does not exceed [£1,000,000][12] (hereafter referred to in this subsection as the **"threshold"**).

  (*b*) Where a taxable person is required by the provisions of paragraph (*a*) to pay an advance payment to the Collector-General by the due date in any year and fails to pay the advance payment by that date, he shall be liable to an additional amount (hereafter referred to in this subsection as the 'surcharge') calculated in accordance with paragraph (*d*):

Provided that no surcharge shall be payable under this paragraph in respect of a failure to pay the advance payment by the due date where, prior to that date, the taxable person by whom the advance payment is payable enters into an arrangement, by agreement with the Collector-General, which guarantees payment of the advance payment by the immediately following 21st day of December and the taxable person pays the advance payment by that 21st day of December .

  (*c*) Notwithstanding the provisions of paragraph (*b*), where a taxable person has complied with the provisions of paragraph (*a*) as respects any advance payment due by the due date in any year, he shall nevertheless be liable to the surcharge, calculated in accordance with paragraph (*d*), as if he had not paid the advance payment, if he has failed to pay to the Collector-General—

(i) any amount of tax payable by him,

(ii) any amount payable by him pursuant to Chapter IV of Part V of the Income Tax Act, 1967, and the regulations made thereunder, or

(iii) any amount of employment contributions payable by him under the Social Welfare Acts,

where the date for payment of such amount fell on or before the 21st day of December immediately following the due date, unless any such amount referred to in subparagraph (i), (ii) or (iii) is the subject of an agreed payment arrangement with the Collector-General and the terms of that arrangement have been complied with by the taxable person as of the 21st day of December following the due date:

Provided that where the only amount payable referred to in—

(I) subparagraph (i) is consequent to an assessment under section 23, or

(II) subparagraph (ii) or (iii) is consequent to an estimate under section 8 of the Finance Act, 1968,

determined after the 21st day of December immediately following the due date, no surcharge shall be payable under this paragraph where the amount payable referred to in subparagraph (i), (ii) or (iii) is less than **10 per cent** of the advance payment due at that due date, or where the Revenue Commissioners consider that, having regard to the circumstances of the case, the adjustment arose from an accidental or genuine misunderstanding or error and should be disregarded for the purposes of the application of the provisions relating to the advance payment and to the application of the surcharge.

(*d*) The surcharge referred to in paragraphs (*b*) and (*c*) shall be calculated at the rate of **0.25 per cent** per day on the amount of the advance payment with effect from and including the due date until the day immediately preceding the day which is—

(i) the day on which the advance payment is paid,

(ii) the day on which the Collector-General receives a return for the taxable period during which the advance payment is due together with the tax, if any, payable for that period, or

(iii) the 20th day of January immediately following the date on which the advance payment is due,

whichever is the earliest:

Provided that the provisions of subparagraph (i) or (ii) shall only apply where the provisions of paragraph (*c*) do not apply.

(*e*) The Revenue Commissioners may, where they consider that an advance payment is payable by a taxable person and where they consider it appropriate to do so, estimate the amount of the advance payment and serve notice on him of the amount so estimated, and the Commissioners may, where they consider it appropriate to do so, vary the amount originally estimated.

(*f*) All the provisions of this Act shall apply to an estimate under paragraph (*e*) as if it were the advance payment and, where at any time after the service of the notice the taxable person declares the actual advance payment, the declared amount shall supersede the estimated amount for the purposes of the application of the provisions of this Act.

(*g*)   The provisions of this Act in relation to the recovery of tax shall apply to the advance payment and the surcharge as if they were tax.

(*h*)   (i)   The Minister may, as respects any due date, by order—

          (I)   increase the threshold to be applied for the purposes of this subsection to that due date, or

          (II)   increase, reduce or revoke an increase in the threshold resulting from any previous order under this subparagraph, including an order relating to this clause:

            Provided that where the threshold is so reduced, it shall not be reduced below £120,000.

      (ii)   An order under subparagraph (i) shall be laid before Dáil Éireann as soon as may be after it is made and, if a resolution annulling the order is passed by Dáil Éireann within the next twenty one sitting days on which Dáil Éireann has sat after the order is laid before it, the order shall be annulled accordingly, but without prejudice to the validity of anything previously done thereunder.

(*i*).   Following payment of the advance payment, any subsequent increase of a taxable person's total net tax, whether by way of assessment or otherwise, for the relevant period shall be disregarded for the purposes of the application of the provisions relating to the advance payment and to the application of the surcharge where—

      (i)   the effect of such increase is to increase the amount of the advance payment by less than 10 per cent, or

      (ii)   the Revenue Commissioners consider that, having regard to the circumstances of the case, the adjustment arose from an accidental or genuine misunderstanding or error and should be disregarded for the purposes of the application of the provisions relating to the advance payment and to the application of the surcharge.

(*j*)   For the purposes of this subsection and subject to the direction and control of the Revenue Commissioners, any power, function or duty conferred or imposed on them may be exercised or performed on their behalf by an officer of the Revenue Commissioners.

(*k*)   In this subsection—

"due date" means the date on which, in accordance with paragraph (*a*), the advance payment is due;

"relevant period" means, as respects a taxable person in relation to the 1st day of December in any year, the period ending on the 30th day of June in that year and commencing on the 1st day of July in the immediately preceding year:

Provided that where a person became a taxable person in that period, the relevant period shall be deemed to commence on the date on which the person first became a taxable person;

"total net tax" means the total tax payable by the taxable person on supplies, importations and intra Community acquisitions less the amount which may be deducted by him in accordance with section 12.][13]

Amendments

1   Substituted by VATAA 1978 s 30(2) with effect from 1 March 1979; previously "goods are delivered or the services are rendered".

2   Subs (1)(proviso) repealed by VATAA 1978 s 30(1) with effect from 1 March 1979.

3   Subs (1A) inserted by FA 1992 s 182(*a*) with effect from 1 January 1993.

4   Inserted by FA 1992 s 182(*b*) with effect from 1 January 1993.

5   Substituted by VATAA 1978 s 30(2) with effect from 1 March 1979; previously "delivery of the goods or the rendering of the service".

6   Substituted by VATAA 1978 s 30(2) with effect from 1 March 1979; previously "delivery or rendering".

7   Subs (3)(*a*)(proviso) inserted by FA 1993 s 92(*a*).

8   Substituted by FA 1995 s 134 as on and from such day or days as the Minister for Finance may by order or orders appoint, either generally or with reference to any particular category of taxable person to whom VATA 1972 s 19(3)(*aa*) applies.

9   Subs (3)(*aa*) inserted by FA 1989 s 58 with effect from 24 May 1989.

10   Subs (3) substituted by FA 1983 s 84 with effect from 1 September 1983.

11   Subs (4) substituted by FA 1993 s 92(*b*) with effect from 1 September 1993.

12   Effectively substituted by Value Added Tax (Threshold for Advance Payment) (Amendment) Order 1994 (SI 342/1994) in respect of payments to be made in December 1994 and subsequently; previously £300,000 (Value Added Tax (Threshold for Advance Payment) Order 1993 (SI 303/1993)).

13   Subs (5) substituted and subs (6) inserted by FA 1993 s 92(*c*).

Cross-references

Advance payment (subs (6)), European Communities (Value Added Tax) Regulations 1993 (SI 345/1993).

Alcohol products (subss (1)-(1A)): s 3B(2), (3).

Fraud, negligence; penalties: s 27(1).

Intra-Community acquisition of goods: s 3A.

Refund of tax (subs (6)(*a*)): s 20(1)(proviso).

Returns, particulars required, Revenue may prescribe: s 32(1)(*j*); details: VATR 1979 r 12; statement of intra-EU supplies: Value Added Tax (Statement of Intra Community Supplies) Regulations 1993 (SI 54/1993).

Time and manner in which tax payable (subs (4)), Revenue may prescribe: s 32(1)(*ae*).

Narrative

Irish Value Added Tax, Chapters 5, 9; *Guide to Value Added Tax (Revenue Commissioners)*: Chapter 7.

Definition

"business": s 1(1); "Collector-General": s 1(1); "goods": ss 1(1), 32; "new means of transport": s 1(1);"person": IA 1937 s 11(*c*); "registered person": s 1(1); "regulations": s 1(1); "supply": s 1(1); "tax": s 1(1); "taxable period": s 1(1); "taxable person": s 1(1), 8; "writing": IA 1937 Sch.

Personal notes

19A Statement of intra-Community supplies

a 22(6),
22(12)
[(1) Subject to subsections (2) and (3), a taxable person shall by the last day of the month immediately following the end of each calendar quarter, furnish to the Revenue Commissioners a statement of his intra-Community supplies in that quarter prepared in accordance with, and containing such other particulars as may be specified in, regulations.

(2) The Revenue Commissioners shall, on request, authorise a taxable person to furnish by the last day of each month a statement of his intra-Community supplies in the previous month prepared in accordance with, and containing such other particulars as may be specified in, regulations.

(3) The Revenue Commissioners may, on request, authorise a taxable person, whose supplies do not exceed or are not likely to exceed, in a calendar year, an amount or amounts specified in regulations, to furnish by the last day of January following that calendar year a statement of such intra-Community supplies prepared in accordance with and containing such other particulars as may be specified in regulations.

(4) Notwithstanding the provisions of subsections (1), (2) and (3), a taxable person who made no intra-Community supplies in the relevant period, but who was liable to furnish a statement in respect of a previous period, shall, unless authorised by the Revenue Commissioners, furnish to them within the relevant time limit a statement indicating that he made no such supplies in that period.

(5) The Revenue Commissioners may, in accordance with regulations, cancel an authorisation under subsection (2) or (3).

(6) In this section **"intra-Community supplies"** means:

   (*a*) supplies of goods to a person registered for value added tax in another Member State, and

   (*b*) transfers of the kind referred to in section 3(1)(*g*)(iii).][1]

Amendments
1   Section 19A inserted by FA 1992 s 183 with effect from 1 January 1993.

Cross-references
Form of statement, Revenue may prescribe: s 32(1)(*af*).
Fraud, negligence; penalties: s 27(1).
Return, particulars required, Revenue may prescribe: s 32(1)(*j*); details: Value Added Tax (Statement of Intra-Community Supplies) Regulations 1993 (SI 54/1993).

Narrative
Guide to Value Added Tax (Revenue Commissioners): Chapter 11.

Definition
"person": IA 1937 s 11(*c*); "a person registered for value added tax": s 1(1); "regulations": s 1(1), 32; "taxable person" ss 1(1), 8.

Personal notes

---

20 Refund of tax

(1) [[Subject to subsections (1A) and (1B)]¹, where]² in relation to a return lodged under section 19 or a claim made in accordance with regulations, it is shown to the satisfaction of the Revenue Commissioners that, as respects any taxable period, the amount of tax, if any, actually paid to the Collector-General in accordance with section 19 together with the amount of tax, if any, which qualified for deduction under section 12 exceeds the tax, if any, which would properly be payable if no deduction were made under the said section 12, they shall refund the amount of the excess less any sums previously refunded under this subsection or repaid under section 12 and may include in the amount refunded any interest which has been paid under section 21.]³

[Provided that where the taxable period is the period ending on the 31st day of December in any year, the amount of tax to be refunded shall be increased by the amount paid, if any, in accordance with paragraph (*a*) of subsection (6) of section 19 where that amount was due during that taxable period.]⁴

[(1A) Where the Revenue Commissioners apply the provisions of section 8(8) to a number of persons they may defer repayment of all or part of any tax refundable under subsection (1) to any one or more of the said persons prior to the application of those provisions, where any one or more of the said persons have not furnished all returns and remitted all amounts of tax referred to in section 19(3) at the time of such application.]⁵

[(1B) The Revenue Commissioners may, where it appears requisite to them to do so for the protection of the revenue, require as a condition for making a refund in accordance with subsection (1) the giving of security of such amount and in such manner and form as they may determine:

Provided that the amount of such security shall not, in any particular case, exceed the amount to be refunded.]⁶

(2) Notwithstanding anything in this Act, a refund of the tax paid in respect of radio broadcasting reception apparatus and parts thereof belonging to an institution or society may be made to the institution or society if, but only if—

> (*a*) in the opinion of the Revenue Commissioners, it has for its primary object the amelioration of the lot of blind persons, and

> (*b*) it shows, to the satisfaction of the Revenue Commissioners, that the goods in question are intended for the use of blind persons.

(3) [(*a*) The Minister may by order provide that a person who fulfils to the satisfaction of the Revenue Commissioners such conditions as may be specified in the order shall be entitled to be repaid so much, as is specified in the order, of any tax borne or paid by him as does not qualify for deduction under section 12.]⁷

> (*b*) The Minister may by order amend or revoke an order under this subsection, including an order under this paragraph.

> (*c*) An order under this subsection shall be laid before Dáil Éireann as soon as may be after it is made and, if a resolution annulling the order is passed by Dáil Éireann within the next twenty-one days on which Dáil Éireann has sat after the order is laid before it, the order shall be annulled accordingly, but without prejudice to the validity of anything previously done thereunder.

(4) No refund shall be made under this section or under [any other provision of this Act or regulations]⁸ unless the claim is made within the period of ten years from the end of the taxable period to which the claim relates.

[(5) (*a*) If a person pays an amount of tax which was not properly due by him, he may claim a refund of the amount and the Revenue Commissioners shall, subject to the provisions of this section, refund to him that amount.

    (*b*)   It shall be a defence in relation to a claim under this subsection or under any other provision of this Act or regulations for a refund that payment of the refund would unjustly enrich the claimant.][9]

[(6) Where the Revenue Commissioners refund any amount due under subsection (1) or subsection (5), they may if they so determine refund any such amount directly into an account, specified by the person to whom the amount is due, in a financial institution.][10]

Amendments

1   Substituted by FA 1992 s 184(1)(*a*) with effect from 28 May 1992; previously "Subject to subsection (1A)" .
2   Substituted by FA 1986 s 87 with effect from 27 May 1986; previously "Where".
3   Subs (1) substituted by FA 1981 s 45 with effect from 28 May 1981.
4   Subs (1)(proviso) inserted by FA 1993 s 93.
5   Subs (1A) substituted by FA 1991 s 83 with effect from 29 May 1991.
6   Subs (1B) inserted by FA 1992 s 184(1)(*b*) with effect from 28 May 1992 .
7   Subs (3)(*a*) substituted by FA 1992 s 184(1)(*c*) with effect from 1 January 1993.
8   Substituted by VATAA s 30(2) with effect from 1 March 1979; previously "section 5(4)".
9   Subs (5) inserted by FA 1992 s 184(1)(*d*) with effect from 28 May 1992.
10   Subs (6) inserted by FA 1995 s 135 with effect from 2 June 1995.

Cross-references

Disabled driver vehicles: Disabled Drivers and Disabled Passengers (Tax Concessions) Regulations 1994 (SI 353/1994).
Disabled persons' aids: Value Added Tax (Refund of Tax)(No 15) Order 1981 (SI 428/1981).
EuroControl (purchases by): Value Added Tax (Refund of Tax)(No 7) Order 1974 (SI 290/1974).
European Space Agency (purchases by): Value Added Tax (Refund of Tax) (No 11) Order 1980 (SI 239/1980).
Existing orders under this section remain valid: FA 1992 s 184(2).
Farm buildings and drainage (unregistered farmers): Value Added Tax (Refund of Tax)(No 25) Order 1993 (SI 266/1993).
Fishermen, boats: VATR 1979 r 29; marine diesel: Value Added Tax (Refund of Tax)(No 16) Order 1983 (SI 234/1983).
Fraud, negligence; penalties: s 27(1).
Hospital equipment (bought through voluntary donations): Value Added Tax (Refund of Tax)(No 23) Order 1992 (SI 58/1992).
Medical research equipment: Value Added Tax (Refund of Tax)(No 27) Order 1995 (SI 38/1995).
Mobile home (to be used as residence): Value Added Tax (Refund of Tax)(No 12) Order 1980 (SI 262/1980).
Philanthropic organisations (exported goods): Value Added Tax (Refund of Tax)(No 21) Order 1987 (SI 308/1987).
Revenue power to make regulations: s 32(1)(*m*); refund procedures: VATR 1979 r 17.
Sea rescue groups (boats and boat houses): Value Added Tax (Refund of Tax)(No 18) Order 1985 (SI 192/1985).
Touring coaches: Value Added Tax (Refund of Tax)(No 28) Order 1996 (SI 98/1996).

Case law

A disabled plaintiff who obtained a VAT refund on a specially adapted car was refused an excise duty refund on the basis that he was not wholly without the use of his legs (as required by regulations). His claim (by judicial review) that he had a "legitimate expectation" to a refund was refused as he should have known he did not meet the requirements: *Wiley v Revenue Commissioners* IV ITR 170.

Narrative

Irish Value Added Tax, Chapter 7.

Statement of practice

Repayments to unregistered persons: SP VAT 2/94.

Definition

"Collector-General": s 1(1); "Dáil Éireann": IA 1937 Sch; "goods": s 1(1); "the Minister": s 1(1); "person": IA 1937 s 11(*c*); "regulations": ss 1(1), 32; "supply": s 1(1); "tax": s 1(1); "taxable period": s 1(1).

Personal notes

---

21 Interest

(1) Where any amount of tax becomes payable under section 19(3) and is not paid, simple interest on the amount shall be paid by the [taxable person]¹, and such interest shall be calculated from the date on which the amount became payable and at a rate of [**1.25 per cent**]² for each month or part of a month during which the amount remains unpaid:

Provided that if the amount of the interest as so calculated is less than £5, the amount of interest payable shall be £5.

(2) Subsection (1) shall apply—

  (*a*) to tax recoverable by virtue of a notice under section 22 as if the tax were tax which the person was liable to pay for the respective taxable period or periods comprised in the notice, and

  [(*b*) to tax recoverable by virtue of a notice under section 23 as if (whether a notice of appeal under that section is received or not) the tax were tax which the person was liable to pay for the taxable period or, as the case may be, the later or latest taxable period included in the period comprised in the notice]³.

Amendments
1 Words substituted by VATAA 1978 s 30(2) with effect from 1 March 1979; previously "accountable person".
2 Substituted by FA 1978 s 46(1) with effect from 5 July 1978; previously "1.5 per cent".
3 Subs (2)(*b*) substituted by FA 1976 s 56 with effect from 27 May 1976.
Cross-references
Revenue may make regulations allowing remission of small amounts of interest: s 32(1)(*o*); regulations: VATR 1979 r 18.
Narrative
Irish Value Added Tax, Chapter 12; *Guide to Value Added Tax (Revenue Commissioners)*: Chapter 7.7.
Definition
"person": IA 1937 s 11(*c*); "tax": s 1(1); "taxable period": s 1(1); "taxable person": ss 1(1), 8.

Personal notes

22 Estimation of tax due for a taxable period

(1) If within the time prescribed by section 19(3) [a taxable person][1] fails to furnish in accordance with the relevant regulations a return of the tax payable by him in respect of any taxable period, then, without prejudice to any other action which may be taken, the Revenue Commissioners may, in accordance with regulations, but subject to section 30, estimate the amount of tax payable by him in respect of that taxable period and serve notice on him of the amount estimated.

[Provided that where the Revenue Commissioners are satisfied that the amount so estimated is excessive, they may amend the amount so estimated by reducing it and serve notice on the person concerned of the revised amount estimated and such notice shall supersede any previous notice issued under this subsection.][2]

(2) Where a notice is served under subsection (1) on a person, the following provisions shall apply:

    (*a*)   the person may, if he claims that he is not [a taxable person][1], by giving notice in writing to the Revenue Commissioners within the period of twenty-one days from the date of the service of the notice, require the claim to be referred for decision to the Appeal Commissioners and their decision shall, subject to section 25, be final and conclusive,

    (*b*)   on the expiration of the said period, if no such claim is required to be so referred, or if such a claim is required to be so referred, on final determination against the claim, the estimated tax specified in the notice shall be recoverable in the same manner and by the like proceedings as if the person had furnished, within the prescribed period, a true and correct return, in accordance with regulations, for the taxable period to which the estimate relates, showing as due by him such estimated tax,

    (*c*)   if at any time after the service of the notice the person furnishes a return, in accordance with regulations, in respect of the taxable period specified in the notice and pays tax in accordance with the return, together with any interest and costs which may have been incurred in connection with the default, the notice shall, subject to paragraph (*d*), stand discharged and any excess of tax which may have been paid shall be repaid,

    (*d*)   where action for the recovery of tax specified in a notice under subsection (1), being action by way of the institution of proceedings in any court or the issue of a certificate under section 485 of the Income Tax Act, 1967, has been taken paragraph (*c*) shall not, unless the Revenue Commissioners otherwise direct, apply in relation to that notice until the said action has been completed.

(3) A notice given by the Revenue Commissioners under subsection (1) may extend to two or more taxable periods.

Amendments

1   Substituted by VATAA 1978 s 30(2) with effect from 1 March 1979; previously "an accountable person".

2   Subs (1)(proviso) inserted by FA 1995 s 136 with effect from 2 June 1995.

Cross-references

Appeal: s 25(2)(*k*).

Estimates, Revenue may accept: s 32(1)(*r*); acceptance: VATR 1979 r 13; Revenue may make: s 32(1)(*u*); regulations: Value Added Tax (Estimation and Assessment of Tax Due) Regulations 1992 (SI 277/1992).

Service of notices, Revenue may make regulations: s 32(1)(*q*).

Time limits for estimates: s 30(4)-(5).

Narrative

Irish Value Added Tax, Chapter 12; *Guide to Value Added Tax (Revenue Commissioners):* Chapter 7.9.

Definition

"Appeal Commissioners": s 1(1); "person": IA 1937 s 11(*c*); "regulations": ss 1(1), 32; "tax": s 1(1); "taxable period": ss 1(1), 8; "taxable person": s 1(1); "writing": IA 1937 Sch.

23 Assessment of tax due for any period

[(1) Where, in relation to any period consisting of one taxable period or of two or more consecutive taxable periods, [the inspector of taxes, or such other officer as the Revenue Commissioners may authorise to exercise the powers conferred by this section (hereafter referred to in this section as **"other officer"**), has reason to believe][1] that an amount of tax is due and payable to [the Revenue Commissioners][2] by a person in any of the following circumstances:

(a) the total amount of tax payable by the person was greater than the total amount of tax (if any) paid by him,

(b) the total amount of tax refunded to the person in accordance with section 20(1) was greater than the amount (if any) properly refundable to him, or

(c) an amount of tax is payable by the person and a refund under section 20(1) has been made to the person,

then, without prejudice to any other action which may be taken, [the inspector or other officer may][3], in accordance with regulations but subject to section 30, make an [assessment][4] in one sum of the total amount of tax which in [his][5] opinion should have been paid or the total amount of tax (including a nil amount) which in accordance with section 20(1) should have been refunded, as the case may be, in respect of the taxable period or periods comprised in such period and may serve a notice on the person specifying—

(i) the total amount of tax so [assessed][6],

(ii) the total amount of tax (if any) paid by the person or refunded to the person in relation to the said period, and

(iii) the total amount so due and payable as aforesaid (referred to subsequently in this section as **"the amount due"**).

(2) Where notice is served on a person under subsection (1), the following provisions shall apply:

(a) the person may, if he claims that the amount due is excessive, on giving notice to the Revenue Commissioners within the period of twenty-one days from the date of the service of the notice, appeal to the Appeal Commissioners, and

(b) on the expiration of the said period, if no notice of appeal is received or, if notice of appeal is received, on determination of the appeal by agreement or otherwise, the amount due, or the amended amount due as determined in relation to the appeal, shall become due and payable as if the tax were tax which the person was liable to pay for the taxable period during which the period of fourteen days from the date of the service of the notice under subsection (1) expired or the appeal was determined by agreement or otherwise, whichever taxable period is the later.

[(3) Where a person appeals an assessment under subsection (1), within the time limits provided for in subsection (2), he shall pay to the Revenue Commissioners the amount which he believes to be due, and if—

(a) the amount paid is greater than **80 per cent** of the amount of the tax found to be due on the determination of the appeal, and

(b) the balance of the amount found to be due on the determination of the appeal is paid within one month of the date of such determination, interest in accordance with section 21 shall not be chargeable from the date of raising of the assessment.][7][8]

Amendments

1 Substituted by FA 1985 s 47 with effect from 30 May 1985; previously "Revenue Commissioners have reason to believe".

2 Substituted by FA 1985 s 47 with effect from 30 May 1985; previously "them".

3 Substituted by FA 1985 s 47 with effect from 30 May 1985; previously "they may".
4 Substituted by FA 1992 s 185(*a*)(i) with effect from 28 May 1992; previously "estimate".
5 Substituted by FA 1985 s 47 with effect from 30 May 1985; previously "their".
6 Substituted by FA 1992 s 185(*a*)(ii) with effect from 28 May 1992; previously "estimated".
7 Subs (3) inserted by FA 1992 s 185(*b*) with effect from 28 May 1992.
8 Section 23 substituted by VATAA 1978 s 17 with effect from 1 March 1979.

Cross-references
Advance payment of tax (year end): s 19(6)(*c*)(proviso).
Appeal: s 25(2)(*k*).
Estimates, Revenue may accept: s 32(1)(*r*); acceptance: VATR 1979 r 13; Revenue may make: s 32(1)(*u*); regulations: Value Added Tax (Estimation and Assessment of Tax Due) Regulations 1992 (SI 277/1992).
Service of notices, Revenue may make regulations: s 32(1)(*g*).
Time limits for estimates: s 30(4)-(5).

Narrative
Irish Value Added Tax, Chapter 12; *Guide to Value Added Tax (Revenue Commissioners)*: Chapter 7.9.

Definition
"Appeal Commissioners": s 1(1); "inspector of taxes": s 1(1); "person": IA 1937 s 11(*c*); "regulations": ss 1(1), 32; "tax": s 1(1); "taxable period": s 1(1).

Personal notes

23A Security to be given by certain taxable persons

[(1) The Revenue Commissioners may, where it appears requisite to them to do so for the protection of the revenue, require a taxable person, as a condition of his supplying goods or services under a taxable supply, to give security, or further security, of such amount and in such manner and form as they may determine, for the payment of any tax which is, or may become, due from him from the date of service on him of a notice in writing to that effect.

(2) Where notice is served on a person in accordance with subsection (1) the person may, on giving notice to the Revenue Commissioners within the period of twenty-one days from the date of the service of the notice, appeal the requirement of giving any security under subsection (1) to the Appeal Commissioners.][1]

Amendments
1   Section 23A inserted by FA 1992 s 186 with effect from 28 May 1992.
Cross-references
Appeal: s 25(2)(*k*).
Non compliance, penalty: s 26(3B).
Service of notices, Revenue may make regulations: s 32(1)(*g*).
Definition
"Appeal Commissioners": s 1(1); "person": IA 1937 s 11(*c*); "supply": s 1(1); "tax": s 1(1); "taxable person": ss 1(1), 8: "writing": 1A 1937 Sch.

Personal notes

24 Recovery of tax

(1) (*a*)   Without prejudice to any other mode of recovery the provisions of any enactment relating to the recovery of income tax and the provisions of any rule of court so relating shall apply to the recovery of any tax payable in accordance with this Act and the regulations thereunder as they apply in relation to the recovery of income tax.

(*b*)   In particular and without prejudice to the generality of paragraph (*a*), that paragraph applies the provisions of sections 480, 485, 486, 487, 488 and 491 of the Income Tax Act, 1967.

(*c*)   Provisions as applied by this section shall so apply subject to any modifications specified by regulations under this Act.

(2) In proceedings instituted under this section or any regulations for the recovery of any amount of tax—

(*a*)   a certificate signed by an officer of the Revenue Commissioners which certifies that a stated amount of tax is due and payable by the defendant shall be evidence, until the contrary is proved, that that amount is so due and payable, and

(*b*)   a certificate certifying as aforesaid and purporting to be signed by an officer of the Revenue Commissioners may be tendered in evidence without proof and shall be deemed, until the contrary is proved, to have been signed by an officer of the Revenue Commissioners.

(3) Any reference in the foregoing subsections to an amount of tax includes a reference to interest payable in the case in question under section 21.

(4) Subject to this section, the rules of the court concerned for the time being applicable to civil proceedings shall apply to proceedings by virtue of this section or any regulation under this Act.

(5) Where an order which was made before the passing of this Act under section 12 of the Court Officers Act, 1945, contains a reference to levy under a certificate issued under section 485 of the Income Tax Act, 1967, that reference shall be construed as including a reference to levy under a certificate issued under the said section 485 as extended by this section.

Cross-references
Adaptation of income tax provisions: VATR 1979 r 15.
Subs (1)(*b*): ITA 1967 s 480: distraint (by Collector General) repealed by FA 1996 s 132 and Sch 5 Pt II; ITA 1967 s 485: enforcement by sheriff or county registrar; ITA 1967 s 486: District Court proceedings; ITA 1967 s 487: continuance of pending proceedings: ITA 1967 s 488: High Court proceedings; ITA 1967 s 491: tax owed is a debt due to the Central Fund.
Revenue may prescribe manner of recovery of arrears: s 32(1)(*l*).
Narrative
Irish Value Added Tax, Chapter 12.
Definition
"person": IA 1937 s 11(*c*); "regulations": ss 1(1), 32; "rule of court": IA 1937 Sch; "tax": s 1(1).

Personal notes

---

25 Appeals

(1) Any person aggrieved by a determination of the Revenue Commissioners in relation to—

    (*a*)   a liability to tax under subsection (5) or (6) of section 17,

    [(*aa*)   the treatment of one or more persons as a single taxable person in accordance with section 8(8),][1]

    [(*ab*)   the deeming, in accordance with section 37, of a person to have made supplies in the course or furtherance of business,][2]

    [(*ac*)   a determination under section 8(3E),][3]

    (*b*)   a charge of tax in accordance with regulations, or

    (*c*)   a claim for repayment of tax,

against which an appeal to the Appeal Commissioners is not otherwise provided for under this Act may, on giving notice in writing to the Revenue Commissioners within twenty-one days after the notification to the person aggrieved of the determination, appeal to the Appeal Commissioners.

[(1A) Where a person is aggrieved by a decision of the Revenue Commissioners that such person is not a taxable person then such person may, on giving notice in writing to the Revenue Commissioners within twenty-one days after the notification of that decision to such person, appeal to the Appeal Commissioners.][4]

(2) The provisions of the Income Tax Acts relating to—

    (*a*)   the appointment of times and places for the hearing of appeals;

    (*b*)   the giving of notice to each person who has given notice of appeal of the time and place appointed for the hearing of his appeal;

    (*c*)   the determination of an appeal by agreement between the appellant and an inspector of taxes or other officer appointed by the Revenue Commissioners in that behalf;

    (*d*)   the determination of an appeal by the appellant giving notice of his intention not to proceed with the appeal;

    [(*dd*)   the refusal of an application for an appeal hearing;][5]

    (*e*)   the hearing and determination of an appeal by the Appeal Commissioners, including the hearing and determination of an appeal by one Appeal Commissioner;

    [(*f*)   the determination of an appeal through the failure of a person who has given notice of appeal to attend before the Appeal Commissioners at the time and place appointed;

    (*ff*)   the refusal of an application for the adjournment of any proceedings in relation to an appeal, and the dismissing of an appeal, by the Appeal Commissioners;][6]

    (*g*)   the extension of the time for giving notice of appeal, and the readmission of appeals by the Appeal Commissioners;

    (*h*)   the rehearing of an appeal by a judge of the Circuit Court and the statement of a case for the opinion of the High Court on a point of law;

    (*i*)   the payment of tax in accordance with the determination of the Appeal Commissioners notwithstanding that an appeal is required to be reheard by a judge of the Circuit Court or that a case for the opinion of the High Court on a point of law has been required to be stated or is pending;

    (*j*)   the payment of tax which is agreed not to be in dispute in relation to an appeal; and

    (*k*)   the procedures for appeal;

[shall, subject to the modifications set out hereunder and to other necessary modifications, apply to a claim under section 22 or an appeal under [section 11(1B), 23 or 23A][7] or this section as if the claim or appeal were an appeal against an assessment to income tax:

> (i)   a reference to a year of assessment shall include a reference to the taxable periods concerned,
>
> (ii) a reference to a return of income shall include a reference to a return required to be made under section 19,
>
> (iii) a reference to interest shall include a reference to interest payable under section 21][8].

Amendments

1   Subs (1)(*aa*) inserted by FA 1991 s 84 with effect from 29 May 1991.
2   Subs (1)(*ab*) inserted by FA 1992 s 187(*a*) with effect from 28 May 1992.
3   Subs (1)(*ac*) inserted by FA 1995 s 137(*a*) with 1 January 1996.
4   Subs (1A) inserted by FA 1995 s 137(*b*) with effect from 2 June 1995.
5   Subs (2)(*dd*) inserted by FA 1995 s 137(*c*) with effect from 2 June 1995.
6   Subs (2)(*f*) - (*ff*) substituted by FA 1983 s 85 with effect from 8 June 1983.
7   Substituted by FA 1992 s 187(*b*) with effect from 28 May 1992; previously "section 11(1B) or 23".
8   Substituted by FA 1983 s 85 with effect from 8 June 1983.

Cross-references

Subs (2)(*a*): ITA 1967 s 416(2)(*a*).
Subs (2)(*b*): ITA 1967 s 416(2)(*b*).
Subs (2)(*c*): ITA 1967 s 416(3)(*a*)-(*c*).
Subs (2)(*d*): ITA 1967 s 416(3)(*d*).
Subs (2)(*e*): ITA 1967 s 416(4)-(5).
Subs (2)(*f*): ITA 1967 s 416(6).
Subs (2)(*g*): ITA 1967 s 416(7).
Subs (2)(*h*): ITA 1967 s 429.
Subs (2)(*i*): ITA 1967 s 428.
Subs (2)(*k*): ITA 1967 s 421.

Narrative

Irish Value Added Tax, Chapter 13; *Guide to Value Added Tax (Revenue Commissioners)*: Chapter 7.9.

Definition

"Appeal Commissioner": s 1(1); "the Circuit Court": IA 1937 Sch; "the High Court": IA 1937 Sch; "inspector of taxes": s 1(1); "person": IA 1937 s 11(*c*); "regulations": ss 1(1), 32; "tax": s 1(1); "taxable period": s 1(1); "writing": IA 1937 Sch; "year of assessment": ITA 1967 s 1(1).

Personal notes

26 Penalties generally

[(1) A person who does not comply with section 9(2), 11(7), 12A, 16, 17, ...[1] [, 19 or 19A][2] or any provision of regulations in regard to any matter to which the foregoing sections relate shall be liable to a penalty of [£1,200][3].][4]

(2) A person who is not a registered person and who, on or after the specified day, ...[5] issues an invoice in which an amount of tax is stated shall be liable to a penalty of [£750][6].

[(2A) Any person who, otherwise than under and in accordance with section 12A or 17(4)(*a*), issues an invoice in which an amount of flat-rate addition is stated shall be liable to a penalty of [£750][7].][8]

(3) Where a person mentioned in subsection (1) or (2) [or (2A)][9] is a body of persons, the secretary shall be liable to a separate penalty of [£750][10].

[(3A) A person who does not comply with [subsection (3) of section 18 or with a requirement of an authorised officer under that section][11] shall be liable to a penalty of [£1,000][12].][13]

[(3B) A person who supplies taxable goods or services in contravention of the requirement of security specified in section 23A shall be liable to a penalty of £1,200 in respect of each such supply.][14]

(4) All penalties under this section may, without prejudice to any other method of recovery, be proceeded for and recovered summarily in the same manner as in summary proceedings for recovery of any penalty under any Act relating to the excise, and, notwithstanding section 10(4) of the Petty Sessions (Ireland) Act, 1851, summary proceedings under this section may be instituted within three years from the date of the incurring of the penalty.

(5) ...[15].

(6) In proceedings for recovery of a penalty under this section—

    (*a*)   a certificate signed by an officer of the Revenue Commissioners which certifies that he has inspected the relevant records of the Revenue Commissioners and that it appears from them that, during a stated period, stated particulars or stated returns were not furnished by the defendant shall be evidence until the contrary is proved that the defendant did not, during that period, furnish the particulars or return,

    (*b*)   a certificate signed by an officer of the Revenue Commissioners which certifies that he has inspected the relevant records of the Revenue Commissioners and that it appears from them that a stated document was duly sent to the defendant on a stated day shall be evidence until the contrary is proved that that person received that document in the ordinary course,

    (*c*)   a certificate signed by an officer of the Revenue Commissioners which certifies that he has inspected the relevant records of the Revenue Commissioners and that it appears from them that a stated notice was not issued by them to the defendant shall be evidence until the contrary is proved that the defendant did not receive the notice in question,

    [(*d*)   a certificate signed by an officer of the Revenue Commissioners which certifies that he has inspected the relevant records of the Revenue Commissioners and that it appears from them that, during a stated period, the defendant was [a taxable person][16] or was a registered person or was not a registered person shall be evidence until the contrary is proved that, during that period, the defendant was [a taxable person][15] or was a registered person or was not a registered person, as the case may be,

    (*e*)   a certificate certifying as provided for in paragraph (*a*), (*b*), (*c*) or (*d*) and purporting to be signed by an officer of the Revenue Commissioners may be tendered in evidence without proof and shall be deemed, until the contrary is proved, to have been signed by an officer of the Revenue Commissioners][17].

(7) Subject to this section, the rules of the court concerned for the time being applicable to civil proceedings shall apply to proceedings pursuant to this section.

Amendments

1   Words "18(2)" deleted by FA 1984 s 90 with effect from 23 May 1984.
2   Substituted by FA 1992 s 188(*a*)(i) with effect from 1 January 1993; previously "or 19" .
3   Substituted by FA 1992 s 188(*a*)(ii) with effect from 28 May 1992; previously "£800".
4   Subs (1) substituted by FA 1982 s 86 with effect from 1 September 1982.
5   Words "otherwise than under and in accordance with section 13," deleted by FA 1976 s 81 with effect from 1 March 1976.
6   Substituted by FA 1992 s 188((*b*) with effect from 28 May 1992; previously "£500".
7   Substituted by FA 1992 s 188(*c*) with effect from 28 May 1992; previously "£500".
8   Subs (2A) inserted by VATAA 1978 s 18 with effect from 1 March 1979.
9   Inserted by VATAA 1978 s 18 with effect from 1 March 1979.
10 Substituted by FA 1992 s 188(*d*) with effect from 28 May 1992; previously "£500".
11 Substituted by FA 1984 s 90 with effect from 23 May 1984; previously "section 18(3)".
12 Substituted by FA 1992 s 188(*e*) with effect from 28 May 1992; previously "£800".
13 Subs (3A) inserted by FA 1973 s 83 with effect from 3 September 1973.
14 Subs (3B) inserted by FA 1992 s 188(*f*) with effect from 28 May 1992.
15 Subs (5) deleted by FA 1982 s 86 with effect from 1 September 1982.
16 Substituted by VATAA 1978 s 30(2) with effect from 1 March 1979; previously "an accountable person".
17 Subs (6)(*d*)-(*e*) substituted by FA 1976 s 57 with effect from 27 May 1976.

Cross-references

Fraud, negligence; penalties: s 27(1).
Revenue offences: FA 1983 s 94; tax defaulters, publication of names: FA 1983 s 23.
Time limits: s 30(1).

Narrative

Irish Value Added Tax, Chapter 12.

Definition

"body of persons": s 1(1); "flat-rate addition": ss 1(1, 12A; "person": IA 1937 s 11(*c*); "registered person": s 1(1); "regulations": ss 1(1), 32; "rule of court": IA 1937 Sch; "secretary": s 1(1); "the specified day": s 1(1); "tax": s 1(1); "taxable person": ss 1(1), 8.

Personal notes

27 Fraudulent returns, etc

(1) Where a person fraudulently or negligently, for the purposes of this Act or of regulations, produces, furnishes, gives, sends or otherwise makes use of, any incorrect return, invoice, [registration number, monthly control statement, claim,][1] credit note, debit note, receipt, account, voucher, bank statement, estimate, statement, information, book, document, record or declaration, he shall, subject to subsection (2), be liable to a penalty of—

    (*a*)   £100, and

    [(*b*)   the amount, or in the case of fraud, twice the amount of the difference between—

        (i)   the amount of tax properly payable by, or refundable to, such person if the said return, invoice, registration number, monthly control statement, claim, credit note, debit note, receipt, account, voucher, bank statement, estimate, statement, information, book, document, record or declaration had been correct, and

        (ii)   the amount of tax (if any) paid, or claimed by way of refund.][2]

(2) Where a person mentioned in the foregoing subsection is a body of persons—

    (*a*)   the reference in paragraph (*a*) of that subsection to £100 shall be construed as a reference to £500, or, in the case of fraud, £1,000, and

    (*b*)   the secretary shall be liable to a separate penalty of £100, or, in the case of fraud, £200.

(3) Where any such return, invoice, [registration number, monthly control statement, claim,][3] credit note, debit note, receipt, account, voucher, bank statement, estimate, statement, information, book, document, record or declaration as is mentioned in subsection (1) was made or submitted by a person neither fraudulently nor negligently and it comes to his notice (or, if he has died, to the notice of his personal representative) that it was incorrect, then, unless the error is remedied without unreasonable delay, the return, invoice, [registration number, monthly control statement, claim,][3] credit note, debit note, receipt, account, voucher, bank statement, estimate, statement, information, book, document, record or declaration shall be treated for the purposes of this section as having been negligently made or submitted by him.

[(4) If a person, in a case in which he represents that he is a registered person or that goods imported by him were so imported for the purposes of a business carried on by him, improperly procures the importation of goods without payment of tax in circumstances in which tax is chargeable, he shall be liable to a penalty of £500, and, in addition, he shall be liable to pay to the Revenue Commissioners the amount of any tax that should have been paid on the importation.][4]

[(5) A person who fraudulently or negligently—

    (*a*)   issues an invoice in which an amount of tax is stated, in such circumstances that, apart from his liability under subsection (5) or (6) of section 17, the said amount does not represent the amount of tax (if any) which becomes due by him in respect of the transaction to which the invoice relates, or

    (*b*)   issues a credit note showing an amount of tax other than that properly applicable to the transaction to which the credit note relates,

shall be liable to a penalty of

        (i)   £100, and

        (ii)   the amount, or, in the case of fraud, twice the amount of his liability under the said subsection (5) or (6), as the case may be, in respect of the issue of any such invoice or credit note.][5]

(6) Notwithstanding anything in section 30, proceedings for the recovery of any penalties under this section shall not be out of time by reason that they are commenced after the time allowed by the said section 30.

(7) For the purposes of this section, any return, invoice, [registration number, monthly control statement, claim,]⁶ credit note, debit note, receipt, account, voucher, bank statement, estimate, statement, information, book document, record or declaration submitted on behalf of a person shall be deemed to have been submitted by that person unless he proves that it was submitted without his consent or knowledge.

(8) Any reference in the foregoing subsections to an amount of tax includes a reference to interest payable in the case in question under section 21.

[(9) Where, in the pursuance of regulations made for the purposes of section 13(1)(a), tax on the supply of any goods has been remitted or repaid and—

> (a) the goods are found in the State after the date on which they were alleged to have been or were to be exported, or

> (b) any condition specified in the regulations or imposed by the Revenue Commissioners is not complied with,

and the presence of the goods in the State after that date or the non-compliance with the condition has not been authorised for the purposes of this subsection by the Revenue Commissioners, the goods shall be liable to forfeiture and the tax which was remitted or repaid shall be charged upon and become payable forthwith by the person to whom the goods were supplied or any person in whose possession the goods are found in the State and the provisions of section 24(1) shall apply accordingly, but the Revenue Commissioners may, if they think fit, waive payment of the whole or part of that tax.]⁷

[(9A) (1)   Where goods—

> (a) were supplied at the rate of **zero per cent**. subject to the condition that they were to be dispatched or transported outside the State in accordance with subparagraph (a), (b) or (c) of paragraph (i) of the Second Schedule and the goods were not so dispatched or transported,

> (b) were acquired without payment of value added tax referred to in Council Directive No. 77/388/EEC of 17 May 1977 in another Member State as a result of the declaration of an incorrect registration number, or

> (c) are being supplied by a taxable person who has not complied with the provisions of section 9(2),

> the goods shall be liable to forfeiture.

> (2)   Whenever an officer authorised by the Revenue Commissioners reasonably suspects that goods are liable to forfeiture in accordance with subsection (1) the goods may be detained by the said officer until such examination, enquiries or investigations as may be deemed necessary by the said officer, or by another authorised officer of the Revenue Commissioners, have been made for the purpose of determining to the satisfaction of either officer whether or not the goods were so supplied or acquired.

> (3)   When a determination referred to in subsection (2) has been made in respect of any goods, or upon the expiry of a period of two months from the date on which the said goods were detained under the said subsection, whichever is the earlier, the said goods shall be seized as liable to forfeiture or released.]⁸

> [(4)   or the purposes of subparagraph (b) of paragraph (1), "the declaration of an incorrect registration number" means–

(*a*)   the declaration by a person of another person's registration number,

(*b*)   the declaration by a person of a number which is not an actual registration number which he purports to be his registration number,

(*c*)   the declaration by a person of a registration number which was obtained from the Revenue Commissioners by supplying incorrect information, or

(*d*)   the declaration by a person of a registration number which was obtained from the Revenue Commissioners for the purposes of acquiring goods without payment of value-added tax referred to in Council Directive No. 77/388/EEC of 17 May, 1977, and not for any bona fide business purpose.][9]

(10) The provisions of the Customs Acts relating to forfeiture and condemnation of goods shall apply to goods liable to forfeiture under [subsection (9) or (9A)][10] as if they had become liable to forfeiture under those Acts and all powers which may be exercised by an officer of Customs and Excise under those Acts may be exercised by officers of the Revenue Commissioners authorised to exercise those powers for the purposes of [the said subsections and any provisions in relation to offences under those Acts shall apply, with any necessary modifications, in relation to the said subsections][11].][12]

[(11) Where an officer authorised by the Revenue Commissioners for the purposes of this subsection or a member of the Garda Síochána has reasonable grounds for suspecting that a criminal offence has been committed under the provisions of section 94 (as amended by section 243 of the Finance Act, 1992) of the Finance Act, 1983, in relation to tax, by a person who is not established in the State, or whom he believes is likely to leave the State, he may arrest that person.][13]

Amendments
1   Inserted by FA 1992 s 189(*a*)(i) with effect from 1 November 1992.
2   Subs (1)(*b*) substituted by FA 1992 s 189(*a*)(ii) with effect from 1 November 1992.
3   Inserted by FA 1992 s 189(*b*) with effect from 1 November 1992.
4   Subs (4) substituted by VATAA 1978 s 19 with effect from 1 March 1979.
5   Subs (5) substituted by FA 1973 s 84 with effect from 3 September 1973.
6   Inserted by FA 1992 s 189(*b*) with effect from 1 November 1992.
7   Subs (9) inserted by VATAA 1978 s 19 with effect from 1 March 1979.
8   Subs (9A) inserted by FA 1992 s 189 with effect from 1 January 1993.
9   Subs (9A)(4) inserted by FA 1994 s 98 with effect from 23 May 1994.
10   Substituted by FA 1992 s 189(*d*)(i) with effect from 1 January 1993; previously "subsection (9)".
11   Substituted by FA 1992 s 189(*d*)(ii) with effect from 1 January 1993 previously "the said subsection".
12   Subs (10) inserted by VATAA 1978 s 19 with effect from 1 March 1979.
13   Subs (11) inserted by FA 1992 s 189(*e*) with effect from 1 January 1993.

Cross-references
Revenue offences: FA 1983 s 94; tax defaulters, publication of names: FA 1983 s 23.
Time limits: s 30(1).

Case law
Subs (9A): No grounds for seizure of oil tanker lorry (alleged breach of Hydrocarbon Oil (Rebated Oil) Regulations 1961 r 8): *McCrystal Oil Company Ltd v Revenue Commissioners,* IV ITR 386.

Narrative
Irish Value Added Tax, Chapter 12.

Definition
"body of persons": s 1(1); "business": s 1(1); "goods": s 1(1); "monthly control statement": ss 1(1), 17; "person": IA 1937 s 11(*c*); "registered person": ss 1(1), 9; "regulations": ss 1(1), 32; "secretary": s 1(1); "supply": s 1(1); "tax": s 1(1).

Personal notes

---

28 Assisting in making incorrect returns, etc

Any person who assists in or induces the making or delivery, for the purposes of tax, of any return, invoice, [monthly control statement, claim,][1] credit note, debit note, receipt, account, voucher, bank statement, estimate, statement, information, book, document, record or declaration which he knows to be incorrect shall be liable to a penalty of [£750][2].

Amendments
1 Inserted by FA 1992 s 190(*a*) with effect from 1 November 1992.
2 Substituted by FA 1992 s 190(*b*) with effect from 28 May 1992; previously "£500" .
Cross-references
Revenue offences: FA 1983 s 94; tax defaulters, publication of names: FA 1983 s 23.
Narrative
Irish Value Added Tax, Chapter 12.
Definition
"monthly control statement": ss 1(1), 17: "person": IA 1937 s 11(*c*); "tax": s 1(1).

Notes

29 Proceedings in High Court in respect of penalties

(1) Without prejudice to any other mode of recovery of a penalty under this Act, an officer of the Revenue Commissioners, authorised by them for the purposes of this subsection, may sue in his own name by civil proceedings for the recovery of the penalty in the High Court as a liquidated sum and the provisions of section 94 of the Courts of Justice Act, 1924, shall apply accordingly.

(2) If an officer who has commenced proceedings pursuant to this section, or who has continued the proceedings by virtue of this subsection, dies or otherwise ceases for any reason to be an officer authorised for the purposes of subsection (1) of this section—

    (*a*)   the right of such officer to continue the proceedings shall cease and the right to continue them shall vest in such other officer so authorised as may be nominated by the Revenue Commissioners,

    (*b*)   where such other officer is nominated under paragraph (*a*) of this subsection, he shall be entitled accordingly to be substituted as a party to the proceedings in the place of the first mentioned officer, and

    (*c*)   where an officer is so substituted, he shall give notice in writing of the substitution to the defendant.

(3) In proceedings pursuant to this section, a certificate signed by a Revenue Commissioner certifying the following facts, namely, that a person is an officer of the Revenue Commissioners and that he has been authorised by them for the purposes of subsection (1), shall be evidence until the contrary is proved of those facts.

(4) In proceedings pursuant to this section, a certificate signed by a Revenue Commissioner certifying the following facts, namely, that the plaintiff has ceased to be an officer of the Revenue Commissioners authorised by them for the purposes of subsection (1), that another person is an officer of the Revenue Commissioners, that such other person has been authorised by them for the purposes of subsection (1) and that he has been nominated by them in relation to the proceedings, for the purposes of subsection (2), shall be evidence until the contrary is proved of those facts.

(5) In proceedings pursuant to this section, a certificate certifying the facts referred to in subsection (3) or (4) and purporting to be signed by a Revenue Commissioner may be tendered in evidence without proof, and shall be deemed, until the contrary is proved, to have been so signed.

(6) Subject to this section, the rules of the High Court for the time being applicable to civil proceedings shall apply to proceedings pursuant to this section.

Narrative
Irish Value Added Tax, Chapter 12.
Definition
"the High Court": IA 1937 Sch; "person": IA 1937 s 11(*c*); "writing": IA 1937 Sch.

Personal notes

30 Time limits

(1) Subject to subsection (3) and sections 26(4) and 27(6), proceedings for the recovery of any penalty under this Act may be commenced at any time within six years next after the date on which it was incurred.

(2) Where the person who has incurred any penalty has died, any proceedings under this Act which have been or could have been commenced against him may be continued or commenced against his personal representative and any penalty awarded in proceedings so continued or commenced shall be a debt due from and payable out of his estate.

[(3) Proceedings may not be commenced by virtue of subsection (2) against the personal representative of a deceased person at a time when, by virtue of paragraph (*b*) of subsection (5), an estimation [or assessment]¹ of tax may not be made on the said personal representative in respect of tax which became due by such person before his death.]²

(4)   (*a*)   An estimation [or assessment]¹ of tax under section 22 or 23 may be made at any time not later than ten years after the end of the taxable period to which the estimate [or assessment]³ relates or, where the period in respect of which the estimate [or assessment]³ is made consists of two or more taxable periods, after the end of the earlier or earliest taxable period comprised in such period:

Provided that in a case in which any form of fraud or neglect has been committed by or on behalf of any person in connection with or in relation to tax, an estimate [or assessment]³ as aforesaid may be made at any time for any period for which, by reason of the fraud or neglect, tax would otherwise be lost to the Exchequer.

     (*b*)   In this subsection **"neglect"** means negligence or a failure to give any notice, to furnish particulars, to make any return or to produce or furnish any invoice, [monthly control statement,]⁴ credit note, debit note, receipt, account, voucher, bank statement, estimate [or assessment]³, statement, information, book, document, record or declaration required to be given, furnished, made or produced by or under this Act or regulations:

Provided that a person shall be deemed not to have failed to do anything required to be done within a limited time if he did it within such further time, if any, as the Revenue Commissioners may have allowed; and where a person had a reasonable excuse for not doing anything required to be done, he shall be deemed not to have failed to do it if he did it without unreasonable delay after the excuse had ceased.

(5)   (*a*)   Where a person dies, an estimation [or assessment]¹ of tax under section 22 or 23 (as the case may be) may be made on his personal representative for any period for which such an estimation [or assessment]¹ could have been made upon him immediately before his death, or could be made upon him if he were living, in respect of tax which became due by such person before his death, and the amount of tax recoverable under any such estimation [or assessment]¹ shall be a debt due from and payable out of the estate of such person.

     [(*b*)   No estimation [or assessment]¹ of tax shall be made by virtue of this subsection later than three years after the expiration of the year in which the deceased person died, in a case in which the grant of probate or letters of administration was made in that year, and no such estimation [or assessment]¹ shall be made later than two years after the expiration of the year in which such grant was made in any other case, but the foregoing provisions of this subsection shall have effect subject to the proviso that where the personal representative—

(i)   after the year in which the deceased person died, lodges a corrective affidavit for the purposes of assessment of estate duty or delivers an additional affidavit under section 38 of the Capital Acquisitions Tax Act, 1976, or

(ii)   is liable to deliver an additional affidavit under the said section 38, has been so notified by the Revenue Commissioners and did not deliver the said additional affidavit in the year in which the deceased person died,

such estimation [or assessment][1] may be made at any time before the expiration of two years after the end of the year in which the corrective affidavit was lodged or the additional affidavit was or is delivered][5].

Amendments
1   Inserted by FA 1992 s 191(*a*) with effect from 28 May 1992.
2   Subs (3) substituted by VATAA 1978 s 20 with effect from 1 March 1979.
3   Inserted by FA 1992 s 191(*b*) with effect from 28 May 1992.
4   Inserted by FA 1992 s 191(*c*) with effect from 1 November 1992.
5   Subs (5)(*b*) substituted by VATAA 1978 s 20 with effect from 1 March 1979.

Cross-references
Fraud, negligence; proceedings not "out of time" in such cases: s 27(6).

Narrative
Irish Value Added Tax, Chapter 12.

Definition
"affidavit": IA 1937 Sch; "monthly control statement": ss 1(1),17; "person": IA 1937 s 11(*c*); "regulations": ss 1(1), 32; "tax": s 1(1); "taxable period": s 1(1); "year": IA 1937 Sch .

Personal notes

_____

_____

_____

_____

_____

_____

_____

_____

_____

_____

_____

_____

_____

_____

_____

_____

_____

31 Application of section 512 of the Income Tax Act, 1967

The provisions of section 512 of the Income Tax Act, 1967, shall apply to any penalty incurred under this Act.

Note

This section allows the Revenue Commissioners to mitigate penalties awarded by a court or to order the release from jail of a convicted tax defaulter.

Narrative

Irish Value Added Tax, Chapter 12.

Personal notes

32 Regulations

(1) The Revenue Commissioners shall make such regulations as seem to them to be necessary for the purpose of giving effect to this Act and of enabling them to discharge their functions thereunder and, without prejudice to the generality of the foregoing, the regulations may make provision in relation to all or any of the following matters—

    (*a*)   the manner in which exemption in respect of certain services may be waived under section 7 and any such waiver may be cancelled, and the adjustments, including a charge of tax, which may be made as a condition of any such cancellation;

    [(*aa*)   the deduction of tax chargeable in respect of intra-Community acquisitions;

    (*ab*)   the manner in which residual tax referred to in section 12(1)(*a*)(ii*b*) may be calculated and deducted;

    (*ac*)   the manner in which residual tax referred to in section 13(3A) may be calculated and repaid;

    (*ad*)   the repayment, in accordance with section 15(5A), of tax chargeable on the importation of goods;

    (*ae*)   the time and manner in which tax shall be payable in respect of the goods referred to in section 19(4);

    (*af*)   the form particulars to be specified therein and the amount or amounts to be applied for the purposes of section 19A(3);

    (*ag*)   the supply of goods by tax-free shops in accordance with paragraph (i*a*) of the Second Schedule;

    (*ah*)   the importation of goods consigned to another Member State in accordance with paragraph (iii*b*) of the Second Schedule;

    (*ai*)   the circumstances in which a person may elect not to apply the proviso to subsection (6)(*d*) of section 3;][1]

    [(*b*)   the treatment under section 5(3) of the use and services specified therein as services supplied by a person for consideration in the course of business;][2]

    (*c*)   the particulars required for registration and the manner in which registration may be effected and cancelled;

    (*d*)   the manner in which a person may elect to be [a taxable person][3] and any such election may be cancelled, the treatment of [a taxable person][3] as a person who is [not a taxable person][4], and the adjustments, including a charge of tax, which may be made as a condition of any such cancellation or treatment;

    [(*da*)   the conditions for a taxable dealer to opt to apply the margin scheme to certain supplies in accordance with section 10A(4);

    (*db*)   the determination of the aggregate margin in accordance with section 10A(8);

    (*dc*)   the form of the invoice or other document that shall be issued in accordance with section 10B(4);

    (*dd*)   the manner in which residual tax referred to in section 12(1)(*a*)(vi) may be deducted;

    (*de*)   the particulars to be furnished in relation to antiques as specified in paragraph (xvia) of the Sixth Schedule or paragraph (iii) of the Eighth Schedule;][5]

[(*e*)   the manner in which notwithstanding section 11(3), any amount may be apportioned;][6]

(*f*)   ...[7];

[(*g*)   the determination, under section 14, of a person's tax liability for any period by reference to moneys received and the adjustments, including a charge of tax, which may be made when a person becomes entitled to determine his tax liability in the manner aforesaid or, having been so entitled, ceases to be so entitled or ceases to be a taxable person;][8]

(*h*)   the keeping by [taxable persons][9] of records and the retention of such records and supporting documents [or other recorded data][10];

[(*i*)   the form of invoice, [monthly control statement,][11] credit note, debit note and settlement voucher, including electronic form, required to be used for the purposes of this Act, the particulars required to be inserted in such documents or electronically recorded and the period within which such documents or electronic data are required to be issued or transmitted and such other conditions in relation to the issue or receipt, in any form, of an invoice, [monthly control statement,][11] credit note, debit note and settlement voucher as may be imposed by the Revenue Commissioners;][12]

(*j*)   the furnishing of returns and the particulars to be shown thereon;

(*k*)   the nomination by the Revenue Commissioners of officers to perform any acts and discharge any functions authorised by this Act to be performed or discharged by the Revenue Commissioners;

(*l*)   the manner in which tax is to be recovered in cases of default of payment;

(*m*)   the refund of tax in excess of the amount required by law to be borne, or paid to the Revenue Commissioners;

(*n*)   disclosure to the Revenue Commissioners of such information as they may require for the ascertainment of liability to tax;

(*o*)   the remission at the discretion of the Revenue Commissioners of small amounts of tax and interest;

[(*p*)   matters consequential on the death of a registered person or his becoming subject to any incapacity including the treatment of a person of such class or classes as may be specified in the regulations as a person carrying on the business of the deceased or incapacitated person;][13]

(*q*)   service of notices;

(*r*)   the acceptance of estimates (whether or not subject to subsequent review) of the amount of tax payable or of any amounts relating to such tax;

(*s*)   the adjustment of the liability of [a taxable person][3] who [supplies goods or services][14] and of the liability of [a taxable person][3] to whom [goods or services are supplied][15] where goods are returned, the consideration is reduced, a bad debt is incurred or a discount is allowed;

(*t*)   the valuation of interests in or over immovable goods;

(*u*)   the estimation of tax due for a taxable or other period;

[(*uu*)   the adjustments to be made by [a taxable person][3] of any apportionment referred to in paragraph (*x*) or deduction under section 12 previously made, being adjustments by reference to changes, occurring not later than five years from the end of the taxable period to which the original apportionment or deduction relates, in any of the matters by reference to which the apportionment or deduction was made or allowed, and the determination of the taxable period in and from which or in which any such adjustment is to take effect;][16]

(v) the relief for stock-in-trade held on the specified day;

[(w) the determination of average build for the purposes of paragraph (xvii) of the Second Schedule;][17]

[(ww) the determination of average foot size for the purposes of paragraph (xix) of the Second Schedule;][18]

(x) the apportionment between the tax which may be deducted under section 12 and tax which may not be deducted under that section, the review, by reference to the circumstances obtaining in any period not exceeding one year, of any such apportionment previously made, the charge or repayment of tax consequent on any such review and the furnishing of particulars by [a taxable person][3] to the Revenue Commissioners for the purpose of any such review;

[(xx) the relief (if any) to be given to [a taxable person][3] in respect of tax borne or paid by him on stock-in-trade held by him immediately before the commencement of the first taxable period for which he is deemed to become [a taxable person][3];

(xxx) the manner in which a determination may be made for the purposes of section 11(1B);][19]

(y) the particulars to be furnished and the manner in which notification is to be given to the Revenue Commissioners by a person who intends to promote a dance, and the manner in which the Revenue Commissioners shall notify the proprietor of any premises in regard to dances proposed to be promoted in such premises.

(2) Regulations under this section may make different provisions in relation to different cases and may in particular provide for differentiation between different classes of persons affected by this Act and for the adoption of different procedures for any such different classes.

[(2A) Regulations under this section for the purposes of section 5(7), [subsection 1(a)(vi) of section 12][20] subsection (1) or (2) of section 13 [subsection (6) or (7) of section 15 or paragraph (ia) of the Sixth Schedule][21] [or in relation to the [matters specified in subsection (1)(w) or (1)(ww)][22]][23] shall not be made without the consent of the Minister for Finance.][24]

(3) Every regulation made under this section shall be laid before Dáil Éireann as soon as may be after it is made and, if a resolution annulling the regulation is passed by Dáil Éireann within the next twenty-one days on which Dáil Éireann has sat after the regulation is laid before it, the regulation shall be annulled accordingly, but without prejudice to the validity of anything previously done thereunder.

Amendments
1   Subs (1)(aa)-(ai) inserted by FA 1992 s 192(a) with effect from 1 January 1993.
2   Subs (1) substituted by VATAA 1978 s 21 with effect from 1 March 1979.
3   Substituted by VATAA 1978 s 30(2) with effect from 1 March 1979; previously "an accountable person".
4   Substituted by VATAA 1978 s 30(2) with effect from 1 March 1979; previously "not accountable".
5   Subs (1)(da)-(de) inserted by FA 1995 s 138 with effect from 2 June 1995.
6   Subs (1)(e) substituted by VATAA 1978 s 21 with effect from 1 March 1979.
7   Subs (1)(f) repealed by FA 1976 s 81 with effect from 1 March 1976.
8   Subs (1)(g) substituted by VATAA 1978 s 21 with effect from 1 March 1979.
9   Words substituted by VATAA 1978 s 30(2) with effect from 1 March 1979; previously "accountable persons".
10   Inserted by FA 1986 s 88 with effect from 27 May 1986.
11   Inserted by FA 1992 s 192(b) with effect from 1 November 1992.
12   Subs (1)(i) substituted by FA 1986 s 88 with effect from 27 May 1986.
13   Subs (1)(p) substituted by VATAA 1978 s 21 with effect from 1 March 1979.
14   Substituted by VATAA 1978 s 30(2) with effect from 1 March 1979; previously "delivers goods or renders services".
15   Substituted by VATAA 1978 s 30(2) with effect from 1 March 1979; previously "goods are delivered or services are rendered".
16   Subs (1)(uu) inserted by FA 1976 s 58 with effect from 27 May 1976.

17   Subs (1)(*w*) inserted by FA 1984 s 91 with effect from 1 May 1984.
18   Subs (1)(*ww*) inserted by FA 1985 s 48 with effect from 1 March 1985.
19   Subs (1)(*xx*)-(*xxx*) inserted by FA 1973 s 85 with effect from 3 September 1973.
20   Inserted by FA 1987 s 44 with effect from 9 July 1987.
21   Substituted by FA 1989 s 60 with effect from 24 May 1989; previously "or subsection (6) or (7) of section 15".
22   Substituted by FA 1985 s 48 with effect from 1 March 1985; previously "matter specified in subsection (1)(*w*)".
23   Inserted by FA 1984 s 91 with effect from 1 May 1984.
24   Subs (2A) inserted by VATAA 1978 s 21 with effect from 1 March 1976.

Cross-references
Subs (1)(*a*): Waiver of exemption: VATR 1979 r 4.
Subs (1)(*aa*): Intra-Community acquisitions, deduction of tax:
Subs (1)(*ab*): residual tax, calculations:
Subs (1)(*ac*): residual tax, calculation:
Subs (1)(*ad*): repayment of tax on imports:
Subs (1)(*af*): Form of statement of Intra-Community supplies:
Subs (1)(*ag*): supply of goods by tax free shops:
Subs (1)(*ah*): Imported goods consigned to another EC State:
Subs (1)(*ai*): Goods supplied where transport ends:
Subs (1)(*b*): Self-supplied services: VATR 1979 r 24.
Subs (1)(*c*): Registration particulars: Value Added Tax (Registration) Regulations 1993 (SI 30/1993).
Subs (1)(*d*): Election to be taxable: VATR 1979 r 3.
Subs (1)(*e*): Apportionment of amounts: VATR 1979 r 34.
Subs (1)(*g*): Cash basis: Value Added Tax (Determination of Tax Due by Reference to Moneys Received) Regulations 1992 (SI 306/1992).
Subs (1)(*h*): Books, records to be kept: VATR 1979 r 9.
Subs (1)(*i*): Invoice etc, particulars: Value Added Tax (Invoices and Other Documents) Regulations 1992 (SI 275/1992), Value Added Tax (Monthly Control Statement) Regulations 1992 (SI 230/1992), Value Added Tax (Time Limits for Issuing Certain Documents) Regulations 1992 (SI 276/1992), Value Added Tax (Electronic Data Exchange and Storage Regulations, 1992 (SI 269/1992).
Subs (1)(*j*): Return, particulars: VATR 1979 r 12; Value Added Tax (Statement of Intra-Community Supplies) Regulations 1993 (SI 54/1993).
Subs (1)(*k*): Nomination of officers: VATR 1979 r 38.
Subs (1)(*l*): Recovery of tax arrears: VATR 1979 r 15.
Subs (1)(*m*): Repayment of tax: VATR 1979 r 17.
Subs (1)(*n*): Disclosure of information to Revenue: VATR 1979 r 35.
Subs (1)(*o*): Remission of small amounts of tax: VATR 1979 r 18.
Subs (1)(*p*): Personal representatives: VATR 1979 r 36.
Subs (1)(*q*): Service of notices: VATR 1979 r 37.
Subs (1)(*r*): Acceptance of estimates: VATR 1979 r 13.
Subs (1)(*s*): Adjustments for goods returned, bad debts, discounts: VATR 1979 r 8.
Subs (1)(*t*): Valuation of interest in land and buildings: VATR 1979 r 19.
Subs (1)(*u*): Estimates of tax due: Value Added Tax (Estimation and Assessment of Tax Due) Regulations 1992 (SI 277/1992).
Subs (1)(*v*): Stock relief (1 November 1972): VATR 1979 r 21.
Subs (1)(*w*): Clothing, determination of average build:
Subs (1)(*ww*): Footwear, determination of average foot size:
Subs (1)(*x*): Apportionment between taxable and exempt turnover: VATR 1979 r 16.
Subs (1)(*xx*): Stock relief: VATR 1979 r 22.
Subs (1)(*xxx*): Determination of tax rate, manner of: Value Added Tax (Determination in Regards to Tax) Regulations 1992 (SI 278/1992).
Subs (1)(*y*): Dance promotions, particulars: VATR 1979 r 20.

Narrative
Irish Value Added Tax, Chapter 12.

Definition
"antiques": s 1(1); "business": s 1(1); "commencement": IA 1937 Sch; "Dáil Éireann": IA 1937 Sch; "goods": s 1(1); "immovable goods": s 1(1); "monthly control statement": ss 1(1),17; "the Minister": s 1(1); "person": IA 1937 s 11(*c*); "registered person": s 1(1); "regulations": ss 1(1), 32; "the specified day": s 1(1); "tax": s 1(1); "taxable dealer": s 1(1); "taxable period": s 1(1); "taxable person": ss 1(1), 8.

Personal notes

33 Officer responsible in case of body of persons

(1) The secretary or other officer acting as secretary for the time being of any body of persons shall be answerable in addition to the body for doing all such acts as are required to be done by the body under any of the provisions relating to tax.

(2) Every such officer as aforesaid may from time to time retain out of any money coming into his hands, on behalf of the body, so much thereof as is sufficient to pay the tax due by the body and shall be indemnified for all such payments made in pursuance of this section.

(3) Any notice required to be given to a body of persons under any of the provisions relating to tax may be given to the secretary or other officer acting as secretary for the time being of such body.

(4) In this section **"the provisions relating to tax"** means—

    (*a*)   the provisions of this Act and regulations, and

    (*b*)   the provisions relating to tax of any subsequent Act.

Definition
"body of persons": s 1(1); "person": IA 1937 s 11(*c*); "secretary": s 1(1); "tax": s 1(1).

Personal notes

131

34 Relief for stock-in-trade held on the specified day

(1) In computing the amount of tax payable by [a taxable person][1], the following amounts may, subject to subsections (3) and (4), in addition to the deductions authorised by section 12, be deducted on account of stock-in-trade which has been [supplied][2] to, and has not been [supplied][2] by, him before the specified day and which is held by him at the commencement of that day, or incorporated in other stock-in-trade held by him at such commencement, that is to say:

> (*a*)   in case the [taxable person][3] was, immediately before the specified day, not registered for turnover tax under the provision of section 49 of the Finance Act, 1963, nor required under the provisions of that section to furnish the particulars specified for registration, and was not registered for wholesale tax under the provisions of section 4 of the Finance (No. 2) Act, 1966, nor required under the provisions of that section to furnish the particulars specified for registration, an amount equal to the sum of the amounts which he would be liable to pay on account of turnover tax and wholesale tax if,

>> (i)   he had been accountable for each of those taxes,

>> (ii)   he had on the day immediately preceding the specified day sold the whole of his stock-in-trade aforesaid in the course of business to a person who was carrying on the same activities as his own and who had not given him, in accordance with section 50 of the Finance Act, 1963, a statement in writing quoting the turnover tax registration number of the person nor given him, in accordance with section 5 of the Finance (No. 2) Act, 1966, a statement in writing quoting the wholesale tax registration number of the person, and

>> (iii)   he had on the said day immediately preceding the specified day received from the person mentioned in subparagraph (ii) payment for the stock-in-trade so deemed to have been sold of an amount equal to the cost to the [taxable person][3] of such stock or the market value thereof, whichever is the lower, and

> (*b*)   in case, immediately before the specified day the [taxable person][3] was registered for turnover tax under the provisions of section 49 of the Finance Act, 1963, or required under the provisions of that section to furnish the particulars specified for registration, but was not registered for wholesale tax under the provisions of section 4 of the Finance (No.2) Act, 1966, nor required under the provisions of that section to furnish the particulars specified for registration, an amount equal to the amount of wholesale tax which he would be liable to pay if,

>> (i)   he had been [a taxable person][1] for the purposes of wholesale tax

>> (ii)   he had on the day immediately preceding the specified day sold the whole of his stock-in-trade aforesaid in the course of business to a person who was carrying on the same activities as his own and who had in accordance with section 50 of the Finance Act, 1963, given him a statement in writing quoting the registration number of the person but had not given him, in accordance with section 5 of the Finance (No. 2) Act, 1966, a statement in writing quoting the wholesale tax registration number of such person, and

>> (iii)   he had on the said day immediately preceding the specified day received from the person mentioned in subparagraph (ii) payment for the stock-in-trade so deemed to have been sold of an amount equal to the cost to the [taxable person][3] of such stock or the market value thereof, whichever is the lower.

(2) Where [a taxable person]¹—

- (a) is not such a person as is mentioned in paragraph (a) or (b) of subsection (1) but was such a person at any time during the year ended the day immediately preceding the specified day or

- (b) is such a person as is mentioned in paragraph (a) or (b) of subsection (1) and was such a person during a part of the year ended the day immediately preceding the specified day but was not such a person during another part of that year,

the Revenue Commissioners may allow such deduction or make such restriction in the deduction which would otherwise be allowable as in their opinion is just and reasonable having regard to the nature of the business carried on, the period during the year ended on the day immediately preceding the specified day during which the business was carried on and the period during the said year during which the person was such a person as is mentioned in the said paragraph (a) or (b) of subsection (1).

(3) A claim for a deduction under this section shall be made in accordance with regulations and the amount authorised to be deducted may be deducted by equal instalments in computing the amount of tax payable in respect of each of the taxable periods beginning on the first day of the first and second taxable periods next following that in which the specified day occurs.

(4) No deduction shall be granted under this section for any amount which is referable to turnover tax or wholesale tax on immovable goods on the [supply]⁵ of which tax is, by virtue of section 4(6), not chargeable or to wholesale tax on newspapers or periodicals, [or second-hand goods]⁴.

(5) In this section—

"stock-in-trade" means, in relation to any person, goods which are either—

- [(a) movable goods of a kind that are [supplied]⁸ by the person in the ordinary course of his business being goods which are actually held for [supply]⁵ (otherwise than by virtue of section 3(1)(e)) or which would be so held if they were mature or if their manufacture, preparation or construction were complete, or]⁶

- (b) materials incorporated in immovable goods of a kind that are [supplied]⁸ by the person in the ordinary course of his business and that have not been [supplied]⁸ by him since the goods were developed, but are actually held for [supply]⁵ or would be so held if their development were complete, or

- (c) consumable materials incorporated in immovable goods by the person in the course of a business consisting of the [supply]⁷ of a service of constructing, repairing, painting or decorating immovable goods where that service has not been completed, or

- (d) materials which have not been incorporated in goods and are such as are used by the person in the manufacture or construction of goods of a kind that are delivered by the person in the ordinary course of his business or, where his ordinary business consists of repairing, painting or decorating immovable goods, are used by him as consumable materials in the course of that business;

materials referred to in paragraph (b) of the definition of **"stock-in-trade"** shall, for the purposes of subsection (1), be regarded as having been [supplied]⁸ to the same extent as the immovable goods into which they have been incorporated can be regarded as having been [supplied]⁸;

materials referred to in paragraph (c) of the definition of **"stock-in-trade"** shall be regarded as having been [supplied]⁸ to the extent that the service in relation to which they have been used has been [supplied]⁸;

"cost" means, in relation to stock-in-trade, the total of the money payable by the person for the [supply]⁵ of the stock, including any addition made for turnover tax or wholesale tax, but excluding any discount or allowance deducted or deductible on payment for the stock.

Amendments

1 Substituted by VATAA 1978 s 30(2) with effect from 1 March 1979; previously "an accountable person".
2 Substituted by VATAA 1978 s 30(2) with effect from 1 March 1979; previously "delivered".
3 Substituted by VATAA 1978 s 30(2) with effect from 1 March 1979; previously "accountable person".
4 Substituted by VATAA 1978 s 30(2) with effect from 1 March 1979; previously "second-hand goods or any goods of a kind specified in the Fourth Schedule".
5 Word substituted by VATAA 1978 s 30(2) with effect from 1 March 1979; previously "delivery".
6 Substituted by FA 1976 s 59 with effect from 27 May 1976.
7 Substituted by VATAA 1978 s 30(2) with effect from 1 March 1979; previously "rendering".
8 Substituted by VATAA 1978 s 30(2) with effect from 1 March 1979; previously "rendered".

Cross-references

Revenue may make provision for stock relief: s 32(1)(v), (xx).

Regulations

Form of claim for deduction: VATR 1979 r 21.
Relief for stock in trade held at commencement of taxability: VATR 1979 r 22.

Orders

Specified day: 1 November 1972, Value Added Tax (Specified Day) Order 1972 (SI 180/1972).

Definition

"business": s 1(1); "development": s 1(1); "developed": s 1(1); "goods": s 1(1); "immovable goods": s 1(1); "movable goods": s 1(1); "person": IA 1937 s 11(c); "regulations": ss 1(1), 32; "second-hand": s 1(1); "the specified day": s 1(1); "supply": s 1(1); "tax": s 1(1); "taxable period": s 1(1); "taxable person": ss 1(1), 8; "writing": IA 1937 Sch.

Personal notes

_____

_____

_____

_____

_____

_____

_____

_____

_____

_____

_____

_____

_____

_____

_____

_____

_____

_____

35 Special provisions for adjustment and recovery of consideration

(1)   (*a*)   Notwithstanding the repeal by this Act of the provisions relating to turnover tax and wholesale tax, sums due on account of turnover tax or wholesale tax under a contract entered into before the specified day, together with any additional sums which might be recoverable by virtue of the provisions of section 9 of the Finance (No. 2) Act, 1966, section 7 of the Finance (No. 2) Act, 1968, section 58 of the Finance Act, 1969, section 51 of the Finance Act, 1970, or section 4 of the Finance (No.2) Act, 1970, shall, in the absence of agreement to the contrary, but subject to subsection (2), be recoverable as if the said provisions relating to turnover tax and wholesale tax had not been repealed.

    (*b*)   (i)   Subject to subparagraph (ii), where, under an agreement made before the specified day, [a taxable person][1] [supplies goods or services][2] on or after that day in such circumstances that tax is chargeable, the consideration provided for under the agreement shall, in the absence of any agreement to the contrary, be adjusted by excluding therefrom the amount, if any, included on account of turnover tax or wholesale tax or both of those taxes, as the case may be, and including therein an amount equal to the amount of the tax so chargeable, and the consideration as so adjusted shall be deemed to be the consideration provided for under the agreement.

        (ii)   The consideration provided for under an agreement for the delivery of immovable goods or the rendering of a service consisting of a development made before the specified day shall, in the absence of agreement to the contrary, be deemed, for the purposes of this paragraph, to include an amount of turnover tax and wholesale tax combined equal to the amount of tax chargeable in respect of the transaction.

    (*c*)   ...[3].

[(1A) (*a*)   Where, after the making of an agreement for the [supply of goods or services][4] and before the date on which under subsection (1) or (2), as may be appropriate, of section 19 any tax in respect of the transaction [falls due][5], there is a change in the amount of tax chargeable on the [supply][6] in question, then, in the absence of agreement to the contrary, there shall be added to or deducted from the total amount of the consideration and any tax stated separately under the agreement an amount equal to the amount of the change in the tax chargeable.

    (*b*)   References in this subsection to a change in the amount of tax chargeable on the [supply of goods or services][4] include references to a change to or from a situation in which no tax is being charged on the [supply][6].][7]

(2) Where, in relation to a [supply of goods or services][8] by [a taxable person][1], the person issues an invoice in which the tax chargeable in respect of the transaction is stated separately, the tax so stated shall, for the purpose of its recovery, be deemed to be part of the consideration for the transaction and shall be recoverable accordingly by the person:

Provided that, if the invoice is issued pursuant to section 17(1), this subsection shall not apply unless it is in the form and contains the particulars specified by regulations.

[(3)   (*a*)   Where, under an agreement made before the commencement of section 12A, a flat-rate farmer supplies agricultural produce or an agricultural service after such commencement to any person, the consideration provided for under the agreement shall, in the absence of agreement to the contrary, be increased by an amount equal to the flat-rate addition appropriate to the said consideration.

(*b*)   Where, in relation to a supply of agricultural produce or an agricultural service by a flat-rate farmer, the flat-rate farmer issues an invoice in which the flat-rate addition is stated separately, the flat-rate addition so stated shall, for the purpose of its recovery, be deemed to be part of the consideration for the transaction and shall be recoverable accordingly by the flat-rate farmer.][9]

Amendments

1   Substituted by VATAA 1976 s 30(2) with effect from 1 March 1979; previously "an accountable person".
2   Substituted by VATAA 1978 s 30(2) with effect from 1 March 1979; previously "delivers goods or renders services".
3   Subs (1)(*c*) repealed by FA 1976 s 81 with effect from 1 March 1976.
4   Substituted by VATAA 1978 s 30(2) with effect from 1 March 1979; previously "delivery of goods or the rendering of services".
5   Substituted by VATAA 1978 s 30(2) with effect from 1 March 1979; previously "would, if the proviso to the said subsection (1) were disregarded, fall due".
6   Substituted by VATAA 1978 s 30(2) with effect from 1 March 1979; previously "delivery or rendering".
7   Subs (1A) inserted by FA 1973 s 86 with effect from 3 September 1973.
8   Substituted by VATAA 1978 s 30(2) with effect from 1 March 1979; previously "delivery of goods or a rendering of services".
9   Subs (3) inserted by VATAA 1978 s 22 with effect from 1 March 1979.

Cross-references

Specified day: 1 November 1972, Value Added Tax (Specified Day) Order 1972 (SI 180/1972).

Definition

"agricultural produce": s 1(1); "agricultural service": 1(1); "commencement": IA 1937 Sch; "development": s 1(1); "farmer": s 1(1); "flat-rate addition": s 1(1); "flat-rate farmer": ss 1(1), 12A; "goods": s 1(1); "immovable goods": s 1(1); "person": IA 1937 s 11(*c*); "regulations": ss 1(1), 32; "the specified day": s 1(1); "supply": s 1(1); "tax": s 1(1); "taxable person": ss 1(1), 8.

Personal notes

36 Special provision for deliveries made prior to the specified day

Amendments

Section 36 repealed by VATAA 1978 s 30(1) with effect from 1 March 1979.

Personal notes

a 21(1)(a) **37 Substitution of agent, etc., for person not resident in State**

[Where a taxable person not established in the State supplies goods or services, the Revenue Commissioners may, where it appears requisite to them to do so for the protection of the revenue, deem a person who—

    (*a*)   acts or has acted on behalf of the taxable person in relation to such supplies, or

    (*b*)   allows or has allowed such supplies to be made on land owned, occupied or controlled by him,

to have made such supplies in the course or furtherance of business from the date of service on him of a notice in writing to that effect.][1]

Amendments
1   Section 37 substituted by FA 1992 s 193 with effect from 28 May 1992.
Cross-references
Right of appeal: s 25(1)(*ab*).
Sixth Directive
Persons liable to pay tax to the authorities: a 21.
Narrative
Irish Value Added Tax, Chapter 12.
Definitions
"business": s 1(1); "land": IA 1937 Sch; "person": IA 1937 s 11(*c*); "tax": s 1(1); "taxable person": s 1(1), 8; "writing": IA 1937 Sch.

Personal notes

38 Extensions of certain Acts

(1) Section 1 of the Provisional Collection of Taxes Act, 1927, is hereby amended by the insertion of "and value added tax" before "but no other tax or duty".

(2) Section 1 of the Imposition of Duties Act, 1957, is hereby amended by the insertion in paragraph (*gg*) (inserted by the Finance Act, 1963) after "turnover tax" of "or value added tax", but no order shall be made under that Act for the purposes of increasing any of the rates of tax or extending the classes of activities or goods in respect of which tax is for the time being chargeable.

(3) Section 39 of the Inland Revenue Regulations Act, 1890, is hereby amended by the insertion of "value added tax," before "stamp duties".

(4) The First Schedule to the Stamp Act, 1891, shall have effect as if the following exemption were inserted therein under the heading "Bill of Exchange or Promissory Note":

> "Bill drawn on any form supplied by the Revenue Commissioners for the purpose of remitting amounts of value added tax".

Definitions
"goods": s 1(1); "tax": s 1(1).

39 Consequential adjustments in regard to capital allowances

Amendments
Repealed by FA 1975 s 29(3) with effect from 6 April 1975.

40 Increase of excise duty on betting

Note
This section is not relevant for Value Added Tax.

41 Repeals

Note
This section refers to repeals in Sch 5, this is not the existing Sch 5 but an earlier one. The section has no significance in relation to the existing Sch 5.

42 Collection of tax

Tax shall be paid to and collected and levied by the Collector-General.

Definition
"Collector-General": s 1(1); "tax": s 1(1).

43 Care and management of tax

Tax is hereby placed under the care and management of the Revenue Commissioners.

Definitions
"tax": s 1(1).

44 Short title

This Act may be cited as the Value Added Tax Act, 1972.

FIRST SCHEDULE
Exempted activities

a 13B(*d*) [(i) Financial services consisting of—

    (*a*)   the issue, transfer or receipt of, or any dealing in, stocks, shares, debentures and other securities, other than documents establishing title to goods,

    (*b*)   the arranging for, or the underwriting of, an issue specified in subparagraph (*a*),

    (*c*)   the operation of any current, deposit or savings account [and the negotiation of, or any dealings in, payments, transfers, debts, cheques and other negotiable instruments excluding debt collection and factoring][1],

    (*d*)   the issue, transfer or receipt of, or any dealing in, currency, bank notes and metal coins, in use as legal tender in any country, excluding such bank notes and coins when supplied as investment goods or as collectors' pieces,

a 13B(*d*)(1) [(*e*)   the granting and the negotiation of credit and the management of credit by the person granting it,][2]

    (*f*)   the granting of, or any dealing in, credit guarantees or any other security for money and the management of credit guarantees by the person who granted the credit,

    [(*g*)   the management of an undertaking which is—

        (I)   a collective investment undertaking within the meaning of section 18 of the Finance Act, 1989, or

        (II)   administered by the holder of an authorisation granted pursuant to the European Communities (Life Assurance) Regulations, 1984 (S.I. No. 57 of 1984), or by a person who is deemed, pursuant to Article 6 of those regulations, to be such a holder, the criteria in relation to which are the criteria specified in relation to an arrangement administered by the holder of a licence under the Insurance Act, 1936, in section 9(2) of the Unit Trusts Act, 1990, or

        (III)   a unit trust scheme established solely for the purpose of superannuation fund schemes or charities, or

        (IV)   determined by the Minister for Finance to be a collective investment undertaking to which the provisions of this subparagraph apply;][3]

    (*gg*)   ...[4];

    (*h*)   services supplied to a person under arrangements which provide for the reimbursement of the person in respect of the supply by him of goods or services in accordance with a credit card, charge card or similar card scheme;][5]

a 13A(1)(*i*),(*j*) (ii)   school or university education, and vocational training or retraining (including the supply of goods and services incidental thereto), provided by educational establishments recognised by the State, and education, training or retraining of a similar kind [, excluding instruction in the driving of mechanically propelled road vehicles other than vehicles designed or constructed for the conveyance of goods with a capacity of 1.5 tonnes or more,][6] provided by other persons;

13A(1)(*b*) [(iii)   professional services of a medical nature, other than services speci-
(*c*)(*e*) fied in paragraph (iii*b*), but excluding such services supplied in the

course of carrying on a business which consists in whole or in part of selling goods;][7]

[(iiia) supply by dental technicians of services of a dental nature and of dentures or other dental prostheses;][8]   13A(1)(*e*)

[(iiib) professional services of a dental or optical nature;][9]   13A(1)(*b*)
(*c*)(*e*)

(iv) letting of immovable goods with the exception of—   a 13B(*b*)

   (*a*) letting of machinery or business installations when let separately from any other immovable goods of which such machinery or installations form part;

   [(*b*) letting of the kind to which [paragraph (ii) of the Third Schedule or paragraph (xiii) of the Sixth Schedule][10] refers;][11]

   [(*bi*) provision of facilities of the kind to which paragraph (viia) of the Sixth Schedule refers;][12]

   (*c*) provision of parking accommodation for vehicles by the operators of car parks; and

   (*d*) hire of safes;

(v) hospital and medical care or treatment provided by a hospital, nursing home, clinic or similar establishment;   a 13A(1)(*b*), (*c*), (*d*), (*e*)

(vi) services for the protection or care of children and young persons, and the provision of goods closely related thereto, provided otherwise than for profit;   a 13A(1)(*h*)

(vii) supply of goods and services closely related to welfare and social security by non-profit making organisations;   a 13(1)(*g*)

[(viii) promotion of and admissions to live theatrical or musical performances, including circuses, but not including—   a 13A(1)(*n*)

   (*a*) dances ...[13], or

   (*b*) performances in conjunction with which facilities are available for the consumption of food or drink during all or part of the performance by persons attending the performance;][14]

[(viiia) supply of cultural services and of goods closely linked thereto by any cultural body, whether established by or under statute or otherwise, which is recognised as such a body by the Revenue Commissioners for the purposes of this paragraph, not being services to which paragraph (viii) relates;][15]   a 13A(1)(*n*)

(ix) agency services in regard to—

   (*a*) the arrangement of passenger transport or accommodation for persons, ...[16]   Annex F 27

   [(*b*) the collection of insurance premiums,][17]   a 13B(*a*)

   [(*c*) insurance services, and   a 13B(*a*)

   (*d*) services specified in paragraph (i),][18]

[excluding [the services of loss adjusters and excluding][19] management and safekeeping services in regard to the services specified in paragraph (i)(*a*), not being services specified in [subparagraph [(g)][20] of paragraph (i)][21];][22]

(x) ...[23]

(xi) ...[24] insurance services;   a 13B(*a*)

[(xia) public postal services (including the supply of goods and services incidental thereto) supplied by An Post including postmasters, or by persons licensed in accordance with section 73 or subsection (1) of   a 13A(1)(*a*) section 111 of the Postal and Telecommunications Services Act, 1983;][25]

(xii) ...[26]

a 13A(1)(*q*)   (xiii) the national broadcasting and television services, excluding advertising;

Annex F 17   (xiv) transport of passengers and their accompanying baggage;

a 13B(*f*)   [(xv) the acceptance of bets subject to the duty of excise imposed by section 24 of the Finance Act, 1926, [of bets of the kind referred to in section 89 of the Finance Act, 1994,][27] and of bets where the event which is the subject of the bet is either a horse race or a greyhound race and the bet is entered into during the meeting at which such race takes place and at the place at which such meeting is held;][28]

a 13B(*f*)   (xvi) issue of tickets or coupons for the purpose of a lottery;

Annex F 1   [(xvii) promotion of (other than in the course of the provision of facilities of the kind specified in paragraph (viia) of the Sixth Schedule), or the admission of spectators to, sporting events;][29]

a 13A(1)(*d*)   (xviii) collection, storage [, supply, intra-Community acquisition or importation][30] of human organs, human blood and human milk;

Annex F 6   (xix) funeral undertaking;

(xx) ...[31]

(xxi) ...[31]

a 13A(1)(*g*)   (xxii) supply of services and of goods closely related thereto for the benefit of their members by non-profit making organisations whose aims are primarily of a political, trade union, religious, patriotic, philosophical, philanthropic or civic nature where such supply is made without payment other than the payment of any membership subscription;

a 13A(1)(*f*)   [(xxii*a*) supply of services by an independent group of persons (being a group which is an independent entity established for the purpose of administrative convenience by persons whose activities are exempt from or are not subject to tax) for the purpose of rendering its members the services directly necessary for the exercise of their activities and where the group only recovers from its members the exact reimbursement of each member's share of the joint expenses;][32]

a 13A(1)(*m*)   (xxiii) provision of facilities for taking part in sporting and physical education activities, and services closely related thereto, provided ...[33] by non-profit making organisations [with the exception of facilities to which paragraph (viib) or (viic) of the Sixth Schedule refers][34];

a 13B(*c*)   (xxiv) supply of goods [other than a supply of goods of a kind specified in section 3(1)(*g*),][35] by a person being goods—

(*a*) which were used by him for the purposes of a business carried on by him,

(*b*) in relation to the acquisition or application of which he had borne tax, and

(*c*) which are of such a kind or were used in such circumstances that no part of the said tax was deductible under section 12;

a 13A(1)(*b*)   (xxv) catering services supplied—

(*a*) to patients of a hospital or nursing home in the hospital or nursing home, and

(*b*) to students of a school in the school.][36]

Amendments

1   Inserted by FA 1991 s 85 with effect from 29 May 1991.
2   Para (i)(*e*) substituted by FA 1995 s 139(*a*) with effect from 2 June 1995.
3   Para (i)(*g*) substituted by FA 1991 s 85 with effect from 29 May 1991.
4   Para (i)(*gg*) deleted by FA 1991 s 85 with effect from 29 May 1991.
5   Para (i) substituted by FA 1987 s 45 with effect from 1 November 1987
6   Inserted by FA 1990 s 106 with effect from 30 May 1990.
7   Para (iii) substituted by FA 1989 s 61 with effect from 1 November 1989.
8   Para (iii*a*) inserted by FA 1986 s 89 with effect from 1 July 1986
9   Para (iii*b*) inserted by FA 1989 s 61 with effect from 1 November 1989.
10 Substituted by FA 1993 s 94 with effect from 1 March 1993; previously "paragraph (vi) of the Third Schedule".
11 Para (iv)(*b*) inserted by FA 1991 s 85 with effect from 29 May 1991.
12 Para (iv)(*bi*) inserted by FA 1992 s 194(1)(*a*) with effect from 1 July 1992.
13 Words "to which section 11(7) relates" deleted by FA 1992 s 194(1)(*b*) with effect from 28 May 1992.
14 Para (viii) inserted by FA 1985 s 49 with effect from 1 March 1985.
15 Para (viii*a*) inserted by FA 1990 s 106 with effect from 30 May 1990.
16 Word "and" deleted by FA 1987 s 45 with effect from 1 November 1987.
17 Para (i)(*b*) substituted by FA 1982 s 87 with effect from 1 September 1982.
18 Para (ix)(*c*), (*d*) substituted by FA 1987 s 45 with effect from 1 November 1987.
19 Inserted by FA 1994 s 99(*a*) with effect from 1 September 1994.
20 Substituted by FA 1991 s 85 with effect from 29 May 1991; previously "(*g*) or (*gg*)".
21 Substituted by FA 1989 s 61 with effect from 1 July 1989; previously "paragraph (i)(*g*)".
22 Words inserted by FA 1987 s 45 with effect from 1 November 1987.
23 Para (x) deleted by FA 1991 s 85 with effect from 1 January 1992.
24 Words "banking and" deleted by FA 1987 s 45 with effect from 1 November 1987.
25 Para (xi*a*) inserted by FA 1991 s 85 with effect from 1 January 1992.
26 Para (xii) deleted by FA 1987 s 45 with effect from 1 November 1987.
27 Inserted by FA 1994 s 99(*b*) with effect from the commencement of s 89.
28 Para (xv) substituted by FA 1980 s 82 with effect from 1 July 1980.
29 Para (xvii) substituted by FA 1992 s 194(1)(*c*) with effect from 1 July 1992.
30 Substituted by FA 1992 s 194(2)(*a*) with effect from 1 July 1992; previously "supply and importation".
31 Paras (xx) and (xxi) deleted by FA 1990 s 106 with effect from 1 January 1991.
32 Para (xxii*a*) inserted by FA 1990 s 106 with effect from 30 May 1990.
33 Words "for its members" deleted by FA 1992 s 194(1)(*e*) with effect from 1 July 1992.
34 Inserted by FA 1992 s 194(2)(*b*) with effect from 1 January 1993.
35 Inserted by FA 1995 s 139(*b*) with effect from 1 January 1996.
36 Sch 1 substituted by VATAA 1978 s 24 with effect from 1 March 1979.

Cross-references

Apportionment of tax, Revenue may specify method: s 32(1)(*x*); method: VATA 1979 r 16.
Para (i)(*e*) taxable amount: s 10(4C); invoice requirements: s 17(1)(proviso).
Para (i)(*gg*): special investment schemes: FA 1993 s 13(6)(*a*)(i) (see *Tax Acts*).
Para (xxiii): Minister may provide that State and local authority may be taxable persons: s 8(2A)(*a*)(proviso); Revenue may make determination regarding such services: s 8(3E)(*a*).
Para (xxiv): margin scheme goods: s 10A(13); auctioneers, special scheme: s 10B(10); taxable dealers supplying means of transport: s 12B(10).

Case law

Para (i)(*h*): Charge card company denied judicial review of its exempt status: *The Diners Club Ltd. v Revenue Commissioners*, III ITR 680.

Statement of practice

Shares, VAT not deductible: SP VAT 2/90.
Sports facilities: persons liable, "sport facilities" defined etc: SP VAT 2/90 SP VAT 4/92.

Narrative

Irish Value Added Tax, Chapter 8; *Guide to Value Added Tax (Revenue Commissioners)*: Chapter 15.

Definition

"business": s 1(1); "goods": s 1(1); "hire": s 1(1); "immovable goods": s 1(1); "the Minister": s 1(1); "establishment": s 1(1); "person": IA 1937 s 11(*c*); "regulations": ss 1(1), 32; "statute": IA 1937 s 3; "supply": s 1(1); "tax": s 1(1).

SECOND SCHEDULE

Goods and services chargeable at the rate of zero per cent

a 15, 16, 28

[(i)   The supply of goods—

       (*a*)   subject to a condition that they are to be transported directly by or on behalf of the person making the supply—

            (I)   outside the Community, or

            (II)   to a registered person within the customs-free airport,

a 28cA(*a*)   (*b*)   dispatched or transported from the State to a person registered for value added tax in another Member State,

a 28cA(*b*)   (*c*)   being new means of transport dispatched or transported directly by or on behalf of the supplier to a person in the territory of another Member State,

a 28cA(*c*)   [(*cc*)   being excisable products dispatched or transported from the State to a person in another Member State when the movement of the goods is subject to the provisions of Chapter II of Part II of the Finance Act, 1992, and any other enactment which is to be construed together with that Chapter, which implement the arrangements specified in paragraph 4 and 5 of Article 7, or Article 16, of Council Directive No. 92/12/EEC of 25 February 1992,][1]

       (*d*)   by a registered person within a free port to another registered person within a free port,

       (*e*)   by a registered person within the customs-free airport to another registered person within the customs-free airport or a free port;

[(*ia*)   subject to such conditions and in such amounts as may be specified in regulations, the supply of goods–

       (*a*)   to travellers departing the State, in a tax-free shop approved by the Revenue Commissioners, or

       (*b*)   to travellers on board vessels or aircraft, where the goods are deemed to be supplied in the State in accordance with section 3 (6)(*cc*);][2]][3]

(ii)   ...[4];

(iii)   the carriage of goods in the State by or on behalf of a person in execution of a contract to transfer the goods to ...[5] a place [outside the Community][6];

[(iii*a*)   intra-Community transport services involving the carriage of goods to and from the Azores or Madeira;

(iii*b*)   subject to and in accordance with regulations, the importation of goods which, at the time of the said importation, are consigned to another Member State;][7]

(iv)   the provision of docking, landing, loading or unloading facilities, including customs clearance, directly in connection with the disembarkation or embarkation of passengers or the importation or exportation of goods;

a 15   [(v)   the supply, modification, repair, maintenance and hiring of—

       (*a*)   sea-going vessels of a gross tonnage of more than 15 tons being vessels used or to be used—

a 15   (I)   for the carriage of passengers for reward,

            (II)   for the purposes of a sea fishing business,

(III)   for other commercial or industrial purposes, or

(IV)   for rescue or assistance at sea, or

(*b*)   aircraft used or to be used by a transport undertaking operating for reward chiefly on international routes;][8]

[(v*a*)   the supply repair, maintenance and hiring of equipment incorporated or used in aircraft to which subparagraph (*b*) of paragraph (v) relates;][9]

[(v*b*)   the supply of goods for the fuelling and provisioning of sea-going vessels and aircraft of the kind specified in paragraph (v);][10]

[(vi)   services, supplied by an agent acting in the name and on behalf of another person, in procuring—

(*a*)   the export of goods ...[11];

(*b*)   services specified in paragraphs (iii), [(iii*a*)][12] (iv), (v) or (x), or

(*c*)   the supply of goods or services outside the [Community][13];][14]

[(vi*a*)   subject to and in accordance with section 13A, the supply of qualifying goods and qualifying services to, or the intra-Community acquisition or importation of qualifying goods by, an authorised person in accordance with that section, excluding supplies of goods within the meaning of paragraph (*e*) or (*f*) of subsection (1) of section 3;][15]

(vii)   animal feeding stuff, excluding feeding stuff which is packaged, sold or otherwise designated for the use of dogs, cats, cage birds or domestic pets;

(viii)   fertiliser (within the meaning of the Fertilisers, Feeding Stuffs and Mineral Mixtures Act, 1955) which is [supplied][16] in units of not less than 10 kilograms and the sale or manufacture for sale of which is not prohibited under section 4 or 6 of the said Act;

(ix)   services provided by the Commissioners of Irish Lights in connection with the operation of lightships, lighthouses or other navigational aids;

[(x)   gold supplied to the Central Bank of Ireland;][17]

(xi)   life saving services provided by the Royal National Lifeboat Institution including the organisation and maintenance of the lifeboat service;

[(xii)   food and drink of a kind used for human consumption, other than the supply thereof specified in [paragraph (iv) of the Sixth Schedule][18], excluding—

(*a*)   beverages chargeable with any duty of excise specifically charged on spirits, beer, wine, cider, perry or Irish wine, and preparations thereof,

[(*b*)   other beverages, including water and syrups, concentrates, essences, powders, crystals or other products for the preparation of beverages, but not including—

(I)   tea and preparations thereof,

(II)   cocoa, coffee and chicory and other roasted coffee substitutes, and preparations and extracts thereof,

(III)   milk and preparations and extracts thereof, or

(IV)   preparations and extracts of meat, yeast, or egg;][19]

[(*c*)   ice cream, ice lollipops, water ices, frozen desserts, frozen yoghurts and similar frozen products, and prepared mixes and powders for making any such product or such similar product;]²⁰

(d)   (I)   chocolates, sweets and similar confectionery (including ...²¹, glacé or crystallized fruits), biscuits, crackers and wafers of all kinds, and all other confectionery and bakery products [, whether cooked or uncooked,]²² excluding bread,

(II)   in this subparagraph **"bread"** means food for human consumption manufactured by baking dough composed exclusively of a mixture of cereal flour and any one or more of the ingredients mentioned in the following subclauses in quantities not exceeding the limitation, if any, specified for each ingredient—

(1)   yeast or other leavening or aerating agent, salt, malt extract, milk, water, gluten,

(2)   fat, sugar and bread improver, subject to the limitation that the weight of any ingredient specified in this subclause shall not exceed **2 per cent** of the weight of flour included in the dough,

(3)   dried fruit, subject to the limitation that the weight thereof shall not exceed **10 per cent** of the weight of flour included in the dough,

other than food packaged for sale as a unit (not being a unit designated as containing only food specifically for babies) containing two or more slices, segments, sections or other similar pieces, having a crust over substantially the whole of their outside surfaces, being a crust formed in the course of baking [, or frying]²³ or toasting, and

[(e)   any of the following when supplied for human consumption without further preparation, namely—

(I)   potato crisps, potato sticks, potato puffs and similar products made from potato, or from potato flour or from potato starch,

(II)   savoury products made from cereal or grain, or from flour or starch derived from cereal or grain, pork scratchings, and similar products,

(III)   popcorn, and

(IV)   salted or roasted nuts whether or not in shells;]²⁴]²⁵

(xiii)   medicine of a kind used for human oral consumption;

(xiv)   medicine of a kind used for animal oral consumption, excluding medicine which is packaged, sold or otherwise designated for the use of dogs, cats, cage birds or domestic pets;

(xv)   seeds, plants, trees, spores, bulbs, tubers, tuberous roots, corms, crowns and rhizomes, of a kind used for sowing in order to produce food;

[(xva)   printed books and booklets including atlases but not including newspapers, periodicals, brochures, catalogues, programmes, books of stationery, cheque books, diaries, albums, books of stamps, of tickets or of coupons;]²⁶

[(xvi)   the supply of services consisting of work on mov-able goods acquired or imported for the purpose of undergoing such work within the Community and dispatched or transported out of the Community by or on behalf of the person providing the services]²⁷ [(xvi*a*) the supply of transport services relating to the importation of goods where the value of such services is included in the taxable amount in accordance with section 15(3);][28]

[(xvii) articles of children's personal clothing of sizes which do not exceed the sizes of those articles appropriate to children of average build of 10 years of age (a child whose age is 10 years or 10 years and a fraction of a year being taken for the purposes of this paragraph to be a child of 10 years of age), but excluding—

    (*a*) articles of clothing made wholly or partly of fur skin other than garments merely trimmed with fur skin, unless the trimming has an area greater than one-fifth of the area of the outside material, and

    (*b*) articles of clothing which are not described, labelled, marked or marketed on the basis of age or size;][29]

[(xviii) sanitary towels and sanitary tampons;][30]

[(xix) articles of children's personal footwear of sizes which do not exceed the size appropriate to children of average foot size of 10 years of age (a child whose age is 10 years or 10 years and a fraction of a year being taken for the purposes of this paragraph to be child of 10 years of age), but excluding footwear which is not described, labelled, marked or marketed on the basis of age or size;][31]

[(xix*a*) medical equipment and appliances being—

    (*a*) invalid carriages, and other vehicles (excluding mechanically propelled road vehicles), of a kind designed for use by invalids or infirm persons,

    (*b*) orthopaedic appliances, surgical belts, trusses and the like, deaf aids, and artificial limbs and other artificial parts of the body excluding artificial teeth [, corrective spectacles and contact lenses][32],

    (*c*) walking frames and crutches,

    (*d*) parts or accessories suitable for use solely or principally with any of the goods specified in subparagraphs (*a*), (*b*) and (*c*) of this paragraph;][33]

[(xx) (*a*) ...[34],

    (*b*) wax candles and night-lights which are white and cylindrical, excluding candles and night-lights which are decorated, spiralled, tapered or perfumed.][35]][36]

Amendments

1 Para (i)(*cc*) inserted by EC(VAT)R 1992 r 14 with effect from 1 January 1993.
2 Para (i*a*) substituted by FA 1994 s 100 with effect 23 May 1994.
3 Para (i) substituted by FA 1992 s 195(2)(*a*) with effect from 1 January 1993.
4 Para (ii) repealed by VATAA 1978 s 30(1) with effect from 1 March 1979.
5 Words "or from" deleted by FA 1996 s 98(*a*) with effect from 15 May 1996.
6 Substituted by FA 1992 s 195(2)(*b*) with effect from 1 January 1993, previously "outside the State".
7 Paras (iii*a*)-(iii*b*) inserted by FA 1992 s 195(2)(*c*) with effect from 1 January 1993.
8 Para (v) substituted by VATAA 1978 s 25 with effect from 1 March 1979.
9 Para (v*a*) inserted by FA 1992 s 195(1)(*a*) with effect from 28 May 1992.
10 Para (v*b*) inserted by FA 1993 s 95(*a*).
11 Words "from the State" deleted by FA 1992 s 195(2)(*d*)(i) with effect from 1 January 1993.
12 Inserted by FA 1992 s 195(2)(*d*)(ii) with effect from 1 January 1993.
13 Substituted by FA 1992 s 195(2)(*d*)(iii) with effect from 1 January 1993; previously "State" .
14 Para (vi) substituted by VATAA 1978 s 25 with effect from 1 March 1979.
15 Para (vi*a*) inserted by FA 1993 s 95(*b*).
16 Substituted by VATAA 1978 s 30(2) with effect from 1 March 1979; previously "delivered".
17 Para (x) substituted by VATAA 1978 s 25 with effect from 1 March 1979.
18 Substituted by FA 1992 s 195(1)(*b*)(i) with effect from 28 May 1992; previously "paragraph (xi*c*) of the Sixth Schedule".
19 Para (xii)(*b*) substituted by FA 1992 s 195(1)(*b*)(ii) with effect from 1 November 1992.

20   Para (xii)(*c*) substituted by FA 1992 s 195(1)(*b*)(iii) with effect from 1 July 1992.
21   Word "drained" deleted by FA 1987 s 46 with effect from 1 July 1987.
22   Inserted by FA 1992 s 195(1)(*b*)(iv)(I) with effect from 1 July 1992.
23   Inserted by FA 1992 s 195(1)(*b*)(iv)(II) with effect from 1 July 1992.
24   Para (xii)(*e*) substituted by FA 1992 s 195(1)(*b*)(v) with effect from 1 July 1992.
25   Para (xii) substituted by FA 1985 s 50 with effect from 1 March 1985.
26   Para (xv*a*) inserted by FA 1982 s 88 with effect from 1 September 1982.
27   Para (xvi) substituted by FA 1996 s 98(*b*) with effect from 1 January 1996.
28   Para (xvi*a*) inserted by FA 1996 s 98(*c*) with effect from 1 January 1996.
29   Para (xvii) substituted by FA 1984 s 92 with effect from 1 May 1984.
30   Para (xviii) substituted by FA 1984 s 92 with effect from 1 May 1984.
31   Para (xix) substituted by FA 1985 s 50 with effect from 1 March 1985; previously "(xviii*a*) and (xix)".
32   Words ", corrective spectacles and contact lenses" inserted by FA 1989 s 63 with effect from 1 November 1989.
33   Para (xix*a*) inserted by Value Added Tax (Reduction of Rate) (No 5) Order 1981 (SI 53/1981) with effect from 1 March 1981.
34   Para (xx)(*a*) deleted by FA 1988 s 63 with effect from 1 March 1992.
35   Para (xx) substituted by FA 1983 s 86 with effect from 1 May 1983.
36   Sch 2 substituted by FA 1976 s 60(*b*) with effect from 1 March 1976.

Cross-references
Para (i)(*a*)(I): alcohol products: s 3B(2); zero rating of sales to authorised exporters: s 13A(1).
Para (i)(*b*): alcohol products: s 3B(2); zero rating of sales to authorised exporters: s 13A(1); margin scheme goods: s 10A(10); auctioneers, special scheme: s 10B(7).
Para (i)(*cc*): alcohol products: s 3B(2).
Para (i*a*): alcohol products: s 3B(2); tax free shops, Revenue may regulate: s 32(1)(*ag*).
Para (iii*b*): import of goods consigned to another EC State: s 32(1)(*ah*).
Para (v): repair etc of movable goods: Sch 6 para (xviii)(*b*).
Para (v*a*): repair etc of movable goods: Sch 6 para (xviii)(*b*).
Para (vi*a*): zero rating of sales to authorised exporters: s 13A(5)-(8).
Para (xii) (other than (subparas (*c*) or (*e*)(II)): rate on food: Sch 6 para (xxxi).
Para (xvi): repair etc of movable goods: s 11(1AB) and Sch 6 para (xviii)(*b*).
Para (xvii): clothing, average size, Revenue may determine: s 32(1)(*w*).
Para (xix): footwear, average size, Revenue may determine: s 32(1)(*ww*).

Narrative
Irish Value Added Tax, Chapter 8; *Guide to Value Added Tax (Revenue Commissioners)*: Chapter 15.

Definition
"business": s 1(1); "Community": s 1(1); "clothing": s 1(1); "the customs-free airport": s 1(1); "establishment": s 1(1); "excisable products": s 1(1); "exportation of goods": s 1(1); "footwear": s 1(1); "free port": s 1(1); "fur skin": s 1(1); "goods": s 1(1); "movable goods": s 1(1); "new means of transport": s 1(1);"person": IA 1937 s 11(*c*); "a person registered for value added tax": s(1); "registered person": s 1(1); "supply": s 1(1); "vessel": s 1(1).

Statement of practice
Agricultural services: SP VAT 5/92.
Intra-community zero rating: SP VAT 8/92.
Food and drink: SP VAT 10/92.
Services: SP VAT 1/92.

THIRD SCHEDULE
Goods and services chargeable at the rate specified in section 11(1)(*c*)

[(i)   Immovable goods being a domestic dwelling for which a contract with a private individual has been entered into before the 25th day of February, 1993, for such supply;

(ii)   services specified in paragraph (xiii) of the Sixth Schedule, under an agreement made before the 25th day of February, 1993, and at charges fixed at the time of the agreement for such supply;

(iii)   services specified in subparagraph (*a*) of paragraph (xv) of the Sixth Schedule, under an agreement made before the 25th day of February, 1993, and at charges fixed at the time of the agreement for such supply.][1]

Amendments
1   Sch 3 substituted by FA 1993 s 96 with effect from 1 March 1993.
Statement of practice
Agricultural services: VAT 5/92.
Services: SP VAT 1/92.
Definition
"development": s 1(1); "goods": s 1(1); "immovable goods": s 1(1); "movable goods": s 1(1); "establishment": s 1(1); "person": IA 1937 s 11(*c*); "tax": s 1(1); "vessel": s 1(1); "week": IA 1937 Sch.

FOURTH SCHEDULE
Services that, where taxable are taxed where received

[(i)   Transfers and assignments of copyright, patents, licences, trade marks and similar rights;

[(i*a*)   hiring out of movable goods other than means of transport;][1]

(ii)   advertising services;

(iii)   services of consultants, engineers, consultancy bureaux, lawyers, accountants and other similar services, data processing and provision of information (but excluding services connected with immovable goods);

(iv)   acceptance of any obligation to refrain from pursuing or exercising in whole or in part, any business activity or any such rights as are referred to in paragraph (i);

(v)   banking, financial and insurance services (including re-insurance, but not including the provision of safe deposit facilities);

(vi)   the provision of staff;

(vii) the services of agents who act in the name and for the account of a principal when procuring for him any services specified in paragraphs (i) to (vi).][2]

Amendments
1 Para (i*a*) inserted by FA 1985 s 52 with effect from 30 May 1985.
2 Sch 4 substituted by VATAA 1978 s 27 with effect from 1 March 1979.
Cross-references
Para (iii): professional services in connection with land etc are taxed where the land etc is located: s 5(6)(*a*).
Place of supply of Fourth Schedule services: s 5(6)(*e*).
Sixth Directive
Supply of services: art 9(2)(*e*).
Statement of practice
Advertising: SP VAT 3/92.
Services received from abroad: SP VAT 1/90.
Narrative
Irish Value Added Tax, Chapter 9; *Guide to Value Added Tax (Revenue Commissioners)*: Chapter 4.8.
Definition
"business": s 1(1); "goods": s 1(1); "immovable goods": s 1(1); "movable goods": s 1(1).

FIFTH SCHEDULE

PART I

Annex A of Council Directive No 77/388/EEC of 17 May, 1977
List of agricultural production activities

[I. CROP PRODUCTION

1. General agriculture, including viticulture

2. Growing of fruit (including olives) and of vegetables, flowers and ornamental plants, both in the open and under glass

3. Production of mushrooms, spices, seeds and propagating materials; nurseries

II. STOCK FARMING TOGETHER WITH CULTIVATION

1. General stock farming

2. Poultry farming

3. Rabbit farming

4. Beekeeping

5. Silkworm farming

6. Snail farming

III. FORESTRY

IV. FISHERIES

1. Fresh-water fishing

2. Fish farming

3. Breeding of mussels, oysters and other molluscs and crustaceans

4. Frog farming

V. Where a farmer, processes, using means normally employed in an agricultural,
forestry or fisheries undertaking, products deriving essentially from his
agricultural production, such processing shall also be regarded as agricultural
production.

PART II

Annex B of Council Directive No.77/388/EEC of 17 May, 1977
List of agricultural services

Supplies of agricultural services which normally play a part in agricultural
production shall be considered the supply of agricultural services, and include the
following in particular:

—field work, reaping and mowing, threshing, baling, collecting, harvesting,
sowing and planting

—packing and preparation for market, for example drying, cleaning, grinding, disinfecting and ensilage of agricultural products

—storage of agricultural products

—stock minding, rearing and fattening

—hiring out, for agricultural purposes, of equipment normally used in agricultural, forestry or fisheries undertakings

—technical assistance

—destruction of weeds and pests, dusting and spraying of crops and land

—operation of irrigation and drainage equipment

—lopping, tree felling and other forestry services.][1]

Amendments

1   Sch 5 inserted by VATAA 1978 s 28 with effect from 1 March 1979.

Cross-references

A "farmer" is defined as a person who carries on at least one Annex A activity: s 8(9).

Definition

"farmer": ss 1(1), 8(*a*); "land": IA 1937 Sch; "supply": s 1(1).

SIXTH SCHEDULE
Goods and services chargeable at the rate specified in section 11(1)(d)[12.5%]

[(i)   (*a*)   Coal, peat and other solid substances held out for sale solely as fuel,

       (*b*)   electricity:

            Provided that this subparagraph shall not apply to the distribution of any electricity where such distribution is wholly or mainly in connection with the distribution of communications signals,

       (*c*)   gas of a kind used for domestic or industrial heating or lighting, whether in gaseous or liquid form, but not including [motor vehicle gas within the meaning of section 42(1) of the Finance Act, 1976][1], gas of a kind normally used for welding and cutting metals or gas sold as lighter fuel,

       (*d*)   hydrocarbon oil of a kind used for domestic or industrial heating, excluding gas oil (within the meaning of the Hydrocarbon (Heavy) Oil Regulations, 1989 (S.I. No. 121 of 1989)), other than gas oil which has been duly marked in accordance with Regulation 6(2) of the said Regulations;

(ii)   the provision of food and drink of a kind specified in paragraph (xii) of the Second Schedule in a form suitable for human consumption without further preparation—

       (*a*)   by means of a vending machine,

       (*b*)   in the course of operating a hotel, restaurant, cafe, refreshment house, canteen, establishment licensed for the sale for consumption on the premises of intoxicating liquor, catering business or similar business, or

       (*c*)   in the course of operating any other business in connection with the carrying on of which facilities are provided for the consumption of the food or drink supplied;

(iii)   the supply, in the course of the provision of a meal, of goods of a kind specified in subparagraph (*c*), (*d*) or (*e*) of paragraph (xii) of the Second Schedule, and fruit juices other than fruit juices chargeable with a duty of excise—

       (*a*)   in the course of operating a hotel, restaurant, cafe, refreshment house, canteen, establishment licensed for the sale for consumption on the premises of intoxicating liquor, catering business or similar business, or

       (*b*)   in the course of operating any other business in connection with the carrying on of which facilities are provided for the consumption of the food or drink supplied;

(iv)   the supply of food and drink (other than beverages specified in subparagraph (*a*) or (*b*) of paragraph (xii) of the Second Schedule) which is, or includes, food and drink which—

       (*a*)   has been heated for the purpose of enabling it to be consumed at a temperature above the ambient air temperature, or

       (*b*)   has been retained heated after cooking for the purpose of enabling it to be consumed at a temperature above the ambient air temperature, or

       (*c*)   is supplied, while still warm after cooking, for the purpose of enabling it to be consumed at a temperature above the ambient air temperature, and is above the ambient air temperature at the time of supply;

(v)   promotion of and admissions to cinematographic performances;

(vi)   promotion of and admissions to live theatrical or musical perform-ances, excluding—

    (*a*)   dances, and

    (*b*)   performances specified in paragraph (viii) of the First Sched-ule;

[(vii)   amusement services of the kind normally supplied in fairgrounds or amusement parks:

    Provided that this paragraph shall not apply to–

    (I)   services consisting of dances,

    (II)   services consisting of circuses,

    (III)   services consisting of gaming, as defined in section 2 of the Gaming and Lotteries Act, 1956 (including services provided by means of a gaming machine of the kind referred to in section 43 of the Finance Act, 1975), or

    (IV)   services provided by means of an amusement machine of the kind referred to in section 120 of the Finance Act. 1992;][2]

[(vii*a*)   the provision by a person other than a non-profit making organisation of facilities for taking part in sporting activities;][3]

[(vii*b*)   the provision by a member-owned golf club of facilities for taking part in golf to any person, other than an individual whose membership sub-scription to that club at the time the facilities are used by that individ-ual entitles that individual to use such facilities without further charge on at least 200 days (including the day on which such facilities are used by that individual) in a continuous period of twelve months, where the total consideration received by that club for the provision of such facilities has exceeded or is likely to exceed £20,000 in any con-tinuous period of twelve months and, for the purposes of this para-graph, the provision of facilities for taking part in golf shall not include the provision of facilities for taking part in pitch and putt;

(vii*c*)   the provision by a non-profit making organisation, other than an or-ganisation referred to in paragraph (vii*b*), of facilities for taking part in golf to any person where the total consideration received by that or-ganisation for the provision of such facilities has exceeded or is likely to exceed £20,000 in any continuous period of twelve months and, for the purposes of this paragraph, the provision of facilities for taking part in golf shall not include the provision of facilities for taking part in pitch and putt;][4]

(viii)   services consisting of the acceptance for disposal of waste material;

(ix)   admissions to exhibitions, of the kind normally held in museums and art galleries, of objects of historical, cultural, artistic or scientific interest, not being services of the kind specified in paragraph (viii*a*) of the First Schedule;

(x)   services [of a kind][5] supplied in the course of their profession by vet-erinary surgeons;

(xi)   agricultural services consisting of—

    (*a*)   field work, reaping, mowing, threshing, baling, harvesting, sowing and planting, [(*ai*) stock-minding, stock-rearing, farm relief services and farm advisory services [(other than farm accountancy or farm management services)]⁶,]⁷

    (*b*) disinfecting and ensilage of agricultural products,

    (*c*) destruction of weeds and pests and dusting and spraying of crops and land,

[(*d*) lopping, tree felling and similar forestry services;]⁸

[(xii) newspapers and periodicals, normally published at least fortnightly, the contents of each issue of which consist, wholly or mainly, as regards the quantity of printed matter contained in them, of information on the principal current events and topics of general public interest;

(xiii) (*a*) letting of immovable goods (other than in the course of the provision of facilities of the kind specified in paragraph (vii*a*)—

    (I) by a hotel or guesthouse, or by a similar establishment which provides accommodation for visitors or travellers,

    (II) in a house, apartment or other similar establishment which is advertised or held out as being holiday accommodation or accommodation for visitors or travellers, or

    (III) in a caravan park, camping site or other similar establishment,

    or

    (*b*) the provision of accommodation which is advertised or held out as holiday accommodation;

(xiv) tour guide services;

(xv) the hiring (in this paragraph referred to as **"the current hiring"**) to a person of—

    (*a*) a vehicle designed and constructed, or adapted, for the conveyance of persons by road,

    (*b*) a ship, boat or other vessel designed and constructed for the conveyance of passengers and not exceeding 15 tonnes gross,

    (*c*) a sports or pleasure boat of any description, or

    (*d*) a caravan, mobile home, tent or trailer tent,

under an agreement, other than an agreement of the kind referred to in section 3(1)(*b*), for any term or part of a term which, when added to the term of any such hiring (whether of the same goods or of other goods of the same kind) to the same person during the period of 12 months ending on the date of the commencement of the current hiring, does not exceed 5 weeks;

[(xvi) a work of art being—

    (*a*) a painting, drawing or pastel, or any combination thereof, executed entirely by hand, excluding hand-decorated manufactured articles and plans and drawings for architectural, engineering, industrial, commercial, topographical or similar purposes,

    (*b*) an original lithograph, engraving, or print, or any combination thereof, produced directly from lithographic stones, plates or other engraved surfaces, which are executed entirely by hand, or (*c*)   an original sculpture or statuary, excluding mass-produced reproductions and works of craftsmanship of a commercial character,

but excluding the supply of such work of art by a taxable dealer in accordance with the provisions of subsection (3) or (8) of section 10A or by an auctioneer within the meaning of section 10B and in accordance with the provisions of subsection (3) of section 10B;]⁹

[(xvi*a*) antiques being, subject to and in accordance with regulations, articles of furniture, silver, glass or porcelain, whether hand-decorated or not, specified in the said regulations, which are shown to the satisfaction of the Revenue Commissioners to be more than 100 years old, other than goods specified in paragraph (xvi), but excluding the supply of such antiques by a taxable dealer in accordance with the provisions of subsection (3) or (8) of section 10A or by an auctioneer within the meaning of section 10B and in accordance with the provisions of subsection (3) of section 10B;]¹⁰

(xvii) literary manuscripts certified by the Director of the National Library as being of major national importance and of either cultural or artistic importance;

(xviii) services consisting of—

(*a*)   the repair or maintenance of movable goods, or

(*b*)   the alteration of [used]¹¹ movable goods, other than [contract work or]¹² such services specified in paragraph (v), (v*a*) or (xvi) of the Second Schedule, but excluding the provision in the course of any such repair, maintenance or alteration service of—

(I)   accessories, attachments or batteries, or

(II) tyres, tyre cases, interchangeable tyre treads, inner tubes and tyre flaps, for wheels of all kinds;

(xix) services consisting of the care of the human body, excluding such services specified in the First Schedule, but including services supplied in the course of a health studio business or similar business;

(xx) services supplied in the course of their profession by jockeys;

[(xx*a*) greyhound feeding stuff, which is packaged, advertised or held out for sale solely as greyhound feeding stuff, and which is supplied in units of not less than 10 kilograms;]¹³

(xxi) the supply to a person of photographic prints (other than goods produced by means of a photocopying process), slides or negatives, which have been produced from goods provided by that person;

(xxii) goods being—

(*a*)   photographic prints (other than goods produced by means of a photocopying process), mounted or unmounted, but unframed,

(*b*)   slides and negatives, and

(*c*)   cinematographic and video film,

which record particular persons, objects or events, supplied under an agreement to photograph those persons, objects or events;

(xxiii) the supply by a photographer of—

(*a*)   negatives which have been produced from film exposed for the purpose of his business, and

(*b*)   film which has been exposed for the purposes of his business;

(xxiv) photographic prints produced by means of a vending machine which

156

incorporates a camera and developing and printing equipment;

(xxv) services consisting of—

(*a*)　the editing of photographic, cinematographic and video film, and

(*b*)　microfilming;

(xxvi) agency services in regard to a supply specified in paragraph (xxi);

(xxvii) instruction in the driving of mechanically propelled road vehicles, not being education, training or retraining of the kinds specified in paragraph (ii) of the First Schedule;

(xxviii) immovable goods;

(xxix) services consisting of the development of immovable goods and work on immovable goods including the installation of fixtures, where the value of movable goods (if any) provided in pursuance of an agreement in relation to such services does not exceed two-thirds of the total amount on which tax is chargeable in respect of the agreement;

(xxx) services consisting of the routine cleaning of immovable goods;

[(xxxi) food of a kind used for human consumption, other than that included in paragraph (xii) of the Second Schedule, being flour or egg based bakery products including cakes, crackers, wafers and biscuits, but excluding—

(*a*)　wafers and biscuits wholly or partly covered or decorated with chocolate or some other product similar in taste and appearance,

(*b*)　food of a kind specified in subparagraph (*c*) or (*e*)(II) of paragraph (xii) of the Second Schedule, and

(*c*)　chocolates, sweets and similar confectionery;][14]

(xxxii) concrete ready to pour [but excluding the supply of such goods by a taxable dealer in accordance with the provisions of subsection (3) or (8) of section 10A or by an auctioneer within the meaning of section 10B and in accordance with the provisions of subsection (3) of section 10B][15];

(xxxiii) blocks, of concrete, of a kind which comply with the specification contained in the Standard Specification (Concrete Building Blocks, Part 1, Normal Density Blocks) Declaration, 1987 (Irish Standard 20: Part 1: 1987) [but excluding the supply of such goods by a taxable dealer in accordance with the provisions of subsection (3) or (8) of section 10A or by an auctioneer within the meaning of section 10B and in accordance with the provisions of subsection (3) of section 10B][16].][17][18]

Amendments

1　Substituted by FA 1993 s 97(1)(*a*) with effect from 1 March 1993; previously "gas of a kind specified in paragraph (i) of the Seventh Schedule".

2　Para (vii) substituted by FA 1994 s 101(*a*) with effect from 1 July 1994.

3　Para (vii*a*) inserted by FA 1992 s 197(3)(*a*) with effect from 1 July 1992.

4　Paras (vii*b*)-(vii*c*) inserted by FA 1995 s 140(*a*) with effect from 1 January 1996.

5　Inserted by FA 1994 s 101(*b*) with effect from 1 July 1994.

6　Substituted by FA 1994 s 101(*c*) with effect from 23 May 1994; previously "(not being services of the kind specified in paragraph (xxii) of the Seventh Schedule)".

7　Para (xi)(*ai*) inserted by FA 1992 s 197(3)(*b*) with effect from 1 July 1992.

8　Para (xi)(*d*) substituted by FA 1993 s 97(1)(*b*) with effect from 1 March 1993; previously "lopping, tree felling and similar forestry services.".

9　Para (xvi) substituted by FA 1995 s 140(*b*) with effect from 1 July 1995.

10　Para (xvi*a*) inserted by FA 1995 s 140(*c*) with effect from 1 July 1995.

11　Substituted by FA 1995 s 140(*d*) with effect from 1 July 1995; previously "second-hand".

12　Inserted by FA 1996 s 99 with effect from 1 January 1996.

13　Para (xx*a*) inserted by FA 1995 s 140(*e*) with effect from 1 July 1995.

14　Paras (xii)-(xxxi) inserted by FA 1993 s 97(1)(*c*).

15　Inserted by FA 1995 s 140(*f*) with effect from 1 July 1995.

16   Words "but excluding the supply of such goods by a taxable dealer in accordance with the provisions of subsection (3) or (8) of section 10A or by an auctioneer within the meaning of section 10B and in accordance with the provisions of subsection (3) of section 10B" inserted by FA 1995 s 140(*g*) with effect from 1 July 1995.

17   Para (xxxi) substituted and paras (xxxii)-(xxxiii) inserted by FA 1993 97(2) with effect from 1 July 1993.

18   Sch 6 substituted by FA 1992 s 197(2) with effect from 28 May 1992.

Cross-references

Para (vii*c*): Minister may provide that State and local authority may be taxable persons: s 8(2A)(proviso).

Para (xiii): agreements prior to 25 February 1993: Sch 3 para (ii).

Para (xvi): margin scheme goods: s 10A(1).

Para (xvi*a*): margin scheme goods: s 10A(1), Sch 8 para (iii); Revenue may make regulations as regards particulars to be furnished in relation to antiques: s 32(1)(*de*).

Para (xv)(*a*): agreements prior to 25 February 1993: Sch 3 para (iii).

Para (xxii): margin scheme goods: s 10A(1), Sch 8 paras (i)(*f*), (iii).

Case law

Para (i)(*b*): Transmission of cable television and radio signals not supply of electricity: *Brosnan v Cork Communications Ltd.*, IV ITR 349.

Narrative

Irish Value Added Tax, Chapter 8; *Guide to Value Added Tax (Revenue Commissioners):* Chapter 15.

Definitions

"antiques": s 1(1); "business": s 1(1); "clothing": s 1(1); "footwear": s 1(1); "fur skin": s 1(1); "goods": s 1(1); "immovable goods": s 1(1); "land": IA 1937 Sch; "movable goods": s 1(1); "establishment": s 1(1); "person": IA 1937 s 11(*c*); "regulations": ss 1(1), 32; "second-hand": s 1(1); "supply": s 1(1); "taxable dealer": s 1(1); "works of art": s 1(1).

SEVENTH SCHEDULE

Amendments
1   Sch 7 repealed by FA 1993 s 98 with effect from 1 March 1993.

EIGHTH SCHEDULE
Works of art, collectors' items and antiques chargeable at the rate specified in section 11(1)(*d*) in the circumstances specified in section 11(1AA)

[(i)   Works of art:

      Every work of art being—

      (*a*)   a picture (other than a painting, drawing or pastel specified in paragraph (xvi) of the Sixth Schedule), collage or similar decorative plaque, executed entirely by hand by an artist, other than—

          (I)   plans and drawings for architectural, engineering, industrial, commercial, topographical or similar purposes,

          (II)   hand-decorated manufactured articles, and

          (III)   theatrical scenery, studio back cloths or the like of painted canvas,

      (*b*)   a sculpture cast the production of which is limited to eight copies and supervised by the artist or by the artist's successors in title provided that, in the case of a statuary cast produced before the 1st day of January, 1989, the limit of eight copies may be exceeded where so determined by the Revenue Commissioners,

      (*c*)   a tapestry or wall textile made by hand from original designs provided by an artist, provided that there are not more than eight copies of each,

      (*d*)   individual pieces of ceramics executed entirely by an artist and signed by the artist,

      (*e*)   enamels on copper, executed entirely by hand, limited to eight numbered copies bearing the signature of the artist or the studio, excluding articles of jewellery, goldsmiths' wares and silversmiths' wares, or

      (*f*)   a photograph taken by an artist, printed by the artist or under the artist's supervision, signed and numbered and limited to 30 copies, all sizes and mounts included, other than photographs specified in paragraph (xxii)(*a*) of the Sixth Schedule;

    (ii)   Collectors' items:

      Every collectors' item being one or more—

      (*a*)   postage or revenue stamps, postmarks, first-day covers, pre-stamped stationery and the like, franked, or if unfranked not being of legal tender and not being intended for use as legal tender, or

      (*b*)   collections and collectors' pieces of zoological, botanical, mineralogical, anatomical, historical, archaeological, palaeontological, ethnographic or numismatic interest;

    (iii)   Antiques:

      Every antique being, subject to and in accordance with regulations, one or more goods which are shown to the satisfaction of the Revenue Commissioners to be more than 100 years old, other than goods specified in paragraph (xvi), (xvi*a*) or (xxii)(*a*) of the Sixth Schedule or in paragraph (i) or (ii) of this Schedule.][1]

Amendments
1   Sch 8 inserted by FA 1995 s 141 with effect from 1 July 1995.
Cross-references
Para (i): margin scheme goods: s 10A(1); rate of tax: s 11(1AA)(*b*)-(*c*).
para (iii): margin scheme goods: s 10A(1); Revenue may make regulations as regards particulars to be furnished in relation to antiques s 32(1)(*de*).
Definitions
"antiques": s 1(1); "collectors' items": s 1(1); "works of art": s 1(1).

FINANCE ACT 1973

(Number 19 of 1973)

ARRANGEMENT OF SECTIONS

PART V
Value added tax

An Act to charge and impose certain duties of customs and inland revenue (including excise), to amend the law relating to customs and inland revenue (including excise) and to make further provisions in connection with finance. [4th August 1973]

PART V
Value added tax

76 Commencement (Part V)

This Part (other than section 90, in so far as it amends the definition of **"manufacturer"** in section 1(1) of the Principal Act) shall come into operation on the 3rd day of September, 1973.

77 "Principal Act"

In this Part **"the Principal Act"** means the Value Added Tax Act, 1972.

78 Amendment of section 3 (supply of goods) of Principal Act

Notes
This amendment provided that the supply of food and drink by means of a vending machine, or in the course of a catering service was to be treated as the supply of a service. It has since been superseded.

---

79 Amendment of section 5 (supply of services) of Principal Act

---

Notes
This amendment provided that certain services (staff meals) self supplied by a taxable person, in connection with his business activities, were to be taxable. The two thirds rule was not to apply to catering services. The changes have since been superseded.

---

80 Amendment of section 11 (rates of tax) of Principal Act

Notes
Paras (*a*)-(*c*), by amending VATA 1972 s 11, increased the VAT rates from 5.26% to 6.75%, 16.37% to 19.5% and 30.26% to 36.75% and imposed VAT on dinner dances. These rate changes have since been superseded.
Para (*d*), by inserting VATA 1972 s 11(1A) provided rules for determining the VAT rate when a change in rate takes place. A new VATA 1972 s 11(1B) empowered the Revenue Commissioners to make determinations regarding the VAT rate applicable to a supply of goods or services (or whether a supply was exempt) and provided a right of appeal against such determinations. Para (*e*), by inserting VATA 1972 s 11(4A)introduced a tax charge on food provided by a customer but prepared by a caterer. Para (*f*) substituted VATA 1972 s 11(8)(*a*) empowered the Minister for Finance to reduce VAT rates.

---

81   Amendment of section 12 (deduction for tax borne or paid) of Principal Act

Notes
Para (*a*) by inserting VATA 1972 s 12(1A) introduced stock relief on commencement for newly registered traders.

82   Amendment of section 19 (tax due and payable) of Principal Act

Notes
This amendment has been superseded.

83   Amendment of section 26 (penalties generally) of Principal Act

Notes
This amendment has been superseded.

84   Amendment of section 27 (fraudulent returns etc) of Principal Act

Notes
This section substituted VATA 1972 s 27(5).

85   Amendment of section 32 (regulations) of Principal Act

Notes
This section inserted VATA 1972 s 32(1)(*xx*) and (*xxx*).

86   Amendment of section 35 (special conditions for adjustment and recovery of consideration) of Principal Act

Notes
This section by inserting VATA 1972 s 35(1A) provided rules for dealing with adjustments in contract prices following a change in the VAT rate.

87   Amendment of First Schedule (exempted activities) to Principal Act

Notes
This section exempted catering services in hospitals and schools, the supply and importation of live horses and greyhounds, and the insemination of cattle, sheep and pigs. The changes have since been superseded.

88   Amendment of Second Schedule (goods and services chargeable at the rate of zero per cent) to Principal Act

Notes
The net effect of these changes was to extend the 0% rate to most food and drink for human consumption, oral medicines, animal feed, food producing seeds etc, and life saving services provided by the Royal National Lifeboat Institution.

89   Amendment of Third Schedule to Principal Act

Notes
This amendment has been superseded.

90   Miscellaneous amendments of Principal Act

The Principal Act is hereby amended as specified in column (3) of the Tenth Schedule to this Act.

97   Care and management of taxes and duties

All taxes and duties (except the excise duties on mechanically propelled vehicles) imposed by this Act are hereby placed under the care and management of the Revenue Commissioners.

98 Short title, construction and commencement

(1) This Act may be cited as the Finance Act, 1973.

...

(5) Part V of this Act shall be construed together with the Value Added Tax Act, 1972.

...

(7) Any reference in this Act to any other enactment shall, except so far as the context otherwise requires, be construed as a reference to that enactment as amended by or under any other enactment including this Act.

TENTH SCHEDULE
Amendment of Enactments

Notes

Amended: definitions of "livestock" and "taxable period" in VATA 1972 s 1(1); inserted "for the time being specified in section 11(1)(*c*)" in VATA 1972 s 3(5)(*b*); inserted "at any of the rates specified in section 11(1)..." in VATA s 17(1). Other amendments in this Schedule are now superseded by subsequent legislation.

FINANCE ACT 1975

(Number 6 of 1975)

ARRANGEMENT OF SECTIONS

PART I
Income tax, sur-tax and corporation profits tax

CHAPTER V
Miscellaneous

PART V
Value added tax

PART VI
Miscellaneous

Section

An Act to charge and impose certain duties of customs and inland revenue (including excise) to amend the law relating to customs and inland revenue (including excise) and to make further provisions in connection with finance. [14th May, 1975]

PART I
Income tax, sur-tax and corporation profits tax

CHAPTER V
Miscellaneous

28 Interest on unpaid taxes

(1) This section applies to interest chargeable under —

    (*a*) ...[1],

    (*b*) section 129 of the Income Tax Act, 1967,

    (*c*) section 550 of the said Income Tax Act, 1967,

    (*d*) section 17(6A) of the Finance Tax Act, 1970,

    (*e*) section 20(2) ...[2] of the Finance Act, 1971, and

    (*f*) section 21 of the Value Added Tax Act, 1972.

(2) Where any interest to which this section applies is chargeable for any month commencing on or after the 6th day of April, 1975, or any part of such a month, in respect of tax due to be paid or remitted whether before, on or after such date, such interest shall be chargeable at the rate of **1.5 per cent** for each month or part of a month instead of at the rate specified in the said sections and those sections shall have effect as if the rate aforesaid were substituted for the rates specified in those sections.

(3) In this section **"tax"** means income tax, sur-tax, ...[3] or value added tax, as may be appropriate.

Amendments
1 Words "section 14 of the Finance Act, 1962" repealed by CTA 1976 s 164 and Sch 3 Pt II.

2   Words "and 50(2)" repealed by CTA 1976 s 164 and Sch 3 Pt II.
3   Words "corporation profits tax" repealed by CTA 1976 s 164 and Sch 3 Pt II.
Cross-references
Corporation tax, collection, this section applied by CTA 1976 s 145(3).
Definition
"month": IA 1937 Sch.

29 Adjustment of capital allowances by reference to value added tax

(1) In computing any deduction, allowance or relief, for any of the purposes of —

    (*a*)   Parts XIII to XVIII, inclusive, of the Income Tax Act, 1967,

    (*b*)   section 22 of the Finance Act, 1971,

    (*c*)   the Finance (Taxation of Profits of Certain Mines) Act, 1974, or

    (*d*)   section 22 of the Finance Act, 1974,

the cost to a person of any machinery or plant, or the amount of any expenditure incurred by him, shall not take account of any amount included in such cost or expenditure for value added tax in respect of which the person may claim —

    (i)   a deduction under section 12 of the Value Added Tax Act, 1972, or

    (ii)   a refund of value added tax under an order under section 20(3) of that Act.

(2) In calculating, for any of the purposes of Part XVI of the Income Tax Act, 1967, the amount of sale, insurance, salvage or compensation moneys to be taken into account in computing a balancing allowance or balancing charge to be made to or on a person, no account shall be taken of the amount of value added tax (if any) chargeable to the person in respect of those moneys.

Cross-references
Petroleum taxation, exploration expenditure: this section applied by FA 1992 s 84(15).
Definition
"person": IA 1937 s 11(*c*).

PART V
Value added tax

50 Amendment of section 10 (amount on which tax is chargeable) of Value Added Tax Act, 1972

Notes
This amendment was an anti avoidance provision dealing with sales by manufacturers to associated companies of televisions, record players etc (old Sch 4). It has since been superseded.

51 Amendment of section 11 (rates of tax) of Value Added Tax Act, 1972

Notes
Para (*a*), which imposed an additional tax on supplies by manufacturers of goods produced from materials supplied by customers, is now irrelevant as VATA 1972 s 11(2) was subsequently deleted by FA 1985 s 43. Para (*b*) substituted VATA 1972 s 4.

52 Amendment of section 13 (special provisions for tax invoiced by farmers and fishermen) of Value Added Tax Act, 1972

Notes
This amendment, which suspended the then 1% flat rate credit for unregistered farmers, has been superseded.

53 Amendment of Third Schedule to Value Added Tax Act, 1972

Notes
This amendment is now irrelevant as VATA 1972 Sch 3 was replaced by FA 1991 s 86.

PART VI
Miscellaneous

55 Amendment of Provisional Collection of Taxes Act, 1927

Notes
This section amended PCTA 1927 s 4(*a*).

---

56 Care and management of taxes and duties

All taxes and duties imposed by this Act are hereby placed under the care and management of the Revenue Commissioners.

57 Short title, construction and commencement

(1) This Act may be cited as the Finance Act, 1975.

...

(6) Any reference in this Act to any other enactment shall, except so far as the context otherwise requires, be construed as a reference to that enactment as amended by or under any other enactment including this Act.

Definition
"commencement" IA 1937 Sch.

FINANCE (No 2) ACT 1975

(Number 19 of 1975)

ARRANGEMENT OF SECTIONS

An Act to charge and impose certain duties of inland revenue, to amend the law relating to inland revenue and to make further provisions in connection with finance. [30th July, 1975]

2 Amendment of Value Added Tax Act, 1972

Notes

This section extended the 0% rate to certain clothing, material for clothing, footwear and fuel. The changes have since been superseded.

169

FINANCE ACT 1976

(Number 16 of 1976)

ARRANGEMENT OF SECTIONS

PART IV
Value added tax

An Act to charge and impose certain duties of customs and inland revenue (including excise),to amend the law relating to customs and inland revenue (including excise) and to make further provisions in connection with finance. [27th May, 1976]

PART IV
Value added tax

49 Commencement

This Part, other than sections 51, 52, 54 to 62, shall be deemed to have come into operation as on and from the 1st day of March, 1976.

50 Definitions (Part IV)

In this Part—

"the Act of 1973" means the Finance Act, 1973;

"the Principal Act" means the Value Added Tax Act, 1972.

51 Amendment of section 3 (delivery of goods) of Principal Act

---

Notes
This section which substituted VATA 1972 s 3(1)(*e*) (self supply to exempt activity) has been superseded.

171

52 Amendment of section 10 (amount on which tax is chargeable) of Principal Act

Notes
This amendment, which provided that potential customs or excise duty was part of the chargeable consideration for VAT has since been superseded.

53 Amendment of section 11 (rates of tax) of Principal Act

Notes
This section by amending VATA 1972 s 11(1), changed the 6.75% VAT rate to 10%, the 19.5% VAT rate to 20% and the 36.75% VAT rate to 35% and 40%. New provisions for VAT on dances were also introduced. The changes have since been superseded.

54 Amendment of section 12 (deduction for tax borne or paid) of Principal Act

Notes
This section restricted the right to a purchases VAT deduction on televisions, radios, records, record players (old Sch 4). The changes have since been superseded.

55 Amendment of section 15 (charge of tax on imported goods) of Principal Act

Notes
This section provided a new method of calculating the tax value of imported goods. The change has since been superseded by FA 1985 s 46.

56 Amendment of section 21 (interest) of Principal Act

Notes
This section substituted VATA 1972 s 21(2)(*b*).

57 Amendment of section 26 (penalties generally) of Principal Act

Notes
This section, by substituting VATA 1972 s 26(6)(*e*)-(*f*), provided a revised wording for form of evidence in connection with recovery of penalties.

58 Amendment of section 32 (regulations) of Principal Act

Notes
This section, by inserting VATA 1972 s 32(1)(*uu*), allowed the Revenue Commissioners to make regulations relating to certain purchases tax credit apportionments.

59 Amendment of section 34 (relief for stock-in-trade held on the specified day) of Principal Act

Notes
This section substituted VATA 1972 s 34(5)(*a*).

60 Substitution of new Schedules for First, Second, Third and Fourth Schedules (exempted activities and rates of tax) to Principal Act

Notes
These amendments listed the goods liable at 0%, 10% and 20% with effect from 1 March 1976. The changes have since been superseded.

61 Consequential amendments

In consequence of the amendments specified in sections 53 and 60 and the repeals specified in Part II of the Fifth Schedule, the Principal Act is hereby further amended as specified in Part II of the First Schedule.

62 Priority in bankruptcy and winding-up

(1) There shall be included among the debts which, under section 4 of the Preferential Payments in Bankruptcy (Ireland) Act, 1889, are to be paid in priority to all other debts in the distribution of the property of a person, being a bankrupt, arranging debtor, or person

dying insolvent, any tax for which the person is liable in relation to taxable periods which shall have ended within the period of 12 months next before the date on which the order of adjudication of the bankrupt was made, the petition of arrangement of the debtor was filed, or, as the case may be, the person died insolvent and any interest payable by the person under section 21 of the Principal Act.

(2)   (*a*)   There shall be included among the debts which, under section 285 of the Companies Act, 1963, are to be paid in priority to all other debts in the winding-up of a company any tax for which the company is liable in relation to taxable periods which shall have ended within the period of 12 months next before the relevant date and any interest payable by the company under section 21 of the Principle Act.

       (*b*)   Paragraph (*a*) shall, for the purposes of section 98 of the Companies Act, 1963, be deemed to be contained in section 285 of that Act.

       (*c*)   In paragraph (*a*) **"the relevant date"** has the same meaning as it has in section 285 of the Companies Act, 1963.

Definition
"taxable period": VATA 1972 s 1(1).

---

63 Transitional provisions in respect of motor vehicles

(1) In this section—

"qualified vehicles" means vehicles which, on or before the 29th day of February, 1976, were delivered to or imported by a person other than a manufacturer of goods of the kind so delivered or imported in such circumstances that tax at the rate of 36.75 per cent. was chargeable in relation to such delivery or importation;

"relevant delivery" means a delivery of any qualified vehicles in such circumstances that, but for this section, tax at the rate of 10 per cent. would be chargeable;

"vehicles" means goods (other than second-hand goods) of a kind specified in Part I of the Fourth Schedule (inserted by this Act) to the Principal Act.

(2) During the period which commenced on the 1st day of March, 1976, and ended on the 30th day of April, 1976, notwithstanding the provisions of section 11 of the Principal Act, tax shall, in relation to a relevant delivery, be chargeable and be deemed to have been chargeable at the rate of 6.75 per cent.

(3) Notwithstanding the provisions of section 12(1) of the Principal Act, the amount deductible by a person under that section in relation to—

    (*a*)   any qualified vehicles, and

    (*b*)   the delivery or importation of any vehicles (not being qualified vehicles) in relation to the consideration for a delivery of which by him tax was charged at the rate of 6.75 per cent.,

shall not exceed, in the case of a delivery of such goods to him, 6.75 per cent. of the consideration payable by him exclusive of any tax payable in respect of the delivery by the person making the delivery and, in the case of an importation, 6.75 per cent. of the value of the goods calculated in accordance with section 15(4) of the said Act.

PART VI
Miscellaneous

81 Repeals

...

(2) The enactment mentioned in column (2) of Part II of the Fifth Schedule to this Act is hereby repealed to the extent specified in column (3) of that Schedule.

(3) ...

    (*b*)   Subsection (2) of this section shall be deemed to have come into operation on the 1st day of March, 1976.

82 Care and management of taxes and duties

All taxes and duties (except the excise duties on mechanically propelled vehicles) imposed by this Act are hereby placed under the care and management of the Revenue Commissioners.

83 Short title, construction and commencement

(1) This Act may be cited as the Finance Act, 1976.

...

(5) Part IV of this Act shall be construed together with the Value Added Tax Act, 1972, and the enactments amending or extending that Act

...

(7) Any reference in this Act to any other enactment shall, except so far as the context otherwise requires, be construed as a reference to that enactment as amended by or under any other enactment including this Act.

FIRST SCHEDULE

Amendment of enactments

PART II

Amendments consequential on certain amendments of Value Added Tax Act, 1972

Notes

Inserted definition of **"fur skin"** in VATA 1972 s 1(1); substituted "either of the rates" in VATA 1972 s 3(5)(*b*).
Other amendments in this schedule are now irrelevant having been superseded by subsequent legislation.

FIFTH SCHEDULE

Enactments repealed

PART II

Notes

Repealed: VATA 1972 ss 11(1)(*b*), 12(1)(*b*), 13, 17(2) and (4), 17(6) [words "otherwise than as required by section 13,"], 17(7) [words from "and an amendment of an invoice" to the end of the subsection]; 17(10)(*a*) [words from "or goods or services" to "to a registered person]; 26(1) [numerals 13], 26(2) [words "otherwise than under and in accordance with section 13"]; 32(1)(*f*); 35(1)(*c*).

VALUE ADDED TAX (AMENDMENT) ACT 1978

(Number 19 of 1978)

ARRANGEMENT OF SECTIONS

Section

FIRST SCHEDULE
Enactments repealed

SECOND SCHEDULE
Consequential amendments

An Act to amend the Value Added Tax Act, 1972, and the Acts amending that Act and to provide for related matters. [20th December, 1978]

1 Principal Act

In this Act **"the Principal Act"** means the Value Added Tax Act, 1972.

2 Amendment of section 1 (interpretation) of Principal Act

Notes

This Act implemented in the State the provisions of the Sixth Council Directive 77/388/EEC on the harmonisation of VAT regimes in EC Member States, with effect from 1 March 1979.

This section deleted the definitions of "accountable person", "established", "manufacturer", "rendering" and "residing" from VATA 1972 s 1. The section also substituted "establishment" for "permanent establishment" and inserted definitions of "agricultural produce", "agricultural service", "community", "farmer", "flat-rate addition", "flat-rate farmer", "supply" and "taxable person" in VATA 1972 s 1.

The main change is that an "accountable person" became a "taxable person" and the old terms "delivery of goods" and rendering of services" have been replaced by the new term "supply" which is used in relation to goods and services throughout the EC.

3 Amendment of section 2 (charge of value added tax) of Principal Act

---

Notes

This section substituted in VATA s 2(1)(a). The charge of tax is restricted to transactions within the State.

4 Amendment of section 3 (supply of goods) of Principal Act

Notes

Para (a) amended VATA 1972 s 3(1) and substituted VATA 1972 s 3(1)(e) - (f) (self supply of goods to exempt activity, self supply of goods to non business use); para (b) substituted VATA 1972 s 3(1A) (small business gifts relieved of tax); para (c) by inserting VATA 1972 s 3(1B) provided that electricity, gas, power etc are deemed to be supplies of goods, not services. Para (d) by substituting VATA 1972 s 3(3) provided that auctioneers fees on auctioned livestock, greyhounds, fruit, vegetables, poultry,

175

fish and eggs are to be taxed at the same rate as the rate applicable to the goods. Similarly an agent dealing in livestock or greyhounds has his fee or commission taxed on at the rate applicable to the goods he is selling.

5 Supply of services

Notes
This section substituted VATA 1972 s 5, providing new rules for place of supply of services, and providing that certain services supplied through an undisclosed agent are deemed to have been supplied by that agent.

6 Amendment of section 8 (taxable persons) of Principal Act

Notes
This section substituted VATA 1972 s 8(1), (2), (7), (8) and (9) and inserted VATA 1972 s 8(2A), redefining the old "accountable person" as "taxable person". Also by amending VATA 1972 s 8(3), the section increased the registration limits: this change has since been superseded.

7 Amendment of section 9 (registration) of Principal Act

Notes
This section substituted VATA 1972 s 9(1).

8 Amount on which tax is chargeable

Notes
This section substituted VATA 1972 s 10.

9 Amendment of section 11 (rates of tax) of Principal Act

Notes
This section substituted VATA 1972 s 11(3) and (4A). The main effect was to abolish the 35% and 40% VAT rates, with effect from 1 March 1979.

10 Amendment of section 12 (deduction for tax borne or paid) of Principal Act

Notes
This section substituted VATA 1972 s 12(1) and (3). VATA 1972 s 12(1) was subsequently substituted by FA 1987 s 41.

11 Special provisions for tax invoiced by flat rate farmers

Notes
This section by inserting VATA 1972 s 12A restored the 1% flat rate credit for unregistered farmers with effect from 1 March 1979.

12 Remission of tax on goods exported, etc.

Notes
This section inserted VATA 1972 s 13.

13 Determination of tax due by reference to cash receipts

Notes
This section, by substituting VATA 1972 s 14, provided new rules for deciding entitlement to the cash basis.

14 Charge of tax on imported goods

Notes
This section, by substituting VATA 1972 s 15, introduced "postponed accounting" for VAT at import with effect from 1 March 1979.

15 Amendment of section 17 (invoices) of Principal Act

Notes
Para (*a*) inserted VATA 1972 s 17(2); para (*b*) inserted VATA 1972 s 17(4); para (*c*) inserted VATA 1972 s 17(6A) para (*d*) amended VATA 1972 s 17(8); para (*e*) inserted VATA 1972 s 17(9)(*aa*); para (*f*) amended VATA 1972 s 17(10)(*a*); para (*g*) inserted VATA 1972 s 17(11A), para (*h*) amended VATA 1972 s 17(12)(*a*)(ii); para (*i*) inserted VATA 1972 s 17(13).

The changes in invoicing procedures are to harmonise Irish invoicing procedures with the stricter provisions of the Sixth Directive.

16 Amendment of section 19 (tax due and payable) of Principal Act

Notes
This amendment which introduced penalties for import/export offences, has been superseded as VATA 1972 s 19(3) was subsequently substituted by FA 1983 s 84.

17 Determination of tax due

Notes
This section substituted VATA 1972 s 23.

18 Amendment of section 26 (penalties generally) of Principal Act

Notes
This section amended VATA 1972 s 26(1); inserted VATA 1972 s 26(2A) and amended VATA 1972 s 26(3). Thr new penalties relate to invoices etc (see s 15).

19 Amendment of section 27 (fraudulent returns, etc) of Principal Act

Notes
This section substituted VATA 1972 s 27(4) and inserted VATA 1972 s 27(9)-(10) (penalties for import/export offences).

20 Amendment of section 30 (time limits) of Principal Act

Notes
This section substituted VATA 1972 s 30(3) and (5)(*b*).

21 Amendment of section 32 (regulations) of Principal Act

Notes
This section substituted VATA 1972 s 32(1)(*b*), (*e*), (*g*) and (*p*), deleted VATA 1972 s 32(1)(*w*) and inserted VATA 1972 s 32(2A). A new VATA 1972 s 32(1)(*w*) was subsequently inserted by FA 1984 s 91.

22 Amendment of section 35 (special provisions for adjustment and recovery of consideration) of Principal Act

Notes
This section inserted VATA 1972 s 35(3).

23 Amendment of section 29 (adjustment of capital allowances by reference to value added tax) of Finance Act 1975

Notes
This section substituted FA 1975 s 29(1) para (ii) .

24 Exempted activities

Notes
This section substituted VATA 1972 Sch 1.

25 Amendment of Second Schedule to Principal Act

Notes
This section substituted VATA 1972 Sch 2 paras (v), (vi) and (x). Amendments to paras (i) and (xvi) have been superseded by FA 1992 s 195.

26 Amendment of Third Schedule to Principal Act

Notes
This amendment is now irrelevant as VATA 1972 Sch 3 was replaced by FA 1991 s 86.

27 Services that are taxed where received

Notes
This section substituted VATA 1972 Sch 4. The old Sch 4 listed "luxury" goods: televisions, radios, record players and records liable at 35%/40%.

28 "Annex A activities" and "Annex B services"

Notes
This section substituted VATA 1972 Sch 5.

28 Amendment of Imposition of Duties Act, 1957

30 Repeals and consequential amendments

(1) The enactment mentioned in column (2) of the First Schedule is hereby repealed to the extent specified in column (3) of that Schedule.

(2) In consequence of the amendments of the Principal Act and of the repeals specified in the First Schedule, the Principal Act is hereby further amended by the substitution of the word or expression mentioned in column (3) of the Second Schedule at any reference number for the word or expression mentioned in column (2) of that Schedule at that reference number wherever it occurs in the provision of the Principal Act mentioned in column (4) of that Schedule at that reference number.

31 Transitional provisions

(1) (a) The register that immediately before the commencement of this Act, was the register of persons who may become or who are accountable persons shall, as on and from such commencement, become and be the register of persons who may become or are taxable persons under section 9 of the Principal Act as amended by this Act and the persons who, immediately before such commencement, were registered in the former register shall, upon such commencement, stand registered in the latter register.

(b) A person who, immediately before the commencement of this Act, was authorised to treat-

   (i)   the moneys which he received in respect of the delivery of taxable goods or rendering of taxable services as the consideration in respect of such delivery of goods or rendering of services, and

   (ii) the moneys he received in respect of the rendering of taxable services as the consideration for the rendering of such services, shall be deemed (if he could be so authorised) to have been so authorised to determine his tax liability in respect of supplies of goods and services or supplies of services, as the case may be, under section 14 of the Principal Act as amended by this Act.

(c) A person who, immediately before the commencement of this Act, was an accountable person and who, upon such commencement, would not, unless he so elected under section 8(3) of the Principal Act, be a taxable person, shall, upon such commencement, be deemed to have so elected and shall be a taxable person until the time when the election is cancelled or he permanently ceases to supply taxable goods and services, whichever is the later.

(2) In relation to a person who, immediately before the commencement of this Act, was an accountable person—

   (a) references in subsection (3) of section 7 of the Principal Act to a waiver shall be deemed to include references to a waiver made under subsection (1) of the said section 7 before such commencement,

   (b) references in subsection (5) of section 8 of the Principal Act to an election shall be deemed to include references to an election made under subsection (3) of the said section 8, (*c*)   references in the said subsection (3) of the said section 7 to the supply of services shall be deemed to include references to the rendering of services before such commencement, and

(*d*)   references in the said subsection (5) and subsection (6)(*b*) of the said section 8 to the supply of goods or services shall be deemed to include references to the delivery of goods, or the rendering of services, before such commencement.

32 Short title, commencement, collective citation and commencement

(1) This Act may be cited as the Value Added Tax (Amendment) Act, 1978.

(2) The Value Added Tax Act, 1972, and (in so far as they relate to value added tax) the Finance Act, 1973, the Finance Act, 1975, the Finance (No. 2) Act 1975, the Finance Act, 1976, the Finance Act, 1978 and this Act shall be construed together as one Act and may be cited together as the Value Added Tax Acts, 1972 to 1978.

(3) This Act, other than section 29 shall come into operation on such day as the Minister may by order appoint.

FIRST SCHEDULE
Enactments repealed

Notes

Repealed : VATA 1972 s 2(2); VATA 1972 s 4(2) [words "section 2(2)"]; VATA 1972 s 11(8)(*a*) [words "and may, in like manner, vary the Fourth Schedule by deleting therefrom descriptions of goods of any kind or by varying any description of goods for the time being specified therein,"]; VATA 1972 s 11(9), VATA 1972 s 19(1)(proviso), VATA 1972 s 36 and VATA 1972 Sch 2 para (ii). Other repeals have been superseded by subsequent legislation.

SECOND SCHEDULE
Consequential amendments

Notes

This schedule is principally concerned with setting out the changes in terminology introduced by this Act. "Supply", "supplied", "supplying" and "supplies" are substituted throughout VATA 1972 in place of "delivery", "delivered", "delivering" and "delivers" respectively in relation to goods and in place of "render", "rendered", "rendering" and "renders" respectively in relation to services. Similarly "taxable person" is substituted for "accountable person" throughout VATA 1972. Other amendments relate to cross-references in VATA 1972.

FINANCE ACT 1978

(Number 21 of 1978)

ARRANGEMENT OF SECTIONS

PART VII
Miscellaneous

An Act to charge and impose certain duties of customs and inland revenue (including excise), to amend the law relating to customs and inland revenue (including excise) and to make further provisions in connection with finance. [5th July 1978]

46 Interest on unpaid taxes

(1) This section applies to interest chargeable under —

(*a*) section 14 of the Finance Act, 1962,

(*b*) sections 129 and 550 of the Income Tax Act, 1967,

(*c*) section 17(6A) of the Finance Act, 1970,

(*d*) sections 20(2) and 50(2) of the Finance Act, 1971,

(*e*) section 21 of the Value-Added Tax Act, 1972,

(*f*) sections 145 and 152 of the Corporation Tax Act, 1976.

(2) Where any interest to which this section applies is chargeable for any month commencing on or after the date of the passing of this Act, or any part of such a month, in respect of tax due to be paid or remitted whether before, on or after such date, such interest shall, notwithstanding the provisions of section 28 of the Finance Act, 1975, be chargeable at the rate of **1.25 per cent** for each month or part of a month instead of at the rate specified in the said sections and those sections shall have effect as if the rate aforesaid were substituted for the rates specified in those sections.

(3) In this section **"tax"** means income tax, sur-tax, capital gains tax, corporation profits tax, corporation tax or value-added tax, as may be appropriate.

Definition
"month": IA 1937 Sch.

---

53 Care and management of taxes and duties

All taxes and duties imposed by this Act are hereby placed under the care and management of the Revenue Commissioners.

54 Short title, construction and commencement

(1) This Act may be cited as the Finance Act, 1978.

...

(9) Any reference in this Act to any other enactment shall, except so far as the context otherwise requires, be construed as a reference to that enactment as amended by or under any other enactment including this Act.

FINANCE ACT 1979

(Number 11 of 1979)

ARRANGEMENT OF SECTIONS

PART III
Value added tax

An Act to charge and impose certain duties of customs and inland revenue (including excise), to amend the law relating to customs and inland revenue (including excise) and to make further provisions in connection with finance. [1st June 1979]

PART III
Value added tax

48 Amendment of section 18 (inspection and removal of records) of Value Added Tax Act 1972

Notes

This amendment is now irrelevant as VATA 1972 s 18(1) was subsequently substituted by FA 1984 s 89.

---

49 Amendment of Third Schedule to Value Added Tax Act 1972

Notes

This amendment is now irrelevant as VATA 1972 Sch 3 was replaced by FA 1991 s 86.

PART V
MISCELLANEOUS

58 Care and management of taxes and duties

All taxes and duties imposed by this Act are hereby placed under the care and management of the Revenue Commissioners.

59 Short title, construction and commencement

(1) This Act may be cited as the Finance Act, 1979.

...

(4) *Part III* of this Act shall be construed together with the Value Added Tax Acts, 1972 to 1978, and may be cited together therewith as the Value Added Tax Acts, 1972 to 1979.

...

(7) Any reference in this Act to any other enactment shall, except so far as the context otherwise requires, be construed as a reference to that enactment as amended by or under any other enactment including this Act.

FINANCE ACT 1980

(Number 14 of 1980)

ARRANGEMENT OF SECTIONS

PART III
Value added tax

Section

80 Increase of rate of tax on certain goods and services
81 Amendment of section 8 (taxable persons) of Value Added Tax Act, 1972
82 Amendment of First Schedule to Value Added Tax Act, 1972

An Act to charge and impose certain duties of customs and inland revenue (including excise), to amend the law relating to customs and inland revenue (including excise) and to make further provisions in connection with finance. [25th June, 1980]

PART III
Value added tax

80 Increase of rate of tax on certain goods and services

Notes
This section, by amending VATA 1972 s 11(1)(*c*) increased the standard rate from 20% to 25% with effect from 1 May 1980. The change has since been superseded.

---

81 Amendment of section 8 (taxable persons) of Value Added Tax Act, 1972

Notes
This amendment, which provided increased registration limits, has since been superseded.

---

82 Amendment of First Schedule to Value Added Tax Act, 1972

Notes
This section, by substituting VATA 1972 Sch 1 para (xv), restricted the scope of the exemption for betting businesses.

PART VI
Miscellaneous

95 Care and management of taxes and duties

All taxes and duties imposed by this Act are hereby placed under the care and management of the Revenue Commissioners.

96 Short title, construction and commencement

(1) This Act may be cited as the Finance Act, 1980.

...

(4) *Part III* of this Act shall be construed together with the Value Added Tax Acts, 1972 to 1979, and may be cited together therewith as the Value Added Tax Acts, 1972 to 1980.

...

(8) Any reference in this Act to any other enactment shall, except so far as the context otherwise requires, be construed as a reference to that enactment as amended by or under any other enactment including this Act.

FINANCE ACT 1981

(Number 16 of 1981)

ARRANGEMENT OF SECTIONS

PART III
Value added tax

An Act to charge and impose certain duties of customs and inland revenue (including excise), to amend the law relating to customs and inland revenue (including excise) and to make further provisions in connection with finance. [28th May 1981]

PART III

42 Principal Act

In this Part "the Principal Act" means the Value Added Tax Act, 1972.

43 Amendment of section 1 (interpretation) of Principal Act

Notes
This section extended the definition of "development" in VATA 1972 s 1(1). to include prefabricated buildings.

---

44 Amendment of section 12 (deduction for tax borne or paid) of Principal Act

---

Notes
This section made a technical amendment to VATA 1972 s 12(2) to provide that repayments formerly dealt with under VATA 1972 s 12(2) are now dealt with under VATA 1972 s 20(2).

---

45 Amendment of section 20 (refund of tax) of Principal Act

Notes
This section made a technical amendment to VATA 1972 s 20(2) to provide that repayments formerly dealt with under VATA 1972 s 12(2) are now dealt with under VATA 1972 s 20(2).

PART VI
Miscellaneous

53 Care and management of taxes and duties

All taxes and duties imposed by this Act are hereby placed under the care and management of the Revenue Commissioners.

54   Short title, construction and commencement

(1) This Act may be cited as the Finance Act, 1981.

...

(4) *Part III* of this Act shall be construed together with the Value Added Tax Acts, 1972 to 1980, and may be cited together therewith as the Value Added Tax Acts, 1972 to 1981.

...

(8) Any reference in this Act to any other enactment shall, unless the context otherwise requires, be construed as a reference to that enactment as amended by or under any other enactment including this Act.

FINANCE (No 2) ACT 1981

(Number 28 of 1981)

ARRANGEMENT OF SECTIONS

PART II
Value added tax

An Act to charge and impose certain duties of customs and inland revenue (including excise), to amend the law relating to customs and inland revenue (including excise) and to make further provisions in connection with finance.   [20th November, 1981]

PART II
Value added tax

10 Definitions (Part II)

In this Part—

"the Act of 1978" means the Value Added Tax (Amendment) Act, 1978;

" the Principal Act" means the Value Added Tax Act, 1972.

11 Amendment of section 8 (taxable persons) of Principal Act

Notes
This section substituted VATA 1972 s 8(4) (turnover limits for compulsory registration). Other amendments have been superseded.

---

12 Amendment of section 11 (rates of tax) of Principal Act

Notes
This section increased the 10% VAT rate to 15% with effect from 1 September 1981 . The change has since been superseded.

---

13 Amendment of section 12A (special provisions for tax invoiced by flat-rate farmers) of Principal Act

---

Notes
This section increased the 1% flat rate credit for unregistered farmers to 1.5% with effect from 1 September 1981. The change has since been superseded.

---

14 Relief for hotels etc

(1) In this section "qualifying service" means a service consisting of the supply, for the benefit of persons not resident in the State, under an agreement made before the 1st day of January, 1981, of sleeping accommodation, with or without board or of motor cars upon hire, boats upon hire or entertainment, at charges fixed at the time of the making of the

189

agreement, to persons carrying on the business of travel agent, tour operator or the hiring out of motor cars or boats.

(2) In respect of taxable periods commencing on the 1st day of November, 1981, notwithstanding the provisions of section of the Principal Act (as amended by this Act) tax shall, in relation to the supply of a qualifying service, be chargeable, and be deemed to have been chargeable, at the rate of 10 per cent.

15 Transitional provisions

A person who, immediately after the passing of this Act, was a taxable person and who, upon such passing, would not, unless he so elected under section 8(3) of the Principal Act, be such a person, shall, upon such passing, be deemed to have so elected and shall be a taxable person until the time when the election is cancelled or he permanently ceases to supply taxable goods and services, whichever is earlier.

PART IV

Miscellaneous

19 Care and management of taxes and duties

All taxes and duties imposed by this Act are hereby placed under the care and management of the Revenue Commissioners.

20 Short title, construction and commencement

(1) This Act may be cited as the Finance (No 2) Act, 1981.

...

(3) *Part II* of this Act shall be construed together with the Value Added Tax Acts, 1972 to 1981, and shall be included in the collective citation "the Value Added Tax Acts, 1972 to 1981".

...

(5) Any reference in this Act to any other enactment shall, except so far as the context otherwise requires, be construed as a reference to that enactment as amended by or under any other enactment including this Act.

FINANCE ACT 1982

(Number 14 of 1982)

ARRANGEMENT OF SECTIONS

PART III
Value added tax

An Act to charge and impose certain duties of customs and inland revenue (including excise), to amend the law relating to customs and inland revenue (including excise) and to make further provisions in connection with finance. [17th July, 1982]

PART III
Value added tax

74 Interpretation (Part III)

In this Part—

"the Principal Act" means the Value Added Tax Act, 1972;

"the Act of 1976" means the Finance Act, 1976;

"the Act of 1978" means the Value Added Tax (Amendment) Act, 1978;

"the Act of 1981" means the Finance Act, 1981.

75 Amendment of section 3 (delivery of goods) of Principal Act

---

Notes
This section substituted VATA 1972 s 3(3) (land and buildings supplied through auctioneer or estate agent no longer taxed at 3%).

---

76 Amendment of section 5 (rendering of services) of Principal Act

---

Notes
This section inserted VATA 1972 s 5(4A). Barristers' services, the fees for which are not technically recoverable in law, (as the barrister cannot sue for unpaid fees) are taxable (with effect from 1 September 1982: see s 87).

---

77 Amendment of section 8 (accountable persons) of Principal Act

---

Notes
This section, by inserting VATA 1972 s 8(3A), provided that a racehorse trainer is a taxable person when his turnover from racehorse training exceeds (or is likely to exceed) £15,000 per annum. The section also substituted a revised definition of "farmer" in VATA 1972 s 8(9).

---

78 Amendment of section 10 (amount on which tax is chargeable) of Principal Act

---

Notes
This section inserted VATA 1972 s 10(4A) to clarify the chargeable amount on sales (of dutiable goods: beer, whiskey etc) "in warehouse", to unregistered persons.

---

79 Amendment of section 11 (rates of tax) of Principal Act

Notes

This section increased the 15% VAT rate to 18% and the 25% VAT rate to 30% with effect from 1 May 1982. The 3% effective rate was applied to professional services supplied to farmers.

80 Amendment of section 12 (deduction for tax borne or paid) of Principal Act

Notes

This amendment, which is connected with s 15, provided a deduction in the VAT return for VAT paid at import (after 1 September 1982) for registered traders.

81 Amendment of section 12A (special provisions for tax invoiced by flat-rate farmers) of Principal Act

Notes

This section, by substituting VATA 1972 s 12A(2) increased the flat rate compensation for unregistered farmers from 1.5% to 1.8% with effect from 1 May 1982, and introduced a new definition of "flat rate farmer".

82 Amendment of section 13 (remission of tax on goods exported etc) of Principal Act

Notes

This section deleted VATA 1972 s 13(4)-(5) (sales in bond).

83 Amendment of section 14 (determination of tax due by reference to cash receipts) of Principal Act

Notes

This change has since been superseded.

84 Amendment of section 15 (charge of tax on imported goods) of Principal Act

Notes

This section reintroduced VAT at import with effect from 1 September 1982.

85 Amendment of section 16 (duty to keep records) of Principal Act

Notes

Para (*a*) amended VATA 1972 s 16(2), to provided that importers must keep copies of customs documents to verify claims for deduction for VAT paid at import. Para (*b*) amended VATA 1972 s 16(3) to provide that the customs documents must be kept for six years.

86 Amendment of section 26 (penalties generally) of Principal Act

Notes

This section substituted VATA 1972 s 26(1) and deleted VATA 1972 s 26(5) (General increase in penalties).

87 Amendment of First Schedule to Principal Act

Notes

The net effect of the changes is that services provided by actuaries, accountants, barristers, solicitors etc and debt collectors are no longer exempt, with effect from 1 September 1982.

88 Amendment of Second Schedule to Principal Act

Notes

This section reduced the scope of the 0% rate for sales by VAT registered persons in the Shannon customs free airport and the section also reduced the rate of VAT on books to 0% .

89 Amendment of Third Schedule to Principal Act

Notes

This amendment reduced the VAT rate on furniture, carpets, lino and coffins from 25% to 18% with effect from 1 May 1982.

---

90 Relief for hotels etc

(1) In this section **"qualifying service"** means a service consisting of the supply, for the benefit of persons not resident in the State, under an agreement made before the 1st day of January, 1982, of sleeping accommodation, with or without board, or of motor cars upon hire, boats upon hire or entertainment, at charges fixed at the time of the making of the agreement, to persons carrying on the business of travel agent, tour operator or the hiring out of motor cars or boats.

(2) In respect of the taxable periods commencing on the 1st day of May, 1982, the 1st day of July, 1982, the 1st day of September, 1982 and the 1st day of November, 1982, notwithstanding the provisions of section 11 of the Principal Act (as amended by this Act), tax shall, in relation to the supply of a qualifying service, be, and be deemed to have been, chargeable, at the rate of **15 per cent**.

PART VI
Miscellaneous

104 Care and management of taxes and duties

All taxes and duties imposed by this Act are hereby placed under the care and management of the Revenue Commissioners.

105 Short title, construction and commencement

(1) This Act may be cited as the Finance Act, 1982.

...

(4) *Part III* of this Act shall be construed together with the Value Added Tax Acts, 1972 to 1981, and may be cited together therewith as the Value -Added Tax Acts, 1972 to 1982.

...

(8) *Part III* of this Act shall, save as is otherwise expressly provided therein, come into force as on and from the 1st day of September, 1982.

(9) Any reference in this Act to any other enactment shall, except so far as the context otherwise requires, be construed as a reference to that enactment as amended by or under any other enactment including this Act.

FINANCE ACT 1983

(Number 15 of 1983)

ARRANGEMENT OF SECTIONS

An Act to charge and impose certain duties of customs and inland revenue (including excise), to amend the law relating to customs and inland revenue (including excise) and to make further provisions in connection with finance. [8th June, 1983]

PART I
Income tax, income levy, corporation tax and capital gains tax

CHAPTER IV
Anti-avoidance and anti-evasion

22 Obligation to show tax reference number on receipts, etc

(1) In this section —

"business" means —

    (*a*)   a profession, or

    (*b*)   a trade consisting solely of the supply (which word has in this paragraph the same meaning as in the Value-Added Tax Acts, 1972 to 1983) of a service and includes, in the case of a trade part of which consists of the supply of a service, that part, and also includes, in the case of a trade the whole or part of which consists of the supply of a service which incorporates the supply of goods in the course of the supply of that service, that trade or that part, as the case may be;

"specified person", in relation to a business, means —

    (*a*)   in case the business is carried on by an individual, that individual, and

    (*b*)   in case the business is carried on by a partnership, the precedent partner;

"tax reference number", in relation to a specified person, means each of the following:

    (*a*)   the Revenue and Social Insurance (RSI) Number stated on any certificate of tax-free allowances issued to that person by an inspector, not being a certificate issued to an employer in respect of an employee of that employer,

    (*b*)   the reference number stated on any return of income form or notice of assessment issued to that person by an inspector, and

    (*c*)   the registration number of that person for the purposes of value-added tax.

(2) The specified person in relation to a business shall ensure that his tax reference number or, if he has more than one tax reference number, one of his tax reference numbers or, if he has not got a tax reference number, his full names and his address is or are stated on any document (being an invoice, credit note, debit note, receipt, account, statement of account, voucher or estimate relating to an amount of £5 or more) issued on or after the 1st day of September, 1983, in the course of that business.

(3) ...

Cross-references
Collective investment undertakings (returns by intermediaries) , tax reference number, definition applied: FA 1989 s 19(1).
Definition
"inspector": CGTA 1975 s 2(1), ITA 1967 ss 1(1), 161; "profession": ITA 1967 s 1(1); "trade": ITA 1967 s 1(1).
Notes
Subs (3) inserted a reference to this section in ITA 1967 Sch 15 col 3 (penalties).

---

23 Publication of names of tax defaulters

(1) In this section **"the Acts"** means —

    (*a*)   the Tax Acts,

    (*b*)   the Capital Gains Tax Acts,

    (*c*)   the Value-Added Tax Act, 1972, and the enactments amending or extending that Act,

    (*d*)   the Capital Acquisitions Tax Act, 1976, and the enactments amending or extending that Act,

    (*e*)   the statutes relating to stamp duty and to the management of that duty, and

    (*f*)   Part VI,

and any instruments made thereunder.

(2) The Revenue Commissioners shall, as respects each year [or any part of a year as they see fit][1] (being the year 1984 or a subsequent year), compile a list of the names and addresses and the occupations or descriptions of every person —

    (*a*)   upon whom a fine or other penalty was imposed by a court under any of the Acts during that year,

    (*b*)   upon whom a fine or other penalty was otherwise imposed by a court during that year in respect of an act or omission by the person in relation to tax, or

    (*c*)   in whose case the Revenue Commissioners, pursuant to an agreement made with the person in that year, refrained from initiating proceedings for recovery of any fine or penalty of the kind mentioned in paragraphs (*a*) and (*b*) and, in lieu of initiating such proceedings, accepted, or undertook to accept, a specified sum of money in settlement of any claim by the Revenue Commissioners in respect of any specified liability of the person under any of the Acts for —

        (i)   payment of any tax,

        (ii)   payment of interest thereon, and

(iii)   a fine or other monetary penalty in respect thereof.

(3) Notwithstanding any obligation as to secrecy imposed on them by the Acts or the Official Secrets Act, 1963 —

(*a*)   the Revenue Commissioners shall include in their annual report to the Minister for Finance, commencing with the report for the year 1984, the list [or lists]² referred to in subsection (2) for the year in respect of which the report is made, and

(*b*)   the Revenue Commissioners may, at any time, cause any such list as is referred to in subsection (2) to be published in *Iris Oifigiúil.*

(4) Paragraph (*c*) of subsection (2) does not apply in relation to a person in whose case —

(*a*)   the Revenue Commissioners are satisfied that, before any investigation or inquiry had been commenced by them or by any of their officers into any matter occasioning a liability referred to in the said paragraph of the person, the person had voluntarily furnished to them complete information in relation to and full particulars of the said matter, or

[(*aa*)   the provisions of section 72 of the Finance Act, 1988, or section 3 of the Waiver of Certain Tax, Interest and Penalties Act, 1993, apply, or]³

(*b*)   the specified sum referred to in the said paragraph (*c*) does not exceed £10,000 or was paid on or before the 31st day of December, 1983.

(5) Any such list as is referred to in subsection (2) shall specify in respect of each person named in the list such particulars as the Revenue Commissioners think fit —

(*a*)   of the matter occasioning the fine or penalty of the kind referred to in subsection (2) imposed on the person or, as the case may be, the liability of that kind to which the person was subject, and

(*b*)   of any interest, fine or other monetary penalty, and of any other penalty or sanction, to which that person was liable, or which was imposed on him by a court, and which was occasioned by the said matter.

(6) In this section **"tax"** means income tax, capital gains tax, corporation tax, value-added tax, gift tax, inheritance tax, residential property tax and stamp duty.

Amendments
1   Inserted by FA 1992 s 240(*a*) for 1992 and later years.
2   Inserted by FA 1992 s 240(*b*) for 1992 and later years.
3   Subs (4)(*aa*) substituted by WCTIPA 1993 s 3(7); originally inserted by FA 1988 s 72(7).
Definition
"statute": IA 1937 s 3; ITA 1967 s 1(1); "the Tax Acts": CTA 1976 s 155(2).

PART III
Value added tax

77 Interpretation (Part III)

In this Part—

"the Principal Act" means the Value Added Tax Act, 1972;

"the Act of 1976" means the Finance Act, 1976;

"the Act of 1978" means the Value Added Tax (Amendment) Act, 1978;

"the Act of 1981" means the Finance (No 2) Act, 1981;

"the act of 1982" means the Finance Act, 1982.

78 Amendment of section 3 (delivery of goods) of Principal Act

---

Notes
This section, by inserting VATA 1972 s 3(7), provided that the disposal of business assets by a liquidator or receiver in the course of winding up the business, is taxable.

---

79 Amendment of section 8 (accountable persons) of Principal Act

Notes
This amendment, which reduced the VAT registration limits, has been superseded.

80 Amendment of section 9 (registration) of Principal Act

Notes
Para (*a*), by amending VATA 1972 s 9(1), and para (*b*), by inserting VATA 1972 s 9(2A), provided that liquidators, receivers etc who dispose of taxable goods in the course of winding up a business, must register for VAT.

81 Amendment of section 11 (rates of tax) of Principal Act

Notes
This section increased the effective 3% rate to 5%, the 18% rate to 23% ,and the 30% rate to 35%, with effect from 1 March 1983. Fuels for home heat etc, previously liable at 0% became taxed at 5%.

82 Amendment of section 12A (special provisions for tax invoiced by flat-rate farmers) of Principal Act

Notes
This section increased the farmers flat rate VAT compensation from 1.8% to 2.3% with effect from 1 March 1983.

83 Amendment of section 15 (charge of tax on imported goods) of Principal Act

Notes
This amendment provided that heating fuels, liable at 5% with effect from 1 March 1983, would be liable at 5% at importation.

84 Amendment of section 19 (tax due and payable) of Principal Act

Notes
This section, by substituting VATA 1972 s 19(3), provides that when a liquidator disposes of taxable goods in the course of winding up a business, he must make the necessary VAT returns, and pay any tax arising on the disposal of the goods by the due date.

85 Amendment of section 25 (appeals) of Principal Act

Notes
This section substituted VATA 1972 s 25(2)(*f*), (*ff*) and (*k*). The changes correspond to the income tax changes made by FA 1983 s 9, which were intended to prevent the appeal procedure being used to delay payment of tax.

86 Amendment of Second Schedule to Principal Act

Notes
This section removed heating fuels that were made taxable at 5% with effect from 1 March 1983 (s 81) from the list of zero rated goods.

87 Amendment of Third Schedule to Principal Act

Notes
This amendment has been superseded.

88 Insertion of Sixth Schedule to Principal Act

Notes
This section inserted VATA 1972 Sch 6, listing goods liable at the new 5% rate. The change has since been superseded.

89 Relief for hotels etc

(1)   (*a*)   In this section **"qualifying service"** means a service consisting of the supply, for the benefit of persons not resident in the State, under an agreement made before the 1st day of January, 1983, of sleeping accommodation, with or without board, or of motor cars upon hire, boats upon hire or entertainment, at

charges fixed at the time of the making of the agreement, to persons carrying on the business of travel agent, tour operator or the hiring out of motor cars or boats.

(*b*)   In respect of the taxable periods commencing on the 1st day of March, 1983, the 1st day of May, 1983, the 1st day of July, 1983, the 1st day of September, 1983 and the 1st day of November, 1983, notwithstanding the provisions of section 11 of the Principal Act (as amended by this Act), tax shall, in relation to the supply of a qualifying service, be, and be deemed to have been, chargeable at the rate of 18 per cent.

(2) Notwithstanding the provisions of section 11 of the Principal Act (as amended by this Act), the rate of tax chargeable in relation to the letting of immovable goods specified in paragraph (iv)(*b*) of the First Schedule to the Principal Act shall be **18 per cent**.

PART V
Revenue offences

94 Revenue offences

(1) In this Part —

"the Acts" means —

(*a*)   the Customs Acts,

(*b*)   the statutes relating to the duties of excise and to the management of those duties,

(*c*)   the Tax Acts,

(*d*)   the Capital Gains Tax Acts,

(*e*)   the Value-Added Tax Act, 1972, and the enactments amending or extending that Act,

(*f*)   the Capital Acquisitions Tax Act, 1976, and the enactments amending or extending that Act,

(*g*)   the statutes relating to stamp duty and to the management of that duty, and

(*h*)   Part VI,

and any instruments made thereunder and any instruments made under any other enactment and relating to tax;

[**"an authorised officer"** means an officer of the Revenue Commissioners authorised by them in writing to exercise any of the powers conferred by the Acts;][1]

"tax" means any tax, duty, levy or charge under the care and management of the Revenue Commissioners.

(2) A person shall, without prejudice to any other penalty to which he may be liable, be guilty of an offence under this section if, after the date of the passing of this Act, he —

(*a*)   knowingly or wilfully delivers any incorrect return, statement or accounts or knowingly or wilfully furnishes any incorrect information in connection with any tax,

(*b*)   knowingly aids, abets, assists, incites or induces another person to make or deliver knowingly or wilfully any incorrect return, statement or accounts in connection with any tax,

(*c*)   claims or obtains relief or exemption from, or repayment of, any tax, being a relief, exemption or repayment to which, to his knowledge, he is not entitled,

(*d*)   knowingly or wilfully issues or produces any incorrect invoice, receipt, instrument or other document in connection with any tax,

[(*dd*)   (i)   fails to make any deduction required to be made by him under section 32(1) of the Finance Act, 1986,

      (ii)   fails, having made the deduction, to pay the sum deducted to the Collector-General within the time specified in that behalf in section 33(3) of that Act, or

      (iii) fails to pay to the Collector-General an amount on account of appropriate tax (within the meaning of Chapter IV of Part I of that Act) within the time specified in that behalf in section 33(4) of that Act,][2]

[(*ddd*) (i)   fails to make any deduction required to be made by him under section 18(5) of the Finance Act, 1989, or

      (ii) fails, having made the deduction, to pay the sum deducted to the Collector-General within the time specified in paragraph 1(3) of the First Schedule to that Act][2],

  (*e*) knowingly or wilfully fails to comply with any provision of the Acts requiring —

      (i)   the furnishing of a return of income, profits or gains, or of sources of income, profits or gains, for the purposes of any tax,

      (ii) the furnishing of any other return, certificate, notification, particulars, or any statement or evidence, for the purposes of any tax,

      (iii) the keeping or retention of books, records, accounts or other documents for the purposes of any tax, or

      (iv) the production of books, records, accounts or other documents, when so requested, for the purposes of any tax,

[(*ee*) knowingly or wilfully, and within the time limits specified for their retention, destroys, defaces, or conceals from an authorised officer—

      (i)   any documents, or

      (ii) any other written or printed material in any form, including any information stored, maintained or preserved by means of any mechanical or electronic device, whether or not stored, maintained or preserved in a legible form, which a person is obliged by any provision of the Acts to keep, to issue or to produce for inspection,][4]

  (*f*) fails to remit any income tax payable pursuant to Chapter IV of Part V of the Income Tax Act, 1967, and the regulations thereunder, or section 7 of the Finance Act, 1968, and the said regulations, or value-added tax within the time specified in that behalf in relation to income tax or value-added tax, as the case may be, by the Acts, or

  (*g*) obstructs or interferes with any officer of the Revenue Commissioners, or any other person, in the exercise or performance of powers or duties under the Acts for the purposes of any tax.

(3) A person guilty of an offence under this section shall be liable —

  [(*a*) on summary conviction to a fine of £1,000 which may be mitigated to not less than one fourth part thereof or, at the discretion of the court, to imprisonment for a term not exceeding 12 months or to both the fine and the imprisonment, or][5]

  (*b*) on conviction on indictment, to a fine not exceeding £10,000 or, at the discretion of the court, to imprisonment for a term not exceeding 5 years or to both the fine and the imprisonment.

(4) Section 13 of the Criminal Procedure Act, 1967, shall apply in relation to an offence under this section as if, in lieu of the penalties specified in subsection (3) of the said section 13, there were specified therein the penalties provided for by subsection (3) (*a*) of this section, and the reference in subsection (2)(*a*) of the said section 13 to the penalties provided for in the said subsection (3) shall be construed and have effect accordingly.

(5) Where an offence under this section is committed by a body corporate and the offence is shown to have been committed with the consent or connivance of any person who,

when the offence was committed, was a director, manager, secretary or other officer of the body corporate, or a member of the committee of management or other controlling authority of the body corporate, that person shall also be deemed to be guilty of the offence and may be proceeded against and punished accordingly.

(6) In any proceedings under this section, a return or statement delivered to an inspector or other officer of the Revenue Commissioners under any provision of the Acts and purporting to be signed by any person shall be deemed, until the contrary is proved, to have been so delivered, and to have been signed, by that person.

(7) Notwithstanding the provisions of any other enactment, proceedings in respect of an offence under this section may be instituted within 10 years from the date of the commission of the offence or incurring of the penalty (as the case may be).

(8) Section 1 of the Probation of Offenders Act, 1907, shall not apply in relation to offences under this section.

(9) The provisions of section 128(4), 500(4), 501(3), 502(3), 506 and 507 of the Income Tax Act, 1967, and sections 26(6) and 27(7) of the Value-Added Tax Act, 1972, shall, with any necessary modifications, apply for the purposes of this section as they apply for the purposes of those provisions, including, in the case of such of those provisions as were applied by the Capital Gains Tax Act, 1975, the Corporation Tax Act, 1976, or Part VI, the purposes of those provisions as so applied.

Amendments
1 Definition inserted by FA 1992 s 243(a)(i).
2 Subs (2)(dd) inserted by FA 1986 s 40(2).
3 Subs (2)(ddd) inserted by FA 1989 Sch 1 para 3(2).
4 Subs (2)(ee) inserted by FA 1992 s 243(a)(ii).
5 Subs (3)(a) substituted by FA 1992 s 243(b).

Case law
Meaning of "criminal matter": *Director of Public Prosecutions v Seamus Boyle*, IV ITR 395.
Subs (2)(e): District Justice not entitled to conclude, on basis of Revenue certificate, that taxpayer had "knowingly and wilfully" failed to submit return of income; taxpayer not present at District Court hearing and was entitled to defend himself: IV ITR 478.

Cross-references
Collective investment undertakings, failure to deduct tax from payment to unit holder: FA 1989 s 18(5).
Self-assessment, notice of attachment, incorrect debtor's return treated (in cases of fraud or negligence) as a Revenue offence: FA 1988 s 73(5); failure to make debtor's return not a Revenue offence: FA 1988 s 73(9).
Subss (4), (6), (7), (8): tax amnesty, penalties applied by: WCTIPA 1993 s 9(2); false statement to obtain allowance: WCTIPA 1993 s 11(3).

Definition
"inspector": CGTA 1975 s 2(1), ITA 1967 ss 1(1), 161; "month": IA 1937 Sch; "profits": CTA 1976 s 1(5)(c); "statute": IA 1937 s 3; ITA 1967 s 1(1); "the Tax Acts": CTA 1976 s 155(2).

PART VII
Miscellaneous

121 Care and management of taxes and duties

All taxes and duties imposed by this Act (apart from income levy collected by health boards) are hereby placed under the care and management of the Revenue Commissioners.

122 Short title, construction and commencement

(1) This Act may be cited as the Finance Act, 1983.

...

(4) Part III and (so far as relating to value added tax) *Parts I* and *V* shall be construed together with the Value Added Tax Acts, 1972 to 1982, and maybe cited therewith as the Value Added Tax Acts, 1972 to 1983.

...

(7) Part III (other than sections 77 to 80, 81(1), 82, 84 and 85) shall be deemed to have come into force and shall take effect as on and from the 1st day of May, 1983, and the said sections 77, 81(1) and 82 shall be deemed to have come into force and shall take effect as on and from the 1st day of March, 1983, and the said sections 78, 80, and 84 shall come into force and shall take effect as on and from the 1st day of September, 1983.

(8) Any reference in this Act to any other enactment shall, unless the context otherwise requires, be construed as a reference to that enactment as amended by or under any other enactment including this Act.

(9) In this Act, a reference to a Part, section or schedule is to a Part or section of, or schedule to, this Act, unless it is indicated that reference to some other enactment is intended.

(10) In this Act, a reference to a subsection, paragraph or sub-paragraph is to the subsection, paragraph or subparagraph of the provision (including a schedule) in which the reference occurs, unless it is indicated that reference to some other provision is intended.

FINANCE ACT 1984

(Number 9 of 1984)

ARRANGEMENT OF SECTIONS

PART III
Value added tax

An Act to charge and impose certain duties of customs and inland revenue (including excise), to amend the law relating to customs and inland revenue (including excise) and to make further provisions in connection with finance. [23rd May 1984]

PART III
Value added tax

84 Interpretation (Part III)

In this Part—

"the Act of 1976" means the Finance Act, 1976;

"the Act of 1983" means the Finance Act, 1983;

"the Principal Act" means the Value Added Tax Act, 1972.

85 Amendment of section 1 (interpretation) of Principal Act

Notes
This section inserted definitions of "clothing" and "footwear" in VATA 1972 s 1(1).

86 Amendment of section 8 (Accountable persons) of Principal Act

Notes
Para (*a*) amended VATA 1972 s 8(1) and para (*c*) inserted VATA 1972 s 8(3B), an anti avoidance provision to counteract "turnover splitting" between controlled businesses. Other changes have since been superseded.

87 Amendment of section 11 (rates of tax) of Principal Act

Notes
This section introduced VAT on adult clothes at 8% with effect from 1 May 1984.

88 Amendment of section 15 (charge of tax on imported goods) of Principal Act

Notes
This section introduced VAT on imported adult clothes at 8% with effect from 1 May 1984.

89 Amendment of section 18 (inspection and removal of records) of Principal Act

Notes
This section substituted VATA 1972 s 18(1) and deleted VATA 1972 s 18(2).

90 Amendment of section 26 (penalties generally) of Principal Act

Notes
This section amended VATA 1972 s 26(1) and (3A), providing revised penalties in relation to the new powers for authorised officers.

91 Amendment of section 32 (regulations) of Principal Act

Notes
This section inserted VATA 1972 s 32(1)(w) (power to make regulations determining the average build of a child of 10 years of age: the cut-off age for children's clothes, which are still liable at 0%).

92 Amendment of Second Schedule to Principal Act

Notes
This section removed adult clothing (other than sanitary towels, tampons etc) from the list of goods liable at 0%, with effect from 1 May 1984.

93 Amendment of Third Schedule to Principal Act

Notes
This section removed concrete from the list of goods liable at 23% (to be liable at 5%). The hire of clothes remained liable at 23%.

94 Amendment of Sixth Schedule to Principal Act

Notes
This section included concrete, and live theatrical and musical performances in the list of goods/services liable at 5%.

95 Insertion of Seventh Schedule to Principal Act

Notes
This inserted VATA 1972 Sch 7 (since deleted) listing adult clothes as liable at 8%.

96 Rate of tax in relation to short-term hiring of certain goods

Notwithstanding the provisions of section 11 of the Principal Act, the rate of value added tax chargeable on the following services shall be **18 per cent** of the amount in respect of which tax is chargeable in relation to those services:

(*a*) the service specified in paragraph (ii) of Part II of the Third Schedule to the Principal Act, and

(*b*) the service consisting of the hiring to a person, under an agreement of the kind specified in the said paragraph (ii) of a tent or of a vehicle designed and constructed, or adapted , for the conveyance of persons by road.

PART VI
Miscellaneous

115 Care and management of taxes and duties

All taxes and duties imposed by this Act are hereby placed under the care and management of the Revenue Commissioners.

116 Short title, construction and commencement

(1) This Act may be cited as the Finance Act, 1984.

...

(4) *Part III* shall be construed together with the Value Added Tax Acts, 1972 to 1983, and maybe cited therewith as the Value Added Tax Acts, 1972 to 1984.

...

(8) *Part III* other than sections 84, 86, 89, 90, 93(*a*)(i), 94 and 96 shall be deemed to have come into force and shall take effect as on and from the 1st day of May, 1984, and the said sections 84, 93(*a*)(i), 94 and 96 shall be deemed to have come into force and shall take effect as on and from the 1st day of March, 1984.

(9) Any reference in this Act to any other enactment shall, unless the context otherwise requires, be construed as a reference to that enactment as amended by or under any other enactment including this Act.

(10) In this Act, a reference to a Part, section or schedule is to a Part or section of, or schedule to, this Act, unless it is indicated that reference to some other enactment is intended.

(11) In this Act, a reference to a subsection, paragraph or sub-paragraph is to the subsection, paragraph or subparagraph of the provision (including a Schedule) in which the reference occurs, unless it is indicated that reference to some other provision is intended.

FINANCE ACT 1985

(Number 10 of 1985)

ARRANGEMENT OF SECTIONS

PART III
Value added tax

Section

PART VI
Miscellaneous

An Act to charge and impose certain duties of customs and inland revenue (including excise), to amend the law relating to customs and inland revenue (including excise) and to make further provisions in connection with finance. [30th May 1985]

41　Interpretation (Part III)

In this Part—

"the Principal Act" means the Value Added Tax Act, 1972;

"the Act of 1976" means the Finance Act, 1976;

"the Act of 1978" means the Value Added Tax (Amendment) Act, 1978;

"the Act of 1983" means the Finance Act, 1983;

"the Act of 1984" means the Finance Act, 1984.

42　Amendment of section 5 (rendering of services) of Principal Act

---

Notes
This section implemented the Tenth Directive 84/386/EEC (place of hire of movable goods) in Irish VAT law. The change as since been superseded.

43　Amendment of section 11 (rates of tax) of Principal Act

Notes
With effect from 1 March 1985, this section abolished the 5%, 8%, 18% and 35% VAT rates, replacing them with 10% and 25%. Goods and services, the supply of which was liable at 5% (other than live theatre etc) or 8% became taxed at 10%, and goods and services the supply of which was liable at 23% or 35% became taxed a t 25%. Concrete blocks and newspapers (previously liable at 23%) became taxed at 10%. Adult footwear, previously liable at 0%, became taxed at 10%. Section 54 below provided a two month deferment of the 5% increase on houses under construction.
A new 2.2% rate was introduced for livestock.

44　Amendment of section 12A (special provisions for tax invoiced by flat-rate farmers) of Principal Act

---

Notes
This section provided a 2.2% flat rate compensation for unregistered farmers, with effect from 1 March 1985.

---

45 Amendment of section 13 (remission of tax on goods exported etc) of Principal Act

Notes
This section amended VATA 1972 s 13(3)(c), dealing with repayment of tax to traders not established in the State, implementing the Tenth Directive (place of hire of movable goods).

46 Amendment of section 15 (charge of tax on imported goods) of Principal Act

Notes
This amendment provided that VAT would be charged at import on goods at the new VAT rates of 2.2%, 10% and 25% introduced by s 43.

47 Amendment of section 23 (determination of tax due) of Principal Act

Notes
This section amended VATA 1972 s 23(1) and VATA 1972 s 23(2)(a) to transfer the power to make VAT estimates from the Revenue Commissioners to inspectors of taxes and other authorised Revenue officers.

48 Amendment of section 32 (regulations) of Principal Act

Notes
This section inserted VATA 1972 s 32(1)(ww) and amended VATA 1972 s 32(2A), enabling the Revenue Commissioners to make regulations determining the average foot size of a child of 10 years of age (the cut off age for children's shoes: liable at 0%).

49 Amendment of First Schedule to Principal Act

Notes
This section inserted VATA 1972 Sch 1 para (viii) to exempt live theatre and music performances, previously liable at 5%.

50 Amendment of Second Schedule to Principal Act

Notes
This section substituted VATA 1972 Sch 2 paras (xii) and (xix) to remove adult shoes from the list of goods liable to VAT at the 0% rate.

51 Miscellaneous amendments (Third, Sixth and Seventh Schedules) to the Principal Act

Notes
This section deleted VATA 1972 Sch 3 (23% rate goods and services) and Sch 7 (8% rate goods: adult clothes) and substituted VATA 1972 Sch 6 (new list of goods liable at 10%).

52 Amendment of Fourth Schedule to Principal Act

Notes
This section inserted VATA 1972 Sch 4 para (ia) (hire of movable goods), implementing the terms of the Tenth Directive 84/386/EEC in the State.

53 Repeals

Section 89(2) of the Act of 1983 and section 92 of the Act of 1984 are hereby repealed.

54 Deferment of increase in rate of tax (private dwellings)

(1) For the purposes of this section-

"dwelling" means a house, or an apartment, flat, penthouse or similar unit of accommodation;

"qualifying supply" means the supply on or before the 30th day of April, 1985, to a person, being an individual acting on his own behalf, of a service consisting of the development of immovable goods, being the construction of a dwelling designed for the private use of, and occupation by , such person, and includes a supply of immovable goods to that person on or before the said date in connection with the supply of the said service.

(2) In this section reference to the construction of a dwelling does not include reference to the conversion, reconstruction, alteration or enlargement of any existing building or buildings.

(3) In respect of the taxable period commencing on the 1st day of March, 1985, notwithstanding the provisions of section 11 of the Principal Act (as amended by this Act), value added tax shall, in relation to a qualifying supply, be, and be deemed to have been, chargeable, at the rate of **5 per cent**.

PART VI
Miscellaneous

70 Care and management of taxes and duties

All taxes and duties imposed by this Act are hereby placed under the care and management of the Revenue Commissioners.

71 Short title, construction and commencement

(1) This Act may be cited as the Finance Act, 1985.

...

(4) *Part III* shall be construed together with the Value Added Tax Acts, 1972 to 1984, and maybe cited therewith as the Value Added Tax Acts, 1972 to 1985.

...

(8) *Part III* (other than sections 42, 45, 47 and 52) shall be deemed to have come into force and shall take effect as on and from the 1st day of May, 1985.

(9) Any reference in this Act to any other enactment shall, unless the context otherwise requires, be construed as a reference to that enactment as amended by or under any other enactment including this Act.

(10) In this Act, a reference to a Part, section or schedule is to a Part or section of, or schedule to, this Act, unless it is indicated that reference to some other enactment is intended.

(11) In this Act, a reference to a subsection, paragraph or sub-paragraph is to the subsection, paragraph or subparagraph of the provision (including a Schedule) in which the reference occurs, unless it is indicated that reference to some other provision is intended.

FINANCE ACT 1986

(Number 13 of 1986)

ARRANGEMENT OF SECTIONS

PART III
Value added tax

Section

PART VI
Miscellaneous

An Act to charge and impose certain duties of customs and inland revenue (including excise), to amend the law relating to customs and inland revenue (including excise) and to make further provisions in connection with finance.   [27th May, 1986]

PART III
Value added tax

79 Interpretation (Part III)

In this Part—

"the Principal Act" means the Value Added Tax Act, 1972;

"the Act of 1978" means the Value Added Tax (Amendment) Act, 1978;

"the Act of 1985" means the Finance Act, 1985.

80 Amendment of section 1 (interpretation) of Principal Act

Notes
This section inserted definition of "free port" in VATA 1972 s 1(1).

---

81 Amendment of section 5 (rendering of services) of Principal Act

---

Notes
Para (*a*) inserted VATA 1972 s 5(3A). Para (*b*) (i) inserted VATA 1972 s 5(6)(*d*) and para (*b*)(ii) substituted VATA 1972 s 5(6)(*e*). The changes dealt with the place of supply of services received from abroad.

---

82 Amendment of section 8 (accountable persons) of Principal Act

---

Notes
This amendment dealt with the accountability for tax of persons in receipt of services from abroad.

---

83 Amendment of section 11 (rates of tax) of Principal Act

Notes
Para (*a*) increased the livestock rate from 2.2% to 2.4% and the standard rate from 23% to 25% with effect from 1 March 1986.

---

84 Amendment of section 12 (deduction for tax borne or paid) of Principal Act

Notes
This section inserted VATA 1972 12(1)(*dd*) to allow a purchases VAT deduction for taxable persons in respect of certain services received from abroad.

85 Amendment of section 12A (special provisions for tax invoiced by flat-rate farmers) of Principal Act

Notes
This section increased the flat rate deduction for unregistered farmers from 2.2% to 2.4% with effect from 1 March 1986.

86 Amendment of section 17 (invoices) of Principal Act

Notes
This section inserted VATA 1972 s 17(1A) to provide for electronic invoicing.

87 Amendment of section 20 (refund of tax) of Principal Act

Notes
This section by inserting VATA 1972 s 20(1A), provides the Revenue Commissioners with power to defer repayment in certain circumstances.

88 Amendment of section 32 (regulations) of Principal Act

Notes
Para (*a*) amended VATA 1972 s 32(1)(*h*) and para (*b*) substituted VATA 1972 s 32(1)(*i*). The changes allow the Revenue to make regulations regarding electronic invoicing.

89 Amendment of First Schedule to Principal Act

Notes
This section inserted VATA 1972 Sch 1 para (iiia), exempting the services (and related goods) supplied by dental technicians.

90 Amendment of Second Schedule to Principal Act

Notes
This section provided that sales within a free port would be liable at 0%, and removed take away food from list of goods liable at 0%.

91 Amendment of Sixth Schedule to Principal Act

Notes
This section included catering services, hot take away food, cinema admissions, repair of movable goods, and body care services in the list of goods and services liable at 10%, and provided a revised definition of "newspapers".

PART VI
Miscellaneous

113 Use of electronic data processing

(1) In this section —

"the Acts" means

    (*a*)   the Tax Acts,

    (*b*)   the Capital Gains Tax Acts,

    [(*c*)   the Value-Added Tax Act, 1972,][1]

    (*d*)   the Capital Acquisitions Tax Act, 1976, and the enactments amending or extending that Act, and

    (*e*)   Part VI of the Finance Act, 1983,

and any instruments made thereunder;

"records" means documents which a person is obliged by any provision of the Acts to keep, to issue or to produce for inspection, and any other written or printed material;

"tax" means income tax, corporation tax, capital gains tax, value added tax or residential property tax, as the case may be.

(2) Subject to the agreement of the Revenue Commissioners, records may be stored, maintained, transmitted, reproduced or communicated, as the case may be, by any electronic, photographic or other process approved of by the Revenue Commissioners, and in circumstances where the use of such process has been agreed by them and subject to such conditions as they may impose.

(3) Where, in pursuance of subsection (2), records are preserved by electronic, photographic or other process, a statement contained in a document produced by any such process shall, subject to the rules of court, be admissible in evidence in any proceedings, whether civil or criminal, to the same extent as the records themselves.

(4) Notwithstanding anything in the Tax Acts, duplicates of assessments need not be made, transmitted or delivered.

(5) The entering by an inspector or other authorised officer of details of an assessment and the tax charged therein in an electronic, photographic or other record from which the Collector-General may extract such details by electronic, photographic or other process shall constitute transmission of such details by the inspector or other authorised officer to the Collector-General.

(6) In any proceedings in the Circuit Court, the District Court or the High Court for or in relation to the recovery of any tax, a certificate signed by the Collector-General or other authorised officer certifying that, before the institution of proceedings, a stated sum of tax as so transmitted became due and payable by the defendant —

> (*a*)　(i)　under an assessment which had become final and conclusive,
>
> 　　　(ii)　under the provisions of section 429(4) (inserted by the Finance Act, 1971) of the Income Tax Act, 1967, or
>
> 　　　(iii)　under the provisions relating to the specified amount of tax within the meaning of section 30 of the Finance Act, 1976,
>
> 　　and
>
> (*b*)　that demand for the payment of the tax has been duly made,

shall be *prima facie* evidence, until the contrary has been proved, of those facts and a certificate certifying as aforesaid and purporting to be signed by the Collector-General or other authorised officer may be tendered in evidence without proof and shall be deemed, until the contrary is proved, to have been signed by the Collector-General or other authorised officer.

Amendments
1　Subs (1)(*c*) substituted by FA 1993 s 99.

Definition
"the Circuit Court": IA 1937 Sch; "District Court": IA 1937 Sch; "the High Court": IA 1937 Sch; "inspector": CGTA 1975 s 2(1), ITA 1967 ss 1(1), 161; "person": IA 1937 s 11(*c*); "rules of court": IA 1937 Sch; "the Tax Acts": CTA 1976 s 155(2).

114 Amendment of provisions relating to payment of interest on tax overpaid

---

Notes
This section, by amending ITA 1967 s 429(4)(proviso)(*a*), reduced the general rate of interest chargeable on unpaid tax from 1.25 per cent per month (or part of a month) to 1 per cent; it also inserted ITA 1967 s 429(6) to provide that the Minister for Finance may change, by ministerial order, the rate of interest chargeable on outstanding tax.

---

115 Liability to tax etc, of holder of fixed charge on book debts of company

[(1) Subject to the other provisions of this section, where a person holds a fixed charge (being a fixed charge which is created on or after the passing of this Act) on the book debts of a company (within the meaning of the Companies Act, 1963), such person shall, if the company fails to pay any relevant amount for which it is liable, become liable to pay such relevant amount on due demand, and on neglect or refusal of payment may be proceeded against in like manner as any other defaulter:

Provided that—

    (*a*) this section shall not apply—

        (i) unless the holder of the fixed charge has been notified in writing by the Revenue Commissioners that a company has failed to pay a relevant amount for which it is liable and that, by reason of this section, the holder of the fixed charge—

            (I) may become liable for payment of any relevant amount which the company subsequently fails to pay, and

            (II) where subparagraph (iii) does not apply, has become liable for the payment of the relevant amount that the company has failed to pay,

        (ii) to any amounts received by the holder of the fixed charge from the company before the date on which the holder is notified in writing by the Revenue Commissioners in accordance with subparagraph (i), and

        (iii) where, within 21 days of the passing of the Finance Act, 1995, or of the creation of the fixed charge, whichever is the later, the holder of the fixed charge furnishes to the Revenue Commissioners a copy of the prescribed particulars of the charge delivered or to be delivered to the registrar of companies in accordance with the provisions of section 99 of the Companies Act, 1963, to any relevant amount which the company was liable to pay before the date on which the holder is notified in writing by the Revenue Commissioners in accordance with subparagraph (i),

        and

    (*b*) the amount or aggregate amount which the person shall be liable to pay in relation to a company in accordance with this section shall not exceed the amount or aggregate amount which that person has, while the fixed charge on book debts in relation to the said company is in existence, received, directly or indirectly, from that company in payment or in part payment of any debts due by the company to that person.

(1A) The Revenue Commissioners may, at any time and by notice in writing given to the holder of the fixed charge, withdraw, with effect from a date specified in the notice, a notification issued by them in accordance with the provisions of subsection (1):

Provided that such withdrawal shall not—

    (i) affect in any way any liability of the holder of the fixed charge under this section which arose prior to such withdrawal, or

    (ii) preclude the issue under subsection (1) of a subsequent notice to the holder of the fixed charge.

(1B) The Revenue Commissioners may nominate any of their officers to perform any acts and discharge any functions authorised by this section to be performed or discharged by the Revenue Commissioners.][1]

(2) In this section **"relevant amount"** means any amount which the company is liable to remit —

    (*a*) under Chapter IV of Part V of the Income Tax Act, 1967, and

    (*b*) under the Value-Added Tax Act, 1972.

Notes
1 Subs (1) substituted and subs (1A)-(1B) inserted by FA 1995 s 174 with effect from 6 April 1995.

---

117 Care and management of taxes and duties

All taxes and duties imposed by this Act are hereby placed under the care and management of the Revenue Commissioners.

118 Short title, construction and commencement

(1) This Act may be cited as the Finance Act, 1986.

...

(4) *Part III* shall be construed together with the Value Added Tax Acts, 1972 to 1985, and may be cited therewith as the Value Added Tax Acts, 1972 to 1986.

...

(7) *Part VI* ...(so far as relating to value added tax) shall be construed together with the Value Added Tax Acts, 1972 to 1986.

...

(9) In *Part III* sections 79, 83(*a*) and 85 shall be deemed to have come into force and shall take effect as on and from the 1st day of March, 1986, and sections 83(*b*) and 89 to 91 (other than paragraph (*a*) of section 91) shall come into force on the 1st day of July, 1986.

(10) Any reference in this Act to any other enactment shall, unless the context otherwise requires, be construed as a reference to that enactment as amended by or under any other enactment including this Act.

(11) In this Act, a reference to a Part, section or schedule is to a Part or section of, or schedule to, this Act, unless it is indicated that reference to some other enactment is intended.

(12) In this Act, a reference to a subsection, paragraph or sub-paragraph is to the subsection, paragraph or subparagraph of the provision (including a Schedule) in which the reference occurs, unless it is indicated that reference to some other provision is intended.

FINANCE ACT 1987

(Number 10 of 1987)

ARRANGEMENT OF SECTIONS

PART III
Value added tax

PART VI
Miscellaneous

An Act to charge and impose certain duties of customs and inland revenue including excise), to amend the law relating to customs and inland revenue (including excise) and to make further provisions in connection with finance.   *[9th July, 1987]*

38 Interpretation (Part III)

In this Part—

"the Principal Act" means the Value Added Tax Act, 1972;

"the Act of 1978" means the Value Added Tax (Amendment) Act, 1978;

"the Act of 1985" means the Finance Act, 1985;

"the Act of 1986" means the Finance Act, 1986.

39 Amendment of section 1 (interpretation) of Principal Act

Notes
Para (*a*)(i) amended the definition of "livestock" in VATA 1972 s 1(1) to include goats and deer. Para (*a*)(ii) by inserting VATA 1972 s 1(2)(*c*) revised the definition of "moneys received" to include professional withholding tax. Para (*b*) revoked The Imposition of Duties (No 283)(Value Added Tax) Order 1986 (SI 412/1986) which had provided that live deer were liable at 2.4% with effect from 1 January 1987. The order is no longer necessary following the legislative amendment.

---

40 Amendment of section 11 (rates of tax) of Principal Act

Notes
This section reduced the rate on livestock from 2.4% to 1.7% with effect from 1 May 1987.

---

41 Amendment of section 12 (deduction for tax borne or paid) of Principal Act

---

Notes
Para (*a*) substituted VATA 1972 s 12(1) ; para (*b*) amended VATA 1972 s 12(3)(*a*) and para (*c*) by substituting VATA 1972 s 12(4) provided amended rules of apportionment between taxable and exempt activities.

---

42 Amendment of section 12A (special provisions for tax invoiced by flat-rate farmers) of Principal Act

---

Notes
This amendment reduced the farmer flat rate compensation from 2.4% to 1.7% with effect from 1 May 1987.

---

43 Amendment of section 13 (remission of tax on goods exported etc) of Principal Act

---

Notes
This section amended VATA 1972 s 13(3)(*c*) providing amended rules for repayment of tax to foreign traders.

---

44 Amendment of section 32 (regulations) of Principal Act

Notes

This section amended VATA 1972 s 32(2A) to provide that certain regulations cannot be made without the Minister's consent.

45 Amendment of First Schedule to Principal Act

Notes

Para (*a*) substituted VATA 1972 Sch 1 para (i), extending the definition of exempt financial services. Para (*b*)(i) amended VATA 1972 Sch 1 para (ix)(*a*) redefining insurance agency services. Para (*c*)amended VATA 1972 Sch para (xi)(*d*) (insurance services) and para (*d*) removed VATA 1972 Sch 1 para (xia) which had been inserted by the Value Added Tax (Exempted Activities) (No 1) Order 1985 to exempt credit card company services. The exemption is now contained in the revised VATA 1972 Sch 1 para (i).

46 Amendment of Second Schedule to Principal Act

Notes

This section deleted the word "drained" from VATA 1972 Sch 2 para (xii)(*d*)(I); this means that drained fruit qualifies as zero rated food.

47 Amendment of Sixth Schedule to Principal Act

Notes

This section included driving lessons, exhibition admissions, photographic services, tour guide services and waste disposal services in the list of goods and services liable at 10%.

PART VI
Miscellaneous

54 Care and management of taxes and duties

All taxes and duties imposed by this Act are hereby placed under the care and management of the Revenue Commissioners.

55 Short title, construction and commencement

(1) This Act may be cited as the Finance Act, 1987.

...

(4) *Part III* shall be construed together with the Value Added Tax Acts, 1972 to 1986, and maybe cited therewith as the Value Added Tax Acts, 1972 to 1987.

...

(8) In *Part III* sections 40 and 42 shall be deemed to have come into force and shall take effect as on and from the 1st day of May, 1987, section 39(*a*)(ii) shall be deemed to have come into force and shall take effect as on and from the 6th day of June, 1987, sections 46 and 47 shall be deemed to have come into force and shall take effect as on and from the 1st day of July, 1987, and sections 41 and 45 shall come into force on the 1st day of November, 1987.

(9) Any reference in this Act to any other enactment shall, unless the context otherwise requires, be construed as a reference to that enactment as amended by or under any other enactment including this Act.

(10) In this Act, a reference to a Part, section or schedule is to a Part or section of, or schedule to, this Act, unless it is indicated that reference to some other enactment is intended.

(11) In this Act, a reference to a subsection, paragraph or sub-paragraph is to the subsection, paragraph or subparagraph of the provision (including a Schedule) in which the reference occurs, unless it is indicated that reference to some other provision is intended.

FINANCE ACT 1988

(Number 12 of 1988)

ARRANGEMENT OF SECTIONS

PART III
Value added tax

Section

59 Interpretation (Part III)

PART VI
Miscellaneous

76 Care and management of taxes and duties
77 Short title, construction and commencement

An Act to charge and impose certain duties of customs and inland revenue (including excise), to amend the law relating to customs and inland revenue (including excise) and to make further provisions in connection with finance. [25th May, 1988]

PART III
Value added tax

59 Interpretation (Part III)

In this Part **"the Principal Act"** means the Value Added Tax Act, 1972.

60 Amendment of section 1 (interpretation) of Principal Act

Notes
This section, by inserting VATA 1972 s 1(2)(*bb*) in the definition of "moneys received" provided that money not actually received because it has been paid directly to the Revenue on foot of an attachment notice (in respect of a defaulting taxpayer) is deemed to have been received.

---

61 Amendment of section 11 (rates of tax) of Principal Act

Notes
This section introduced a 5% rate on electricity, and reduced the livestock rate from 1.7% to 1.4%, with effect from 1 March 1988.

---

62 Amendment of section 12A (special provisions for tax invoiced by flat-rate farmers) of Principal Act

---

Notes
This section reduced the farmer flat rate compensation from 1.7% to 1.4% with effect from 1 March 1988.

---

63 Amendment of Second Schedule to Principal Act

Notes
This section, by deleting VATA 1972 Sch 2 para (xx)(*a*), excluded electricity from the list of goods and services liable at 0%.

PART VI
Miscellaneous

76 Care and management of taxes and duties

All taxes and duties imposed by this Act are hereby placed under the care and management of the Revenue Commissioners.

77   Short title, construction and commencement

(1) This Act may be cited as the Finance Act, 1988.

...

(4) *Part III* shall be construed together with the Value Added Tax Acts, 1972 to 1987, and maybe cited therewith as the Value Added Tax Acts, 1972 to 1988.

...

(9) *Part III,* other than section 60 shall be deemed to have come into force and shall take effect as on and from the 1st day of March, 1988, and the said section 60 shall take effect as on and from the 1st day of October, 1988.

(10) Any reference in this Act to any other enactment shall, unless the context otherwise requires, be construed as a reference to that enactment as amended by or under any other enactment including this Act.

(11) In this Act, a reference to a Part, section or schedule is to a Part or section of, or schedule to, this Act, unless it is indicated that reference to some other enactment is intended.

(12) In this Act, a reference to a subsection, paragraph or sub-paragraph is to the subsection, paragraph or subparagraph of the provision (including a Schedule) in which the reference occurs, unless it is indicated that reference to some other provision is intended.

FINANCE ACT 1989

(Number 10 of 1989)

ARRANGEMENT OF SECTIONS

PART III
Value added tax

An Act to charge and impose certain duties of customs and inland revenue (including excise), to amend the law relating to customs and inland revenue (including excise) and to make further provisions in connection with finance.   [24th May, 1989]

PART III
Value added tax

53 Interpretation (Part III)

In this Part—

"the Principal Act" means the Value Added Tax Act, 1972;

"the Act of 1978" means the Value Added Tax (Amendment) Act, 1978;

"the Act of 1985" means the Finance Act, 1985;

"the Act of 1988" means the Finance Act, 1988.

54 Amendment of section 5 (supply of services) of Principal Act

Notes
This section inserted VATA 1972 s 5(4B) to reverse the decision in *Bourke v Bradley and Sons*, HC, 28 July 1988, where it was held that barrister's services were provided to the insurance company and not the insured person. The new provision deems the services to have been supplied to, and received by, the insured person.

55 Amendment of section 8 (accountable persons) of Principal Act

Notes
Para (*a*) (i) substituted "£15,000" for "£12,000" in VATA 1972 s 8(3)(*b*).
Para (*a*) (ii) substituted "£32,000" for "£25,000" in VATA 1972 s 8(3)(*c*).
Para (*a*) (iii) substituted "£15,000" for "£12,000" in VATA 1972 s 8(3)(*e*).
Para (*b*) substituted "£15,000" for "£12,000" in VATA 1972 s 8(3A).
Para (*c*) substituted "£15,000" for "£12,000" in VATA 1972 s 8(9).
The net effect of the changes is to increase, with effect from 1 July 1989, the VAT registration limits from £25,000 to £30,000 (for persons whose turnover in the preceding 12 months derives as to 90% or more from the supply of goods) and from £12,000 to £15,000 (for persons whose turnover does not derive as to 90% or more from the supply of goods - service businesses).

56 Amendment of section 11 (rates of tax) of Principal Act

Notes
This section inserted VATA 1972 s 11(1)(*bb*) (new 5% rate on electricity, but not in connection with communication signals) and increased the rate on livestock from 1.4% to 2% with effect from 1 March 1989.

57 Amendment of section 12A (special provisions for tax invoiced by flat-rate farmers) of Principal Act

Notes

This section increased the farmer flat rate compensation from 1.4% to 2% with effect from 1 March 1989.

58 Amendment of section 19 (tax due and payable) of Principal Act

Notes

This section, by inserting VATA 1972 s 19(3)(3)(*aa*), provided that certain traders, authorised by the Collector General would be permitted to submit annual VAT returns.

59 Amendment of section 20 (refund of tax) of Principal Act

Notes

This is a technical amendment to VATA 1972 s 20(3) which enables the Minister for Finance to make Orders that provide for the repayment of VAT (usually to unregistered persons). The current valid orders are included later in this book.

60 Amendment of section 32 (regulations) of Principal Act

Notes

This section amended VATA 1972 s 32(2A), to provide that regulations made by the Revenue Commissioners in relation to heating fuels etc must have the consent of the Minister for Finance.

61 Amendment of First Schedule to Principal Act

Notes

Para (*a*), by inserting VATA 1972 Sch para (i)(*gg*) added the management of a collective investment undertaking to the list of exempted activities, with effect from 1 July 1989. Paras (*b*) and (*c*), by substituting VATA 1972 Sch 1 para (iii) and inserting VATA 1972 Sch 3 para (iii*b*) with effect from 1 November 1989 provide that professional services of an optical nature continue to be exempt, but the supply of spectacles is not exempt. Such a supply becomes liable at 10% (see ss 62 and 63).

62 Amendment of Second Schedule to Principal Act

Notes

This section, by amending VATA 1972 Sch 2 para (xixa)(*b*), removed spectacles from the category of artificial body parts, thus excluding spectacles from being included at the 0% rate, now that the supply of spectacles as part of a professional optician service, is no longer exempt.

63 Amendment of Sixth Schedule to Principal Act

Notes

This amendment includes antiques, art works, and literary manuscripts in the list of goods and services liable at 10%, with effect from 1 July 1989. Corrective spectacles are included in the list of goods and services liable at 10% with effect from 1 November 1989 (no longer exempt: see s 61; not liable at 0%: see s 62).

PART VII
Miscellaneous

92 Tax concessions for disabled drivers

(1) Notwithstanding anything to the contrary contained in any enactment, the Minister for Finance may, after consultation with the Minister for Health and the Minister for the Environment, make regulations providing for—

    (*a*)   the repayment of excise duty and value added tax and the remission of road tax in respect of a motor vehicle used by, and

    (*b*)   the repayment of excise duty relating to hydrocarbon oil used for combustion in the engines of vehicles, to be specified in the regulations, by, a severely and permanently disabled person-

        (i)   as a driver, where the disablement is of such a nature that the person concerned could not drive any vehicle unless it is specially adapted to take account of that disablement, or

(ii)   as a passenger, where the vehicle has been specially constructed or adapted to take account of the passenger's disablement, and where the vehicle is adapted, the cost of such adaptation consists of not less than [20 per cent][1] of the value of the vehicle excluding tax and excise duty, or such lesser percentage in respect of certain cases as may be specified by regulations in respect of the repayment of any tax relating to adaptation costs only.

(2) Regulations under this section shall provide for—

(a)   the criteria for eligibility for the remission of the taxes specified in subsection (1), including such further medical criteria in relation to disabilities as may be considered necessary,

(b)   subject to subsection (3)(b), the procedures to be used in relation the primary medical certification of a disabled person and to appeals against such certification,

(c)   the procedures for certification of vehicles to which the regulations relate,

(d)   the amount of value added tax and excise duty repayable in respect of a vehicle to which the regulations relate,

(e)   the maximum engine size or sizes to which the regulations relate,

(f)   the limits on the frequency of renewal of a vehicle for the purposes of obtaining a refund of tax or excise duty, and

(g)   in the case of the driver concerned, evidence that the vehicle is for his personal use and evidence of his driving capacity,

and the regulations may provide for such other matters as the Minister for Finance considers necessary or expedient for the purposes of giving effect to this section.

(3)   (a)   Upon the first coming into operation of regulations under this section, section 43(1) of the Finance Act, 1968, shall cease to have effect.

(b)   Any person who, at the passing of this Act, was the registered owner of a motor vehicle, being a motor vehicle in respect of which such a person was entitled to and had received a refund of motor tax or excise duty by reference to section 43(1) of the Finance Act, 1968, shall be deemed to be a person who possesses a primary medical certificate which, subject to compliance with the non medical requirements set out in the regulations, entitles him to a similar repayment of tax or excise duty by reference to this section.

(4) Regulations made under this section shall be laid before Dáil Éireann as soon as may be after they are made, and if a resolution annulling the regulations is passed Dáil Éireann within the next subsequent 21 days on which Dáil Éireann has sat after the regulations have been so laid, the regulations shall be annulled accordingly, but without prejudice to the validity of anything previously done thereunder.

(5) In this section—

"medical practitioner" means a medical practitioner registered under the Medical Practitioners Act, 1978;

"primary medical certification" means medical certification by a medical practitioner who is the holder of a post in a health board, being the post commonly known as the post of Director of Community Care and Medical Officer of Health, in the area in which the person to whom the certification relates ordinarily resides and **"primary medical certificate"** shall be construed accordingly.

Amendments
1   Substituted by FA 1991 s 124; previously "30 per cent".
Regulations
Disabled Drivers (Tax Concessions) Regulations 1989 (SI 340/1989).

99   Care and management of taxes and duties

All taxes and duties imposed by this Act are hereby placed under the care and management of the Revenue Commissioners.

100   Short title, construction and commencement

(1) This Act may be cited as the Finance Act, 1989.

...

(4) *Part III* shall be construed together with the Value Added Tax Acts, 1972 to 1988, and maybe cited therewith as the Value Added Tax Acts, 1972 to 1989.

...

(8) *Part III* other than sections 54, 55, 56(*a*) and 58 to 63 shall be deemed to have come into force and shall take effect as on and from the 1st day of March, 1989, paragraphs (*a*) and (*d*) of section 61 and section 63 shall take effect as on and from the 1st day of July, 1989, and paragraphs (*b*) and (*c*) of section 61 and sections 62 and 63(*b*) shall take effect as on and from the 1st day of November, 1989.

(9) Any reference in this Act to any other enactment shall, unless the context otherwise requires, be construed as a reference to that enactment as amended by or under any other enactment including this Act.

(10) In this Act, a reference to a Part, section or schedule is to a Part or section of, or schedule to, this Act, unless it is indicated that reference to some other enactment is intended.

(11) In this Act, a reference to a subsection, paragraph or sub-paragraph is to the subsection, paragraph or subparagraph of the provision (including a Schedule) in which the reference occurs, unless it is indicated that reference to some other provision is intended.

FINANCE ACT 1990

(Number 10 of 1990)

ARRANGEMENT OF SECTIONS

PART III
Value added tax

An Act to charge and impose certain duties of customs and inland revenue (including excise), to amend the law relating to customs and inland revenue (including excise) and to make further provisions in connection with finance. [30th May, 1990]

PART III
Value added tax

97   Interpretation *(Part III)*

In this Part—

"the Principal Act" means the Value Added Tax Act, 1972;

"the Act of 1978" means the Value Added Tax (Amendment) Act, 1978;

"the Act of 1985" means the Finance Act, 1985;

"the Act of 1986" means the Finance Act, 1986;

"the Act of 1989" means the Finance Act, 1989.

98   Amendment of section 1 (interpretation) of Principal Act

---

Notes
This section, by inserting the word "horses" in the definition of "livestock" in VATA 1972 s 1(1) provided that the supply of live horses became liable at 2.3% with effect from 1 January 1991. This was as a result of the deletion of the Sixth Directive Annex F para 4 (77/388/EEC) by the Eighteenth Directive art 1(2)(c), with effect from 1 January 1991.

---

99   Amendment of section 3 (delivery of goods) of Principal Act

---

Notes
This section deleted the words "live horses" from VATA 1972 s 3(3)(a) and (b). The words are no longer needed as the supply of live horses became liable at 2.3% with effect from 1 January 1991 (see s 98).

---

100   Amendment of section 5 (supply of services) of Principal Act

---

Notes
Para (a) amended VATA 1972 s 5(6)(e)(ii)(II) and para (b) inserted VATA 1972 s 5(6)(e)(ii)(III), to provide that a recipient of services received from abroad who is established in the State and also in the State of the supplier, must "self account" on such services if they are used for the Irish establishment.

---

101   Amendment of section 8 (accountable persons) of Principal Act

Notes

This section deleted the words "live horses and" from the definition of "agricultural produce" in VATA 1972 s 8(9). This amendment is related to ss 98-99. The supply of live horses became liable at 2.3% (as livestock) with effect from 1 January 1991.

102   Amendment of section 11 (rates of tax) of Principal Act

Notes

This section reduced the 25% rate to 23%, increased the 2% rate to 2.3% and increased the (electricity) 5% rate to 10%, with effect from 1 March 1990. The wording for the 2.3% rate was amended to include live greyhounds and horses, with effect from 1 January 1991.

103   Amendment of section 12A (special provisions for tax invoiced by flat-rate farmers) of Principal Act

Notes

This section increased the flat rate compensation for unregistered farmers from 2% to 2.3%, with effect from 1 March 1990.

104   Amendment of section 15 (charge of tax on imported goods) of Principal Act

Notes

This section provided that live greyhounds would be liable to 2.3% VAT at import with effect from 1 January 1991.

105   Non-application for a limited period of section 15 (invoices) of Principal Act

In respect of the period from the 1st day of October, 1990, to the 31st day of December, 1990, the provisions of section 17 of the Principal Act shall not apply in the case of the supply of services specified in paragraph (va) (inserted by this Act) of the Sixth Schedule (inserted by the Act of 1985) to the Principal Act.

Notes

This section gives Bord Telecom Éireann time to adjust to its systems to the strict invoicing requirements of VATA 1972 s 17, following the introduction of VAT at 10% on telecommunications services, with effect from 1 October 1990.

106   Amendment of First Schedule to Principal Act

Notes

Para (*a*), by amending VATA 1972 Sch 1 para (ii) removes general driving lessons (driving lessons other than for goods vehicles with a capacity of 1.5 tonnes or more) from the list of exempted activities. Para (*b*), by inserting VATA 1972 Sch 1 para (viii*a*), provides that the supply of cultural services (and the supply of goods closely related to such services) is exempt from VAT with effect from 1 March 1990. Para (*c*), by deleting VATA 1972 Sch 1 paras (xx) and (xxi), provided that with effect from 1 January 1991 the supply of live horses or greyhounds is no longer included in the list of exempted activities (see ss 98-99). Para (*d*), by inserting VATA 1972 Sch 1 para (xxii*a*) with effect from 1 March 1990 includes services provided by independent administrative entities (set up by persons carrying on exempted activities) in the list of exempted activities.

107   Amendment of Sixth Schedule to Principal Act

Notes

Para (*a*) included electricity (see s 102) in the list of good and services liable at 10% with effect from 1 March 1990. Para (*b*) included telecommunications services (see s 105) in the list of goods and services liable at 10% with effect from 1 October 1990. Para (*c*), with effect from 1 March 1990, excluded services provided by independent administrative entities (set up by persons carrying on exempted activities) from the list of goods and services liable at 10%, as such services are exempt (see s 106).

PART VII
Miscellaneous

139   Care and management of taxes and duties

All taxes and duties imposed by this Act are hereby placed under the care and management of the Revenue Commissioners.

140 Short title, construction and commencement

(1) This Act may be cited as the Finance Act, 1990.

...

(4) *Part III* shall be construed together with the Value Added Tax Acts, 1972 to 1989, and maybe cited therewith as the Value Added Tax Acts, 1972 to 1990.

...

(9) *Part III* (other than sections 98 to 101, paragraph (*c*)(ii) of section 102, sections 104 to 106 and paragraphs (*b*) to (*d*) of section 107) shall be deemed to have come into force and shall take effect as on and from the 1st day of March, 1990, paragraph (*c*) of section 107 shall take effect as on and from the 1st day of July, 1990, paragraph (*c*) of section 107 shall take effect as on and from the 1st day of October, 1990, and sections 98, 99 and 101, paragraph (*c*)(ii) of section 102, section 104 and paragraph (*c*) of section 106 shall take effect as on and from the 1st day of January, 1991.

(10) Any reference in this Act to any other enactment shall, except so far as the context otherwise requires, be construed as a reference to that enactment as amended by or under any other enactment including this Act.

(11) In this Act, a reference to a Part, section or schedule is to a Part or section of, or schedule to, this Act, unless it is indicated that reference to some other enactment is intended.

(12) In this Act, a reference to a subsection, paragraph or sub-paragraph is to the subsection, paragraph or subparagraph of the provision (including a Schedule) in which the reference occurs, unless it is indicated that reference to some other provision is intended.

FINANCE ACT 1991

(Number 13 of 1991)

ARRANGEMENT OF SECTIONS

PART III
Value added tax

An Act to charge and impose certain duties of customs and inland revenue (including excise), to amend the law relating to customs and inland revenue (including excise) and to make further provisions in connection with finance [29th May, 1991]

PART III
Value added tax

76 Interpretation (Part III)

In this Part—

"the Principal Act" means the Value Added Tax Act, 1972;

"the Act of 1978" means the Value Added Tax (Amendment) Act, 1978;

"the Act of 1985" means the Finance Act, 1985;

"the Act of 1986" means the Finance Act, 1986;

"the Act of 1987" means the Finance Act ,1987.

77 Amendment of section 1 (interpretation) of Principal Act

Notes

This section deleted the definition of "hotel" in VATA 1972 s 1(1) with effect from 1 January 1992. A broader definition, which includes guesthouses, holiday home accommodation, campsite facilities, is included in the list of goods and service liable at 10% (new VATA 1972 Sch 3 para (vi)) with effect from 1 January 1992. The old definition did not include short term letting of apartments, holiday cottages etc.

---

78 Amendment of section 7 (waiver of exemption) of Principal Act

---

Notes

This section amended VATA 1972 s 7(1) to provide that after 1 January 1992 veterinary surgeons will no longer have the right to waive their exemption from VAT. This is because services supplied by veterinary surgeons became taxable at the new 12.5% rate with effect from 1 January 1992 (see s 87).

---

79   Amendment of section 8 (accountable persons) of Principal Act

Notes

Para (*a*) amended VATA 1972 s 8(1) and para (*b*) substituted VATA 1972 s 8(8), to provide that where the Revenue take the view that certain persons are "connected" they may "deem" such persons to be members of a VAT group. This section, combined with s 83, allows the Revenue to "defer" VAT repayments to members of such groups.

80   Amendment of section 11 (rates of tax) of Principal Act

Notes

This section reduced the 23% rate to 21%, and increased the 10% rate (on certain goods and services) to 12.5%, with effect from 1 March 1991. The 10% rate remains for goods and services listed in the new VATA 1972 Sch 3.

81   Amendment of section 12 (deduction for tax borne or paid) of Principal Act

Notes

This section inserted VATA 1972 s 12(1)(*a*)(iiia) to provide that VAT charged "in respect of services directly related to" the transfer of a business (or part thereof) to another taxable person (VATA 1972 s 3(5)(*b*)(iii)) is deductible in the purchases part of the VAT return. This means that the VAT on liquidator's fees etc is deductible in purchases part of the liquidator's return (see VATA 1972 s 3(7) and 19(3)((*b*)-(*c*)).

82   Amendment of section 15 (charge of tax on imported goods) of Principal Act

Notes

With effect from 1 March 1991, this section provided that the goods liable at 10% (listed in the new VATA 1972 Sch 3) would be liable at the same rate on importation.

83   Amendment of section 20 (refund of tax) of Principal Act

Notes

This section, by substituting VATA 1972 s 20(1A), provides that where the Revenue take the view that certain persons are "connected" they may "deem" such persons to be members of a VAT group. This section, combined with s 79, allows the Revenue to "defer" VAT repayments to members of such groups.

84   Amendment of section 25 (appeals) of Principal Act

Notes

This section, by inserting VATA 1972 s 25(1)(*aa*), provides a right of appeal against a deemed group registration (see ss 79, 83).

85   Amendment of First Schedule to Principal Act

Notes

Para (*a*) (i), by amending VATA 1972 Sch 1 para (i)(*c*), includes dealing in negotiable instruments in the list of exempted activities (financial services) with effect from 1 March 1991.

Para (*a*), by substituting VATA 1972 Sch 1 para (i)(*g*), deleting VATA 1972 Sch 1 para (i)(*gg*), and amending VATA 1972 Sch 1 para (ix), redefine the management of a unit trust, which is already an exempted activity (financial services), to reflect the repeal of the Unit Trusts Act 1972 and the enactment of the Unit Trusts Act 1990.

Para (*b*), by substituting VATA 1972 Sch 1 para (iv)(*b*) with effect from 1 January 1992, removes the short term letting of land or buildings in a tourist context (hotels, apartments, holiday cottages etc) from the list of exempted activities. Guesthouse accommodation, holiday home accommodation, campsite facilities etc, are included in the list of goods and service liable at 10% (new VATA 1972 Sch 3 para (vi)) with effect from 1 January 1992.

Para (*c*), by deleting VATA Sch 1 para (x), removes professional services supplied by veterinary surgeons from the list of exempted activities, with effect from 1 January 1992. This is because services supplied by veterinary surgeons became taxable at the new 12.5% rate with effect from 1 January 1992 (see s 87).

Para (*d*), by inserting VATA 1972 Sch 1 para (xia) with effect from 1 January 1992, clarifies the fact that services supplied by An Post other than the public postal service, are liable to VAT (not exempt).

86   Insertion of Third Schedule to Principal Act

Notes

This section inserted a new VATA 1972 Sch 3 with effect from 1 March 1991, listing goods and services liable at 10%: building work, concrete blocks, concrete ready to pour, guesthouse accommodation, hotel accommodation, holiday home accommodation, land and buildings (developed), tour guide services, and the short term hire of boats, cars, caravans and tents. It further amended VATA 1972 Sch 3 by substituting para (vi) with effect from 1 January 1992. This latter change includes apartments and holiday cottages under the tourist accommodation heading.

87 Amendment of Sixth Schedule to Principal Act

Notes

Subs (1)(*a*) removed VATA 1972 Sch 6 paras (ii), (iii), (iv), (v) and (x) (goods and services now liable at 10% that are included in new VATA 1972 Sch 3: see s 86).

Subs (1)(*c*), by inserting VATA 1972 Sch 6 para (xii*d*) with effect from 1 July 1991, includes professional services supplied by jockeys in the list of goods and services liable at 12.5% (previously 23%).

Subs (1)(*d*), by inserting VATA 1972 Sch 6 para (xiii*j*) with effect from 1 January 1992, includes professional services supplied by veterinary surgeons in the list of goods and services liable at 12.5% (previously exempt with a right to waive that exemption: see s 78).

Subs (1)(*e*), by amending VATA 1972 Sch 6 para (xiv), removes land drainage and reclamation from the list of goods and services liable at 12.5% (now 10%: s 86).

Subs (2), by substituting VATA 1972 Sch 6 para (xii*b*), provides that the routine cleaning of land or buildings is liable at 12.5%.

PART VII
Miscellaneous

124 Amendment of section 92 (tax concessions for disabled drivers, etc) of Finance Act, 1989

Notes

This section substituted "20 per cent" for "30 per cent" in FA 1989 s 92(1)(ii).

131 Care and management of taxes and duties

All taxes and duties imposed by this Act are hereby placed under the care and management of the Revenue Commissioners.

132 Short title, construction and commencement

(1) This Act may be cited as the Finance Act, 1991.

...

(4) *Part III* shall be construed together with the Value Added Tax Acts, 1972 to 1990, and maybe cited therewith as the Value Added Tax Acts, 1972 to 1991.

...

(9) *Part III* (other than sections 77 to 79, section 81, sections 83 to 85, section 86(2), paragraphs (*c*) to (*e*) of section 87(1) and section 87(2)) shall be deemed to have come into force and shall take effect as on and from the 1st day of March, 1991, paragraph (*c*) of section 87(1) shall take effect as on and from the 1st day of July, 1991, sections 77 and 78, paragraphs (*b*) to (*d*) of section 85, paragraph (*b*) of section 86(2) and paragraph (*d*) of section 87(1) shall take effect as on and from the 1st day of January, 1992.

(10) Any reference in this Act to any other enactment shall, except so far as the context otherwise requires, be construed as a reference to that enactment as amended by or under any other enactment including this Act.

(11) In this Act, a reference to a Part, section or schedule is to a Part or section of, or schedule to, this Act, unless it is indicated that reference to some other enactment is intended.

(12) In this Act, a reference to a subsection, paragraph or sub-paragraph is to the subsection, paragraph or subparagraph of the provision (including a Schedule) in which the reference occurs, unless it is indicated that reference to some other provision is intended.

FINANCE ACT 1992

(Number 9 of 1992)

ARRANGEMENT OF SECTIONS

PART III
Value added tax

An Act to charge and impose certain duties of customs and inland revenue (including excise), to amend the law relating to customs and inland revenue (including excise) and to make further provisions in connection with finance [28th May, 1992]

164 Interpretation (Part III)

In this Part —

"the Principal Act" means the Value Added Tax Act, 1972;

"the Act of 1973" means the Finance Act, 1973;

"the Act of 1976" means the Finance Act, 1976;

"the Act of 1978" means the Value Added Tax (Amendment) Act, 1978;

"the Act of 1981" means the Finance Act, 1981;

"the Act of 1982" means the Finance Act, 1982;

"the Act of 1983" means the Finance Act, 1983;

"the Act of 1984" means the Finance Act, 1984;

"the Act of 1985" means the Finance Act, 1985;

"the Act of 1986" means the Finance Act, 1986;

"the Act of 1987" means the Finance Act, 1987;

"the Act of 1990" means the Finance Act, 1990;

"the Act of 1991" means the Finance Act, 1991.

165 Amendment of section 1 (interpretation) of Principal Act

Notes

Para (*a*) amended VATA 1972 s 1 (1) as follows:

para (*a*)(i), by inserting a definition of "exportation of goods" defines the term as export to a non EC destination;

para (*a*)(ii) deleted the definition of "harbour authority"; para (*a*)(iii), by inserting a definition of "importation of goods" defines the term as import from a non EC location; para (*a*)(iv) inserted the definition of "intra-Community acquisition of goods" (broadly, imports and exports within the EC); para (*a*)(v) inserted the definition of "monthly control statement" with effect from 1 November 1992 (a new document to be issued by taxable persons: see s 180); para (*a*)(vi) inserted the definition of "new means of transport" (new boats, planes and vehicles); para (*a*)(vii) inserted the definition of "a person registered for value added tax" (a person registered for VAT in an EC State); para (*a*)(viii) amended definition of "taxable goods"; para (*a*)(ix) amended definition of taxable services; para (*a*)(x) inserted the definition of "vessel".

Para (*b*), by inserting VATA 1972 s 1(2A), provides that the EC territory is with effect from 1 January 1993, for the purposes of Irish VAT, the same as the EC territory detailed in the Sixth Directive art 3.

---

166   Amendment of section 2 (charge of value added tax) of Principal Act

Notes

This section, by inserting VATA 1972 s 2(1A) with effect from 1 January 1993, provides that intra Community acquisitions of goods (other than new, boats, planes and vehicles) by taxable persons are liable to VAT. A taxable person who does not carry on any exempt activities will self account for the "EC import" in both the purchases part of his VAT return and the sales part of the VAT return, with no net tax due (postponed accounting).

Intra Community acquisitions of new boats, planes and vehicles by all persons including private individuals (not just taxable persons: VAT registered persons) are also liable to VAT.

167   Amendment of section 3 (supply of goods) of Principal Act

Notes

Para (*a*)(i) adjusts VATA 1972 s 3 (1)(*e*) (self supply to exempt activity) to provide that such a self supply may arise where goods imported VAT free from another EC State (intra Community acquisitions of goods) are diverted to an exempt activity; para (*a*)(ii) adjusts VATA 1972 s 3 (1)(*f*)(ii) (self supply to non business use) to provide that such a self supply may arise where goods imported VAT free (intra Community acquisition of goods) are diverted to a non business use; para (*a*)(iii), by inserting VATA 1972 s 3 (1)(*g*), provides that the transfer of goods which remain in the possession of the same legal entity (intra branch transfer) within the EC is a supply, and the goods will therefore be taxed as an intra Community acquisition in the EC State of arrival; para (*b*) made related changes to VATA 1972 s 3 (1A); para (*c*), by substituting VATA 1972 s 3 (6), provides new rules for place of supply of dispatched goods, and turnover limits for distance sellers.

168   Intra-Community acquisition of goods

Notes

This section inserted VATA 1972 s 3A which defines the new term "Intra Community acquisition of goods" for the transitional period of the single market.

169   Amendment of section 5 (supply of services) of Principal Act

Notes

Para (*a*) amended VATA 1972 s 5(3A) (which provides that persons must self account on certain services received from abroad) to exclude intra EC haulage services from that subsection; para (*b*)(i), by substituting VATA 1972 s 5(6)(*b*) provides that haulage services (other than intra EC haulage services) are deemed to be supplied where the transport takes place; para (*b*)(i), by substituting VATA 1972 s 5(6)(*c*)(ii) provides that services ancillary to haulage (loading etc) other than intra EC haulage are deemed to take place where physically performed; and para (*c*), by substituting VATA 1972 s 5(6)(*f*)-(*h*), provides new place of supply rules for intra EC haulage services and related loading etc service. In essence, where the recipient of such services is VAT registered, the services are deemed to be supplied in the EC State that issued the recipient's VAT number; if the recipient is not registered the haulage service is taxed in the EC State of departure, and the loading etc ancillary services are taxed where physically performed.

170   Amendment of section 8 (taxable persons) of Principal Act

Notes

Subs (1)(*a*), by substituting VATA 1972 s 8(3)(*a*), provided that a farmer is not obliged to register for VAT unless his turnover from agricultural services exceeds £15,000 in any continuous 12 month period; subs (1)(*b*), by inserting VATA 1972 s 8(3C) provided that the liquor license holder of a licensed premises where a dance takes place will be regarded as accountable for VAT on the dance takings.

Subs (2)(*a*) and (*b*) by amending VATA 1972 s 8(1) and inserting VATA 1972 s 8(1A), provide that persons engaging in the intra Community acquisition of goods are taxable persons, but such persons are not obliged to register (see above) unless the value of the intra Community acquisitions exceeds £32,000 in any continuous 12 month period; subs (2)(*c*) amended VATA 1972 s 8(2) to provide that intra EC haulage services received by VAT registered persons, like Fourth Schedule services, must be "self accounted" for by the recipient; subs (2)(*d*) by inserting VATA 1972 s 8(2B) provided that persons who are taxable only because of an intra Community acquisition of a new boat, plane or vehicle are not taxable unless they elect; subs (2)(*e*), by substituting VATA 1972 s 8(3), includes persons whose intra Community acquisitions of goods do not exceed £32,000 in any continuous 12 month period in the list of persons who are not taxable unless they elect to be taxable; subs (2)(*f*) by substituting VATA 1972 s 8(6), allows the Revenue Commissioners to cancel a VAT registration where the person is no longer taxable.

171   Amendment of section 9 (registration) of Principal Act

Notes

This section, by inserting VATA 1972 s 9(1A), obliges the Revenue Commissioners to issue a VAT number to persons they have registered for VAT.

172   Amendment of section 10 (amount on which tax is chargeable) of Principal Act

Notes

Para (*a*) by inserting VATA 1972 s 10(1A) details the taxable amount for intra Community acquisitions; para (*b*) made a corresponding referential amendment to VATA 1972 s 10(2); para (*c*) by amending VATA 1972 s 10(2)(proviso) prevents a trade in allowance being given in computing the taxable amount of an intra Community acquisition of goods; para (*d*), by substituting VATA 1972 s 10(3)(*a*) provides that intra Community acquisitions of goods acquired for less than market value are taxed on their open market value; para (*e*) by amending VATA 1972 s 10(4) provides that the taxable amount on self supplied goods may include the value of an intra Community acquisition; para (*f*) by inserting VATA 1972 s 10(4B) provides that the taxable amount on intra EC branch transfers of goods is the open market price of the goods; para (*g*) by inserting VATA 1972 s 10(5A), allows an Irish taxable person to reduce to nil the taxable amount on an intra Community acquisition the VAT on which has already been accounted for in another EC State (triangulation); para (*h*) by amending VATA 1972 s 10(10) includes a reference to intra Community acquisition of goods in the definition of open market price.

173 Amendment of section 11 (rates of tax) of Principal Act

Notes

Subs (1)(*a*), by substituting VATA 1972 s 11(1)(*c*) provided that the 12.5% rate would continue to apply to goods listed in VATA 1972 Sch 6 other than those specified in VATA 1972 s 11(1)(*c*)(ii), which would be liable at the new 16% rate; subs (1)(*b*) increased the rate on livestock from 2.3% to 2.7% with effect from 1 March 1992.
Subs (2)(*a*) by substituting VATA 1972 s 11(1) provides rates of 21%, 0%, 10%, 12.5% 16% and 2.7% with effect from 28 May 1992; subs (2)(*b*) deleted VATA 1972 s 11(7) (VAT on dance takings: now taxed at 21% with the liquor license holder as the accountable person: see s 170); subs (2)(*c*) made a referential amendment to VATA 1972 s 11(8)(*a*).
Subs (3)(*a*) amended VATA 1972 s 11(1) to apply the new VAT rates to intra Community acquisitions of goods after 1 January 1993; subs (3)(*b*) made a referential amendment in VATA 1972 s 11(1A)(*a*); subs (3)(*c*) by substituting VATA 1972 s 11(1B)(*a*)(ii), (*b*)(ii) and amending VATA 1972 s 11(1B)(*g*) allows the Revenue Commissioners to make determinations regarding the VAT rates or VAT status applicable to intra Community acquisitions of goods and provides equivalent appeal procedures; subs (3)(*d*) by amending VATA 1972 s 11(3), includes intra Community acquisitions of goods in the package rule. Broadly, that rule provides that if a package comprising goods and/or services chargeable at different VAT rates is sold as a unit, the package is liable at the highest VAT rate applicable to any item in the package.

174 Amendment of section 12 (deductions of tax borne or paid) of Principal Act

Notes

Para (*a*), by inserting VATA 1972 s 12(1)(*a*)(iia) allows taxable persons a purchases VAT deduction for intra Community acquisitions of goods; para (*a*), by inserting VATA 1972 s 12(1)(*a*)(iib) allows taxable persons a purchases VAT deduction (equal to the residual VAT) for intra EC branch transfers of goods.
Para (*b*), by amending VATA 1972 s 12(3)(*a*)(iii) and VATA 1972 s 12(3)(*a*)(iv) denies a purchases VAT deduction for intra Community acquisitions of passenger motor vehicles other than as stock in trade.

175 Amendment of section 12A (special provisions for tax invoiced by flat-rate farmers) of Principal Act

Notes

This section increased the farmer flat rate compensation from 2.3% to 2.7% with effect from 1 March 1992 and with effect from 1 January 1993 allows a flat rate addition to be paid to non Irish farmers, in which case the addition should be reclaimed from the VAT authorities of the EC State in which the farmer is based. Similarly unregistered Irish farmers may take a flat rate addition from an EC based customer. That EC based customer may then reclaim the flat rate addition paid to the Irish farmer from the Revenue Commissioners.

176 Amendment of section 13 (remission of tax on goods exported, etc.) of Principal Act

Notes

Para (*a*) amended VATA 1972 s 13(3)(*c*) to allow the repayment an EC based customer of an Irish farmer the flat rate addition paid to that farmer; para (*b*) by inserting VATA 1972 s 13(3A), allows the Revenue Commissioners to repay (to persons other than traders in the goods in question) the residual VAT contained in the value of a new boat, plane or vehicle that has been dispatched to another EC State.

177 Amendment of section 14 (determination of tax due by reference to cash receipts) of Principal Act

Notes

Subs (1)(*a*), by amending VATA 1972 s 14(1) and deleting VATA 1972 s 14(1)(*d*) restricts the cash basis to traders whose turnover derives as to 90% (either from goods or services) from trade with other taxable persons; subs (1)(*b*) by inserting VATA 1972 s 14(1A) provides that VAT is chargeable at the rate applicable when the goods or services were supplied and is not chargeable more than once on the same supply; subs(1)(*c*) made referential amendments to VATA 1972 s 14(2); subs (1)(*d*) by inserting VATA 1972 s 14(3) provides that the cash basis does not apply to imports.
Subs (2) amended VATA 1972 s 14(3) to provide that the cash basis does not apply to intra Community acquisitions of goods.

178 Amendment of section 15 (charge of tax on imported goods) of Principal Act

Notes

Para (*a*) substituted VATA 1972 s 15(1) to provide that VAT on imported goods is chargeable at 0%, 2.7%, 10%, 12.5%, 16% or 21% as applicable; para (*b*) deleted VATA 1972 s 15(2); para (*c*) by inserting VATA 1972 s 11(5A) allows the Revenue Commissioners to repay VAT at imported paid on goods which are subsequently dispatched (or transported) to another EC State, provided the VAT is accounted for in that EC State as an intra Community acquisition.

179 Amendment of section 16 (duty to keep records) of Principal Act

Notes

Para (*a*) by amending VATA 1972 s 16(2), deleted the requirement to keep copies of customs entries; para (*b*) by amended VATA 1972 s 16(3), includes monthly control statements and documents relating to intra Community acquisitions of goods must be kept for six years.

180 Amendment of section 17 (invoices) of Principal Act

Notes

Para (*a*), by amending VATA 1972 s 17(1) provides that VAT invoices etc must be issued to persons other than individuals in other EC States; para (*b*) by substituting VATA 1972 s 17(1A)(*b*)-(*d*), provides that only Revenue authorised traders may engage in electronic invoicing; para (*c*) by inserting VATA 1972 s 17(1B) provides that taxable persons with turnover in excess of £2,000,000 from taxable supplies in any continuous 12 month period must issue their customers with monthly control statements; para (*d*) amended VATA 1972 s 17(2) to allow flat rate farmers to issue flat rate VAT invoices to EC customers; para (*e*) amended VATA 1972 s 17(3) to provide that VAT credit notes and supplementary VAT invoices must be issued to customers (non individuals) in other EC States; para (*f*) amended VATA 1972 s 17(4)(*b*) to allow flat rate farmers to issue flat rate VAT credit notes and supplementary flat rate VAT invoices to customers in EC States; para (*g*) amended VATA 1972 s 17(8) to provide that a VAT invoice need not be issued for an advance payment received for an intra Community supply; para (*h*) inserted VATA 1972 s 17(12)(*ai*) and amended VATA 1972 s 17(12)(*b*) to provide that flat rate farmer must issue a flat rate VAT invoice to EC customers on request.

181 Amendment of section 18 (inspection and removal of records) of Principal Act

Notes

Para (*a*)(i), by inserted VATA 1972 s 18(1)(*a*)(iia) gives new powers of search to authorised Revenue officers; para (*a*)(ii), by amending VATA 1972 s 18(1)(*a*)(iii), allows authorised Revenue officers to remove records and take copies and extracts from such records for the purposes of any court proceedings (not just penalty proceedings); para (*a*)(iii), by amending VATA 1972 s 18(1)(*a*)(iv) allows Revenue officials to inspect goods connected with intra Community acquisitions on a trader's premises; para (*a*)(iv), by amending VATA 1972 s 18(1)(*a*)(v)allows authorised Revenue officials to require the person carrying on the business to provide information on request.

Para (*b*), by inserting VATA 1972 s 18(1A), requires taxable persons to provide customer lists and information to an authorised Revenue officer on request; para (*b*), by inserting VATA 1972 s 18(1B), redefines "records" to include computer discs, microfilmed records etc.

182 Amendment of section 19 (tax due and payable) of Principal Act

Notes

Para (*a*), by inserting VATA 1972 s 19(1A) provides that tax chargeable on intra Community acquisitions becomes due on the 15th day of the month following the month in which the intra Community acquisition took place;

para (*b*), by amending VATA 1972 s 19(2) provides that, in relation to advance payments, tax becomes due at the time the payment is received, but this does not apply to advance payments in respect of intra Community acquisitions;

para (*c*), by inserting VATA 1972 s 19(4), provides that tax on intra Community acquisitions of motor vehicles (by persons other than motor dealers), tax is payable under the rules laid down in the Value Added Tax (Payment of Tax on Intra Community Acquisitions of Means of Transport) Regulations 1992 (SI 412/1992).

183 Statement of intra-Community supplies

Notes

This section, by inserting VATA 1972 s 19A, provides that taxable persons with sales to other EC States must make quarterly returns (export sales listings) detailing such sales.

184 Amendment of section 20 (refund of tax of Principal Act

(1) ....

(2) Every order made under section 20(3)(*a*) of the Principal Act which is a subsisting order immediately before the commencement of this section shall, upon such commencement, continue in force as if made under the said section 20(3)(*a*) as amended by this section.

Notes

Subs (1)(*a*) and (*b*), by amending VATA 1972 s 20(1) and inserting VATA 1972 s 20(1B) allow the Revenue Commissioners to request security from a trader before making a refund; subs (1)(*c*) substituted VATA 1972 s 20(3)(*a*) which allows the Minister for Finance to make repayments to unregistered person; subs (1)(*d*), by inserting VATA 1972 s 20(5) allows the Revenue Commissioners to argue that they need not make a refund to taxpayer where that refund would "unjustly enrich" the taxpayer.

185 Amendment of section 23 (determination of tax due) of Principal Act

Notes

Para (*a*) made minor changes to VATA 1972 s 23(1) which have the effect of redefining inspector's "estimates" of tax due as "assessments" of tax due, to distinguish such assessments from automatic estimates issued where a VAT return has not been received (VATA 1972 s 22); para (*b*), by inserting VATA 1972 s 23(3), allows a taxpayer to make an advance payment in relation to an inspector's assessment that is under appeal; if the payment is 80% or more of the amount finally found to be due, no interest will accrue.

186 Security to be given by certain taxable persons

Notes

This section, by inserting VATA 1972 s 23A, allows the Revenue Commissioners to request security from certain traders.

187 Amendment of section 25 (appeals) of Principal Act

Notes

Para (*a*), by inserting VATA 1972 s 25(1)(*ab*), grants a right of appeal against a Revenue decisions to substitute an persons for a foreign trader doing business in the State; para (*b*) made referential amendments to VATA 1972 s 25(2)(*k*).

188 Amendment of section 26 (penalties generally) of Principal Act

Notes

Para (*a*)(i), by amending VATA 1972 s 26(1), provides a £1,200 penalty for failure to submit a statement of intra Community supplies; para (*a*)(ii) increased the general penalty to £1,200 (from £800); para (*b*), by amending VATA 1972 s 26(2), increased the penalty for issue of an invoice by an unregistered person from £500 to £750; para (*c*), by amending VATA 1972 s 26(2A) increased the penalty for unauthorised issue of a flat rate VAT invoice from £500 to £750; para (*d*), by amending VATA 1972 s 26(3), increased the corresponding penalties for a company secretary from £500 to £750; para (*e*) by amending VATA 1972 s 26(3A) increased the penalties for obstruction of an authorised officer from £800 to £1,000; para (*f*), by inserting VATA 1972 s 26(3B), provides a new penalty of £1,200 (in respect of each supply) for persons who supply taxable goods in contravention of a Revenue security request.

189 Amendment of section 27 (fraudulent returns etc) of Principal Act

Notes

Para (*a*), by amending VATA 1972 s 27(1), and substituting VATA 1972 s 27(1)(*b*), extended the fraud provisions to monthly control statements and misuse of a VAT number.

Para (*b*), by amending VATA 1972 s 27(3), allows persons who have submitted incorrect monthly control statements, or misused a VAT number to correct the error that has come to the person's notice provided the error is corrected without unreasonable delay; para (*b*), by amending VATA 1972 s 27(7), provides that a monthly control statement or VAT number submitted on behalf of a person is deemed to have been submitted by that person unless he proves it was issued without his consent.

Para (*c*) by inserting VATA 1972 s 27(9A), empowers the Revenue Commissioners to seize allegedly exported goods if the goods are found in the State after the alleged date of export; para (*d*) made referential amendments to VATA 1972 s 27(10); para (*e*) by inserting VATA 1972 s 27(11), gives authorised Revenue officers a limited power of arrest.

190 Amendment of section 28 (assisting in making incorrect returns) of Principal Act

Notes

This section by amending VATA 1972 s 28, provides a penalty for assisting in making an incorrect monthly control statement. The general penalty for assisting in making incorrect returns etc is increased from £500 to £750.

191 Amendment of section 30 (time limits) of Principal Act

Notes

This section changed reference to "estimates" to "assessments" in VATA 1972 s 30 (see s 185) and extended the meaning of "neglect" to include neglect in relation to a monthly control statement.

192 Amendment of section 32 (regulations) of Principal Act

Notes

Para (*a*) inserted VATA 1972 s 32(1)(*aa*)-(*ai*), which allow the Revenue Commissioners power to make regulations regarding: tax deductible on intra Community acquisitions, how residual tax is to be calculated, repayment of import VAT on goods dispatched to another EC State, payment of tax on intra Community acquisitions of boats, plane and vehicles, supplies in tax free shops and distance selling.

193 Substitution of certain persons for persons not established in the State

Notes
This section substituted VATA 1972 s 37, which allows the Revenue Commissioners to substitute an Irish trader for a foreign trader who is not established in the State.

194 Amendment of First Schedule to Principal Act

Notes
Subs (1)(*a*) by inserting VATA 1972 Sch 1 para (iv)(*bi*), excludes the provision of commercial sports facilities (now 12.5%) from the list of exempted activities; subs (1)(*b*) made a referential amendment to VATA 1972 Sch 1 para (viii); subs(1)(*c*) substituted VATA 1972 Sch 1 para (xvii) (revised definition of promotion of sporting events which excludes provision of commercial sports facilities that are taxed at 12.5%; subs(1)(*e*), by amending VATA 1972 Sch 1 para (xxiii), removed the requirement that the provision of sports facilities must, to be exempt, be supplied to the members of the non profit making organisation.

Subs (2)(*a*), by amending VATA 1972 Sch 1 para (xviii), provides that the intra Community acquisition of human organs, blood and milk is an exempted activity; subs (2)(*b*) amended VATA 1972 Sch 1 para (xxiv) to provide that the supply of non deductible goods (cars etc), other than by way of intra EC branch transfer, is exempt.

195 Amendment of Second Schedule to Principal Act

Notes
Subs (1)(*a*), by inserting VATA 1972 Sch 2 para (*va*), provides that international aircraft equipment repairs are included in the list of goods and services liable at 0%; subs (1)(*b*)(i) made a referential amendment to VATA 1972 Sch 2 para (xii); subs (1)(*b*)(ii), by substituting VATA 1972 Sch 2 para (xii)(*b*) with effect from 1 November 1992, restricts the drinks liable at 0% to cocoa, coffee, coffee substitutes, egg preparations, milk, milk extracts, meat preparations ("Bovril" type drinks), tea, tea preparations, and yeast preparations: this means that bottled waters etc are liable to VAT with effect from 1 November 1992; subs (1)(*b*)(iii), by substituting VATA 1972 Sch 2 para (xii)(*c*),with effect from 1 July 1992, excludes frozen desserts etc from the list of goods and services liable at 0%: this means such goods become liable at 21%; subs (1)(*b*)(iv)(I) amended VATA 1972 Sch 2 para (xii)(*d*) with effect from 1 July 1992 to exclude confectionery and bakery products (whether cooked or uncooked) from the list of goods and services liable at 0%; subs (1)(*b*)(iv)(II) amended VATA 1972 Sch 2 para (xii)(*d*) with effect from 1 July 1992 to allow bread with a crust formed by a frying process to qualify for the 0% rate; subs (1)(*b*)(v), by substituting VATA 1972 Sch 2 para (xii)(*e*) with effect from 1 July 1992, excludes crisp like snack food products from the list of goods and services liable at 0%.

Subs (2)(*a*), by substituting VATA 1972 Sch 2 para (i)-(*ai*), includes intra Community supplies in the list of goods and services liable at 0%; subs (2)(*b*), by amending VATA 1972 Sch 2 para (iii), provides that only goods haulage to non EC destinations will be liable at 0% on or after 1 January 1993; subs (2)(*c*) by inserting VATA 1972 Sch 2 para (iii*a*), provides that intra EC goods transport to or from the Azores or Madeira is liable at 0%; subs (2)(*c*) by inserting VATA 1972 Sch 2 para (iii*b*), provides that the goods may be imported from outside the EC VAT free provided the goods are consigned to another EC State; subs (2)(*d*) made referential amendments to VATA 1972 Sch 2 para (vi)(*a*), para (vi)(*b*) and para (vi)(*c*) (export agent services); and subs (2)(*c*), by substituting VATA 1972 Sch 2 para (xvi) with effect from 1 January 1993, provides that after that date repair etc work on imported goods will only be liable at 0% where the goods are temporarily arriving from a non EC State.

196 Amendment of Third Schedule to Principal Act

Notes
Para (*a*) made a referential amendment to VATA 1972 Sch 3 para (ii); para (*b*), amended VATA 1972 Sch 3 para (vi)(*a*) with effect from 1 July 1992, .to provide that commercial sports facilities provided by hotels etc would be taxable at 12.5% (Sch 6) rather than the existing rate on accommodation etc (10%).

197 Amendment of Sixth Schedule to Principal Act

Notes
Subs (2) by substituting VATA 1972 Sch 6 with effect from 28 May 1992, provides a new list of goods and services liable at 12.5%: agricultural services, cinema admissions, exhibition admissions (cultural etc), fairground entertainment services, fuel (heating), meals (restaurant etc), meals (take away etc), musical show admissions, theatre admissions, veterinary services, waste disposal services.

Subs (3)(*a*) inserted Sch 6 para (vii*a*) with effect from 1 July 1992 to provide that the commercial sports facilities is included in the list of goods and services liable at 12.5%; subs (3)(*b*), by inserting VATA 1972 Sch 6 para (xi)(ai) with effect from 1 July 1992 excludes farm advisory services liable at 16% from the 12.5% rate.

198 Insertion of Seventh Schedule in Principal Act

Notes
This section, by inserting VATA 1972 Sch 7 with effect from 28 May 1992, provides a new list of goods and services liable at 16%: adult clothes and clothing materials, adult footwear and footwear leather, art works, car gas, cleaning services (land and buildings), driving lessons, farm advisory services, jockey services, photographic goods, photographic services, photographic editing services, photographic agency services, repair services, telecommunications services.

PART VIII
Miscellaneous

253 Care and management of taxes and duties

All taxes and duties imposed by this Act are hereby placed under the care and management of the Revenue Commissioners.

254 Short title, construction and commencement

(1) This Act may be cited as the Finance Act, 1992.

...

(4) Part III shall be construed together with the Value Added Tax Acts, 1972 to 1991, and maybe cited therewith as the Value Added Tax Acts, 1972 to 1992.

...

(11) In relation to Part III:

     (*a*)   sections 164, 173(1), 175(1) and 197(1) shall be deemed to have come into force and shall take effect as on and from the 1st day of march, 1992;

     (*b*)   subparagraph (ii) of paragraph (*a*) of section 165, paragraph (*b*) of subsection (1) and paragraph (*f*) of subsection (2) of section 170, section 171, section 173(2), paragraphs (*b*) and (*d*) of subsection (1) of section 177, paragraphs (*a*) and (*b*) of section 178, paragraph (*a*) and subparagraph (i) of paragraph (*b*) of section 179, paragraph (*b*) of section 180, subparagraphs (ii) and (iv) of paragraph (*a*) and paragraph (*b*) of section 181, paragraphs (*a*), (*b*) and (*d*) of subsection (1) of section 184, sections 185, 186 and 187, subparagraph (ii) of paragraph (*a*) and paragraphs (*b*), (*c*), (*d*), (*e*) and (*f*) of section 188, paragraph (*b*) of section 190, paragraphs (*a*) and (*b*) of section 191, section 193, paragraphs (*b*) and (*d*) of subsection (1) of section 195 and paragraph (*a*) of section 196, sections 197(2) and 198 shall have effect as on and from the date of passing of this Act;

     (*c*)   paragraph (*a*) of subsection (1) of section 170, paragraphs (*a*), (*c*) and (*e*) of subsection (1) of section 194, subparagraphs (iii), (iv) and (v) of paragraph (*b*)of subsection (1) of section 195, paragraph (*b*) of section 196 and section 197(3) shall take effect as on and from the 1st day of July, 1992;

     (*d*)   subparagraph (v) of paragraph (*a*) of section 165, subparagraphs (iii), (iv) and (v) of paragraph (*b*) of section 179, paragraph (*c*) of section 180, paragraphs (*a*) and (*b*) of section 189, paragraph (*a*) of section 190, paragraph (*c*) of section 191, paragraph (*b*) of section 192 and subparagraph (ii) of paragraph (*b*) of subsection (1) of section 195 shall take effect as on and from the 1st day of November, 1992; and

     (*e*)   the provisions of this Part, other than those specified in paragraphs (*a*) to (*d*), shall take effect as on and from the 1st day of January, 1993.

(12) Any reference in this Act to any other enactment shall, unless the context otherwise requires, be construed as a reference to that enactment as amended by or under any other enactment including this Act.

(13) In this Act, a reference to a Part, section or schedule is to a Part or section of, or schedule to, this Act, unless it is indicated that reference to some other enactment is intended.

(14) In this Act, a reference to a subsection, paragraph or sub-paragraph is to the subsection, paragraph or subparagraph of the provision (including a Schedule) in which the reference occurs, unless it is indicated that reference to some other provision is intended.

FINANCE ACT 1993

(Number 13 of 1993)

ARRANGEMENT OF SECTIONS

PART III
Value added tax

Section

81   Interpretation (Part III)

An Act to charge and impose certain duties of customs and inland revenue (including excise), to amend the law relating to customs and inland revenue (including excise) and to make further provisions in connection with finance [17th June, 1993]

PART III
Value added tax

81 Interpretation (Part III)

In this Part—

"the Principal Act" means the Value Added Tax Act, 1972;

"the Act of 1973" means the Finance Act, 1973;

"the Act of 1976" means the Finance Act, 1976;

"the Act of 1978" means the Value added tax (Amendment) Act, 1978;

"the Act of 1981" means the Finance Act, 1981;

"the Act of 1982" means the Finance Act, 1982;

"the Act of 1991" means the Finance Act, 1991;

"the Act of 1992" means the Finance Act, 1992.

82 Amendment of section 3 (supply of goods) of Principal Act

Note

This section, by amending VATA 1972 s 3(1)(*g*) with effect from 17 June 1993, treats the intra EC transfer of a new boat, plane or vehicle as a supply.

---

83 Amendment of section 3A (intra-Community acquisition of goods) of Principal Act

---

Note

Para (*a*), by amending VATA 1972 s 3A(1)(*a*), redefines "intra Community acquisition of goods" to include the acquisition of goods from a person who carries on an exempted activity in an EC State. Para (*b*) substituted VATA 1972 s 3A(1)(*b*) to take account of the change made by para (*a*).

---

84 Alcohol products

Note

This section by inserting VATA 1972 s 3B with effect from 1 August 1993, provides that, for alcohol products under duty suspension arrangements, only the last supply is a supply for VAT purposes and the VAT is due when the excise is due.

---

85 Amendment of section 8 (taxable persons) of Principal Act

Note
Para (*a*) provides that a farmer or sea fisherman who is only a taxable person because of intra Community acquisitions or services received from abroad, may elect not to be taxable in respect of intra Community acquisitions of goods made by him (VATA 1972 s 8(1A)(*c*)); a farmer whose turnover derived from the supply of racehorse training services has exceeded £15,000 in any continuous 12 month period, who is only a taxable person because of intra Community acquisitions or services received from abroad, may elect not to be taxable in respect of intra Community acquisitions of goods made by him (VATA 1972 s 8(1A)(*d*)).
Para (*b*) provides that a farmer or sea fisherman who is only a taxable person because of intra Community acquisitions or services received from abroad by him, may elect not to be taxable in respect of service received from abroad by him (VATA 1972 s 8(2)(*b*)); a farmer whose turnover derived from the supply of racehorse training services has exceeded £15,000 in any continuous 12 month period, who is only a taxable person because of intra Community acquisitions or services received from abroad, may elect not to be taxable in respect of services received from abroad by him (VATA 1972 s 8(2)(*c*)).
Para (*c*)(i) made a referential amendment in VATA 1972 s 8(3); para (*c*)(ii) made a referential amendment in VATA 1972 s 8(3)(*c*)(ii); para (*c*)(iii) deleted VATA 1972 s 8(3)(*d*) (no longer needed because of the restructuring of the section); para (*c*)(iv) substituted VATA 1972 s 8(3)(proviso)(ii) to reflect the foregoing changes.
Para (*d*), by amending VATA 1972 s 8(3A) provides that a farmer whose turnover derived from the supply of racehorse training services has exceeded £15,000 in any continuous 12 month period will only be a taxable person in respect of such services and intra Community acquisitions of goods or services received from abroad.
Para (*e*) amended VATA 1972 s 8(5) to provide that when a person who has elected to be a taxable person wishes to deregister, any review of the liability for the election period must take account of intra Community acquisitions.

86 Amendment of section 10 (amount on which tax is chargeable) of principle Act

Note
VATA 1972 s 10(4A) provides that where goods in warehouse are sold to an unregistered person while "in warehouse", VAT is chargeable on the full dutiable amount. This section excludes alcohol products (VATA 1972 s 3B) from such treatment.

87 Amendment of section 11 (rates of tax) of Principal Act

Note
With effect from 1 March 1993: this section abolished the 16% VAT rate, and reduced the livestock rate from 2.7% to 2.5%.

88 Amendment of section 12 (deductions for tax borne or paid) of Principal Act

Note
Para (*a*), by inserting VATA 1972 s 12(1)(*a*)(iic), allows a purchases VAT deduction for alcohol products (in accordance with regulations); para (*b*) made a technical amendment to VATA 1972 s 12(1)(*a*)(viii); para (*c*), by inserting VATA 1972 s 12(1)(*a*)(proviso), disallows purchases VAT deductions to farmers and sea fishermen who are only taxable persons because of intra Community acquisitions of goods or services received from abroad; this amendment also disallows purchases VAT deductions to farmers who are also racehorse trainers that are only taxable persons because of racehorse training services, intra Community acquisitions of goods, or services received from abroad.

89 Amendment of section 12A (special provisions for tax invoiced by flat-rate farmers) of Principal Act

Note
This section reduced the flat rate compensation for unregistered farmers from 2.7% to 2.5% with effect from 1 March 1993.

90 Supplies to, and intra-Community acquisitions and imports by, certain taxable persons

Note
This section, by inserting VATA 1972 s 13A with effect from 1 August 1993, allows authorised persons to zero rate supplies to qualifying exporters (taxable persons whose turnover is derived as to 75% or more from exports).

91 Amendment of section 17 (invoices) of Principal Act

Note
Para (*a*), by amending VATA 1972 s 17(1) provides that a taxable person making distance sales to a customer in another EC State must issue that customer with a VAT invoice.
Para (*b*), by inserting VATA 1972 s 17(3A), provides that where a person issued a VAT invoice showing a higher rate of tax than the correct rate, the invoice is nullified, and the issuer must issue a VAT credit note followed by a replacement VAT invoice.

92 Amendment of section 19 (tax due and payable) of Principal Act

Note
Para (*a*), by inserting VATA 1972 s 19(3)(*a*)(proviso) provides that the tax payable for the November December VAT period may be reduced by the amount of the advance payment (see below).

Para (*b*), by substituting VATA 1972 s 19(4), provides that tax on new vehicles is payable at the time of payment of vehicle registration tax, and the tax on intra Community acquisitions of new boats and planes (by non taxable persons) is payable in a manner determinable by regulations.

Para (*c*), by substituting VATA 1972 s 19(5) provides that a where a person is a taxable person only because of an intra Community acquisition of excise products, the VAT is payable in a manner determinable by regulations.

Para (*c*), by inserting VATA 1972 s 19(6) provides that taxable persons with annual VAT liability in excess of £120,000 must, on 1 December in each calendar year, make an advance payment equal to one twelfth of the VAT due for the year ended 30 June immediately preceding the 1 December payment date. The advance payment is then offset against liability shown due on the November December VAT return (which is due on or before 19 January).

93 Amendment of section 20 (refund of tax) of Principal Act

Note

This section, by inserting VATA 1972 s 20(1)(proviso), provides that if an advance payment (see s 92) was made for a November December VAT period which turns out to be a repayment VAT period, the advance payment is to be refunded with the repayment.

94 Amendment of First Schedule to principal Act

Note

This section made a referential amendment to VATA 1972 Sch 1 para (iv)(*b*).

95 Amendment of Second Schedule to Principal Act

Note

Para (*a*), by inserting VATA 1972 Sch 2 para (v*b*), provides that the fuelling and provisioning of seagoing ships and aircraft (operating for reward chiefly on international routes) is liable at 0%.

Para (*b*), by inserting VATA 1972 Sch 2 para (vi*a*), provides that the supply of qualifying goods and services by an authorised person to a qualifying exporter is liable at 0%.

96 Goods and services chargeable at the rate specified in section 11(1)(*c*) of Principal Act

Note

This section substituted VATA 1972 Sch 3, which now lists remaining goods and services liable at 10%.

97 Amendment of Sixth Schedule to Principal Act

Note

These amendments restructured VATA 1972 Sch 6, so that it lists the goods and service liable at 12.5% with effect from 1 March 1993. Those goods and services are listed alphabetically in the table at the start of this book.

98 Repeal of Seventh Schedule to Principal Act

Note

This section repealed VATA 1992 Sch 7 (goods and services that were liable at 16%) with effect from 1 March 1993.

99 Amendment of section 113 (use of electronic data processing) of Finance Act, 1986

Note

This section substituted FA 1986 s 113(1)(*c*).

142 Care and management of taxes and duties

All taxes and duties imposed by this Act are hereby placed under the care and management of the Revenue Commissioners.

143 Short title, construction and commencement

(1) This Act may be cited as the Finance Act, 1993.

(2) ...

(3) Part III shall be construed together with the Value Added Tax Acts, 1972 to 1992, and may be cited together therewith as the Value Added Tax Acts, 1972 to 1993.

(4) ...

(5) ...

(6) ...

(7) ...

(8) ...

(9) In relation to Part III:

- (*a*) section 81, subparagraph (ii) of paragraph (*c*) of section 85, paragraphs (*a*) and (*c*) of section 87, paragraph (*a*) of section 89, sections 94 and 96, subsection (1) of section 97 and section 98 shall be deemed to have come into force and shall take effect as on and from the 1st day of March, 1993;

- (*b*) subsection (2) of section 97 shall take effect as on and from the 1st day of July, 1993;

- (*c*) sections 84 and 86, paragraph (*a*) of section 88, section 90 and paragraph (*b*) of section 95 shall take effect as on and from the 1st day of August 1993;

- (*d*) paragraph (b) of section 92 shall take effect as on and from the 1st day of September, 1993; and

- (*e*) the provisions of this Part, other than those specified in paragraphs (*a*) to (*d*), shall have effect as on and from the date of passing of this Act.

(10) Any reference in this Act to any other enactment shall, except so far as the context otherwise requires, be construed as a reference to that enactment as amended by or under any other enactment including this Act.

(11) In this Act, a reference to a Part, section or Schedule is to a Part or section of, or Schedule to, this Act, unless it is indicated that reference to some other enactment is intended.

(12) In this Act, a reference to a subsection, paragraph, subparagraph or clause is to the subsection, paragraph, subparagraph or clause of the provision (including a Schedule) in which the reference occurs, unless it is indicated that reference to some other provision is intended.

Definitions
"Income Tax Acts": ITA 1967 s 3; "the Corporation Tax Acts": CTA 1976 s 155(1).

FINANCE ACT 1994

(Number 13 of 1994)

ARRANGEMENT OF SECTIONS

PART III
Value added tax

An Act to charge and impose certain duties of customs and inland revenue (including excise), to amend the law relating to customs and inland revenue (including excise) and to make further provisions in connection with finance [23rd May 1994]

PART III
Value added tax

90 Interpretation (Part III)

In this Part–

"**the Principal Act**" means the Value-Added Tax Act, 1972;

"**the Act of 1978**" means the Value-Added Tax (Amendment) Act, 1978;

"**the Act of 1982**" means the Finance Act, 1982;

"**the Act of 1989**" means the Finance Act, 1989;

"**the Act of 1992**" means the Finance Act. 1992.

91 Amendment of section 1 (interpretation) of Principal Act

Notes
Para (*a*) substituted VATA 1972 s 1 definition of "new means of transport" para (*b*)(i) with effect from 1 January 1995.
Para (*b*) substituted "6,000 kilometres" for "3,000 kilometres" in VATA 1972 s 1 definition of "new means of transport" with effect from 1 January 1995.
After 1 January 1995, a vehicle will be regarded as new if it is less than six months old or if it has not travelled more than 6,000 km.

---

92 Amendment of section 3 (supply of goods) of Principal Act

Notes
This section inserted "(*vb*)" in VATA 1972 s 3(*g*)(ii) 23 May 1994.
Intra EU branch transfers are regarded as Intra EU supplies, with several exception, for example, goods transferred to another EU State to have contract work performed on them.
This amendment provides that the transfer of goods to another EU State to be used there in fuelling or provisioning a seagoing vessel will not be regarded as an Intra EU supply.

---

93 Person liable to pay tax in relation to certain supplies of immovable goods

Notes

This section inserted VATA 1972 s 4A. Upon the creation of a long lease, a VAT registered lessee may agree with a VAT registered lessor that the lessee will be accountable for the VAT on the creation of the lease; the lessee will also be entitled to take a simultaneous VAT deduction in the purchases VAT return. In the case of a lessee who only carries on taxable activities, this will mean that he will be entitled to an equivalent purchases VAT deduction and he will have no net payment of VAT. The provision is subject to EU approval.

94 Amendment of section 8 (taxable persons) of Principal Act

Notes

Para (*a*) substituted "specified in the First Schedule" for "specified in paragraph (vi), (vii), (xxii) or (xxiii) of the First Schedule" in VATA 1972 s 8 subs (1A)(*e*)(iii) with effect from 23 May 1994.

Para (*b*)(i) substituted "£20,000" for "£15,000" in VATA 1972 s 8(3)(*a*).with effect from 1 July 1994.

Para (*b*)(ii) substituted VATA 1972 s 8(3)(*b*)(ii) with effect from 1 July 1994.

Para (*b*)(iii) substituted "£40,000" for "£32,000" in VATA 1972 s 8(3)(*c*)(i) with effect from 1 July 1994.

Para (*b*)(iv) substituted "£20,000" for "£15,000" in VATA 1972 s 8(3)(*e*) with effect from 1 July 1994.

Para (*c*) substituted "£20,000" for "£15,000" in VATA 1972 s 8(3A)with effect from 1 July 1994.

Para (*d*)(i) substituted "£20,000" for "£15,000" in VATA 1972 s 8(9)(*b*)(ii) definition of "farmer" with effect from 1 July 1994

Para (*d*)(ii) substituted VATA 1972 s 8(9)(*b*)(iii) definition of "farmer" with effect from 1 July 1994.

The net effect of these changes is to increase, with effect from 1 July 1994, the registration threshold to £40,000 for traders (deriving 90% or more of their turnover from supply of goods) in any continuous 12 month period, and to £20,000 for traders (deriving 10% or more of their turnover from supply of services) in any continuous 12 month period.

95 Amendment of section 10 (amount on which tax is chargeable) of Principal Act

Notes

This section inserted VATA 1972 s 10(3)(*c*)(proviso) with effect from 23 May 1994. Bad debt relief will not apply in the case of long term leases of property.

96 Amendment of section 12 (deductions for tax borne or paid) of Principal Act

Notes

Para (*a*) inserted VATA 1972 s 12(1)(*a*)(iii*b*). This gives the simultaneous VAT deduction in the purchases part of a VAT return of a lessee who has opted, by agreement with his lessor, to account for the VAT on the creation of a long lease.

Para (*b*)(i) inserted VATA 1972 s 12(3)(*a*)(i*a*) with effect from 23 May 1994. Advertising-related food and drink expenditure will not be deductible in the purchases part of the VAT return.

Para (*b*)(ii) inserted VATA 1972 s 12(3)(*c*)-(*d*) with effect from 23 May 1994. Expenditure on a building, or fitting out a building that will be used for entertainment is not deductible for VAT purposes.

97 Amendment of section 14 (determination of tax due by reference to cash receipts) of Principal Act

Notes

Para (*a*) substituted VATA 1972 s 14(1) .with effect from 23 May 1994.

Para (*b*)(i) deleted "paragraph (*a*) of" in VATA 1972 s 14(2) with effect from 23 May 1994. Persons with annual turnover beneath £250,000 are to be entitled to the cash basis.

Para (*b*)(ii) substituted "that subsection" for "the said paragraphs (*a*)" in VATA 1972 s 14(2) with effect from 23 May 1994. This is a consequential technical change.

98 Amendment of section 27 (fraudulent returns etc. of Principal Act

Notes

This section inserted VATA 1972 s 27(9A)(4) with effect from 23 May 1994. The declaration of an incorrect VAT number, and consequent penalties, is not restricted to a taxpayer's own VAT number. Using another person's VAT number, or a fictitious VAT number, or a fraudulently obtained VAT number, constitutes "declaration of an incorrect VAT number" for VAT purposes and may give rise to penalty proceedings etc.

99 Amendment of First Schedule to Principal Act

Notes

Para (*a*) inserted "the services of loss adjusters and excluding" in VATA 1972 Sch 1 para (ix) with effect from 1 September 1994.

Para (*b*) inserted "of bets of the kind referred to in section 89 of the Finance Act, 1994," in VATA 1972 Sch 1 para (xv) with effect from the commencement of s 89.

The services of loss adjuster, previously exempt, are liable to VAT with effect from 1 September 1994. Betting remains exempt from VAT, despite technical changes (FA 1994 s 89) which relate to betting tax.

100 Amendment of Second Schedule to Principal Act

Notes

This section substituted VATA 1972 Sch 2 para (*ia*) with effect from 23 May 1994. Only sales in Revenue-approved tax-free shops will qualify for zero-rating.

---

101 Amendment of Sixth Schedule to Principal Act

Notes

Para (*a*) substituted VATA Sch 6 para (vii) with effect from 1 July 1994.

Para (*b*) inserted "of a kind" in VATA Sch 6 para (x) with effect from 1 July 1994.

Para (*c*) substituted "(other than farm accountancy or farm management services)" for "(not being services of the kind specified in paragraph (xxii) of the Seventh Schedule)"in VATA Sch 6 para (*ai*) with effect from 23 May 1994.

To qualify for the 12.5% rate, previously, fairground entertainment services (swings, roundabouts etc) could not be provided in the same location for more than 19 days; this generally meant that only travelling fairs could avail of the 12.5% rate. The 12.5% rate now applies to all fairground services, whether travelling or not.

Dance takings, slot machine and amusement machine takings remain liable at 21%. Circus activities remain exempt (Sch 1 para (viii) where no food or drink is provided in the course of the performance).

Veterinary technician services (veterinary services provided by a person other than a fully qualified veterinary surgeon) are liable at 12.5%.

PART VII
Miscellaneous

CHAPTER II
General

165 Care and management of taxes and duties

All taxes and duties imposed by this Act are hereby placed under the care and management of the Revenue Commissioners.

166 Short title, construction and commencement

(1) This Act may be cited as the Finance Act, 1994.

....

(4) Part III shall be construed together with the Value-Added Tax Acts, 1972 to 1993, and may be cited together therewith as the Value-Added Tax Acts, 1972 to 1994.

....

(9) In relation to Part III:

(*a*)   paragraphs (*b*), (*c*) and (*d*) of section 94, section 97 and paragraphs (*a*) and (*b*) of section 101 shall take effect as on and from the 1st day of July, 1994;

(*b*)   paragraph (*a*) of section 99 shall take effect as on and from the 1st day of September, 1994;

(*c*)   section 91 shall take effect as on and from the 1st day of January, 1995;

(*d*)   section 93 and paragraph (*a*) of section 96 shall take effect as on and from such date as the Minister for Finance may, by order, appoint;

(*e*)   paragraph (*b*) of section 99 shall take effect as on and from the commencement of section 89;

(*f*)   the provisions of this Part, other than those specified in paragraphs (*a*) to (*e*), shall have effect as on and from the date of passing of this Act.

(10) Any reference in this Act to any other enactment shall, except so far as the context otherwise requires, be construed as a reference to that enactment as amended by or under any other enactment including this Act.

(11) In this Act, a reference to a Part, section or Schedule is to a Part or section of, or Schedule to, this Act, unless it is indicated that reference to some other enactment is intended.

(12) In this Act, a reference to a subsection, paragraph, subparagraph, clause or subclause is to the subsection, paragraph, subparagraph, clause or subclause of the provision (including a Schedule) in which the reference occurs, unless it is indicated that reference to some other provision is intended.

FINANCE ACT 1995

(Number 8 of 1995)

ARRANGEMENT OF SECTIONS

PART III
Value added tax

An Act to charge and impose certain duties of customs and inland revenue (including excise), to amend the law relating to customs and inland revenue (including excise) and to make further provisions in connection with finance [2nd June 1995]

PART III
Value added tax

118 Intepretation (Part III)

In this Part —

"the Principal Act" means the Value Added Tax Act, 1972;

"the Act of 1978" means the Value Added Tax (Amendment) Act, 1978;

"the Act of 1992" means the Finance Act, 1992.

119 Amendment of section 1 (interpretation) of Principal Act

Notes

Para (*a*) inserted the definition of "antiques" in VATA 1972 s 1(1) with effect from 1 July 1995.

Para (*b*) inserted the definition of "collectors' items" in VATA 1972 s 1(1) with effect from 1 July 1995.

Para (*c*) inserted the definition of "margin scheme" in VATA 1972 s 1(1) with effect from 1 July 1995.

Para (*d*) substituted the definition of "second-hand goods" for "second-hand" in VATA 1972 s 1(1) with effect from 1 July 1995.

Para (*e*) inserted the definition of "taxable dealer" in VATA 1972 s 1(1) with effect from 1 July 1995.

Para (*f*) inserted the definition of "works of art" in VATA 1972 s 1(1) with effect from 1 July 1995.

These new definitions are required to facilitate the implementation of the Seventh Directive (94/5/EC) which has amended the Sixth Directive (77/388/EEC).

The essence of the changes is that, after 1 July 1995, certain dealers in second-hand goods, in particular antique dealers and auctioneers, need only account for VAT on the gross profit margin that arises when they sell on goods acquired from unregistered persons. Motor dealers (suppliers of means of transport) will have a separate scheme under which they will be entitled, when selling a vehicle that has been acquired from an unregistered person, to a deduction for the residual VAT included in the price.

---

120 Amendment of section 3 (supply of goods) of Principal Act

Notes

Para (*a*) inserted "other than the transfer of ownership of the goods to a person supplying financial services of the kind specified in subparagraph (i)(*e*) of the First Schedule, where those services are supplied as part of an agreement of the kind referred to in paragraph (*b*) in respect of those goods" in VATA 1972 s 3(1)(*a*) with effect from 2 June 1995. Interest income from the granting of credit is to remain exempt from VAT, but hire purchase transaction remain liable as supplies of goods.

Para (*b*) inserted VATA 1972 s 3(1)(*aa*) with effect from 1 July 1995. The supply by an agent or auctioneer of tangible movable goods is a supply for VAT purposes.

121 Amendment of section 3A (intra-Community acquisition of goods) of Principal Act

Notes

This section inserted VATA 1972 s 3A(1A) with effect from 1 July 1995. (Second-hand) goods arriving in the State from another EU State that have already been subject to the margin scheme, the special scheme for auctioneers, or the special scheme for means of transport in another EU State will not be liable to VAT in Ireland, unless resold.

122 Amendment of section 4 (special provisions in relation to the supply of immovable goods) of Principal Act

Notes

Para (*a*) substituted VATA 1972 s 4(5) with effect from 2 June 1995. VAT is chargeable on the full value, including the site value, of a new house.

Para (*b*) inserted "other than a supply of immovable goods to which the provisions of subsection (5) apply" in VATA 1972 s 4(6)(*b*) with effect from 2 June 1995. This is a technical amendment which relates to para (*a*).

123 Amendment of section 5 (supply of services) of Principal Act

Notes

This section inserted "has established his business or" after "the service" in VATA 1972 s 5(5) with effect from 2 June 1995. In general, the place of supply of services is where the supplier has established his business, or where he has his fixed establishment.

124 Amendment of section 8 (taxable persons) of Principal Act

Notes

Para (*a*) inserted VATA 1972 s 8(2A)(*a*)(proviso) with effect from 1 January 1996. Member-owned golf-clubs and sports clubs will no longer be able to claim exemption on the grounds that they are not profit-making, if this results in distortion of competition. Local authority sports facilities will no longer be able to claim exemption on the basis that the State is not a taxable person, if this results in distortion of competition.

Para (*b*) inserted VATA 1972 s 8(3E) with effect from 1 January 1996. The Revenue Commissioners are empowered to determine that for example, a local authority-owned sports facility which places a similar commercially run business at a disadvantage is a taxable person. The Revenue Commissioners may also determine that, for example, a member-owned golf-club, which claims to be non-profit making while operating as a commercial enterprise, is a taxable person.

125 Amendment of section 10 (amount on which tax is chargeable) of Principal Act

Notes

Para (*a*) deleted VATA 1972 s 10(2)(proviso) with effect from 1 July 1995. The old "trade-in" rule is deleted as its provisions have been superseded by the Seventh Directive (see s 119).

Para (*b*) inserted VATA 1972 s 10(4C) with effect from 1 July 1995. Where goods are sold under a hire purchase agreement, the taxable amount is the total amount received by the supplier, or the open market price of the goods, whichever is higher.

126 Margin scheme goods

Notes

This section inserted VATA 1972 s 10A with effect from 1 July 1995. Certain dealers in second-hand goods, in particular antique dealers, need only account for VAT on the gross profit margin that arises when they sell on goods acquired from unregistered persons. The margin is treated as VAT-inclusive. The dealer may opt to apply the normal VAT rules if he wishes.

127 Special scheme for auctioneers

Notes

This section inserted VATA 1972 s 10B with effect from 1 July 1995. Auctioneers need only account for VAT on the gross profit margin that arises when they sell on goods acquired from unregistered persons. The margin is treated as VAT-inclusive.

128 Amendment of section 11 (rates of tax) of Principal Act

Notes

Para (*a*) inserted VATA 1972 s 11(1AA) with effect from 1 July 1995. The 12.5% rate is to apply to works of art, antiques and collectors' items.

Para (*b*) deleted VATA 1972 s 11(5) with effect from 1 July 1995. Interest charges arising in a hire purchase or credit sale transaction are no longer liable to VAT; see ss 120, 139.

129 Amendment of section 12 (deductions for tax borne or paid) of Principal Act

Notes

Para (*a*) substituted VATA 1972 s 12(1)(*a*)(vi) with effect from 1 July 1995. Taxable dealers who supply means of transport (for example motor dealers) are entitled to deduct the residual VAT included in the price of second-hand vehicles acquired from unregistered persons.

Para (*b*) inserted VATA 1972 s 12(3A) with effect from 1 July 1995. If the margin scheme is being used by a trader, and as a result he need only account for VAT on the transaction margin, he is not entitled to a purchases VAT credit on the same transaction.

130 Special scheme for means of transport supplied by taxable dealers

Notes

This section inserted VATA 1972 s 12B with effect from 1 July 1995. Taxable dealers who supply means of transport (for example motor dealers) are entitled to deduct the residual VAT included in the price of second-hand vehicles acquired from unregistered persons. This section sets how the residual VAT is calculated.

131 Amendment of section 14 (determination of tax due by reference to cash receipts) of Principal Act

Notes

This section inserted VATA 1972 s 14(1B) with effect from 2 June 1995. Traders whose annual turnover is below the annual threshold (currently £250,000) may opt to account for VAT on the cash receipts basis. The Minister for Finance may, by order, increase this annual turnover limit.

132 Amendment of section 17 (invoices) of Principal Act

Notes

This section inserted VATA 1972 s 17(1B)(proviso) with effect from 2 June 1995. Taxable persons, the value of whose supplies to other taxable persons has not exceeded £2m in the previous 12 months, need not issue monthly control statements.

133 Amendment of section 18 (inspection and removal of records) of Principal Act

Notes

This section inserted of "and the value and description of any gifts or promotional items given by him to any person in connection with such supplies or any other payments made by him to any person in connection with such supplies" after "thereon" in VATA 1972 s 18(1A)(*a*) with effect from 2 June 1995.

This section is related to the previous section. With the relaxation of the requirement for certain traders to supply monthly control statements to other taxable persons, any taxable person may be required to provide full details to the inspector of taxes of promotional schemes which he uses.

134 Amendment of section 19 (tax due and payable) of Principal Act, etc

Notes

This section substituted VATA 1972 s 19(3)(*aa*)(i) definition of "accounting period" as on and from such day or days as the Minister for Finance may by order or orders appoint, either generally or with reference to any particular category of taxable person to whom VATA 1972 s 19(3)(*aa*) applies.

Traders who submit an annual VAT return may opt to align that VAT return with their annual accounts year, subject to authorisation from the Collector General.

135 Amendment of section 20 (refund of tax) of Principal Act

Notes

This section inserted VATA 1972 s 20(6) with effect from 2 June 1995. The Collector General may make VAT repayments directly into a bank or building society account nominated by the trader.

136 Amendment of section 22 (estimation of tax due for a taxable period) of Principal Act

Notes

This section inserted VATA 1972 s 22(1)(proviso) with effect from 2 June 1995. The Revenue Commissioners may reduce a section 22 estimate of tax due if they believe the initial estimate was too high.

137 Amendment of section 25 (appeals) of Principal Act

Notes

Para (*a*) inserted VATA 1972 s 25(1)(*ac*) with effect from 1 January 1996. Persons deemed taxable (see s 124), for example member-owned golf clubs, or local authority sports facilities, are entitled to appeal the Revenue decision.

Para (*b*) inserted VATA 1972 s 25(1A) with effect from 2 June 1995. If the Revenue refuse to regard a person as a taxable person, that person may appeal.

Para (*c*) inserted VATA 1972 s 25(2)(*dd*) with effect from 2 June 1995.

See *WLD Worldwide Leather Diffusion Ltd v Revenue Commissioners* [1994] ITR 165.

138 Amendment of section 32 (regulations) of Principal Act.

Notes

This section inserted VATA 1972 s 32(1)(*da*)-(*de*) with effect from 2 June 1995. The Revenue Commissioners are entitled to make regulations relating to the Seventh Directive, in relation to the conditions for the margin scheme, the method of calculation of the margin, the form of invoices and documents required to be issued, the method for calculating residual tax included in the price of second-hand vehicles, and details to be provided in relation to antiques.

139 Amendment of First Schedule to Principal Act

Notes

Para (*a*) substituted VATA 1972 Sch 1 para (i)(*e*) with effect from 2 June 1995. The net effect is that in so far as hire purchase and credit sale transactions amount to "the granting and the negotiation of credit", in other words, the interest arising on such transactions, is exempt from VAT. This section is linked to section 120 above.

Para (*b*) inserted "with the exception of facilities to which paragraph (vii*b*) or (vii*c*) of the Sixth Schedule refers" after "organisations" in VATA 1972 Sch 1 para (xxiii) with effect from 1 January 1996. Member-owned golf clubs will no longer be exempt in relation to income from non-members, for example, in relation to green fees, where that income exceeds or is likely to exceed £20,000 in any continuous 12 month period.

140 Amendment of Sixth Schedule to Principal Act

Notes

Para (*a*) inserted VATA 1972 Sch 6 paras (vii*b*)-(vii*c*) with effect from 1 January 1996. The income from member-owned golf clubs that was previously exempt, for example, in relation to green fees, will now be liable at 12.5%.

Para (*b*) substituted VATA 1972 Sch 6 para (xvi) with effect from 1 July 1995. The current definition of "work of art" is separated into works of art, and "antiques" which are transferred to the new VATA 1972 Sch 6 para (xvi*a*) (see below).

Para (*c*) inserted VATA 1972 Sch 6 para (xvi*a*) with effect from 1 July 1995. Antiques that qualify for the margin scheme or auction scheme do not qualify for the 12.5% rate.

Para (*d*) substituted "used" for "second-hand" in VATA 1972 Sch 6 para (xviii)(*b*) with effect from 1 July 1995. This is a technical amendment.

Para (*e*) inserted VATA 1972 Sch 6 para (xx*a*) with effect from 1 July 1995. Greyhound feeding stuff is now liable at 12.5% (previously 21%).

Para (*f*) inserted "but excluding the supply of such goods by a taxable dealer in accordance with the provisions of subsection (3) or (8) of section 10A or by an auctioneer within the meaning of section 10B and in accordance with the provisions of subsection (3) of section 10B" after "pour" in VATA 1972 Sch 6 para (xxxii) with effect from 1 July 1995.

Para (*g*) inserted "but excluding the supply of such goods by a taxable dealer in accordance with the provisions of subsection (3) or (8) of section 10A or by an auctioneer within the meaning of section 10B and in accordance with the provisions of subsection (3) of section 10B" after "(Irish Standard 20: Part I: 1987)" in VATA 1972 Sch 6 para (xxxiii) with effect from 1 July 1995.

Concrete ready to pour and concrete blocks that qualify for the margin scheme or auction scheme do not qualify for the 12.5% rate.

141 Addition of Eighth Schedule to Principal Act

Notes

This section inserted VATA 1972 Sch 8 with effect from 1 July 1995.

PART VII
Miscellaneous

CHAPTER II
General

172 Duties of a relevant person in relation to certain revenue offences

(1) In this section—

"the Acts" means—

    (*a*)   the Customs Acts,

    (*b*)   the statutes relating to the duties of excise and to the management of those duties,

    (*c*)   the Tax Acts,

    (*d*)   the Capital Gains Tax Acts,

    (*e*)   the Value Added Tax Act, 1972, and the enactments amending or extending that Act,

    (*f*)   the Capital Acquisitions Tax Act, 1976, and the enactments amending or extending that Act,

    (*g*)   the statutes relating to stamp duty and to the management of that duty,

and any instruments made thereunder and any instruments made under any other enactment and relating to tax;

"appropriate officer" means any officer nominated by the Revenue Commissioners to be an appropriate officer for the purposes of this section;

"company" means any body corporate;

"relevant person", in relation to a company, means a person who—

    (*a*)   (i)   is an auditor to the company appointed in accordance with section 160 of the Companies Act, 1963 (as amended by the Companies Act, 1990), or

            (ii)   in the case of an industrial and provident society or a friendly society, is a public auditor to the society for the purposes of the Industrial and Provident Societies Acts, 1893 to 1978, and the Friendly Societies Acts, 1896 to 1977,

        or

    (*b*)   with a view to reward assists or advises the company in the preparation or delivery of any information, declaration, return, records, accounts or other document which he or she knows will be, or is likely to be, used for any purpose of tax:

        Provided that a person who would, but for this proviso, be treated as a relevant person in relation to a company shall not be so treated if the person assists or advises the company solely in the person's capacity as an employee of the said company, and a person shall be treated as assisting or advising the company in that capacity where the person's income from assisting or advising the company consists solely of emoluments to which Chapter IV of Part V of the Income Tax Act, 1967, applies;

"relevant offence" means an offence committed by a company which consists of the company—

    (*a*)   knowingly or wilfully delivering any incorrect return, statement or accounts or knowingly or wilfully furnishing or causing to be furnished any incorrect information in connection with any tax,

253

(*b*) knowingly or wilfully claiming or obtaining relief or exemption from, or repayment of, any tax, being a relief, exemption or repayment to which there is no entitlement,

(*c*) knowingly or wilfully issuing or producing any incorrect invoice, receipt, instrument or other document in connection with any tax,

(*d*) knowingly or wilfully failing to comply with any provision of the Acts requiring the furnishing of a return of income, profits or gains, or of sources of income, profits or gains, for the purposes of any tax:

Provided that an offence under this paragraph committed by a company shall not be a relevant offence if the company has made a return of income, profits or gains to the Revenue Commissioners in respect of an accounting period falling wholly or partly into the period of 3 years immediately preceding the accounting period in respect of which the offence was committed;

"**tax**" means tax, duty, levy or charge under the care and management of the Revenue Commissioners.

(2) If, having regard solely to information obtained in the course of examining the accounts of a company, or in the course of assisting or advising a company in the preparation or delivery of any information, declaration, return, records, accounts or other document for the purposes of tax, as the case may be, a person who is a relevant person in relation to the company becomes aware that the company has committed, or is in the course of committing, one or more relevant offences, the person shall, if the offence or offences are material—

(*a*) communicate particulars of the offence or offences in writing to the company without undue delay and request the company to—

(i) take such action as is necessary for the purposes of rectifying the matter, or

(ii) notify an appropriate officer of the offence or offences,

not later than 6 months after the time of communication, and

(*b*) (i) unless it is established to the person's satisfaction that the necessary action has been taken or notification made, as the case may be, under paragraph (*a*), cease to act as the auditor to the company or to assist or advise the company in such preparation or delivery as is specified in paragraph (*b*) of the definition of relevant person, and

(ii) shall not so act, assist or advise before a time which is—

(I) 3 years after the time at which the particulars were communicated under paragraph (*a*), or

(II) the time at which it is established to the person's satisfaction that the necessary action has been taken or notification made, as the case may be, under paragraph (*a*),

whichever is the earlier:

Provided that nothing in this paragraph shall prevent a person from assisting or advising a company in preparing for, or conducting, legal proceedings, either civil or criminal, which are extant or pending at a time which is 6 months after the time of communication under paragraph (*a*).

(3) Where a person, being in relation to a company a relevant person within the meaning of paragraph (*a*) of the definition of relevant person, ceases under the provisions of this section to act as auditor to the company, then the person shall deliver—

(*a*) a notice in writing to the company stating that he or she is so resigning, and

(*b*) a copy of the notice to an appropriate officer not later than 14 days after he or she has delivered the notice to the company.

(4) A person shall be guilty of an offence under this section if the person—

    (*a*)   fails to comply with subsection (2) or (3), or

    (*b*)   knowingly or wilfully makes a communication under subsection (2) which is incorrect.

(5) Where a relevant person is found guilty of an offence under this section the person shall be liable—

    (*a*)   on summary conviction to a fine of £1,000 which may be mitigated to not less than one-fourth part thereof, or

    (*b*)   on conviction on indictment, to a fine not exceeding £5,000 or, at the discretion of the court, to imprisonment for a term not exceeding 2 years or to both the fine and the imprisonment.

(6) Section 13 of the Criminal Procedure Act, 1967, shall apply in relation to this section as if, in lieu of the penalties specified in subsection (3) of the said section 13, there were specified therein the penalties provided for by subsection (5)(*a*) of this section, and the reference in subsection (2)(*a*) of the said section 13 to the penalties provided for in the said subsection (3) shall be construed and have effect accordingly.

(7) Notwithstanding the provisions of any other enactment, proceedings in respect of this section may be instituted within 6 years from the time at which a person is required under subsection (2) to communicate particulars of an offence or offences in writing to a company.

(8) It shall be a good defence in a prosecution for an offence under subsection (4)(*a*) in relation to a failure to comply with subsection (2) for an accused (being a person who is a relevant person in relation to a company) to show that he or she was, in the ordinary scope of professional engagement, assisting or advising the company in preparing for legal proceedings and would not have become aware that one or more relevant offences had been committed by the company if he or she had not been so assisting or advising.

(9) If a person who is a relevant person takes any action required by subsection (2) or (3), no duty to which the person may be subject shall be regarded as contravened and no liability or action shall lie against the person in any court for so doing.

(10) The Revenue Commissioners may nominate an officer to be an appropriate officer for the purposes of this section and the name of an officer so nominated and the address to which copies of notices under subsection (2) or (3) shall be delivered shall be published in the Iris Oifigiúil.

(11) This section shall have effect as respects a relevant offence committed by a company in respect of tax which is—

    (*a*)   assessable by reference to accounting periods, for any accounting period beginning after the 30th day of June, 1995,

    (*b*)   assessable by reference to years of assessment, for the year of assessment 1995-96 and subsequent years,

    (*c*)   payable by reference to a taxable period, for a taxable period beginning after the 30th day of June, 1995,

    (*d*)   chargeable on gifts or inheritances taken on or after the 30th day of June, 1995,

    (*e*)   chargeable on instruments executed on or after the 30th day of June, 1995, or

    (*f*)   payable in any other case, on or after the 30th day of June, 1995.

Definitions
"month": IA 1937 Sch; "person": IA 1937 s 11(*c*); "writing": IA 1937 Sch; "year": IA 1937 Sch; "year of assessment": CGTA 1975 s 2(1), ITA 1967 s 1(1).

---

174 Amendment of section 115 (liability to tax, etc., of holder of fixed charge on book debts of company) of Finance Act, 1986

Notes
With effect from 6 April 1995:
this section substituted FA 1986 s 115(1).

175 Power to obtain information

(1) For the purposes of the assessment, charge, collection and recovery of any tax or duty placed under their care and management, the Revenue Commissioners may, by notice in writing, request any Minister of the Government to provide them with such information in the possession of the Minister in relation to payments for any purposes made by the Minister, whether on his own behalf or on behalf of any other person, to such persons or classes of persons as the Revenue Commissioners may specify in the notice and a Minister so requested shall provide such information as may be specified.

(2) The Revenue Commissioners may nominate any of their officers to perform any acts and discharge any functions authorised by this section to be performed or discharged by the Revenue Commissioners.

Definitions
"person": IA 1937 s 11(*c*); "tax": s 1(1); "writing": IA 1937 Sch

177 Tax clearance certificates in relation to public sector contracts

(1) In this section—

"the Acts" means—

> (*a*)　the Tax Acts,
>
> (*b*)　the Capital Gains Tax Acts,
>
> (*c*)　the Value Added Tax Act, 1972, and the enactments amending or extending that Act,

and any instruments made thereunder;

"the scheme" means a scheme of the Department of Finance for the time being in force for requiring persons to show, by means of tax clearance certificates, compliance with the obligations imposed by the Acts in relation to the matters specified in subsection (2) before the award to them of contracts that are specified in a circular of the Department of Finance entitled "Tax Clearance Procedures — Public Sector Contracts", numbered F 49/24/84 and issued on the 30th day of July, 1991, or any such circular amending or replacing that circular;

"tax clearance certificate" shall be construed in accordance with subsection (2).

(2) Subject to the provisions of this section, where a person who is in compliance with the obligations imposed on the person by the Acts in relation to—

> (*a*)　the payment or remittance of any taxes, interest or penalties required to be paid or remitted under the Acts to the Revenue Commissioners, and
>
> (*b*)　the delivery of any returns required to be made under the Acts,

applies to the Collector-General in that behalf for the purposes of the scheme, the Collector-General shall issue to the person a certificate (in this section referred to as "a tax clearance certificate") stating that the person is in compliance with the obligations aforesaid.

(3) A tax clearance certificate shall not be issued to a person unless—

> (*a*)　the person, and any partnership of which the person is or was a member, in respect of the period of the person's membership thereof,
>
> (*b*)　in a case where the person is a partnership, each person who is a member of the partnership, and

    (*c*)   in a case where the person is a company, each person who is either the beneficial owner of, or able directly or indirectly, to control, more than 50 per cent. of the ordinary share capital of the company,

is in compliance with the obligations imposed on the person and each other person (including any partnership) by the Acts in relation to the matters specified in paragraphs (*a*) and (*b*) of subsection (2).

(4) Where a person (hereafter in this subsection referred to as "the first-mentioned person") applies for a tax clearance certificate in accordance with subsection (2) and the business activity to which the application relates was previously carried on by, or was previously carried on as part of a business activity carried on by, another person (hereafter in this subsection referred to as "the second-mentioned person") and—

    (*a*)   the second-mentioned person is a company which is connected within the meaning of section 16(3) of the Finance (Miscellaneous Provisions) Act, 1968, with the first-mentioned person or would have been such a company but for the fact that the company has been wound up or dissolved without being wound up, or

    (*b*)   the second-mentioned person is a company and the first-mentioned person is a partnership and—

        (i)   a member of the partnership is or was able, or

        (ii)   where more than one such member is a shareholder of the company, those members acting together are or were able,

directly or indirectly, either on his, her or their own, or with a connected person or connected persons within the meaning of the said section 16(3), to control more than 50 per cent. of the ordinary share capital of the company, or

    (*c*)   the second-mentioned person is a partnership and the first-mentioned person is a company and—

        (i)   a member of the partnership is or was able, or

        (ii)   where more than one such member is a shareholder of the company, those members acting together are or were able,

        directly or indirectly, either on his, her or their own, or with a connected person or connected persons within the meaning of the said section 16(3), to control more than 50 per cent. of the ordinary share capital of the company,

then, a tax clearance certificate shall not be issued to the first-mentioned person unless, in relation to the business activity to which the application relates, the second-mentioned person is in compliance with the obligations imposed on that person by the Acts in relation to the matters specified in paragraphs (*a*) and (*b*) and subsection (2):

Provided that this subsection shall not apply to a business the transfer of which was effected before the 9th day of May, 1995, or a business the transfer of which is or was effected after that date if a contract for the transfer was made before that date.

(5) Subsections (4), (5) and (6) of section 242 of the Finance Act, 1992, shall, with any necessary modifications, apply to an application for a tax clearance certificate under this section as they apply to an application for a tax clearance certificate under that section.

(6) A tax clearance certificate shall be valid for the period specified therein.

(7) This section shall come into operation on the 1st day of July, 1995.

Definitions
"business": s 1(1); "person": IA 1937 s 11(*c*); "tax": s 1(1).

---

178 Care and management of taxes and duties

All taxes and duties (except the excise duties on mechanically propelled vehicles imposed by section 117) imposed by this Act are hereby placed under the care and management of the Revenue Commissioners.

179 Short title, construction and commencement

(1) This Act may be cited as the Finance Act, 1995.

...

(4) Part III shall be construed together with the Value Added Tax Acts, 1972 to 1994, and may be cited together therewith as the Value Added Tax Acts, 1972 to 1995.

...

...

(10) In relation to Part III:

(*a*)   section 119, paragraph (*b*) of section 120, section 121, paragraph (*a*) of section 125, sections 126 and 127, paragraph (*a*) of section 128, sections 129 and 130, paragraphs (*b*), (*c*), (*d*), (*e*), (*f*) and (*g*) of section 140 and section 141 shall take effect as on and from the 1st day of July, 1995;

(*b*)   section 124, paragraph (*a*) of section 137, paragraph (*b*) of section 139 and paragraph (*a*) of section 140 shall take effect as on and from the 1st day of January, 1996;

(*c*)   the provisions of this Part, other than those specified in paragraphs (*a*) and (*b*), shall have effect as on and from the date of passing of this Act.

(11) Any reference in this Act to any other enactment shall, except so far as the context otherwise requires, be construed as a reference to that enactment as amended by or under any other enactment including this Act.

(12) In this Act, a reference to a Part, section or Schedule is to a Part or section of, or Schedule to, this Act, unless it is indicated that reference to some other enactment is intended.

(13) In this Act, a reference to a subsection, paragraph, subparagraph, clause or subclause is to the subsection, paragraph, subparagraph, clause or subclause of the provision (including a Schedule) in which the reference occurs, unless it is indicated that reference to some other provision is intended.

FINANCE ACT 1996

(Number 9 of 1996)

PART III
Value added tax

PART VII
Miscellaneous

An Act to charge and impose certain duties of customs and inland revenue (including excise), to amend the law relating to customs and inland revenue (including excise) and to make further provisions in connection with finance. [*15th May, 1996*]

PART III
Value added tax

87 Interpretation (Part III)

In this Part (

"the Principal Act" means the Value Added Tax Act, 1972;

"the Act of 1978" means the Value Added Tax (Amendment) Act, 1978;

"the Act of 1992" means the Finance Act, 1992;

"the Act of 1993" means the Finance Act, 1993;

"the Act of 1995" means the Finance Act, 1995.

88 Amendment of section 1 (interpretation) of Principal Act

General note

The Second Simplification Directive (Council Directive 95/7/EC of 10 April 1995) introduced changes which were initially given effect in Irish law from 1 January 1996 by the European Communities (Value Added Tax) Regulations 1995 (SI 363/1995). FA 1996 now confirms the changes, and repeals those regulations. The changes mean that intra EU cross border contract work on movable goods is now treated as a service - and no VAT is chargeable where the customer is VAT registered within the EU.

Notes

Para (*a*) inserted definitions of "contractor" and "contract work" in VATA 1972 s 1(1) with effect from 1 January 1996 - these definitions are needed for the for the simplified treatment of contract work.

Para (*b*), by substituting "used" for "second-hand" in the definition of "goods" in VATA 1972 s 1(1) with effect from 15 May 1996 ensures that the more restrictive definition of "second-hand" is not applied to goods that are to be the subject of contract work.

Para (*c*) substituted "the State" for "a Member State" in the definition of "importation of goods" in VATA 1972 s 1(1) with effect from 15 May 1996. This is a technical amendment to facilitate the simplified procedure for contract work.

---

89 Amendment of section 3 (supply of goods) of Principal Act

Notes

Para (*a*)(i) substituted VATA 1972 s 3(1)(*aa*) with effect from 15 May 1996; all commission sales of movable goods by auctioneers and agents are treated as supplies of goods for VAT purposes.

Para (*a*)(ii) substituted VATA 1972 s 3(1)(*c*) with effect from 1 January 1996; contract work on movable goods is now a supply of a service, and not a supply of goods. Intra EU cross border contract work (now a service) need not be reported on the quarterly EU sales listing.

Para (*a*)(iii)(I) deleted VATA 1972 s 3(1)(*g*)(iii) with effect from 1 January 1996 - that paragraph is redundant because the contract work is no longer regarded as a supply of goods.

Para (*a*)(iii)(II) substituted VATA 1972 s 3(1)(*g*)(iiia) with effect from 1 January 1996; a transfer of goods from Ireland to another EU State in order to have contract work carried out on them is not a supply for VAT purposes, provided the goods are later returned to Ireland.

Para (*b*) deleted VATA 1972 s 3(3), which dealt with certain auction sales, with effect from 1 January 1996; the relevant transactions are now included in VATA 1972 s 3(1)(*aa*).

Para (*c*) substituted VATA 1972 s 3(4) with effect from 15 May 1996. An auctioneer selling goods on a commission basis is regarded as having been supplied with the goods when he sells them - this means that the auctioneer will effectively be taxed on his commission margin, but the transaction will be regarded as a simultaneous supply of goods to, and by, the auctioneer.

90 Amendment of section 5 (supply of services) of Principal Act

Notes

Para (*a*)(i) inserted "except where the provisions of subparagraph (iv) of paragraph (*f*) apply" after "movable goods" in VATA 1972 s 5(6)(*c*)(iii) with effect from 1 January1996; para (*a*)(ii) inserted ", including contract work, except where the provisions of subparagraph (iv) of paragraph (*f*) apply" after "movable goods" in VATA 1972 s 5(6)(*c*)(iv) with effect from 1 January 1996; these changes ensure that the normal place of taxation rules do not apply in the case of valuation services relating to, or work on, movable goods.

Para (*b*) inserted VATA 1972 s 5(6)(*f*)(iv) with effect from 1 January 1996. The place of taxation for intra EU cross border work on movable goods, or valuation services on movable goods, is the EU State in which the customer is VAT registered, if the goods have been sent back from the country in which the repair or valuation work was performed.

91 Amendment of section 10B (special scheme for auctioneers) of Principal Act

Notes

This section substituted "auction scheme goods" for "tangible movable goods" in VATA 1972 s 10B(9) with effect from 15 May 1996. This is a technical amendment to correct a drafting inconsistency.

92 Amendment of section 11 (rates of tax) of Principal Act

Notes

Para (*a*), by substituting "2.8 per cent" for "2.5 per cent" in VATA 1972 s 11(1)(*f*) with effect from 1 March 1996, increases the rate applicable to the supply of livestock, live greyhounds and the hire of horses.

Para (*b*), by inserting VATA 1972 s 11(1AB) with effect from 1 January 1996, provides that although contract work is now a supply of services (see s 89(*a*)(ii) above), the tax rate applicable is the rate that would apply to the supply of the finished goods.

93 Amendment of section 12 (deductions for tax borne or paid) of Principal Act

Notes

Para (*a*), by inserting VATA 1972 s 12(1)(*a*)(ia) with effect from 1 July 1996, ensures that a taxable person acquiring goods from a finance company will be entitled to a VAT deduction on the basis of the document issued by the finance company.

Para (*b*) deleted "or" at the end of VATA 1972 s 12(3)(*a*)(iii) and inserted VATA 1972 s 12(3)(*a*)(iva) with effect from 15 May 1996. This is a technical amendment to ensure that a VAT deduction does not become available to traders as a consequence of the redefining of contract work as a supply of services.

94 Amendment of section 12A (special provisions for tax invoiced by flat-rate farmers) of Principal Act

Notes

This section, by substituting "2.8 per cent" for "2.5 per cent" in VATA 1972 s 12A(1) with effect from 1 March 1996, increased the farmers' flat rate addition.

95 Amendment of section 13A (supplies to, and intra-Community acquisitions and imports by, certain taxable persons) of Principal Act

Notes

This section inserted ", supplies of contract work where the place of supply is deemed to be a Member State other than the State and supplies of contract work made in accordance with paragraph (xvi) of the Second Schedule" after "Second Schedule" in the definition of "qualifying person" in VATA 1972 s 13A(1) with effect from 1 January 1996.

This change is intended to ensure that exporting firms are not affected by the redefinition of contract work as a supply of services.

96 Amendment of section 15 (charge of tax on imported goods) of Principal Act

Notes

This section inserted ", expenses resulting from the transport of the goods to another place of destination within the Community, if that destination is known at the time of the importation," after "duties" in VATA 1972 s 15(3) with effect from 1 January 1996. Where imported goods are sent to another EU State, the intra EU transport cost is to be included on the value for assessment of VAT at import.

97 Amendment of section 17 (invoices) of Principal Act

Notes

Para (*a*) added VATA 1972 s 17(1)(proviso) with effect from 1 July 1996; the person supplying goods that the subject of a finance (HP) agreement must invoice the finance company and not the person acquiring the goods.

Para (*b*) inserted VATA 1972 s 17(1AA)-(1AB) with effect from 1 July 1996; the finance company must provide VAT-invoice type details in its agreement with the person acquiring the goods. The finance company is also obliged to maintain, and make available for inspection, proper books and records.

Para (*c*) inserted VATA 1972 s 17(3AB) with effect from 1 July 1996; where a finance company that has already supplied goods to a customer under a HP agreement subsequently receives a credit note from the supplier, it must issue a corresponding credit note to its customer.

Para (*d*) inserted VATA 1972 s 17(5A) with effect from 1 July 1996; if a finance company shows a greater amount of tax on its VAT-invoice type agreement, it is liable for that amount.

Para (*e*) inserted VATA 1972 s 17(7A) with effect from 1 July 1996. The VAT-invoice type agreement must be issued on or before the 22nd of the month following the month in which the goods were supplied.

98 Amendment of Second Schedule to the Principal Act

Notes

Para (*a*) deleted "or from" after "goods to" in VATA 1972 Sch 2 para (iii) with effect from 15 May 1996; transport of imported goods is no longer zero-rated under this paragraph, but under paragraph (xvi*a*), as inserted by paragraph (*b*).

Para (*b*) substituted VATA 1972 Sch 2 para (xvi) with effect from 1 January 1996; a service consisting of work on movable goods that have been brought into the EU for the purposes of such work is zero-rated, provided the goods are subsequently re-exported from the EU.

Para (*c*) inserted VATA 1972 Sch 2 para (xvi*a*) with effect from 1 January 1996. Intra EU transport of goods imported from outside the EU is zero-rated, provided the transport costs have been included in the value for VAT at importation.

99 Amendment of Sixth Schedule to the Principal Act

Notes

This section, by inserting "contract work or" after "other than" in VATA 1972 Sch 6 para (xviii)(*b*) with effect from 1 January 1996, provides that contract work will not be liable at 12.5% unless the goods subject to contract work are liable at 12.5%.

100 Revocation (Part III)

Notes

This section revoked the European Communities (Value Added Tax) Regulations 1995 (SI 363/1995).

PART VII
Miscellaneous

142 Care and management of taxes and duties

All taxes and duties (except the excise duties on mechanically propelled vehicles imposed by section 86) imposed by this Act are hereby placed under the care and management of the Revenue Commissioners.

143 Short title, construction and commencement

...

(4) Part III shall be construed together with the Value-Added Tax Acts, 1972 to 1995, and may be cited together therewith as the Value-Added Tax Acts, 1972 to 1996.

(10) In relation to Part III:

    (*a*)   section 87, paragraph (*a*) of section 88, subparagraphs (ii) and (iii) of paragraph (*a*) of section 89, section 90, paragraph (*b*) of section 92, sections 95 and 96, paragraphs (*b*) and (*c*) of section 98 and section 99 shall be deemed to have come into force and shall take effect as on and from the 1st day of January, 1996;

    (*b*)   paragraph (*a*) of section 92 and section 94 shall be deemed to have come into force and shall take effect as on and from the 1st day of March, 1996;

    (*c*)   paragraph (*a*) of section 93 and section 97 shall take effect as on and from the 1st day of July, 1996;

    (*d*)   the provisions of this Part, other than those specified in paragraphs (*a*), (*b*) and (*c*), shall have effect as on and from the date of passing of this Act.

(11) Any reference in this Act to any other enactment shall, except so far as the context otherwise requires, be construed as a reference to that enactment as amended by or under any other enactment including this Act.

(12) In this Act, a reference to a Part, section or Schedule is to a Part or section of, or Schedule to, this Act, unless it is indicated that reference to some other enactment is intended.

(13) In this Act, a reference to a subsection, paragraph, subparagraph, clause or subclause is to the subsection, paragraph, subparagraph, clause or subclause of the provision (including a Schedule) in which the reference occurs, unless it is indicated that reference to some other provision is intended.

REGULATIONS

VALUE ADDED TAX REGULATIONS 1979

(SI No 63 of 1979)

Short title and commencement

1. (1) These Regulations may be cited as the Value Added Tax Regulations, 1979.

(2) These Regulations shall come into operation on the 1st, day of March, 1979.

Cross-reference
VATA 1972 s 32.

Notes
These regulations which came into effect on 1 March 1979 prescribe the manner in which VAT is to be operated in respect of elections for taxability, waiver of exemptions and the treatment of two or more taxable persons as a single taxable person; registration and cancellation; cash receipts basis; accounts to be kept, invoices credit notes etc; returns, payments, apportionments, estimates etc; refunds and remissions of tax; valuation of interests in immovable goods; dances; relief for stock in trade held at commencement of taxability; determination of tax; supply of certain services; treatment of certain gifts and trading stamps exchanged for goods.

Interpretation

2. (1) In these Regulations—

"the Act" means the Value Added Tax Act, 1972;

"taxable turnover", in relation to any period, means the total of the amounts on which tax is chargeable for that period at any of the rates specified in section 11(1) of the Act;

"turnover", in relation to any period, means the amount on which tax would be chargeable for that period in accordance with section 10 of the Act if section 6 of the Act were disregarded.

(2) In these Regulations—

> (a)   a reference to a regulation is to a regulation of these Regulations, and

> (b)   a reference to a paragraph, subparagraph or clause is to a paragraph, subparagraph or clause of the regulation in which the reference occurs,

unless it is indicated that reference to some other provision is intended.

Election to be a taxable person

3. (1) A person who, in accordance with section 8(3) of the Act is not a taxable person but who desires to elect to be such a person shall furnish to the Revenue Commissioners the particulars for registration specified in Regulation 6.

(2) The furnishing of the particulars referred to in paragraph (1) shall constitute an election to be a taxable person and such election shall have effect as from the end of the taxable period during which such particulars are received by the Revenue Commissioners, or, by agreement between the person and the Revenue Commissioners, as from the end of the next preceding taxable period, until the date on which the person permanently ceases to supply taxable goods or services in the course or furtherance of business or until the date on which his election is cancelled in accordance with paragraph (3), whichever date is the earlier.

(3) A person who is a taxable person by reason only of an election in that behalf made in accordance with paragraphs (1) and (2) shall be entitled to have such election cancelled and to be treated, as from the date specified in paragraph (4), as a person who had not made such an election provided he fulfils all of the following conditions; and a person who satisfies the Revenue Commissioners in regard to his turnover in accordance with section 8(6)(a) of the Act may be treated as a person who is not a taxable person provided he fulfils similar conditions:

> (a)   he shall notify the Revenue Commissioners in writing that he desires to have his election cancelled or that he desires to be treated as a person who is not a taxable person;

> (b)   he shall furnish to the Revenue Commissioners particulars of—

>> (i)   the total amount of tax paid by him in accordance with section 19(3) of the Act in respect of whichever of the following periods is the lesser:

>>> (I)   all the taxable periods comprised in the period commencing with the beginning of the first taxable period for which his election had effect or he was treated as a taxable person and ending with the termination of the taxable period immediately preceding that during which he notifies the Revenue Commissioners that he wishes to have his election cancelled or be treated as a person who is not a taxable person, or

>>> (II)   the eighteen consecutive taxable periods next before the taxable period during which he so notifies the Revenue Commissioners,

>> and

>> (ii)   the total amount of tax refunded to him in accordance with section 20(1) of the Act in respect of whichever of the periods referred to in clause (i) is appropriate;

(*c*)   he shall pay to the Collector-General an amount equal to the excess (if any) of the total amount referred to in clause (ii) of the preceding subparagraph over the total amount referred to in clause (i) of that subparagraph.

(4) If the conditions specified in the preceding paragraph have been fulfilled to the satisfaction of the Revenue Commissioners, they shall so notify the person concerned in writing and, on receipt by the person of such notice, his election shall be cancelled or he shall be treated as a person who is not a taxable person with effect as on and from the end of the taxable period during which the conditions have been so fulfilled; and as on and from the end of such taxable period, the person shall be treated as a person who had not elected to be a taxable person or as a person who is not a taxable person.

(5) A person who notifies the Revenue Commissioners during any taxable period (in this paragraph referred to as the final taxable period) of his desire to have his election cancelled or to be treated as a person who is not a taxable person shall not be entitled, under section 20(1) of the Act to any refund of tax, other than a refund referable solely to an error or mistake made by him, in excess of whichever of the following amounts is appropriate —

(*a*)   in a case in which there is an excess of the amount referred to in paragraph (3)(*b*)(i) over the amount referred to in paragraph (3)(*b*)(ii), an amount for the final taxable period and for any subsequent taxable period consisting of the amount of such excess, increased by the amounts paid under section 19(3) of the Act, for the final taxable period and any subsequent taxable periods up to and including the taxable period to which the claim relates and reduced by the total of the refunds under Section 20(1) of the Act previously made for any of those taxable periods, and

(*b*)   in any other case, an amount for the final taxable period or for any subsequent taxable period consisting of the excess of the total of the amounts paid under section 19(3) of the Act for the final and all subsequent taxable periods up to and including the taxable period to which the claim relates reduced by the total of the refunds under section 20(1) of the Act previously made for any of those taxable periods.

(6) In the case of a person who, in the absence of an election to be a taxable person, would (in accordance with section 8(3)(*a*) of the Act) not be such a person, paragraph (3)(*b*) shall apply as if —

(i)   the amount of tax paid by him in accordance with section 19(3) of the Act in respect of each of the taxable periods comprised in whichever of the periods referred to in clause (i) is appropriate were increased by an amount equal to 1 per cent. of the consideration on which tax was chargeable for each of those taxable periods in respect of transactions specified in section 8(9) of the Act other than in paragraph (*d*) of the definition of farmer, and

(ii)   the total amount of tax refunded to him in respect of all the taxable periods comprised in the period referred to in clause (ii) were reduced by the total amount of tax which qualified for deduction under section 12 of the Act in respect of those taxable periods and which, in accordance with any order made under section 20(3) of the Act would fall to be refunded to him if he were not a taxable person.

Waiver of exemption

4.(1) A person who, in accordance with section 7(1) of the Act desires to waive his right to have the supply by him of the services specified in paragraph (iv) or (x) of the First Schedule to the Act regarded as exempted activities shall furnish the following particulars in writing to the Revenue Commissioners:—

(*a*)   his name and address;

(*b*)   whether he is registered for value added tax and if so, his registration number;

(*c*)   the paragraph or paragraphs in the said First Schedule in which are specified the services in respect of which it is desired that the right to exemption should be waived;

and

(*d*)   the taxable period as from the commencement of which he desires that the waiver should have effect, not being earlier than the current taxable period.

(2) The Revenue Commissioners shall acknowledge receipt of the particulars referred to in the preceding paragraph and shall specify the taxable period, not being earlier than the taxable period referred to in subparagraph (*d*) of the said preceding paragraph, as from the commencement of which the waiver of exemption in respect of the services specified in the paragraph or paragraphs referred to in subparagraph (*c*) of the said preceding paragraph shall have effect; and as from the commencement of the taxable period so specified and until the date upon which the person permanently ceases to supply taxable goods or services (including services to which the waiver of exemption applies), in the course or furtherance of business, or until his waiver is cancelled in accordance with paragraph (3), the provisions of the Act shall apply to him as if the services specified in the paragraph or paragraphs referred to in paragraph (1)(*c*) were not specified in the said First Schedule.

(3) A person who, in accordance with paragraph (1), waives his right to exemption in respect of the services specified in paragraph (iv) or (x) of the First Schedule to the Act shall be entitled to have such waiver cancelled and to be treated, as from the date specified in paragraph (4), as a person who had not so waived his right to exemption, provided he fulfils all of the following conditions:—

(*a*)   he shall notify the Revenue Commissioners in writing of the paragraph or paragraphs of the First Schedule to the Act in which are specified the services in respect of which it is desired that the waiver of his right to exemption should be cancelled;

(*b*)   he shall furnish particulars of—

     (i)   the tax, or, in case he is chargeable with tax on the supply of goods or services other than those specified in the paragraphs referred to in the notification aforesaid, the additional tax paid by him in accordance with section 19(3) of the Act in respect of the services so specified for all of the taxable periods comprised in the period commencing with the beginning of the first taxable period for which his waiver had effect and ending with the termination of the taxable period immediately preceding that during which he notifies the Revenue Commissioners that he desires to have his waiver cancelled, and

     (ii)   the total amount of tax refunded to him in accordance with section 20(1) of the Act in respect of all of the taxable periods comprised in the period referred to in clause (i), or in case such total amount is referable partly to services specified in the paragraphs referred to in the notification aforesaid and partly to the supply of goods or other services, the amount included in such total amount which is referable to the services so specified;

(*c*)   he shall pay to the Collector General an amount equal to the excess (if any) of the total amount or of the amount referred to in subparagraph (*b*)(ii), as the case may be, over the total amount of tax or of the additional tax, as may be appropriate, referred to in subparagraph (*b*)(i).

(4) If the conditions specified in the preceding paragraph are fulfilled to the satisfaction of the Revenue Commissioners, they shall so notify the person concerned in writing and, on receipt by the person of such notice, his waiver shall be cancelled with effect as on and from the end of the taxable period during which he is so notified; and as on and from the end of such taxable period the person shall be treated as a person who had not waived his right to exemption in respect of services specified in the paragraph or paragraphs referred to in the notification given by the person pursuant to paragraph (3)(*a*).

(5) A person who notifies the Revenue Commissioners during any taxable period (in this paragraph referred to as the final taxable period) of his desire to have his waiver of exemption cancelled shall not be entitled, under section 20(1) of the Act to any refund of tax, other than a refund referable solely to some error or mistake made by him, in excess of whichever of the following amounts is appropriate:

(*a*)   in a case in which there is an excess of the amount referred to in paragraph (3)(*b*)(i) over the amount referred to in paragraph (3)(*b*)(ii), an amount for the final taxable period and for any subsequent taxable period consisting of such excess, increased by the amounts paid under section 19(3) of the Act, for the final taxable period and any subsequent taxable periods up to and including the taxable period to which the claim relates and reduced by the total of the refunds under section 20(1) of the Act previously made for any of those taxable periods, and

(*b*)   in any other case, an amount for the final taxable period or for any subsequent taxable period consisting of the excess of the total of the amounts paid under section 19(3) of the Act for the final and all subsequent taxable periods up to and including the taxable period to which the claim relates, reduced by the total of the refunds under section 20(1) of the Act previously made in respect of any of those taxable periods.

(6) Where the period referred to in paragraph (3)(*b*)(i) exceeds ten years, reference therein to the first taxable period for which his waiver had effect shall be construed as a reference to the taxable period the beginning of which is ten years earlier than the date of commencement of the taxable period during which he notifies the Revenue Commissioners that he desires to have his waiver cancelled.

Treatment of two or more taxable persons as a single taxable person

5. (1) If two or more taxable persons desire that all the business activities carried on by each of them shall, in accordance with section 8(8) of the Act be deemed, for the purposes of the Act to be carried on by any one of those persons, each of them shall furnish the following particulars in writing to the Revenue Commissioners:—

(*a*)   his name, address and registration number;

(*b*)   the nature of the business activities carried on by him;

(*c*)   in case the person desires that all the business activities carried on by him should be deemed to be carried on by another person, the name, address and registration number of that other person;

(*d*)   in case the person desires that all the business activities carried on by another person or two or more other persons should be deemed to be carried on by the first-mentioned person, the name, address and registration number of that other person or of each of those other persons; and

(*e*)   such other information about the business activities of the person or about the business or financial relationship between him and each of the other persons carrying on the business activities aforesaid as the Revenue Commissioners may, by notice in writing, require.

(2) The Revenue Commissioners shall, in their absolute discretion, determine—

(*a*)   whether all the business activities carried on by two or more persons who have furnished the particulars specified in paragraph (1) shall be deemed to be carried on by any one of those persons;

(*b*)   in case all the business activities referred to in subparagraph (*a*) are deemed to be carried on by any one of the persons referred to in the said subparagraph (*a*):—

(i)   the person by whom the said activities are deemed to be carried on;

(ii)   the person or each of the persons all of whose business activities are deemed to be carried on by the person referred to in clause (i);

    (*c*)   the date, not being earlier than the commencement of the taxable period during which the particulars referred to in paragraph (1) are furnished, as from which all of the business activities of the person or persons concerned are deemed to be carried on by one of them, and shall notify each of the persons concerned in writing of the matters so determined.

(3) Upon the issue of a notification to a person in accordance with paragraph (2) of a determination that all the business activities referred to in the determination are deemed to be carried on by one person, the following provisions shall apply from the date specified in the notification pursuant to paragraph (2)(*c*) until the notification is cancelled in accordance with paragraph (5):

    (*a*)   in case the person to whom the notification is issued is the person by whom all the business activities referred to in the notification are deemed to be carried on, the provisions of the Act shall, subject to paragraph (4), apply to the person as if all transactions by or between himself and the other person or persons carrying on the said business activities were transactions by himself, and all other rights and obligations under the Act shall be determined accordingly,

    (*b*)   in case the person to whom the notification is issued is not the person by whom all the business activities referred to in the notification are deemed to be carried on, the provisions of the Act shall, subject to paragraph (4), apply to him as if all transactions by or between himself and the person by whom the said business activities are deemed to be carried on (in this subparagraph referred to as the last-mentioned person) were transactions by the last-mentioned person, but the person shall be jointly liable with the last-mentioned person and any other person specified in the notification to comply with all the provisions of the Act and regulations (including the provisions requiring payment of tax) that apply to him and the last-mentioned person and any other person so specified and shall be subject to the penalties under the Act to which he and the last-mentioned person and any other person so specified would be liable if they were liable to pay to the Revenue Commissioners the whole of the tax chargeable, apart from this Regulation, in respect of himself and the last-mentioned person and any other person so specified.

(4) Notwithstanding anything in paragraph (3), each of the persons all of whose business activities are during any period deemed, in accordance with this Regulation, to be carried on by one of them shall be deemed to be a registered person during the whole of that period, and the provisions of section 17 of the Act shall apply to each of those persons as if a notification under paragraph (3) had not been issued.

(5) The Revenue Commissioners may, in their absolute discretion, by notice in writing addressed to each of a group of persons all of whose business activities are, by virtue of a notification issued in accordance with paragraph (2), deemed to be carried on by one of those persons, and as on and from the date specified in the notice (which shall not be earlier than the date of the notice) cancel the notification under the said paragraph (2); and as on and from the date specified in the said notice the provisions of the Act and Regulations shall apply to all the persons aforesaid as if a notification under the said paragraph (2) had not been issued, but without prejudice to the liability of any of the persons for tax or penalties in respect of anything done or not done during the period for which the said notification was in force.

Registration

6. ...

Notes

Revoked by Value Added Tax (Registration) Regulations 1993 r 7 (SI 30/1993).

Determination of tax due by reference to cash receipts

7. ...

Notes
Revoked by Value Added Tax (Determination of Tax Due by Reference to Moneys Received) Regulations 1986 r 4 (SI 298/1986).

Adjustments for returned goods, discounts, and price alterations

8. Where, in a case in which section 10(3)(*c*) of the Act applies and section 17(9) of the Act does not apply, by reason of the return of goods, the allowance of discount, a reduction in price or the default of a debtor, the consideration exclusive of tax actually received by a taxable person in respect of the supply by him of any goods or services is less than the amount on which tax has become chargeable in respect of such supply, or no consideration is actually received, the following provisions shall apply:

(*a*)   the amount of the deficiency in respect of any supply shall be ascertained by deducting from the amount of consideration actually chargeable with tax, the amount exclusive of tax, or where a percentage only of the consideration is actually chargeable with tax, a corresponding percentage of the amount actually received, in respect of such supply,

(*b*)   the sum of the deficiencies, ascertained in accordance with subparagraph (*a*), incurred in each taxable period and relating to consideration chargeable at each of the various rates of tax (including the zero rate) specified in section 11(1) of the Act shall be deducted from the amounts ascertained in accordance with section 10 of the Act which would otherwise be chargeable with tax at each of those rates and the net amounts as so ascertained shall be the amounts on which tax is chargeable for the taxable period:

Provided that if the sum of the deficiencies as ascertained in accordance with subparagraph (*b*) in relation to tax chargeable at any of the rates so specified exceeds the amount on which but for this Regulation tax would be chargeable at that rate, or no tax is chargeable at that rate, the tax appropriate to the excess or to the sum of the deficiencies, if no tax is chargeable, shall be treated as tax deductible in accordance with section 12 of the Act,

(*c*)   the taxable person to whom a credit note is, in accordance with section 17 of the Act, issued by another taxable person in respect of an adjustment under this Regulation shall reduce the amount which would otherwise be deductible under section 12 of the Act for the taxable period during which the credit note is issued (in this Regulation referred to as the tax deduction) by the amount of tax shown thereon or by the amount of tax appropriate to the amount of the reduction of consideration shown thereon whichever is the greater (in this subparagraph referred to as the appropriate tax reduction) and if the appropriate tax reduction exceeds the tax deduction the excess shall be carried forward and deducted from the tax deduction for the next taxable period and so on until the appropriate tax reduction is exhausted.

(2) Where, in accordance with section 17(4)(*b*) of the Act a farmer credit note is issued by a flat-rate farmer, the taxable person to whom the credit note is issued shall reduce the amount which would otherwise be deductible under section 12(1)(f) of the Act for the taxable period during which the farmer credit note is issued (in this Regulation referred to as the flat-rate deduction) by the amount of the flat-rate addition shown thereon (in this subparagraph referred to as the appropriate flat-rate reduction) and, if the appropriate flat-rate reduction exceeds the flat-rate deduction, the excess shall be carried forward and deducted from the flat-rate deduction for the next taxable period and so on until the appropriate flat-rate reduction is exhausted.

Accounts

9. (1) Every taxable person shall keep full and true accounts entered up to date of—

(*a*)   in relation to consideration receivable from registered persons, the amount receivable from each such person in respect of each transaction for which an invoice is required to be issued under section 17 of the Act together with a cross-reference to the copy of the relevant invoice,

(b) in relation to consideration receivable from unregistered persons, a daily total of the consideration receivable from all such persons together with a cross-reference to the relevant counter books, copies of sales dockets, cash register tally rolls or other documents which are in use for the purposes of the business,

(c) in relation to importations, a description of the goods imported together with particulars of the value thereof as determined in accordance with section 15 of the Act, the amount of the consideration relating to the purchase of the goods if purchased in connection with the importation, the amount of tax, if any, paid on importation and a cross-reference to the invoices and customs documents used in connection with the importation,

(d) in relation to goods, being goods developed, constructed, assembled, manufactured, produced, extracted, purchased or imported by the taxable person or by another person on his behalf and applied by him (otherwise than by way of disposal to another person) for the purposes of any business carried on by him, a description of the goods in question and the cost excluding tax, to the taxable person of acquiring or producing them except where tax chargeable in relation to the application of the goods would, if it were charged, be wholly deductible under section 12 of the Act,

(e) in relation to goods, being goods which were appropriated by a taxable person for any purpose other than the purpose of his business or disposed of free of charge, where tax chargeable in relation to the goods, upon their acquisition by the taxable person, if they had been so acquired, or upon their development, construction, assembly, manufacture, production, extraction, importation or application in accordance with paragraph (d), as the case may be, was wholly or partly deductible under section 12 of the Act, a description of the goods in question and the cost, excluding tax, to the taxable person, of acquiring or producing them,

(f) in relation to services regarded in accordance with section 5(3) of the Act as supplied by a person in the course or furtherance of business, a description of the services in question together with particulars of the cost, excluding tax, to the taxable person of supplying the services and of the consideration, if any, receivable by him in respect of the supply,

(g) in relation to services referred to in section 5(6)(e)(ii) of the Act in respect of which a person is liable to pay tax in accordance with section 8(2) of the Act, a description of the services in question together with particulars of the cost to the person of acquiring the service,

(h) in the case of services deemed, in accordance with clause (i) or (ii) of subparagraph 5(6)(e) of the Act to be supplied at places outside the State, the name and address of the person to whom the service is supplied, the nature of the service and the amount of the consideration receivable in respect of the supply,

(i) in relation to discounts allowed or price reductions made to a registered person subsequent to the issue of an invoice to such person, the amount credited to such person and, except in a case in which section 17(9)(a) of the Act applies, a cross-reference to the corresponding credit note,

(j) in relation to discounts allowed or price reductions made to unregistered persons, a daily total of the amount so allowed together with a cross-reference to the goods returned book, cash book or other record used in connection with the matter,

(k) in relation to bad debts written off, particulars of the name and address of the debtor, the nature of the goods or services to which the debt relates and the date or dates upon which the debt was incurred, (*l*)   in relation to goods and services supplied to the taxable person by another taxable person, the amount of the consideration, the corresponding tax invoiced by the other taxable person and a cross-reference to the corresponding invoice,

(*m*)   in relation to goods and services supplied by unregistered persons, other than goods and services in respect of which flat-rate farmers are required, in accordance with section 12A (1) of the Act to issue invoices, a daily total of the consideration payable to such persons and a cross-reference to the purchases book, cash book, purchases dockets or other records which are in use in connection with the business,

(*n*)   in relation to goods and services supplied by flat-rate farmers but in respect of which such persons are required, in accordance with section 12A(1) of the Act, to issue invoices, the amount of the consideration (exclusive of the flat-rate addition) and of the flat-rate addition invoiced by each such person and a cross-reference to the corresponding invoice,

(*o*)   in relation to discounts or price reductions received from registered persons, subsequent to the receipt of invoices from such persons, except in a case in which section 17(9)(*a*) of the Act applies, the amount of the discount or price reduction and the corresponding tax received from each such person and a cross-reference to the corresponding credit note,

(*p*)   in relation to discounts or price reductions in relation to goods and services referred to in subparagraph (*n*), the amount of the discount or price reduction (exclusive of the flat-rate addition) and of the flat-rate addition and a cross-reference to the invoice issued in connection with the goods and services in question,

(*q*)   in relation to discounts or price reductions received other than those referred to in subparagraphs (*o*) and (*p*), a daily total of the amounts so received and a cross-reference to the cash book or other record used in connection with such matters,

(*r*)   in relation to dances—

    (i)   the date upon which each dance was held and the address of the place at which it was held,

    (ii)   the charge for admission to each dance,

    (iii) the number of persons admitted to each dance,

    (iv) the total amount of money received or receivable from the persons admitted to each dance in respect of admission, and

    (v)   where goods or services are supplied in connection with a dance and payment of the consideration therefor is a condition of admission to the dance, the amount of such consideration in respect of each dance,

(*s*)   in respect of supplies of goods specified in paragraph (i) of the Second Schedule to the Act, the name and address of the person to whom the goods are supplied, a description of the goods supplied, the amount of the consideration, a cross-reference to the copy of the relevant invoice and a cross-reference to the relevant Customs and transport documents, and

(*t*)   in the case of the supply of services in circumstances that, by virtue of any of the provisions of section 5 of the Act, are deemed to be supplied outside the State, the name and address of the person to whom the services are supplied, the amount of the consideration and a cross-reference to the copy of the relevant invoice or other document.

(2) The accounts kept in accordance with paragraph (1) shall set out separately, the consideration, discounts, price reductions, bad debts and values at importation under separate headings in relation to—

    (*a*)   exempted activities,

(b)   goods and services chargeable at each rate of tax, including the zero rate, and

(c)   goods and services a percentage only of the consideration for the supply of which is chargeable to tax.

(3)   (a)   In relation to a person for the time being authorised in accordance with section 14(1)(a) of the Act to determine the amount of tax which becomes due by him by reference to the amount of moneys which he receives, references in this Regulation to consideration in respect of the supply of goods or services shall be construed as references to the moneys received in respect of such supply, whether made before, on or after the specified day.

(b)   In relation to a person for the time being authorised, in accordance with section 14(1)(b) of the Act, to determine the amount of tax referable to taxable services which becomes due by him by reference to the amount of moneys which he receives in respect of such supply, references in this Regulation to consideration in respect of the supply of services shall be construed as references to the moneys received in respect of such supply, whether made before, on or after the specified day.

(4) Where the Revenue Commissioners are satisfied that the accounts of a taxable person are kept in such a form as to enable his liability to tax to be computed accurately and verified by them, they may, by notice in writing given to the taxable person, dispense him from keeping accounts in the form prescribed by paragraphs (1) and (2), and any such dispensation may be cancelled by them by notice in writing given to the taxable person.

Invoices and other documents

10.

Notes
Revoked with effect from 1 January 1993 by Value Added Tax (Invoices and other Documents) Regulations 1992 r 6 (SI 275/1992).

Time limits for issuing certain documents

11.

Notes
Revoked with effect from 1 January 1993 by Value Added Tax (Time Limits for Issuing Certain Documents) Regulations 1992 r 7 (SI 276/1992).

Returns

12.

Notes
Revoked by Value-Added Tax (Returns) Regulations, 1993 (SI No 247 of 1993) r 5.

Acceptance of estimates

13. (1) The Revenue Commissioners may, if they so think proper and until they otherwise decide, accept estimates, based on procedures approved of by them, of the tax for any taxable period which a person is required to pay by reference to a return furnished in accordance with section 19(3) of the Act and may impose in relation to any such acceptance the condition (which shall be fulfilled by the person) that the person shall, within such period as may be specified, furnish a return in accordance with the said section 19(3) or furnish such further particulars as may be specified to enable the estimates to be reviewed.

(2) Where an estimate of the tax payable for any taxable period has been accepted in accordance with paragraph (1), the estimate may be reviewed by reference to the return or other particulars furnished in accordance with the arrangement and any necessary adjustment may be made by way of additional charge of tax or repayment of tax as the circumstances may require.

(3) If a person in respect of whom an estimate of the tax payable by him has been accepted for any taxable period fails to furnish the return or other particulars the furnishing of which is a condition of acceptance of the estimate in accordance with paragraph (1), or fails to pay any additional tax found to be payable as a result of a review of an estimate for any taxable period made in accordance with paragraph (2), any additional tax which the Revenue Commissioners have reason to believe may be due may be included in an estimate of tax made in accordance with section 23 of the Act.

(4) The provisions of section 21 of the Act shall not apply to any additional charge of tax arising out of a review made in accordance with paragraph (2) if the return or other particulars referred to in that paragraph are furnished within the time specified in the condition governing the acceptance of the estimate and payment of the additional tax is made not later than the end of the time so specified.

(5) A review in accordance with paragraph (2) may extend to a period consisting of two or more consecutive taxable periods and any additional tax or repayment of tax arising out of such review shall be regarded as referable to the latest taxable period in such period.

Estimation of tax due

14.

Notes
Revoked with effect from 1 January 1993 by Value Added Tax (Estimation and Assessment of Tax Due) Regulations 1992 r 6 (SI 277/1992).

Modification of certain provisions

15. (1) Section 480 of the Income Tax Act, 1967 (No. 6 of 1967), as applied by section 24 of the Act shall so apply subject to the following modifications:

(*a*)   in subsection (1)—

   (i)   the expression "the sum charged" shall be construed as referring to value added tax payable by the person concerned,

   (ii)   the expression "the Collector" shall be construed as referring to the Collector-General,

   (iii)   the words "in accordance with the assessments and warrants delivered to him" shall be disregarded,

   (iv)   the words "the warrant delivered to him on his appointment" shall be construed as referring to the nomination given to the Collector-General on his being nominated by the Revenue Commissioners as the Collector-General,

(*b*)   in subsection (4) the words "a distress levied by the Collector" shall be construed as referring to a distress levied by the Collector-General or by a person nominated by the Collector-General to represent him at the execution,

(*c*)   in subsection (5) references to the Collector or his deputy shall be construed as references to the Collector-General or to a person nominated by him for the purpose of the subsection and the requirement of appraisal of the distress shall be disregarded.

(2) Section 485 of the Income Tax Act, 1967, as applied by section 24 of the Act shall so apply subject to the following modifications in subsection (1):

(*a*)   the words "any sum which may be levied on him in respect of income tax" shall be construed as referring to value added tax payable by the person concerned,

(*b*)   the expression "the Collector" shall be construed as referring to the Collector-General.

(3) Section 486 of the Income Tax Act, 1967, as applied by section 24 of the Act shall so apply subject to the following modifications:

(a) the words "income tax or sur-tax" in subsection (1) shall be construed as referring to value added tax,

(b) the expression "the Collector or other officer of the Revenue Commissioners, duly authorised to collect the said tax" in subsections (1) and (2) and "the Collector or other officer under this section" in subsection (3) shall each be construed as referring to the Collector-General.

(4) Section 487 of the Income Tax Act, 1967, as applied by section 24 of the Act shall so apply subject to the modification that the references to income tax shall be construed as references to value added tax.

(5) Section 488 of the Income Tax Act, 1967, as applied by section 24 of the Act shall so apply subject to the following modifications:

(a) the references in subsections (1) and (5) to income tax or sur-tax shall be construed as references to value added tax,

(b) in subsection (5) the references to an inspector and to the Collector shall each be construed as a reference to the Collector-General and the words "under an assessment which has become final and conclusive" shall be disregarded.

(6) Section 491 of the Income Tax Act, 1967, as applied by section 24 of the Act shall so apply subject to the modification that the expression "income tax or sur-tax" shall be construed as referring to value added tax.

Apportionment of amounts

16. (1) Where, in relation to the computation of the tax payable by a taxable person in respect of any taxable period, it is necessary to apportion an amount of tax between tax which may be deducted under section 12(1) of the Act and tax which may not be deducted under that section, the apportionment shall be made on the basis of the ratio which the amount of the taxable turnover in the taxable period in question bears to the total turnover in that period, and the amount so ascertained which is referable to the amount of the taxable turnover shall be the amount deductible under the said section 12(1).

(2) Notwithstanding anything in paragraph (1), an apportionment of an amount of tax between tax which may be deducted under the said section and tax which may not be deducted under that section may be made upon any basis, other than that referred to in paragraph (1), which may be agreed between the taxable person and the Revenue Commissioners.

(3) An apportionment of tax made in accordance with paragraph (1) or (2) may be reviewed by reference to the ratio which the total amount of the taxable turnover in the year in which the taxable period in question occurs bears to the total turnover in that year and any necessary adjustment may be made by way of additional charge of tax or repayment of tax as the circumstances may require.

(4) The year referred to in paragraph (3) is a period of twelve months beginning on the 1st day of January in any year, but if the taxable person customarily makes up accounts for periods of twelve months ending on a fixed date, the year referred to is a period of twelve months ending—

(a) in case the fixed date coincides with the end of a taxable period, on the fixed date, and

(b) in any other case, on the last day of the taxable period during which the fixed date occurs.

(5) The provisions of section 21 of the Act shall not apply to an additional charge of tax referable to a review under this Regulation unless the additional charge is the subject of an estimation of tax under section 22 or 23 of the Act.

Refund of tax

17. A claim for refund of tax shall be furnished in writing to the Revenue Commissioners and shall —

    (*a*)   set out the grounds on which the refund is claimed,

    (*b*)   contain a computation of the amount of the refund claimed, and

    (*c*)   if so required by the Revenue Commissioners, be vouched by the receipts for tax paid and such other documents as may be necessary to prove the entitlement to a refund of the amount claimed.

Remission of small amounts of tax

18. The Revenue Commissioners may, at their discretion, remit the amount of tax, together with interest thereon, payable by a person in respect of goods and services supplied by him during any taxable period, if the total amount of the tax, exclusive of any interest chargeable thereon does not exceed £15.

Valuation of interests in immovable goods

19. (1) Where —

    (*a*)   it is necessary to value an interest in immovable goods for the purposes of section 10(9) of the Act,

    (*b*)   the disposal of such interest consists of or includes the creation of an interest,

    (*c*)   a rent is payable in respect of the interest so created, and

    (*d*)   the terms under which the interest is created do not provide for an increase in the rent to take effect earlier than the end of the fifth year after the interest was created,

the value of such rent to be included in the consideration for the purpose of ascertaining the open market price of the interest disposed of shall, in the absence of other evidence of the amount of that price, be—

    (i)   three-quarters of the annual amount of the rent multiplied by the number of complete years for which the rent has been created, or

    (ii)   the annual amount of the rent multiplied by the fraction of which the numerator is 100 and the denominator is the rate of interest (before deduction of income tax, if any) on the security of the Government which was issued last before the date of the creation of the rent for subscription in the State, and which is redeemable not less than five years after the date of issue (allowance having been made in calculating the interest for any profit or loss which will occur on the redemption of the security), whichever is the lower.

(2) Where a person having an interest in immovable goods (in this paragraph referred to as "the disponor") disposes as regards the whole or any part of those goods of an interest which derives from that interest in such circumstances that he retains the reversion on the interest disposed of (in this paragraph referred to as the reversionary interest), the following provisions shall apply:

    (*a*)   the value of the reversionary interest shall be ascertained by deducting the value of the interest disposed of from the value of the full interest which the disponor had in the goods or the part thereof disposed of at the time the disposition was made, and

    (*b*)   if, under the terms of the disposition, the reversionary interest could not, except through the default of the person in whose favour the disposition was made or a person deriving his title through him, revert to the disponor within a period of 20 years from the date of the disposition—

        (i)   the disponor shall be deemed to have disposed of his full interest in the goods or the part thereof disposed of, and

        (ii)   the value of the reversionary interest shall be disregarded.

Procedures regarding dances

20. (1) Every person who intends to promote a dance (other than a dance to which the number of persons to be admitted is limited to one hundred and the consideration for admission to which does not exceed twenty pence), or a series of such dances, shall, not later than fourteen days before the date on which the dance, or the first dance of the series, as the case may be, is to be held, send to the Collector-General a notification in writing containing the following particulars:

    (*a*)   the name and address of the person,

    (*b*)   the address of the premises in which the dance or dances is or are to be held,

    (*c*)   the name and address of the proprietor of the premises mentioned in subparagraph (*b*),

    (*d*)   as respects the dance or each of the series of dances, the date and time of the dance or of each dance within the series of dances and the proposed admission charge, and

    (*e*)   where the person promoting the dance or dances is a body of persons other than a body corporate, the name and address of the individual who will be responsible for payment of the tax.

(2) On receipt of a notification in accordance with paragraph (1), the Collector-General shall forthwith acknowledge it and shall at the same time send a notice in writing to the proprietor of the premises mentioned in the notification, specifying the dance or dances so mentioned and stating that notification in respect thereof has been received in accordance with this Regulation.

(3) The proprietor of any premises shall not promote a dance therein, or allow a dance to be promoted therein by any other person, unless he has received notice from the Revenue Commissioners that they have been notified in accordance with section 11(7)(*c*) of the Act.

(4) If any alteration is made or occurs as respects any of the particulars contained in a notification sent to the Collector-General under paragraph (1), the person responsible for sending the notification under that paragraph shall immediately notify the Collector-General in writing of the alteration.

Notes
This regulation is effectively inapplicable following repeal of VATA 1972 s 11(7) by FA 1992 s 173(2).

Relief for stock-in trade held on 1st November 1972

21. A claim for deduction under section 34(1) of the Act in respect of stock-in-trade held at the commencement of the 1st day of November, 1972, shall be supported by a statement in writing of all stock-in-trade held at that time setting out details of the stock-in-trade so held under the following headings—

    (*a*)   stocks which have borne turnover tax and wholesale tax on purchase or importation other than—

        (i)   second-hand goods;

        (ii)   newspapers and periodicals;

        (iii)   motor vehicles designed and constructed for the conveyance of persons by road, and sports motor vehicles, estate cars, station wagons, motor cycles, motor scooters, mopeds and auto cycles, whether or not designed and constructed for the purpose aforesaid, excluding vehicles designed and constructed for the carriage of more than sixteen persons (inclusive of the driver), invalid carriages and other vehicles of a type designed for use by invalids or infirm persons;

        (iv)   radio receiving sets and television receiving sets which are of the domestic or portable type or which are of a kind suitable for use in road vehicles;

(v)   gramophones, radiogramophones, record reproducers;

(vi)   gramophone records,

(*b*)   stocks which have borne wholesale tax only on purchase, other than goods of a kind specified in clauses (i) to (vi) of subparagraph (*a*),

(*c*)   (i)   goods which suffered turnover tax only on purchase,

(ii)   second-hand goods which were purchased from persons accountable for turnover tax and on which turnover tax was borne on purchase,

(iii)   goods of a kind specified at (iii), (iv), (v) and (vi) of subparagraphs (*a*) and (*b*),

(iv)   newspapers and periodicals which suffered turnover tax on purchase, and

(*d*)   stocks which do not qualify for relief.

Relief for stock-in-trade held at commencement of taxability

22. (1) A claim by a taxable person for a deduction under section 12(1) of the Act of an amount authorised to be so deducted by section 12(1A) of the Act shall be made to the Collector General and shall be supported by a statement in writing of all stock-in-trade held by him at the commencement of the first taxable period for which he is deemed to be a taxable person (in this Regulation referred to as the relevant day) setting out details of stock-in-trade so held by him under the following headings:

(*a*)   stocks supplied to him by taxable persons and in respect of which, if supplied immediately before the relevant day, tax would be chargeable on the full amount of the consideration at the rate specified in section 11(1)(*a*) of the Act;

(*b*)   stocks supplied to him by taxable persons and in respect of which, if supplied immediately before the relevant day, tax would be chargeable on the full amount of the consideration at the rate specified in section 11(1)(*c*) of the Act;

(*c*)   stocks supplied to him by taxable persons and in respect of which, if supplied immediately before the relevant day, tax would be chargeable on the percentage of the total consideration specified in section 11(2)(*a*) of the Act at the rate specified in section 11(1)(*a*) of the Act;

(*d*)   agricultural produce supplied by flat-rate farmers; and

(*e*)   stocks, other than stocks referred to in subparagraph (d), in respect of which, if supplied immediately before the relevant day, tax would not be chargeable or would be chargeable at the zero rate.

(2)   (*a*)   The deduction in respect of stocks specified in subparagraph (*a*) or (*b*) of paragraph (1) shall be ascertained in the following manner:

(i)   the stocks shall be valued at cost inclusive of tax, or market value, whichever is the lower,

(ii)   there shall be deducted from the total value of stocks ascertained in accordance with clause (i) the value of any stocks included therein in respect of which an invoice issued in accordance with subsection (1), (2), (3) or (4) of section 17 of the Act has been or is likely to be received on or after the relevant day,

(iii)   the amount of the deduction shall be the amount of tax which would be chargeable if the stocks were supplied immediately before the relevant day by a taxable person in the course or furtherance of business for a consideration inclusive of tax equal to the amount of their value after making the deduction specified in clause (ii) and the tax fell due on the date of supply;

(*b*)   the deduction in respect of stocks specified in subparagraph (*c*) or (*d*) of paragraph (1) shall be ascertained in the following manner:

(i)   the stocks shall be valued at cost inclusive of tax, or market value, whichever is the lower,

(ii) there shall be deducted from the total value of stocks ascertained in accordance with clause (i) the value of any stocks included therein in respect of which an invoice issued in accordance with subsection (1), (2), (3) or (4) of section 17 of the Act has been or is likely to be received on or after the relevant day,

(iii) the amount of the deduction shall be **1 per cent** of their value after making the deduction specified in clause (ii).

(3) Relief claimed in accordance with this Regulation shall be distinguished if included in a return made in accordance with section 19(3) of the Act.

Determination in regard to tax

23.

Notes

Revoked with effect from 1 January 1993 by Value Added Tax (Determination in Relation to Tax Due) Regulations 1992 r 6 (SI 278/1992).

Supply of certain services

24. (1) Subject to paragraph (2) and in accordance with section 5(3)(*c*) of the Act, the following services shall be deemed to be a supply of services by a person for consideration in the course or furtherance of his business, that is to say, the supply of catering services for his own private or personal use or that of his staff for the supply of which he provides materials or facilities or towards the cost of which he contributes in whole or in part.

(2)This Regulation shall not apply to any such supplies as are referred to in paragraph (1) if the total cost of providing them has not exceeded and is not likely to exceed £500 in any taxable period.

Postponement of payment of tax on goods supplied while warehoused

25. (1) Where goods chargeable with a duty of excise on their manufacture or production are supplied while warehoused to a registered person for the purposes of his business, they may, in accordance with section 13(5) of the Act be removed from warehouse without payment of the tax chargeable on the supply.

(2) Where goods have been supplied while warehoused to a registered person without payment of the tax chargeable on the supply in accordance with paragraph (1), the tax chargeable in accordance with section 13(5)(*b*) of the Act in relation to the said supply shall be accounted for by that person together with any tax chargeable on the supply of goods or services by him in a return furnished by him in accordance with these Regulations for the taxable period during which the goods were removed from warehouse.

(3) Where goods have been supplied while warehoused to a registered person without payment of the tax chargeable on the supply in accordance with paragraph (1) and the tax is not accounted for in a return lodged for the period in question in accordance with paragraph (2), or the person fails to lodge a return due for that period, the tax chargeable in respect of the supply shall become due.

(4) Where—

(*a*) tax due by a person in accordance with paragraph (2) has not been accounted for, or

(*b*) tax due by a person in accordance with paragraph (3) has not been paid or accounted for, the said Commissioners may direct that as from a specified date paragraph (1) shall not apply to that person.

Postponement of payment of tax on goods imported by registered persons

26.

Notes
Repealed by FA 1982 s 84 with effect from 1 September 1982.

Repayment of tax on certain importations of goods

27.

Notes
Revoked with effect from 25 October 1985 by Value Added Tax (Remission and Repayment of Tax on Certain Exportations) Regulations 1985 (SI 344/1985).

Limitation of application of customs law to imported goods

28.

Notes
Revoked with effect from 1 September 1982 by Value Added Tax (Imported Goods) Regulations 1983 (SI 279/1982).

Remission or repayment of tax on fishing vessels and equipment

29. (1) Tax is, in accordance with section 13(1)(*c*) of the Act, hereby remitted in respect of the supply or importation of fishing nets, and sections thereof, of a kind used by commercial sea fishermen for the purposes of their occupation and not commonly used for any other purpose.

(2) A person who establishes to the satisfaction of the Revenue Commissioners that he has borne or paid tax on—

(*a*)   the supply or hire to him, the importation by him or the maintenance or repair for him of a commercial sea fishing vessel of a gross tonnage of not more than 15 tons, on the acquisition of which he received from An Bord Iascaigh Mhara a grant or loan of money, or

(*b*)   the supply or hire to him, the importation by him or the repair, modification or maintenance for him of goods specified in the Schedule to this Regulation for use exclusively in the operation by him of a commercial sea fishing vessel of a gross tonnage of not more than 15 tons, on the acquisition of which he received from An Bord Iascaigh Mhara a grant or loan of money, or

(*c*)   the hire to him, or the repair or maintenance for him of goods specified in the Schedule to this Regulation for use exclusively in the operation by him of a commercial sea fishing vessel of a gross tonnage of more than 15 tons, whether or not the subject of a grant or loan of money from An Bord Iascaigh Mhara, or

(*d*)   the repair or maintenance for him of a fishing net specified in paragraph (1) for use exclusively in the course of a commercial sea fishing business carried on by him,

and who fulfils to the satisfaction of the said Commissioners the conditions specified in paragraph (3) shall be entitled to be repaid the tax borne or paid.

(3) The conditions to be fulfilled by a person specified in paragraph (2) are—

(*a*)   he shall claim a refund of tax by completing such claim form as may be provided for the purpose by the Revenue Commissioners and he shall certify the particulars shown on such claim form to be correct,

(*b*)   he shall, by production of sufficient documentary evidence, establish that the outlay in relation to which his claim for a refund of tax arises was incurred in the operation by him of a vessel specified in paragraph (2) for the purposes of a commercial sea fishing business,

281

(c)   he shall, by production of an invoice provided in accordance with section 17(12)(a)(ii) of the Act or by the production of a receipt for tax paid on goods imported, establish the amount of tax borne or paid in relation to the outlay referred to in paragraph (2),

(d)   he shall, by the production of a certificate from An Bord Iascaigh Mhara or such other documentary evidence as may be acceptable to the Revenue Commissioners, establish where appropriate that the outlay in relation to which his claim for a refund of tax arises relates to a commercial sea fishing vessel in respect of which he qualified for financial assistance by grant or loan from An Bord Iascaigh Mhara,

(e)   he shall establish that he is not a person registered in the register maintained under section 9 of the Act nor a person required under the provisions of that section to furnish the particulars specified for registration.

SCHEDULE

Anchors, autopilots, bilge and deck pumps, buoys and floats, compasses, cranes, echo graphs, echo sounders, electrical generating sets, fish boxes, fish finders, fishing baskets, life boats and life rafts, marine lights, marine engines, net drums, net haulers, net sounders, radar apparatus, radio navigational aid apparatus, radio telephones, refrigeration plant, trawl doors, trawl gallows, winches.

Refund to foreign traders

30. (1) A person who establishes to the satisfaction of the Revenue Commissioners that he carries on a business outside the State and that he supplies no goods or services in the State shall, subject to paragraph (2), be entitled, in accordance with section 13(3) of the Act, to be repaid tax borne by him on the purchase of goods or services or in respect of goods imported by him if he fulfils to the satisfaction of the said Commissioners the following conditions, that is to say:

(a)   he shall claim a refund by completing such claim form as may be provided for the purpose by the Revenue Commissioners and he shall certify the particulars shown on such claim form to be correct;

(b)   he shall, by the production of invoices or import documents, establish the amount of tax borne;

(c)   in the case of a person having an establishment in another Member State of the Community he shall produce a certificate from the relevant official department of that State that he is a person subject, under the laws of that State, to value added tax referred to in Council Directive No. 77/388/EEC of 17 May, 1977 [OJ No. L145/1 of 13.6.1977.]; and

(d)   he shall establish that he is not entitled to repayment of the tax under any other provision of the Act or Regulations or of any other Act or instrument made under statute administered by the Revenue Commissioners.

(2) No repayment of tax under this Regulation shall be made in respect of—

(a)   the provision of food or drink, or accommodation or other personal services,

(b)   entertainment expenses,

(c)   the acquisition (including hiring) of motor vehicles,

(d)   the purchase of petrol,

(e)   the acquisition of goods for supply within the State or for hiring out for utilisation within the State, or

(f)   goods or services acquired or goods imported in connection with an activity which, if it took place within the State, would be an exempted activity.

(3) For the purposes of this Regulation the services specified in paragraph (iii) of the Second Schedule to the Act shall be deemed to be not supplied in the State.

Exemption of certain business gifts

31. For the purposes of section 3(1A)(*a*) of the Act a gift of goods made in the course or furtherance of business (otherwise than as one forming part of a series or succession of gifts made to the same person) the cost of which to the donor does not exceed £15 exclusive of tax shall not be deemed to have been effected for consideration.

Supplies of stamps, coupons, tokens and vouchers

32. The amount on which tax is chargeable by virtue of section 2(1)(*a*) of the Act in relation to supplies of stamps, coupons, tokens or vouchers specified in section 10(7)(*b*) of the Act shall be nil where the supplies are made by a person in relation to the operation of a business consisting mainly of the supply of goods or services in exchange for the stamps, coupons, tokens or vouchers, and the goods or services are of a kind which the person to whom the stamps, coupons, tokens or vouchers are surrendered does not supply except in relation to the operation of such a scheme.

Supplies of goods or services in exchange for stamps, coupons, tokens or vouchers

33. The amount on which tax is chargeable by virtue of section 2(1)(*a*) of the Act in relation to supplies of goods or services to which section 10(7)(*c*) of the Act relates shall be the cost, excluding tax, to the supplier of producing or acquiring the goods or providing the services, as the case may be, increased by such amount as is reasonable having regard to the open market value of similar goods or services.

Apportionment of consideration

34. For the purposes of section 11(3) of the Act—

    (*a*)   the consideration in respect of the provision of board and lodging, otherwise than in the course of carrying on a hotel business, shall be apportioned as to the amount which relates to the supply of services under section 5(2)(*c*) of the Act and the amount which relates to the letting of immovable goods specified in paragraph (iv) of the First Schedule to the Act;

    (*b*)   where a service consisting of the transport of passengers and the provision of hotel accommodation is supplied for a single consideration, such consideration shall be apportioned as to the amounts which relate to such transport of passengers and such provision of accommodation, respectively.

Disclosure of information to the Revenue Commissioners

35. Any person engaged in the supply of goods or services in the course or furtherance of business shall, when required to do so by notice in writing served on him by the Revenue Commissioners, disclose to the Revenue Commissioners such particulars of any goods or services supplied to him as may be required by such notice.

Death or incapacity of taxable person

36. If a taxable person dies, becomes bankrupt, or, being a body corporate, goes into liquidation, anything which he would have been liable to do under the Act or these Regulations shall be done by his personal representative, assignee, trustee, committee or liquidator, as the case may be.

Service of notices

37. Any notice, notification or requirement which is authorised or required to be given, served, made, sent or issued under the Act or under these Regulations may be sent by post.

Nomination of officers

38. The Revenue Commissioners may nominate any of their officers to perform any acts and discharge any functions authorised by the Act to be performed or discharged by the Revenue Commissioners.

Revocation

39. The Value Added Tax Regulations, 1972 (S.I. No. 177 of 1972), and the Value Added Tax Regulations, 1973 (S.I. No. 254 of 1973), are hereby revoked

EUROPEAN COMMUNITIES (VALUE ADDED TAX)(MUTUAL ASSISTANCE AS REGARDS THE RECOVERY OF CLAIMS) REGULATIONS 1980

(SI No 406 of 1980)

1. These Regulations may be cited as the European Communities (Value Added Tax)(Mutual Assistance as Regards the Recovery of Claims) Regulations, 1980.

Note

These regulations implement in the State the relevant EC Directives to allow mutual assistance between Member States for recovery of VAT claims.

---

2. (1) In these regulations--

"another Member State" means a Member State of the European Communities other than the State;

"the Commission Directive" means Commission Directive No 77/794/EEC of 4 November, 1977;

"the Council Directive" means Council Directive No 76/308/EEC of 15 March, 1976, as amended by Council Directive No 79/1071/EEC of 6 December, 1979.

(2) A word or expression that is used in these regulations and is also used in the Council Directive or in the Commission Directive has, unless the contrary intention appears, the meaning in these regulations that it has in the Council Directive or the Commission Directive, as the case may be.

3. The amount of value added tax specified in any request duly made pursuant to the Council Directive by an authority in another Member State for the recovery in the State of any amount claimed by that authority in such Member State pursuant to a claim referred to in Article to of the said Directive shall be recoverable in any court of competent jurisdiction by the Minister for Finance and for the purposes of the foregoing the amount shall be regarded as being a debt due to the Minister for Finance, by the person against whom the claim is made by such authority, in respect of a duty or tax under the care and management of the Revenue Commissioners or a simple contract debt due by such person to the aforesaid Minister, as may be appropriate.

4. The rules laid down in---

    (*a*)   Articles 4 to 12 and 14 to 17 of the Council Directive, and

    (*b*)   Articles 2 to 21 of the Commission Directive,

shall apply in relation to claims in respect of value added tax referred to in Article 2 of the Council Directive which arise in another Member State and which are the subject of legal proceedings instituted in pursuance of these regulations.

5. In any legal proceedings instituted in pursuance of these regulations any document which is in the form specified in Annex III to the Commission Directive and which purports to be authenticated in the manner specified in Article II of that Directive shall be received in evidence without proof of any seal or signature thereon or that any signatory thereto was the proper person to sign it, and such document shall, until the contrary is shown, be sufficient evidence of the facts therein stated.

6. (1) Legal proceedings instituted in pursuance of these regulations for the recovery of any sum shall be stayed if the defendant satisfies the court that legal proceedings relevant to his liability on the claim to which the proceedings so instituted relate are pending, or are about to be instituted, before a court, tribunal or other competent body in another Member State; but any such stay may be removed if the legal proceedings in such Member State are not prosecuted or instituted with reasonable expedition.

(2) In any legal proceedings instituted in pursuance of these regulations it shall be a defence for the defendant to show that a final decision on the claim to which the proceedings relate has been given in his favour by a court, tribunal or other body of competent jurisdiction in another Member State, and, in relation to any part of a claim to which such legal proceedings relate, it shall be a defence for the defendant to show that such a decision has been given in relation to that part of the claim.

(3) No question shall be raised in any legal proceedings instituted in pursuance of these regulations as to the defendant's liability on the claim to which the proceedings relate except as provided in paragraph (2) of this regulation.

(4) For the purposes of this regulation legal proceedings shall be regarded as pending so long as an appeal may be brought against any decision in the proceedings; and for the said purposes a decision against which no appeal lies or against which an appeal lies within a period which has expired without an appeal having been brought shall be regarded as being a final decision.

EUROPEAN COMMUNITIES (MUTUAL ASSISTANCE IN THE FIELD OF VALUE ADDED TAX) REGULATIONS 1980

(SI No 407 of 1980)

1. These Regulations may be cited as the European Communities (Mutual Assistance in the Field of Value Added Tax) Regulations, 1980.

Note

These Regulations provide for the extension at national level of the EEC Council Directive of 19 December 1977 concerning mutual assistance (exchange of information) by the competent authorities of the Member States in the field of direct taxation to VAT, as required by an amending Council Directive of 6 December 1979.

---

2. In these Regulations–

"authorised officer" means an officer of the Revenue Commissioners authorised in writing by the Revenue Commissioners for the purposes of these Regulations;

"the Council Directive" means Council Directive No. 77/799/EEC of 19 December, 1977, as amended by Council Directive No. 79/1070/EEC of 6 December, 1979.

3. (1) The Revenue Commissioners and authorised officers of those Commissioners may disclose to the competent authorities of another Member State any information concerning value added tax required to be so disclosed by virtue of the Council Directive.

(2) Neither the Revenue Commissioners nor an authorised officer of those Commissioners shall disclose any information in pursuance of the Council Directive unless satisfied that the competent authorities of the other Member State concerned are bound by, or have undertaken to observe, rules of confidentiality with respect to the information which are not less strict than those applying to it in the State.

(3) Nothing in this section shall permit the Revenue Commissioners or an authorised officer of those Commissioners to authorise the use of information disclosed by virtue of the Council Directive to the competent authorities of another Member State other than for the purposes of taxation or to facilitate legal proceedings for failure to observe the tax laws of that State.

VALUE ADDED TAX (IMPORTED GOODS) REGULATIONS 1982

(SI No 279 of 1982)

Amendments

Revoked by Value Added Tax (Imported Goods)(No 2) Regulations 1992 (SI 440/1992) with effect from 1 January 1993.

Notes

These regulations which came into effect on 1 September 1982 modify or exclude for VAT purposes various customs provisions which apply to the payment of VAT on imported goods by registered persons.

VALUE ADDED TAX (IMPORTED GOODS) REGULATIONS 1983

(SI No 129 of 1983)

Amendments
Revoked by Value Added Tax (Imported Goods) Regulations 1992 (SI 439/1992) with effect from 1 January 1993.

Notes
These regulations, which came into effect on 1 April 1983, deal with relief from payment of VAT at importation on raw materials and components for certain manufacturers. To qualify for relief an importer must (*a*) be registered for VAT, (*b*) be in the business of manufacturing goods in the State and (*c*) export at least 75 per cent in value of his total manufactured output.

EUROPEAN COMMUNITIES (EXEMPTION FROM IMPORT CHARGES OF CERTAIN VEHICLES ETC, TEMPORARILY IMPORTED) REGULATIONS, 1983

(SI No 422 of 1983)

Cross-references
VATA 1972 s 32.

Notes
These regulations, which came into force on 1 January 1984, implement in Ireland EC Council Directive 83/182/EEC of 28 March 1983 which provides relief from import charges for certain vehicles temporarily imported from another Member State of the EC. Importations of vehicles not covered by these regulations continue to be governed by Motor Vehicles (Temporary Importation) Regulations 1970 (SI 54/1970).
Council Directive 83/182/EEC of 28 March 1983 ceased to have effect on 31 December 1992 as regards its provisions on VAT: Council Directive 91/680/EEC of 16 December 1991 art 2(2).

Case law
Temporary importation of car: whether for private use, taxable amount*: Keller v Revenue Commissioners, Ireland and Attorney General*, HC Murphy J, 22 June 1993

EUROPEAN COMMUNITIES (EXEMPTION FROM IMPORT CHARGES OF CERTAIN PERSONAL PROPERTY) REGULATIONS 1983

(SI No 423 of 1983)

Notes

These regulations, which came into force on 1 January 1984, implement in Ireland EC Council Directive 83/183 of 28 March 1983 which provides relief from imported charges for personal property imported in connection with: a transfer of normal residence; the furnishing or relinquishing of a secondary residence; a marriage and an inheritance where property is permanently imported from another Member State of the EC. The appropriate exemptions are now contained in the European Communities (Exemption from Value Added Tax on the Permanent Importation of CErtain Goods) Regulations 1985 (SI 183/185).

Council Directive 83/183/EEC of 28 March 1983 ceased to have effect on 31 December 1992 as regards its provisions on VAT: Council Directive 91/680/EEC of 16 December 1991 art 2(2).

VALUE ADDED TAX (EXPORTED GOODS) REGULATIONS 1984

(SI No 230 of 1984)

Amendments

Revoked by Value Added Tax (Exported Goods) Regulations 1992 (SI 438/1992) with effect from 1 January 1993.

Notes

These regulations, which have effect as from 1 March 1984, provide for relief from VAT on certain supplies of goods to foreign visitors and to Irish residents departing the State for more than a year. The relevant goods must be shipped out of the State on board an aircraft or ship (other than private aircraft or vessels).

VALUE ADDED TAX (GOODS EXPORTED IN BAGGAGE) REGULATIONS 1984

(SI No 231 of 1984)

Amendments

Revoked by Value Added Tax (Exported Goods) Regulations 1992 (SI 438/1992) with effect from 1 January 1993.

Notes

These regulations, which have effect as from 1 March 1984, provide for relief from VAT on certain supplies of goods to foreign visitors and to Irish residents departing the State for more than a year. The relevant goods must be exported as personal baggage of the purchaser.

EUROPEAN COMMUNITIES (EXEMPTION FROM VALUE ADDED TAX ON THE PERMANENT IMPORTATION OF CERTAIN GOODS) REGULATIONS 1985

(SI No 183 of 1985)

1. (1) These Regulations may be cited as the European Communities (Exemption from Value Added Tax on the Permanent Importation of Certain Goods) Regulations, 1985.

Cross-reference
VATA 1972 s 32.
Notes
These regulations which came into force on 1 July 1984, give effect to the Council Directive of 28 March 1983 (83/181/EEC) and provide, subject to certain conditions, for exemption from VAT of certain importations of personal property from outside the Community. Also included are importations of scholastic materials and household effects of students coming to study on a full time basis, imports of certain goods on the transfer of undertakings to the State, imports of certain agricultural and medical products, laboratory animals, certain goods for charitable organisations or the promotion of trade and goods imported for examination, analysis or test purposes and a number of other miscellaneous exemptions.

---

(2) These Regulations shall be construed together with the Act and the Customs Acts (other than the provisions thereof specified in Regulation 30 of these Regulations) and any instrument relating to the customs made under statute (other than the instrument specified in the said Regulation 30).

2. These Regulations shall be deemed to have come into operation on the 1st day of July, 1984.

3. (1) In these Regulations—

"the Act" means the Value Added Tax Act, 1972 (No. 22 of 1972);

"the Community" means the territory of the Member States where Council Directive No. 77/388/EEC of 17 May 1977 (OJ L 145, 13.6.77, p1), applies;

"ECU" means the unit of account as defined in Council Regulation No. 3180/78 of 18 December, 1978 (OJ L 379, 30.12.78, p1);

"importation", in relation to goods, has the meaning assigned to it by Article 7 of the Council Directive No. 77/388/EEC of 17 May, 1977, and cognate words shall be construed accordingly;

"Member State" means Member State of the European Economic Community;

"tax" means value added tax.

(2) In Regulations 4, 5 and 6 of these Regulations—

"alcoholic products" means products (beer, wine, aperitifs with a wine or alcohol base, brandies, liqueurs and spirituous beverages, etc.) falling within headings 22.03 to 22.09 of the Common Customs Tariff;

"household effects" means personal effects, household linen and furnishings and items of equipment intended for the personal use of the persons concerned or for meeting their household needs;

"personal property" means any property intended for the personal use of the persons concerned or for meeting their household needs, and includes—

    (*a*)   household effects,

    (*b*)   cycles and motor-cycles, private motor vehicles and their trailers, camping caravans, pleasure craft and private aeroplanes,

    (*c*)   household provisions appropriate to normal family requirements, household pets and saddle animals,

    (*d*)   portable instruments of the applied or liberal arts required by the person concerned for the pursuit of his trade or profession, but does not include property whose nature or quantity reflects a commercial interest or property intended for an economic activity within the meaning of Article 4 of Council Directive No. 77/388/EEC of 17 May, 1977;

"value for the purposes of tax chargeable at importation" means the value of imported goods for the purposes of section 15 of the Act as specified in subsections (3) and (4) of that section.

(3) A word or expression that is used in these Regulations and is also used in Council Directive No. 83/181/EEC of 28 March, 1983, shall, unless the context otherwise requires, have the meaning in these Regulations that it has in that Directive.

4. (1) Subject to paragraphs (2) to (8) of this Regulation, tax shall not be charged on goods, being the personal property of any person, other than—

    (*a*)   alcoholic products,

    (*b*)   tobacco and tobacco products,

    (*c*)   commercial means of transport,

    (*d*)   articles for use in the exercise of a trade or profession, excluding portable instruments of the applied or liberal arts,

imported from a country outside the Community by a natural person transferring his normal place of residence to the State and which—

    (i)   except in special cases justified by the circumstances, have been in the possession of, and, in the case of durable goods, used by that person for a minimum period of six months before the date on which he ceases to have his normal place of residence outside the Community;

    (ii)   are intended to be used at his normal place of residence in the State for the purpose for which they were used immediately before such importation;

    (iii)   have borne either in the country of origin or in the country from which he is departing any customs or fiscal charges to which they are normally liable and are not the subject, on the grounds of exportation, of any exemption from or refund of such charges;

    (iv)   are the personal property of that person, being a person whose normal place of residence has been outside the Community for a continuous period of at least 12 months, or who shows to the satisfaction of the Revenue Commissioners that his intention was to reside outside the Community for a continuous period of at least 12 months;

    (v)   except in special cases justified by the circumstances, are entered for customs purposes, for permanent importation within 12 months of the date of establishment in the State by that person of his normal place of residence.

(2) In the case of goods which are—

    (*a*)   supplied under diplomatic or consular arrangements,

    or

    (*b*)   supplied to international organisations, recognised as such by the public authorities in the State, or to members of such organisations within the limits and under the conditions laid down by the international conventions establishing the organisations or by headquarters agreements,

the reference in subparagraph (i) of paragraph (1) of this Regulation to six months shall be construed as a reference to twelve months, and the conditions specified in subparagraph (iii), of the said paragraph shall be deemed to have been complied with.

(3) Goods the subject of relief under paragraphs (1) or (2) of this Regulation may be imported in several separate consignments within the period specified in subparagraph (v) of the said paragraph (1).

(4) Until 12 months have elapsed from the date of the declaration for their final importation, goods which have been imported tax-free under this Regulation may not be lent, given as security, hired out or transferred, whether for a consideration or free of charge, except in circumstances duly justified to the satisfaction of, and with the prior sanction of the Revenue Commissioners.

(5) Any lending, giving as security, hiring out or transfer before the expiry of the period referred to in paragraph (4) of this Regulation shall entail payment of the relevant tax on the goods concerned, at the rate applying on the date of such loan, giving as security, hiring out or transfer, on the basis of the type of goods and the value for the purposes of tax chargeable at importation as ascertained or accepted on that date by the Revenue Commissioners.

(6)   (*a*)   Relief under this Regulation shall also apply in respect of personal property permanently imported before the person concerned establishes his normal place of residence in the State, provided that he gives an undertaking in writing to the Revenue Commissioners that he will actually establish his normal place of residence in the State within a period of 6 months after the importation. Such undertaking shall be accompanied by security, the form and amount of which shall be determined by the Revenue Commissioners.

       (*b*)   For the purpose of subparagraph (*a*) of this paragraph the period specified in paragraph (1)(i) of this Regulation shall be calculated from the date of the importation of the personal property into the State.

(7)   (*a*)   Subject to subparagraphs (*b*) and (*c*) of this paragraph, where the person concerned leaves the country situated outside the Community where he had his normal place of residence and, because of occupational commitments, does not simultaneously establish his normal place of residence in the State, although having the intention of ultimately doing so, relief under this Regulation shall apply in respect of the personal property which he transfers into the State for this purpose.

       (*b*)   Relief in respect of the personal property referred to in subparagraph (1)(*a*) of this paragraph shall be granted in accordance with the conditions laid down in this Regulation on the basis that:

          (i)   the periods specified in paragraphs (1)(i) and (v) of this Regulation shall be calculated from the date of importation;

         (ii)   the period specified in paragraph (4) of this Regulation shall be calculated from the date when the person concerned actually established his normal place of residence in the State.

       (*c*)   Relief under this paragraph shall not be given unless the person concerned gives an undertaking in writing to the Revenue Commissioners that he will actually establish his normal place of residence in the State within such period as may be specified by the Revenue Commissioners having regard to the circumstances. Such undertaking shall, if the Revenue Commissioners so require, be accompanied by security, the form and amount of which shall be determined by the Revenue Commissioners.

(8) Where, owing to exceptional political circumstances, a person has to transfer his normal place of residence from a country situated outside the Community to the State, the Revenue Commissioners may in their absolute discretion waive or modify the requirements of paragraph (1) of this Regulation, in so far as it refers to use of the goods prior to and subsequent to importation, subparagraph (*b*) of that paragraph, the conditions of the said paragraph relating to commercial means of transport and to articles for use in the exercise of a trade or profession and the requirements of paragraph (4) of this Regulation.

5. (1) Subject to paragraphs (3) to (7) of this Regulation, tax shall not be charged on the importation of trousseaux and household effects, whether or not new, belonging to a person transferring his or her normal place of residence from a country outside the Community to the State on the occasion of his or her marriage.

(2) (*a*) Subject to subparagraphs (*b*) and (*c*) of this paragraph, relief under this Regulation shall also apply to presents customarily given on the occasion of a marriage which are sent to a person fulfilling the conditions laid down in paragraph (1) of this Regulation by persons having their normal place of residence in a country situated outside the Community.

(*b*) The exemption shall apply to presents of a unit value not exceeding 200 ECU.

(*c*) However, where the value of a present is more than 200 ECU, but less than 1,000 ECU, the Revenue Commissioners may, in their absolute discretion, grant the exemption.

(3) Relief in respect of the goods referred to in paragraph (1) of this Regulation shall be conditional on the goods having borne, either in the country of origin or in the country from which the person concerned is departing, any customs or fiscal charges to which they are normally liable.

(4) Relief under this Regulation shall apply only to a person:

(*a*) whose normal place of residence has been outside the Community for a continuous period of at least twelve months, or where it is shown to the satisfaction of the Revenue Commissioners that the intention of the person concerned was clearly to reside outside the Community for a continuous period of at least 12 months, and

(*b*) who produces evidence of the marriage.

(5) Relief under this Regulation shall not apply to alcoholic products, tobacco or tobacco products.

(6) Save in exceptional cases justified by the circumstances, relief under this Regulation shall be granted only in respect of goods permanently imported—

(*a*) not earlier than two months before the date fixed for the wedding; in such case the Revenue Commissioners may make the granting of relief dependent on the provision of security in such form and of such amount as the Revenue Commissioners may determine, and

(*b*) not later than four months after the date of the wedding.

(7) Goods the subject of relief under this Regulation may be imported in several separate consignments within the period specified in paragraph (6) of this Regulation.

(8) Until 12 months have elapsed from the date of the declaration for their final importation, goods which have been imported tax-free under this Regulation may not be lend, given as security, hired out or transferred, whether for a consideration or free of charge, except in circumstances duly justified to the satisfaction of, and with the prior sanction of the Revenue Commissioners.

(9) Any lending, giving as security, hiring out or transfer before the expiry of the period referred to in paragraph (8) of this Regulation shall entail payment of the relevant tax on the goods concerned, at the rate applying on the date of such loan, giving as security, hiring out or transfer, on the basis of the type of goods and the value for the purposes of tax chargeable at importation ascertained or accepted on that date by the Revenue Commissioners.

6. (1) Subject to paragraphs (2) and (3) of this Regulation, tax shall not be charged on personal property of a deceased person imported from a country outside the Community by a person, being an individual resident in the State who either has acquired by inheritance (*causa mortis*) the ownership or the beneficial ownership of such property or who is the personal representative of such deceased person, if—

(*a*) such individual or personal representative provides the Revenue Commissioners with a statutory declaration or a corresponding declaration made under the laws of the country of exportation that the property he is importing was acquired by inheritance or that he is the personal representative of the deceased person, as the case may be,

(b)   the property is imported not more than two years, or such longer period, in special cases, as the Revenue Commissioners may determine, after the date on which such individual enters into possession of the property or such personal representative takes control of the property, and

(c)   the property is personal property other than

     (i)   alcoholic products,

     (ii)   tobacco or tobacco products,

     (iii)   commercial means of transport,

     (iv)   articles for use in the exercise of a trade or profession, other than portable instruments of the applied or liberal arts, which were required for the exercise of the trade or profession of the deceased,

     (v)   stocks of raw materials and finished or semi-finished products,

     (vi)   livestock and stocks of agricultural products exceeding the quantities appropriate to normal family requirements.

(2) Goods the subject of relief under this Regulation may be imported in several separate consignments within the period provided for in subparagraph (b) of paragraph (1) of this Regulation.

(3) Paragraph (1) of this Regulation shall apply *mutatis mutandis* to personal property acquired by inheritance by a body of persons engaged in a non-profit making activity and established in the State.

7. Tax shall not be charged on articles of clothing, scholastic materials or household effects imported for their personal use during the period of their studies by persons not normally resident in the State who are enrolled in an educational establishment in the State in order to attend full-time educational courses.

8. Tax shall not be charged on the importation of goods (other than alcoholic products, perfumes, toilet waters, tobacco and tobacco products) not exceeding a total value of 10 ECU which —

(a)   are delivered to a consignee by letter or parcel post in a single postal delivery,

(b)   are despatched to him by a single consignor, and

(c)   do not form part of grouped consignments from the same consignor to the same consignee.

9. (1) Subject to paragraph (2) to (5) of this Regulation tax shall not be charged on—

(a)   machinery, plant or equipment imported by a person on cessation of his business activity abroad in order to carry on a similar activity within the State:

     Provided that the following conditions are complied with in relation to the goods, namely, the goods have been used in his business for a period of at least 12 months or such shorter period as the Revenue Commissioners consider reasonable prior to the date on which the business ceased to operate in the country of departure, are intended for the same purposes after transfer and are for use in the State in an agricultural activity or in an activity in respect of which he would be a taxable person in accordance with section 8 of the Act; or

(b)   livestock imported by a farmer on the transfer to the State of an activity carried on in an agricultural holding:

     Provided that the following conditions are complied with in relation to livestock, namely, the livestock are owned by the farmer for at least 12 months or such shorter period as the Revenue Commissioners consider reasonable prior to the importation and are intended to be used for farming after importation and their number is appropriate to the nature and size of the farming enterprise undertaken by the person in the State.

(2) Paragraph (1) of this Regulation shall not apply to importations by persons established outside the State the transfer of whose business to the State is consequent upon or is for the purpose of merging with, or being absorbed by, a person or persons in the State in circumstances in which a new activity is not, or is not intended to be, commenced.

(3) Notwithstanding the provisions of paragraph (1) of this Regulation, relief may be granted in respect of machinery, plant or equipment imported from another Member State by charitable or philanthropic organisations at the time of the transfer of their principal place of business to the State if the goods were not exempt under Article 15 (12) of Council Directive No. 77/388/EEC of 17 May, 1977.

(4) Relief under this Regulation shall not apply to—

(a) means of transport which are not used in the production process of the business concerned nor, in the case of a service business, used directly in the provision of the service;

(b) food supplies intended for human consumption or for animal feed;

(c) fuel and stocks of raw materials or finished or semi-finished products;

(d) livestock in the possession of dealers.

(5) Except in special cases justified by the circumstances, relief under this Regulation shall be granted only in respect of machinery, plant or equipment imported before the expiry of a period of 12 months from the date when the importer ceased his activities in the country of departure.

(6) Where the Revenue Commissioners are satisfied that there are special circumstances justifying it, they may grant relief under this Regulation notwithstanding that the conditions specified in paragraph (1) or (2), as may be appropriate, of this Regulation are not complied with.

10. (1) Subject to paragraphs (2) to (6) of this Regulation tax shall not be charged on the importation of agricultural, stock-farming, bee-keeping, horticultural or forestry products from land situated in Northern Ireland and occupied and operated by farmers having their principal farms in the State adjacent to the land frontier of the State.

(2) Subject to paragraph (1) of this Regulation **"stock-farming products"** means such products obtained from animals reared or acquired in the State or imported in accordance with the general tax arrangements applicable in the State.

(3) Relief under this Regulation shall also apply to purebred horses of not more than 6 months of age and born outside the State of an animal covered in the State and then exported temporarily to give birth.

(4) Relief under this Regulation shall apply only to products which have not undergone any treatment other than that which normally follows their harvesting or production.

(5) Relief under this Regulation shall apply only in respect of products imported by the farmer concerned or expressly on his behalf.

(6) Relief under this Regulation shall apply, *mutatis mutandis*, to the products of fishing or fish-farming activities carried out in the lakes or waterways bordering or crossing the land frontier of the State by persons established in the State, and to the products of hunting activities carried out on such lakes or waterways by persons established in the State.

11. (1) Subject to paragraph (2) of this Regulation, tax shall not be charged on the importation from Northern Ireland of seeds, fertilizers and products for the treatment of soil and crops and intended for use on land situated in the State and operated by farmers having their principal farms in Northern Ireland adjacent to the land frontier of the State.

(2) Relief under this Regulation shall apply only to the quantities of seeds, fertilisers or other products—

(a) required for the purpose of operating the land concerned;

(b) imported directly into the State by the farmer or expressly on his behalf.

12. (1) Subject to the provisions of this Regulation, tax shall not be charged on the importation of the following goods:

(*a*) live animals specially prepared and sent free of charge for laboratory use;

(*b*) biological or chemical substances—

(i) which are imported free of charge from another Member State, or

(ii) which are imported from countries outside the Community subject to the limits and conditions laid down in Article 60(1)(*b*) of Council Regulation No. 918/83/EEC of 28 March 1983 (OJ 1105, 23.4.1983, p1), setting up a Community system of reliefs from customs duty;

(*c*) therapeutic substances of human origin, being human blood and its derivatives (whole human blood, dried human plasma, human albumin and fixed solutions of human plasma protein, human immunoglobulin and human fibrinogen);

(*d*) blood-grouping reagents whether of human, animal, plant or other origin used for blood-type grouping and for the detection of blood incompatibilities;

(*e*) tissue-typing reagents whether of human, animal plant or other origin used for the determination of human tissue-types;

(*f*) pharmaceutical products for human or veterinary medical use by persons or animals participating in international sports events, within the limits necessary to meet their requirements during their stay in the State.

(2) (*a*) Relief under subparagraphs (*a*) or (*b*) of paragraph (1) of this Regulation shall apply only to animals and biological and chemical substances intended for—

(i) public establishments, or departments of public establishments, principally engaged in education or scientific research, or

(ii) private establishments principally engaged in education or scientific research and approved by the Revenue Commissioners for the purposes of this Regulation.

(*b*) Relief under subparagraphs (*c*), (*d*) or (*e*) of paragraph (1) of this Regulation shall apply only to—

(i) goods that—

(I) are intended for institutions or laboratories approved by the Revenue Commissioners for the purposes of this Regulation for use exclusively for non-commercial medical or scientific purposes,

(II) are accompanied by a certificate of conformity of a duly authorised body in the country of departure, and

(III) are in containers bearing a special label identifying them,

and

(ii) special packaging essential for the transport of therapeutic substances of human origin or blood-grouping or tissue-typing reagents, and

(iii) solvents and accessories needed for their use and included in consignments of the goods.

13. (1) Subject to paragraphs (2) to (7) of this Regulation, and to any limit as to quantity or value that the Revenue Commissioners may impose in order to remedy any abuse and to combat major distortions of competition tax shall not be charged on the importation of—

(*a*) basic human necessities obtained free of charge by State organisations or by charitable or philanthropic organisations approved by the Revenue Commissioners for distribution free of charge to needy persons, (*b*) goods sent free of charge by a person or organisation established abroad, and without any commercial intent on the part of the sender, to State organisations or charitable or philanthropic organisations approved by the Revenue Commissioners, for the purpose of fund-raising at occasional charity events for the benefit of needy persons,

(*c*) equipment and office materials sent free of charge by a person or organisation established abroad, and without any commercial intent on the part of the sender, to charitable or philanthropic organisations approved by the Revenue Commissioners, for use solely for the purpose of meeting their operating needs or carrying out their stated charitable or philanthropic aims.

(2) Relief under this Regulation shall not apply to—

(*a*) alcoholic products,

(*b*) tobacco or tobacco products,

(*c*) motor vehicles other than ambulances.

(3) Relief under this Regulation shall be granted only to organisations the accounting procedures of which enable the Revenue Commissioners to supervise their operations and which provide such guarantees as the Revenue Commissioners may consider necessary.

(4) (*a*) Goods the subject of relief under paragraph (1) of this Regulation shall not be lent, hired out or otherwise disposed of, whether for consideration or free of charge, for purposes other than those laid down in the said paragraph except in circumstances duly justified to the satisfaction of and with the prior sanction of the Revenue Commissioners.

(*b*) Goods and equipment may be lent, hired out or transferred to an organisation entitled to benefit from relief under paragraph (1) of this Regulation where the latter body uses the goods and equipment for purposes specified in subparagraphs (*a*) and (*b*) of the said paragraph.

(*c*) Goods the subject of relief under this Regulation which are lent, hired out or transferred otherwise than in accordance with subparagraph (*a*) or (*b*) of this paragraph shall be subject to payment of tax at the rate applying on the date of the loan, hiring out or transfer, on the basis of the type of goods and equipment and the value for the purposes of tax chargeable at importation ascertained or accepted on that date by the Revenue Commissioners.

(5) Organisations referred to in paragraph (1) of this Regulation which cease to fulfil the conditions giving entitlement to relief under that paragraph, or which propose to use goods and equipment imported without payment of tax for purposes other than those provided for by the said paragraph (1), shall so inform the Revenue Commissioners.

(6) Goods remaining in the possession of organisations which cease to fulfil the conditions giving entitlement to relief under this Regulation shall be liable to the relevant tax payable on importation at the rate applying on the date on which those conditions cease to be fulfilled, on the basis of the type of goods and equipment and the value for the purposes of tax chargeable at importation as ascertained or accepted on that date by the Revenue Commissioners.

(7) Goods used by an organisation benefiting from relief under this Regulation for purposes other than those provided for in paragraph (1) of this Regulation shall be liable to the relevant tax payable on importation at the rate applying on the date on which they are put to such other use on the basis of the type of goods and equipment and the value for the purposes of tax chargeable at importation ascertained on that date by the Revenue Commissioners.

14. (1) Subject to paragraphs (2) to (6) of this Regulation, tax shall not be charged on the importation of—

(*a*) articles specially designed for the education, employment or social advancement of blind or other physically or mentally handicapped persons which are—

    (i)   imported by institutions or organisations principally engaged in the education of or the provision of assistance to handicapped persons, and approved by the Revenue Commissioners for the purposes of this Regulation, and

    (ii)   donated to such institutions or organisations free of charge and with no commercial intent on the part of the donor;

(b)   specific spare parts, components or accessories specifically for such articles as aforesaid and tools for use for the maintenance, checking, calibration and repair of the said articles:

Provided that such spare parts, components, accessories or tools are imported at the same time as the said articles or, if imported subsequently, that they can be identified as being intended for articles previously imported tax-free or which would be eligible for tax-free importation at the time when such entry is requested for the said spare parts, components or accessories and tools.

(2) Goods the subject of relief under this Regulation shall not be used for purposes other than the education, employment or social advancement of blind or other physically or mentally handicapped persons.

(3)   (a)   Goods the subject of relief under paragraph (1) of this Regulation may be lent, hired out or transferred, whether for a consideration or free of charge, by the institutions or organisations referred to in the said paragraph on a non-profit making basis to other such institutions or organisations with whom they are associated.

    (b)   No loan, hiring out or transfer of goods the subject of relief under this Regulation may be effected under conditions other than those provided for in subparagraph (a) except in special cases justified by the circumstances and with the prior sanction of the Revenue Commissioners:

Provided that—

    (i)   goods may be lent, hired out or transferred to an institution or organisation itself entitled to benefit from relief under this Regulation where the latter body uses the article for purposes specified in paragraph (1) of this Regulation,

    (ii)   goods the subject of relief under this Regulation which are lent, hired out or transferred otherwise than in accordance with the preceding provision of this subparagraph shall be subject to payment of tax, at the rate applying on the date of the loan, hiring out or transfer, on the basis of the type of goods and the value for the purposes of tax chargeable at importation ascertained or accepted on that date by the Revenue Commissioners.

(4) Institutions or organisation referred to in paragraph (1) of this Regulation which cease to fulfil the conditions giving entitlement to relief under the said paragraph or which propose to use such goods for purposes other than those provided for by the said paragraph shall so inform the Revenue Commissioners.

(5) Goods remaining in the possession of institutions or organisations which cease to fulfil the conditions giving entitlement to relief under paragraph (1) of this Regulation shall be liable to tax at the rate applying on the date on which those conditions cease to be fulfilled, on the basis of the type of goods and the value for the purposes of tax chargeable at importation ascertained or accepted on that date by he Revenue Commissioners.

(6) Goods used by an institution or organisation benefiting from relief under this Regulation for purposes other than those provided for in paragraph (1) of this Regulation shall be liable to tax payable on importation at the rate applying on the date on which they are put to such other use on the basis of the type of goods and the value for the purposes of tax chargeable at importation ascertained or accepted on that date by the Revenue Commissioners.

15. (1) Subject to paragraphs (2) to (8) of this Regulation, tax shall not be charged on—

  (*a*)   goods, other than building materials or equipment intended for rebuilding disaster areas, imported by State organisations, or charitable or philanthropic organisations, approved of by the Revenue Commissioners for the purposes of this Regulation—

  (i)   for distribution free of charge to victims of natural disasters affecting the territory of any Member State of the Community, or

  (ii)   for making available free of charge to the victims of such disasters, while remaining the property of the importer,

  or

  (*b*)   goods imported by disaster-relief agencies in order to meet their needs during the period of their activity in connection with such disasters.

(2) The granting of relief under paragraph (1) of this Regulation shall be subject to a decision by the Commission of the European Communities, acting at the request of the State or other Member States concerned in accordance with an emergency procedure entailing the consultation of the other Member States:

Provided that, pending notification of the Commission's decision, the Revenue Commissioners may grant relief under paragraph (1) subject to an undertaking by the organisation concerned to pay the relevant tax if relief is not granted.

(3) Entitlement to relief under this Regulation may be granted only to disaster-relief organisations the accounting procedures of which enable the Revenue Commissioners to supervise their operations and which provide such security as the Revenue Commissioners may consider necessary.

(4) The organisations benefiting from relief under paragraph (1) of this Regulation shall not lend, hire out or transfer, whether for a consideration or free of charge, the goods referred to in that paragraph under conditions other than those laid down in that paragraph except in special cases justified by the circumstances and with the prior sanction of the Revenue Commissioners:

Provided that—

  (*a*)   goods may be lent, hired out or transferred to an organisation itself entitled to benefit from relief under this Regulation where the latter body uses the goods for purposes specified in paragraph (1) of this Regulation, and

  (*b*)   goods the subject of relief under this Regulation which are lent, hired out or transferred otherwise than in accordance with the preceding provisions of this subparagraph shall be subject to prior payment of tax, at the rate applying on the date of the loan, hiring out or transfer, on the basis of the type of goods and the value for the purposes of tax chargeable at importation ascertained or accepted on that date by the Revenue Commissioners.

(5) The goods referred to in paragraph (1)(*a*)(ii) of this Regulation, after they cease to be used by disaster victims, may not be lent, hired out or transferred, whether for a consideration or free of charge, except in special cases justified by the circumstances and with the prior sanction of the Revenue Commissioners:

Provided that—

  (*a*)   goods may be lent, hired out or transferred to an organisation itself entitled to benefit from relief pursuant to the said paragraph (1) or, if appropriate, to an organisation entitled to benefit from relief pursuant to Regulation 13(1)(*a*) of these Regulations where such organisations use them for purposes specified in the said paragraph (1) or Regulation 13(1)(*a*),

  (*b*)   goods the subject of loan, hiring out or transfer otherwise than in accordance with subparagraph (i) of this proviso shall be subject to payment of tax, at the rate applying on the date of the loan, hiring out or transfer, on the basis of the type of goods and the value for the purposes of tax chargeable at importation ascertained or accepted on that date by the Revenue Commissioners.

(6) Organisations referred to in paragraph (1) of this Regulation which cease to fulfil the conditions giving entitlement to relief or which propose to use such goods for purposes other than those provided for by that paragraph shall so inform the Revenue Commissioners.

(7) In the case of goods remaining in the possession of organisations which cease to fulfil the conditions giving entitlement to relief under this Regulation when these are transferred to an organisation itself entitled to benefit from relief pursuant to this Regulation or, if appropriate, to an organisation entitled to relief pursuant to Regulation 13 of these Regulations, the appropriate relief shall be granted, if the organisation uses the goods in question for purposes which confer the right to such relief. In other cases, the goods shall be liable to the relevant tax at the rate applying on the date on which those conditions cease to be fulfilled, on the basis of the type of goods and the value for the purposes of tax chargeable at importation ascertained or accepted on that date by the Revenue Commissioners.

(8) Goods used by an organisation benefiting from relief under this Regulation for purposes other than those provided for in paragraph (1) of this Regulation shall be liable to the relevant tax at the rate applying on the date on which they are put to such other use, on the basis of the type of goods and the value for the purposes of tax chargeable at importation ascertained or accepted on that date by the Revenue Commissioners.

16. (1) Tax shall not be charged on the importation of—

   (*a*)   decorations conferred by foreign governments on persons normally resident in the State,

   (*b*)   cups, medals and similar articles of an essentially symbolic nature awarded in a foreign country to persons normally resident in the State in connection with their activities in fields such as the arts, science, sport, the public service, or in recognition of merit at a particular event and imported by such persons, or

   (*c*)   cups, medals and similar articles of an essentially symbolic nature awarded in a foreign country to or other persons established in a foreign country for presentation in the State for the same purposes as those specified in subparagraph (*b*) of this paragraph:

Provided that satisfactory evidence as the facts is produced to the Revenue Commissioners by the importer and the operations involved are not in any way of a commercial character.

   (2)   (*a*)   Without prejudice, where relevant, to the provisions applicable to the international movement of travellers, tax shall not be charged on the importation of—

      (i)   goods imported by

         (I)   persons normally resident in the State, being goods presented to them as gifts by the host authorities, during the course of an official visit paid in a foreign country, or

         (II)   persons not normally resident in and paying an official visit in the State, being goods intended to be offered as gifts on that occasion to the host authorities; or

      (ii)   goods sent as gifts, in token of friendship or goodwill, by an official body, public authority or group carrying on an activity in the public interest which is located in another country, to an official body, public authority or group carrying on an activity in the public interest which is located in the State and approved by the Revenue Commissioners for the purposes of this Regulation to receive such goods free of tax.

   (*b*)   Relief under subparagraph (*a*) of this paragraph shall apply only to goods, other than alcoholic products, tobacco and tobacco products, which

      (i)   are offered on an occasional basis,

      (ii)   do not, by their nature, value or quantity, reflect any commercial interest, and

        (iii)   are not used for commercial purposes.

(3)   (*a*)   Within the limits and subject to the conditions laid down by the Revenue Commissioners tax shall not be charged on the importation of—

        (i)   gifts to reigning monarchs and heads of State, or

        (ii)   goods to be used or consumed by reigning monarchs and foreign heads of State, or by persons officially representing them, during their official stay in the State.

    (*b*)   Subparagraph (*a*) of this paragraph shall apply also to persons enjoying prerogatives at international level analogous to those enjoyed by reigning monarchs or heads of State.

17. (1) Without prejudice to Regulation 19(1)(*a*)(i) of these Regulations and subject to paragraphs (2) and (3) of this Regulation, tax shall not be charged on the importation of samples of goods of negligible value which can be used only to solicit orders for goods of the type they represent.

(2) The Revenue Commissioners may, if they think fit, require that, in order to qualify for relief, articles be rendered permanently unusable by being torn, perforated, or clearly and indelibly marked, or by any other process, provided such operation does not destroy their character as samples.

(3) In this Regulation **"samples of goods"** means any article representing a type of goods whose manner of presentation and quantity for goods of the same type or quality, rule out its use for any purpose other than that of seeking orders.

18. (1)(*a*)   Subject to subparagraph (*b*) of this paragraph, tax shall not be charged on the importation of printed advertising matter such as catalogues, price lists, directions for use or brochures relating to—

        (i)   goods for sale or hire, or

        (ii)   transport, commercial insurance or banking services offered, by a person established outside the State.

    (*b*)   Relief under subparagraph (*a*) of this paragraph shall apply only to printed advertisement which fulfil the following conditions:

        (i)   printed matter shall clearly display the name of the undertaking which produces, sells or hires out the goods, or which offers the services, to which it refers,

        (ii)   each consignment shall contain no more than one document or a single copy of each document if it is made up of several documents; however, tax shall not be charged on the importation of consignments comprising several copies of the same document if their total gross weight does not exceed 1 kilogram, and

        (iii)   printed matter shall not be the subject of grouped consignments from the same consignor to the same consignee.

(2) Tax shall not be charged on the importation of articles for advertising purposes, of no intrinsic commercial value, sent free of charge by suppliers to their customers which, apart from their advertising function, are not capable of being used.

19. (1)(*a*)   Subject to paragraphs (2) to (5), tax shall not be charged on the importation of—

        (i)   small representative samples of goods intended for a trade fair or similar event,

        (ii)   goods imported solely in order to be demonstrated or in order to demonstrate machines and apparatus displayed at a trade fair or similar event, (iii)　materials such as paints, varnishes and wallpaper, of such value and quantity as are appropriate for the purposes of building, fitting-out and decorating of a temporary stand at a trade fair or similar event, and which are incapable of further use, or

(iv)　printed matter, catalogues, prospectuses, price lists, advertising posters, calendars, whether or not illustrated, unframed photographs and other article supplied free of charge in order to advertise goods displayed at a trade fair or similar event.

(*b*)　In subparagraph (*a*) of this paragraph **"trade fair or similar event"** means:

(i)　exhibitions, fairs, shows and similar events connected with trade, industry, agriculture or handicrafts;

(ii)　exhibitions and events held mainly for charitable purposes;

(iii)　exhibitions and events held mainly for scientific, technical, handicraft, artistic, educational or cultural or sporting purposes, for religious reasons or for reasons of worship, trade union activity or tourism, or in order to promote international understanding,

(iv)　meetings of representatives of international organisations or collective bodies, and

(v)　official or commemorative ceremonies and gatherings,

but not exhibitions staged for private purposes in commercial stores or premises to sell goods.

(2) Paragraph (1)(*a*)(i) of this Regulation shall apply only to samples which:

(*a*)　are imported free of charge as such or are obtained at the exhibition from goods imported in bulk;

(*b*)　are used only for distribution free of charge to the public at the exhibition for use or consumption by the persons to whom they are offered;

(*c*)　are identifiable as advertising samples of low unitary value;

(*d*)　are not readily marketable and, where appropriate, are packaged in such a way that the quantity of the item involved is less than the smallest quantity of the same item normally sold on the market;

(*e*)　in the case of foodstuffs and beverages not packaged in the manner specified in subparagraph (*d*) of this paragraph, are intended for consumption during the exhibition;

(*f*)　in their total value and quantity, are appropriate to the nature of the exhibition, the number of visitors, and the extent of the exhibitor's participation.

(3) Paragraph (1)(*a*)(ii) of this Regulation shall apply only to goods which are:

(*a*)　consumed or destroyed during the exhibition, and

(*b*)　appropriate, in their total value and quantity, to the nature of the exhibition, the number of visitors, and the extent of the exhibitor's participation.

(4) Paragraph (1)(*a*)(iv) of this Regulation shall apply only to printed matter and articles for advertising purposes which:

(*a*)　are intended solely for distribution free of charge to the public at the exhibition;

(*b*)　in their total value and quantity, are appropriate to the nature of the exhibition, the number of visitors, and the extent of the exhibitor's participation.

(5) Clauses (i) and (ii) of paragraph (1)(*a*) of the Regulation shall not apply to—

(*a*)　alcoholic products,

(*b*)　tobacco or tobacco products, or

(*c*)　fuels, whether solid, liquid or gaseous.

20. (1) Subject to paragraphs (2) to (7) of this Regulation, tax shall not be charged on the importation of goods imported for examination, analysis or tests to determine their composition, quality or other technical characteristics for purposes of information or industrial or commercial research.

(2) Subject to the provisions of paragraph (5) of this Regulation, paragraph (1) of this Regulation shall apply to goods only if they are completely used up or destroyed in the course of the examination, analysis or test for which they are imported.

(3) This Regulation shall not apply to goods used in examinations, analysis or tests which in themselves constitute sales promotion operations.

(4) This Regulation shall apply only to the quantities of goods which are strictly necessary for the purpose for which they are imported. These quantities shall in each case be determined by the Revenue Commissioners, taking into account the said purpose.

(5)   (*a*)   This regulation shall apply to goods which are not completely used up or destroyed during examination, analysis or testing if the products remaining are, with the agreement and under the supervision of the Revenue Commissioners:

        (i)   completely destroyed or rendered commercially valueless on completion of the examination, analysis or testing concerned,

        (ii)   surrendered to the State without causing it any expense and comply with such other conditions (if any) as the Revenue Commissioners may determine, or

        (iii)   in duly justified circumstances, exported.

    (*b*)   In subparagraph (*a*) of this paragraph **"products remaining"** means products resulting from the examinations, analyses or tests or goods not actually used.

(6) Save where paragraph (5)(*a*) applies, products remaining at the end of the examinations, analyses or tests referred to in paragraph (1) shall be subject to the relevant tax, at the rate applying on the date of completion of the examinations, analyses or tests concerned, on the basis of the type of goods and the value for the purposes of tax chargeable at importation ascertained or accepted on that date by the Revenue Commissioners; however, the person concerned may, with the agreement and under the supervision of the Revenue Commissioners, convert products remaining to waste or scrap, in which case the appropriate amount of tax shall be that applying to such waste or scrap at the time of conversion.

(7) The period within which the examinations, analyses or tests referred to in this Regulation are to be carried out and the administrative formalities completed in order to ensure the use of the goods concerned for the purposes intended shall be determined in each case by the Revenue Commissioners.

21. Tax shall not be charged on the importation of trademarks, patterns or designs or their supporting documents or on applications for patents for invention or the like for submission to the bodies competent to deal with the protection of copyrights or the protection of industrial or commercial patent rights.

22. Tax shall not be charged on the importation of:

    (*a*)   documentation, being leaflets, brochures, books, magazines, guidebooks, posters, whether or not framed, unframed photographs and photographic enlargements, maps, whether or not illustrated, window transparencies and illustrated calendars for distribution free of charge whose principal purpose is to encourage the public to visit foreign countries, in particular in order to attend cultural, tourist, sporting, religious or trade or professional meetings or events and which contain not more than **25 per cent** of private commercial advertising and the general nature of whose promotional aims is evident.

    (*b*)   foreign hotel lists and yearbooks published by official tourist agencies, or under their auspices, and timetables for foreign transport services that are for distribution free of charge and contain not more than **25 per cent** of private commercial advertising, or

(c)   reference material supplied to accredited representatives or correspondents appointed by official national tourist agencies and not intended for distribution such as yearbooks, lists of telephone or telex numbers, hotel lists, fairs catalogues, specimens, of craft goods of negligible value, and literature on museums, universities, spas or other similar establishments.

23. Tax shall not be charged on the importation of—

(a)   documents sent free of charge to the public service of the State,

(b)   publications of foreign governments and publications of official international bodies for distribution free of charge,

(c)   ballot papers for elections organised by bodies set up outside the State,

(d)   objects to be submitted as evidence or for like purposes to the courts or other official agencies of the State,

(e)   specimen signatures and printed circulars concerning signatures sent as part of customary exchanges of information between public services or banking establishments,

(f)   official printed matter sent to the Central Bank of Ireland,

(g)   reports, statements, notes, prospectuses, application forms and other documents drawn up by companies whose headquarters are outside the State and sent to the bearers or subscribers of securities issued by such companies,

(h)   recorded media, such as punched cards, sound recordings, microfilms and the like, which contain information sent free of charge to the addressee where such relief does not give rise to abuses or to major distortion of competition,

(i)   files, archives, printed forms and other documents to be used in international meetings, conferences or congresses, and reports on such gatherings,

(j)   plans, technical drawings, traced designs, descriptions and other similar documents imported with a view to obtaining or fulfilling orders outside the State or to participating in a competition held in the State,

(k)   documents to be used in examinations held in the State by institutions set up outside the State,

(l)   printed forms to be used as official documents in the international movement of vehicles or goods, within the framework of international conventions,

(m)   printed forms, labels, tickets and similar documents sent by transport undertakings or by undertakings of the hotel industry located outside the State to travel agencies set up in the State,

(n)   printed forms and tickets, bills of lading, way-bills and other commercial or office documents which have been used,

(o)   official printed forms from national or international authorities and printed matter conforming to international standards sent for distribution by associations of another country to corresponding associations located in the State,

(p)   photographs, slides and stereotype mats for photographs, whether or not captioned, sent to press agencies or newspaper or magazine publishers,

(q)   visual and auditory materials of an educational, scientific or cultural character specified in the Schedule to these Regulations which are produced by the United Nations or one of its specialised agencies, whatever the use for which they are intended,

(r)   collectors' pieces and works of art of an educational scientific or cultural character which are not intended for sale and which are imported by museums, galleries and other institutions approved of by the Revenue Commissioners for the purposes of this Regulation and on condition that the articles in question are imported free of charge or, if they are imported against payment, are not supplied by a taxable person.

24. Tax shall not be charged on the importation of—

(*a*) material such as rope, straw, cloth, paper, cardboard, wood and plastics used in the stowage and protection, including heat protection, of imported goods during their transportation to the State, where such materials are not normally re-usable and where the consideration for their supply forms part of the taxable amount as defined in Article 11 of the Sixth Council Directive No. 77/388/EEC of 17 May 1977,

(*b*) litter, fodder and feeding stuffs put on board means of transport used to convey animals to the territory of the State for distribution to the said animals during the journey.

25. (1) Subject to paragraphs (2) to (4) of this Regulation, tax shall not be charged on the importation of—

(*a*) fuel contained in the standard tanks of private and commercial motor vehicles, including motor cycles,

(*b*) fuel contained in portable tanks carried by private motor vehicles and motor cycles, with a maximum of 10 litres per vehicle,

(*c*) lubricants carried in motor vehicles and required for their normal operation during the journey in question.

(2) In paragraph (1) of this Regulation—

"commercial motor vehicle" means any motorised road vehicle which by its type of construction and equipment is designed for and capable of transporting, whether for payment or not:

(*a*) more than nine persons including the driver, or

(*b*) goods,

and any road vehicle for a special purpose other than transport as such;

"private motor vehicle" means any motor vehicle not covered by the definition in (*a*);

"standard tanks" means the tanks permanently fixed by the manufacturer to all motor vehicles of the same type as the vehicle in question and whose permanent fitting enables fuel to be used directly, both for the purposes of propulsion and, where appropriate, for the operation of a refrigeration system;

gas tanks fitted to motor vehicles designed for the direct use of gas as a fuel shall also be considered to be standard tanks.

(3) Fuel the subject of relief under paragraph (1) of this Regulation shall not be used in a vehicle other than that in which it was imported nor be removed from that vehicle and stored, except during necessary repairs to that vehicle, or transferred for a consideration or free of charge by the importer.

(4) Non-compliance with the provisions of paragraph (3) shall give rise to application of tax on the goods at the rate in force on the date of such non-compliance, on the basis of the type of goods and the value for the purposes of tax chargeable at importation ascertained or accepted on that date by the Revenue Commissioners.

26. Tax shall not be charged on the importation of—

(*a*) goods for use by organisations approved by the Revenue Commissioners for the purposes of this Regulation for construction, upkeep or ornamentation of cemeteries and tombs of, and memorials to, war victims of a foreign country who are buried in the State,

(*b*) coffins containing bodies and urns containing the ashes of deceased persons, and flowers, funeral wreaths and other ornamental objects normally accompanying them, or

(*c*) flowers, wreaths and other ornamental objects imported by persons resident in another Member State of the Community attending a funeral in or visiting the state to decorate graves if such importations do not reflect, either by their nature or their quantity, any commercial intent.

27. (1) The value in Irish currency of the ECU to be applied in each year for the purposes of these Regulations shall be calculated by reference to the official rate of exchange between the currencies obtaining on the first working day of October of the previous year.

(2) The amounts in Irish currency arrived at by converting the amounts of ECU shall be rounded off to the nearest IR£.

(3) The said value applying in a particular year shall continue in force in the following year, if, without taking into account the rounding off aforesaid, the difference between the values applicable to those years is less than **5 per cent** of the earlier year's value.

28. Nothing in these Regulations shall be construed as affecting—

(*a*) the privileges and immunities granted under cultural, scientific or technical cooperation agreements concluded between the State and other countries;

(*b*) the special exemptions justified by the nature of frontier traffic which are granted under frontier arrangements concluded between the State and other countries.

29. Nothing in these Regulations shall be construed as exempting an importer from compliance with any legal requirement, obligation, restriction or prohibition other than the requirement of payment of tax on goods which, but for these Regulations, would be chargeable to tax on importation.

30. The following provisions shall not apply in relation to goods relieved from tax by virtue of these Regulations:

section 17 of the Finance Act, 1936 (No.31 of 1936), as amended by section 13 of the Finance Act, 1957 (No. 20 of 1957),

paragraphs (*a*),(*b*),(*d*) and (*e*) of section 18 of the Finance Act, 1936 (No.31 of 1936),

section 18 of the Finance Act, 1938 (No. 25 of 1938),

section 17 of the Finance Act, 1946 (No. 15 of 1946),

Relief from Customs Duties (Fairs, Exhibitions, and Similar Events) Order, 1965 (S.I. No. 143 of 1965),

section 76 of the Finance Act, 1974 (No. 27 of 1974),

Council Regulation No. 918/83/EEC of 28 March, 1983.

31. A person who, after the date of the making of these Regulations, contravenes a provision thereof, shall be guilty of an offence and shall, without prejudice to any other penalty to which he may be liable, be liable, on summary conviction, to a fine not exceeding £500.

SCHEDULE
Goods referred to in Regulation 23(*q*)

Visual and auditory materials of an educational, scientific or cultural character

Common Tariff Number	Custom Heading Description
37.04	Sensitized plates and film, exposed but not developed, negative or positive:
	A. Cinematograph film:
	ex II. Other positives, of an educational , scientific or cultural character
3x 37.05	Plates, unperforated film and perforated film (other than cinematograph film), exposed and developed, negative or positive, of an educational, scientific or cultural character
37.07	Cinematograph film, exposed and developed, whether or not incorporating sound track or consisting only of sound track, negative or positive:

B. II. Other positives:

ex A. Newsreels (with or without sound track) depicting events of current news value at the time of importation, and imported up to a limit of two copies of each subject for copying purposes.

ex B. Other:

—Archival film material (with or without sound track) intended for use in connection with newsreel films

—Recreational films particularly suited for children and young people

—Other films of an educational, scientific or cultural character

49.11 Other printed matter including printed pictures and photographs:

ex B. Other:

—Microcards or other information storage media required in computerized information and documentation services, of an educational scientific or cultural character.

—Wall charts designed solely for demonstration and education

ex 90.21 Instruments, apparatus or models, designed solely for demonstrational purposes (for example, in education or exhibition), unsuitable for other uses:

—Patterns, models and wall charts of an educational, scientific or cultural character, designed solely for demonstration and education

—Mock-ups or visualisations of abstract concepts such as molecular structures or mathematical formulae

92.12 Gramophone records and other sound or similar recordings, matrices for the production of records, prepared record blanks, film for mechanical sound recordings, prepared tapes, wires, strips and like articles of a kind commonly used for sound or similar recording

ex B. Recorded

—Of an educational, scientific or cultural character

Various

—Holograms for laser projection

—Multi-media kits

—Materials for programmed instruction, including materials in kit form, with the corresponding printed materials.

VALUE ADDED TAX (PLACE OF SUPPLY OF CERTAIN SERVICES) REGULATIONS 1985

(SI No 343 of 1985)

Notes
Revoked with effect from 27 May 1986 by VATA 1972 s 5(6)(*d*) (inserted by FA 1986 s 81(*b*)(i))

VALUE ADDED TAX (REMISSION AND REPAYMENT OF TAX ON CERTAIN IMPORTATIONS) REGULATIONS 1985

(SI No 344 of 1985)

Notes

Prior to the implementation of the single market (1 January 1993), these regulations (with effect from 25 October 1985) provided relief from VAT on (*a*) goods re imported after undergoing work in another EC Member State and (*b*) goods imported on hire, lease or loan, or for use in connection with the supply of taxable services where the goods are subsequently exported. Where goods in (*a*) exported by a non taxable person to another EC State for repair, maintenance etc exclusively in that State were subject to non recoverable VAT in that other EC State, the reimportation of the goods to Ireland was be exempt from VAT at importation.

Where goods in (*b*) were imported by a non taxable person the excess (if any) of VAT paid at importation over the VAT attributable to the hiring or leasing of the goods or their use for the supply of taxable services was repayable.

EUROPEAN COMMUNITIES (VALUE ADDED TAX) (EXEMPTION ON TEMPORARY IMPORTATIONS OF CERTAIN GOODS) REGULATIONS 1986

(SI No 264 of 1986)

Cross-reference
VATA 1972 s 32.

Notes
These regulations, which come into operation on 1 January 1986, gave effect in Ireland to the Seventeenth Council Directive (85/362/EEC) of 16 July 1985. They provided for relief from VAT for most goods, other than consumable goods and means of transport, temporarily imported into Ireland from anther EC State.
The Seventeenth Council Directive (85/362/EEC) of 16 July 1985 ceased to have effect on 31 December 1992 as regards relations between Member States: Council Directive 91/680/EEC of 16 December 1991 art 2(1).

VALUE ADDED TAX (DETERMINATION OF TAX DUE BY REFERENCE TO MONEYS RECEIVED) REGULATIONS 1986

(SI No 298 of 1986)

Amendments

Revoked by Value Added Tax (Determination of Tax Due by Reference to Moneys Received) Regulations 1992 r 13 (SI 306/92).

Notes

These regulations, which come into force on 2 September 1986, amended the terms and conditions, formerly contained in VATR 1979 r 7 relating to the operation of the cash received basis of accounting for VAT. The regulations extended the definition of "connected persons" (transactions between such persons do not qualify for the cash received basis). They also gave the inspector power to withdraw the cash received basis where he was satisfied that it did not provide a reliable measure of the true liability.

VALUE ADDED TAX (FREE PORTS) REGULATIONS 1987

(SI No 275 of 1987)

1. These Regulations may be cited as the Value Added Tax (Free Ports) Regulations, 1987.

Cross-references
VATA 1972 s 32.
Notes
These regulations, which came into force on 24 July 1987, deal with relief from payment of VAT at importation of goods for use in a free port established in accordance with the Free Ports Act 1986. To qualify for relief an importer must be registered for VAT, licensed to carry on business in the free port and import the goods for the purposes of his business in the free port. Relief is not given for imports of food, drink, motor vehicles or petrol unless VAT on such imports would be deductible in normal circumstances. Relief may be withdrawn if the regulations are not complied with.

---

2. These Regulations shall be deemed to have come into operation on the 24th day of July, 1987.

3. In these Regulations—

"the Act" means the Value Added Tax Act, 1972;

"control" has the meaning ascribed to it by section 8(3B) (inserted by the Finance Act, 1984 (No. 9 of 1984)) of the Act.

4. (1) Subject to paragraph (2) of this Regulation, goods that are imported by a registered person may be delivered, or removed, directly to a free port without payment of the tax chargeable on the importation if that person complies with—

    (*a*)   the condition that he show to the satisfaction of the Revenue Commissioners that—

        (i)   he is a person who has, under section 4 of the Free Ports Act, 1986 (No. 6 of 1986), been granted a licence authorising him to carry on within that free port any trade, business or manufacture and

        (ii) the goods are being imported for the purposes of his trade, business or manufacture in that free port,

    and

    (*b*)   such other conditions as the Revenue Commissioners may impose.

(2) This Regulation shall not apply to the importation of food, drink, motor vehicles or petrol except where tax on the importation of those goods would, if it were paid, be wholly deductible under section 12 of the Act.

5. (1) Without prejudice to paragraph (2) of this Regulation, goods, which have been imported by a registered person without payment of the tax chargeable on the importation in accordance with Regulation 4 of these Regulations, may not be removed from the free port concerned to any other part of the State (other than into another free port or the customs-free airport), in circumstances in which such removal is not in relation to a supply of those goods or, if it is in relation to a supply of those goods, is in relation to a supply to a person who exercises control over the registered person, or over whom the registered person exercises control, or over whom and the registered person another person exercises control.

(2)   (*a*)   The removal of goods, precluded by paragraph (1) of this Regulation, may be allowed, with the prior agreement in writing of the Revenue Commissioners, in such exceptional cases as may be determined by them in their absolute discretion.

    (*b*)   Where, by virtue of this paragraph, the removal of goods is allowed, tax which would, but for these Regulations, have been payable on the importation of the goods, shall be payable at the time of the removal by the registered person specified in paragraph (1) of this Regulation.

6. Where goods have been imported by a registered person without payment of the tax chargeable on the importation in accordance with Regulation 4 of these Regulations, details of the goods, including the value by reference to each rate of tax (including the zero rate) shall, if so required, be included in the return for the taxable period during which the importation took place required to be furnished by that person under section 19 of the Act and the regulations made thereunder.

7. Where, in the opinion of the Revenue Commissioners, a person does not, or has ceased to, satisfy a condition referred to, or specified, in Regulation 4 of these Regulations, or has failed to comply with Regulation 5 or 6 of these Regulations, the Revenue Commissioners shall send to such person by post notification of their opinion and the relief provided for by the said Regulation 4 shall not apply in relation to goods imported by that person during the period from the date on which such notification would be delivered in the ordinary course of post until the time when the person concerned shows to the satisfaction of the Revenue Commissioners that he intends to comply with the conditions referred to, or specified, in the said Regulation 4 and with the said Regulations 5 and 6.

VALUE ADDED TAX (SECOND-HAND MOTOR VEHICLES) REGULATIONS 1988

(SI No 121 of 1988)

Notes

These regulations were revoked by the Value Added Tax (Special Scheme for Means of Transport: Documentation) Regulations 1996 (SI 201/1996) r 9 with effect from 1 July 1996. They provided for VAT relief in case of the acquisition for resale of certain second hand road motor vehicles by taxable persons from non-taxable persons.

VALUE ADDED TAX (FURNITURE, SILVER, GLASS AND PORCELAIN) REGULATIONS 1989

(SI No 304 of 1989)

1. These Regulations may be cited as the Value Added Tax (Furniture, Silver, Glass and Porcelain) Regulations, 1989.

Cross-reference

Enabling legislation: VATA 1972 s 32 , Sch 6 para (xvi)(*d*).

With effect from 1 January 1993, "importation" means importation from a non EC country and "exportation" means exportation to a non EC country: VATA 1972 s 1(1).

Notes

These regulations, which came into effect on 1 November 1989, provide, subject to conditions, for the reduction from 21% to 12.5% in the rate of VAT applicable to the supply and importation of certain articles of furniture, silver, glass and porcelain more than 100 years old.

---

2. (1) In these Regulations—

"the Act" means the Value Added Tax Act, 1972;

"qualifying goods" means articles of the kind specified in Regulation 3 which are more than 100 years old, where such evidence, as specified in Regulation 4, is produced which satisfies the Revenue Commissioners that the articles concerned are more than 100 years old.

(2) In these Regulations a reference to a Regulation is to a Regulation of these Regulations.

3. (1) Paragraph (i*a*)(*d*)(inserted by the Finance Act, 1989 (No. 10 of 1989)) of the Sixth Schedule to the Act shall have effect subject to and in accordance with these Regulations.

(2) For the purposes of giving effect by these Regulations to the said paragraph (i*a*)(*d*), the following articles of furniture, silver, glass and porcelain are hereby specified to be the articles to which the said paragraph (i*a*)(*d*) of these Regulations apply, that is to say:

(*a*)   in the case of furniture, any article being movable goods which have been manufactured wholly or mainly from wood, metal (other than silver), marble or other stone, or any combination thereof, and which were designed for use as furnishings, fitments or decoration for private, commercial or public buildings, or for gardens, and to which subparagraphs (*a*), (*b*) and (*c*) of paragraph (i*a*) of the Sixth Schedule to the Act do not relate;

(*b*)   in the case of silver, any article manufactured wholly or mainly from silver, not being jewellery, coins, medals, ingots or bars;

(*c*)   in the case of glass, any article manufactured wholly or mainly from glass, including mirrors, chandeliers and leaded or stained glass windows;

(*d*)   in the case of porcelain, any article being a cup, saucer, bowl, plate, dish, jug, vase, pot, urn or similar goods, or a statue or statuary other than an article to which paragraph (i*a*)(*c*) of the Sixth Schedule to the Act relates), manufactured wholly or mainly from porcelain, china, terracotta, clay, ceramics or similar materials, or any combination thereof.

4. Evidence that qualifying goods are more than 100 years old shall consist of—

(*a*)   a certificate issued by a member of the association known as the Irish Antique Dealers' Association, or of an equivalent trade association recognised by the Revenue Commissioners for the purpose of issuing such a certificate, or

(*b*)   a certificate issued on behalf of the National Museum of Ireland, or

(*c*)   a statutory declaration by a person recognised, for the purpose of making such a declaration, as a connoisseur by the Revenue Commissioners in respect of articles of the type concerned, or (*d*)   in the case of imported goods, a certificate, declaration or other document made under the laws of the country of exportation which in the opinion of the Revenue Commissioners correspond to any of the foregoing provisions of this Regulation, or

(*e*)   an invoice issued in accordance with Regulation 6 or a certification made in accordance with Regulation 7.

5. A non-taxable person who supplies qualifying goods to a taxable person who is acquiring such goods for resale shall on the date of such supply, or within the ten days next following that date, issue to the taxable person who acquires the goods an invoice in respect of that supply, which sets out the following particulars:

(*a*)   the name and address of the person who is supplying the goods to which the invoice relates,

(*b*)   the name, address and tax registration number of the said taxable person,

(*c*)   the date upon which the invoice is issued,

(*d*)   the date upon which the goods to which the invoice relates are supplied,

(*e*)   a description of the goods including details of the quantity, type, apparent material of construction, possible origin and identifying features,

(*f*)   the consideration for the supply, and

(*g*)   the signature or acknowledgement of the person by whom the invoice is issued,

and the taxable person to whom the qualifying goods are supplied shall provide the form for the purpose of the said invoice, enter the appropriate particulars thereon, and give a copy of the invoice to the supplier of the goods.

6. A taxable person who supplies qualifying goods to another taxable person shall include on the invoice concerned, which he is required to issue in accordance with section 17 (1) of the Act, a declaration to the effect that the goods are more than 100 years old.

7. A taxable person who supplies qualifying goods to a non-taxable person shall, for the purposes of Regulation 8, certify in writing in respect of each such supply that the said goods are more than 100 years old.

8. Every taxable person shall, in relation to qualifying goods which he has acquired or supplied, keep full and true records, entered up to date, of the acquisition and resale of such goods, together with cross-references between all such records, the relevant invoices issued in accordance with Regulations 5 and 6, and the certification made in accordance with Regulation 7.

DISABLED DRIVERS (TAX CONCESSIONS) REGULATIONS 1989

(SI No 340 of 1989)

Notes

Revoked by Disabled Drivers and Disabled Passengers (Tax Concessions) Regulations 1994 (SI 353/1994) r 19 with effect from 1 December 1994.

VALUE ADDED TAX (DETERMINATION OF TAX DUE BY REFERENCE TO MONEYS RECEIVED) (AMENDMENT) REGULATIONS 1992

(SI No 93 of 1992)

Amendments
Revoked by Value Added Tax (Determination of Tax Due by Reference to Moneys Received) Regulations 1992 r 13 (SI 306/1992) with effect from 28 October 1992.
Cross-references
VATA 1972 ss 14 and 32.
Notes
These regulations provided that an adjustment to take account of an increase in debtors during the period of use of the moneys received basis must now be made in all cases (previously only required where moneys received basis was in use for six years). The adjustment is to be calculated by reference to the debtors position at the time of authorisation to use the moneys received basis or the position six years previous to the change of basis, whichever is the later. No adjustment will be required if the cessation of use of the moneys received basis results from the death of the taxable person.

2. ....

Notes
These regulations substituted Value Added Tax (Determination of Tax Due by Reference to Moneys Received) Regulations 1986 r 3(10) (SI 298/1986) with effect from 16 April 1992.

VALUE ADDED TAX (MONTHLY CONTROL STATEMENT) REGULATIONS 1992

(SI No 230 of 1992)

1. These regulations may be cited as the Value Added Tax (Monthly Control Statement) Regulations, 1992.

2. These regulations shall come into operation on the 1st day of November, 1992.

Notes

These regulations (which came into effect on 1 November 1992) specify the details required to be shown in the monthly control statement that must be issued by suppliers (whose annual turnover from the supply of taxable goods exceeds £2m) to their customers. The regulations also specify the time limits within which the monthly control statement must be issued, and provide that each supplier must retain a copy of any monthly control statements he has issued.

---

3. In these regulations—

"the Act" means the Value Added Tax Act, 1972;

"monthly control statement" means the monthly control statement which is required to be issued in accordance with section 17(1B) of the Act.

4. Every monthly control statement issued by a taxable person shall set out the following particulars:

(*a*) the name, address and registration number of the person by whom the goods referred to in the statement were supplied,

(*b*) the name and address of the person to whom the goods referred to in the statement were supplied,

(*c*) the date of issue of the statement,

(*d*) the calendar month to which the statement refers,

(*e*) in relation to supplies of goods for which an invoice, credit note, debit note or settlement voucher was issued in accordance with section 17 of the Act, the total amount of the consideration inclusive of tax shown on each of those documents,

(*f*) in relation to supplies of goods for which an invoice, credit note, debit note or settlement voucher was not issued,

    (i) the date of each such supply,

    (ii) a description of the goods supplied,

    (iii) the consideration, exclusive of tax, for each supply,

    (iv) the rate or rates of tax and amount of tax at each rate chargeable to the person who has supplied the goods,

(*g*) in relation to any adjustment of the consideration for the supplies referred to in paragraph (*e*) or (*f*) agreed between the supplier of the goods and the taxable person and for which a credit note was not issued under section 17 of the Act,

    (i) the amount of such adjustment,

    (ii) the date of such adjustment,

(*h*) where, in respect of the supply referred to in paragraph (*e*) or (*f*), any payment has been or will be made by the person by whom the goods were supplied,

    (i) the amount of such payment or payments

    (ii) the date or dates when such payment or payments were or will be made

337

     (iii)   the person or persons to whom such payment or payments have been or will be made

and

   (*i*)   in relation to any gifts or promotional items given in connection with the supplies referred to in paragraph (*e*) or (*f*),

     (i)   a description of such gifts or promotional items

     (ii)   the value of such gifts or promotional items

     (iii)   the date of provision of such gifts or promotional items.

5. A monthly control statement required to be issued in accordance with section 17(1B) of the Act shall be issued not later than the last day of the month following the month during which goods are supplied.

6. Every person issuing a monthly control statement shall keep a copy thereof and references in these regulations to any such statement, other than references to its issue, shall include references to a copy thereof.

VALUE ADDED TAX (ELECTRONIC DATA EXCHANGE AND STORAGE) REGULATIONS 1992

(SI No 269 of 1992)

1. These Regulations may be cited as the Value Added Tax (Electronic Data Exchange and Storage) Regulations, 1992.

Notes

These regulations specify the requiements that must be fulfilled by traders who wish (in accordance with VATA 1972 s 17(1A)) to issue or receive electronic VAT invoices, credit notes etc..

---

2. (1) In these Regulations—

"the Act" means the Value Added Tax Act, 1972 (No 22 of 1972);

"message" means an invoice, credit note, debit note or settlement voucher, required to be issued in accordance with section 17 of the Act;

"file" means a computer record consisting of a number of messages;

"registration number", in relation to a person, means the number assigned to the person for the purposes of registration under section 9 of the Act;

"transmission file" means a file that is constructed in a definitive format for electronic transmission to a particular trading partner;

"transmission sequence number" means a number, being one of a series of numbers which is unique to particular trading partners, generated sequentially at the time of preparation of a transmission file;

"trading partners" means any two taxable persons engaged in the electronic exchange of messages;

"transaction log" means a record of transmission sequence numbers between particular trading partners.

(2) In these Regulations—

(*a*) a reference to a Regulation is to a Regulation of these Regulations, and

(*b*) a reference to a paragraph, subparagraph or clause is to a paragraph, subparagraph or clause of the provision in which the reference occurs,

unless it is indicated that reference to some other provision is intended.

3. (1) Where, by virtue of section 17(1A) of the Act, a taxable person proposes to issue or receive messages by electronic means, he shall apply in writing to the Revenue Commissioners to be authorised to so issue and receive messages and shall at the same time furnish to the Revenue Commissioners—

(*a*) the following particulars:

(i) his name and address,

(ii) his registration number,

(iii) the name, address and registration number of each of his trading partners, and

(iv) the date from which he intends, if authorised by the Revenue Commissioners, to issue or receive messages by electronic means, being a date not less than one month after the date he so applies to the Revenue Commissioners,

and

339

(*b*) a declaration that the electronic data exchange system to be used by him is capable of satisfying the requirements specified in subparagraphs (*a*), (*b*), (*c*), (*d*), (*e*) and (*f*) of Regulation 4(1).

(2) Where a change occurs in any of the particulars furnished in accordance with clauses (i), (ii) and (iii) of subparagraph (*a*) of paragraph (1), the taxable person shall furnish to the Revenue Commissioners particulars of the change within thirty days following the date of the change.

4. (1) Where the Revenue Commissioners consider that it is expedient in the interests of the efficient administration of the tax, they shall authorise in writing, where appropriate from a specified or ascertainable date, a taxable person who has furnished the particulars required in accordance with paragraphs (1) and (2) of Regulation 3 to issue or receive messages by electronic means, to or from another taxable person who has also been so authorised, subject to the condition that the electronic data exchange system to be used by the trading partners concerned is capable of—

(*a*) producing, retaining and storing a record of such messages in such form and containing such particulars as are required in accordance with section 17 of the Act and regulations under the Act,

(*b*) reproducing on paper any file, message, transmission file or any other document required to be produced, retained or stored in accordance with regulations under the Act,

(*c*) generating transmission sequence numbers,

(*d*) precluding the repeated issue of any particular transmission sequence number,

(*e*) precluding the omission of any particular number in the sequence of issue of transmission sequence numbers, and

(*f*) maintaining records required to be retained or stored in accordance with paragraph (2) in such manner as will allow their retrieval by reference either to the date or the transmission sequence number of the transmission.

(2) A taxable person who is authorised in accordance with paragraph (1) to issue or receive messages by electronic means shall, in addition to the documents required to be issued, retained and stored in accordance with the Act and regulations under the Act, issue, retain and store the following documents:

(*a*) in the case of an authorised issuer, a record capable of being reproduced on paper, made at the time of construction of a transmission file and issued to a trading partner, containing the following particulars:

(i) the name, address and registration number of the issuer,

(ii) the name, address and registration number of the recipient,

(iii) the date of transmission of the transmission file,

(iv) the transmission sequence number, and

(v) for each type of message in the transmission file the following particulars:

(I) the total number of messages in the file,

(II) the total consideration, exclusive of tax, in respect of which the messages were issued by him,

(III) the amount of the said consideration liable to tax at each rate including the zero rate,

(IV) the amount of tax appropriate to the said consideration at each rate, and

(V) the total consideration for exempt supplies, if any, in the file;

(*b*) in the case of an authorised recipient, a record, capable of being reproduced on paper, made at the time of receipt of a transmission file, the file having been converted from the issuer's transmission file format to the recipient's own file format, and containing the following particulars:

    (i)   the name, address and registration number of the issuer,

    (ii)   the name, address and registration number of the recipient,

    (iii)   the date of transmission of the transmission file,

    (iv)   the transmission sequence number, and

    (v)   for each type of message in the file the following particulars:

        (I)   the total number of messages in the file,

        (II)   the total consideration exclusive of tax in respect of which the messages were received by him,

        (III)   the amount of the said consideration liable at each rate including the zero rate, and

        (IV)   the amount of tax appropriate to the said consideration at each rate, and

        (V)   the total consideration for exempt supplies, if any, in the file;

(c)   in the case of an authorised issuer and an authorised recipient, a summary document produced at the end of each calendar month by each of them of a transmission file, containing the following particulars:

    (i)   the name, address and registration number of the issuer,

    (ii)   the name, address and registration number of the recipient,

    (iii)   the calendar month to which the document relates, and

    (iv)   in respect of that month the following particulars:

        (I)   each transmission sequence number,

        (II)   the total consideration, exclusive of tax, to which the document relates,

        (III)   the amount of the consideration liable at each rate of tax including the zero rate,

        (IV)   the amount of tax appropriate to the said consideration at each rate,

        (V)   the total consideration for exempt supplies, if any,

        and

    (v)   in the case of the authorised issuer, the sequence numbers of faulty or failed transmissions;

(d)   in the case of an authorised recipient, a document produced by him and issued to a trading partner giving details of any discrepancy between the documents specified in paragraphs (a) and (b);

(e)   in all cases, a transaction log.

5. An authorisation issued under Regulation 4 may be withdrawn by the Revenue Commissioners where—

(a)   the condition specified in paragraph (1) of Regulation 4 ceases to be met,

(b)   the requirements of paragraph (2) of Regulation 4 are not being carried out,

(c)   the provisions of Regulation 3 have not been complied with, or

(d)   they consider that such an authorisation is no longer expedient in the interests of the efficient administration of the tax.

VALUE ADDED TAX (INVOICES AND OTHER DOCUMENTS) REGULATIONS 1992

(SI No 275 of 1992)

1. (1) These Regulations may be cited as the Value Added Tax (Invoices and other Documents) Regulations, 1992.

(2) These Regulations shall come into operation on the 1st day of January, 1993.

Notes

These regulations specify the details that must be shown on VAT invoices, credit notes etc for those documents to be valid.

---

2. In these Regulations—

"the Act" means the Value Added Tax Act, 1972;

"registration number", in relation to a person, means the number assigned to the person for the purpose of registration under section 9 of the Act;

"value added tax registration number in another Member State" means the registration number issued to a person by the authorities of another Member State of the Community for the purposes of value added tax referred to in Council Directive No 77/388/EEC of 17 May, 1977.

3.   (*a*)   Every invoice issued by a taxable person in accordance with section 17(1) of the Act shall set out the following particulars:

      (i)   the name, address and registration number of the person who supplied the goods or services to which the invoice relates,

      (ii)   the name and address of the person to whom the goods or services have been supplied,

      (iii)   in the case of a supply of goods to a person, other than an individual who does not engage in the supply of goods or services in the course or furtherance of business, in another Member State:

          (I)   the name,

          (II)   the address, and

          (III)   where the person is a person registered for value added tax in that other Member State, the value added tax registration number in that Member State,

      of the person to whom the goods or services have been supplied,

      (iv)   the date of issue of the invoice,

      (v)   the date on which the goods or services were supplied,

      (vi)   a description of the goods or services supplied and, in the case of services consisting of the hiring or leasing of movable goods, a description of the goods,

      (vii)   the quantity or volume of the goods supplied,

      (viii)   the consideration exclusive of tax for the supply,

      (ix)   a description of any goods given in exchange or part exchange for the goods referred to in paragraph (*a*)(vi) of this Regulation,

      (x)   the amount of the deduction made in respect of the goods referred to in paragraph (*a*)(ix) of this Regulation and the amount on which tax becomes chargeable after making such deduction,

(xi)   the rate or rates of tax, and amount of tax at each rate, chargeable in respect of the supply of goods or services.

(*b*)   Every invoice issued by a flat-rate farmer in accordance with section 17(2) of the Act shall be signed or acknowledged by him and shall set out the following particulars:

    (i)   the name and address of the person who supplied the goods or services to which the invoice relates,

    (ii)   the name address and registration number of the person to whom the goods or services were supplied,

    (iii)   in the case of a supply of goods to a person registered for value added tax in another Member State the name, address and value added tax registration number in that Member State of the person to whom the goods or services have been supplied,

    (iv)   the date of issue of the invoice,

    (v)   the date on which the goods or services were supplied,

    (vi)   a description of the goods or services supplied,

    (vii)   the quantity or volume of the goods supplied,

    (viii)   the consideration, exclusive of the flat-rate addition, for the supply, and

    (ix)   the rate and amount of the flat-rate addition.

(*c*)   Every invoice issued by a taxable person in accordance with section 17(3) of the Act shall set out the following particulars:

    (i)   the name, address and registration number of the person who supplied the goods or services to which the invoice relates,

    (ii)   the name and address of the person to whom the goods or services were supplied,

    (iii)   in the case of a supply of goods to a person, other than an individual who does not engage in the supply of goods or services in the course or furtherance of business, in another Member State:

        (I)   the name,

        (II)   the address, and

        (III)   where the person is a person registered for value added tax in that other Member State, the value added tax registration number in that Member State,

    of the person to whom the goods or services have been supplied,

    (iv)   the date of issue of the invoice,

    (v)   the amount, exclusive of tax, of the increase in consideration for the supply,

    (vi)   the rate or rates of tax and amount of tax at each rate, appropriate to the increase in consideration chargeable in respect of the supply of goods or services, and

    (ix)   a cross-reference to every other invoice issued by the taxable person in respect of the total consideration for the supply of the goods or services.

(*d*)   Every invoice issued by a flat-rate farmer in accordance with section 17(4) of the Act shall be signed or acknowledged by him and shall set out the following particulars:

    (i)   the name and address of the person who supplied the goods or services to which the invoice relates,

(ii)   the name, address and registration number of the person to whom the goods or services were supplied,

(iii)   in the case of a supply of goods to a person registered for value added tax in another Member State the name, address and value added tax registration number in that Member State of the person to whom the goods or services have been supplied,

(iv)   the date of issue of the invoice,

(v)   the amount, exclusive of the flat-rate addition, of the increase in consideration for the supply of goods or services,

(vi)   the rate and amount of the flat-rate addition,

(vii)   a cross-reference to every other invoice issued by the flat-rate farmer in respect of the total consideration for the supply of goods or services.

(*e*)   Every credit note issued by a taxable person in accordance with section 17(3) of the Act shall set out the following particulars:

(i)   the name, address and registration of the person issuing the credit note,

(ii)   the name and address of the person to whom the credit note is issued,

(iii)   in the case of a supply of goods to a person, other than an individual who does not engage in the supply of goods or services in the course or furtherance of business, in another Member State:

(I)   the name,

(II)   the address, and

(III)   where the person is a person registered for value added tax in that other Member State, the value added tax registration number in that Member State,

of the person to whom the goods or services have been supplied,

(iv)   the date of issue of the credit note,

(v)   the reason why the credit note is being issued and a cross-reference to the corresponding invoice,

(vi)   the amount of the consideration, exclusive of tax, in respect of which the credit note is being issued, and

(vii)   the relevant rate or rates of tax, current on the date upon which the credit note is issued, and the amount of tax at each rate appropriate to the consideration for which credit is being given.

(*f*)   Every farmer credit note issued in accordance with section 17(4) of the Act shall set out the following particulars:

(i)   the name and address of the person issuing the credit note,

(ii)   the name, address and registration number of the person to whom the credit note is being issued,

(iii)   in the case of a supply of goods to a person registered for value added tax in another Member State the name, address and value added tax registration number in that Member State of the person to whom the goods or services have been supplied,

(iv)   the date of issue of the credit note,

(v)   the reason why the credit note is being issued and a cross-reference to the corresponding invoice,

(vi)   the amount of the consideration exclusive of the flat-rate addition in respect of which the credit note is being issued, and

(vii)   the rate and amount of the flat-rate addition.

(g) Every settlement voucher issued in accordance with section 17(10) of the Act in respect of goods or services supplied to a registered person by another registered person shall set out the following particulars:

    (i) the name, address and registration number, of the registered person who supplied the goods or services to which the settlement voucher relates,

    (ii) the name, address and registration number of the person to whom the goods or services were supplied,

    (iii) the date of issue of the settlement voucher,

    (iv) the date on which the goods or services were supplied,

    (v) a description of the goods or services supplied, and in the case of services consisting of the hiring or leasing of movable goods, a description of the goods,

    (vi) the quantity or volume of goods supplied,

    (vii) the consideration, exclusive of tax, for the supply,

    (viii) a description of any goods given in exchange or part exchange for the goods referred to in paragraph (g)(v) of this Regulation,

    (ix) the amount of the deduction made in respect of the goods referred to in paragraph (g)(viii) of this Regulation, and

    (x) the rate or rates of tax and amount of tax at each rate chargeable in respect of the supply of goods or services.

(h) Every settlement voucher issued in accordance with section 17(10) of the Act in respect of agricultural produce or agricultural services supplied to a registered person by flat-rate farmer shall be signed or acknowledged by the flat-rate farmer and shall set out the following particulars:

    (i) the name and address of the person who supplied the goods or services to which the settlement voucher relates,

    (ii) the name, address and registration number of the person to whom the goods or services have been supplied,

    (iii) the date of issue of the settlement voucher,

    (iv) the date on which the goods or services were supplied,

    (v) a description of the goods or services supplied,

    (vi) the quantity or volume of goods supplied,

    (vii) the amount of the consideration, exclusive of the flat-rate addition, for the supply and

    (viii) the rate and amount of the flat-rate addition.

(i) Every debit note issued in accordance with section 17(11) of the Act shall set out the following particulars:

    (i) the name, address and registration number of the person issuing the debit note,

    (ii) the name, address, and registration number, of the person to whom the debit note is being issued,

    (iii) the date of issue of the debit note,

    (iv) the reason why the debit note is being issued and a cross-reference to the corresponding invoice or settlement voucher,

    (v) the amount of the consideration, exclusive of tax, in respect of which the debit note is being issued, and

    (vi) the relevant rate or rates of tax and the amount of tax at each rate appropriate to the consideration shown on the debit note.

(*j*)　Every farmer debit note issued in accordance with section 17(11A) of the Act shall be signed or acknowledged by the flat-rate farmer and shall set out the following particulars:

　　(i)　the name, address and registration number of the person issuing the debit note,

　　(ii)　the name and address of the person to whom the debit note is being issued,

　　(iii)　the date of issue of the debit note,

　　(iv)　the reason why the debit note is being issued and a cross-reference to the corresponding invoice or settlement voucher,

　　(v)　the amount of the consideration, exclusive of the flat-rate addition, in respect of which the debit note is being issued, and

　　(vi)　the rate and the amount of the flat-rate addition appropriate to the consideration shown on the debit note.

4. Any person issuing in accordance with section 17 of the Act an invoice, credit note, settlement voucher or debit note shall keep an exact copy thereof and references in these Regulations to any such document include references to a copy thereof.

5. An invoice, credit note, settlement voucher or debit note issued in accordance with section 17 of the Act shall show separate totals for consideration, discounts and price reductions, as appropriate, and the corresponding tax, if any, in relation to —

(*a*)　exempted activities, and

(*b*)　goods and services chargeable at each rate of tax including the zero rate.

6. Regulation 10 of the Value Added Tax Regulations, 1979 (SI No 63 of 1979) is hereby revoked.

VALUE ADDED TAX (TIME LIMITS FOR ISSUING CERTAIN DOCUMENTS) REGULATIONS 1992

(SI No 276 of 1992)

1. (1) These Regulations may be cited as the Value Added Tax (Time Limits for Issuing Certain Documents) Regulations, 1992.

(2) These Regulations shall come into operation on the 1st day of January, 1993.

Notes

These regulations specify the time limits within which VAT invoices, credit notes etc must be issued.

---

2. In these Regulations **"the Act"** means the Value Added Tax Act, 1972.

3. An invoice, required to be issued in accordance with sections 12A or 17(1) of the Act, shall be issued within fifteen days next following the month during which the goods or services were supplied.

4. An invoice, required to be issued in accordance with sections 17(3)(*a*) or 17(4)(*a*) of the Act, shall be issued within fifteen days next following the day upon which the increased consideration is paid or the increase in consideration is agreed between the parties, whichever day is the earlier.

5. A credit note, required to be issued in accordance with sections 17(3)(*b*) or 17(4)(*b*) of the Act, shall be issued—

    (*a*)   in the case of a decrease because of an allowance of a discount, within fifteen days of the date of receipt of the money to which the discount relates, or

    (*b*)   in any other case, within fifteen days next following the day on which the decrease in consideration is agreed between the parties.

6. An invoice, required pursuant to section 17(8) of the Act, to be issued in respect of a payment for supply of goods or services before the supply is completed shall to be issued within fifteen days next following the month during which the payment was received.

7. Regulation 11 of the Value Added Tax Regulations, 1979 (SI No 63 of 1979) is hereby revoked.

VALUE ADDED TAX (ESTIMATION AND ASSESSMENT OF TAX DUE) REGULATIONS 1992

(SI No 277 of 1992)

1. These Regulations may be cited as the Value Added Tax (Estimation and Assessment of Tax Due) Regulations, 1992.

Notes

These regulations specify the method by which the Revenue Commissioners may issue automatic estimates where no VAT return has been received (VATA 1972 s 22). The regulations also specify the method by which the Revenue Commissioners may issue an inspector's asssesssment (VATA 1972 s 23) where the inspector has reason to believe that tax may have been underpaid.

---

2. These Regulations shall come into operation on the 1st day of January, 1993.

3. In these Regulations **"the Act"** means the Value Added Tax Act, 1972.

4. (1) An estimation of tax due for a taxable period for the purposes of section 22 of the Act may be made by an officer of the Revenue Commissioners, authorised by them in that behalf. The authorised officer shall sign a list containing the relevant particulars of the persons to whom the estimates relate and enter on the list the date of such signing and the list shall be retained by the Revenue Commissioners for a period of not less than ten years from the date of such signing.

(2) The relevant particulars are —

> (*a*)   the name, address and registration number of each person in respect of whom an estimate or two or more estimates is or are made,

> (*b*)   the taxable period to which each estimate relates, and

> (*c*)   the amount of tax estimated to be payable in respect of each taxable period referred to in subparagraph (*b*) of this paragraph.

5. (1) An assessment of tax due or refundable for a taxable period or other period consisting of two or more taxable periods for the purposes of section 23 of the Act may be made by an inspector of taxes or such other officer as the Revenue Commissioners may authorise in that behalf. The inspector of tax or other authorised officer shall sign a list containing the relevant particulars of the persons to whom the assessments relate and enter on the list the date of such signing and the list shall be retained by the Revenue Commissioners for a period of not less than ten years from the date of such signing.

(2) The Relevant particulars are—

> (*a*)   the name, address and registration number of each person in respect of whom an assessment or two or more assessments is or are made,

> (*b*)   the period consisting of one taxable period or two or more consecutive taxable periods to which each assessment relates,

> (*c*)   the total amount of tax which it is assessed should have been paid or the total amount of tax (including a nil amount) which in accordance with section 20(1) of the Act should have been refunded, as the case may be, in respect of the taxable period or periods comprised in each period referred to in subparagraph (*b*) of this paragraph,

> (*d*)   the total amount of tax (including a nil amount) paid by the person or refunded to the person, as the case may be, in respect of the taxable period or periods concerned, and

> (*e*)   the net amount due in respect of the taxable period or periods comprised in each period referred to in subparagraph (*b*) of this paragraph.

6. Regulation 14 of the Value Added Tax Regulations, 1979 (SI No 63 of 1979) is hereby revoked.

VALUE ADDED TAX (DETERMINATION IN REGARD TO TAX) REGULATIONS 1992

(SI No 278 of 1992)

1. These Regulations may be cited as the Value Added Tax (Determination in Regard to Tax) Regulations, 1992.

Notes

These regulations specify the form and contents of a declaration (of the VAT rate applicable to a particular supply of goods or services) made by the Revenue Commissioners under VATA 1972 s 11(1B).

---

2. These Regulations shall come into operation on the 1st day of January, 1993.

3. In these Regulations —

"the Act" means the Value Added Tax Act, 1972;

"a determination" means a determination made for the purposes of section 11(1B) of the Act.

4. A determination shall be in writing, shall contain the particulars of the determination, shall be signed by the officer making the determination and shall bear the date upon which it is so signed.

5. Determinations concerning two or more matters may be included in the same document.

6. Regulation 23 of the Value Added Tax Regulations, 1979 (SI No 63 of 1979) is hereby revoked.

VALUE ADDED TAX (DETERMINATION OF TAX DUE BY REFERENCE TO MONEYS RECEIVED) REGULATIONS 1992

(SI No 306 of 1992)

1. These Regulations may be cited as the Value Added Tax (Determination of Tax Due by Reference to Moneys Received) Regulations, 1992.

Notes

These regulations specify the requirements to be met by a trader who wishes to account for VAT on the cash receipts basis (VATA 1972 s 14).

---

2. (1) In these Regulations —

"the Act" means the Value Added Tax Act, 1972;

"moneys received basis of accounting" means the method of determining, in accordance with section 14(1) of the Act, the amount of tax which becomes due by a taxable person;

"turnover from taxable supplies", in relation to any period, means the total of the amounts on which tax is chargeable for that period at any of the rates specified in section 11(1) of the Act.

(2) In these Regulations —

    (*a*)   a reference to a regulation is to a regulation of these Regulations, and

    (*b*)   a reference to a paragraph or subparagraph is to a paragraph or subparagraph of the provision in which it occurs, unless it is indicated that reference to some other provision is intended.

3. For the purposes of [section 14(1)(*a*)][1] of the Act and for the purposes of these Regulations supplies to [persons who are not registered persons][2] shall be deemed to include any supplies to a taxable person where the said taxable person is not entitled to claim, under section 12 of the Act, a full deduction of the tax chargeable in relation to the said supply.

Amendments

1 Substituted by Value Added Tax (Determination of Tax Due by Reference to Moneys Received) Regulations 1994 (SI 259/1994) para 3; previously "section 14(1)".

2 Substituted by Value Added Tax (Determination of Tax Due by Reference to Moneys Received) Regulations 1994 (SI 259/1994) para 3; previously "unregistered persons".

[**4.** (1) An application by a taxable person (hereafter referred to in this Regulation as the "applicant") for authorisation to use the moneys received basis of accounting shall be made in writing to the Revenue Commissioners and shall include(

    (*a*)   the applicant's name and address;

    (*b*)   the number assigned, if any, to the applicant for the purposes of registration under section 9 of the Act (the VAT registration number);

    (*c*)   the nature of the business activities carried on by the applicant.

(2) An applicant who claims eligibility under section 14(1)(*a*) of the Act shall include in any application made in accordance with this Regulation particulars of(

    (*a*)   the percentage of the applicant's turnover from taxable supplies, if any, which related to supplies to persons who are not registered persons(

        (i)   in the period of 12 months ended on the last day of the taxable period prior to the application, or

    (ii)   in the period from the commencement of his business activities to the last day of the taxable period referred to in clause (i) of this subparagraph,

whichever is the shorter; and,

    (*b*)   the applicant's estimate of the percentage of the said applicant's turnover from taxable supplies which will relate to supplies to persons who are not registered persons in the period of 12 months commencing with the beginning of the taxable period during which the application is made.

(3) An applicant who claims eligibility under section 14(1)(*b*) of the Act shall include in any application made in accordance with this Regulation particulars of(

    (*a*)   the amount of the applicant's turnover from taxable supplies in the period of 12 months ended on the last day of the taxable period prior to the application; and

    (*b*)   the applicant's estimate of the said applicant's turnover from taxable supplies in the period of 12 months commencing with the beginning of the taxable period during which the application is made.][1]

Amendments

1 Para 4 substituted by Value Added Tax (Determination of Tax Due by Reference to Moneys Received) Regulations 1994 (SI 259/1994) para 4.

---

5. (1) The Revenue Commissioners shall, if they consider that a person satisfies the requirements of section 14(1) of the Act, authorise the person, by notice in writing, to use the moneys received basis of accounting.

(2) An authorisation given under paragraph (1) shall have effect from the commencement of the taxable period during which it is given or from such other date as may be specified in the authorisation.

6. An authorisation to use the moneys received basis of accounting given by the Revenue Commissioners before the coming into force of these Regulations shall be deemed to have been issued in accordance with Regulation 5.

7. (1) An authorisation under Regulation 5 shall not apply to tax chargeable on any supply where the person to whom or to whose order the supply is made is a connected person.

(2) For the purposes of this Regulation any question of whether a person is connected with another person shall be determined in accordance with the following provisions:

    (*a*)   a person is connected with an individual if that person is the individual's husband or wife, or is a relative, or the husband or wife of a relative, of the individual or of the individual's husband or wife;

    (*b*)   a person is connected with any person with whom he is in partnership, and with the husband or wife or a relative of any individual with whom he is in partnership;

    (*c*)   subject to subparagraphs (*d*) and (*e*), a person is connected with another person if he has control over that other person, or if the other person has control over the first-mentioned person, or if both persons are controlled by another person or persons;

    (*d*)   a body corporate is connected with another person if that person, or persons connected with him, have control of it, or the person and persons connected with him together have control of it;

    (*e*)   a body corporate is connected with another body corporate —

        (i)   if a person has control of one and persons connected with him or he and persons connected with him have control of the other, or

        (ii)   if a group of two or more persons has control of each body corporate and the groups either consist of the same persons or could be regarded as consisting of the same persons by treating (in one or more cases) a member of either group as replaced by a person with whom he is connected;

(*f*)   in this paragraph **"relative"** means brother, sister, ancestor or lineal descendant.

(3) In this Regulation **"control"**, in relation to a body corporate or in relation to a partnership, has the meaning assigned to it by section 8(3B) of the Act.

8. An authorisation under Regulation 5 shall not affect the amount on which tax is chargeable in any of the circumstances referred to in subsections (2) to (9) of section 10 of the Act or tax chargeable on supplies referred to in Regulation 7.

9. [(1) A taxable person authorised in accordance with Regulation 5 shall notify the Revenue Commissioners in writing whenever, for any period of four consecutive calendar months during the validity of such authorisation, the following occurs:

(*a*)   the percentage of the taxable person's turnover from taxable supplies to persons who are not registered persons is less than 90 per cent; and

(*b*)   the taxable person's turnover from taxable supplies is such that in the twelve months immediately following such four months period it is likely to exceed £250,000,

and notification in accordance with this Regulation shall be made within 30 days of the end of such four month period.][1]

(2) Where a taxable person fails to notify the Revenue Commissioners in accordance with paragraph (1), the authorisation under Regulation 5 shall be deemed to be cancelled in accordance with Regulation 10. Such cancellation shall have effect for the purposes of section 14 of the Act from the commencement of the taxable period during which the taxable person should have notified the Revenue Commissioners in accordance with paragraph (1).

Amendments

1   Para 9(1) substituted by Value Added Tax (Determination of Tax Due by Reference to Moneys Received) Regulations 1994 (SI 259/1994) para 5.

---

10. (1) The Revenue Commissioners shall cancel an authorisation under Regulation 5:

(*a*)   if the person so authorised requests the cancellation by notice in writing given to the Revenue Commissioners, or

(*b*)   they consider that the person no longer satisfies the requirements of section 14(1) of the Act.

(2) An authorisation under Regulation 5 shall be cancelled by notice in writing given by the Revenue Commissioners to the person who was the subject of the authorisation. Without prejudice to Regulation 9, such cancellation shall have effect for the purposes of section 14 of the Act from the commencement of the taxable period during which notice is given or from the commencement of such later taxable period as may be specified in the notice.

11.(1) (*a*)   Where a person, who for any period is authorised under Regulation 5 and such authorisation was issued prior to 28 May, 1992, ceases to be so authorised or ceased to be a taxable person, the tax payable by him for the taxable period during which such cessation occurs shall be adjusted in accordance subparagraphs (*b*) and (*c*).

(*b*)   An amount shall be established and apportioned between each rate of tax specified in section 11(1) of the Act in accordance with the following formula—

$$(B - A) \times \frac{C}{D}$$

where —

A is the total amount due to the person at the beginning of the authorised period for goods and services supplied by him,

B is the total amount due to the person at the end of the authorised period for goods and services supplied by him,

C is the chargeable amount in respect of taxable supplies at each such rate of tax in the 12 months prior to the date of cessation or in the authorised period, whichever is the shorter, and

D is the chargeable amount in respect of total taxable supplies in the 12 months prior to the date of cessation or in the authorised period, whichever is the shorter:

Provided that —

    (i)   no adjustment of liability shall be made where A is greater than B, and

    (ii) the apportionment between the various rates of tax may be made in accordance with any other basis which may be agreed between the taxable person and the Revenue Commissioners.

  (c)   The amount so apportioned at each rate shall be a tax-inclusive amount and the tax therein shall be payable during the taxable period in which the cessation occurs.

(2) (a)   Where a person, who for any period is authorised under Regulation 5 and such authorisation was issued on or after 28 May, 1992, ceases to be so authorised or ceases to be a taxable person, the tax payable by him for the taxable period during which the cessation occurs shall be adjusted in accordance with subparagraphs (b) and (c).

  (b)   The total amount due to the person at the end of the authorised period for goods and services supplied by him shall be apportioned between each rate of tax specified in section 11(1) of the Act in accordance with the following formula —

$$B \times \frac{C}{D}$$

where B, C and D have the same meaning as in subparagraph (b) of paragraph (1):

Provided that the apportionment between the various rates of tax may be made in accordance with any other basis which may be agreed between the taxable person and the Revenue Commissioners.

  (c)   The amount so apportioned at each rate shall be a tax-inclusive amount and the tax therein shall be payable during the taxable period in which the cessation occurs.

(3) No adjustment of liability as provided for in this Regulation shall be made if the cessation referred to in subparagraph 11(1)(a) or 11(2)(a) was occasioned by the death of the taxable person.

(4) For the purposes of this Regulation —

  (a)   **"the authorised period"** means the period during which the person was authorised to apply the moneys received basis of accounting:

Provided that where the person was authorised to apply the moneys received basis of accounting for more than six years the authorised period shall be deemed to be for a period of six years ending on the date on which the cancellation of the authorisation has effect.

  (b)   **"the tax therein"** shall be established at the rates specified in section 11(1) of the Act

    (i)   applicable on the date the authorised period ends or,

    (ii)   applicable at the time the relevant goods and services were supplied where such details can be established to the satisfaction of the Revenue Commissioners.

12. For the purposes of these Regulations and subject to the direction and control of the Revenue Commissioners, any power, function or duty conferred or imposed on the Revenue Commissioners may be exercised or performed on their behalf by an officer of the Revenue Commissioners.

13. The Value Added Tax (Determination of Tax due by reference to Moneys Received) Regulations, 1986 (SI No 298 of 1986) and the Value Added Tax (Determination of Tax Due by Reference to Moneys Received)(Amendment) Regulations, 1992 (SI No 93 of 1992) are hereby revoked.

VALUE ADDED TAX (PAYMENT OF TAX ON INTRA-COMMUNITY ACQUISITIONS OF MEANS OF TRANSPORT) REGULATIONS 1992

(SI No 412 of 1992)

Notes

Revoked with effect from 1 September 1993 by Value-Added Tax (Payment of Tax on Intra-Community Acquisition of Certain New Means of Transport) Regulations 1993 (SI No 248 of 1993) r 5

EUROPEAN COMMUNITIES (VALUE ADDED TAX) REGULATIONS 1992

(SI No 413 of 1992)

1. (1) These Regulation may be cited as the European Communities (Value Added Tax) Regulations, 1992.

(2) These Regulations shall be construed together with the Value Added Tax Acts 1972 to 1992.

2. These Regulations shall come into operation on the 1st day of January, 1993.

3. In these Regulations—

"the Principal Act" means the Value Added Tax Act, 1972;

"the Act of 1978" means the Value Added Tax (Amendment) Act, 1978;

"the Act of 1992" means the Finance Act, 1992.

4. ....

Note

This para amended VATA 1972 s 1(1)(*a*).

5.

Note

This para amended VATA 1972 s 3 (1)(*g*)(i) , inserted VATA 1972 s 3(1)(*g*)(iiia), (6)(*a*)(proviso) and (6)(*cc*), amended VATA 1972 s 3(6)(*d*)(ii) , substituted VATA 1972 s 3(6)(*d*)(proviso), and added VATA 1972 s 3(8).

6.

Note

This para amended VATA 1972 s 3A(1)(*a*), inserted VATA 1972 s 3A(3)(*aa*), (*ab*) and added VATA 1972 s 3A(5).

7.

Note

This para amended VATA 1972 s 8(1A), substituted VATA 1972 s 8(2B), inserted VATA 1972 s 8(3D) and inserted VATA 1972 s 8(8)(*a*)(IA)-(IB).

8.

Note

This para inserted VATA 1972 s 10(9A).

9.

Note

This para amended VATA 1972 s 11(1)(*b*).

10.

Note

This para inserted VATA 1972 s 12(1)(*b*)(i*a*) and amended VATA 1972 s 12(1)(*b*)(iii).

11.

Note
This para inserted VATA 1972 s 15A.

12.

Note
This para amended VATA 1972 s 17(1).

13.

Note
This para inserted VATA 1972 s 19(5).

14.

Note
This para inserted VATA 1972 Sch 2 para (i)(*cc*).

VALUE ADDED TAX (EXPORTED GOODS) REGULATIONS 1992

(SI No 438 of 1992)

1. (1) These Regulations may be cited as the Value Added Tax (Exported Goods) Regulations, 1992.

(2) These Regulations shall come into operation on the 1st day of January, 1993.

Notes

These regulations provide relief from VAT on goods bought by visiting (non EC) tourists or by Irish residents who are departing the EC for more than one year. The goods must be exported with the purchaser's personal baggage or put on board a ship or plane that is travelling to a non EC destination.

---

2. (1) In these Regulations—

"goods" means any article, and includes a group of articles normally supplied as a set;

"qualifying goods" means goods other than mechanically propelled road vehicles or goods for the equipping, fuelling or provisioning of any means of transport for private use;

"qualifying person" means any person who, at the time of the supply to him of qualifying goods,—

    (*a*)   was not normally resident in the Community or, if he was normally resident in the Community at that time, intended at the time to depart from the Community for a period of at least twelve consecutive months, and

    (*b*)   was not a member of the crew of a ship, aircraft or other conveyance engaged in the transport of passengers or goods into or out of the Community.

(2) In these Regulations—

    (*a*)   a reference to a Regulation is to a Regulation of these Regulations, and

    (*b*)   a reference to a paragraph or subparagraph is to a paragraph or subparagraph of the provision in which the reference occurs,

unless it is indicated that reference to some other provision is intended.

3. The tax, if any, chargeable on the supply of qualifying goods—

(1) to a qualifying person who intended at the time of the supply to export the said goods in his personal baggage, or

(2) which are delivered, by or on behalf of a qualifying person, on board a ship or aircraft (other than a private ship or aircraft) proceeding to a place outside the Community for export in that ship or aircraft,

shall be remitted, provided that the said goods are exported within two months of the date of their supply and subject to the conditions set out in Regulation 4.

4. (1) The supplier of the qualifying goods shall—

    (*a*)   satisfy himself that the person to whom the goods are being supplied is a qualifying person,

    (*b*)   issue to the qualifying person at the time of the supply of the qualifying goods an invoice in respect of that supply setting out the following particulars:

        (i)   the name, address and tax registration number of the supplier,

        (ii)   the name and address of the qualifying person,

        (iii)   the date upon which the invoice is issued,

        (iv)   a description of and the quantity of the qualifying goods,

        (v)   the consideration for the supply,

      (vi)   an indication of the basis on which the supplier satisfied himself in accordance with subparagraph (1)(*a*), including details of any relevant document inspected, and

     (vii) the signature or acknowledgement of the qualifying person,

    and

  (*c*)   retain in his records a copy of the said invoice together with documentary proof of export of the goods in accordance with paragraphs (2) or (3).

(2) Where the provisions of paragraph (1) of Regulation 3 apply, the qualifying person shall return to the supplier of the qualifying goods the invoice issued in accordance with subparagraph (1)(*b*) on which the export of the goods is duly certified by—

  (*a*)   a customs officer in the State, or

  (*b*)   where the goods have been exported via another Member State of the Community, a customs officer in that Member State, or

  (*c*)   an equivalent official in the country to which the said goods have been exported,

or in such other manner as the Revenue Commissioners may deem acceptable for that purpose.

(3) Where the provisions of paragraph (2) of Regulation 3 apply, the supplier shall obtain documentary evidence, certified by a customs officer in the State, that the qualifying goods have been exported.

5. The Value Added Tax (Exported Goods) Regulations, 1984 (SI No 230 of 1984) and the Value Added Tax (Goods Exported in Baggage) Regulations, 1984 (SI No 231 of the 1984) are hereby revoked.

VALUE ADDED TAX (IMPORTED GOODS) REGULATIONS 1992

(SI No 439 of 1992)

1. These Regulations may be cited as the Value Added Tax (Imported Goods) Regulations, 1992.

Notes

These regulations allow manufacturers whose exports (including exports to EC States: intra-Community supplies) represent at least 75% in value of their total manufacturing output to import raw materials etc VAT free (from non EC countries).

---

2. These Regulations shall come into operation on the 1st day of January, 1993.

3. (1) In these Regulations—

"the Act" means the Value Added Tax Act, 1972.

"qualifying goods" means goods imported and entered for the purpose of undergoing a process of manufacture or for the purpose of being incorporated with other goods as a part or ingredient of a manufactured product.

(2) In these Regulations a reference to a Regulation is to a Regulation of these Regulations, unless it is indicated that reference to some other provision is intended.

4. Qualifying goods that are imported by a registered person may, subject to compliance with the requirement of these Regulations, be delivered or removed without payment of the tax chargeable on the importation where the person shows to the satisfaction of the Revenue Commissioners—

    (*a*)   that he is in the business of manufacturing goods in the State,

    (*b*)   that the goods are being imported for the purposes of the business, and

    (*c*)   that the consideration relating to supplies specified in subparagraphs (i)(*a*)(I), (i)(*b*) or (i)(*c*) of the Second Schedule to the Act made by him of goods manufactured by him in the State, taking one taxable period with another, amounts to and is likely to continue to amount to not less than **75 per cent** of the consideration, excluding tax, relating to the total of his supplies of goods manufactured by him.

5. A person who wishes to import qualifying goods without payment of the tax chargeable on their importation, in accordance with Regulation 4, shall apply in writing to the Revenue Commissioners for authorisation to do so. He shall complete such form as is provided for that purpose by the Revenue Commissioners and he shall certify the particulars shown on such form to be correct. He shall in addition provide such further documentation in support of the application as the Revenue Commissioners may request.

6. Where they consider that a person satisfies the requirements of Regulation 4, the Revenue Commissioners shall authorise that person, by notice in writing, to have qualifying goods delivered or removed without payment of the tax chargeable on the importation of those goods.

7. Registered persons who, before the coming into force of these Regulations, have been authorised by the Revenue Commissioners to deliver or remove goods without payment of the tax chargeable on the importation in accordance with the Value Added Tax (Imported Goods) Regulations, 1983 (SI No 129 of 1983) shall be deemed to have been authorised in accordance with Regulation 6.

8. In relation to each consignment of goods to be imported by a person authorised under Regulation 6 without payment of the tax chargeable on the importation, the following conditions shall be complied with—

    (*a*)   the authorisation or, by agreement with a customs officer in the State, a copy thereof shall be produced with the relevant customs entry, and (*b*)   the relevant customs entry shall incorporate

        (i)   a declaration by the authorised person, or by his representative duly authorised by him in writing for this purpose, that the goods are raw materials and components for use in the authorised person's manufacturing business, and

        (ii) a claim for VAT-free importation.

9. Where goods have been imported by a person without payment of the tax chargeable on the importation in accordance with these Regulations, the tax so chargeable shall be accounted for by the authorised person in the return required to be furnished by him under section 19 of the Act for the taxable period during which the importation took place.

10. (1) A person authorised in accordance with Regulation 6 shall notify the Revenue Commissioners in writing where he no longer satisfies the requirements of Regulation 4. Such notification shall be made within 30 days of the person no longer satisfying the requirements of Regulation 4.

(2) Where a person fails to notify the Revenue Commissioners in accordance with paragraph (1) of this Regulation, the authorisation under Regulation 6 shall be deemed to be cancelled in accordance with Regulation 11. Such cancellation shall have effect from the date on which the person no longer satisfies the requirements of Regulation 4.

11. (1) The Revenue Commissioners shall cancel an authorisation under Regulation 6 where they consider that the person no longer satisfies the requirements of Regulation 4.

(2) An authorisation under Regulation 6 shall be cancelled by notice in writing given by the Revenue Commissioners to the person who was the subject of the authorisation. Such cancellation shall have effect from the date of the notice or from such later date as may be specified in the notice.

12. The Value Added Tax (Imported Goods) Regulations, 1983 (SI No 129 of 1983) are hereby revoked.

VALUE ADDED TAX (IMPORTED GOODS) (No 2) REGULATIONS 1992

(SI No 440 of 1992)

1. These Regulations may be cited as the Value Added Tax (Imported Goods) (No 2) Regulations, 1992.

Notes

These regulations modify the application of customs law as regards VAT at importation:

(*a*) on goods imported for warehousing (or for processing or re-export);
(*b*) on goods reimported by the person who exported them;
(*c*) in relation to customs drawback and repayments;
(*d*) on goods brought from the Shannon customs free airport into other parts of the State;
(*e*) in relation to the deferred payment of VAT at import;
(*f*) in relation to the application of EC customs law to VAT at import.

---

2. These Regulations shall come into operation on the 1st day of January, 1993.

3. In these Regulations—

(*a*)　a reference to a Regulation is to a Regulation of these Regulations, and

(*b*)　a reference to a paragraph is to a paragraph of the provision in which it occurs,

unless it is indicated that reference to some other provision is intended.

4. Without prejudice to Regulation 9, the provisions of the Customs Consolidation Act, 1876 as amended relating to the warehousing of imported goods, section 11 of the Finance (Miscellaneous Provisions) Act, 1958 (No 28 of 1958), and section 38 of the Finance Act, 1932 (No 20 of 1932), as amended by section 17 of the Finance Act, 1965 (No 22 of 1965), and the European Communities (Customs) Regulations, 1972 (SI No 334 of 1972), shall not apply to tax chargeable at importation.

5. Section 6 of the Customs and Inland Revenue Act, 1879, and section 25(2) of the Finance Act, 1933 (No 15 of 1933), shall, insofar as they apply to tax, have effect in relation to goods which are being re-imported into the State after exportation therefrom only if they are re-imported into the State by the person who exported them from the State.

6. Section 24 and 28 of the Finance Act, 1933 (No 15 of 1933), shall apply to tax chargeable at importation only insofar as the tax is not deductible under section 12 of the Act.

7. Without prejudice to Regulation 9, section 5(1) of the Customs-Free Airport Act, 1947 (No 5 of 1947), shall not, insofar as it applies to tax, have effect in relation to goods brought from the Customs-free airport (within the meaning of that Act) into any other part of the State where it is established to the satisfaction of the Revenue Commissioners that the goods are Community goods or that the tax has already been borne or paid on the goods.

8. Section 29(7) of the Finance Act, 1978 (No 21 of 1978), shall apply in relation to tax payable at importation with the modification that the reference to goods entered for home use shall be deemed to include a reference to imported goods entered for free circulation or for processing under customs control.

9. Legislation relating to customs adopted by the European Communities concerning the placing of goods under—

(*a*)　arrangements for temporary importation with total exemption from customs duty,

(*b*)　external transit arrangements,

(*c*)　temporary storage arrangements,

(*d*)   free zone or free warehouse arrangements,

(*e*)   customs warehousing arrangements,

(*f*)   inward processing (suspension) arrangements, or

(*g*)   arrangements for the admission of goods into territorial waters in connection with drilling or production platforms,

shall only apply in relation to tax chargeable at importation where, and for such time as, goods are held under those arrangements for the purpose of compliance with and implementation of the Community rules relating to customs.

10. Without prejudice to Regulation 9, legislation relating to customs adopted by the European Community concerning suspension of customs duties, reduction in customs duties, or repayment or remission of customs duties shall not apply to tax chargeable at importation.

11. The Value Added Tax (Imported Goods) Regulations, 1982 (SI No 279 of 1982) are hereby revoked.

VALUE ADDED TAX (REGISTRATION) REGULATIONS 1993

(SI No 30 of 1993)

1. These Regulations may be cited as the Value Added Tax (Registration) Regulations, 1993.

Notes

These regulations set out the details to be supplied (and the procedures to be followed) when registering (or deregistering) for VAT.

---

2. In these Regulations **"the Act"** means the Value Added Tax Act, 1972.

3. A taxable person, or a person who in accordance with section 8(3) of the Act desires to elect to be a taxable person, shall register for tax by completing such form as is provided for that purpose by the Revenue Commissioners and he shall certify the particulars shown on such form to be correct.

4. Where a change occurs in any of the particulars furnished in the form referred to in Regulation 3 of these Regulations -

    (*a*)   the registered person,

    (*b*)   if the registered person is dead, his personal representative, or

    (*c*)   if the registered person is a body of persons which is in liquidation or is otherwise being wound up, the liquidator or any other person who is carrying on business during such liquidation or, as the case may be, winding up,

shall, within thirty days immediately following the date of the change, furnish to the Revenue Commissioners particulars of the change.

5. A person who is registered in accordance with section 9 of the Act and who ceases—

    (*a*)   to supply taxable goods or services, and

    (*b*)   to make intra-Community acquisitions,

in the State shall notify the Revenue Commissioners in writing of such cessation. Such written notification must be furnished by the end of the taxable period following that in which the cessation occurred.

6. The Revenue Commissioners may, by notice in writing, cancel the registration of a person who does not become, or who ceases to be, a taxable person, and such cancellation shall have effect as on and from the date of the notice, or as on and from such date as may be specified in the notice.

7. Regulation 6 of the Value Added Tax Regulations 1979 (S.I. No. 63 of 1979) is hereby revoked.

VALUE ADDED TAX (STATEMENT OF INTRA-COMMUNITY SUPPLIES) REGULATIONS 1993

(SI No 54 of 1993)

1. These Regulations may be cited as the Value Added Tax (Statement of Intra-Community Supplies) Regulations, 1993.

Notes
These regulations set out the details to be shown on the EC export sales listing (VAT Information Exchange Systeom return - VIES return - officially described as the statement of intra-Community supplies) that must be submitted by taxable persons. The regulations also specify how such statements may sent to the Revenue Commissioners and the frequency of such returns.

---

2. These Regulations shall be deemed to have come into operation on the 1st day of January, 1993.

3. (1)In these Regulations–

"the Act" means the Value Added Tax Act 1972;

"correction statement" means a statement of corrective details furnished in relation to a statement previously supplied;

"intra-Community supplies" has the meaning assigned to it by section 19A(6) of the Act;

"statement" means a statement of intra-Community supplies required to be furnished to the Revenue Commissioners by a taxable person in accordance with section 19A of the Act;

"working day" means a day other than–

(*a*) a Saturday or Sunday,

(*b*) a day that is a public holiday (within the meaning of the Holidays (Employees) Act, 1973 (No. 25 of 1973)), or

(*c*) any other day when the offices of the Revenue Commissioners are closed to the public.

(2) In these Regulations–

(*a*) a reference to a Regulation is to a Regulation of these Regulations, and

(*b*) a reference to a paragraph or subparagraph is to a paragraph or subparagraph of the provision in which it occurs,

unless it is indicated that reference to some other provision is intended.

4. (1) Subject to Regulation 5 a taxable person who is required in accordance with section 19A of the Act to furnish a statement of intra-Community supplies shall complete to the satisfaction of the Revenue Commissioners such forms as are provided for that purpose by them.

(2) Where for any reason a taxable person becomes aware of an error in a statement furnished in accordance with paragraph (1) he shall, within five working days, furnish a correction statement on the form provided for that purpose by the Revenue Commissioners.

5. (1) Notwithstanding the provisions of Regulation 4, a taxable person may, on written application to the Revenue Commissioners, be authorised by them to furnish a statement or correction statement on a document or in a manner other than by use of the forms referred to in Regulation 4.

(2) Where a taxable person is authorised in accordance with paragraph (1), the statement or correction statement shall be furnished in a format specified by the Revenue

Commissioners and shall include all the particulars that would have been provided had the person completed the relevant form referred to in Regulation 4.

6. In furnishing a statement or correction statement in accordance with Regulation 4 or 5 a taxable person shall, in respect of the period covered by the statement–

(*a*)   make a separate entry in respect of his intra-Community supplies to each person registered for value-added tax in another Member State,

(*b*)   include in each entry referred to in subparagraph (*a*) the indicator "P" where the intra-Community supplies include–

(i)   goods which have been returned by him to that person having undergone contract work in the State, or

(ii)   goods dispatched or transported by him to that person for the purposes of having contract work carried out on the goods,

(*c*)   in the case of intra-Community supplies referred to in paragraph (*b*)(ii), omit in the entry any indication of the value of the goods and

(*d*)   make a separate entry including the indicator "T" in respect of any supplies of the type referred to in section 3A(5)(iii) of the Act to each person registered for value-added tax in another Member State,

and shall also furnish such other particulars of his intra-Community supplies as are requested on the appropriate form.

7. (1) (*a*)   A statement or correction statement may be prepared and furnished to the Revenue Commissioners by a person other than the taxable person where that person has been authorised by the taxable person to act on his behalf in that regard.

(*b*)   Where a statement or correction statement is prepared and furnished to the Revenue Commissioners by virtue of subparagraph (*a*), the provisions of the Act shall apply as if it had been prepared and furnished to the Revenue Commissioners by the taxable person.

(2) A statement or correction statement purporting to be prepared and furnished to the Revenue Commissioners by or on behalf of any taxable person shall, for all the purposes of the Act, be deemed to have been prepared and furnished to the Revenue Commissioners by that taxable person, or by his authority, as the case may be, unless the contrary is proved.

(3) A taxable person who authorises another person in accordance with paragraph (1) shall notify the Revenue Commissioners in writing of such authorisation.

(4) A taxable person shall, on cancelling an authorisation referred to in paragraph (1), advise the Revenue Commissioners in writing of the cancellation within five working days of such cancellation.

(5) The Revenue Commissioners may by notice in writing exclude a taxable person from the provisions of this Regulation.

8. (1) Subject to paragraph (2) and save as may be otherwise permitted by the Revenue Commissioners under these Regulations, every statement and correction statement shall be completed otherwise than in handwriting by means of typing or other similar process.

(2) Every statement and correction statement shall be signed and dated by the taxable person or the person authorised by him in accordance with paragraph (1) of Regulation 7.

(3) Where a taxable person has been authorised in accordance with Regulation 5 to furnish a statement or correction statement by electronic means or through magnetic media, any such statement shall have the same effect as if it were a signed statement or correction statement, as the case may be.

9. (1) A taxable person may, on written application to the Revenue Commissioners, be authorised by the Commissioners to submit an annual statement in accordance with section 19A(3) of the Act where the taxable person's supplies of goods and services do not exceed or are not likely to exceed £60,000 in a calendar year, and his intra-

Community supplies do not exceed or are not likely to exceed £12,000 in that calendar year and provided such intra-Community supplies do not include the supply of new means of transport.

(2) A taxable person authorised to submit a return in accordance with section 19(3)(*aa*) of the Act may, on written application to the Revenue Commissioners, be authorised by the Commissioners to submit an annual statement in accordance with section 19A(3) of the Act where the taxable person's supplies of goods and services do not exceed or are not likely to exceed £150,000 in a calendar year, and his intra-Community supplies do not exceed or are not likely to exceed £12,000 in that calendar year and provided such intra-Community supplies do not include the supply of new means of transport.

10. An authorisation under subsection (2) or (3) of section 19A of the Act shall be cancelled by notice in writing given by the Revenue Commissioners to the person who was the subject of the authorisation and any such cancellation shall have effect from the date of the notice or from such later date as may be specified in the notice.

11. The provisions of Regulations 4, 5, 6, 7 and 8 shall apply to a statement or correction statement furnished on a monthly or annual basis as the case may be: Provided that the taxable person referred to in paragraph (1) of Regulation 9 shall not be obliged to furnish details of the value of his intra-Community supplies or to comply with subparagraphs (*b*) or (*d*) of paragraph (1) of Regulation 6.

EUROPEAN COMMUNITIES (INTRASTAT) REGULATIONS 1993

(SI No 136 of 1993)

1. These Regulations may be cited as the European Communities (Intrastat) Regulations, 1993.

2. These Regulations shall come into operation on the 22 day of May, 1993.

3. (1) In these Regulations—

"authorised officer" means an officer of the Revenue Commissioners authorised by them in writing to exercise the powers of an authorised officer referred to in these Regulations;

"the basic Regulation" means Council Regulation (EEC) No 3330/91 of 7 November, 1991;

"the Community Regulations" means the basic Regulation, Commission Regulation (EEC) No 3046/92 of 22 October 1992 and Commission Regulation (EEC) No 2256/92 of 31 July 1992 and Commission Regulation (EEC) No 3590/92 of 11 December 1992;

"the Intrastat system" means the Intrastat system referred to in the basic Regulation in so far as that system applies to trade between Member States pursuant to Articles 17 to 28 of that Regulation;

"Member State" means a Member State of the European Economic Community;

"officer of statistics" has the meaning assigned to it by the Statistics Act, 1926 (No 12 of 1926);

"records" means any document or other written or printed material in any form as well as information (including statistical information) stored, maintained or preserved by means of any mechanical or electronic device, whether or not stored, maintained or preserved in a legible form;

"trader" means a person referred in Article 20(5) of the basic Regulation of Article 4 of Commission Regulation (EEC) No 3046/92 of 22 October 1992.

Subject to paragraph (1) of this Regulation, a word or expression that is used in these Regulations and is also used in the Community Regulations shall, unless the context otherwise requires, have the same meaning in these Regulations that it has in those Regulations.

4. (1) The statistical information required by the Intrastat system which a trader is responsible for providing in respect of each month in accordance with the provisions of the Community Regulations shall be furnished to the Revenue Commissioners, on forms provided by them for that purpose, by or on behalf of that trader not later than the 10th working day immediately following the end of the month concerned and the said forms shall be completed in accordance with, as appropriate:—

(*a*) the terms of the manual entitled "VIES and INTRASTAT Traders Manual" published by the Revenue Commissioners in October, 1992, (hereafter in this Regulation referred to as the "relevant manual") and any document published by them for the time being amending the relevant manual,

(*b*) the terms of any subsequent edition of the relevant manual published by the Revenue Commissioners that is the current such edition (hereafter in this Regulation referred to as a "replacement manual") and any document published by them for the time being amending the replacement manual.

(2) A document referred to in subparagraph (*a*) or (*b*) of paragraph (1) of this Regulation is referred to hereafter in this Regulation as a "supplement".

(3) The Revenue Commissioners may, on written application being made to them by a trader, authorise the furnishing of the statistical information referred to in paragraph (1) of this Regulation by or on behalf of that trader in a manner other than by use of the forms

referred to in the said paragraph (1) and the manner to be so authorised shall be one that is specified in the relevant manual, a replacement manual or a supplement.

(4) A trader to whom on authorisation as aforesaid has been given shall furnish or cause to be furnished on his behalf the statistical information referred to in paragraph (1) of this Regulation to the Revenue Commissioners in the manner specified in the authorisation not later than the 10th working day immediately following the end of the month concerned and the information so furnished shall include all the particulars that would have been provided had the trader, or the person acting on his behalf, completed the forms referred to in the said paragraph (1).

(5) The furnishing of statistical information in accordance with paragraph (4) of this Regulation shall have the same effect as if the statistical information was furnished on the forms referred to in paragraph (1) of this Regulation.

(6) A trader who fails to comply with paragraph (1) or (4) of this Regulation shall be guilty of an offence under these Regulations.

(7) *Prima facie* evidence of the relevant manual, a replacement manual or a supplement may be given in proceedings for an offence under these Regulations by the production of a copy of the relevant manual, replacement manual or supplement purporting to be published by the Revenue Commissioners together with a certificate purporting to be signed by an officer of the Revenue Commissioners certifying that the relevant manual, replacement manual or supplement, as the case may be, contains the relevant matters as respects the obligations of the trader concerned (who shall be named in the certificate) under paragraph (1) or (4), as the case may be, of this Regulation.

(8) In proceedings for an offence under these Regulations:—

    (*a*)   it shall be presumed until the contrary is proved that no authorisation has been given by the Revenue Commissioners under paragraph (3) of this Regulation, and

    (*b*)   *prima facie* evidence of such an authorisation may be given by the production of a document purporting to be a written application by the trader concerned for the authorisation and of a document purporting to be a copy of the authorisation granted by the Revenue Commissioners.

(9) A certificate referred to in paragraph (7) of this Regulation shall:—

    (*a*)   indicate the rank or position in the Office of the Revenue Commissioners of the officer who has signed it.

    (*b*)   be admitted in evidence without proof of the signature of that officer.

(10) (*a*)   Notice of the publication of the relevant manual shall be published in the Irish Oifigiúil as soon as may be after the commencement of these Regulations.

    (*b*)   Notice of the publication of a replacement manual or a supplement shall be published in the Irish Oifigiúil as soon as may be after the publication of the replacement manual or supplement, as the case may be.

    (*c*)   A notice under this paragraph shall indicate that a member of the public shall be entitled to be supplied by the Revenue Commissioners free of charge with a copy of the relevant manual, replacement manual or supplement, as the case may be, on request being made by him therefor.

    (*d*)   *Prima facie* evidence of the publication of a notice under this paragraph may be given in proceedings for an offence under these Regulations by the production of a copy of the Irish Oifigiúil purporting to contain the notice.

(11) The Revenue Commissioners shall supply to a member of the public, free of charge, a copy of the relevant manual, replacement manual or supplement on request being made by him therefor.

5. (1) The Taoiseach shall specify from time to time assimilation thresholds for the purposes of Article 28 of the basic Regulation.

(*a*)   A specification by the Taoiseach of assimilation thresholds for the purposes of aforesaid shall be published in the Irish Oifigiúil as soon as may be after it is made.

(*b*)   *Prima facie* evidence of a specification as aforesaid may be given in proceedings for an offence under these Regulations by the production of a copy of the Iris Oifigiúil purporting to contain the specification.

6. A trader who, in purported compliance with Regulation 4 of these Regulations, furnishes or causes or permits to be furnished to the Revenue Commissioners information which is false, misleading or incomplete in any respect shall be guilty of an offence under these Regulations.

7. (1) An authorised officer may at all reasonable times enter any premises or place where he reasonably believes records relating to goods to which the intrastat system applies are kept and may require any person on those premises or in that place to produce to him the said records or such of them as he specifies and may search for, inspect and take copies, or extracts from, the said records and may remove the said records from those premises or that place for further inspection.

(2) A person who obstructs, hinders or interferes with an authorised officer in the exercise of the powers conferred on him by paragraph (1) of this Regulation or who refuses without lawful excuse to produce to such an officer records which he is required by such an officer to produce under the said paragraph shall be guilty of an offence under these Regulations.

8. (1) All records received or kept by a trader relating to goods in respect of which he is responsible for furnishing statistical information to the Revenue Commissioners under Regulation 4 of these Regulations shall be preserved by him for a period of not less than 2 years from the end of the month to which they relate.

(2) A trader shall produce or cause to be produced to an authorised officer upon request by that officer the records referred to in paragraph (1) of this Regulation or such of them as that officer specifies.

(3) A trader who fails to comply with paragraph (1) of this Regulation or with a request under paragraph (2) of this Regulation shall be guilty of an offence under these Regulations.

9. An officer of statistics shall:—

(*a*)   have access to, and, on request, be given by the Revenue Commissioners copies of, the statistical information furnished to the Revenue Commissioners by or on behalf of traders under Regulation 4 of these Regulations,

(*b*)   on request, be given such information by the Revenue Commissioners as they deem fit to give relating to goods to which the Intrastat system applies and which has come into their possession through the exercise by an authorised officer of his powers under Regulation 7 or 8 of these Regulations.

10. (1) Statistical information furnished by or on behalf of a trader under Regulation 4 of these Regulations shall not, save with the consent of that trader or for the purposes of a prosecution under these Regulations, be shown or communicated to any person other than an officer of the Revenue Commissioners or an officer of statistics in the course of his official duties.

(2) As far as practicable statistics derived from statistical information furnished by or on behalf of a trader under Regulation 4 of these Regulations shall not be published or disseminated in a manner that would result directly or indirectly in the disclosure of details relating to any business of that trader but nothing in this paragraph shall be held to impose a duty owed to a trader to avoid such a disclosure.

11. (1) A trader who by act or omission fails to comply with a provision of the Community Regulations shall be guilty of an offence under these Regulations.

(2) A person who is guilty of an offence under these Regulations shall be liable on summary conviction to a fine of £1,000.

(3) Where a trader is convicted of an offence under Regulation 4 of these Regulations he shall, if the failure in respect of which he is convicted of the offence is continued after conviction, be guilty of a further offence on every day on which the failure continues and for each such offence he shall be liable on summary conviction to a fine of £50.

(4) Proceedings for an offence under these Regulations may be brought and prosecuted by the Revenue Commissioners.

12. (1) Where an offence under these Regulations is committed by a body corporate and is proved to have been committed with the consent or connivance of or be attributable to any neglect on the part of a person being a director, manager, secretary or other similar officer of the body corporate, or a person who was purporting to act in any such capacity, that person as well as the body corporate shall be guilty of an offence and shall be liable to be proceeded against and punished as if he were guilty of the first-mentioned offence.

(2) Where the affairs of a body corporate are managed by its members, paragraph (1) of this Regulation shall apply in relation to the acts and defaults of a member in connection with his functions of management as if he were a director of the body corporate.

13. (1) Subject to the provisions of this Regulation, in proceedings for an offence under these Regulations a certificates signed by an officer of the Revenue Commissioners which certifies that he has inspected the relevant records of the Revenue Commissioners and that it appears from them that the trader concerned (who shall be named in the certificate):—

    (*a*)   was required under Regulation 4 of these Regulations to provided statistical information of a kind and at a time or times specified in the certificate, and failed to do so, or

    (*b*)   failed, in a manner specified in the certificate, to do a stated act or furnish stated records or particulars in accordance with any of the provisions of these Regulations, shall be *prima facie* evidence that the trader concerned was so required to provide statistical information as aforesaid or, as the case may be, failed to do a stated act or furnish stated records or particulars as aforesaid.

(2) A certificate referred to in paragraph (1) of this Regulation shall:—

    (*a*)   indicate the rank or position in the Office of the Revenue Commissioners of the officer who has signed it,

    (*b*)   be admitted in evidence without proof of the signature of that officer.

(3) If in proceedings against a person for an offence under these Regulations it is proposed to tender in evidence a certificate referred to in paragraph (1) of this Regulation the prosecution shall cause to be served on the person not less than 21 days after the commencement of the trial of the offence a copy of the certificate together with a notice informing the person:—

    (*a*)   that it is proposed to tender the certificate in evidence in the proceedings,

    (*b*)   that the certificate shall not, without the leave of the Court, be admitted in evidence if the person serves on the solicitor for the prosecution not later than 7 days before the commencement of the trial of the offence a notice objecting to the admissibility of the certificate.

    (*c*)   that if the person serves a notice as aforesaid and the facts stated in the certificate are required to be proved, wholly or partly, by oral evidence at the trial of the offence the person shall be liable to pay to the prosecution the costs and witness expenses incurred in so proving the said facts unless, in the opinion of the Court, the person had good grounds for serving the said notice.

(4)   (*a*)   A certificate referred to in paragraph (1) of this Regulation shall not, without the leave of the Court, be admitted in evidence if the defendant concerned has served on the solicitor for the prosecution a notice referred to in paragraph (3)(*b*) of this Regulation within the period mentioned in that provision.

    (*b*)   If the defendant concerned has served a notice as aforesaid and the facts stated in the certificate are required to be proved, wholly or partly, by oral evidence at the trial of the offence in question the Court shall, unless it is of the opinion that the defendant had good grounds for serving the said notice, order him to pay to the prosecution the costs and witness expenses incurred in so proving the said facts.

14. The Revenue Commissioners may, in their discretion, mitigate any fine incurred under these Regulations, or stay or compound any proceedings for recovery thereof, and may also, after judgement, further mitigate or entirely remit such a fine.

VALUE ADDED TAX (RETURNS) REGULATIONS 1993

(SI No 247 of 1993)

The Revenue Commissioners, in exercise of the powers conferred on them by sections 19 and 32 of the Value-Added Tax Act, 1972 (No 22 of 1972), hereby make the following Regulations:

1. These Regulations may be cited as the Value Added Tax (Returns) Regulations, 1993.

2. In these Regulations **"the Act"** means the Value Added Tax Act, 1972.

3. A taxable person who is required in accordance with section 19(3)(*a*) of the Act to furnish a return, shall complete such form as is issued to him for that purpose by the Collector-General in respect of the taxable person in question and he shall certify the particulars shown on that form to be correct:

Provided that where the form issued to the said taxable person by the Collector-General specifies supplementary trading details to be furnished in respect of preceding taxable periods as well as the taxable period in question, such supplementary trading details shall be part of the return which is required to be furnished in respect of that taxable period.

4. A taxable person who is required in accordance with section 19(3)(*aa*) of the Act to furnish a return, shall complete such form as is issued to him for that purpose by the Collector-General and he shall certify the particulars shown on that form to be correct.

5. Regulation 12 of the Value Added Tax Regulations, 1979 (SI No 63 of 1979), is hereby revoked.

VALUE ADDED TAX (PAYMENT OF TAX ON INTRA-COMMUNITY ACQUISITION OF CERTAIN NEW MEANS OF TRANSPORT) REGULATIONS 1993

(SI No 248 of 1993)

The Revenue Commissioners, in exercise of the powers conferred on them by sections 19(4) and 32 of the Value Added Tax Act, 1972 (No 22 of 1972), hereby make the following Regulations:

1. These Regulation may be cited as the Value Added Tax (Payment of Tax on Intra-Community Acquisitions of Certain New Means of Transport) Regulations, 1993.

2. These Regulations shall come into operation on the 1st day of September, 1993.

3. In these Regulations—

"the Act" means the Value Added Tax Act, 1972;

"new aircraft" means a new means of transport other than a motorised land vehicle or a vessel;

"new vessel" means a new means of transport other than a motorised land vehicle or an aircraft.

4. Where a person makes an intra-Community acquisition of a new aircraft or a new vessel, in respect of which he is not entitled to a deduction of tax under section 12 of the Act, the person shall—

(*a*)   complete such form as may be provided by the Revenue Commissioners for the purpose of this Regulation,

(*b*)   provide such further documentation in support of the details provided on the form as the Revenue Commissioners may request,

(*c*)   certify that the particulars and documentation provided are true and accurate,

(*d*)   not later than three days after the due date furnish, to the Collector of Customs and Excise for the area in which he is resident, the completed form and supporting documentation referred to in paragraph (*a*) and (*b*) of this Regulation and at the same time pay to that Collector the amount of tax due,

(*e*)   if requested to do so, make the new aircraft or the new vessel, as appropriate, available for inspection in the State by an officer of the Revenue Commissioners.

5. The Value Added Tax (Payment of Tax on Intra-Community Acquisitions of Means of Transport) Regulations, 1992 (SI No 412 of 1992), are hereby revoked.

EUROPEAN COMMUNITIES (VALUE ADDED TAX) REGULATIONS 1993

(SI No 345 of 1993)

1. (1) These Regulations may be cited as the European Communities (Value Added Tax) Regulations, 1993.

(2) These Regulations shall be construed together with the Value Added Tax Acts 1972 to 1993.

2. In these Regulations—

"advance payment" means the advance payment referred to in section 19(6) of the Principal Act;

"due date" means the due date referred to in section 19(6) of the Principal Act;

"November liability" means—

- (*a*)   the amount of tax which would be payable in accordance with section 19(3) of the Principal Act, or
- (*b*)   nil, where an amount of tax would be repayable in accordance with section 20(1) of the Principal Act,

if the November period were to be treated as a taxable period;

"November period" means the month of November immediately preceding a due date;

"the Principal Act" means the Value-Added Tax Act, 1972.

3. Notwithstanding the provisions of section 19(6) of the Principal Act, for the purposes of the application of the said section 19(6) and of these Regulations, all references in the said section 19(6) to the 1st day of December shall be construed as references to the 10th day of December.

4. Subject to his complying with Regulation 5, a taxable person who is liable to pay an advance payment in accordance with section 19(6) of the Principal Act may opt, as an alternative, to pay his November liability and in such circumstances all the provisions of the said section 19(6) shall apply to the November liability as if it were advance payment.

5. Where a taxable person desires to avail of the option provided for in Regulation 4, he shall, by the due date, notify the Collector-General accordingly in writing and declare his November liability to the Collector-General in writing.

VALUE ADDED TAX (DETERMINATION OF TAX DUE BY REFERENCE TO MONEYS RECEIVED) (AMENDMENT) REGULATIONS 1994

(SI No 259 of 1994)

1. (1) These Regulations may be cited as the Value Added Tax (Determination of Tax Due by Reference to Moneys Received) (Amendment) Regulations, 1994.

(2) The Principal Regulations and these Regulations shall be construed together as one and may be cited together as the Value Added Tax (Determination of Tax Due by Reference to Moneys Received) Regulations, 1992 and 1994.

2. In these Regulations—

"the Act" means the Value Added Tax Act, 1972;

"the Principal Regulations" means the Value Added Tax (Determination of Tax Due by Reference to Moneys Received) Regulations 1992 (SI No 306 of 1992).

3.

Notes

Para 3 substituted "section 14(1)(*a*)" for "section 14(1)" and "persons who are not registered persons" for "unregistered persons" in Value Added Tax (Determination of Tax Due by Reference to Moneys Received) Regulations 1992 (SI 306/1992) para 3.

This regulation is made to take account of the fact that traders with annual turnover below £250,000 may now avail of the cash receipts basis of accounting for VAT.

4.

Notes

Para 4 substituted Value Added Tax (Determination of Tax Due by Reference to Moneys Received) Regulations 1992 (SI 306/1992) para 4.

5.

Notes

Para 5 substituted Value Added Tax (Determination of Tax Due by Reference to Moneys Received) Regulations 1992 (SI 306/1992) para 9(1).

DISABLED DRIVERS AND DISABLED PASSENGERS (TAX CONCESSIONS) REGULATIONS 1994

(SI No 353 of 1994)

1. These Regulations may be cited as the Disabled Drivers and Disabled Passengers (Tax Concessions) Regulations, 1994, and shall come into operation on the 1st day of December, 1994.

Cross-references
FA 1989 s 92.

Notes
These regulations, which came into force on 1 December 1994, set out the medical criteria, certification procedures, repayment limits and other matters necessary to give effect to FA 1989 s 92 which provides for tax concessions for disabled drivers and disabled passengers.

---

2. (1) In these Regulations —

"adapted", in relation to a vehicle, does not include adaptations of production line models which are available from the manufacturer or assembler thereof as an optional extra, and "adaptation" shall be construed accordingly;

"authorised person" means a person authorised under section 136 of the Finance Act, 1992 (No 9 of 1992);

"Board medical certificate" means a certificate duly completed in the form prescribed in the Second Schedule and issued by the Disabled Drivers Medical Board of Appeal or a certificate duty completed in the form prescribed in the Second Schedule to the Disabled Drivers (Tax Concessions) Regulations, 1989 (S.I. No 340 of 1989), and so issued under those regulations;

"conversion" has the meaning assigned to it in section 130 of the Finance Act, 1992;

"disabled driver" means a severely and permanently disabled person who possesses a certificate of the kind referred to in paragraph (*a*) or (*b*) of Regulation 4 and whose disablement is of such a nature that the person concerned could not drive a vehicle unless it is specially constructed or adapted to take account of that disablement;

"disabled passenger" means a severely and permanently disabled person who possesses a certificate of the kind referred to in paragraph (*a*) or (*b*) of Regulation 4 and for whom a vehicle has been specially constructed or adapted to the extent prescribed in Regulation 10 (1)(*a*), to take account of that passenger's disablement;

"disabled person" means a person who is severely and permanently disabled, fulfilling one or more of the medical criteria set out in Regulation 3;

"licensing authority" has the meaning assigned to it in section 130 of the Finance Act, 1992;

"purchased" does not include any form of lease arrangement;

"qualifying organisation" means a philanthropic organisation which is not funded primarily by—

    (*a*)   the State,

    (*b*)   any board established by statute, or

    (*c*)   any public or local authority,

which organisation is chiefly engaged, in a voluntary capacity on a non-commercial basis, in the care and transport of severely and permanently disabled persons and which is recognised as such, for the purposes of these Regulations, by the Revenue Commissioner;

"registered" has the meaning assigned to it in section 130 of the Finance Act, 1992;

"**residual value added tax**" means an amount determined by the Revenue Commissioners as being equivalent to the amount of value-added tax which would be included in the open market selling price of a vehicle if it were sold by an authorised person at the time specified in these Regulations;

"**residual vehicle registration tax**" means an amount determined by the Revenue Commissioners as being equivalent to the amount of vehicle registration tax which would be chargeable if that vehicle were liable for such tax at the time specified in these Regulations;

"**vehicle**" has the meaning assigned to it in section 130 of the Finance Act, 1992.

(2) In these Regulations a reference to a Regulation or Schedule is to a Regulation of, or Schedule to, these Regulations and a reference to a paragraph or subparagraph is to a paragraph or subparagraph of the provision in which the reference occurs.

Medical criteria

3. For the purposes of section 92(2)(*a*) of the Finance Act, 1989, the eligibility on medical ground of disabled persons who are severely and permanently disabled shall be assessed by reference to any one or more of the following medical criteria:

    (*a*)   persons who are wholly or almost wholly without the use of both legs;

    (*b*)   persons wholly without the use of one of their legs and almost wholly without the use of the other leg such that they are severely restricted as to movement of their lower limbs;

    (*c*)   persons without both hands or without both arms;

    (*d*)   persons without one or both legs;

    (*e*)   persons wholly or almost wholly without the use of both hands or arms and wholly or almost wholly without the use of one leg;

    (*f*)   persons having the medical condition of dwarfism and who have serious difficulties of movement of the lower limbs.

4. Without prejudice to Regulation 5, a claim for repayment or remission under these Regulations shall be allowed only where the person who makes the claim, or in connection with whom the claim is made, is in possession of either —

    (*a*)   a primary medical certificate duly completed in the form prescribed in the First Schedule as evidence of qualifying disablement, signed, dated and endorsed with the official stamp by the appropriate Director of Community Care and Medical Officer of Health, or

    (*b*)   a Board medical certificate duly completed in the form prescribed in the Second Schedule as evidence of qualifying disablement, signed and dated by a member of the Disabled Drivers Medical Board of Appeal:

Provided that compliance with this Regulation may be waived by the Revenue Commissioners in the case of a claim made by a qualifying organisation.

5. Any person who is deemed, by virtue of section 92(3)(*b*) of the Finance Act, 1989, to be a person who possesses a primary medical certificate shall be deemed to have satisfied the Revenue Commissioners and the licensing authority concerned that that person is a disabled driver or a disabled passenger as the case may be.

Medical Board of Appeal

6. (1) Subject to Regulation 19(3), on the nomination of the Minister for Health the Minister for Finance shall appoint, for a period in each case of 4 years, three medical practitioners to the Disabled Drivers Medical Board of Appeal (in these Regulations referred to as "the Board") and any such practitioner may be reappointed by the Minister for Finance on the nomination of the Minister for Health for a further such period or periods.

(2) Every vacancy on the Board shall be filled by the appointment by the Minister for Finance of a medical practitioner, nominated for that purpose by the Minister for Health,

for the remainder of the period to which the former member's appointment to the Board had related.

(3) Whenever the Minister for Health so requests, the Minister for Finance shall remove any named person from the Board.

(4) A person who is dissatisfied by a decision of a Director of Community Care and Medical Officer of Health in respect of primary medical certification may appeal to the Board within 28 days, or such longer period as it may allow, of the person first being informed of that decision.

(5) Where the Board adjudicates in favour of the disabled driver or disabled passenger concerned, as the case may be, it shall issue a Board medical certificate.

7. Where a licensing authority or the Revenue Commissioners have reason to believe that the person named on a primary medical certificate or a Board medical certificate or who was deemed to have satisfied the said authority or Commissioners under the terms of Regulation 5, does not fulfil any one of the criteria set out in Regulation 3, they shall refer such person to the Board who shall cancel the primary medical certificate or Board medical certificate in question, if they consider it appropriate to do so.

Reliefs for disabled drivers

8. (1) Where a person satisfied the Revenue Commissioners that that person is a disabled driver and has borne or paid value-added tax, vehicle registration tax or residual vehicle registration tax in respect of a vehicle or in respect of the adaptation of a vehicle which —

    (*a*)   is specially constructed or adapted to take account of that person's disablement,

    (*b*)   is purchased by that person,

    (*c*)   is registered in the name of that person, and

    (*d*)   is fitted with an engine whose capacity is not greater than 2,000 cubic centimetres,

that person shall be entitled to be repaid the said amounts of tax and residual vehicle registration tax, subject to the limit specified in Regulation 9 for the purposes of this Regulation:

Provided that the Revenue Commissioners shall repay residual vehicle registration tax only where the person concerned has purchased the vehicle in question from an authorised person.

(2) Where at the time of registration of a vehicle in the name of a person who satisfies the Revenue Commissioners that that person is a disabled driver and the vehicle in question complies with the provisions set out at subparagraphs (*a*) (*b*) and (*d*) of paragraph (1), the Revenue Commissioners shall remit the vehicle registration tax payable, subject to the limit specified in Regulation 9 for the purposes of this Regulation.

(3) Where, after these Regulations come into force, a person becomes a severely and permanently disabled person who fulfils one of the medical criteria set out in Regulation 3 after that person has purchased a vehicle which complies with the provisions set out at subparagraphs (*c*) and (*d*) of paragraph (1), and the vehicle is specially adapted to take account of that person's disablement, that person shall be entitled to be repaid —

    (*a*)   the amount of residual value-added tax and residual vehicle registration tax appropriate to the vehicle at the time such person lodges a claim with the Revenue Commissioners, and

    (*b*)   the value-added tax charged in respect of the adaptation of that vehicle,

subject to the limit specified in Regulation 9 for the purposes of this Regulation.

(4) Where a person receives a repayment or remission under paragraph (1) or (2), that person shall undertake —

    (*a*)   to use the vehicle in question for a period of 2 years from the date of purchase, and to inform the Revenue Commissioners immediately if any circumstances arise during that period where the vehicle is sold or otherwise disposed of by that person, and

(*b*)   to abide by the provisions of Regulation 15.

(5) Where a person receives a repayment or remission under paragraph (3), that person shall undertake —

(*a*)   to use the vehicle in question for a period of 2 years from the date on which the Revenue Commissioners receive the application for the repayment, and to inform the Revenue Commissioners immediately if any circumstances arise during that period where the vehicle is sold or otherwise disposed of by that person, and

(*b*)   to abide by the provisions of Regulation 15.

9. The total amount to be repaid and remitted under Regulation 8 or under paragraph (3) and, in so far as it relates to that paragraph, paragraph (4) of Regulation 12 shall not exceed £7,500 in respect of any vehicle.

Reliefs for disabled passengers

10. (1) Where a person satisfies the Revenue Commissioners that that person is a severely and permanently disabled passenger or a family member of such a disabled passenger residing with and responsible for the transportation of that disabled passenger and such person has borne or paid value-added tax, vehicle registration tax or residual vehicle registration tax in respect of a vehicle or in respect of the adaptation of a vehicle which —

(*a*)   has been specially constructed or adapted for use by that disabled passenger, and where the vehicle is so adapted, the cost of such adaptation excluding value-added tax consists of not less than the amount specified for the purpose in section 92(1) of the Finance Act, 1989:

Provided that in calculating the cost of adaptation of such vehicle, if the Revenue Commissioners so approve, there shall be included —

(i)   the cost of conversion of that vehicle, excluding the additional vehicle registration tax incurred in such conversion, and

(ii)   the purchase cost excluding value-added tax of any adaptations previously fitted to another vehicle adapted for use by that disabled passenger, and refitted to the vehicle in question,

(*b*)   has been purchased by the disabled passenger or by the said family member of that disabled passenger for the purpose of transporting that person, and

(*c*)   is fitted with an engine whose capacity is not greater than 4,000 cubic centimetres,

the person who has borne or paid the said amounts of tax and residual vehicle registration tax shall be entitled to be repaid same, subject to the limit specified in Regulation 11 for the purposes of this Regulation:

Provided that the Revenue Commissioners shall repay residual vehicle registration tax only where the said person has purchased the vehicle in question from an authorised person.

(2) Where at the time of registration of a vehicle by a severely and permanently disabled passenger or by a family member of a severely and permanently disabled passenger residing with the responsible for the transportation of that disabled person and the vehicle in question complies with the provisions set out at subparagraphs (*a*),(*b*) and (*c*) of paragraph (1), the Revenue Commissioners shall remit the vehicle registration tax payable, subject to the limit specified in Regulation 11 for the purposes of this Regulation.

(3) Where, after these Regulations come into force, a person becomes a severely and permanently disabled person who fulfils one of the medical criteria set out in Regulation 3 after that person or a family member of that person residing with and responsible for the transportation of that person has purchased a vehicle which complies with the provision set out at paragraph (1)(*c*) and the vehicle is adapted to the extent outlined in paragraph

(1)(*a*) for the disabled person's use as a passenger, the person who has purchased the vehicle shall be entitled to be repaid —

    (*a*)   the amount of residual value-added tax and residual vehicle registration tax appropriate to the vehicle at the time such person lodges a claim with the Revenue Commissioners, and

    (*b*)   the value-added tax charged in respect of the adaptation of that vehicle,

subject to the limit specified in Regulation 11 for the purposes of this Regulation.

(4)   (*a*)   Where a person receives a repayment or remission under paragraph (1) or (2) of this Regulation that person shall undertake —

      (i)   to use the vehicle in question for the transportation of the disabled passenger in question, for a period of 2 years from the date of purchase, and to inform the Revenue Commissioners immediately if any circumstances arise during that period where the vehicle is sold or otherwise disposed of by that person, and

      (ii)   to abide by the provisions of Regulation 15.

   (*b*)   Where a person receives a repayment or remission under paragraph (3) that person shall undertake —

      (i)   to use the vehicle in question for the transportation of the disabled passenger in question, for a period of 2 years from the date on which the Revenue Commissioners receive the application for repayment, and to inform the Revenue Commissioners immediately if any circumstances arise during that period where the vehicle is sold or otherwise disposed of by that person, and

      (ii)   to abide by the provisions of Regulation 15.

   (*c*)   Where the Revenue Commissioners accept a claim under this Regulation in respect of the transport of a disabled passenger, they shall not accept a claim (other than in the circumstances to which Regulation 15 applies) relating to any further vehicle in respect of the transport of the same passenger for a period of 2 years from the date of purchase of the vehicle for which the claim was accepted where such claim was made under the provisions of paragraph (1) or (2), and a period of 2 years from the date of receipt of the application by the Revenue Commissioners, where such application was made under the provisions of paragraph (3).

   (*d*)   Where the Revenue Commissioners have accepted a claim for repayment of vehicle registration tax in respect of the transport of a disabled person as passenger under the Disabled Drivers (Tax Concessions) Regulations, 1989, they shall not accept a claim relating to any further vehicle in respect of the transport of the same passenger for a period of 2 years from the date of purchase of the vehicle for which the claim was accepted:

      Provided that the Revenue Commissioners may waive this provision in exceptional circumstances subject to the refund of a portion of the repayment, calculated in accordance with the formula set out in Regulation 15 (1).

(5)   (*a*)   In exceptional circumstances, the Revenue Commissioners may waive the condition concerning residency of a claimant under Regulation 10.

   (*b*)   The Revenue Commissioners shall waive the conditions concerning both family membership and residency of a claimant under Regulation 10 in the case of a claim lodged by a person appointed by the President of the High Court to act on behalf of a disabled passenger who is a Ward of Court.

11. The total amount to be repaid and remitted under Regulation 10 shall not exceed £12,500 in respect of any vehicle.

Reliefs for qualifying organisations

12. (1) Where a qualifying organisation satisfied the Revenue Commissioners that it has borne or paid value-added tax, vehicle registration tax or residual vehicle registration tax in respect of a vehicle or in respect of the adaptation of a vehicle which, subject to paragraph (2)—

   (*a*)   is specially constructed or adapted for the transport of disabled persons, and where the vehicle is so adapted the cost of such adaptation, excluding value-added tax, consists of not less than the amount specified for the purpose in subsection 92 (1) of the Finance Act, 1989:

   Provided that in calculating the cost of adaptation of such vehicle, if the Revenue Commissioners so approve, there shall be included —

   (i)   the cost of conversion of that vehicle, excluding the additional vehicle registration tax incurred in such conversion, and

   (ii)   the purchase cost excluding value-added tax of any adaptations previously fitted to another vehicle adapted for use by that qualifying organisation, and refitted to the vehicle in question,

   (*b*)   is purchased by that organisation,

   (*c*)   is registered in the name of that organisation, and

   (*d*)   is fitted with an engine whose capacity is not greater than 4,000 cubic centimetres,

that organisation shall be entitled to be repaid the said amounts of tax and residual vehicle registration tax, subject to the limit specified in Regulation 13 for the purposes of this paragraph:

Provided that the Revenue Commissioners shall repay residual vehicle registration tax only where the said organisation has purchased the vehicle in question from an authorised person.

(2) Where the vehicle referred to in paragraph (1) has been specially constructed or adapted for the transport of 5 or more disabled persons, the provisions of subparagraph (1)(*d*) and of Regulation 13 shall not apply where the seating capacity in the vehicle for passengers who are not disabled persons is not greater than twice the seating capacity for disabled passengers.

(3) Where a qualifying organisation satisfies the Revenue Commissioners that it has borne or paid value-added tax, vehicle registration tax or residual vehicle registration tax in respect of a vehicle or in respect of the adaptation of a vehicle which —

   (*a*)   is specially constructed or adapted to take account of the disablement of a disabled person as driver,

   (*b*)   is purchased by that organisation,

   (*c*)   is registered in the name of that organisation, and

   (*d*)   is fitted with an engine whose capacity is not greater then 2,000 cubic centimetres,

that organisation shall be entitled to be repaid the said amounts of tax and residual vehicle registration tax, subject to the limit specified in Regulation 9 for the purposes of this paragraph:

Provided that the Revenue Commissioners shall repay residual vehicle registration tax only where the said organisation has purchased the vehicle in question from an authorised person.

(4) Where, at the time of registration of a vehicle by a qualifying organisation, the Revenue Commissioners are satisfied that the vehicle in question complies with the provisions set out at subparagraphs (*a*), (*b*) and (*d*) of paragraph (1) or set out at subparagraphs (*a*), (*b*) and (*d*) of paragraph (3), as appropriate, they shall remit the vehicle registration tax payable.

(5) The Revenue Commissioners shall give a repayment of remission under this Regulation only where they are satisfied that the vehicle in question is a reasonable requirement of the organisation making the claim, having regard, inter alia, to the number of disabled persons being transported by that organisation, and the number and capacity of vehicles already owned by that organisation.

(6) Where an organisation receives a repayment or remission under paragraph (1) or (3) that organisation shall undertake —

(*a*)   to use the vehicle in question for a period of 2 years from the date of purchase, and to inform the Revenue Commissioners immediately if any circumstances arise during that period where the vehicle is sold or otherwise disposed of by that organisation, and

(*b*)   to abide by the provisions of Regulation 15.

(7) The Revenue Commissioners shall consult the National Rehabilitation Board in respect of each organisation which applies to them under these Regulations.

(8) Where the Revenue Commissioners have reasonable cause to believe that a qualifying organisation should no longer be entitled to the benefit of these Regulations, they shall consult the National Rehabilitation Board and may withdraw the concessions from such organisation.

13. The total amount to be repaid and remitted under paragraph (1) and, in so far as it relates to that paragraph, paragraph (4) of Regulation 12 shall not exceed £12,500 in respect of any vehicle.

Passenger vehicles qualifying more than once

14. Where a repayment or remission has been granted under Regulation 10 or 12 in respect of a vehicle which is subsequently purchased for the transport of a different disabled passenger or by a different qualifying organisation, and the adaptations remain in the vehicle at the time of such subsequent purchase, the requirements set out at Regulation 10(1)(*a*) or 12(1)(*a*), as the case may be, shall be deemed to be fulfilled.

Refunds to the Revenue Commissioners

15.   (1) Where a beneficiary of a repayment or remission under Regulation 8 or 10 in respect of a vehicle (in this Regulation referred to as "the first-mentioned vehicle")—

(*a*)   sells it or otherwise disposes of it within 2 years of the date of purchase or, in the case of a person referred to in Regulation 8(3) or 10(3), within 2 years of the date on which the Revenue Commissioners receive the application for repayment, or

(*b*)   claims a repayment or remission under the same Regulation in respect of a subsequent vehicle purchased by that person within 2 years of purchasing the first-mentioned vehicle, or, in the case of a person referred to in Regulation 8(3) or 10(3), within 2 years of the date on which the Revenue Commissioners receive the application for repayment,

such person shall refund to the Revenue Commissioners a portion of the amount which was either or both repaid and remitted on the first-mentioned vehicle, calculated by the Revenue Commissioners according to the following formula:

$$A \times \frac{B}{(C+D)}$$

where:

A   is the open market selling price of the first-mentioned vehicle on the date of its sale or disposal or on the date of purchase of the subsequent vehicle, whichever is applicable,

B   is the total amount repaid or remitted in respect of the first-mentioned vehicle and any adaptations thereto,

C   is the open market selling price of the first-mentioned vehicle at the time of its purchase by the beneficiary, and

D   is the cost including value-added tax of any adaptations to the first-mentioned vehicle on which repayment was claimed by the beneficiary.

(2) The refund referred to in paragraph (1) shall be paid to the Revenue Commissioners within one month of the sale or disposal of the first-mentioned vehicle, but where the circumstances referred to at paragraph (1)(*b*) apply, not later than the time of the repayment or remission of any tax in respect of the subsequent vehicle.

(3) Where a qualifying organisation which receives a repayment or remission under Regulation 12 in respect of a vehicle sells it or otherwise disposes of it within 2 years of the date of purchase such organisation shall refund to the Revenue Commissioners a portion of the amount which was either or both repaid and remitted on the vehicle, calculated by the Revenue Commissioners according to the following formula:

$$A \times \frac{B}{(C+D)}$$

where:

A   is the open market selling price of the vehicle on the date of its sale or disposal,

B   is the total amount repaid or remitted in respect of the vehicle and any adaptations thereto,

C   is the open market selling price of the vehicle at the time of its purchase by the organisation, and

D   is the cost including value-added tax of any adaptations to the vehicle on which repayment was claimed by the organisation.

(4) The refund referred to in paragraph (3) shall be paid to the Revenue Commissioners within one month of the sale or disposal of the vehicle in question.

(5) The Revenue Commissioners shall not repay or remit any tax or residual vehicle registration tax under Regulation 8, 10 or 12 in respect of any vehicle unless the provisions of paragraph (2) or (4), as the case may be, have been fulfilled.

(6) In exceptional cases, and subject to such conditions as they consider necessary in each such case, the Revenue Commissioners may reduce the amount of the refund required under this Regulation.

Fuel repayments

16. (1) The excise duty paid on any fuel used for combustion in the engine of a vehicle on which repayment or remission of tax, or residual vehicle registration tax has been granted in accordance with these Regulations shall be repaid by the Revenue Commissioners where the use of the fuel was related to the transportation of the disabled person or persons concerned whether as driver or passenger.

(2) Where the repayment or remission of tax or residual vehicle registration tax was made under Regulation 8 or 10, the repayment of excise duty on fuel referred to in paragraph (1) shall be limited to the duty on an annual maximum of 600 gallons per beneficiary.

(3) Where the repayment or remission of tax or residual vehicle registration tax was made under Regulation 12, the repayment of excise duty on fuel referred to in paragraph (1) shall be limited to the duty on an annual maximum of 900 gallons per vehicle.

(4) The excise duty paid on any fuel used for combustion in the engine of a vehicle which would have qualified for repayment or remission of value-added tax, vehicle registration tax or residual vehicle registration tax in accordance with these Regulations but for the fact that the vehicle was purchased prior to the coming into effect of these Regulations, shall be repaid by the Revenue Commissioners where the use of the fuel was related to the transportation of the disabled person or persons concerned whether as driver or passenger, and the provisions of paragraphs (2) and (3) shall apply with any necessary modifications.

Road Tax

17. The licensing authority shall remit the excise duty which would, but for this provision, be payable under section 1 of the Finance (Excise Duties) (Vehicles) Act, 1952 (No 24 of 1952) (being the duty known as road tax), on any vehicle which qualifies for relief under regulation 8, 10 or 12.

General

18. (1) A person or organisation wishing to avail of the provisions of Regulation 8, 10 or 12 shall complete the Declaration in the Third Schedule in respect of each vehicle involved, and such claim form as may be provided for the purpose by the Revenue Commissioners and present them to the Revenue Commissioners, together with such documentary evidence as they shall require.

(2) A person or organisation wishing to avail of the provisions of Regulation 17 shall apply to the appropriate licensing authority and produce to it evidence that the vehicle has qualified for relief under Regulation 8, 10 or 12, and, in the case of an applicant who has qualified for relief under Regulation 8, a valid current driving licence.

Revocation and transitional provisions, etc

19. (1) The Disabled Drivers (Tax Concessions) Regulations, 1989 (SI No 340 of 1989), are hereby revoked.

(2) Any primary medical certificate or other certificate issued under the Regulations revoked by paragraph (1) shall be deemed to be a valid certificate for the purposes of these Regulations, and such certificate and person named thereon shall be subject to the provisions of Regulation 7.

(3) Notwithstanding paragraph (1), the Board appointed under Regulation 6 of the Disabled Drivers (Tax Concessions) Regulations, 1989, shall continue for the period of its appointment as if appointed under these Regulations and Regulation 6(1) of these Regulations shall be construed accordingly.

Regulation 4(a)

FIRST SCHEDULE

PRIMARY MEDICAL CERTIFICATE

Issued for the purposes of section 92 of the Finance Act, 1989, and the Disabled Drivers and Disabled Passengers (Tax Concessions) Regulations, 1994.

Name of applicant: Mr./Mrs./Miss/Ms * ....

Normal Address: ....

....

....

I, ..., Director of Community Care and Medical Officer of Health for the .... Health Board area, hereby certify that in my opinion the person named above is a severely and permanently disabled person who meets one or more of the medical criteria set out in the Disabled Drivers and Disabled Passengers (Tax Concessions) Regulations, 1994.

Particulars of the applicant's disablement are as follows:**

- (*a*)   the applicant is wholly or almost wholly without the use of both legs;

- (*b*)   the applicant is wholly without the use of one leg and almost wholly without the use of the other leg such that the applicant is severely restricted as to movement of the lower limbs;

- (*c*)   the applicant is without both hands or without both arms;

- (*d*)   the applicant is without one or both legs;

- (*e*)   the applicant is wholly or almost wholly without the use of both hands or arms and wholly or almost wholly without the use of one leg;

- (*f*)   the applicant has the medical condition of dwarfism and has serious difficulties of movement of the lower limbs.

Date: ....

....(Signature)

Director of Community Care and Medical Officer of Health,

....Health Board.

Official Stamp

*Delete as appropriate.

**Tick as appropriate and cross out particulars that do not apply.

Regulation 4 (b)

SECOND SCHEDULE

BOARD MEDICAL CERTIFICATE

Issued, on appeal, for the purposes of section 92 of the Finance Act, 1989, and the Disabled Drivers and Disabled Passengers (Tax Concessions) Regulations, 1994.

Name of applicant: Mr./Mrs./Miss/Ms * ....

Normal Address: ....

....

....

The Disabled Drivers Medical Board of Appeal hereby certifies that in its opinion the person named above is a severely and permanently disabled person who meets one or more of the medical criteria set out in the Disabled Drivers and Disabled Passengers (Tax Concessions) Regulations, 1994.

Particulars of the applicant's disablement are as follows:**

(a) ☐ the applicant is wholly or almost wholly without the use of both legs;

(b) ☐ the applicant is wholly without the use of one leg and almost wholly without the use of the other leg such that the applicant is severely restricted as to movement of the lower limbs;

(c) ☐ the applicant is without both hands or without both arms;

(d) ☐ the applicant is without one or both legs;

(e) ☐ the applicant is wholly or almost wholly without the use of both hands or arms and wholly or almost wholly without the use of one leg;

(f) ☐ the applicant has the medical condition of dwarfism and has serious difficulties of movement of the lower limbs.

Date: ....

.... (Signature)

For and on behalf of the Disabled Drivers Medical Board of Appeal and a member of that Board.

*Delete as appropriate.

**Tick as appropriate and cross out particulars that do not apply.

Regulation 18

THIRD SCHEDULE

DISABLED DRIVERS AND DISABLED PASSENGERS (TAX CONCESSIONS) REGULATIONS, 1994.

(Every applicant must complete Part I, II or III, as appropriate)

Part I

DECLARATION BY DISABLED DRIVER.

NAME OF DISABLED DRIVER * ....

ADDRESS ....

....

....

I hereby declare as follows:

Vehicle, registration number (if available) ....

engine number .... and

chassis number ....,

is registered or about to be registered in my name, is intended for my personal use as driver and has been specially constructed or adapted to take account of my disablement. I am unable to drive any vehicle not specially adapted for my use. I am the holder of a valid current driving licence for the class to which the vehicle belongs.

Signed: . ... (applicant)

Date: ....

WARNING: ANY PERSON WHO MAKES A FALSE DECLARATION WILL INCUR SEVERE PENALTIES.

PART II

DECLARATION BY OR ON BEHALF OF A DISABLED PASSENGER

NAME OF DISABLED PASSENGER * ....

ADDRESS ....

....

....

Where a family member is applying in respect of the transport of the above-mentioned person:

NAME OF FAMILY MEMBER APPLYING ....

ADDRESS ....

....

....

I hereby declare as follows:

Vehicle, registration number (if available) ....

engine number .... and

chassis number ....,

has been specially constructed or adapted to take account of the disablement of the passenger mentioned above and has been purchased for the purpose of transporting the passenger in question.

Signed: . ... (applicant)

Date: ....

WARNING: ANY PERSON WHO MAKES A FALSE DECLARATION WILL INCUR SEVERE PENALTIES.

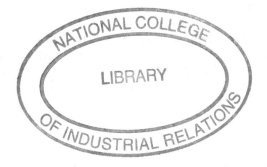

PART III

DECLARATION ON BEHALF OF A QUALIFYING ORGANISATION

NAME OF ORGANISATION ....

ADDRESS ....

....

....

I hereby declare as follows:

Vehicle, registration number (if available) ....

engine number .... and

chassis number ....,

either

has been specially constructed or adapted to take account of the disablement of
.... (specify the number) severely and permanently
disabled passengers, being cared for and transported by this organisation   *

or

has been specially constructed or adapted for the use of a disabled person as driver   *

Signed: .... (applicant)

Position in organisation (e.g. Chairman, Secretary etc.) ....

Date: ....

WARNING: ANY PERSON WHO MAKES A FALSE DECLARATION WILL INCUR SEVERE PENALTIES.

*Tick whichever is appropriate.

EUROPEAN COMMUNITIES (VALUE ADDED TAX) REGULATIONS 1994

(SI No 448 of 1994)

1. (1) These Regulation may be cited as the European Communities (Value Added Tax) Regulations, 1994.

(2) These Regulations shall be construed together with the Value Added Tax Acts 1972 to 1994.

2. These Regulations shall come into operation on the 1st day of January, 1995.

3. In these Regulations **"the Principal Act"** means the Value Added Tax Act, 1972.

4.

Note
This para inserted VATA 1972 s 15B. This new section provides transitional arrangements for the taxation of trade with Austria, Finland, and Sweden, all of whom became EU Member States on 1 January 1995. Goods dispatched prior to 1 January 1995 from those States, to Ireland, remain liable to VAT at point of import if such goods were placed under a tax suspension regime on importation, and remain uncleared on 1 January 1995.

EUROPEAN COMMUNITIES (VALUE ADDED TAX) REGULATIONS 1995

(SI No 363 of 1995)

General note

The Second Simplification Directive (Council Directive 95/7/EC of 10 April 1995) introduced changes which were initially given effect in Irish law from 1 January 1996 by these regulations. The changes mean that intra EU cross border contract work on movable goods is now treated as a service - and no VAT is chargeable where the customer is VAT registered within the EU. These regulations were revoked by FA 1996 s 100, as the necessary changes were replicated in FA 1996 Pt III.

VALUE ADDED TAX (SPECIAL SCHEME FOR MEANS OF TRANSPORT; DOCUMENTATION) REGULATIONS 1996

(SI No 201 of 1996)

1. These Regulations may be cited as the Value Added Tax (Special Scheme for Means of Transport: Documentation) Regulations, 1996.

2. These Regulations shall come into operation on the 1st day of July, 1996.

3. In these Regulations—

"the Act of 1995" means the Finance Act, 1995 (No 8 of 1995);

"taxable dealer" has the meaning assigned to it by section 12B(3) (inserted by the act of 1995) of the Principal Act;

"means of transport" has the meaning assigned to it by section 12B(3) (inserted by the Act of 1995) of the Principal Act;

"the Principal Act" means the Value Added Tax Act, 1972;

"residual tax" has the meaning assigned to it by section 12B(4) (inserted by the Act of 1995) of the Principal Act.

4. (1) A taxable dealer shall deduct residual tax in accordance with section 12(1)(*a*)(vi) of the Principal Act in respect of the acquisition or purchase of a means of transport from a person specified in paragraph (*a*) or (*b*) of subsection (2) of section 12B of that Act, subject to the following conditions:

   (*a*)   that the dealer prepares a document which sets out all the particulars specified in paragraph (2) of this Regulation, in respect of the transaction in question,

   (*b*)   that the document referred to at subparagraph (*a*) of this paragraph is signed and dated by the person who is supplying the means of transport concerned, acknowledging the accuracy of the details therein and declaring that that person is a person of the type referred to in either paragraph (*a*) or (*b*) of subsection (2) of section 12B of the Principal Act, and

   (*c*)   that the dealer gives to the person who is supplying the means of transport concerned a copy of the completed document referred to at subparagraphs (*a*) and (*b*) of this paragraph within 15 days of the date of the acquisition or purchase of that means of transport.

(2) The particulars in respect of the means of transport concerned which are to be included in the document referred to in paragraph (1) of this Regulation are as follows:

   (*a*)   the name and address of the person who is supplying that means of transport;

   (*b*)   the name and address of the taxable dealer who is purchasing or acquiring that means of transport;

   (*c*)   the date upon which the supply of that means of transport takes place;

   (*d*)   a description of that means of transport, including details of the make, model, engine number, registration number and year of manufacture; and

   (*e*)   the total consideration for the supply of that means of transport.

5. A taxable dealer shall deduct residual tax in accordance with section 12(1)(*a*)(vi) of the Principal Act in respect of the acquisition or purchase of a means of transport from a person specified in paragraph (*c*) of subsection (2) of section 12B of that Act, subject to the condition that such dealer shall be in possession of an invoice issued by that person in accordance with the provisions of sections 12B(5) and 17(1) of that Act.

6. A taxable dealer shall deduct residual tax in accordance with section 12(1)(*a*)(vi) of the Principal Act in respect of the acquisition or purchase of a means of transport from a person specified in paragraph (*d*) of subsection (2) of section 12B of that Act, subject to the condition that such dealer shall be in possession of an invoice issued by that person which indicates that the supply by that person was subject to value added tax in accordance with the provisions implementing Article 26*a* or 28*o* of Council Directive 77/388/EEC of 17 May 1977 (OJ No L145, 13 June 1977, p 1) in the Member State in which the supply took place.

7. An invoice issued in accordance with the provisions of sections 12B(5) and 17(1) of the Principal Act shall show the following endorsement:

"Special Scheme - this invoice does not give the right to an imput credit of VAT".

8. A taxable dealer shall keep full and true records, entered up to date, of the acquisition and disposal of a means of transport, in respect of which that dealer has deducted residual tax in accordance with section 12(1)(*a*)(vi) of the Principal Act, together with appropriate cross-references between all such records.

9. The Value Added Tax (Second-hand Motor Vehicles) Regulations 1988 (SI No 121 of 1988) are hereby revoked.

ORDERS

VALUE ADDED TAX (SPECIFIED DAY) ORDER 1972

(SI No 180 of 1972)

Date of imposition of the tax

1. This Order may be cited as the Value Added Tax (Specified Day) Order, 1972.

Cross-references
VATA 1972 s 1(1).
Notes
This order appoints 1 November 1972 as the day on which VAT comes into operation in place of turnover tax and wholesale tax.

---

2. The 1st day of November, 1972, is hereby appointed to be the specified day for the purposes of the Value Added Tax Act, 1972.

VALUE ADDED TAX (APPOINTED DAY) ORDER 1972

(SI No 192 of 1972)

Date for registration

1. This order may be cited as the Value Added Tax (Appointed Day) Order, 1972.

Cross-references
VATA 1972 s 9(4).
Notes
This Order appoints 1 September 1972 as the date from which taxable persons may register for VAT.

---

2. The 1st day of September, 1972, is hereby appointed to be the appointed day for the purpose of section 9 of the Value Added Tax Act, 1972.

VALUE ADDED TAX (REFUND OF TAX) (No 1) ORDER 1972

(SI No 267 of 1972)

Notes

Revoked by Value Added Tax (Refund of Tax) (No 25) Order 1993 (SI No 266 of 1993) r 9.

VALUE ADDED TAX (REDUCTION OF RATE) (No 1) ORDER 1972

(SI No 268 of 1972)

Amendments
Revoked by FA 1973 s 80(*f*) with effect from 3 September 1973.

Notes
Where the rate of tax chargeable on the delivery of goods was 16.37%, that rate also applied to the hire of such goods. This order reduced the VAT rate applicable to the hire of such goods to 5.26%. The reduction in rate only applied where the goods were in the possession of the person (to whom the goods were hired) on 1 November 1972.

VALUE ADDED TAX (REFUND OF TAX) (No 2) ORDER 1972

(SI No 269 of 1972)

Notes
Revoked by Value Added Tax (Refund of Tax) (Revocation) Order 1979 (SI 232/1979) with effect from 1 March 1979.

VALUE ADDED TAX (REDUCTION OF RATE) (No 2) ORDER 1972

(SI No 326 of 1972)

Amendments
Revoked by FA 1973 s 80(*f*) with effect from 3 September 1973.
Notes
This order enabled unregistered sea fishermen to reclaim VAT on fishing boats the purchase of which had been grant aided (or loan financed) by Bord Iascaigh Mhara.

VALUE ADDED TAX (REFUND OF TAXING) (No 3) ORDER 1972

(SI No 327 of 1972)

Amendments

Revoked by Value Added Tax (Refund of Tax)(No 12) Order 1980 (SI 262/1980) with effect from 1 March 1979.

Notes

This order enabled the Revenue Commissioners to repay VAT (in excess of the 3% rate applicable to fixed buildings) to the purchaser of a mobile home or similar structure where the mobile home etc was used (or provided for use by a local authority) as a residence.

VALUE ADDED TAX (REFUND OF TAX) (No 4) ORDER 1972

(SI No 328 of 1972)

Amendments

Revoked by Value Added Tax (Refund of Tax) (No 13) Order (SI 263/1980).

Notes

This order enabled the Revenue Commissioners to repay VAT paid on specially constructed or adapted motor vehicles for use by disabled drivers.

VALUE ADDED TAX (REDUCTION OF RATE)
(No 3) ORDER 1973

(SI No 69 of 1973)

Amendments
Revoked by FA 1973 s 80(*f*) with effect from 3 September 1973.
Notes
With effect from 1 November 1972, this order applied the 0% rate to life saving services provided by the Royal National Lifeboat Institution.

VALUE ADDED TAX (REFUND OF TAX) (No 5) ORDER 1973

(SI No 70 of 1973)

Amendments

Revoked by Value Added Tax (Refund of Tax) (No 14) Order 1980 (SI 264/1980) with effect from 1 March 1979.

Notes

With effect from 1 November 1972, this order allowed the repayment of VAT paid (in excess of 5.26%) on medical and laboratory appliances bought by hospitals. colleges etc..

VALUE ADDED TAX (REFUND OF TAX) (No 6) ORDER 1973

(SI No 238 of 1973)

Notes

This order made consequential amendments to existing Orders arising out of changes in the rates of tax made by FA 1973. Para 2 substituted Value Added Tax (Refund of Tax)(No 3) Order 1972 r 5 (SI 327/1972); para 3(*a*) amended Value Added Tax (Refund of Tax)(No 4) Order 1972 r 4 (*c*)(i)(I) and substituted r 5 (*a*)(iii)(SI 328/1972); para 4(*a*) amended Value Added Tax (Refund of Tax)(No 5) Order 1973 r 4 and substituted r 6 (SI 70/1973).

VALUE ADDED TAX (REFUND OF TAX) (No 7) ORDER 1974

(SI No 290 of 1974)

Eurocontrol purchases

1. This Order may be cited as the Value Added Tax (Refund of Tax) (No 7) Order, 1974.

Cross-references
VATA 1972 s 20(3).
Notes
This Order enables repayment of VAT on purchases of goods by Eurocontrol to be made subject to certain conditions.

---

2. This Order shall be deemed to have come into operation on the 1st day of November, 1972.

3. In this Order **"the Organisation"** means the European Organisation for the Safety of Air Navigation (Eurocontrol) established by the International Convention relating to Cooperation for the Safety of Air Navigation signed at Brussels on the 13th day of December, 1960, and references to the Organisation include references to the Permanent Commission for the Safety of Air Navigation comprised in the Organisation and to the Air Traffic Services Agency comprised in the Organisation.

4. Where the Organisation establishes to the satisfaction of the Revenue Commissioners that, in connection with its official activities it has borne tax on the delivery to it of goods or on the rendering to it of services, and those goods or services are of substantial value, and fulfils to the satisfaction of the said Commissioners all the conditions which are specified in paragraph 5 of this Order it shall be entitled to be repaid the tax so established as having been borne or paid.

5.   (*a*)   The Organisation shall claim a refund of the tax by completing such claim form as may be provided for the purpose by the Revenue Commissioners and it shall certify the particulars shown on such claim form to be correct.

       (*b*)   The Organisation shall, by the production of an invoice provided in accordance with section 17(12)(*a*)(i) of the Value Added Tax Act, 1972, establish the amount of tax borne in relation to such delivery or rendering.

VALUE ADDED TAX (REFUND OF TAX) (No 8) ORDER 1978

(SI No 145 of 1978)

Notes
Revoked by Value-Added Tax (Refund of Tax) (No 25) Order 1993 (SI No 266 of 1993) r 9.

VALUE ADDED TAX (REDUCTION OF RATE) (No 4) ORDER 1978

(SI No 146 of 1978)

Candles

1.(1) This Order may be cited as the Value Added Tax (Reduction of Rate) (No 4) Order, 1978.

(2) This Order shall come into operation on the 1st day of July, 1978.

Cross-references
VATA 1972 s 11(8).

2.

Notes
This Order, by inserting VATA 1972 Sch 2 para (xx)(*cc*) adds plain white candles and night lights to the list of zero rated goods.

VALUE ADDED TAX (AMENDMENT) ACT, 1978 (COMMENCEMENT) ORDER 1979

(SI No 8 of 1979)

Date of implementation of Value Added Tax (Amendment) Act, 1978

1. This Order may be cited as the Value Added Tax (Amendment) Act, 1978 (Commencement) Order, 1979.

Cross reference
VATAA 1978 s 32(3).
Notes
This Order brings VAT(A)A 1978 into operation on 1 March 1979.

---

2. The 1st day of March, 1979, is hereby appointed as the day on which sections 1 to 28 and 30 to 32 of the Value Added Tax (Amendment) Act, 1978, shall come into operation.

VALUE ADDED TAX (REFUND OF TAX) (No 9) ORDER 1979

(SI No 59 of 1979)

Stocks of radios and record players

1. This Order may be cited as the Value Added Tax (Refund of Tax) (No 9) Order, 1979.

Cross-references
VATA 1972 s 20(3).

Notes
This Order allows traders in radio receivers and record players (other than manufacturers) to claim a refund of VAT on stocks purchased before 1 March 1979 and held for resale on that date.

---

2. This Order shall come into operation on the 1st day of March, 1979.

3. Where a person, other than a manufacturer of goods of the kind in question, registered in accordance with section 9 of the Value Added Tax Act, 1972 (No 22 of 1972), establishes to the satisfaction of the Revenue Commissioners that—

    (*a*)   he holds at the commencement of the 1st day of March, 1979, a stock of radio receiving sets that are of the domestic or portable type or of a type suitable for use in road vehicles; or a stock of gramophones, radiogramophones or record players, for supply in the course of a business carried on by him, and

    (*b*)   he has purchased or imported the goods in question prior to the 1st day of March, 1979, in such circumstances that tax at the rate specified in section 11(1)(*c*)(ii) of the said Act was borne or paid on the goods either by him or by a previous purchaser or importer of the goods and that the tax did not qualify for deduction under subsection (1) of section 12 of the Act except to the extent specified in the proviso to that subsection,

he shall, subject to the conditions specified in Article 4 of this Order, be entitled to be repaid such of the following amounts as are appropriate:

    (i)   in a case where the goods in questions were imported by or delivered to the person in such circumstances that tax at the rate specified in section 11(1)(*c*)(ii) of the said Act was charged on the importation or delivery, an amount equal to **30 per cent** of the amount on which tax was so charged, and

    (ii)   in any other case, the amount of tax which the Revenue Commissioners are satisfied has been borne on the acquisition of the goods and which does not qualify for deduction under section 12(1)(*a*) of the Act.

4. The conditions referred to in Article 3 of this Order are:

    (*a*)   the person concerned shall claim a refund of the tax by completing such form as may be provided for the purpose by the Revenue Commissioners showing, if requested, the total number of items of each description of goods, the number of different makes and models within each description, the name of the supplier and the number and date of invoice in relation to each item or group of items and the relative amounts of consideration or value at importation and he shall certify the particulars shown on such claim form to be correct,

    (*b*)   the person concerned shall, if requested by the Revenue Commissioners, by the production of invoices issued in accordance with section 17(1) of the Act or by the production of customs documents, establish to them the amount of the consideration or the value at importation, as the case may be, in relation to which a refund is claimed.

443

VALUE ADDED TAX (REFUND OF TAX) (REVOCATION) ORDER 1979

(SI No 232 of 1979)

Revocation of SI No 269 of 1972

1.(1) This Order may be cited as the Value Added Tax (Refund of Tax) (Revocation) Order, 1979.

(2) This Order shall be deemed to have come into operation on the 1st day of March, 1979.

Cross-reference
VATA 1972 s 20(3).

Notes
This Order revokes Value Added Tax (Refund of Tax) (No 2) Order 1972 (SI 269/1972) which enabled commercial sea fishermen who were not registered for VAT to reclaim VAT on fishing boats for which they received a grant or loan from An Bord Iascaigh Mhara. This relief is now given by VATR 1979 r 29.

---

2. The Value Added Tax (Refund of Tax) (No 2) Order, 1972 (S.I. No 269 of 1972), is hereby revoked.

VALUE ADDED TAX (REFUND OF TAX) (No 10) ORDER 1979

(SI No 275 of 1979)

Vehicles for disabled persons

Amendments
Revoked by Value Added Tax (Refund of Tax) (Revocation) Order 1989 (SI 351/1989).

Notes
This order enabled the Revenue Commissioners to repay VAT paid on the purchase or importation of vehicles built (or adapted) to carry disabled persons.

VALUE ADDED TAX (REFUND OF TAX) (No 11) ORDER 1980

(SI No 239 of 1980)

European Space Agency

1. This Order may be cited as the Value Added Tax (Refund of Tax) (No 11) Order, 1980.

Cross-references
VATA 1972 s 20(3).

Notes
This Order permits repayment of VAT on purchase of goods and services by the European Space Agency subject to certain conditions. The Order came into operation on 29 November 1976.

---

2. This Order shall be deemed to have come into operation on the 29th day of November, 1976.

3. In this Order **"the Agency"** means the European Space Agency established by the Convention for the Establishment of a European Space Agency signed at Paris on the 30th day of May, 1975.

4. Where the Agency establishes to the satisfaction of the Revenue Commissioners that it has borne tax on the supply to it of goods or services of substantial value which are strictly necessary for the exercise of its official activities and fulfils to the satisfaction of the said Commissioners all the conditions which are specified in paragraph 5 of this Order it shall be entitled to be repaid the tax so established as having been borne.

5.   (*a*)   The agency shall claim a refund of the tax by completing such claim form as may be provided for the purpose by the Revenue Commissioners and it shall certify the particulars shown on such claim form to be correct.

   (*b*)   The agency shall, by the production of an invoice, provided in accordance with section 17(12)(*a*)(i) of the Value Added Tax Act, 1972, establish the amount of tax borne in relation to such supply.

VALUE ADDED TAX (REFUND OF TAX) (No 12) ORDER 1980

(SI No 262 of 1980)

Mobile homes

1. (1) This Order may be cited as the Value Added Tax (Refund of Tax) (No 12) Order, 1980.

(2) This Order shall be deemed to have come into operation on the 1st day of March, 1979.

Cross-references
VATA 1972 s 20(2).

Notes
This Order, which came into operation on 1 March 1979, enables repayment of VAT to be made in respect of caravans, mobile homes or similar structures purchased by a person (or local authority) for use as a residence. The refund will be such as to adjust the rate of VAT to the same effective rate as applies to the construction of permanent buildings. It is a condition for repayment that the caravan or mobile home be rated.
This Order revokes Value Added Tax (Refund of Tax) (No 3) Order 1972 (SI 327/1972) with effect from 1 March 1979.

---

2. (1) In this Order **"the Act"** means the Value Added Tax Act, 1972 (No 22 of 1972).

(2) A reference in this Order to a caravan includes a reference to a mobile home or any similar structure designed primarily for residential purposes.

3. A person who establishes to the satisfaction of the Revenue Commissioners that he has borne or paid tax in relation to the supply to or importation by him of a caravan and who fulfils to the satisfaction of the said Commissioners the conditions which are specified in paragraph 4 of this Order shall be entitled to be repaid so much of such tax as is specified in paragraph 5 of this Order.

4. The conditions to be fulfilled by a person referred to in paragraph 3 of this Order are—

    (*a*)   he shall claim a refund of the tax by completing such claim form as may be provided for the purpose by the Revenue Commissioners and he shall certify the particulars shown in such claim form to be correct;

    (*b*)   he shall establish that the caravan in relation to which a claim for a refund of the tax arises—

        (i)   is used by him as a permanent residence for himself and that neither he nor (if he is a married man having his spouse living with him) his spouse has any other place of abode within the State available for his occupation, or

        (ii)   is, in the case of a local authority, occupied as a residence by a tenant of the local authority;

    (*c*)   he shall, in the case of a person other than a local authority, by the production of a certificate from the appropriate local authority or such other documentary evidence as may be acceptable to the Revenue Commissioners, establish that the caravan has been rated under the Valuation Acts;

    (*d*)   he shall, by the production of invoices, provided in accordance with section 17(12)(*a*)(i) of the Act, or by the production of receipts for tax paid on importation, establish the amount of tax borne or paid by him in relation to the caravan excluding any amount referable to articles of furniture or equipment which would not be regarded as fixtures if the caravan were regarded as immovable goods at the time of its supply or importation;

    (*e*)   he shall establish the net tax-exclusive amount of the consideration for the supply to him of the caravan, or, if the caravan was imported by him, its net tax-exclusive value, exclusive, in either case, of the amount, if any, included in such consideration or value for the supply or importation of such articles as are referred to in subparagraph (*d*) of this paragraph;

451

    (*f*)   he shall establish that he is not entitled to a deduction under section 12 of the Act for any portion of the tax specified in subparagraph (*d*) of this paragraph.

5. The amount of tax to be repaid to a person referred to in paragraph 3 of this Order shall be so much of the amount of tax specified in paragraph 4(*d*) of this Order as the person shows to the satisfaction of the Revenue Commissioners to be in excess of the amount which would have been borne or paid by him if the rate and percentage for the time being referred to in section 11(2)(*b*) of the Act had applied to the supply or importation in question.

Cross-references
FA 1985 s 43(*b*).

---

6. The Value Added Tax (Refund of Tax) (No 3) Order, 1972 (S.I. No 327 of 1972), is hereby revoked with effect as on and from the 1st day of March 1979.

VALUE ADDED TAX (REFUND OF TAX) (No 13) ORDER 1980

(SI No 263 of 1980)

Disabled drivers' vehicles

Notes

This Order, which revoked and replaced Value Added Tax (Refund of Tax) (No 4) Order 1972 (SI 328/1972), was itself revoked by the Value Added Tax (Refund of Tax) (Revocation) Order 1989 (SI 351/1989). Refunds of tax and excise duty to disabled drivers are now governed by the Disabled Drivers (Tax Concessions) Regulations 1989 (SI 340/1989).

VALUE ADDED TAX (REFUND OF TAX) (No 14) ORDER 1980

(SI No 264 of 1980)

Certain hospital equipment

1. (1) This Order may be cited as the Value Added Tax (Refund of Tax) (No 14) Order, 1980.

(2) This Order shall be deemed to have come into operation on the 1st day of March, 1979.

Cross-references
VATA 1972 s 20(3).

Notes
This Order, which came into force on 1 March 1979, provides for a refund of the excess of VAT paid over the low rate on medical or research equipment by hospitals, universities, colleges, schools or similar educational bodies operating medical research laboratories (including veterinary research). This Order revokes the Value Added Tax (Refund of Tax) (No 5) Order 1973 (SI 70/1973).
With effect from 1 January 1993, "importation" means importation from a non EC country: VATA 1972 s 1(1).

---

2. In this Order **"the Act"** means the Value Added Tax Act, 1972.

3. This Order applies to the following persons:

    (*a*)   a body of persons in its capacity as a person operating a hospital;

    (*b*)   a university, college, school or similar educational body in its capacity as a person operating a medical research laboratory;

    (*c*)   a research institution in its capacity as a person operating a medical research laboratory.

4. A person to whom this Order applies who establishes to the satisfaction of the Revenue Commissioners that he has borne or paid tax at a rate in excess of the rate per cent. for the time being specified in section 11(1)(*a*) of the Act in relation to the supply to or importation by him of any instrument or appliance of a kind commonly used to make a diagnosis, to prevent or treat an illness, to carry out a surgical operation or to carry out scientific research and who fulfils to the satisfaction of the Revenue Commissioners the conditions which are specified in paragraph 5 of this Order shall be entitled to be repaid so much of such tax as is specified in paragraph 6 of this Order.

5. The conditions to be fulfilled by a person referred to in paragraph 4 of this Order are—

    (*a*)   he shall claim a refund of the tax by completing such claim form as may be provided for the purpose by the Revenue Commissioners and he shall certify the particulars shown on such form to be correct;

    (*b*)   he shall establish that he is a person to whom this Order applies and that the instruments or appliances on the supply or importation of which the tax was borne or paid by him were used by him in the capacity in relation to which this Order applies to him;

    (*c*)   he shall establish, by the production of invoices, provided in accordance with section 17(12)(*a*)(i) of the Act, or by the production of receipts for tax paid on imported goods, the amount of tax borne or paid by him in relation to the goods specified in paragraph 4 of this Order;

    (*d*)   he shall establish that he is not entitled to a deduction under section 12 of the Act for any portion of the tax specified in subparagraph (*c*) of this paragraph.

6. The amount of tax to be repaid to the claimant shall be so much of the amount of tax specified in paragraph 5(c) of this Order as the person shows to the satisfaction of the Revenue Commissioners to be in excess of the amount of tax which would have been borne or paid by him if the rate specified in section 11(1)(*a*) of the Act had applied to the supply or importation in question.

7. The Value Added Tax (Refund of Tax) (No 5) Order, 1973 (S.I. No 70 of 1973) is hereby revoked with effect as on and from the 1st day of March, 1979.

VALUE ADDED TAX (REDUCTION OF RATE) (No 5) ORDER 1981

(SI No 53 of 1981)

Certain medical goods used by disabled persons

1. (1) This Order may be cited as the Value Added Tax (Reduction of Rate) (No 5) Order, 1981.

Cross-references
VATA 1972 s 11(8).
Notes
This Order, which came into effect on 1 March 1981, applies the zero rate of VAT to a variety of medical goods used by disabled or infirm people.

---

(2) This Order shall come into operation on the 1st day of March, 1981.

2.

Notes
This para inserted VATA 1972 Sch 2 para (xix*a*).

3.

Notes
This para deleted VATA 1972 Sch 3 para (xvii)(*c*) and substituted VATA 1972 Sch 3 para (xvii)(*f*).

VALUE ADDED TAX (REFUND OF TAX) (No 15) ORDER 1981

(SI No 428 of 1981)

Certain goods for use by disabled persons

1. This Order may be cited as the Value Added Tax (Refund of Tax)(No 15) Order, 1981.

Cross-references
VATA 1972 s 20(3).
Notes
This Order provides for repayment of VAT on certain goods and applications which assist disabled people where such goods are purchased after 1 March 1981.

---

2. In this Order—

"the Act" means the Value Added Tax Act, 1972;

"disabled person" means a person who, as a result of an injury, disease, congenital deformity or physical or mental illness, or defect, suffers from a loss of physical or mental faculty resulting in a specified degree of disablement; and cognate words shall be construed accordingly;

"qualified goods" means goods other than mechanically propelled road vehicles which are aids or appliances, including parts and accessories, specially constructed or adapted for use by a disabled person and includes goods which, although not so specially constructed or adapted, are of such a kind as might reasonably be treated as so constructed or adapted having regard to the particular disablement of that person;

"specified degree of disablement" means, as regards a disablement to which the provisions of the Social Welfare (Occupational Injuries) Regulations, 1967 (No 77 of 1967), apply, a degree of disablement which, if assessed in accordance with those provisions, would be not less than **30 per cent**, and, as regards any other disablement, a degree of disablement of equivalent extent.

3. Where a person establishes to the satisfaction of the Revenue Commissioners that—

    (*a*)   he has borne or paid tax which became chargeable on or after the 1st day of March, 1981, in respect of the supply to or importation by him of qualifying goods, and

    (*b*)   he fulfils the conditions which are specified in paragraph 4 of this Order, and such other conditions as the said Commissioners may impose, he shall be entitled to repayment of the amount of tax so borne or paid.

4. The conditions to be fulfilled by a person referred to in paragraph 3 of this Order are—

    (*a*)   he shall claim a refund of the tax by completing such claim form as may be provided for the purpose by the Revenue Commissioners and he shall certify the particulars shown on such claim form to be correct;

    (*b*)   (i)   in case he is the person for whose use the goods referred to in paragraph 3 of this Order were supplied or imported, he shall, by the production of such evidence as may be acceptable to the said Commissioners, establish that he is a disabled person and that the goods are for the purpose of assisting him to overcome his disability in the performance of essential daily functions or in the exercise of a vocation, and that the goods are so used by him;

        (ii)   in case he is not the person for whose use the said goods were supplied or imported, he shall, by the production of such evidence as may be acceptable to the said Commissioners, establish that the goods were supplied by him, other than in the course of business, to a particular person who is a disabled person for the purpose of assisting that person to overcome his disability in the performance of essential daily

459

functions or in the exercise of a vocation, and that the goods are so used by that other person;

(c) he shall by the production of invoices, provided in accordance with section 17(12)(a)(i) of the Act, or by the production of receipts for tax paid on goods imported, establish the amount of tax borne or paid to which the claim relates;

(d) he shall establish that he is not entitled to a deduction under section 12 of the Act or a repayment under section 20(2) of the Act or under a regulation or order, other than this Order, made under the Act in respect of any portion of the tax specified in subparagraph (c) of this paragraph;

(e) he shall establish that the tax specified in subparagraph (c) of this paragraph does not form any part of expenditure incurred by him which has been or will be met, directly or indirectly, by the State, by any board established by statute, or by any public or local authority.

VALUE ADDED TAX (REFUND OF TAX) (No 16) ORDER 1983

(SI No 324 of 1983)

1. (1) This Order may be cited as the Value Added Tax (Refund of Tax) (No 16) Order, 1983.

(2) This Order shall be deemed to have come into operation on the 1st day of May, 1983.

Cross-references

VATA 1972 s 20(3).

Notes

This Order, which came into operation on 1 May 1983, enables sea-fishermen to reclaim VAT on importation of marine diesel for use on a registered sea-fishing vessel.

---

2. In this Order—

    (*a*) **"the Act"** means the Value Added Tax Act, 1972;

    (*b*) **"sea-fishing vessel"** means a sea-fishing boat which —

        (i) is registered in accordance with the Merchant Shipping (Registry, Lettering and Numbering of Fishing Boats) (Regulations) Order, 1927 (S.R. & O., No 105 of 1927),

        and

        (ii) is registered under the Mercantile Marine Act, 1955 (No 29 of 1955);

    (*c*) **"hydrocarbon oil"** means hydrocarbon oil of a kind specified in paragraph (i)(*c*) of the Sixth Schedule to the Act.

3. A person who establishes to the satisfaction of the Revenue Commissioners that he has borne or paid tax on the supply to or importation by him of hydrocarbon oil used for combustion in the engine of a sea-fishing vessel in the course of a sea-fishing business carried on by him and who fulfils to the satisfaction of the said Commissioners the conditions which are specified in paragraph 4 of this Order, shall be entitled to be repaid the amount of tax so borne or paid.

4. The conditions to be fulfilled by a person referred to in paragraph 3 of this Order are—

    (*a*) he shall claim a refund of the tax concerned by completing such claim form as may be provided for the purpose by the Revenue Commissioners and he shall certify the particulars shown on such claim form to be correct;

    (*b*) he shall, by the production of invoices, provided in accordance with section 17(12)(*a*)(i) of the Act, or by the production of receipts for tax paid on goods imported, establish the amount of tax borne or paid to which the claim relates;

    (*c*) he shall establish that he is not a person who is registered in the register maintained under section 9 of the Act, nor a person required under the provisions of that section to furnish the particulars specified for registration;

    (*d*) except where the Revenue Commissioners otherwise allow, the claim for a refund of tax shall be made in respect of hydrocarbon oil used within a period or periods of three months.

VALUE ADDED TAX (REFUND OF TAX) (No 17) ORDER 1984

(SI No 249 of 1984)

Notes
Revoked by Value-Added Tax (Refund of Tax) (No 25) Order 1993 (SI No 266 of 1993) r 9.

VALUE ADDED TAX (REFUND OF TAX) (No 18) ORDER 1985

(SI No 192 of 1985)

1. (1) This Order may be cited as the Value Added Tax (Refund of Tax) (No 18) Order, 1985.

(2) This Order shall be deemed to have come into operation on the 1st day of January, 1979.

Notes

This Order, which has effect from 1 January 1979, enables VAT on certain small reserve craft, ancillary equipment and special boat buildings to be repaid to qualifying sea rescue groups subject to certain conditions. The Order is retrospective. With effect from 1 January 1993, "importation" means importation from a non EC country: VATA 1972 s 1(1).

---

2. In this Order —

"the Act" means the Value Added Tax Act, 1972, (No 22 of 1972);

"the Irish Water Safety Association" means the body established under the Irish Water Safety Association (Establishment) Order, 1980 (S.I. No 244 of 1980).

3. A body of persons which establishes to the satisfaction of the Revenue Commissioners that it has borne or paid tax in relation to the supply or hire to it, the importation by it or the repair, modification or maintenance for it of a boat or similar craft of a gross tonnage of 15 tons or less, designed and constructed, or adapted, for the purpose of rescue or assistance at sea, of equipment for use in or in conjunction with any such boat or craft, or of a building or structure for housing or operating such boat, craft or equipment, and which fulfils to the satisfaction of the said Commissioners the conditions specified in paragraph 4 of this Order shall be entitled to be repaid such tax.

4. The conditions to be fulfilled by a body of persons referred to in paragraph 3 of this Order are:

(*a*) it shall claim a refund of the tax by completing such form as may be provided for the purpose by the Revenue Commissioners and shall certify the particulars shown on such form to be correct;

(*b*) it shall, by the production of documentary evidence establish that the outlay in relation to which the claim for a refund of tax arises was incurred in respect of the supply or hire to it, the importation by it or the repair, modification or maintenance for it of a boat or similar craft of a gross tonnage of 15 tons or less designed and constructed, or adapted, for the purpose of rescue or assistance at sea, of equipment for use in or in conjunction with such boat or craft, or of a building or structure for housing or operating such boat, craft or equipment;

(*c*) it shall, by the production of invoices provided in accordance with section 17(12)(*a*)(i) of the Act, or by the production of a receipt for tax paid on importation, establish the amount of tax borne or paid in relation to the outlay referred to in subparagraph (*b*) of this paragraph;

(*d*) subject to paragraph 5 of this Order, it shall, by the production of documentary evidence from the Irish Water Safety Association, establish to the satisfaction of the Revenue Commissioners that it provides services of rescue or assistance at sea and that the nature and extent of such services meet the requirements of the said Association in relation to the organisation and functioning of bodies of persons providing services of rescue or assistance at sea;

(*e*) it shall establish to the satisfaction of the Revenue Commissioners that the boat or craft, the equipment, and the building or structure specified in paragraph 3 of this Order are not used for any purpose other than in relation to rescue or assistance at sea or the training of persons in connection therewith;

(f)   it shall establish that it is not a person who is registered in the register maintained under section 9 of the Act, nor a person required under the provisions of that section to furnish the particulars specified for registration;

(g)   except where the Revenue Commissioners otherwise allow, the claim for a refund of tax shall be made only in respect of outlay incurred within a period of twelve months or more.

5. The provisions of this Order, other than paragraph 4(*d*), shall apply to claims for refund of tax made by the Irish Water Safety Association.

6. The secretary, or other officer acting as secretary for the time being, of a body of persons which makes a claim for refund of tax under this Order shall be answerable in addition to the body for doing all such acts as are required to be done by the body in relation to the making of such a claim.

VALUE ADDED TAX (EXEMPTED ACTIVITIES)
(No 1) ORDER 1985

(SI No 430 of 1985)

1. This Order may be cited as the Value Added Tax (Exempted Activities) (No 1) Order,
1985.

Cross-references
VATA 1972 s 6(2).
Notes
This Order exempts from VAT the reimbursement by credit card companies of traders for goods and services supplied to card
holders.

2. ...

Notes
This para inserted VATA 1972 Sch 1 para (xi*a*).

VALUE ADDED TAX (REFUND OF TAX) (No 19) ORDER 1986

(SI No 68 of 1986)

1. (1) This Order may be cited as the Value Added Tax (Refund of Tax) (No 19) Order, 1986.

(2) This Order shall be deemed to have come into operation on the 1st day of March, 1986.

Cross-references
VATA 1972 s 20(3).
Notes
This Order, which came into operation on 1 March 1986, enables VAT in excess of the low rate on certain touring coaches to be repaid subject to certain conditions.

2. In this Order **"the Act"** means the Value Added Tax Act, 1972.

[**3.** A person who establishes to the satisfaction of the Revenue Commissioners that he had borne or paid tax in relation to the acquisition, including the hiring (other than the hiring for a period of less than 6 consecutive months), by him of a passenger road motor vehicle not more than 24 months old, being—

    (*a*)   a single-deck touring coach having dimensions as designated by the manufacturer of not less than 3,350 millimetres in height, not less than 10,000 millimetres in length and not less than 1,400 millimetres in floor height, or

    (*b*)   a double-deck touring coach having dimensions as designated by the manufacturer of not more than 4,300 millimetres in height and not less than 10,000 millimetres in length, for use by him for the purposes of the business referred to in subparagraph (*b*) of paragraph 4 of this Order, and who fulfils to the satisfaction of the said Commissioners the conditions that are specified in the said paragraph 4 and such other conditions as the said Commissioners may impose, shall be entitled to be repaid so much of such tax as is specified in paragraph 5 of this Order.][1]

Amendments
1 Para 3 substituted by Value Added Tax (Refund of Tax) (No 22) Order 1988 (SI 262/1988)

4. The conditions to be fulfilled by a person referred to in paragraph 3 of this Order are:—

    (*a*)   he shall claim a refund of the tax by completing such claim form as may be provided for the purpose by the Revenue Commissioners and he shall certify the particulars shown on such form to be correct;

    (*b*)   he shall, by the production of such evidence as the Revenue Commissioners may require, establish that he is engaged in the business of carriage of persons, including tourists, by road under contracts for group transport;

    (*c*)   he shall, by the production of invoices, provided in accordance with section 17(12)(*a*)(i) of the Act, or by the production of receipts for the tax paid on importation of the vehicle, establish the amount of tax borne or paid by him in relation to the acquisition by him of the vehicle;

    (*d*)   he shall establish that he is not entitled to a deduction under section 12 of the Act in respect of any portion of the tax specified in subparagraph (*c*) of this paragraph.

5. The amount of tax to be repaid under this Order shall be so much of the amount of tax specified in paragraph 4(*c*) of this Order as is shown to the satisfaction of the Revenue Commissioners to be in excess of the amount which would have been borne or paid if the rate and percentage for the time being specified in section 11(1)(*c*) of the Act had applied in relation to the acquisition in question.

IMPOSITION OF DUTIES (No 283) (VALUE ADDED TAX) ORDER 1986

(SI No 412 of 1986)

Amendments
Revoked by FA 1987 s 39(*b*) with effect from 9 July 1987.

Notes
This order, which came into effect on 1 January 1987, by including "deer" in the definition of livestock in VATA 1972 s 1, provided that the VAT rate on the supply of live deer was reduced from 25% to 2.4%.

VALUE ADDED TAX (REFUND OF TAX) (No 20) ORDER 1987

(SI No 10 of 1987)

Notes
Revoked with effect from 29 January 1992, by Value Added Tax (Refund of Tax) (No 23) Order 1992 (SI 58/1992).

VALUE ADDED TAX (REFUND OF TAX) (No 21) ORDER 1987

(SI No 308 of 1987)

1. (1) This Order may be cited as the Value Added Tax (Refund of Tax) (No 21) Order, 1987.

(2) This Order shall be deemed to have come into operation on the 1st day of July, 1987.

Cross-references

VATA 1972 s 20(3).

Notes

This Order, which has effect from 1 July 1987, provides relief from tax for goods purchased for export by philanthropic organisations for use in their activities abroad.

With effect from 1 January 1993, "exportation" means exportation to a non EC country: VATA 1972 s 1(1).

---

2. In this Order—

    (*a*) **"the Act"** means the Value Added Tax Act, 1972;

    (*b*) **"qualifying body"** means any non-profit making body of persons with aims of a philanthropic nature, engaged in humanitarian, charitable or teaching activities abroad;

    (*c*) **"qualifying goods"** means goods which, within four months of their supply in, or importation into, the State, have been exported, by or on behalf of a qualifying body, for use in its humanitarian, charitable or teaching activities abroad.

3. A person, who establishes to the satisfaction of the Revenue Commissioners that—

    (*a*) he is a qualifying body, or that he is acting on behalf of a qualifying body,

    (*b*) the goods to which the claim relates are qualifying goods,

    (*c*) he has borne or paid tax on the supply to, or importation by, him of those qualifying goods,

and who fulfils, to the satisfaction of the said Commissioners, the conditions specified in paragraph 4 of this Order, shall be entitled to be repaid such tax.

4. The conditions to be fulfilled by a person referred to in paragraph 3 of this Order are that he shall—

    (*a*) claim a refund of the tax by completing such claim form as may be provided for the purpose by the Revenue Commissioners, and certify the particulars shown on such claim form to be correct;

    (*b*) establish the amount of tax borne or paid to which the claim relates by the production of invoice or other documents, provided in accordance with section 17(12)(*a*)(i) of the Act, or by the production of receipts for tax paid on goods imported;

    (*c*) establish that he is not entitled to remission, repayment or deduction of the tax under any other provision of the Act, or under any instrument made under statute administered by the Revenue Commissioners in respect of the supply or importation of the qualifying goods.

VALUE ADDED TAX (REFUND OF TAX) (No 22) ORDER 1988

(SI No 262 of 1988)

1.(1) This Order may be cited as the Value Added Tax (Refund of Tax) (No 22) Order, 1988.

(2) This Order shall be deemed to have come into operation on the 1st day of October, 1988.

Cross-references
VATA 1972 s 20(3).
Notes
This Order extends the existing VAT refund scheme to luxury touring coaches.

---

2. ...

Note
Para 2 substituted Value Added Tax (Refund of Tax) (No 19) Order 1986 (SI 68/1986) para 3.

VALUE ADDED TAX (REFUND OF TAX) (REVOCATION) ORDER 1989

(SI No 351 of 1989)

1. (1) This Order may be cited as the Value Added Tax (Refund of Tax) (Revocation) Order, 1989.

(2) This Order shall come into operation on the 21st day of December 1989.

2. The Value Added Tax (Refund of Tax) (No 10) Order, 1979, (SI No 275 1979) and the Value Added Tax (Refund of Tax) (No 13) Order, 1980 (SI No 263 of 1980), are hereby revoked.

Notes
These orders are revoked as the Disabled Drivers (Tax Concessions) Regulations (SI 340/1989) now provides equivalent relief.

VALUE ADDED TAX (REFUND OF TAX) (No 23) ORDER 1992

(SI No 58 of 1992)

1.(1) This Order may be cited as the Value Added Tax (Refund of Tax) (No 23) Order, 1992.

(2) This Order shall be deemed to have come into operation on the 29th day of January, 1992.

Cross-references
VATA 1972 s 20(3).

Notes
This Order, which came into operation on 29 January 1992, provides for a full refund of VAT paid on qualifying medical equipment purchased through voluntary donations. It replaces and revokes the Value Added Tax (Refund of Tax) (No 20) Order 1987 (SI 10/1987).

---

2. In this Order—

"the Act" means the Value Added Tax Act, 1972 (No 22 of 1972), and every enactment which is to be construed together with that Act;

"qualifying goods" means any new instrument or new appliance, excluding means of transport—

    (*a*)   in relation to which the amount on which tax is chargeable by virtue of the Act is £20,000 or more,

    (*b*)   which has been designed and manufactured for use solely in medical research or in diagnosis, prevention, or treatment of illness,

    (*c*)   which has been the subject of a recommendation by the Minister for Health that, having regard to the requirements of the health services in the State, a refund of tax under this Order would be appropriate;

"qualifying body" means any body of persons engaged in the operation of a hospital.

3. Where a person establishes to the satisfaction of the Revenue Commissioners that—

    (*a*)   he has borne or paid tax which became chargeable on or after the 29th day of January, 1992, in respect of the supply to, or the importation by, him of qualifying goods,

    (*b*)   he is a qualifying body or, if he is not such a body, the qualifying goods have been, or are to be, donated by him to a qualifying body,

    (*c*)   no part of the funds used, or to be used, in the purchase of the qualifying goods was, or is to be, provided, directly or indirectly, by the State, or by any board established by or under statute, or by any public or local authority, or by the qualifying body which has purchased the qualifying goods or to which they have been, or are to be, donated, or by any body of persons associated with such qualifying body in the operation of a hospital, or by any body of persons operating a hospital, and

    (*d*)   in respect of the supply or importation of qualifying goods, he is not entitled to repayment of the tax under any provision of the Act or under any instrument other than this Order made under statute administered by the Revenue Commissioners,

and the person completes such claim form as may be provided for the purpose by the Revenue Commissioners and certifies the particulars shown on such claim form to be correct, he shall be entitled to be repaid the full tax so borne or paid.

(4) The Value Added Tax (Refund of Tax) (No 20) Order, 1987 (SI No 10 of 1987), is hereby revoked.

VALUE ADDED TAX (REFUND OF TAX) (No 24) ORDER 1993

(SI No 134 of 1993)

Amendments

Revoked by Value-Added Tax (Refund of Tax) (No 26) Order 1994 (SI No 165 of 1994) para 6.

VALUE ADDED TAX (REFUND OF TAX) (No 25) ORDER 1993

(SI No 266 of 1993)

1. This Order may be cited as the Value Added Tax (Refund of Tax) (No 25) Order, 1993.

2. (1) In this Order—

"the Act" means the Value Added Tax Act, 1972;

"flat-rate farmer" has the meaning assigned to it by section 12A(2) of the Act,

"qualifying person" means a flat-rate farmer who has borne or paid tax in relation to outlay on the construction, extension, alteration or reconstruction of any building or structure which is designed for use solely or mainly for the purpose of a farming business, or on the fencing, drainage or reclamation of any land intended for use for the purposes of such a business;

"registered person" means a flat-rate farmer who is a taxable person referred to in subsection (1A)(c) or (2)(b) of section 8 of the Act and who is included on the register of taxable persons maintained by the Revenue Commissioners pursuant to section 9 of the Act;

"structure" includes a farmyard, a farm road and a concrete path adjacent to farm buildings;

"unregistered person" means a flat-rate farmer other than a registered person.

(2) In this Order a reference to a paragraph is to a paragraph of this Order, unless it is indicated that reference to some other provision is intended.

3. An unregistered person who establishes to the satisfaction of the Revenue Commissioners that he is a qualifying person, and who fulfils to the satisfaction of the said Commissioners the conditions which are specified in paragraph 4, shall be entitled to be repaid so much of such tax as is specified in paragraph 7.

4. The conditions to be fulfilled by an unregistered person are as follows:

    (*a*)   he shall claim a repayment of the tax by completing such claim form as may be provided for that purpose by the Revenue Commissioners and he shall certify the particulars shown on such claim form to be correct;

    (*b*)   he shall produce—

        (i)   the invoices or other documents, issued or given to him for the purposes of section 17 of the Act, or

        (ii)   the receipts for tax paid on goods imported,

    showing the tax borne or paid by him which is the subject of the refund claim;

    (*c*)   he shall, if requested to do so by the Revenue Commissioners, produce the plans, specifications or other documentary evidence in relation to—

        (i)   the construction, extension, alteration or reconstruction of a building or structure which is designed for use solely or mainly for the purposes of a farming business, or

        (ii)   the fencing, drainage of reclamation of any land intended for use for the purposes of such a business,

    in respect of which his claim for a refund of tax is being made; and

    (*d*)   he shall have complied with all the obligations imposed on him by the Act, the Income Tax Acts, the Corporation Tax Acts or the Capital Gains Tax Act, and any instruments made thereunder, in relation to—

        (i)   the payment or remittance of the taxes, interest and penalties required to be paid or remitted thereunder, and

     (ii)   the delivery of returns.

5. A registered person who is a qualifying person shall, subject to the conditions which are specified in paragraph 6, be entitled to reclaim so much of such tax as is specified in paragraph 7 as if such tax were deductible tax under section 12 of the Act.

6. The conditions to be fulfilled by a registered person are as follows:

    (*a*)   he shall reclaim the tax in the return which he is obliged to furnish in accordance with section 19(3) of the Act and he shall certify the particulars shown on the relevant return form to be correct;

    (*b*)   he shall retain all the documents referred to in subparagraphs (*b*) and (*c*) of paragraph 4 which are relevant to his claim as if they were records to be kept in accordance with section 16 of the Act; and

    (*c*)   he shall have compiled with all the obligations imposed on him by the Act, the Income Tax Acts, the Corporation Tax Acts or the Capital Gains Tax Act, and any instruments made thereunder, in relation to—

        (i)   the payment or remittance of the taxes, interest and penalties required to be paid or remitted thereunder, and

       (ii)   the delivery of returns.

7. The amount of tax to be repaid in accordance with paragraph 3 or reclaimed in accordance with paragraph 5 shall, subject to paragraph 8, be the tax borne or paid which the qualifying person shows to the satisfaction of the Revenue Commissioners to be referable solely to outlay which relates to—

    (*a*)   the construction, extension, alteration or reconstruction of that part of the building or structure which was designed solely for the purposes of a farming business and has actually been put to use in such a business carried on by him, or

    (*b*)   the fencing, drainage or reclamation of any land which has actually been put to use in such a business carried on by him.

8. A claim for repayment of tax under subparagraph (*a*) of paragraph 4 shall be made only in respect of outlay involving a total amount of tax of more than £100.

9. The Value Added Tax (Refund of Tax) (No 1) Order, 1972 (SI 267 of 1972), the Value Added Tax (Refund of Tax) (No 8) Order, 1978 (SI 145 of 1978) and the Value Added Tax (Refund of Tax) (No 17) Order, 1984 (SI 249 of 1984), are hereby revoked.

VALUE ADDED TAX (THRESHOLD FOR ADVANCE PAYMENT) ORDER 1993

(SI No 303 of 1993)

1. This Order may be cited as the Value Added Tax (Threshold for Advance Payment) Order, 1993.

2. In this Order—

"the Act" means the Value Added Tax Act, 1972 (No 22 of 1972);

"threshold" means a threshold for the purposes of section 19(6) of the Act;

"due date" means a due date for the purposes of section 19(6) of the Act.

3. The threshold to be applied for the purposes of section 19(6) of the Act to the due date which is the 1st day of December, 1993, and to each successive due date thereafter, shall be £300,000.

VALUE ADDED TAX (REFUND OF TAX) (No 26) ORDER 1994

(SI No 165 of 1994)

Amendments

Revoked by Value Added Tax (Refund of Tax) (No 28) Order 1996 (SI 98/1996) r 6.

VALUE ADDED TAX (THRESHOLD FOR ADVANCE PAYMENT) (AMENDMENT) ORDER 1994

(SI No 342 of 1994)

1. This Order may be cited as the Value Added Tax (Threshold for Advance Payment) (Amendment) Order, 1994.

2. In this Order—

"the Act" means the Value Added Tax Act, 1972 (No 22 of 1972);

"due date" means a due date (as construed by reference to the European Communities (Vaule Added Tax) Regulations, 1993 (SI No 345 of 1993) for the purposes of section 19(6) of the Act.

"threshold" means a threshold for the purposes of section 19(6) of the Act;

3. The threshold to be applied for the purposes of section 19(6) of the Act to the due date which is the 10th day of December, 1994, and to each successive due date thereafter, shall be £1,000,000 and accordingly, for the purposes of section 19(6)(*h*)(i)(II) of the Act the threshold of £300,000 specified in Article 3 of the Value Added Tax (Threshold for Advance Payment) Order, 1993 (SI No 303 of 1993), is hereby increased to £1,000,000.

VALUE ADDED TAX (REFUND OF TAX) (No 27) ORDER 1995

(SI No 38 of 1995)

1. (1) This Order may be cited as the Value Added Tax (Refund of Tax) (No 27) Order, 1995.

(2) This Order shall be deemed to have come into operation on the 27th day of January, 1994.

2. In this Order—

"the Act" means the Value Added Tax Act, 1972 (No 22 of 1972), and every enactment which is to be construed together with that Act;

"qualifying body" means—

> (*a*)   a research institution, or

> (*b*)   a university, college, school or similar educational body,

which conducts medical research in a laboratory;

"qualifying goods" means any new instrument or new appliance, excluding means of transport—

> (*a*)   in relation to which the amount on which tax is chargeable by virtue of the Act is £20,000 or more,

> (*b*)   which has been designed and manufactured for use in medical research, and

> (*c*)   which has been the subject of a recommendation by the Health Research Board that, having regard to the requirements of medical research in the State, a refund of tax under this Order would be appropriate.

3. Where a person establishes to the satisfaction of the Revenue Commissioners that—

> (*a*)   such person has borne or paid tax which became chargeable on or after the 27th day of January, 1994, in respect of the supply of goods to, the intra-Community acquisition of goods by, or the importation of goods by, such person where such goods are qualifying goods,

> (*b*)   such person is a qualifying body or, if such person is not a qualifying body, the qualifying goods have been, or are to be, donated by such person to a qualifying body,

> (*c*)   no part of the funds used, or to be used, in the purchase of the qualifying goods was, or is to be, provided, directly or indirectly, by the State, or by any board established by or under statute, or by any public or local authority, or by the qualifying body which has purchased the qualifying goods or to which they have been, or are to be, donated, or by any body or persons associated with such qualifying body in the operation of a medical research laboratory or by any other body of persons operating a medical research laboratory, and

> (*d*)   such person is not entitled, under any provision of the Act or under any instrument other than this Order made under statute administered by the Revenue Commissioners, to a deduction or repayment of the tax borne or paid in respect of the supply of goods to, the intra-Community acquisition of goods by or the importation of goods by such person where such goods are qualifying goods,

and the person completes such claim form as may be provided for the purpose by the Revenue Commissioners and certifies the particulars shown on such claim form to be correct, such person shall be entitled to be repaid the full tax so borne or paid.

FINANCE ACT 1994 (COMMENCEMENT OF SECTIONS 93 AND 96(*a*)) ORDER 1995

(SI No 184 of 1995)

1. This Order may be cited as the Finance Act, 1994 (Commencement of Sections 93 and 96(*a*)) Order, 1995.

2. The 7th day of July, 1995 is hereby appointed as the date on which section 93 and 96(*a*) of the Finance Act, 1994 (No 13 of 1994), shall take effect.

VALUE ADDED TAX (REFUND OF TAX) (No 28) ORDER 1996

(SI No 98 of 1996)

1. (1) This Order may be cited as the Value Added Tax (Refund of Tax) (No 28) Order, 1996.

(2) This Order shall be deemed to have came into operation on the 23rd day of January, 1996.

Notes

The Order provides for a full repayment of VAT to exempt coach operators, subject to certain conditions, in respect of the tax paid on touring coaches of certain age and dimensions.

---

2. (1) In this Order—

"the Act" means the Value Added Tax Act, 1972 (No 22 of 1972);

"qualifying person" means a person who—

    (*a*)   is engaged in the business of carriage for reward of tourists by road under contracts for group transport, and

    (*b*)   has complied with all the obligations imposed on the person by the Act, the Income Tax Acts, the Corporation Tax Acts or the Capital Gains Tax Acts, and any instruments made thereunder, in relation to

        (i)   the payment or remittance of taxes, interest the penalties required to be paid or remitted thereunder, and

        (ii)   the delivery of returns;

"qualifying vehicle" means—

    (*a*)   a single-deck touring coach having dimensions as designated by the manufacturer of not less than 3,000 millimetres in height, not less than 8,000 millimetres in length, not less than 1,000 millimetres in floor height and with an underfloor luggage capacity of not less than 3 cubic metres, or

    (*b*)   a double-deck touring coach having dimensions as designated by the manufacturer of not more than 4,300 millimetres in height and not less than 10,000 millimetres in length.

(2) In this Order a reference to a paragraph or subparagrpah is to a paragraph or subparagraph of this Order, unless it is indicated that reference to some other provision is intended.

3. (1) Unless the provisions in subparagraph (2) are applied, a qualifying person who has bone or paid tax on—

    (*a*)   the supply to such person or the hiring or leasing (other than hiring or leasing for a period of less than six consecutive months) to such person, or

    (*b*)   the intra-Community acquisition or importation by such person,

of a qualifying vehicle which is for use by such person in the State in the business of the carriage for reward of tourists by road under contracts for group transport shall, subject to the conditions specified in paragraph 4, be repaid the full tax so borne or paid provided that—

        (i)   the supply, intra-Community acquisition or importation of the vehicle which gave rise to such tax occurred when the vehicle was not more than two years old, or

        (ii)   the hiring or leasing of the vehicle (other than hiring or leasing for a period of less than six consecutive months) which gave rise to such tax was on the basis of a contract for such hire or lease first entered into when the vehicle was not more than two years old.

(2) A qualifying person who is a taxable person and who becomes liable for tax in the State in respect of the intra-Community acquisition of a qualifying vehicle may, in lieu of claiming repayment under subparagraph (1), elect to deduct the tax chargeable in respect of that acquisition in the return which such person is obliged to furnish, concerning that acquisition, in accordance with section 19(3) (inserted by section 84 of the Finance Act, 1983 (No 15 of 1983)) of the Act.

(3) The provisions of this paragraph shall apply only where—

    (*a*)   the supply, hire, lease, intra-Community acquisition or importation, as the case may be, referred to in subparagraph (1) or (2) occured on or after the date specified in paragraph 1(2), and

    (*b*)   the qualifying person is not entitled to a deduction or repayment—

        (i)   by any other provision of the Act or regulations made thereunder, or

        (ii)   under any other enactment administered by the Revenue Commissioners,

of any portion of the tax paid or payable in respect of the qualifying vehicle.

4. The conditions to be fulfilled by a person in order to obtain a repayment of tax under this Order in accordance with subparagraph (1) of paragraph 3 are that the person shall:

    (*a*)   complete such form as is provided for that purpose by the Revenue Commissioners, and shall certify the particulars shown on such form to be correct;

    (*b*)   establish to the satisfaction of the Revenue Commissioners that that person is a qualifying person;

    (*c*)   produce—

        (i)   in the case of a supply to that person of a qualifying vehicle, an invoice, issued to that person in accordance with section 17(12)(*a*)(i) (amended by section 30(2) of, and the Second Schedule to, the Value Added Tax (Amendment) Act, 1978 (No 34 of 1978)) of the Act, establishing the amount of tax borne by that person on that supply,

        (ii)   in the case of the hire or lease of a qualifying vehicle, a copy of the hiring agreement or leasing agreement, as may be appropriate, and, in respect of each repayment claim, an invoice, issued to that person in accordance with the said section 17(12)(*a*)(i) establishing the amount of tax borne by that person,

        (iii)   in the case of an intra-Community acquisition of a qualifying vehicle, an official receipt or other document establishing the amount of tax paid by that person in respect of the intra-Community acquisition, together with the invoice issued to that person by the supplier in the Member State of supply, or

        (iv)   in the case of an importation of a qualifying vehicle, an official receipt or other document establishing the amount of tax paid by that person on the importation and indicating the number of the relevant customs entry.

5. This Order shall not apply to vehicles used or intended to be used primarily for the provision of public transport services.

6. The Value Added Tax (Refund of Tax) (No 26) Order, 1994 (SI No 165 of 1994) is hereby revoked.

EUROPEAN UNION DIRECTIVES

The Sixth Council Directive (77/388/EEC) is the cornerstone of the harmonised system of VAT in that it introduced a common system of VAT with a uniform basis in the European Community.

It has been interpreted many times and many of these interpretations have been formulated into other Directives and Regulations (many of these are referred to in the next section of this book). It has been directly amended by the directives listed below. These amendments have been incorporated into the Sixth Directive which is reproduced in this section.

Amending directives and directives that are no longer valid are shown in *italic*.

FIRST COUNCIL DIRECTIVE

of 11 April 1967

67/227/EEC

on the harmonisation of legislation of Member States concerning turnover taxes
(OJ L71, 14.4.1967, p 1301)

THE COUNCIL OF THE EUROPEAN ECONOMIC COMMUNITY,

Having regard to the Treaty establishing the European Economic Community, and in particular Articles 99 and 100 thereof;

Having regard to the proposal from the Commission;

Having regard to the Opinion of the European Parliament;

Having regard to the Opinion of the Economic and Social Committee;

Whereas the main objective of the Treaty is to establish, within the framework of an economic union, a common market within which there is healthy competition and whose characteristics are similar to those of a domestic market;

Whereas the attainment of this objective presupposes the prior application in Member States of legislation concerning turnover taxes such as will not distort conditions of competition or hinder the free movement of goods and services within the common market;

Whereas the legislation at present in force does not meet these requirements; whereas it is therefore in the interest of the common market to achieve such harmonisation of legislation concerning turnover taxes as will eliminate, as far as possible, factors which may distort conditions of competition, whether at national or Community level, and make it possible subsequently to achieve the aim of abolishing the imposition of tax on importation and the remission of tax on exportation in trade between Member States;

Whereas, in the light of the studies made, it has become clear that such harmonisation must result in the abolition of cumulative multi-stage taxes and in the adoption by all Member States of a common system of value added tax;

Whereas a system of value added tax achieves the highest degree of simplicity and of neutrality when the tax is levied in as general a manner as possible and when its scope covers all stages of production and distribution and the provision of services; whereas it is therefore in the interest of the common market and of Member States to adopt a common system which shall also apply to the retail trade;

Whereas, however, the application of that tax to retail trade might in some Member States meet with practical and political difficulties; whereas, therefore, Member States should be permitted, subject to prior consultation, to apply the common system only up to and including the wholesale trade stage, and to apply, as appropriate, a separate complementary tax at the retail trade stage, or at the preceding stage;

Whereas it is necessary to proceed by stages, since the harmonisation of turnover taxes will lead in Member States to substantial alterations in tax structure and will have appreciable consequences in the budgetary, economic and social fields;

Whereas the replacement of the cumulative multi-stage tax systems in force in the majority of Member States by the common system of value added tax is bound, even if the rates and exemptions are not harmonised at the same time, to result in neutrality in competition, in that within each country similar goods bear the same tax burden, whatever the length of the production and distribution chain, and that in international trade the amount of the tax burden borne by goods is known so that an exact equalisation of that amount may be ensured; whereas, therefore, provision should be made, in the first stage, for adoption by all Member States of the common system of value added tax, without an accompanying harmonisation of rates and exemptions;

Whereas it is not possible to foresee at present how and within what period the harmonisation of turnover taxes can achieve the aim of abolishing the imposition of tax on importation and the remission of tax on exportation in trade between Member States; whereas it is therefore preferable that the second stage and the measures to be taken in respect of that stage should be determined later on the basis of proposals made by the Commission to the Council;

Has adopted this Directive

Article 1

Member States shall replace their present system of turnover taxes by the common system of value added tax defined in Article 2.

In each Member State the legislation to effect this replacement shall be enacted as rapidly as possible, so that it can enter into force on a date to be fixed by the Member State in the light of the conjunctural situation; this date shall not be later than [1 January 1972][1].

From the entry into force of such legislation, the Member State shall not maintain or introduce any measure providing for flat-rate equalisation of turnover taxes on importation or exportation in trade between Member States.

Amendments
1 "1 January 1972" substituted for the date "1 January 1970" by Council Directive 69/463/EEC (Third Directive) art 1; see OJ L320, 20.12.1969, p 34.

Article 2

The principle of the common system of value added tax involves the application to goods and services of a general tax on consumption exactly proportional to the price of the goods and services, whatever the number of transactions which take place in the production and distribution process before the stage at which tax is charged.

On each transaction, value added tax, calculated on the price of the goods or services at the rate applicable to such goods or services, shall be chargeable after deduction of the amount of value added tax borne directly by the various cost components.

The common system of value added tax shall be applied up to and including the retail trade stage.

...[1]

Amendments
1 repealed by Council Directive 77/388/EEC (Sixth Directive of 17 May 1977) art 36; see OJ L145, 13.6 1977, p 1, previously it read—
"However, until the abolition of the imposition of tax on importation and the remission of tax on exportation in trade between Member States, Member States may, subject to the consultation provided for in Article 5, apply this system only up to and including the wholesale trade stage, and may apply, as appropriate, a separate complementary tax at the retail trade stage or at the preceding stage."
Case law
Where a farmer received compensation for discontinuing milk production, there was no "consumption" within the meaning of art 2, and therefore no supply of services: *Mohr v Finamzant Bad Segeberg*, ECJ 215/94, [1996] STC 328.

Article 3

The Council shall issue, on a proposal from the Commission, a second Directive concerning the structure of, and the procedure for applying, the common system of value added tax.

Cross references
See Council Directive 67/228/EEC (Second Directive), OJ L71, 14.4.1967, p 1303. This directive ceases to apply in member states in accordance with art 37 of Council Directive 77/388/EEC (Sixth Directive), OJ L145, 13.6.1977, p 1.

Article 4

In order to enable the Council to discuss this, and if possible to take decisions before the end of the transitional period, the Commission shall submit to the Council, before the end of 1968, proposals as to how and within what period the harmonisation of turnover taxes can achieve the aim of abolishing the imposition of tax on importation and the remission of tax on exportation in trade between Member States, while ensuring the neutrality of those taxes as regards the origin of the goods or services.

In this connection, particular account shall be taken of the relationship between direct and indirect taxes, which differs in the various Member States; of the effects of an alteration in tax systems on the tax and budget policy of Member States; and of the influence which tax systems have on conditions of competition and on social conditions in the Community.

Article 5

Amendments
Article 5 repealed by Council Directive 77/388/EEC (Sixth Directive) art 36; see OJ L145, 13.6.1977, p 1, previously it read—
"Article 5
Should a Member State intend to exercise the power provided for in the last paragraph of Article 2, it shall so inform the Commission in good time, having regard to Article 102 of the Treaty."

Article 6

This Directive is addressed to the Member States.

SIXTH COUNCIL DIRECTIVE

of 17 May 1977

77/388/EEC

(OJ L145, 13.6.1977, p 1)

On the harmonization of the laws of the Member States relating to turnover taxes
— Common system of value added tax: uniform basis of assessment

THE COUNCIL OF THE EUROPEAN COMMUNITIES,

Having regard to the Treaty establishing the European Economic Community, and in particular Articles 99 and 100 thereof,

Having regard to the proposal from the Commission,

Having regard to the opinion of the European Parliament, (OJ C40, 8.4.74, p 25)

Having regard to the opinion of the Economic and Social Committee, (OJ C 139, 12.11.74, p 15)

Whereas all Member States have adopted a system of value added tax in accordance with the first and second Council Directives of 11 April 1967 on the harmonization of the laws of the Member States relating to turnover taxes, (OJ 71, 14.4.67, pp 1301-1367)

Whereas the Decision of 21 April 1970 on the replacement of financial contributions from Member States by the Communities' own resources (OJ L94, 28.4.70, p 19) provides that the budget of the Communities shall, irrespective of other revenue, be financed entirely from the Communities' own resources; whereas these resources are to include those accruing from value added tax and obtained by applying a common rate of tax on a basis of assessment determined in a uniform manner according to Community rules;

Whereas further progress should be made in the effective removal of restrictions on the movement of persons, goods, services and capital and the integration of national economies;

Whereas account should be taken of the objective of abolishing the imposition of tax on the importation and the remission of tax on exportation in trade between Member States; whereas it should be ensured that the common system of turnover taxes is non-discriminatory as regards the origin of goods and services, so that a common market permitting fair competition and resembling a real internal market may ultimately be achieved;

Whereas, to enhance the non-discriminatory nature of the tax, the term "taxable person" must be clarified to enable the Member States to extend it to cover persons who occasionally carry out certain transactions;

Whereas the term "taxable transaction" has led to difficulties, in particular as regards transactions treated as taxable transactions; whereas these concepts must be clarified;

Whereas the determination of the place where taxable transactions are effected has been the subject of conflicts concerning jurisdiction as between Member States, in particular as regards supplies of goods for assembly and the supply of services; whereas although the place where a supply of services is effected should in principle be defined as the place where the person supplying the services has his principal place of business, that place should be defined as being in the country of the person to whom the services are supplied, in particular in the case of certain services supplied between taxable persons where the cost of the services is included in the price of the goods;

Whereas the concepts of chargeable event and of the charge to tax must be harmonized if the introduction and any subsequent alterations of the Community rate are to become operative at the same time in all Member States;

Whereas the taxable base must be harmonized so that the application of the Community rate to taxable transactions leads to comparable results in all the Member States;

Whereas the rates applied by Member States must be such as to allow the normal deduction of the tax applied at the preceding stage;

Whereas a common list of exemptions should be drawn up so that the Communities' own resources may be collected in a uniform manner in all the Member States;

Whereas the rules governing deductions should be harmonized to the extent that they affect the actual amounts collected; whereas the deductible proportion should be calculated in a similar manner in all the Member States;

Whereas it should be specified which persons are liable to pay tax, in particular as regards services supplied by a person established in another country;

Whereas the obligations of taxpayers must be harmonized as far as possible so as to ensure the necessary safeguards for the collection of taxes in a uniform manner in all the Member States; whereas taxpayers should, in particular, make a periodic aggregate return of their transactions, relating to both inputs and outputs where this appears necessary for establishing and monitoring the basis of assessment of own resources;

Whereas Member States should nevertheless be able to retain their special schemes for small undertakings, in accordance with common provisions, and with a view to closer harmonization; whereas Member States should remain free to apply a special scheme involving flat rate rebates of input value added tax to farmers not covered by normal schemes; whereas the basic principles of this scheme should be established and a common method adopted for calculating the value added of these farmers for the purposes of collecting own resources;

Whereas the uniform application of the provisions of this Directive should be ensured; whereas to this end a Community procedure for consultation should be laid down; whereas the setting up of a Value Added Tax Committee would enable the Member States and the Commission to cooperate closely;

Whereas Member States should be able, within certain limits and subject to certain conditions, to take or retain special measures derogating from this Directive in order to simplify the levying of tax or to avoid fraud or tax avoidance;

Whereas it might appear appropriate to authorize Member States to conclude with non-member countries or international organizations agreements containing derogations from this Directive;

Whereas it is vital to provide for a transitional period to allow national laws in specified fields to be gradually adapted,

HAS ADOPTED THIS DIRECTIVE:

TITLE I
Introductory provisions

Article 1

Member States shall modify their present value added tax systems in accordance with the following Articles.

They shall adopt the necessary laws, regulations and administrative provisions so that the systems as modified enter into force at the earliest opportunity and by 1 January 1978 at the latest.

TITLE II
Scope

Article 2

The following shall be subject to value added tax:

1. the supply of goods or services effected for consideration within the territory of the country by a taxable person acting as such;   s 2(1)(*a*)

2. the importation of goods.   s 2(1)(*b*)

Cross-references
Intra-Community acquisition of goods and new means of transport: art 28a.

Case law
Busking, non-quantifiable amounts of voluntary donations, not a supply of services effected for consideration: *Tolsma v Inspecteur der Omzetbelasting Leeuwarden* [1994]STI 324, ECJ 16/93.
Greek arrangements whereby petrol was charged to VAT once only on importation (and not along the supply chain) were held to be in breach of art 2: *BP Soupergas Aronimos Etairia Geniki Emporiki Viomichaniki kai Antiprossopeion v Greece* [1995] STC 805, ECJ 62/93.
Person who habitually supplies free services not taxable: *Staatssecretaris van Financiën v Hong Kong Trade Development Council* [1982]ECR 1277, [1983]1 CMLR 73, ECJ 89/81.
Services for which no definite subjective consideration received not taxable: *Staatssecretaris van Financiën v Cooperatieve Aardappelen Bewaarplaats GA* ECJ 154/80.
No rule requiring Member States to tax transport services beyond the territorial limits in international waters: *EC Commission v France* [1991]STI 455, ECJ 30/89.
Illegal activities
No VAT liability on illegal supplies of drugs: *Mol v Inspecteur der Invoerrechten en Accijnzen*; ECJ 269/86; *Vereniging Happy Family v Inspecteur der Omzetbelasting* [1989]3 CMLR 729, ECJ 289/86.
No VAT liability on illegal imports of drugs: *Einberger v Hauptzollamt Freiburg (No 2)* [1984]ECR 1177, (1985) 1 CMLR 765, ECJ 294/82.
No VAT liability on illegal import of counterfeit money: *Witzemann v Hauptzollamt Munchen-Mitte* [1991]STI 60, ECJ 343/89.
By exempting certain professional services, Spain had not complied with art 2: *EC Commission v Spain* (1991) OJ C297/07, ECJ 35/90.

TITLE III
Territorial application

[*Article 3*

1. For the purposes of this Directive,   s 1(2A)

— **"territory of a Member State"** shall mean the territory of the country as defined in respect of each Member State in paragraphs 2 and 3,

— **"Community"** and **"territory of the Community"** shall mean the territory of the Member States as defined in respect of each Member State in paragraphs 2 and 3,

— **"third territory"** and **"third country"** shall mean any territory other than those defined in paragraphs 2 and 3 as the territory of a Member State.

2. For the purposes of this Directive, the **"territory of the country"** shall be the area of application of the Treaty establishing the European Economic Community as defined in respect of each Member State in Article 227.

3. The following territories of individual Member States shall be excluded from the territory of the country: s 1(3)

— Federal Republic of Germany: s 1(4)

the Island of Heligoland,

the territory of Büsingen,

Kingdom of Spain:

Ceuta,

Melilla,

— Republic of Italy:

Livigno,

Campione d'Italia,

the Italian waters of Lake Lugano.

The following territories of individual Member States shall also be excluded from the territory of the country:

— Kingdom of Spain:

the Canary Islands,

— French Republic:

the overseas departments,

— Hellenic Republic

Αγιο Ορος

[**4.** By way of derogation from paragraph 1, in view of the conventions and treaties which they have concluded respectively with the French Republic and the United Kingdom of Great Britain and Northern Ireland, the Principality of Monaco and the Isle of Man shall not be treated for the purposes of the application of this Directive as third territories.

Member States shall take the measures necessary to ensure that transactions originating in or intended for:

— the Principality of Monaco are treated as transactions originating in or intended for the French Republic,

— the Isle of Man are treated as transactions originating in or intended for the United Kingdom of Great Britain and Northern Ireland.][1]

5. If the Commission considers that the provisions laid down in paragraphs 3 and 4 are no longer justified, particularly in terms of fair competition or own resources, it shall submit appropriate proposals to the Council.][2]

Amendments

1 Para (4) substituted by Council Directive 92/111/EEC of 14 December 1992 art 1(1).

2 Art 3 substituted by Council Directive 91/680/EEC of 16 December 1991, art 1(1) with effect from 1 January 1993.

Case law

Transport via international waters from a point in an EC State to a point in the same EC State taxable: *Trans Tirreno Express SpA v Ufficio Provinciale IVA, Sassari* [1986]2 CMLR 100, ECJ 283/84.

Services supplied on board ships over which a member state has jurisdiction taxable even if outside the member State's territorial jurisdiction: *Berkholz v Finanzampt Hamburg-Mitte-Altstadt* [1985]3 CMLR 667, ECJ 168/84.

TITLE IV
Taxable persons

Article 4

_{s 4} **1.** "**Taxable person**" shall mean any person who independently carries out in any place any economic activity specified in paragraph 2, whatever the purpose or results of that activity.

2. The economic activities referred to in paragraph 1 shall comprise all activities of producers, traders and persons supplying services including mining and agricultural activities and activities of the professions. The exploitation of tangible or intangible property for the purpose of obtaining income therefrom on a continuing basis shall also be considered an economic activity.

_{ss 1(1),3(7)} **3.** Member States may also treat as a taxable person anyone who carries out, on an occasional basis, a transaction relating to the activities referred to in paragraph 2 and in particular one of the following:

(*a*) the supply before first occupation of buildings or parts of buildings and the land on which they stand; Member States may determine the conditions of application of this criterion to transformations of buildings and the land on which they stand.

Member States may apply criteria other than that of first occupation, such as the period elapsing between the date of completion of the building and the date of first supply or the period elapsing between the date of first occupation and the date of subsequent supply, provided that these periods do not exceed five years and two years respectively.

"A building" shall be taken to mean any structure fixed to or in the ground;

(b) the supply of building land.

"Building land" shall mean any unimproved or improved land defined as such by the Member States.

4. The use of the word "independently" in paragraph 1 shall exclude employed and other persons from the tax in so far as they are bound to an employer by a contract of employment or by any other legal ties creating the relationship of employer and employee as regards working conditions, remuneration and the employer's liability.

s 8(1), (1A),(8)

Subject to the consultations provided for in Article 29, each Member State may treat as a single taxable person persons established in the territory of the country who, while legally independent, are closely bound to one another by financial, economic and organizational links.

s 8(3)(e), (proviso),((3B)

5. States, regional and local government authorities and other bodies governed by public law shall not be considered taxable persons in respect of the activities or transactions in which they engage as public authorities, even where they collect dues, fees, contributions or payments in connection with these activities or transactions.

s 8(2A) VATR 1979 r 5

However, when they engage in such activities or transactions, they shall be considered taxable persons in respect of these activities or transactions where treatment as non-taxable persons would lead to significant distortions of competition.

In any case, these bodies shall be considered taxable persons in relation to the activities listed in Annex D, provided they are not carried out on such a small scale as to be negligible.

Member States may consider activities of these bodies which are exempt under Article 13 or 28 as activities which they engage in as public authorities.

Cross-references
Person who from time to time supplies a new means of transport: art 28a(4).
Case law
"Building land" includes both prepared and unpreparted sites, and land which is officially designated for building, or for which permission to build has been granted (Advocate General).
"Economic activity" (feasibility study): *Intercommunale voor Zeewaterontzilting v Belgian State*, ECJ 110/94.
Interpretation: *Hamann v Finanzamt Hamburg-Eimsbüttel* [1991]STC 193, [1990]2 CMLR 383, ECJ 51/88; see also ECJ 283/81.
Additional taxation on buildings or building land: *Kerrutt v Finanzamt Mönchengladback-Mitte* [1987]2 CMLR 221, ECJ 73/85.
Interaction of art 4(1) and art 17 (deduction): *Re VAT on leased buildings, EC Commission v France*, [1989]1 CMLR 505, ECJ 50/87.
Taxable persons
Independent third party tax collectors: *Ayuntamiento de Sevilla v Recaudadores de las Zonas Primera y Segunda* [1991]OJ C220/10 ECJ 202/90.
Intending trader: *Rompelman and Rompelman-Van Deelen v Minister van Financiën* ECJ 268/83.
Notaries and bailiffs: *Re notaries and bailiffs: EC Commission v Netherlands* [1988]2 CMLR 921, ECJ 235/85.
Not taxable persons
Person supplying services against a statutory charge: *Apple and Pear Development Council v C & E Commissioners* [1988]STC 221, [1988]2 CMLR 394, [1988]2 All ER 922, ECJ 102/86.
Person habitually supplying free services: *Staatssecretaris van Financiën v Hong Kong Trade Development Council* [1982]ECR 1277, [1983]1 CMLR 73, ECJ 89/81.
Public authorities: *Ufficio Distrettuale delle Imposte Dirette di Fiorenzuola d'Arda v Comune di Carpaneto Piacentino,*[1990]3 CLMR 153, ECJ 4/89; *Ufficio Provinciale Imposta sui Valore Aggiunto di Piacenza v Comune di Rivergaro* [1990]STC 205, ECJ 231/87 and 129/88.
Holding companies: *Polysar Investments Netherlands BV v Inspecteur der Invoerrechten en Accijnzen* [1991]STI 638, ECJ 60/90.

TITLE V
Taxable transactions

Article 5

Supply of goods

1. "Supply of goods" shall mean the transfer of the right to dispose of tangible property as owner.

2. Electric current, gas, heat, refrigeration and the like shall be considered tangible property.

3. Member States may consider the following to be tangible property:

    (*a*)   certain interest in immovable property;

    (*b*)   rights *in rem* giving the holder thereof a right of user over immovable property;

    (*c*)   shares or interests equivalent to shares giving the holder thereof *de jure* or *de facto* rights of ownership or possession over immovable property or part thereof.

4. The following shall also be considered supplies within the meaning of paragraph 1:

    (*a*)   the transfer, by order made by or in the name of a public authority or in pursuance of the law, of the ownership of property against payment of compensation;

    (*b*)   the actual handing over of goods, pursuant to a contract for the hire of goods for a certain period or for the sale of goods on deferred terms, which provides that in the normal course of events ownership shall pass at the latest upon payment of the final instalment;

    (*c*)   the transfer of goods pursuant to a contract under which commission is payable on purchase or sale.

[**5.** Member States may consider the handing over of certain works of construction to be supplies with the meaning of paragraph 1.][1]

6. The application by a taxable person of goods forming part of his business assets for his private use or that of his staff, or the disposal thereof free of charge or more generally their application for purposes other than those of his business, where the value added tax on the goods in question or the component parts thereof was wholly or partly deductible, shall be treated as supplies made for consideration. However, applications for the giving of samples or the making of gifts of small value for the purposes of the taxable person's business shall not be so treated.

7. Member States may treat as supplies made for consideration:

    (*a*)   the application by a taxable person for the purposes of his business of goods produced, constructed, extracted, processed, purchased or imported in the course of such business, where the value added tax on such goods, had they been acquired from another taxable person, would not be wholly deductible;

    (*b*)   the application of goods by a taxable person for the purposes of a non-taxable transaction, where the value added tax on such goods became wholly or partly deductible upon their acquisition or upon their application in accordance with subparagraph (*a*);

    (*c*)   except in those cases mentioned in paragraph 8, the retention of goods by a taxable person or his successors when he ceases to carry out a taxable economic activity where the value added tax on such goods became wholly or partly deductible upon their acquisition or upon their application in accordance with subparagraph (*a*).

8. In the event of a transfer, whether for consideration or not or as a contribution to a company, of a totality of assets or part thereof, Member States may consider that no supply of goods has taken place and in that event the recipient shall be treated as the successor to the transferor. Where appropriate, Member States may take the necessary measures to prevent distortion of competition in cases where the recipient is not wholly liable to tax.

ss 3(1),(5)(*b*)(iii), 5(8)

Amendments
1   Substituted by Council Directive 95/7/EC of 10 April 1995 art 1(1) with effect from 1 January 1996.
Cross-references
Delivery to another taxable person of contract work, and transfer by a taxable person of goods from his undertaking to another member state, regarded as supplies of goods effected for consideration: art 28a(5).
Case law
Para (1): "capital goods", meaning: *Verbond van Nederlandse Ondernemingen v Inspecteur der Invoerrechten en Accijnzen* [1977]ECR 113, [1977]1 CMLR 413, ECJ 51/76.
Para (3)(*b*): Supply of goods not limited to legal transfer of property: *Staatssecretaris van Financiën v Shipping and Forwarding Enterprise Safe BV* [1991]STC 627, ECJ 320/88.
"Exploitation", meaning. Rights in rem tangible property: *W M van Tiem v Staatssecretaris van Financiën* [1991]STI 59, ECJ 186/89.
Para (5)(*a*): "made" and "repair": production of goods from customer's materials, a new article is made when its has a different function from the materials provided: *Van Dijk's Boekhuis BV v Staatssecretaris van Financiën* [1986]2 CMLR 575, ECJ 139/84.
Para (6): A builder (taxable person) who acquired land for his own use and built a house on it only taxable as regards the houses: *P de Jong v Staatssecretaris van Financiën* (1992) OJ C135/p 15 ECJ 20/91; no VAT arises on disposal of asset where deduction not allowed: *H Kühne v Finanzamt München III* [1990]STC 749, [1990]3 CMLR 287, ECJ 50/88.
Taxpayer not a taxable person with regard to sale of private dwelling where it was sold together with business premises: *Finanzamt Uelzen v Armbrecht* [1995] STC 997, ECJ.
Transfer of an undertaking, meaning: *Spijkers (Josef Maria Antonius) v Gebroeders Benedik Abbatoir CV and Alfred Benedik en Zonen BV* ECJ 24/85; *Dr Sophie Redmond Stichting [Foundation]vHendrikus Bartol and others* ECJ 29/91.
Part of a business, meaning: *Commerz-Credit-Bank AG -Europartner v Finamzamt Saarbrücken*ECJ 50/91.

Article 6
Supply of services

1. **"Supply of services"** shall mean any transaction which does not constitute a supply of goods within the meaning of Article 5.

s 5(1)
VATR 1979 r 24

Such transactions may include *inter alia*:

—   assignments of intangible property whether or not it is the subject of a document establishing title,

—   obligations to refrain from an act or to tolerate an act or situation,

—   the performance of services in pursuance of an order made by or in the name of a public authority or in pursuance of the law.

2. The following shall be treated as supplies of services for consideration:

a 5(2), (3)

(*a*)   the use of goods forming part of the assets of a business for the private use of the taxable person or of his staff or more generally for purposes other than those of his business where the value added tax on such goods is wholly or partly deductible;

(*b*)   supplies of services carried out free of charge by the taxable person for his own private use or that of his staff or more generally for purposes other than those of his business.

Member States may derogate from the provisions of this paragraph provided that such derogation does not lead to distortion of competition.

3. In order to prevent distortion of competition and subject to the consultations provided for in Article 29, Member States may treat as a supply of services for consideration the supply by a taxable person of a service for the purposes of his undertaking where the value added tax on such a service, had it been supplied by another taxable person, would not be wholly deductible.

s 5(3)

4. Where a taxable person acting in his own name but on behalf of another takes part in a supply of services, he shall be considered to have received and supplied those services himself.

s 5(4)

5. Article 5(8) shall apply in like manner to the supply of services.

s 5(8)

Case law

Para (1): Where a farmer received compensation for discontinuing milk production, there was no "consumption" within the meaning of article 2 of the First Directive, and therefore no supply of services: *Mohr v Finamzamt Bad Segeberg*, ECJ 215/94, [1996] STC 328.

Para (2): transport company providing transport service and cash collection service, collection charge was regarded as inseparable from and ancillary to the transport service: *NV Nederlandse Spoorwegen v Staatssecretaris van Financiën* [1979] ECR 2041, [1980]1 CMLR 144, ECJ 126/78.

Self-supply, Private use of business-owned car, whether associated expenses part of taxable amount: *Finamzämt München v Mohsche* [1993]STI 945, ECJ 193/91.

Production of goods from customer's materials, a new article is made when its has a different function from the materials provided: *Van Dijk's Boekhuis BV v Staatssecretaris van Financiën* [1986]2 CMLR 575, ECJ 139/84.

[Article 7
Imports

s 15

1. "Importation of goods" shall mean:

    (*a*)   the entry into the Community of goods which do not fulfil the conditions laid down in Articles 9 and 10 of the Treaty establishing the European Economic Community or, where the goods are covered by the Treaty establishing the European Coal and Steel Community, are not in free circulation;

    [(*b*)   the entry into the Community of goods from a third territory, other than the goods covered by (*a*).][1]

2. The place of import of goods shall be the Member State within the territory of which the goods are when they enter the Community.

3. Notwithstanding paragraph 2, where goods referred to in paragraph 1(*a*) are, on entry into the Community, placed under one of the arrangements referred to in Article 16(1)(B)[(*a*), (*b*), (*c*) and (*d*)],[2] under arrangements for temporary importation with total exemption from import duty or under external transit arrangements, the place of import of such goods shall be the Member State within the territory of which they cease to be covered by those arrangements.

[Similarly, when goods referred to in paragraph 1(*b*) are placed, on entry into the Community, under one of the procedures referred to in Article 33a(1)(*b*) or (*c*), the place of import shall be the Member State within whose territory this procedure ceases to apply.][3]][4]

Amendments

1 Para (1)(*b*) substituted by Council Directive 92/111/EEC of 14 December 1992 art 1(3), with effect from 1 January 1993.
2 Added by Council Directive of 14 December 1992 art 1(2), with effect from 1 January 1993.
3 Substituted by Council Directive of 14 December 1992 art 1(1), with effect from 1 January 1993.
4 Art 7 substituted by Council Directive 91/680/EEC of 18 December 1991 art 1(2), with effect from 1 January 1993.

TITLE VI
Place of taxable transactions

Article 8
Supply of goods

s 3(6)(*b*)

1. The place of supply of goods shall be deemed to be:

    (*a*)   in the case of goods dispatched or transported either by the supplier or by the person to whom they are supplied or by a third person: the place where the goods are at the time when dispatch or transport to the person to whom they are supplied begins. Where the goods are installed or assembled, with or without a trial run, by or on behalf of the supplier, the place of supply shall be deemed to be the place where the goods are installed or assembled. In cases where the installation or assembly is carried out [in a Member State other than][1] that of the supplier, [the Member State within the territory of which the installation or assembly is carried out][2] shall take any necessary steps to avoid double taxation in that State;

    (*b*)   in the case of goods not dispatched or transported: the place where the goods are when the supply takes place.

[(*c*) in the case of goods supplied on board ships, aircraft or trains during the part of a transport of passengers effected in the Community: at the point of the departure of the transport of passengers.

For the purposes of applying this provision:

— **"part of a transport of passengers effected in the Community"** shall mean the part of the transport effected, without a stop in a third territory, between the point of departure and the point of arrival of the transport of passengers,

— **"the point of departure of the transport of passengers"** shall mean the first point of passenger embarkation foreseen within the Community, where relevant after a leg outside the Community,

— **"the point of arrival of the transport of passengers"** shall mean the last point of disembarkation of passengers foreseen within the Community of passengers who embarked in the Community, where relevant before a leg outside the Community.

In the case of a return trip, the return leg shall be considered to be a separate transport.

The Commission shall, by 30 June 1993 at the latest, submit to the Council a report accompanied, if necessary, by appropriate proposals on the place of taxation of goods supplied for consumption and services, including restaurant services, provided for passengers on board ships, aircraft or trains.

By 31 December 1993, after consulting the European Parliament, the Council shall take a unanimous decision on the Commission proposal.

Until 31 December 1993, Member States may exempt or continue to exempt goods supplied for consumption on board whose place of taxation is determined in accordance with the above provisions, with the right to deduct the value added tax paid at an earlier stage.]³

[**2.** By way of derogation from paragraph 1(*a*), where the place of departure of the consignment or transport of goods is in a third territory, the place of supply by the importer as defined in Article 21(2) and the place of any subsequent supplies shall be deemed to be within the Member State of import of the goods.]⁴

Amendments
1 Substituted by Council Directive 91/680/EEC of 16 December 1991, art 1(3) with effect from 1 January 1993.
2 Substituted by Council Directive 91/680/EEC of 16 December 1991, art 1(5) with effect from 1 January 1993.
3 Para (1)(*c*) substituted by Council Directive 92/111/EEC of 14 December 1992 art 1(4) with effect from 1 January 1993.
4 Para (2) substituted by Council Directive 91/680/EEC of 16 December 1991, art1(5), with effect from 1 January 1993.
Cross-references
Derogation from art 8(1)(*a*) and (2): art 28b(B).

Article 9
ss 1(1),5(4)
Supply of services

1. The place where a service is supplied shall be deemed to be the place where the supplier has established his business or has a fixed establishment from which the service is supplied or, in the absence of such a place of business or fixed establishment, the place where he has his permanent address or usually resides.

2. However:

(*a*) the place of the supply of services connected with immovable property, including the services of estate agents and experts, and of services for preparing and coordinating construction works, such as the services of architects and of firms providing on-site supervision, shall be the place where the property is situated;
s 5(6)(*a*)

s 5(6)(*b*)

(*b*)   the place where transport services are supplied shall be the place where transport takes place, having regard to the distances covered;

(*c*)   the place of the supply of services relating to:

s 5(6)(*c*)(i), (ii)

—   cultural, artistic, sporting, scientific, educational, entertainment or similar activities, including the activities of the organizers of such activities, and where appropriate, the supply of ancillary services,

s 5(6)(*c*)(iii), (iv)

—   ancillary transport activities such as loading, unloading, handling and similar activities,

—   valuations of movable tangible property,

—   work on movable tangible property,

shall be the place where those services are physically carried out;

(*d*)   ...[1]

s 5(6)(*e*),(*f*), (*g*),(*h*)

(*e*)   the place where the following services are supplied when performed for customers established outside the Community or for taxable persons established in the Community but not in the same country as the supplier, shall be the place where the customer has established his business or has a fixed establishment to which the service is supplied or, in the absence of such a place, the place where he has his permanent address or usually resides:

Sch 4(i)-(v), (vii)

—   transfers and assignments of copyrights, patents, licences, trade marks and similar rights,

—   advertising services,

s 5(6), Sch 4

—   services of consultants, engineers, consultancy bureaux, lawyers, accountants and other similar services, as well as data processing and the supplying of information,

—   obligations to refrain from pursuing or exercising, in whole or in part, a business activity or a right referred to in this point (*e*),

—   banking, financial and insurance transactions including reinsurance, with the exception of the hire of safes,

—   the supply of staff,

—   the services of agents who act in the name and for the account of another, when they procure for their principal the services referred to in this point (*e*).

[—   the hiring out of movable tangible property with the exception of all forms of transport].[2]

3. In order to avoid double taxation, non-taxation or the distortion of competition the Member States may, with regard to the supply of services referred to in 2(*e*) [and the hiring out of forms of transport][3] consider:

(*a*)   the place of supply of services, which under this Article would be situated within the territory of the country, as being situated outside the Community where the effective use and enjoyment of the services take place outside the Community;

(*b*)   the place of supply of services, which under this Article would be situated outside the Community, as being within the territory of the country where the effective use and enjoyment of the services take place within the territory of the country.

Amendments

1   Deleted by Council Directive 84/386/EEC (Tenth Directive) of 31 July 1984, art 1 with effect from 1 July 1985.
2   Inserted by Council Directive 84/386/EEC (Tenth Directive) of 31 July 1984, art 1 with effect from 1 July 1985.
3   Substituted by Council Directive 84/386/EEC (Tenth Directive) of 31 July 1984, art 1 with effect from 1 July 1985.

Cross-references
Derogation from art 9(2)(*b*), 9(2)(*c*) and 9(1) respectively: art 28b(C), (D), (E).
Case law
Para (1): Services (gaming machines) supplied on board ships over which a member state has jurisdiction taxable even if outside the member State's territorial jurisdiction; meaning of "fixed establishment": *Berkholz v Finanzampt Hamburg-Mitte-Altstadt* [1985]3 CMLR 667, ECJ 168/84.
Para (2)(*e*): Advertising services, meaning: *EC Commission v France, Luxembourg, Spain*, [1993]STI 1424, ECJ cases 68, 69 and 73/92.

TITLE VII
Chargeable event and chargeability of tax

Article 10

1.   (*a*) **"Chargeable event"** shall mean the occurrence by virtue of which the legal conditions necessary for tax to become chargeable are fulfilled.

       (*b*) The tax becomes **"chargeable"** when the tax authority becomes entitled under the law at a given moment to claim the tax from the person liable to pay, notwithstanding that the time of payment may be deferred.

ss 15,19(1), 19(3)

2. The chargeable event shall occur and the tax shall become chargeable when the goods are delivered or the services are performed. Deliveries of goods other than those referred to in Article 5(4)(*b*) and supplies of services which give rise to successive statements of account or payments shall be regarded as being completed at the time when the periods to which such statements of account or payments pertain expire.

ss 14,19(2)

However, where a payment is to be made on account before the goods are delivered or the services are performed, the tax shall become chargeable on receipt of the payment and on the amount received.

By way of derogation from the above provisions, Member States may provide that the tax shall become chargeable, for certain transactions or for certain categories of taxable person, either:

—   no later than the issue of the invoice or of the document serving as invoice, or

—   no later than receipt of the price, or

—   where an invoice or document serving as invoice is not issued, or is issued late, within a specified period from the date of the chargeable event.

[3. The chargeable event shall occur and the tax shall become chargeable when the goods are imported. Where goods are placed under one of the arrangements referred to in Article 7(3) on entry into the Community, the chargeable event shall occur and the tax shall become chargeable only when the goods cease to be covered by those arrangements.

However, where imported goods are subject to customs duties, to agricultural levies or to charges having equivalent effect established under a common policy, the chargeable event shall occur and the tax shall become chargeable when the chargeable event for those Community duties occurs and those duties become chargeable.

Where imported goods are not subject to any of those Community duties, Member States shall apply the provisions in force governing customs duties as regards the occurrence of the chargeable event and the moment when the tax becomes chargeable.][1]

Amendments
1 Para (3) substituted by Council Directive 91/680/EEC of 16 December 1991, art 1(6) with effect from 1 January 1993.
Case law
Interim payments of VAT required by Italian law precluded by articles 10 and 22(4): *Balocchi v Ministero delle Finanze dello Stato* [1993] STI 1348, ECJ 10/92.
Italian derogation allowed receipt of price to be the chargeable event: *Ufficio IVA di Trapani v Italittica SpA* [1995] STC 1059, ECJ.

Time when service supplied not to be identified with invoice issue date or date payment on account received (if later): *Impresa Construzioni Comm Quirino Mazzalai v Ferrovia del Renon SpA* [1976]ECR 657, 1977 1 CMLR 105, ECJ 111/75.

Stolen goods: *Les Assurances Du Crédit NV v Bowy and Decoopmann* ECJ 205/90.

TITLE VIII
Taxable amount

s 15
VATR 1979 r 19

Article 11

A. Within the territory of the country

s 10(9)(*b*)

1. The taxable amount shall be:

s 10(9)(*a*)

    (*a*)   in respect of supplies of goods and services other than those referred to in (*b*), (*c*) and (*d*) below, everything which constitutes the consideration which has been or is to be obtained by the supplier from the purchaser, the customer or a third party for such supplies including subsidies directly linked to the price of such supplies;

s 10(4)

    (*b*)   in respect of supplies referred to in Article 5(6) and (7), the purchase price of the goods or of similar goods or, in the absence of a purchase price, the cost price, determined at the time of supply;

    (*c*)   in respect of supplies referred to in Article 6(2), the full cost to the taxable person of providing the services;

s 10(1),(10)

    (*d*) in respect of supplies referred to in Article 6(3), the open market value of the services supplied.

"Open market value" of services shall mean the amount which a customer at the marketing stage at which the supply takes place would have to pay to a supplier at arm's length within the territory of the country at the time of the supply under conditions of fair competition to obtain the services in question.

2. The taxable amount shall include:

    (*a*)   taxes, duties, levies and charges, excluding the value added tax itself;

    (*b*)   incidental expenses such as commission, packing, transport and insurance costs charged by the supplier to the purchaser or customer. Expenses covered by a separate agreement may be considered to be incidental expenses by the Member States.

VATR 1979 r 8 **3.** The taxable amount shall not include:

    (*a*)   price reductions by way of discount for early payment;

    (*b*)   price discounts and rebates allowed to the customer and accounted for at the time of the supply;

    (*c*)   the amounts received by a taxable person from his purchaser or customer as repayment for expenses paid out in the name and for the account of the latter and which are entered in his books in a suspense account. The taxable person must furnish proof of the actual amount of this expenditure and may not deduct any tax which may have been charged on these transactions.

[**4.** By way of derogation from paragraphs 1, 2 and 3, Member States which, on 1 January 1993, did not avail themselves of the option provided for in the third subparagraph of Article 12(3)(*a*) may, where they avail themselves of the option provided for in Title B(6), provide that, for the transactions referred to in the second subparagraph of Article 12(3)(*c*), the taxable amount shall be equal to a fraction of the amount determined in accordance with paragraphs 1, 2 and 3.

That fraction shall be determined in such a way that the value added tax thus due is, in any event, equal to at least 5% of the amount determined in accordance with paragraphs 1, 2 and 3.][1]

B. Importation of goods

[**1.** The taxable amount shall be the value for customs purposes, determined in accordance with the Community provisions in force; this shall also apply for the import of goods referred to in Article 7(1)(*b*).][2]

2. ...[3]

[**3.** The taxable amount shall include, insofar as they are not already included:

(*a*)　taxes, duties, levies and other charges due outside the importing Member State and those due by reason of importation, excluding the value added tax to be levied;

(*b*)　incidental expenses, such as commission, packing, transport and insurance costs, incurred up to the first place of destination within the territory of the importing Member State.

　　"First place of destination" shall mean the place mentioned on the consignment note or any other document by means of which the goods are imported into the importing Member State. In the absence of such an indication, the first place of destination shall be taken to be the place of the first transfer of cargo in the importing Member State.

　　[The incidental expenses referred to above shall also be included in the taxable amount where they result from transport to another place of destination within the territory of the Community if that place is known when the chargeable event occurs.][4]][5]

4. The taxable amount shall not include those factors referred to in A(3)(*a*) and (*b*).

5. When goods have been temporarily exported [from the Community][6] and are re-imported after having undergone [outside the Community][7] repair, processing or adaptation, or after having been made up or reworked [outside the Community][7], ...[8], Member States shall take steps to ensure that the treatment of the goods for value added tax purposes is the same as that which would have applied to the goods in question had the above operations been carried out within the territory of the country.

[**6.** By way of derogation from paragraphs 1 to 4, Member States which, on 1 January 1993, did not avail themselves of the option provided for in the third paragraph of Article 12(3)(*a*) may provide that for imports of the works of art, collectors' items and antiques defined in Article 26*a*(A)(*a*), (*b*) and (*c*), the taxable amount shall be equal to a fraction of the amount determined in accordance with paragraphs 1 to 4.

That fraction shall be determined in such a way that the value added tax thus due on the import is, in any event, equal to at least 5% of the amount determined in accordance with paragraphs 1 to 4.][9]

C. Miscellaneous provisions　　　　　　　　　　　　　　　　　s 10(3)(*c*)

1. In the case of cancellation, refusal or total or partial non-payment, or where the price is reduced after the supply takes place, the taxable amount shall be reduced accordingly under conditions which shall be determined by the Member States.

However, in the case of total or partial non-payment, Member States may derogate from this rule.

[**2.** Where information for determining the taxable amount on importation is expressed in a currency other than that of the Member State where assessment takes place, the exchange rate shall be determined in accordance with the Community provisions governing the calculation of the value for customs purposes.

Where information for the determination of the taxable amount of a transaction other than an import transaction is expressed in a currency other than that of the Member State where assessment takes place, the exchange rate applicable shall be the latest selling rate recorded, at the time the tax becomes chargeable, on the most representative exchange market or markets of the Member State concerned, or a rate determined by reference to that or those markets, in accordance with the procedures laid down by that Member State. However, for some of those transactions or for certain categories of taxable person, Member States may continue to apply the exchange rate determined in accordance with the Community provisions in force governing the calculation of the value for customs purposes.][10]

3. As regards returnable packing costs, Member States may:

— either exclude them from the taxable amount and take the necessary measures to see that this amount is adjusted if the packing is not returned,

— or include them in the taxable amount and take the necessary measures to see that this amount is adjusted where the packing is in fact returned.

Amendments

1 Art 11A(4) inserted by Council Directive 94/5/EC of 14 February 1994 art 1(1)(a) with effect from 1 January 1995.

2 Art 11B(1) substituted by Council Directive 92/111/EEC of 14 December 1992, art 1(5) with effect from 1 January 1993.

3 Art 11B(2) deleted by Council Directive 91/680/EEC of 16 December 1991, art 1(7)(2nd indent) with effect from 1 January 1993.

4 Substituted by Council Directive 95/7/EC of 10 April 1995 art 1(2) with effect from 1 January 1996.

5 Art 11B(3) substituted by Council Directive 91/680/EEC of 16 December 1991, art 1(8) with effect from 1 January 1993.

6 Words in Art 11B(5) added by Council Directive 91/680/EEC of 16 December 1991, art 1(9) with effect from 1 January 1993.

7 Substituted by Council Directive 91/680/EEC of 16 December 1991, art 1(9) with effect from 1 January 1993.

8 Deleted by Council Directive 91/680/EEC of 16 December 1991, art 1(a) with effect from 1 January 1993.

9 Art 11B(6) inserted by Council Directive 94/5/EC of 14 February 1994 art 1(1)(b) with effect from 1 January 1995.

10 Art 11C(2) substituted by Council Directive 91/680/EEC of 16 December 1991, art 1(10) with effect from 1 January 1993.

Case law

Credit card transaction, retailer's gross consideration (including credit card commission) is the taxable amount: *Chaussures Bally SA v Ministry of Finance (Belgium)* [1993]STI 944, ECJ 18/92.

Collection of charge for goods by person delivering them: *NV Nederlandse Spoorwegen v Staatssecretaris van Financiën* [1979]ECR 2041, [1980]1 CMLR 144, ECJ 126/78.

Compensation received for discontinuing milk production did not constitute supply of services (art 6(1)) as there was no "consumption" within the meaning of article 2 of the First Directive, and therefore no taxable amount (11A(1)(a)): *Mohr v Finamzamt Bad Segeberg*, ECJ 215/94, [1996] STC 328.

Gaming machine takings, taxable amount: *Glawe Spiel (HJ) und Unterhaltungsgeräte Aufstellungsgesellschaft mbH & Co KG v Finamzamt Hamburg-Barmbek-Uhlenhorst* [1994] STC 543, ECJ 38/93.

Goods supplied free of charge on introduction of new customer, taxable amount: *Empire Stores Ltd v C & E Commissioners* [1994] STC 638, ECJ 33/93.

Greek arrangements whereby petrol was charged to VAT once only on importation (and not along the supply chain) were held to be in breach of art 11A(1), 11B(1) and (2): *BP Soupgas Anonimos Etairia Geniki Emporiki Viomichaniki Kai Antiprossopeion v Greece*, [1995] STC 805, ECJ 62/93.

No subjective consideration for services: *Staatsecretaris van Financiën v Cooperatieve Aardappelen Bewaarplaats GA* ECJ 154/80.

Interest payable prior to the payment of the full price is regarded as part of the consideration; interest payable after the date of the supply constitutes granting of credit and is exempt: *Muys' en De Winter's Bouw-en Aannwmingsbedrijf BV v Staatsecretaris van Financiën* [1993]STI 1367, ECJ 281/91.

Interest (penalty) on late payment of court judgment not taxable: *BAZ Bausystem AG v Finanzamt München für Körperschaften* [1982]ECR 2527, [1982]3 CMLR 688, ECJ 222/81.

Open market value

Art 11A(1): Wholesaler supplying "inducement" goods to retailer: *Naturally Yours Cosmetics Ltd v C & E Commissioners* [1988]STC [1989]CMLR 797, ECJ 230/87.

Art 11A(3)(b): Coupons accepted in part payment, "open market value" includes the difference between normal retail price and actual sum received where retailer receives a coupon given to the customer on previous purchase a normal retail sale price: *Boots Co plc v C & E Commissioners* [1990]STC 387, ECJ 126/88.

Rounding off of amounts due: *'K' Line Air Service Europe BV v Eulaerts NV and Belgian State Taxation* ECJ 131/91.

Pre-single market (residual VAT)

Residual VAT in imported goods: *Bergeres-Becque v Chef de Service Interregional des Douanes* [1986]2 CMLR 143, ECJ 39/85.

Used goods imported from another EC State: *Gaston Schul, Douane Expediteur BV v Inspecteur der Invoerrechten en Accijnzen* [1982]ECR 1409, [1982]3 CMLR 229, ECJ 15/81.

Failure to comply with judgment of the Court: *Re VAT on Motor Cars, EC Commission v Belgium* [1989]2 CMLR 972, ECJ 391/85.

Taxable amount on imported goods purchased from private individual: *Staatsecretaris van Financiën v Gaston Schul Douane Expediteur BV* [1986]1 CMLR 559, ECJ 47/84.

TITLE IX
Rates

Article 12　　　　　　　　　　　　　　　　s 11

1. The rate applicable to taxable transactions shall be that in force at the time of the chargeable event. However:

　(*a*)　in the cases provided for in the second and third subparagraphs of Article 10(2), the rate to be used shall be that in force when the tax becomes chargeable;

　[(*b*)　in the cases provided for in the second and third subparagraphs of Article 10(3), the rate applicable shall be that in force at the time when the tax becomes chargeable.][1]

2. In the event of changes in the rates, Member States may:　　　　art 28.2

—　effect adjustments in the cases provided for in paragraph 1(*a*) in order to take account of the rate applicable at the time when the goods or services were supplied,

—　adopt all appropriate transitional measures.

3.　[(*a*)The standard rate of value added tax shall be fixed by each Member State as a percentage of the taxable amount and shall be the same for the supply of goods and for the supply of services. From 1 January 1993 until 31 December 1996, this percentage may not be less than 15%.

On the basis of the report on the operation of the transitional arrangements and proposals on the definitive arrangements to be submitted by the Commission pursuant to Article 28l, the Council shall decide unanimously before 31 December 1995 on the level of the minimum rate to be applied after 31 December 1996 with regard to the standard rate.

Member States may also apply either one or two reduced rates. These rates shall be fixed as a percentage of the taxable amount which may not be less than 5% and shall apply only to supplies of the categories of goods and services specified in Annex H.][2]

　(*b*)　Member States may apply a reduced rate to supplies of natural gas and electricity provided that no risk of distortion of completion exists. A Member State intending to apply such a rate must, before doing so, inform the Commission. The Commission shall give a decision on the existence of a risk of distortion of competition. If the Commission has not taken that decision within three months of the receipt of the information a risk of distortion of competition is deemed not to exist.

　[(*c*)　Member States may provide that the reduced rate, or one of the reduced rates, which they apply in accordance with the third paragraph of (*a*) shall also apply to imports of works of art, collectors' items and antiques as referred to in Article 26a(A)(*a*), (*b*) and (*c*).

Where they avail themselves of this option, Member States may also apply the reduced rate to supplies of every work of art, within the meaning of Article 26a(A)(*a*):

—　effected by their creator or his successors in title,

—　effected on an occasional basis by a taxable person other than a taxable dealer, where these works of art have been imported by the taxable person himself or where they have been supplied to him by their creator or his successors in title or where they have entitled him to full deduction of value added tax.][3]

　...[4]

Until 31 December 1994, those Member States currently applying a reduced rate may continue to do so; those currently applying a standard rate may not apply a reduced rate. This will allow a two-year postponement of the application of the standard rate.

(*e*)   The rules concerning the regime and the rates applied to gold shall be determined by a directive relating to special arrangements applicable to gold. The Commission shall make such a proposal in time for its adoption by the Council, acting unanimously, before 31 December 1992.

Member States will take all necessary measures to combat fraud in this area from 1 January 1993. These measures may include the introduction of a system of accounting for VAT on supplies of gold between taxable persons in the same Member State which provides for the payment of tax by the buyer on behalf of the seller and a simultaneous right for the buyer to a deduction of the same amount of tax as input tax.][5]

4. ....[6] Each reduced rate shall be so fixed that the amount of value added tax resulting from the application thereof shall be such as in the normal way to permit the deduction therefrom of the whole of the value added tax deductible under the provisions of Article 17.

[On the basis of a report from the Commission, the Council shall starting in 1994, review the scope of the reduced rates every two years. The Council, acting unanimously on a proposal from the Commission, may decide to alter the list of goods and services in Annex H.][7]

[**5.** Subject to paragraph 3(*c*), the rate applicable on the importation of goods shall be that applied to the supply of like goods within the territory of the country.][8]

[**6.** The Portuguese Republic may apply to transactions carried out in the autonomous regions of the Azores and Madeira and to direct imports to those regions, reduced rates in comparison to those applying on the mainland.][9]

Amendments

1   Para (1)(*b*) substituted by Council Directive 92/111/EEC of 14 December 1992, art 1(6) with effect from 1 January 1993.
2   Para (3)(*a*) substituted by Council Directive 92/111/EEC of 14 December 1992, art 1(7) with effect from 1 January 1993.
3   Para (3)(*b*) substituted by Council Directive 94/5/EEC of 14 February 1994, art 1(2)(*a*) with effect from 1 January 1995.
4   Para (3)(*d*) deleted by Council Directive 96/42/EC of 25 June 1996 with effect from 1 January 1995.
5   Para (3) substituted by Council Directive 92/77/EEC of 19 October 1992, art 1(1).
6   Deleted by Council Directive 92/77/EEC of 19 October 1992, art 1(3) with effect from 1 January 1993.
7   Inserted by Council Directive 92/77/EEC of 19 October 1992, art 1(3) with effect from 1 January 1993.
8   Para (5) substituted by Council Directive 94/5/EC of 14 February 1994 art 1(2)(*b*) with effect from 1 January 1995.
9   Para (6) inserted by the Act of Accession 1985 art 26, Annex I, Part V, point 2.

Case law

Production of goods from customer's materials, a new article is made when its has a different function from the materials provided: *Van Dijk's Boekhuis BV v Staatssecretaris van Financiën* [1986]2 CMLR 575, ECJ 139/84.
"Clearly defined social reasons" for zero rating (VAT on electricity supplied to businesses): *EC Commission v Ireland* [1988]3 CMLR 189, ECJ 415/85; see also *EC Commission v United Kingdom* [1988]STC 456, [1989]1 All ER 364, [1988]3 CMLR 169, ECJ 416/85.

Discriminatory tax rates

Imported works of art: *Krystyna Gmurzynska-Bscher v Oberfinanzdirektion Köln* ECJ 231/89.
Differential taxation: *EC Commission v Greece* ECJ cases 278/83 and 200/85.
Differing VAT rates (under Italian law on) different sparkling wines - the classification used was deemed to discriminate against imports: *Re Italian VAT on sparkling wines, EC Commission v Italy* [1985]3 CMLR 688, ECJ 278/83; see also (no discrimination): *Re VAT on Diesel Cars, EC Commission v Italy* [1988]1 CMLR 97, ECJ 200/85.

TITLE X
Exemptions

s 6(1)

Article 13
Exemptions within the territory of the country

A. Exemptions for certain activities in the public interest

1. Without prejudice to other Community provisions, Member States shall exempt the following under conditions which they shall lay down for the purpose of ensuring the correct and straightforward application of such exemptions and of preventing any possible evasion, avoidance or abuse:

(*a*)　the supply by the public postal services of services other than passenger transport and telecommunications services, and the supply of goods incidental thereto;　　Sch 1(xi*a*)

(*b*)　hospital and medical care and closely related activities undertaken by bodies governed by public law or, under social conditions comparable to those applicable to bodies governed by public law, by hospitals, centres for medical treatment or diagnosis and other duly recognized establishments of a similar nature;　　Sch 1(iii)-(iii*b*), (v),(xxv)

(*c*)　the provision of medical care in the exercise of the medical and paramedical professions as defined by the Member State concerned;　　Sch 1(iii)-(iii*b*),(v)

(*d*)　supplies of human organs, blood and milk;　　Sch 1(iii)-(iii*b*), (v),(xviii)

(*e*)　services supplied by dental technicians in their professional capacity and dental prostheses supplied by dentists and dental technicians;　　Sch 1(iii)-(iii*b*),(v)

(*f*)　services supplied by independent groups of persons whose activities are exempt from or are not subject to value added tax, for the purpose of rendering their members the services directly necessary for the exercise of their activity, where these groups merely claim from their members exact reimbursement of their share of the joint expenses, provided that such exemption is not likely to produce distortion of competition;　　Sch 1(xxii*a*)

(*g*)　the supply of services and of goods closely linked to welfare and social security work, including those supplied by old people's homes, by bodies governed by public law or by other organizations recognized as charitable by the Member State concerned;　　Sch 1(vii)

(*h*)　the supply of services and of goods closely linked to the protection of children and young persons by bodies governed by public law or by other organizations recognized as charitable by the Member State concerned;　　Sch 1(vi)

(*i*)　children's or young people's education, school or university education, vocational training or retraining, including the supply of services and of goods closely related thereto, provided by bodies governed by public law having such as their aim or by other organizations defined by the Member State concerned as having similar objects;　　Sch 1(ii), (xxv)

(*j*)　tuition given privately by teachers and covering school or university education;　　Sch 1(ii)

(*k*)　certain supplies of staff by religious or philosophical institutions for the purpose of subparagraphs (*b*), (*g*), (*h*) and (*i*) of this Article and with a view to spiritual welfare;

(*l*)　supply of services and goods closely linked thereto for the benefit of their members in return for a subscription fixed in accordance with their rules by non-profit-making organizations with aims of a political, trade-union, religious, patriotic, philosophical, philanthropic or civic nature, provided that this exemption is not likely to cause distortion of competition;　　Sch 1(xxii)

(*m*)　certain services closely linked to sport or physical education supplied by non-profit-making organizations to persons taking part in sport or physical education;　　Sch 1(xxiii)

(*n*)　certain cultural services and goods closely linked thereto supplied by bodies governed by public law or by other cultural bodies recognized by the Member State concerned;　　Sch 1(viii), (viii*a*)

(*o*)　the supply of services and goods by organizations whose activities are exempt under the provisions of subparagraphs (*b*), (*g*), (*h*), (*i*), (*l*), (*m*) and (*n*) above in connection with fund-raising events organized exclusively for their own benefit provided that exemption is not likely to cause distortion of competition. Member States may introduce any necessary restrictions in particular as regards the number of events or the amount of receipts which give entitlement to exemption;

(*p*) the supply of transport services for sick or injured persons in vehicles specially designed for the purpose by duly authorized bodies;

Sch 1(xiii) (*q*) activities of public radio and television bodies other than those of a commercial nature.

2. (*a*) Member States may make the granting to bodies other than those governed by public law of each exemption provided for in (1)(*b*), (*g*), (*h*), (*i*), (*l*), (*m*) and (*n*) of this Article subject in each individual case to one or more of the following conditions:

— they shall not systematically aim to make a profit, but any profits nevertheless arising shall not be distributed but shall be assigned to the continuance or improvement of the services supplied,

— they shall be managed and administered on an essentially voluntary basis by persons who have no direct or indirect interest, either themselves or through intermediaries, in the results of the activities concerned,

— they shall charge prices approved by the public authorities or which do not exceed such approved prices or, in respect of those services not subject to approval, prices lower than those charged for similar services by commercial enterprises subject to value added tax,

— exemption of the services concerned shall not be likely to create distortions of competition such as to place at a disadvantage commercial enterprises liable to value added tax.

(*b*) The supply of services or goods shall not be granted exemption as provided for in (1)(*b*), (*g*), (*h*), (*i*), (*l*), (*m*) and (*n*) above if:

— it is not essential to the transactions exempted,

— its basic purpose is to obtain additional income for the organization by carrying out transactions which are in direct competition with those of commercial enterprises liable for value added tax.

B. Other exemptions

Without prejudice to other Community provisions, Member States shall exempt the following under conditions which they shall lay down for the purpose of ensuring the correct and straightforward application of the exemptions and of preventing any possible evasion, avoidance or abuse:

Sch 1(ix)(*b*)-(*c*)
Sch 1(xi) (*a*) insurance and reinsurance transactions, including related services performed by insurance brokers and insurance agents;

Sch 1(iv) (*b*) the leasing or letting of immovable property excluding:

1. the provision of accommodation, as defined in the laws of the Member States, in the hotel sector or in sectors with a similar function, including the provision of accommodation in holiday camps or on sites developed for use as camping sites;

2. the letting of premises and sites for parking vehicles;

3. lettings of permanently installed equipment and machinery;

4. hire of safes.

Member States may apply further exclusions to the scope of this exemption;

(*c*)   supplies of goods used wholly for an activity exempted under this Article or under Article 28(3)(*b*) when these goods have not given rise to the right to deduction, or of goods on the acquisition or production of which, by virtue of Article 17(6), value added tax did not become deductible;

Sch 1(xxiv)

(*d*)   the following transactions:

Sch 1(i)
Sch 1(ix)(*d*)

1.   the granting and the negotiation of credit and the management of credit by the person granting it;

2.   the negotiation of or any dealings in credit guarantees or any other security for money and the management of credit guarantees by the person who is granting the credit;

3.   transactions, including negotiation, concerning deposit and current accounts, payments, transfers, debts, cheques and other negotiable instruments, but excluding debt collection and factoring;

4.   transactions, including negotiation, concerning currency, bank notes and coins used as legal tender, with the exception of collectors' items; "collectors' items" shall be taken to mean gold, silver or other metal coins or bank notes which are not normally used as legal tender or coins of numismatic interest;

s 1(1)

5.   transactions, including negotiation, excluding management and safekeeping, in shares, interests in companies or associations, debentures and other securities, excluding:

—   documents establishing title to goods,

—   the rights or securities referred to in Article 5(3);

6.   management of special investment funds as defined by Member States;

(*e*)   the supply at face value of postage stamps valid for use for postal services within the territory of the country, fiscal stamps, and other similar stamps;

s 1(1)

(*f*)   betting, lotteries and other forms of gambling, subject to conditions and limitations laid down by each Member State;

Sch 1(xv)(xvi)

(*g*)   the supply of buildings or parts thereof, and of the land on which they stand, other than as described in Article 4(3)(*a*);

(*h*)   the supply of land which has not been built on other than building land as described in Article 4(3)(*b*).

C. Options

s 7

Member States may allow taxpayers a right of option for taxation in cases of:

VATR 1979 r 3

(*a*)   letting and leasing of immovable property;

(*b*)   the transactions covered in B(*d*) (*g*) and (*h*) above.

Member States may restrict the scope of this right of option and shall fix the details of its use.

Cross-references

For exemptions not included in this title, see arts 28c and 28k(1), (2).

Case law

Whether postal handling charge a customs charge: *Donner v State of the Netherlands* [1983]ECR 19, [1983]1 CMLR 711, ECJ 39/82.

Art 13A(1)(*c*): meaning of "medical care", corrective spectacles not exempt: *EC Commission v United Kingdom* [1988]STC 251, [1988]2 All ER 557, ECJ 353/85.

Art 13A(1)(*f*): did not apply to non-profit making foundation performing work for another non-profit making foundation (receiving exact reimbursement of expenses): *Stichting Uitvoering Financiële Acties v Staatssecretaris van Financiën* [1991]2 CMLR 429, ECJ 348/87.

Art 13A(1)(*g*): did not apply to profit making creches run by "natural persons": *Bulthuis Griffioen v Inspector der Omzetbelasting* [1995] STC 954, ECJ 453/93.

Art 13B(*b*): Sites for parking vehicles includes covered garages: *Skatteministeriet v Henriksen* [1990]STC 768, [1990]3 CMLR 558, ECJ 173/88.

Payment received by tenant for early surrender of lease, not taxable where grant of lease, and rent paid, were exempt: *Lubbock Fine and Co v Commissioners of Customs & Excise*, [1994]STC 101, ECJ 63/92.

Art 13B(*d*): Credit card transaction, retailer's gross consideration (including credit card commission) is the taxable amount: *Chaussures Bally SA v Ministry of Finance (Belgium)* [1993]STI 944, ECJ 18/92.

Interest payable prior to the payment of the full price is regarded as part of the consideration; interest payable after the date of the supply constitutes granting of credit and is exempt: *Muys' en De Winter's Bouw-en Aannwmingsbedrijf BV v Staatsecretaris van Financiën* [1993]STI 1367, ECJ 281/91.

Transport services provided to (not by) postal services taxable: *Re VAT on Postal Transport, EC Commission v Germany* [1986]2 CMLR 177, ECJ 107/84.

Direct effect of Directives

Member States were to adopt the Sixth Directive by 1 January 1978, but it was not implemented in Germany until 1 January 1980. Nevertheless its exemptions could be relied upon with effect from 1 January 1979 (Ninth Directive): *R A Grendel GmbH v Finanzamt für Körperschaften, Hamburg* [1982]ECR 2301, [1983]1 CMLR 379, ECJ 255/81; but not before 1 January 1979: *Kloppenburg v Finanzamt Leer* [1984]ECR 1075, [1985]1 CMLR 205, ECJ 70/83.

A credit negotiator who had covertly passed on VAT in 1978 and 1979 could not afterwards claim exemption: *Weissgerber v Finanzamt Neustadt an der Weinstraße* [1991]STC 589, ECJ 207/87; see also *EC Commission v Italy* ECJ 104/86; *Bianco and Girard* 331/85, 376/85, 378/85.

Article 14
Exemptions on importation

1. Without prejudice to other Community provisions, Member States shall exempt the following under conditions which they shall lay down for the purpose of ensuring the correct and straightforward application of such exemption and of preventing any possible evasion, avoidance or abuse:

(*a*)   final importation of goods of which the supply by a taxable person would in all circumstances be exempted within the country;

(*b*)   ...[1]

(*c*)   ...[2]

(*d*)   final importation of goods qualifying for exemption from customs duties other than as provided for in the Common Customs Tariff ...[3]. However, Member States shall have the option of not granting exemption where this would be liable to have a serious effect on conditions of competition ...[4];

[This exemption shall also apply to the import of goods, within the meaning of Article 7(1)(*b*), which would be capable of benefiting from the exemption set out above if they had been imported within the meaning of Article 7(1)(*a*);][5]

(*e*)   reimportation by the person who exported them of goods in the state in which they were exported, where they qualify for exemption from customs duties ...[6];

(*f*)   ...[7];

(*g*)   importations of goods:

—   under diplomatic and consular arrangements, which qualify for exemption from customs duties ...[8],

—   by international organizations recognized as such by the public authorities of the host country, and by members of such organizations, within the limits and under the conditions laid down by the international conventions establishing the organizations or by headquarters agreements,

—   into the territory of Member States which are parties to the North Atlantic Treaty by the armed forces of other States which are parties to that Treaty for the use of such forces or the civilian staff accompanying them or for supplying their messes or canteens where such forces take part in the common defence effort;

(*h*)   importation into ports by sea fishing undertakings of their catches, unprocessed or after undergoing preservation for marketing but before being supplied;

(*i*)   the supply of services, in connection with the importation of goods where the value of such services is included in the taxable amount in accordance with Article 11B(3)(*b*);

(*j*)   importation of gold by Central Banks.

2. The Commission shall submit to the Council at the earliest opportunity proposals designed to lay down Community tax rules clarifying the scope of the exemptions referred to in paragraph 1 and detailed rules for their implementation.

Until the entry into force of these rules, Member States may:

—   maintain their national provisions in force on matters related to the above provisions,

—   adapt their national provisions to minimize distortion of competition and in particular the non-imposition or double imposition of value added tax within the Community,

—   use whatever administrative procedures they consider most appropriate to achieve exemption.

Member States shall inform the Commission, which shall inform the other Member States, of the measures they have adopted and are adopting pursuant to the preceding provisions.

Amendments
1   Para (1)(*b*) deleted Council Directive 91/680/EEC of 16 December 1991, art 1(11) with effect from 1 January 1993.
2   Para (1)(*c*) deleted by Council Directive 92/111/EEC of 14 December 1992, art 1(8) with effect from 1 January 1993.
3   Deleted by Council Directive 91/680/EEC of 16 December 1991, art 1(11) with effect from 1 January 1993.
4   Deleted by Council Directive 91/680/EEC of 16 December 1991, art 1(11) with effect from 1 January 1993.
5   Added by Council Directive 92/111/EEC of 14 December 1992, art 1(8) with effect from 1 January 1993.
6   Deleted by Council Directive 91/680/EEC of 16 December 1991, art 1(11) with effect from 1 January 1993.
7   Para (1)(*f*) deleted by Council Directive 91/680/EEC of 16 December 1991, art 1(11) with effect from 1 January 1993.
8   Deleted by Council Directive 91/680/EEC of 16 December 1991, art 1(11) with effect from 1 January 1993.

Cross-references
Goods imported into an EC State other than that of arrival: art 28c(D).
Directives adopted under art 14(2): Council Directive 83/181/EEC (clarifying the scope of art 14(1)(*d*)); Council Directive 85/362/ EEC (Seventeenth Directive)(clarifying the scope of art 14(1)(*c*)).

Case law
Note: the following decisions are less significant following the implementation of the Single Market.
Double imposition of VAT on motor vehicles: *Ministère Publique and Ministere des Finances v Profant* [1986]2 CMLR 378, ECJ 249/84.
"Frontier zone", meaning: *Michael Paul v Hauptzollamt Emmerich* ECJ 54/84.
National rules prohibiting use of temporarily imported motor vehicles, permissible: *Re Carciati* [1980]ECR 2773, [1981]2 CMLR 274, ECJ 823/79; *Abbink (Jan Gerrit, criminal proceedings)* [1984]ECR 4079, [1986]1 CMLR 579, ECJ 134/83.
"Normal residence", meaning, Danish national working in Germany: *Rigsadvokaten v N C Ryborg* [1991]STI 501, ECJ 297/89.
Temporary importation of racehorses: *R v C & E Commissioners, ex parte Tattersalls Ltd* [1988]STC 630, [1988]3 CMLR 113, ECJ 10/87.
Travellers' allowances, Member State not upholding EEC Treaty: *Re border shopping: EC Commission v Ireland* [1990]3 CMLR 103, ECJ 158/88; *EC Commission v Denmark* (1991) OJ C4/2, ECJ 208/88.
Temporary importation of motor vehicle: *Ministère Public des Finances du Royaume de Belgique v Ledoux* [1991]STC 553, ECJ 127/86.

Article 15
[*Exemption of exports from the Community and like transactions and international transport*]¹

s 13(1), (2)

SI 230/1984
SI 231/1984

Without prejudice to other Community provisions Member States shall exempt the following under conditions which they shall lay down for the purpose of ensuring the correct and straightforward application of such exemptions and of preventing any evasion, avoidance or abuse:

1. the supply of goods dispatched or transported to a destination [outside the Community]² by or on behalf of the vendor;

2. the supply of goods dispatched or transported to a destination [outside the Community]² by or on behalf of a purchaser not established within the territory of the country, with the exception of goods transported by the purchaser himself for the equipping, fuelling and provisioning of pleasure boats and private aircraft or any other means of transport for private use;

[[In the case of the supply of goods to be carried in the personal luggage of travellers, this exemption shall apply on condition that:

— the traveller is not established within the Community,

— the goods are transported to a destination outside the Community before the end of the third month following that in which the supply is effected,

— the total value of the supply, including value added tax, is more than the equivalent in national currency of ECU 175, fixed in accordance with Article 7(2) of Directive 69/169/EEC (OJ No l 133, 4.6.1969, p 6. Directive as last amended by Directive 94/4/EC (OJ No L 60, 3.3.1994, p 14)); however, Members States may exempt a supply with a total value of less than that amount.

For the purposes of applying the second subparagraph:

— a traveller not established within the Community shall be taken to mean a traveller whose domicile or habitual residence is not situated within the Community. For the purposes of this provision, "domicile or habitual residence" shall mean the place entered as such in a passport, identity card or other identity documents which the Member State within whose territory the supply takes place recognizes as valid,

— proof of exportation shall be furnished by means of the invoice or other document in lieu thereof, endorsed by the customs office where the goods left the Community.

Each Member State shall transmit to the Commission specimens of the stamps it uses for the endorsement referred to in the second indent of the third subparagraph. The Commission shall transmit this information to the tax authorities in the other Member States.][3]]4

[**3.** The supply of services consisting of work on movable property acquired or imported for the purpose of undergoing such work within the territory of the Community, and dispatched or transported out of the Community by the person providing the services or by the customer if [not established within the territory of the country][5] or on behalf of either of them;][6]

4. the supply of goods for the fuelling and provisioning of vessels:

(*a*) used for navigation on the high seas and carrying passengers for reward or used for the purpose of commercial, industrial or fishing activities;

(*b*) used for rescue or assistance at sea, or for inshore fishing, with the exception, for the latter, of ships' provisions;

(*c*) of war, as defined in subheading 89.01 A of the Common Customs Tariff, leaving the country and bound for foreign ports or anchorages.

[The Commission shall submit to the Council as soon as possible proposals to establish Community fiscal rules specifying the scope of and practical arrangements for implementing this exemption and the exemptions provided for in (5) to (9). Until these rules come into force, Member States may limit the extent of the exemption provided for in this paragraph.][7]

Sch 2(v)(va) **5.** the supply, modification, repair, maintenance, chartering and hiring of the seagoing vessels referred to in paragraph 4(*a*) and (*b*) and the supply, hiring, repair and maintenance of equipment — including fishing equipment — incorporated or used therein;

6. the supply, modification, repair, maintenance, chartering and hiring of aircraft used by airlines operating for reward chiefly on international routes, and the supply, hiring, repair and maintenance of equipment incorporated or used therein;

7. the supply of goods for the fuelling and provisioning of aircraft referred to in paragraph 6;

8. the supply of services other than those referred to in paragraph 5, to meet the direct needs of the sea-going vessels referred to in that paragraph or of their cargoes;

9. the supply of services other than those referred to in paragraph 6, to meet the direct needs of aircraft referred to in that paragraph or of their cargoes;

Sch 2(v*b*)

10. supplies of goods and services:

— under diplomatic and consular arrangements,

— to international organizations recognized as such by the public authorities of the host country, and to members of such organizations, within the limits and under the conditions laid down by the international conventions establishing the organizations or by headquarters agreements,

— effected within a Member State which is a party to the North Atlantic Treaty and intended either for the use of the forces of other States which are parties to that Treaty or of the civilian staff accompanying them, or for supplying their messes or canteens when such forces take part in the common defence effort.

[— to another Member State and intended for the forces of any Member State which is a party to the North Atlantic Treaty, other than the Member State of destination itself, for the use of those forces or of the civilian staff accompanying them, or for supplying their messes or canteens when such forces take part in the common defence effort.]⁸

This exemption shall be [subject to [limitations]⁹ laid down by the host Member State]¹⁰ until Community tax rules are adopted.

[In cases where the goods are not dispatched or transported out of the country, and in the case of services, the benefit of the exemption may be given by means of a refund of the tax.]¹¹

11. supplies of gold to Central Banks;

12. goods supplied to approved bodies which export them [from the Community]¹² as part of their humanitarian, charitable or teaching activities [outside the Community]¹³. This exemption may be implemented by means of a refund of the tax;

[**13.** The supply of services, including transport and ancillary operations, but excluding the supply of services exempted in accordance with Article 13, where these are directly connected with the export of goods or imports of goods covered by the provisions of Article 7(3) or Article 16(1), Title A;]¹⁴

14. services supplied by brokers and other intermediaries, acting in the name and for account of another person, where they form part of transactions specified in this Article, or of transactions carried out [outside the Community]¹⁵.

This exemption does not apply to travel agents who supply in the name and for account of the traveller services which are supplied in other Member States.

[**15.** the Portuguese Republic may treat sea and air transport between the islands making up the autonomous regions of the Azores and Madeira and between those regions and the mainland in the same way as international transport.]¹⁶

Amendments

1   Substituted by Council Directive 91/680/EEC of 16 December 1991, art 1(12) with effect from 1 January 1993.
2   Substituted by Council Directive 91/680/EEC of 16 December 1991, art 1(13) with effect from 1 January 1993.
3   Substituted by Council Directive 95/7/EC of 10 April 1995 art 1(3) with effect from 1 January 1996.
4   Inserted by Council Directive 92/111/EEC of 14 December 1992, art 1(9) with effect from 1 January 1993.
5   Substituted by Council Directive 92/111/EEC of 14 December 1992, art 1(9) with effect from 1 January 1993.
6   Para (3) substituted by Council Directive 91/680/EEC of 16 December 1991, art 1(14) with effect from 1 January 1993.
7   Substituted by Council Directive 92/111/EEC of 14 December 1992, art 1(9) with effect from 1 January 1993.

8   Inserted by Council Directive 91/680/EEC of 16 December 1991, art 1(15) with effect from 1 January 1993.
9   Substituted by Council Directive 92/111/EEC of 14 December 1992, art 1(9) with effect from 1 January 1993.
10   Substituted by Council Directive 91/680/EEC of 16 December 1991, art 1(16) with effect from 1 January 1993.
11   Substituted by Council Directive 92/111/EEC of 14 December 1992, art 1(9) with effect from 1 January 1993.
12   Inserted by Council Directive 91/680/EEC of 16 December 1991, art 1(17) with effect from 1 January 1993.
13   Substituted by Council Directive 91/680/EEC of 16 December 1991, art 1(17) with effect from 1 January 1993.
14   Para (13) substituted by Council Directive 92/111/EEC of 14 December 1992, art 1(9) with effect from 1 January 1993.
15   Substituted by Council Directive 91/680/EEC of 16 December 1991, art 1(19) with effect from 1 January 1993.
16   Para (15) inserted by the Act of Accession 1985 art 26, Annex I, Part V, point 2.

Case law
Para (4): fuelling and provisioning, only direct supplies regarded as exempt; fuelling and provisioning need not be simultaneous: *Staatssecretaris van Financiën v Velker International Oil Co Ltd NV* [1990]STC 640, ECJ 185/89.

---

s 13(1),(2)

Article 16
Special exemptions linked to international goods traffic

[**1.** Without prejudice to other Community tax provisions, Member States may, subject to the consultations provided for in Article 29, take special measures designed to exempt all or some of the following transactions, provided that they are not aimed at final use and/or consumption and that the amount of value added tax due on cessation of the arrangements on situations referred to at A to E corresponds to the amount of tax which would have been due had each of these transactions been taxed within the territory of the country:

A. imports of goods which are intended to be placed under warehousing arrangements other than customs;

B. supplies of goods which are intended to be:

(*a*)   produced to customs and, where applicable, placed in temporary storage;

(*b*)   placed in a free zone or in a free warehouse;

(*c*)   placed under customs warehousing arrangements or inward processing arrangements;

(*d*)   admitted into territorial waters:

— in order to be incorporated into drilling or production platforms, for purposes of the construction, repair, maintenance, alteration or fitting-out of such platforms, or to link such drilling or production platforms to the mainland,

— for the fuelling and provisioning of drilling or production platforms;

(*e*)   placed, within the territory of the country, under warehousing arrangements other than customs warehousing.

For the purposes of this Article, warehouses other than customs warehouses shall be taken to be:

— for products subject to excise duty, the places defined as tax warehouses for the purposes of Article 4(*b*) of Directive 92/12/EEC,

— for goods other than those subject to excise duty, the places defined as such by the Member States. However, Member States may not provide for warehousing arrangements other than customs warehousing where the goods in question are intended to be supplied at the retail stage.

Nevertheless, Member States may provide for such arrangements for goods intended for:

— taxable persons for the purposes of supplies effected under the conditions laid down in Article 28k,

—   tax-free shops within the meaning of Article 28k, for the purpose of supplies to travellers taking flights or sea crossings to third countries, where those supplies are exempt pursuant to Article 15,

—   taxable persons for the purposes of supplies to travellers on board aircraft or vessels during a flight or sea crossing where the place of arrival is situated outside the Community,

—   taxable persons for the purposes of supplies effected free of tax pursuant to Article 15, point 10.

The places referred to in (*a*), (*b*), (*c*) and (*d*) shall be as defined by the Community customs provisions in force;

C. supplies of services relating to the supplies of goods referred to in B;

D. supplies of goods and of services carried out:

(*a*)   in the places listed in B(*a*), (*b*), (*c*) and (*d*) and still subject to one of the situations specified therein;

(*b*)   in the places listed in B(*e*) and still subject, within the territory of the country, to the situation specified therein.

Where they exercise the option provided for in (*a*) for transactions effected in customs warehouses, Member States shall take the measures necessary to ensure that they have defined warehousing arrangements other than customs warehousing which permit the provisions in (*b*) to be applied to the same transactions concerning goods listed in Annex J which are effected in such warehouses other than customs warehouses;

E. supplies:

—   of goods referred to in Article 7(1)(*a*) still subject to arrangements for temporary importation with total exemption from import duty or to external transit arrangements,

—   of goods referred to in Article 7(1)(*b*) still subject to the internal Community transit procedure provided for in Article 33a,

as well as supplies of services relating to such supplies.

By way of derogation from the first subparagraph of Article 21(1)(*a*), the person liable to pay the tax due in accordance with the first subparagraph shall be the person who causes the goods to cease to be covered by the arrangements or situations listed in this paragraph.

When the removal of goods from the arrangements or situations referred to in this paragraph gives rise to importation within the meaning of Article 7(3), the Member State of import shall take the measures necessary to avoid double taxation within the country.][1]

[**1a.** Where they exercise the option provided for in paragraph 1, Member States shall take the measures necessary to ensure that intra-Community acquisitions of goods intended to be placed under one of the arrangements or in one of the situations referred to in paragraph 1(B) benefit from the same provisions as supplies of goods effected within the country under the same conditions.][2]

2. Subject to the consultation provided for in Article 29, Member States may opt to exempt intra-Community acquisitions of goods made by a taxable person and imports for and supplies of goods to a taxable person intending to export them [outside the Community][3] as they are or after processing, as well as supplies of services linked with his export business, up to a maximum equal to the value of his exports during the preceding 12 months.   s 13A

[When they take up this option the Member States shall, subject to the consultation provided for in Article 29, extend the benefit of this exemption to intra-Community acquisitions of goods by a taxable person, imports for and supplies of goods to a taxable person intending to supply them, as they are or after processing, under the conditions laid down in Article 28c(A), as well as supplies of services relating to such supplies, up to a maximum equal to the value of his supplies of goods effected under the conditions laid down in Article 28c(A) during the preceding twelve months.

Member States may set a common maximum amount for transactions which they exempt under the first and second subparagraphs.]⁴

3. The Commission shall submit to the Council at the earliest opportunity proposals concerning common arrangements for applying value added tax to the transactions referred to in paragraphs 1 and 2.

Amendments
1 Para (1) substituted by art 28c(E)(1) which was amended by Council Directive 95/7/EC of 10 April 1995 art 1(9) with effect from 1 January 1996 (1 January 1997 for Germany and Luxembourg).
2 Para (1a) substituted by art 28c(E)(1) which was amended by Council Directive 95/7/EC of 10 April 1995 art 1(9) with effect from 1 January 1996 (1 January 1997 for Germany and Luxembourg).
3 Inserted by art 28c(E)(inserted by Council Directive 92/111/EEC of 14 December 1992 art 1(13)) with effect from 1 January 1993.
4 Inserted by art 28c(E)(inserted by Council Directive 92/111/EEC of 14 December 1992 art 1(13)) with effect from 1 January 1993.

Cross-references
Dispatch or transport of goods to, from or between the Azores and Madeira: arts 28c(C).
Exercise of option under art 16(2): art 28k(4).

TITLE XI
Deductions

Article 17
Origin and scope of the right to deduct

s 12

1. The right to deduct shall arise at the time when deductible tax becomes chargeable.

[**2.** Insofar as the goods and services are used for the purposes of his taxable transactions, the taxable person shall be entitled to deduct from the tax which he is liable to pay:

[(*a*) value added tax due or paid within the territory of the country in respect of goods or services supplied or to be supplied to him by another taxable person;]¹

(*b*) value added tax due or paid in respect of imported goods within the territory of the country;

(*c*) value added tax due pursuant to Articles 5(7)(*a*), (6)(3) and 28a(6);

(*d*) value added tax due pursuant to Article 28a(1)(*a*).]²

[**3.** Member States shall also grant every taxable person the right to the deduction or refund of the value added tax referred to in paragraph 2 insofar as the goods and services are used for the purposes of:

(*a*) transactions relating to the economic activities referred to in Article 4(2), carried out in another country, which would be deductible if they had been performed within the territory of the country;

(*b*) transactions which are exempt under Article 14(1)(i), 15, 16(1)(B), (C), (D) or (E) or (2) or [28c(A) and (C)]³;

s 12(1)(*b*)

(*c*) any of the transactions exempt pursuant to Article 13B(*a*) and (*d*)(1) to (5), when the customer is established outside the Community or when those transactions are directly linked with goods to be exported to a country outside the Community.]⁴

s 13(3)
VATR 1979 r 30

[**4.** The refund of value added tax referred to in paragraph 3 shall be effected:

— to taxable persons who are not established within the territory of the country but who are established in another Member State in accordance with the detailed implementing rules laid down in Directive 79/1072/EEC (OJ L 331, 27.12.1979, p 11);

— to taxable persons who are not established within the territory of the Community, in accordance with the detailed implementing rules laid down in Directive 86/560/EEC (OJ L 326, 21.11.1986, p 40).

[For the purposes of applying the above:

(a) the taxable persons referred to in Article 1 of Directive 79/1072/EEC shall also be considered for the purposes of applying the said Directive as taxable persons who are not established in the country when, inside the territory of the country, they have only carried out supplies of goods and services to a person who has been designated as the person liable to pay the tax in accordance with Article 21(1)(a);

(b) the taxable persons referred to in Article 1 of Directive 86/560/EEC shall also be considered for the purposes of applying the said Directive as taxable persons who are not established in the Community when, inside the territory of the country, they have only carried out supplies of goods and services to a person who has been designated as the person liable to pay the tax in accordance with Article 21(1)(a);

(c) Directives 79/1072/EEC and 86/560/EEC shall not apply to supplies of goods which are, or may be, exempted under Article 28c(A) when the goods supplied are dispatched or transported by the acquirer or for his account.][5][6]

5. As regards goods and services to be used by a taxable person both for transactions covered by paragraphs 2 and 3, in respect of which value added tax is deductible, and for transactions in respect of which value added tax is not deductible, only such proportion of the value added tax shall be deductible as is attributable to the former transactions.

This proportion shall be determined, in accordance with Article 19, for all the transactions carried out by the taxable person.

However, Member States may:

(a) authorize the taxable person to determine a proportion for each sector of his business, provided that separate accounts are kept for each sector;

(b) compel the taxable person to determine a proportion for each sector of his business and to keep separate accounts for each sector;

(c) authorize or compel the taxable person to make the deduction on the basis of the use of all or part of the goods and services;

(d) authorize or compel the taxable person to make the deduction in accordance with the rule laid down in the first subparagraph, in respect of all goods and services used for all transactions referred to therein;

(e) provide that where the value added tax which is not deductible by the taxable person is insignificant it shall be treated as nil.

6. Before a period of four years at the latest has elapsed from the date of entry into force of this Directive, the Council, acting unanimously on a proposal from the Commission, shall decide what expenditure shall not be eligible for a deduction of value added tax. Value added tax shall in no circumstances be deductible on expenditure which is not strictly business expenditure, such as that on luxuries, amusements or entertainment.

Until the above rules come into force, Member States may retain all the exclusions provided for under their national laws when this Directive comes into force.

7. Subject to the consultation provided for in Article 29, each Member State may, for cyclical economic reasons, totally or partly exclude all or some capital goods or other goods from the system of deductions. To maintain identical conditions of competition, Member States may, instead of refusing deduction, tax the goods manufactured by the taxable person himself or which he has purchased in the country or imported, in such a way that the tax does not exceed the value added tax which would have been charged on the acquisition of similar goods.

Amendments

1   Para (2)(*a*) substituted by art 28f(1) which was amended by Council Directive 95/7/EC of 10 April 1995 art 1(10) with effect from 25 May 1995.

2   Para (2) substituted by art 28f(1) which was inserted byCouncil Directive 91/680/EEC of 16 December 1991, art 1(22) with effect from 1 January 1993 for the transitional period specified in art 28l first para.

3   Substituted by Council Directive 92/111/EEC of 14 December 1992, art 1(18) with effect from 1 January 1993.

4   Para (3) substituted by art 28f(1) which was inserted by Council Directive 91/680/EEC of 16 December 1991, art 1(22) with effect from 1 January 1993 for the transitional period specified in art 28l first para.

5   Inserted by Council Directive 92/111/EEC of 14 December 1992, art 1(18) with effect from 1 January 1993.

6   Para (4) substituted by art 28f(1) which was inserted by Council Directive 91/680/EEC of 16 December 1991, art 1(22) with effect from 1 January 1993 for the transitional period specified in art 28l first para.

Cross-references

Right of deduction by person who from time to time supplies a new means of transport: art 28a(4).

Right of deduction in relation to supplies by tax-free shops: art 28k(3).

Case law

Deductibility of VAT on professional fees incurred in connection with disposal of shares in subsidiary: *BLP Group v C & E Commissioners* [1995] STC 424, ECJ 4/94.

Greece held to be in breach of Art 17(1) and (2): *BP Soupergas Anonimos Etairia Geniki Emporiki Viomichaniki v Greece* [1995] STC 805, ECJ 62/93.

Taxpayer not entitled to deduction in relation to sale of private dwelling where it was sold together with business premises: *Finanzampt Uelzen v Armbrecht* [1995] STC 997, ECJ.

Partially taxable holding company, exclusion of dividends (received from group companies) in denominator when computing input credit: *Satam SA v Minister Responsible for the Budget* [1993] STI 1077, ECJ 333/91.

Para (2)(*a*): Although a deduction is only available for goods "supplied", a taxable person may claim a deduction for goods physically supplied to employees (but invoiced to the taxable trader): *Leesportefeuille "Intiem" CV v Staatssecretaris van Financiën* [1989]2 CMLR 856, ECJ 165/86.

---

s 12

Article 18
Rules governing the exercise of the right to deduct

[**1.** To exercise his right of deduction, a taxable person must:

(*a*)   in respect of deductions pursuant to Article 17(2)(*a*), hold an invoice drawn up in accordance with Article 22(3);

(*b*)   in respect of deductions pursuant to Article 17(2)(*b*), hold an import document specifying him as consignee or importer and stating or permitting the calculation of the amount of tax due;

(*c*)   in respect of deductions pursuant to Article 17(2)(*c*), comply with the formalities established by each Member State;

(*d*)   when he is required to pay the tax as a customer or purchaser where Article 21(1) applies, comply with the formalities laid down by each Member State;

(*e*)   in respect of deductions pursuant to Article 17(2)(*d*), set out in the declaration provided for in Article 22(4) all the information needed for the amount of the tax due on his intra-Community acquisitions of goods to be calculated and hold an invoice in accordance with Article 22(3).][1]

s 3(7)

2. The taxable person shall effect the deduction by subtracting from the total amount of value added tax due for a given tax period the total amount of the tax in respect of which, during the same period, the right to deduct has arisen and can be exercised under the provisions of paragraph 1.

However, Member States may require that as regards taxable persons who carry out occasional transactions as defined in Article 4(3), the right to deduct shall be exercised only at the time of the supply.

3. Member States shall determine the conditions and procedures whereby a taxable person may be authorized to make a deduction which he has not made in accordance with the provisions of paragraphs 1 and 2.

[**3a.** Member States may authorise a taxable person who does not hold an invoice in accordance with Article 22(3) to make the deduction referred to in Article 17(2)(*d*); they shall determine the conditions and arrangements for applying this provision.][2]

4. Where for a given tax period the amount of authorised deductions exceeds the amount of tax due, the Member States may either make a refund or carry the excess forward to the following period according to conditions which they shall determine.

s 20(1)
VATR 1979 r 17

However, Member States may refuse to refund or carry forward if the amount of the excess is insignificant.

Amendments
1 Para (1) substituted by art 28f(2) which was inserted by Council Directive 91/680/EEC of 16 December 1991, art 1(22) with effect from 1 January 1993 for the transitional period specified in art 28l first para.
2 Para (3a) inserted by art 28f(3) which was inserted by Council Directive 91/680/EEC of 16 December 1991, art 1(22) with effect from 1 January 1993 for the transitional period specified in art 28l first para.

Article 19
Calculation of the deductible proportion

s 12
VATR 1979 r 16

1. The proportion deductible under the first subparagraph of Article 17(5) shall be made up of a fraction having:

— as numerator, the total amount, exclusive of value added tax, of turnover per year attributable to transactions in respect of which value added tax is deductible under Article 17(2) and (3),

— as denominator, the total amount, exclusive of value added tax, of turnover per year attributable to transactions included in the numerator and to transactions in respect of which value added tax is not deductible. The Member States may also include in the denominator the amount of subsidies, other than those specified in Article 11A(1)(*a*).

The proportion shall be determined on an annual basis, fixed as a percentage and rounded up to a figure not exceeding the next unit.

2. By way of derogation from the provisions of paragraph 1, there shall be excluded from the calculation of the deductible proportion, amounts of turnover attributable to the supplies of capital goods used by the taxable person for the purposes of his business. Amounts of turnover attributable to transactions specified in Article 13B(*d*), in so far as these are incidental transactions, and to incidental real estate and financial transactions shall also be excluded. Where Member States exercise the option provided under Article 20(5) not to require adjustment in respect of capital goods, they may include disposals of capital goods in the calculation of the deductible proportion.

s 12(4)

[not done by Ireland]

3. The provisional proportion for a year shall be that calculated on the basis of the preceding year's transactions. In the absence of any such transactions to refer to, or where they were insignificant in amount, the deductible proportion shall be estimated provisionally, under supervision of the tax authorities, by the taxable person from his own forecasts. However, Member States may retain their current rules.

Deductions made on the basis of such provisional proportion shall be adjusted when the final proportion is fixed during the next year.

Case law
Partially taxable holding company, exclusion of dividends (received from group companies) in denominator when computing input credit: *Satam SA v Minister Responsible for the Budget* [1993]STI 1077, ECJ 333/91.

Article 20
Adjustments of deductions

s 12
VATR 1979 r 1

1. The initial deduction shall be adjusted according to the procedures laid down by the Member States, in particular:

(*a*) where that deduction was higher or lower than that to which the taxable person was entitled;

(*b*) where after the return is made some change occurs in the factors used to determine the amount to be deducted, in particular where purchases are cancelled or price reductions are obtained; however, adjustment shall not be made in cases of transactions remaining totally or partially unpaid and of destruction, loss or theft of property duly proved or confirmed, nor in the case of applications for the purpose of making gifts of small value and giving samples specified in Article 5(6). However, Member States may require adjustment in cases of transactions remaining totally or partially unpaid and of theft.

2. In the case of capital goods, adjustment shall be spread over five years including that in which the goods were acquired or manufactured. The annual adjustment shall be made only in respect of one fifth of the tax imposed on goods. The adjustment shall be made on the basis of the variations in the deduction entitlement in subsequent years in relation to that for the year in which the goods were acquired or manufactured.

By way of derogation from the preceding subparagraph, Member States may base the adjustment on a period of five full years starting from the time at which the goods are first used.

[In the case of immovable property acquired as capital goods, the adjustment period may be extended up to 20 years.][1]

3. In the case of supply during the period of adjustment capital goods shall be regarded as if they had still been applied for business use by the taxable person until expiry of the period of adjustment. Such business activities are presumed to be fully taxed in cases where the delivery of the said goods is taxed; they are presumed to be fully exempt where the delivery is exempt. The adjustment shall be made only once for the whole period of adjustment still to be covered.

However, in the latter case, Member States may waive the requirement for adjustment in so far as the purchaser is a taxable person using the capital goods in question solely for transactions in respect of which value added tax is deductible.

4. For the purposes of applying the provisions of paragraphs 2 and 3, Member States may:

— define the concept of capital goods,

— indicate the amount of the tax which is to be taken into consideration for adjustment,

— adopt any suitable measures with a view to ensuring that adjustment does not involve any unjustified advantage,

— permit administrative simplifications.

s 12(4) **5.** If in any Member State the practical effect of applying paragraphs 2 and 3 would be insignificant, that Member State may subject to the consultation provided for in Article 29 forego application of these paragraphs having regard to the need to avoid distortion of competition, the overall tax effect in the Member State concerned and the need for due economy of administration.

6. Where the taxable person transfers from being taxed in the normal way to a special scheme or vice versa, Member States may take all necessary measures to ensure that the taxable person neither benefits nor is prejudiced unjustifiably.

Amendments
1 Substituted by Council Directive 95/7/EC of 10 April 1995 art 1(2) with effect from 1 January 1996.
Case law
Intending trader a taxable person: *Rompelman and Rompelman-Van Deelen v Minister van Financiën* ECJ 268/83.
Para (4): "capital goods", meaning: *Verbond van Nederlandse Ondernemingen v Inspecteur der Invoerrechten en Accijnzen* [1977]ECR 113, [1977]1 CMLR 413, ECJ 51/76; used for business and non-business purposes: *Lennartz v Finanzamt München III* [1991]STI 700, ECJ 97/90.
Invoices
Particulars required by authorities should not make deduction difficult: *Léa Jeunehomme and Société Anonyme d'Etude et de Gestion Immobiliére "EGI" v Belgian State* [1988]STI 598, ECJ 123 and 330/87.
Taxpayer not entitled to deduction in relation to sale of private dwelling where it was sold together with business premises: *Finamzampt Uelzen v Armbrecht* [1995] STC 997, ECJ.

VAT not deductible solely because it is stated on invoice: *Genius Holding BV v Staatssecretaris van Financiën* [1991]STC 239, ECJ 342/87.

TITLE XII
Persons liable for payment for tax

[Article 21   s 8(3)
Persons liable to pay tax to the authorities

The following shall be liable to pay value added tax:

1. Under the internal system:

[(*a*)   the taxable person carrying out the taxable supply of goods or of   s 37
services, other than one of the supplies of services referred to in (*b*).

Where the taxable supply of goods or of services is effected by a taxable person who is not established within the territory of the country, Member States may adopt arrangements whereby tax is payable by another person. *Inter alios* a tax representative or the person for whom the taxable supply of goods or of services is carried out may be designated as that other person.

However, the tax is payable by the person to whom the supply of goods is made when the following conditions are met:

—   the taxable operation is a supply of goods made under the conditions laid down in paragraph 3 of Title E of Article 28c,

—   the person to whom the supply of goods is made is another taxable person or a non-taxable legal person identified for the purposes of value added tax within the territory of the country,

—   the invoice issued by the taxable person not established within the territory of the country conforms to Article 22(3).

However, Member States may provide a derogation from this obligation in the case where the taxable person who is not established within the territory of the country has appointed a tax representative in that country.

Member States may provide that someone other than the taxable person shall be held jointly and severally liable for payment of the tax;

[(*b*)   persons to whom services covered by Article 9(2)(*e*) are supplied or   s 37
persons who are identified for value added tax purposes within the   art 28g
territory of the country to whom services covered by Article 28b, (C), (D), (E) and (F) are supplied, if the services are carried out by a taxable person established abroad; however, Member States may require that the supplier of services shall be held jointly and severally liable for payment of the tax;]¹]²

(*c*)   any person who mentions the value added tax on an invoice or other document serving as invoice;

(*d*)   any person effecting a taxable intra-Community acquisition of goods. Where an intra-Community acquisition of goods is effected by a person established abroad, Member States may adopt arrangements whereby tax is payable by another person. Inter alios, a tax representative may be designated as that other person. Member States may also provide that someone other than the person effecting the intra-Community acquisition of goods shall be held jointly and severally liable for payment of the tax;

2. on importation: the person or persons designated or accepted as being liable by   s 15
the Member State into which the goods are imported.]³

Amendments
1 Para (1)(b) substituted by art 28g which was amended by Council Directive 95/7/EC of 10 April 1995, art 1(11) with effect from 25 May 1995.
2 Para (1)(a)-(b) substituted by Council Directive 92/111/EEC of 14 December 1992, art 1(19) with effect from 1 January 1993.
3 Art 21 substituted by art 28g which was inserted by Council Directive 91/680/EEC of 16 December 1991, art 1(22) with effect from 1 January 1993 for the transitional period specified in art 28l first para.
Case law
Stolen goods: *Les Assurances Du Crédit NV v Bowy and Decoopman* ECJ 205/90.

VATR 1979 r 6

TITLE XIII
Obligations of persons liable for payment

ss 15,
17(9)-(13)

[Article 22
Obligations under the internal system

1. (a) Every taxable person shall state when his activity as a taxable person commences, changes or ceases.

(b) Without prejudice to (a), every taxable person referred to in Article 28(a)(1)(a), second subparagraph, shall state that he is effecting intra-Community acquisitions of goods when the conditions for application of the derogation provided for in that Article are not fulfilled.

(c) Member States shall take the measures necessary to identify by means of an individual number:

— every taxable person, with the exception of those referred to in Article 28a(4), who within the territory of the country effects supplies of goods or of services giving him the right of deduction, other than provisions of services for which tax is payable solely by the customer in accordance with Article 21(1)(b) [and other than a supply of goods or services to a person who has been designated as the person liable for the tax in accordance with Article 21(1)(a), third paragraph][1]. However, Member States need not identify certain taxable persons referred to in Article 4(3);

— every taxable person referred to in paragraph 1(b) and every taxable person who exercises the option provided for the third subparagraph of Article 28a(1)(a).

[— every taxable person who, within the territory of the country, effects intra-Community acquisitions of goods for the purposes of his operations relating to the economic activities referred to in Article 4(2) carried out abroad,][2]

(d) Each individual identification number shall have a prefix in accordance with ISO International Standard No 3166 —alpha 2 —by which the Member State of issue may be identified.

(e) Member States shall take the measures necessary to ensure that their identification systems distinguish the taxable persons referred to in (c) and to ensure the correct application of the transitional arrangements for the taxation of intra-Community transactions as laid down in this Title.

ss 16(1),
17(8)

2. (a) Every taxable person shall keep accounts in sufficient detail for value added tax to be applied and inspected by the tax authorities.

s 17(2)(4)

[(b) Every taxable person shall keep a register of the goods he has dispatched or transported or which have been dispatched or transported on his behalf out of the territory defined in Article 3 but within the Community for the purposes of the transactions referred to in the fifth, sixth and seventh indents of Article 28a(5)(b).

Every taxable person shall keep sufficiently detailed accounts to permit the identification of goods dispatched to him from another

Member State by or on behalf of a taxable person identified for purposes of value added tax in that other Member State, in connection with which a service has been provided pursuant to the third or fourth indent of Article 9(2)(*c*);]³

Every taxable person shall keep a register of materials dispatched to him from another Member State by or on behalf of a taxable person identified for purposes of value added tax in that other Member State with a view to the supply to that taxable person of contract work.

3. (*a*) Every taxable person shall issue an invoice, or other document serving as invoice, in respect of goods and services which he has supplied or rendered to another taxable person or to a non-taxable legal person. Every taxable person shall also issue an invoice, or other document serving as invoice, in respect of the supplies of goods referred to in Article 28b(B)(1) and in respect of goods supplied under the conditions laid down in Article 28c(A). A taxable person shall keep a copy of every document issued. s 17(1), (4)
SI 279/1992

Every taxable person shall likewise issue an invoice in respect of any payment to account made to him before any supplies of goods referred to in the first subparagraph and in respect of any payment to account made to him by another taxable person or by a non-taxable legal person before the provision of services is completed.

(*b*) The invoice shall state clearly the price exclusive of tax and the relevant tax at each rate as well as any exemptions.

The invoice shall also indicate:

[— in the case of the transactions referred to in Article 28b(C), (D), (E) and (F), the number by which the taxable person is identified in the territory of the country and the number by which the customer is identified and under which the service has been rendered to him.]⁴

— in the case of the transactions referred to in Article 28c(A)(*a*), the number by which the taxable person is identified in the territory of the country and the number by which the person acquiring the goods is identified in another Member State;

— in the case of the supply of new means of transport, the particulars specified in Article 28a(2).

[— where the provisions of Article 28c(E)(3) are applied, an explicit reference to that provision as well as the identification number for value added tax purposes under which the taxable person has carried out the intra-Community acquisition and the subsequent supply of goods and the number by which the person to whom this supply is made is identified for value added tax purposes.]⁵

(*c*) Member States shall lay down the criteria that shall determine whether a document may be considered an invoice.

4. (*a*) Every taxable person shall submit a return by a deadline to be determined by Member States. That deadline may not be more than two months later than the end of each tax period. The tax period shall be fixed by each Member State at one month, two months or a quarter. Member States may, however, set different periods provided that they do not exceed one year.

(*b*) The return shall set out all the information needed to calculate the tax that has become chargeable and the deductions to be made including, where appropriate, and insofar as it seems necessary for the establishment of the basis of assessment, the total value of the transactions relative to such tax and deductions and the value of any exempt transactions.

(c) The return shall also set out:

— on the one hand, the total value, less value added tax, of the supplies of goods referred to in Article 28c(A) on which tax has become chargeable during the period.

[— on the other hand, the total amount, less value added tax, of the intra-Community acquisitions of goods referred to in Article 28a(1) and (6) effected within the territory of the country on which tax has become chargeable.

The following shall also be added: the total value, less value added tax, of the supplies of goods referred to in the second sentence of Article 8(1)(a) and in Article 28(b)(B)(1) effected in the territory of the country on which tax has become chargeable during the return period, where the place of departure of the dispatch or transport of the goods is situated within the territory of another Member State, and the total amount, less value added tax, of the supplies of goods made within the territory of the country for which the taxable person has been designated as the person liable for the tax in accordance with Article 28c(E)(3) and under which the tax has become payable in the course of the period covered by the declaration,][6]

— on the other hand, the total value, less value added tax, of the intra-Community acquisitions of goods referred to in Article 28a(1) and (6) on which tax has become chargeable.

The following shall also be added: the total value, less value added tax, of the supplies of goods referred to in the second sentence of Article 8(1)(a) and in Article 28b(B)(1) effected in the territory of the country on which tax has become chargeable during the return period, where the place of departure of the dispatch or transport of the goods is situated within the territory of another Member State.

s 19(4) **5.** Every taxable person shall pay the net amount of the value added tax when submitting the regular return. Member States may, however, set a different date for the payment of that amount or may demand an interim payment.

ss 17(1B), 19A **6.** (a) Member States may require a taxable person to submit a statement, including all the particulars specified in paragraph 4, concerning all transactions carried out in the preceding year. That statement shall provide all the information necessary for any adjustments.

(b) [Every taxable person identified for value added tax purposes shall also submit a recapitulative statement of the acquirers identified for value added tax purposes to whom he has supplied goods under the conditions provided for in Article 28c(A)(a) and (d), and of consignees identified for value added tax purposes in the transactions referred to in the fifth subparagraph.][7]

The recapitulative statement shall be drawn up for each calendar quarter within a period and in accordance with procedures to be determined by the Member States, which shall take the measures necessary to ensure that the provisions concerning administrative co-operation in the field of indirect taxation are in any event complied with.

The recapitulative statement shall set out:

— the number by which the taxable person is identified for purposes of value added tax in the territory of the country and under which he effected supplies of goods in the conditions laid down in Article [28c(A)(a)][8],

[— the number by which each person acquiring goods is identified for purposes of value added tax in another Member State and under which the goods were supplied to him,]⁹

— for each person acquiring goods, the total value of the supplies of goods effected by the taxable person. Those amounts shall be declared for the calendar quarter during which the tax became chargeable.

The recapitulative statements shall also set out:

— for the supplies of goods covered by Article [28c(A)(d)]¹⁰, the number by means of which the taxable person is identified for purposes of value added tax in the territory of the country, the number by which he is identified in the Member State of arrival of the dispatch or transport [and the total amount of the supplies, determined in accordance with Article 28e(2).]¹¹,

— the amounts of adjustments made pursuant to Article 11(C)(1). Those amounts shall be declared for the calendar quarter during which the person acquiring the goods is notified of the adjustment.

...¹²

[In the cases set out in the third subparagraph of Article 28b(A)(2), the taxable person identified for value added tax purposes within the territory of the country shall mention in a clear way on the recapitulative statement:

— the number by which he is identified for value added purposes within the territory of the country and under which he carried out the intra-Community acquisition and the subsequent supply of goods,

— the number by which, within the territory of the Member State of arrival of the dispatch or transport of the goods, the consignee of the subsequent supply by the taxable person is identified,

— and, for each consignee, the total amount, less value added tax, of the supplies made by the taxable person within the territory of the Member State of arrival of the dispatch or transport of the goods. These amounts shall be declared for the calendar quarter during which the tax became chargeable.]¹³

(c) By way of derogation from (b), Member States may:

— require recapitulative statements to be filed on a monthly basis;

— require that recapitulative statements give additional particulars.

(d) In the case of supplies of new means of transport effected under the conditions laid down in Article 28c(A)(b) by a taxable person identified for purposes of value added tax to a purchaser not identified for purposes of value added tax or by a taxable person as defined in Article 28a(4), Member States shall take the measures necessary to ensure that the vendor communicates all the information necessary for value added tax to be applied and inspected by the tax authority.

(e) Member States may require taxable persons who in the territory of the country effect intra-Community acquisitions of goods as defined in Article 28a(1)(a) and (6) to submit statements giving details of such acquisitions provided, however, that such statements may not be required for a period of less than one month.

Member States may also require persons who effect the intra-Community acquisitions of new means of transport as defined to in Article 28a(1)(b) to provide, when submitting the return referred to in paragraph 4, all the information necessary for value added tax to be applied and inspected by the tax authority.

7. Member States shall take the measures necessary to ensure that those persons who, in accordance with Article 21(1)(*a*) and (*b*), are considered to be liable to pay the tax instead of a taxable person established abroad or who are jointly and severally liable for the payment comply with the above obligations relating to declaration and payment.

ss 16(2),
17(5)-(7)
20(1A)(1B)
SI 275/1992
SI 277/1992

8. Member States may impose other obligations which they deem necessary for the correct collection of the tax and for the prevention of evasion, subject to the requirement of equal treatment for domestic transactions and transactions carried out between Member States by taxable persons and provided that such obligations do not, in trade between Member States, give rise to formalities connected with the crossing of frontiers.

9.　(*a*)　Member States may release from certain or all obligations:

— taxable persons carrying out only supplies of goods or of services which are exempt under Articles 13 and 15,

— taxable persons eligible for the exemption from tax provided for in Article 24 and for the derogation provided for in Article 28a(1)(*a*), second subparagraph;

— taxable persons carrying out none of the transactions referred to in paragraph 4(*c*).

(*b*)　Member States may release taxable persons other than those referred to in (*a*) from certain of the obligations referred to in 2(*a*).

(*c*)　Member States may release taxable persons from payment of the tax due where the amount involved is insignificant.

10. Member States shall take measures to ensure that non-taxable legal persons who are liable for the tax payable in respect of intra-Community acquisitions of goods covered by the first subparagraph of Article 28a(1)(*a*) comply with the above obligations relating to declaration and payment and that they are identified by an individual number as defined in paragraph 1(*c*), (*d*) and (*e*).

[**11.** In the case of intra-Community acquisitions of products subject to excise duty referred to in Article 28a(1)(*c*) as well as][14] In the case of intra-Community acquisitions of new means of transport covered by Article 28a(1)(*b*), Member States shall adopt arrangements for declaration and subsequent payment.

s 19A

12. Acting unanimously on a proposal from the Commission, the Council may authorise any Member State to introduce particular measures to simplify the statement obligations laid down in paragraph 6(*b*). Such simplification measures, which shall not jeopardize the proper monitoring of intra-Community transactions, may take the following forms:

(*a*)　Member States may authorize taxable persons who meet the following three conditions to file one-year recapitulative statements indicating the numbers by which the persons to whom those taxable persons have supplied goods under the conditions laid down in Article 28c(A) are identified for purposes of value added tax in other Member States:

— the total annual value, less value added tax, of their supplies of goods or provisions of services, as defined in Articles 5, 6 and 28a(5), does not exceed ECU 35,000 the amount of the annual turnover which is used as a reference for application of the exemption from tax provided for in Article 24,

— the total annual value, less value added tax, of supplies of goods effected by them under the conditions laid down in Article 28c(A) does not exceed the equivalent in national currency of ECU 15 000,

— supplies of goods effected by them under the conditions laid down in Article 28c(A) are other than supplies of new means of transport;

(*b*)   Member States which set at over three months the tax period for which a taxable person must submit the returns provided for in paragraph 4 may authorize such persons to submit recapitulative statements for the same period where those taxable persons meet the following three conditions:

—   the overall annual value, less value added tax, of the goods and services they supply, as defined in Articles 5, 6 and 28a(5), does not exceed the equivalent in national currency of ECU 200 000,

—   the total annual value, less value added tax, of supplies of goods effected by them under the conditions laid down in Article 28c(A) does not exceed the equivalent in national currency of ECU 15 000,

—   supplies of goods effected by them under the conditions laid down in Article 28c(A) are other than supplies of new means of transport.][15]

Amendments

1   Para (1)(c)(3rd indent) inserted by Council Directive 92/111/EEC of 14 December 1992, art 1(20) with effect from 1 January 1993.

2   Inserted by Council Directive 92/111/EEC of 14 December 1992, art 1(20) with effect from 1 January 1993.

3   Para (2)(*b*) substituted by art 28h which was amended by Council Directive 95/7/EC of 10 April 1995, art 1(12) with effect from 25 May 1995.

4   Para (3)(*b*)(2nd subpara 1st indent) substituted by art 28h which was amended by Council Directive 95/7/EC of 10 April 1995, art 1(12) with effect from 25 May 1995.

5   Para (3)(*b*)(4th indent) inserted by Council Directive 92/111/EEC of 14 December 1992, art 1(20) with effect from 1 January 1993.

6   Para (4)(*c*)(2nd indent) substituted by Council Directive 92/111/EEC of 14 December 1992, art 1(20) with effect from 1 January 1993.

7   Para (6)(*b*)(1st para) substituted by art 28h which was amended by Council Directive 95/7/EC of 10 April 1995, art 1(12) with effect from 25 May 1995.

8   Substituted by Council Directive 92/111/EEC of 14 December 1992, art 1(20) with effect from 1 January 1993.

9   Para (6)(*b*)(3rd subpara)(2nd indent) substituted by art 28h which was amended by Council Directive 95/7/EC of 10 April 1995, art 1(12) with effect from 25 May 1995.

10   Substituted by Council Directive 92/111/EEC of 14 December 1992, art 1(20) with effect from 1 January 1993.

11   Substituted by Council Directive 92/111/EEC of 14 December 1992, art 1(20) with effect from 1 January 1993.

12   Para (6)(*b*)(5th subpara) deleted by art 28h which was amended by Council Directive 95/7/EC of 10 April 1995, art 1(12) with effect from 25 May 1995.

13   Inserted by Council Directive 92/111/EEC of 14 December 1992, art 1(20) with effect from 1 January 1993.

14   Inserted by Council Directive 92/111/EEC of 14 December 1992, art 1(20) with effect from 1 January 1993.

15   Art 22 substituted by Council Directive 91/680/EEC of 16 December 1991, art 28h with effect from 1 January 1993 for the transitional period specified in art 28l first para.

Case law

Interim payments of VAT required by Italian law precluded by articles 10 and 22(4): *Balocchi v Ministero delle Finanze dello Stato* [1993]STI 1348, ECJ 10/92.

Invoices: particulars required by authorities should not make deduction difficult: *Léa Jeunehomme and Société Anonyme d'Etude et de Gestion Immobiliére "EGI" v Belgian State* [1988]STI 598, ECJ 123 and 330/87.

Article 23
Obligations in respect of imports

s 15

As regards imported goods, Member States shall lay down the detailed rules for the making of the declarations and payments.

In particular, Member States may provide that the value added tax payable on importation of goods by taxable persons or persons liable to tax or certain categories of these two need not be paid at the time of importation, on condition that the tax is mentioned as such in a return to be submitted under Article 22(4).

Case law

Differing accounting and payment periods for import VAT and VAT on internal transactions are permissible: *Dansk Denkavit v Ministeriet for Skatter og Afgifter* [1984]ECR 2649, [1985]3 CMLR 729, ECJ 42/83.

Penalties relating to import VAT should not be more severe than penalties relating to internal transactions: *The State (Italy) v Rainer Drexl* [1989]2 CMLR 241, ECJ 299/86.

TITLE XIV
Special schemes

Article 24
Special scheme for small undertakings

1. Member States which might encounter difficulties in applying the normal tax scheme to small undertakings by reason of their activities or structure shall have the option, under such conditions and within such limits as they may set but subject to the consultation provided for in Article 29, of applying simplified procedures such as flat-rate schemes for charging and collecting the tax provided they do not lead to a reduction thereof.

2. Until a date to be fixed by the Council acting unanimously on a proposal from the Commission, but which shall not be later than that on which the charging of tax on imports and the remission of tax on exports in trade between the Member States are abolished:

(*a*) Member States which have made use of the option under Article 14 of the second Council Directive of 11 April 1967 to introduce exemptions or graduated tax relief may retain them and the arrangements for applying them if they conform with the value added tax system.

Those Member States which apply an exemption from tax to taxable persons whose annual turnover is less than the equivalent in national currency of 5,000 European units of account at the conversion rate of the day on which this Directive is adopted, may increase this exemption up to 5,000 European units of account.

Member States which apply graduated tax relief may neither increase the ceiling of the graduated tax reliefs nor render the conditions for the granting of it more favourable;

(*b*) Member States which have not made use of this option may grant an exemption from tax to taxable persons whose annual turnover is at the maximum equal to the equivalent in national currency of 5,000 European units of account at the conversion rate of the day on which this Directive is adopted; where appropriate, they may grant graduated tax relief to taxable persons whose annual turnover exceeds the ceiling fixed by the Member States for the application of exemption;

(*c*) Member States which apply an exemption from tax to taxable persons whose annual turnover is equal to or higher than the equivalent in national currency of 5,000 European units of account at the conversion rate of the day on which this Directive is adopted, may increase it in order to maintain its value in real terms.

3. The concepts of exemption and graduated tax relief shall apply to the supply of goods and services by small undertakings.

Member States may exclude certain transactions from the arrangements provided for in paragraph 2. The provisions of paragraph 2 shall not, in any case, apply to the transactions referred to in Article 4(3).

[In all circumstances supplies of new means of transport effected under the conditions laid down in Article 28c(A) as well as supplies of goods and services effected by a taxable person who is not established in the territory of the country shall be excluded from the exemption from tax under paragraph 2.][1]

4. The turnover which shall serve as a reference for the purposes of applying the provisions of paragraph 2 shall consist of the amount, exclusive of value added tax, of goods and services supplied as defined in Articles 5 and 6, to the extent that they are taxed, including transactions exempted with refund of tax previously paid in accordance with Article 28(2), and the amount of the transactions exempted pursuant to Article 15, the amount of real property transactions, the financial transactions referred to in Article 13B(*d*), and insurance services, unless these transactions are ancillary transactions.

However, disposals of tangible or intangible capital assets of an undertaking shall not be taken into account for the purposes of calculating turnover.

5. Taxable persons exempt from tax shall not be entitled to deduct tax in accordance with the provisions of Article 17, nor to show the tax on their invoices or on any other documents serving as invoices.

6. Taxable persons eligible for exemption from tax may opt either for the normal value added tax scheme or for the simplified procedures referred to in paragraph 1. In this case they shall be entitled to any graduated tax relief which may be laid down by national legislation.

7. Subject to the application of paragraph 1, taxable persons enjoying graduated relief shall be treated as taxable persons subject to the normal value added tax scheme.

8. At four-yearly intervals, and for the first time on 1 January 1982, and after consultation of the Member States, the Commission shall report to the Council on the application of the provisions of this Article. It shall as far as may be necessary, and taking into account the need to ensure the long-term convergence of national regulations, attach to this report proposals for:

    (*a*)   improvements to be made to the special scheme for small undertakings;

    (*b*)   the adaptation of national systems as regards exemptions and graduated value added tax relief;

    (*c*)   the adaptation of the limit of 5,000 European units of account mentioned in paragraph 2.

9. The Council will decide at the appropriate time whether the realization of the objective referred to in Article 4 of the first Council Directive of 11 April 1967 requires the introduction of a special scheme for small undertakings and will, if appropriate, decide on the limits and common implementing conditions of this scheme. Until the introduction of such a scheme, Member States may retain their own special schemes which they will apply in accordance with the provisions of this Article and of subsequent acts of the Council.

Amendments

1 Inserted by art 28i which was inserted by Council Directive 91/680/EEC of 16 December 1991, art 1(22) with effect from 1 January 1993 for the transitional period specified in art 28l first para, and subsequently amended by Council Directive 92/111/EEC of 14 December 1992, art 1(21) with effect from 1 January 1993.

Article 25
Common flat-rate scheme for farmers

ss 8(3),(9), 17(9)-(13)

1. Where the application to farmers of the normal value added tax scheme, or the simplified scheme provided for in Article 24, would give rise to difficulties, Member States may apply to farmers a flat-rate scheme tending to offset the value added tax charged on purchases of goods and services made by the flat-rate farmers pursuant to this Article.

2. For the purposes of this Article, the following definitions shall apply:

—   **"farmer"**: a taxable person who carries on his activity in one of the undertakings defined below,

—   **"agricultural, forestry or fisheries undertakings"**: an undertaking considered to be such by each Member State within the framework of the production activities listed in Annex A,

—   **"flat-rate farmer"**: a farmer subject to the flat-rate scheme provided for in paragraphs 3 et seq.,

— **"agricultural products"**: goods produced by an agricultural, forestry or fisheries undertaking in each Member State as a result of the activities listed in Annex A,

— **"agricultural service"**: any service as set out in Annex B supplied by a farmer using his labour force and/or by means of the equipment normally available on the agricultural, forestry or fisheries undertaking operated by him,

— **"value added tax charge on inputs"**: the amount of the total value added tax attaching to the goods and services purchased by all agricultural, forestry and fisheries undertakings of each Member State subject to the flat-rate scheme where such tax would be deductible under Article 17 by a farmer subject to the normal value added tax scheme,

— **"flat-rate compensation percentages"**: the percentages fixed by Member States in accordance with paragraph 3 and applied by them in the cases specified in paragraph 5 to enable flat-rate farmers to offset at a fixed rate the value added tax charge on inputs,

— **"flat-rate compensation"**: the amount arrived at by applying the flat-rate compensation percentage provided for in paragraph 3 to the turnover of the flat-rate farmer in the cases referred to in paragraph 5.

3. Member States shall fix the flat-rate compensation percentages, where necessary, and shall notify the Commission before applying them. Such percentages shall be based on macro-economic statistics for flat-rate farmers alone for the preceding three years. They may not be used to obtain for flat-rate farmers refunds greater than the value added tax charges on inputs. Member States shall have the option of reducing such percentages to a nil rate. The percentage may be rounded up or down to the nearest half point.

Member States may fix varying flat-rate compensation percentages for forestry, for the different sub-divisions of agriculture and for fisheries.

4. Member States may release flat-rate farmers from the obligations imposed upon taxable persons by Article 22.

[When they exercise this option, Member States shall take the measures necessary to ensure the correct application of the transitional arrangements for the taxation of intra-Community transactions as laid down in Title XVIa.][1]

[**5.** The flat-rate percentages provided for in paragraph 3 shall be applied to the prices, exclusive of tax, of:

    (*a*) agricultural products supplied by flat-rate farmers to taxable persons other than those eligible within the territory of the country for the flat-rate scheme provided for in this Article;

    (*b*) agricultural products supplied by flat-rate farmers, under the conditions laid down in Article 28c(A), to non-taxable legal persons not eligible, in the Member State of arrival of the dispatch or transport of the agricultural products thus supplied, for the derogation provided for in Article 28a(1)(*a*), second subparagraph;

    (*c*) agricultural services supplied by flat-rate farmers to taxable persons other than those eligible within the territory of the country for the flat-rate scheme provided for in this Article.

This compensation shall exclude any other form of deduction.][2]

[**6.** In the case of the supplies of agricultural products and of agricultural services referred to in paragraph 5, Member States shall provide for the flat-rate compensation to be paid either:

    (*a*) by the purchaser or customer. In that event, the taxable purchaser or customer shall be authorized, as provided for in Article 17 and in accordance with the procedures laid down by the Member States, to deduct from the tax for which he is liable within the territory of the country the amount of the flat-rate compensation he has paid to flat-rate farmers.

Member States shall refund to the purchaser or customer the amount of the flat-rate compensation he has paid to flat-rate farmers in respect of any of the following transactions:

—   supplies of agricultural products effected under the conditions laid down in Article 28c(A) to taxable persons, or to non-taxable legal persons acting as such in another Member State within which they are not eligible for the derogation provided for in the second subparagraph of Article 28a(1)(*a*);

—   supplies of agricultural products effected under the conditions laid down in Article 15 and in Article 16(1)(B), (D) and (E) to taxable purchasers established outside the Community, provided that the products are used by those purchasers for the purposes of the transactions referred to in Article 17(3)(*a*) or (*b*) or for the purposes of services which are deemed to be supplied within the territory of the country and on which tax is payable solely by the customers under Article 21(1)(*b*);

—   supplies of agricultural services to taxable customers established within the Community but in other Member States or to taxable customers established outside the Community, provided that the services are used by those customers for the purposes of the transactions referred to in Article 17(3)(*a*) and (*b*) or for the purposes of services which are deemed to be supplied within the territory of the country and on which tax is payable solely by the customers under Article 21(1)(*b*).

Member States shall determine the method by which the refunds are to be made; in particular, they may apply Article 17(4); or

(*b*)   by the public authorities.][3]

7. Member States shall make all necessary provisions to check properly the payment of the flat-rate compensation to the flat-rate farmers.

8. As regards all supplies of agricultural products and agricultural services other than those covered by paragraph 5, the flat-rate compensation is deemed to be paid by the purchaser or customer.

9. Each Member State may exclude from the flat-rate scheme certain categories of farmers and farmers for whom the application of the normal value added tax scheme, or the simplified scheme provided for in Article 24(1), would not give rise to administrative difficulties.

[Whenever they exercise the option provided for in this Article, Member States shall take all measures necessary to ensure that the same method of taxation is applied to supplies of agricultural products effected under the conditions laid down in Article 28b(B)(1), whether the supply is effected by a flat-rate farmer or by a taxable person other than a flat-rate farmer.][4]

10. Every flat-rate farmer may opt, subject to the rules and conditions to be laid down by each Member State, for application of the normal value added tax scheme or, as the case may be, the simplified scheme provided for in Article 24(1).

11. The Commission shall, before the end of the fifth year following the entry into force of this Directive, present to the Council new proposals concerning the application of the value added tax to transactions in respect of agricultural products and services.

12. When they take up the option provided for in this Article the Member States shall fix the uniform basis of assessment of the value added tax in order to apply the scheme of own resources using the common method of calculation in Annex C.

Amendments

1   Inserted by art 28j(1) which was inserted by Council Directive 91/680/EEC of 16 December 1991, art 1(22) with effect from 1 January 1993 for the transitional period specified in art 28l first para.

2   Para (5) substituted by art 28j(2) which was inserted by Council Directive 91/680/EEC of 16 December 1991, art 1(22) with effect from 1 January 1993 for the transitional period specified in art 28l first para.

3   Para (6) substituted by art 28j(2) which was inserted by Council Directive 91/680/EEC of 16 December 1991, art 1(22) with effect from 1 January 1993 for the transitional period specified in art 28l first para.

4   Inserted by art 28j(3) which was inserted by Council Directive 91/680/EEC of 16 December 1991, art 1(22) with effect from 1 January 1993 for the transitional period specified in art 28l first para.

Case law

Flat-rate farmers: *Re Flat-rate VAT for Farmers, EC Commission v Italy* [1989]3 CMLR 748, ECJ 3/86.

Article 26
Special scheme for travel agents

1. Member States shall apply value added tax to the operations of travel agents in accordance with the provisions of this Article, where the travel agents deal with customers in their own name and use the supplies and services of other taxable persons in the provision of travel facilities. This Article shall not apply to travel agents who are acting only as intermediaries and accounting for tax in accordance with Article 11 A (3)(*c*). In this Article travel agents include tour operators.

2. All transactions performed by the travel agent in respect of a journey shall be treated as a single service supplied by the travel agent to the traveller. It shall be taxable in the Member State in which the travel agent has established his business or has a fixed establishment from which the travel agent has provided the services. The taxable amount and the price exclusive of tax, within the meaning of Article 22(3)(*b*), in respect of this service shall be the travel agent's margin, that is to say, the difference between the total amount to be paid by the traveller, exclusive of value added tax, and the actual cost to the travel agent of supplies and services provided by other taxable persons where these transactions are for the direct benefit of the traveller.

3. If transactions entrusted by the travel agent to other taxable persons are performed by such persons outside the Community, the travel agent's service shall be treated as an exempted intermediary activity under Article 15(14). Where these transactions are performed both inside and outside the Community, only that part of the travel agent's service relating to transactions outside the Community may be exempted.

4. Tax charged to the travel agent by other taxable persons on the transactions described in paragraph 2 which are for the direct benefit of the traveller, shall not be eligible for deduction or refund in any Member State.

Case law

Letting of holiday dwellings: *Beheermattschappij van Ginkel Waddinxveen BV, Reisen Passingbureau Ban Ginkel v Inspecteur der Omzetbelasting* ECJ 163/91.

[Article 26a
Special arrangements applicable to second-hand goods, works of art, collectors' items and antiques

A. Definitions

For the purpose of this Article, and without prejudice to other Community provisions:

   (*a*)   *works of art* shall means the objects referred to in (*a*) of Annex I.

   However, Member States shall have the option of not considering as "works of art" the items mentioned in the final three indents in (*a*) in Annex I;

   (*b*)   *collectors items* shall mean the objects referred to in (*b*) of Annex I;

   (*c*)   *antiques* shall mean the objects referred to in (*c*) of Annex I;

(d) *second-hand goods* shall mean tangible movable property that is suitable for further use as it is or after repair, other than works of art, collectors' items or antiques and other than precious metals or precious stones as defined by the Member States;

(e) *taxable dealer* shall mean a taxable person who, in the course of his economic activity, purchases or acquires for the purposes of his undertaking, or imports with a view to resale, second-hand goods and/ or works of art, collectors' items or antiques, whether that taxable person is acting for himself or on behalf of another person pursuant to a contract under which commission is payable on purchase or sale;

(f) *organizer of a sale by public auction* shall mean any taxable person who, in the course of his economic activity, offers goods for sale by public auction with a view to handing them over to the highest bidder;

(g) *principal of an organizer of a sale by public auction* shall mean any person who transmits goods to an organizer of a sale by public auction under a contract under which commission is payable on a sale subject to the following provisions:

— the organizer of the sale by public auction offers the goods for sale in his own name but on behalf of his principal,

— the organizer of the sale by public auction hands over the goods, in his own name but on behalf of his principal, to the highest bidder at the public auction.

B. Special arrangements for taxable dealers

1. In respect of supplies of second-hand goods, works of art, collectors' items and antiques effected by taxable dealers, Member States shall apply special arrangements for taxing the profit margin made by the taxable dealer, in accordance with the following provisions.

2. The supplies of goods referred to in paragraph 1 shall be supplies, by a taxable dealer, of second-hand goods, works of art, collectors' items or antiques supplied to him within the Community:

— by a non-taxable person,

or

— by another taxable person, in so far as the supply of goods by that other taxable person is exempt in accordance with Article 13(B)(c),

or

— by another taxable person in so far as the supply of goods by that other taxable person qualifies for the exemption provided for in Article 24 and involves capital assets,

or

— by another taxable dealer, in so far as the supply of goods by that other taxable dealer was subject to value added tax in accordance with these special arrangements.

3. The taxable amount of the supplies of goods referred to in paragraph 2 shall be the profit margin made by the taxable dealer, less the amount of value added tax relating to the profit margin. That profit margin shall be equal to the difference between the selling price charged by the taxable dealer for the goods and the purchase price.

For the purposes of this paragraph, the following definitions shall apply:

— *selling price* shall mean everything which constitutes the consideration, which has been, or is to be, obtained by the taxable dealer from the purchaser or a third party, including subsidies directly linked to that transaction, taxes, duties, levies and charges and incidental expenses such as commission, packaging, transport and insurance costs charged by the taxable dealer to the purchaser but excluding the amounts referred to in Article 11(A)(3),

— *purchase price* shall mean everything which constitutes the consideration defined in the first indent, obtained, or to be obtained, from the taxable dealer by his supplier.

4. Member States shall entitle taxable dealers to opt for application of the special arrangements to supplies of:

(*a*) works of art, collectors' items or antiques which they have imported themselves;

(*b*) works of art supplied to them by their creators or their successors in title;

(*c*) works of art supplied to them by taxable person other than a taxable dealer where the supply by that other taxable person was subject to the reduced rate pursuant to Article 12(3)(*c*).

Member States shall determine the detailed rules for exercising this option which shall in any event cover a period at least equal to two calendar years.

If the option is taken up, the taxable amount shall be determined in accordance with paragraph 3. For supplies of works of art, collectors' items or antiques which the taxable dealer has imported himself, the purchase price to be taken into account in calculating the margin shall be equal to the taxable amount on importation, determined in accordance with Article 11(B), plus the value added tax due or paid on importation.

5. Where they are effected in the conditions laid down in Article 15, the supplies of second-hand goods, works of art, collectors' item or antiques subject to the special arrangements for taxing the margin shall be exempt.

6. Taxable persons shall not be entitled to deduct from the tax for which they are liable the value added tax due or paid in respect of goods which have been, or are to be, supplied to them by a taxable dealer, in so far as the supply of those goods by the taxable dealer is subject to the special arrangements for taxing the margin.

7. In so far as goods are used for the purposes of supplies by him subject to the special arrangements for taxing the margin, the taxable dealer shall not be entitled to deduct from the tax for which he is liable;

(*a*) the value added tax due or paid in respect of works of art, collectors' items or antiques which he has imported himself;

(*b*) the value added tax due or paid in respect of works of art which have been, or are to be, supplied to him by their creators or their successors in title;

(*c*) the value added tax due or paid in respect of works of art which have been, or are to be, supplied to him by a taxable person other than a taxable dealer.

8. Where he is led to apply both the normal arrangements for value added tax and the special arrangements for taxing the margin, the taxable dealer must follow separately in his accounts the transactions falling under each of these arrangements, according to rules laid down by the Member States.

9. The taxable dealer may not indicate separately on the invoices which he issues, or on any other document serving as an invoice, tax relating to supplies of goods which he makes subject to the special arrangements for taxing the margin.

10. In order to simplify the procedure for charging the tax and subject to the consultation provided for in Article 29, Member States may provide that, for certain transactions or for certain categories of taxable dealers, the taxable amount of supplies of goods subject to the special arrangements for taxing the margin shall be determined for each tax period during which the taxable dealer must submit the return referred to in Article 22(4).

In that event, the taxable amount for supplies of goods to which the same rate of value added tax is applied shall be the total margin made by the taxable dealer less the amount of value added tax relating to that margin.

The total margin shall be equal to the difference between:

— the total amount of supplies of goods subject to the special arrangements for taxing the margin effected by the taxable dealer during the period; that amount shall be equal to the total selling prices determined in accordance with paragraph 3,

and

— the total amount of purchases of goods as referred to in paragraph 2 effected, during that period, by the taxable dealer; that amount shall be equal to the total purchase prices determined in accordance with paragraph 3.

Member States shall take the necessary measures to ensure that the taxable persons concerned do not enjoy unjustified advantages or sustain unjustified loss.

11. The taxable dealer may apply the normal value added tax arrangements to any supply covered by the special arrangements pursuant to paragraph 2 or 4.

Where the taxable dealer applies the normal value added tax arrangements to:

(*a*) the supply of a work of art, collectors' item or antique which he has imported himself, he shall be entitled to deduct from his tax liability the value added tax due or paid on the import of those goods;

(*b*) the supply of a work of art supplied to him by its creator or his successors in title, he shall be entitled to deduct from his tax liability the value added tax due or paid for the work of art supplied to him;

(*c*) the supply of a work of art supplied to him by a taxable person other than a taxable dealer, he shall be entitled to deduct from his tax liability the value added tax due or paid for the work of art supplied to him.

This right to deduct shall arise at the time when the tax due for the supply in respect of which the taxable dealer opts for application of the normal value added tax arrangements become chargeable.

C. Special arrangements for sales by public auction.

1. By way of derogation from B, Member States may determine, in accordance with the following provisions, the taxable amount of supplies of second-hand goods, works of art, collectors' items or antiques effected by an organizer of sales by public auction, acting in his own name, pursuant to a contract under which commission is payable on the sale of those goods by public auction, on behalf of:

— a non-taxable person,

or

— another taxable person, in so far as the supply of goods, within the meaning of Article 5(4)(*c*), by that other taxable person is exempt in accordance with Article 13(B)(*c*),

or

— another taxable person, in so far as the supply of goods, within the meaning of Article 5(4)(*c*), by that other taxable person qualifies for the exemption provided for in Article 24 and involves capital assets,

or

— a taxable dealer, in so far as the supply of goods, within the meaning of Article 5(4)(*c*), by that other taxable dealer, is subject to tax in accordance with the special arrangements for taxing the margin provided for in B.

2. The taxable amount of each supply of goods referred to in paragraph 1 shall be the total amount invoiced in accordance with paragraph 4 to the purchaser by the organizer of the sale by public auction, less:

— the net amount paid or to be paid by the organizer of the sale by public auction to his principal, determined in accordance with paragraph 3,

and

— the amount of the tax due by the organizer of the sale by public auction in respect of his supply.

3. The net amount paid or to be paid by the organizer of the sale by public auction to his principal shall be equal to the difference between:

— the price of the goods at public auction,

and

— the amount of the commission obtained or to be obtained by the organizer of the sale by public auction from his principal, under the contract whereby commission is payable on the sale.

4. The organizer of the sale by public auction must issue to the purchaser an invoice or a document in lieu itemizing:

— the auction price of the goods,

— taxes, dues, levies and charges,

— incidental expenses such as commission, packing, transport and insurance costs charged by the organizer to the purchaser of the goods.

That invoice must not indicate any value added tax separately.

5. The organizer of the sale by public auction to whom the goods were transmitted under a contract whereby commission is payable on a public auction sale must issue a statement to his principal.

That statement must itemize the amount of the transaction, ie the auction price of the goods less the amount of the commission obtained or to be obtained from the principal.

A statement so drawn up shall serve as the invoice which the principal, where he is a taxable person, must issue to the organizer of the sale by public auction in accordance with Article 22(3).

6. Organizers of sales by public auction who supply goods under the conditions laid down in paragraph 1 must indicate in their accounts, in suspense accounts:

— the amounts obtained or to be obtained from the purchase of the goods,

— the amount reimbursed or to be reimbursed to the vendor of the goods.

These amounts must be fully substantiated.

7. The supply of goods to a taxable person who is an organizer of sales by public auction shall be regarded as being effected when the sale of those goods by public auction is itself effected.

D. Transitional arrangements for the taxation of trade between Member States

During the period referred to in Article 28l, Member States shall apply the following provisions:

(*a*) supplies of new means of transport, within the meaning of Article 28a(2), effected within the conditions laid down in Article 28c(A) shall be excluded from the special arrangements provided for in B and C;

(*b*) by way of derogation from Article 28a(1)(*a*), intra-Community acquisition of second-hand goods, works of art, collectors' items or antiques shall not be subject to value added tax where the vendor is a taxable dealer acting as such and the goods acquired have been subject to tax in the Member State of departure of the dispatch or transport, in accordance with the special arrangements for taxing the margin provided for in B, or where the vendor is an organizer of sales by public auction acting as such and the goods acquired have been subject to tax in the Member State of departure of the dispatch or transport, in accordance with the special arrangements provided for in C;

(*c*) Articles 28b(B) and 28c(A)(*a*), (*c*) and (*d*) shall not apply to supplies of goods subject to value added tax in accordance with either of the special arrangements laid down in B and C.]¹

Amendments
1 Article 26a inserted by Council Directive 94/5/EC of 14 February 1994 art 1(3).

TITLE XV
Simplification procedures

Article 27

1. The Council, acting unanimously on a proposal from the Commission, may authorize any Member State to introduce special measures for derogation from the provisions of this Directive, in order to simplify the procedure for charging the tax or to prevent certain types of tax evasion or avoidance. Measures intended to simplify the procedure for charging the tax, except to a negligible extent, may not affect the amount of tax due at the final consumption stage.

2. A Member State wishing to introduce the measures referred to in paragraph 1 shall inform the Commission of them and shall provide the Commission with all relevant information.

3. The Commission shall inform the other Member States of the proposed measures within one month.

4. The Council's decision shall be deemed to have been adopted if, within two

months of the other Member States being informed as laid down in the previous paragraph, neither the Commission nor any Member State has requested that the matter be raised by the Council.

5. Those Member States which apply on 1 January 1977 special measures of the type referred to in paragraph 1 above may retain them providing they notify the Commission of them before 1 January 1978 and providing that where such derogations are designed to simplify the procedure for charging tax they conform with the requirement laid down in paragraph 1 above.

Cross-references
Art 27(1): derogations granted: Authorisation 83/333/EEC (derogations under a draft agreement between Germany and Luxembourg); Authorisation 84/468/EEC (derogations under a draft agreement between Germany and the Netherlands); Decision 89/487/EEC (authorising France to derogate from art 17(6)); Decision 89/488/EEC (authorising France to derogate from art 17(2)).
Case law
Para (1): "special measures": Member State which failed to inform EC Commission of "special measure" could not rely on it in the national court: *Direct Cosmetics Ltd v C & E Commissioners* [1985]STC 479, [1985]2 CMLR 145, ECJ 5/84; *Direct Cosmetics Ltd and Laughtons Photographs Ltd v C & E Commissioners* [1988]STC 540, ECJ 138/139/86.

TITLE XVI
Transitional provisions

Article 28

1. Any provisions brought into force by the Member States under the provisions of the first four indents of Article 17 of the second Council Directive of 11 April

1967 shall cease to apply, in each Member State, as from the respective dates on which the provisions referred to in the second paragraph of Article 1 of this Directive come into force.

[**1a.** Until a date which may not be later than 30 June 1999, the United Kingdom of Great Britain and Northern Ireland may, for imports of works of art, collectors' items or antiques which qualified for an exemption on 1 January 1993, apply Article 11(B)(6) in such a way that the value added tax due on importation is, in any event, equal to 2,5% of the amount determined in accordance with Article 11(B)(1) to (4).][1]

[**2.** Notwithstanding Article 12(3), the following provisions shall apply during the transitional period referred to in Article 281.

(a) Exemptions with refund of the tax paid at the preceding stage and reduced rates lower than the minimum rate laid down in Article 12(3) in respect of the reduced rates, which were in force on 1 January 1991 and which are in accordance with Community law, and satisfy the conditions stated in the last indent of Article 17 of the second Council Directive of 11 April 1967, may be maintained.

Member States shall adopt the measures necessary to ensure the determination of own resources relating to these operations.

In the event that the provisions of this paragraph create for Ireland distortions of competition in the supply of energy products for heating and lighting, Ireland may, on specific request, be authorised by the Commission to apply a reduced rate to such supplies, in accordance with Article 12(3). In that case, Ireland shall submit its request to the Commission together with all necessary information. If the Commission has not taken a decision within three months of receiving the request, Ireland shall be deemed to be authorised to apply the proposed reduced rates.

(b) Member States which, at 1 January 1991 in accordance with Community law, applied exemptions with refund of tax paid at the preceding stage, or reduced rates lower than the minimum laid down in Article 12(3) in respect of the reduced rates, to goods and services other than those specified in Annex H, may apply the reduced rate or one of the two reduced rates provided for in Article 12(3) to any such supplies.

(c) Member States which under the terms of Article 12(3) will be obliged to increase their standard rate as applied at 1 January 1991 by more than 2%, may apply a reduced rate lower than the minimum laid down in Article 12(3) in respect of the reduced rate to supplies of categories of goods and services specified in Annex H. Furthermore, those Member States may apply such a rate to restaurant services, children's clothing, children's footwear and housing. Member States may not introduce exemptions with refund of the tax at the preceding stage on the basis of this paragraph.

(d) Member States which at 1 January 1991 applied a reduced rate to restaurant services, children's clothing, children's footwear and housing, may continue to apply such a rate to such supplies.

(e) Member States which at 1 January 1991 applied a reduced rate to supplies of goods and services other than those specified in Annex H may apply the reduced rate or one of the two reduced rates provided for in Article 12(3) to such supplies, provided that the rate is not lower than 12%.

[This provision may not apply to supplies of second-hand goods, works of art, collectors' items or antiques subject to value added tax in accordance with one of the special arrangements provided for an Article 26a(B) and (C).][2]

(*f*)   The Hellenic Republic may apply VAT rates up to 30% lower than the corresponding rates applied in mainland Greece in the departments of Lesbos, Chios, Samos, the Dodecanese and the Cyclades, and on the following islands in the Aegean: Thasos, Northern Sporades, Samothrace and Skiros.

(*g*)   On the basis of a report from the Commission, the Council shall, before 31 December 1994, re-examine the provisions of subparagraphs (*a*) to (*f*) above in relation to the proper functioning of the internal market in particular. In the event of significant distortions of competition arising, the Council, acting unanimously on a proposal from the Commission, shall adopt appropriate measures.

[(*h*)   Member States which, on 1 January 1993, were availing themselves of the option provided for in Article 5(5)(*a*) as in force on that date, may apply to supplies under contract to make up work the rate applicable to the goods after making up.

For the purposes of applying this provision, supplies under a contract to make up work shall be deemed to be delivery by a contractor to his customer of movable property made or assembled by the contractor from materials or objects entrusted to him by the customer for this purpose, whether or not the contractor has provided any part of the materials used.]³]⁴

[(*i*)   Member States may apply a reduced rate to supplies of live plants (including bulbs, roots and the like, cut flowers and ornamental foliage) and wood for use as firewood.]⁵

3. During the transitional period referred to in paragraph 4, Member States may:

(*a*)   continue to subject to tax the transactions exempt under Article 13 or 15 set out in Annex E to this Directive;

(*b*)   continue to exempt the activities set out in Annex F under conditions existing in the Member State concerned;

(*c*)   grant to taxable persons the option for taxation of exempt transactions under the conditions set out in Annex G;

(*d*)   continue to apply provisions derogating from the principle of immediate deduction laid down in the first paragraph of Article 18(2);

(*e*)   continue to apply measures derogating from the provisions of Articles ...⁶ 6(4) and 11 A(3)(*c*);

(*f*)   provide that for supplies of buildings and building land purchased for the purpose of resale by a taxable person for whom tax on the purchase was not deductible, the taxable amount shall be the difference between the selling price and the purchase price;

(*g*)   by way of derogation from Articles 17(3) and 26(3), continue to exempt without repayment of input tax the services of travel agents referred to in Article 26(3). This derogation shall also apply to travel agents acting in the name and on account of the traveller.

[**3a.** Pending a decision by the Council, which, under to Article 3 of Directive 89/465/EEC (OJ L 3.8.89, p 21), is to act on the abolition of the transitional derogations provided for in paragraph 3, Spain shall be authorized to exempt the transactions referred to in point 2 of Annex F in respect of services rendered by authors and the transactions referred to in points 23 and 25 of Annex F.]⁷

4. The transitional period shall last initially for five years as from 1 January 1978. At the latest six months before the end of this period, and subsequently as necessary, the Council shall review the situation with regard to the derogations set out in paragraph 3 on the basis of a report from the Commission and shall unanimously determine on a proposal from the Commission, whether any or all of these derogations shall be abolished.

5. At the end of the transitional period passenger transport shall be taxed in the country of departure for that part of the journey taking place within the Community according to the detailed rules of procedure to be laid down by the Council acting unanimously on a proposal from the Commission.

Amendments
1 Para (1*a*) inserted by Council Directive 94/5/EC of 14 February 1994, art 1(4).
2 Inserted in para (2)(*e*) by Council Directive 94/5/EC of 14 February 1994, art 1(5).
3 Para (2)(*h*) inserted by Council Directive 95/7/EC of 10 April 1995 art 1(2) with effect from 25 May 1995.
4 Para (2) substituted by Council Directive 92/77/EEC of 19 October 1992, art 1(4) with effect from 1 January 1993.
5 Para (2)(*i*) inserted by Council Directive 96/42/EC of 25 June 1996 with effect from 1 January 1996.
6 Deleted by Council Directive 94/5/EC of 14 February 1994 art 1(8); previously "5(4)(*c*),".
7 Para (3*a*) inserted by Council Directive 91/680/EEC of 16 December 1991, art 1(21) with effect from 1 January 1993.
Cross-references
Application of art 28(3)(*b*) to Greece: Act of Accession 1979 art 128 and Annex VIII Part II point 2(*b*).

TITLE XVI*a*
Transitional arrangements for the taxation of trade between Member States

---

Amendments
1 This title (art 28a-m) inserted by Council Directive 91/680/EEC of 16 December 1991 art 22.
Cross-references
Period of application of this title: art 28l.

[*Article 28a*
Scope

1. The following shall also be subject to value added tax:

s 2(1A)
    (*a*) intra-Community acquisitions of goods for consideration within the territory of the country by a taxable person acting as such or by a non-taxable legal person where the vendor is a taxable person acting as such who is not eligible for the tax exemption provided for in Article 24 and who is not covered by the arrangements laid down in the second sentence of Article 8(1)(*a*) or in Article 28(*b*)(B)(1).

        [By way of derogation from the first subparagraph, intra-Community acquisitions of goods made under the conditions set out in paragraph 1a by a taxable person or non-taxable legal person shall not be subject to value added tax.][1]

        Member States shall grant taxable persons and non taxable legal persons eligible under the second subparagraph the right to opt for the general scheme laid down in the first subparagraph. Member States shall determine the detailed rules for the exercise of that option which shall in any case apply for two calendar years.

    (*b*) intra-Community acquisitions of new means of transport effected for consideration within the country by taxable persons or non-taxable legal persons who qualify for the derogation provided for in the second subparagraph of (*a*) or by any other non-taxable person.

    [(*c*) the intra-Community acquisition of goods which are subject to excise duties effected for consideration within the territory of the country by a taxable person or a non-taxable legal person who qualifies for the derogation referred to in the second subparagraph of point (*a*), and for which the excise duties become chargeable within the territory of the country pursuant to Directive 92/12/EEC (OJ L 76, 23.3.1992, p 1.)][2]

[**1a.** The following shall benefit from the derogation set out in the second subparagraph of paragraph 1(*a*):

    (*a*) intra-Community acquisitions of goods whose supply within the territory of the country would be exempt pursuant to Article 15(4) to (10);

    (*b*) intra-Community acquisitions of goods other than those at (*a*), made:

— by a taxable person for the purpose of his agricultural, forestry or fisheries undertaking, subject to the flat-rate scheme set out in Article 25, by a taxable person who carries out only supplies of goods or services in respect of which value added tax is not deductible, or by a non-taxable legal person,

— for a total amount not exceeding, during the current calendar year, a threshold which the Member States shall determine but which may not be less than the equivalent in national currency of ECU 10,000, and

— provided that the total amount of intra-Community acquisitions of goods did not, during the previous calendar year, exceed the threshold referred to in the second indent.

The threshold which serves as the reference for the application of the above shall consist of the total amount, exclusive of value added tax due or paid in the Member State from which the goods are dispatched or transported, of intra-Community acquisitions of goods other than new means of transport and other than goods subject to excise duty.][3]

2. For the purposes of this Title:

(a) the following shall be considered as **"means of transport"**: vessels exceeding 7.5 metres in length, aircraft the take-off weight of which exceeds 1550 kilograms and motorised land vehicles the capacity of which exceeds 48 cubic centimetres or the power of which exceeds 7.2 kilowatts, intended for the transport of persons or goods, except for the vessels and aircraft referred to in Article 15(5) and (6);   s 1(1)

[(b) the means of transport referred to in (a) shall not be considered to be "new" where both of the following conditions are simultaneously fulfilled:

— they were supplied more than three months after the date of first entry into service. However, this period shall be increased to six months for the motorized land vehicles defined in (a),

— they have travelled more than 6,000 kilometres in the case of land vehicles, sailed for more than 100 hours in the case of vessels, or flown for more than 40 hours in the case of aircraft.

Member States shall lay down the conditions under which the above facts can be regarded as established.][4]

3. "Intra-Community acquisition of goods" shall mean acquisition of the right to dispose as owner of movable tangible property dispatched or transported to the person acquiring the goods by or on behalf of the vendor or the person acquiring the goods to a Member State other than that from which the goods are dispatched or transported.   s 3A(5)

Where goods acquired by a non-taxable legal person are dispatched or transported from a third territory and imported by that non-taxable legal person into a Member State other than the Member State of arrival of the goods dispatched or transported, the goods shall be deemed to have been dispatched or transported from the Member State of import. That Member State shall grant the importer as defined in Article 21(2) a refund of the value added tax paid in connection with the importation of the goods insofar as the importer establishes that his acquisition was subject to value added tax in the Member State of arrival of the goods dispatched or transported.

4. Any person who from time to time supplies a new means of transport under the conditions laid down in Article 28c(A) shall also be regarded as a taxable person.   s 3A(1)

The Member State within the territory of which the supply is effected shall grant the taxable person the right of deduction on the basis of the following provisions:

— the right of deduction shall arise and may be exercised only at the time of the supply;

— the taxable person shall be authorized to deduct the value added tax included in the purchase price or paid on the importation or intra-Community acquisition of the means of transport, up to an amount not exceeding the tax for which he would be liable if the supply were not exempt.

Member States shall lay down detailed rules for the implementation of these provisions.

5. [The following shall be treated as supplies of goods effected for consideration:][5]

...[6]

s 3(1)(g) (*b*) the transfer by a taxable person of goods from his undertaking to another Member State.

The following shall be regarded as having been transferred to another Member State: any tangible property dispatched or transported by or on behalf of the taxable person out of the territory defined in Article 3 but within the Community for the purposes of his undertaking, other than for the purposes of one of the following transactions:

— the supply of the goods in question by the taxable person within the territory of the Member State of arrival of the dispatch or transport under the conditions laid down in the second sentence of Article 8(1)(*a*) and in Article 28b(B)(1),

— the supply of the goods in question by the taxable person under the conditions laid down in Article 8(1)(*c*),

— the supply of the goods in question by the taxable person within the territory of the country under the conditions laid down in Article 15 or in Article 28c(A),

...[7]

[— the supply of a service performed for the taxable person and involving work on the goods in question physically carried out in the Member State in which the dispatch or transport of the goods ends, provided that the goods, after being worked upon, are re-dispatched to that taxable person in the Member State from which they had initially been dispatched or transported,][8]

s 3(1)(g)(iv) — temporary use of the goods in question within the territory of the Member State of arrival of the dispatch or transport of the goods for the purposes of the supply of services by the taxable person established within the territory of the Member State of departure of the dispatch or transport of the goods,

s 3(1)(g)(v) — temporary use of the goods in question, for a period not exceeding 24 months, within the territory of another Member State in which the import of the same goods from a third country with a view to temporary use would be eligible for the arrangements for temporary importation with full exemption from import duties.

[However, when one of the conditions to which the benefit of the above is subordinated is no longer met, the goods shall be considered as having been transferred to a destination in another Member State. In this case, the transfer is carried out at the moment that the conditions is no longer met.][9]

6. The intra-Community acquisition of goods for consideration shall include the use by a taxable person for the purposes of his undertaking of goods dispatched or transported by or on behalf of that taxable person from another Member State within the territory of which the goods were produced, extracted, processed, purchased, acquired as defined in paragraph 1 or imported by the taxable person within the framework of his undertaking into that other Member State.

[The following shall also be deemed to be an intra-Community acquisition of goods effected for consideration: the appropriation of goods by the forces of a State party to the North Atlantic Treaty, for their use or for the use of the civilian staff accompanying them, which they have not acquired subject to the general rules governing taxation on the domestic market of one of the Member States, when the importation of these goods could not benefit from the exemption set out in Article 14(1)(g).][10]

7. Member States shall take measures to ensure that transactions which would have been classed as "supplies of goods" as defined in paragraph 5 or Article 5 if they had been carried out within the territory of the country by a taxable person acting as such are classed as "intra-Community acquisitions of goods".][11]

Amendments

1 Substituted by Council Directive 92/111/EEC of 14 December 1992, art 1(10) with effect from 1 January 1993.

2 Para (1)(c) inserted by Council Directive 92/111/EEC of 14 December 1992, art 1(10) with effect from 1 January 1993.

3 Para (1a) inserted by Council Directive 92/111/EEC of 14 December 1992, art 1(10) with effect from 1 January 1993.

4 Para (2)(b) substituted by Council Directive 94/5/EC of 14 February 1994 art 1 para (6).

5 Substituted by Council Directive 95/7/EC of 10 April 1995 art 1(6) with effect from 25 May 1995.

6 Deleted by Council Directive 95/7/EC of 10 April 1995 art 1(6) with effect from 25 May 1995.

7 Deleted by Council Directive 95/7/EC of 10 April 1995 art 1(6) with effect from 25 May 1995.

8 Substituted by Council Directive 95/7/EC of 10 April 1995 art 1(6) with effect from 25 May 1995.

9 Inserted by Council Directive 92/111/EEC of 14 December 1992, art 1(10) with effect from 1 January 1993.

10 Inserted by Council Directive 92/111/EEC of 14 December 1992, art 1(10) with effect from 1 January 1993.

11 Art 28a inserted by Council Directive 91/680/EEC of 16 December 1991, art 1(22) with effect from 1 January 1993.

Cross-references

Period of application: art 28l.

[*Article 28b*
Place of transactions

A. Place of the intra-Community acquisition of goods

1. The place of the intra-Community acquisition of goods shall be deemed to be the place where the goods are at the time when dispatch or transport to the person acquiring them ends.

s 3A(2)(a)

2. Without prejudice to paragraph 1, the place of the intra-Community acquisition of goods referred to in Article 28a(1)(a) shall, however, be deemed to be within the territory of the Member State which issued the value added tax identification number under which the person acquiring the goods made the acquisition, unless the person acquiring the goods establishes that that acquisition has been subject to tax in accordance with paragraph 1.

ss 3A(2)(b),
5(6)(g)

If, however, the acquisition is subject to tax in accordance with paragraph 1 in the Member State of arrival of the dispatch or transport of the goods after having been subject to tax in accordance with the first subparagraph, the taxable amount shall be reduced accordingly in the Member State which issued the value added tax identification number under which the person acquiring the goods made the acquisition.

[For the purposes of applying the first subparagraph, the intra-Community acquisition of goods shall be deemed to have been subject to tax in accordance with paragraph 1 when the following conditions have been met:

— the acquirer establishes that he has effected this intra-Community acquisition for the needs of a subsequent supply effected in the Member State referred to in paragraph 1 and for which the consignee has been designated as the person liable for the tax due in accordance with Article 28c(E)(3),

— the obligations for declaration set out in the last subparagraph of Article 22(6)(b) have been satisfied by the acquirer.][1]

B. Place of the supply of goods

s 3A(6)(d) **1.** By way of derogation from Article 8(1)(a) and (2), the place of the supply of goods dispatched or transported by or on behalf of the supplier from a Member State other than that of arrival of the dispatch or transport shall be deemed to be the place where the goods are when the dispatch or transport to the purchaser ends, where the following conditions are fulfilled:

— the supply of goods is effected for a taxable person eligible for the derogation provided for in the second subparagraph of Article 28(a)(1)(a), for a non-taxable legal person who is eligible for the same derogation or for any other non-taxable person,

— the supply is of goods other than new means of transport and other than goods supplied after assembly or installation, with or without a trial run, by or on behalf of the supplier.

Where the goods thus supplied are dispatched or transported from a third territory and imported by the supplier into a Member State other than the Member State of arrival of the goods dispatched or transported to the purchaser, they shall be regarded as having been dispatched or transported from the Member State of import.

2. However, where the supply is of goods other than products subject to excise duty, paragraph 1 shall not apply to supplies of goods dispatched or transported to the same Member State of arrival of the dispatch or transport where:

— the total value of such supplies, less value added tax, does not in one calendar year exceed the equivalent in national currency of ECU 100,000 and

s 3(6)(1) — the total value, less value added tax, of the supplies of goods other than products subject to excise duty effected under the conditions laid down in paragraph 1 in the previous calendar year did not exceed the equivalent in national currency of ECU 100,000.

The Member State within the territory of which the goods are when dispatch or transport to the purchaser ends may limit the thresholds referred to above to the equivalent in national currency of ECU 35,000 where that Member State fears that the threshold of ECU 100,000 referred to above would lead to serious distortions of the conditions of competition. Member States which exercise this option shall take the measures necessary to inform the relevant public authorities in the Member State of dispatch or transport of the goods.

Before 31 December 1994, the Commission shall report to the Council on the operation of the special ECU 35,000 thresholds provided for in the preceding subparagraph. In that report the Commission may inform the Council that the abolition of the special thresholds will not lead to serious distortions of the conditions of competition. Until the Council takes a unanimous decision on a Commission proposal, the preceding subparagraph shall remain in force.

3. The Member State within the territory of which the goods are at the time of departure of the dispatch or transport shall grant those taxable persons who effect supplies of goods eligible under paragraph 2 the right to choose that the place of such supplies shall be determined in accordance with paragraph 1.

The Member States concerned shall determine the detailed rules for the exercise of that option, which shall in any case apply for two calendar years.

C. Place of the supply of services in the intra-Community transport of goods

s 5(6)(f)-(g) **1.** By way of derogation from Article 9(2)(b), the place of the supply of services in the intra-Community transport of goods shall be determined in accordance with paragraphs 2, 3 and 4. For the purposes of this Title the following definitions shall apply:

— **"the intra-Community transport of goods"** shall mean transport where the place of departure and the place of arrival are situated within the territories of two different Member States[.][2]

[The transport of goods where the place of departure and the place of arrival are situated within the territory of the country shall be treated as intra-Community transport of goods where such transport is directly linked to transport of goods where the place of departure and the place of arrival are situated within the territories of two different Member States;][2]

— **"the place of departure"** shall mean the place where the transport of goods actually starts, leaving aside distance actually travelled to the place where the goods are,

— **"the place of arrival"** shall mean the place where the transport of goods actually ends.

2. The place of the supply of services in the intra-Community transport of goods shall be the place of departure.   s 5(6)(g)(i)

3. However, by way of derogation from paragraph 2, the place of the supply of services in the intra-Community transport of goods rendered to customers identified for purposes of value added tax in a Member State other than that of the departure of the transport shall be deemed to be within the territory of the Member State which issued the customer with the value added tax identification number under which the service was rendered to him.   s 5(6)(f)(i)

4. Member States need not apply the tax to that part of the transport corresponding to journeys made over waters which do not form part of the territory of the Community as defined in Article 3.

D. Place of the supply of services ancillary to the intra-Community transport of goods

By way of derogation from Article 9(2)(c), the place of the supply of services involving activities ancillary to the intra-Community transport of goods, rendered to customers identified for purposes of value added tax in a Member State other than that within the territory of which the services are physically performed, shall be deemed to be within the territory of the Member State which issued the customer with the value added tax identification number under which the service was rendered to him.   s 5(6)(f)(ii)

E. Place of the supply of services rendered by intermediaries

1. By way of derogation from Article 9(1), the place of the supply of services rendered by intermediaries, acting in the name and for the account of other persons, where they form part of the supply of services in the intra-Community transport of goods, shall be the place of departure.   s 5(6)(g)(iii)

However, where the customer for whom the services rendered by the intermediary are performed is identified for purposes of value added tax in a Member State other than that of the departure of the transport, the place of the supply of services rendered by an intermediary shall be deemed to be within the territory of the Member State which issued the customer with the value added tax identification number under which the service was rendered to him.   s 5(6)(f)(iii)

2. By way of derogation from Article 9(1), the place of the supply of services rendered by intermediaries acting in the name and for the account of other persons, where they form part of the supply of services the purpose of which is activities ancillary to the intra-Community transport of goods, shall be the place where the ancillary services are physically performed.   s 5(6)(g)(ii)

However, where the customer of the services rendered by the intermediary is identified for purposes of value added tax in a Member State other than that within the territory of which the ancillary service is physically performed, the place of supply of the services rendered by the intermediary shall be deemed to be within the territory of the Member State which issued the customer with the value added tax identification number under which the service was rendered to him by the intermediary.

s 5(6)(g)(ii) **3.** By way of derogation from Article 9(1), the place of the supply of services rendered by intermediaries acting in the name and for the account of other persons, when such services form part of transactions other than those referred to in paragraph 1 or 2 or in Article 9(2)(*e*), shall be the place where those transactions are carried out.

s 5(6)(*f*)(iii) However, where the customer is identified for purposes of value added tax in a Member State other than that within the territory of which those transactions are carried out, the place of supply of the services rendered by the intermediary shall be deemed to be within the territory of the Member State which issued the customer with the value added tax identification number under which the service was rendered to him by the intermediary.

[**F.** Place of the supply of services in the case of valuations of or work on movable tangible property

By way of derogation from Article 9(2)(*c*), the place of the supply of services involving valuations or work on movable tangible property, provided to customers identified for value added tax purposes in a Member State other than the one where those services are physically carried out, shall be deemed to be in the territory of the Member State which issued the customer with the value added tax identification number under which the service was carried out for him.

This derogation shall not apply where the goods are not dispatched or transported out of the Member State where the services were physically carried out.][4]][5]

Amendments
1 Inserted by Council Directive 92/111/EEC of 14 December 1992, art 1(11) with effect from 1 January 1993.
2 Substituted by Council Directive 95/7/EC of 10 April 1995 art 1(7) with effect from 25 May 1995.
3 Inserted by Council Directive 95/7/EC of 10 April 1995 art 1(7) with effect from 25 May 1995.
4 Art 28b(F) inserted Council Directive 95/7/EC of 10 April 1995 art 1(7) with effect from 25 May 1995.
5 Art 28*b* inserted by Council Directive 91/680/EEC of 16 December 1991, art 1(22) with effect from 1 January 1993.
Cross-references
Period of application: art 28l.

[*Article 28c*

Exemptions

A. Exempt supplies of goods

Without prejudice to other Community provisions and subject to conditions which they shall lay down for the purpose of ensuring the correct and straightforward application of the exemptions provided for below and preventing any evasion, avoidance or abuse, Member States shall exempt:

Sch 2(i)(*b*)   (*a*)   supplies of goods, [as defined in Article 5][1], dispatched or transported by or on behalf of the vendor or the person acquiring the goods out of the territory referred to in Article 3 but within the Community, effected for another taxable person or a non-taxable legal person acting as such in a Member State other than that of the departure of the dispatch or transport of the goods.

This exemption shall not apply to supplies of goods by taxable persons exempt from tax pursuant to Article 24 or to supplies of goods effected for taxable persons or non-taxable legal persons who qualify for the derogation in the second subparagraph of Article 28a(1)(*a*);

Sch 2(i)(*c*)   (*b*)   supplies of new means of transport, dispatched or transported to the purchaser by or on behalf of the vendor or the purchaser out of the territory referred to in Article 3 but within the Community, effected for taxable persons or non-taxable legal persons who qualify for the derogation provided for in the second subparagraph of Article 28a(1)(*a*), or for any other non-taxable person;

[(*c*) the supply of goods subject to excise duty dispatched or transported or transported to the purchaser, by the vendor, by the purchaser or on his behalf, outside the territory referred to in Article 3 but inside the Community, effected for taxable persons or non-taxable legal persons who qualify for the derogation set out in the second subparagraph of Article 28a(1)(*a*), when the dispatch or transport of the goods is carried out in accordance with Article 7(4) and (5), or Article 16 of Directive 92/12/EEC.   Sch 2(i)(*d*)

This exemption shall not apply to supplies of goods subject to excise duty effected by taxable persons who benefit from the exemption from tax set out in Article 24;]²

[(*d*) the supply of goods, within the meaning of Article 28a(5)(*b*), which benefit from the exemptions set out above if they have been made on behalf of another taxable person.]³

B. Exempt intra-Community acquisitions of goods

Without prejudice to other Community provisions, and subject to conditions which they shall lay down for the purpose of ensuring the correct and straightforward application of the exemptions provided for below and preventing any evasion, avoidance or abuse, Member States shall exempt:

(*a*) the intra-Community acquisition of goods the supply of which by taxable persons would in all circumstances be exempt within the territory of the country;

(*b*) the intra-Community acquisition of goods the importation of which would in all circumstances be exempt under Article 14(1);

(*c*) the intra-Community acquisition of goods where, pursuant to Article 17(3) and (4), the person acquiring the goods would in all circumstances be entitled to full reimbursement of the value added tax due under Article 28a(1).

C. Exempt transport services

The Member States shall exempt the supply of intra-Community transport services involved in the dispatch or transport of goods to and from the islands making up the autonomous regions of the Azores and Madeira as well as the dispatch or transport of goods between those islands.   Sch 2(iii*a*)

D. Exempt importation of goods

Where goods dispatched or transported from a third territory are imported into a Member State other than that of arrival of the dispatch or transport, Member States shall exempt such imports where the supply of such goods by the importer as defined in Article 21(2) is exempt in accordance with paragraph A.   Sch 2(iii*b*)

Member States shall lay down the conditions governing this exemption with a view to ensuring its correct and straightforward application and preventing any evasion, avoidance or abuse.

[E. Other exemptions

1. [*Substitutes art 16(1) and (1a)*]⁴

2. [*Amends art 16(2)*]

3. Member States shall take specific measures to ensure that value added tax is not charged on the intra-Community acquisition of goods effected, within the meaning of Article 28b(A)(1), within its territory when the following conditions are met:

— the intra-Community acquisition of goods is effected by a taxable person who is not established in the territory of the country but who is identified for value added purposes in another Member State,

— the intra-Community acquisition of goods is effected for the purposes of a subsequent supply of goods made by a taxable person in the territory of the country,

— the goods so acquired by this taxable person are directly dispatched or transported from another Member State than that in which he is identified for value added tax purposes and destined for the person for whom he effects the subsequent supply,

— the person to whom the subsequent supply is made is a taxable person or a non-taxable legal person who is identified for value added tax purposes within the territory of the country,

— the person to whom the subsequent supply is made has been designated in accordance with the third subparagraph of Article 21(1)(*a*) as the person liable for the tax due on the supplies effected by the taxable person not established within the territory of the country.][5][6]

Amendments

1   Substituted by Council Directive 95/7/EC of 10 April 1995, art 1(8) with effect from 25 May 1995; previously "as defined in Articles 5 and 28a(5)(*a*)".

2   Art 28c(A)(*c*) substituted by Council Directive 92/111/EEC of 14 December 1992, art 1(12) with effect from 1 January 1993.

3   Art 28c(A)(*d*) inserted by Council Directive 92/111/EEC of 14 December 1992, art 1(12) with effect from 1 January 1993.

4   Art 28c(E)(1) substituted by Council Directive 95/7/EC of 10 April 1995 art 1(9) with effect from 1 January 1996.

5   Art 28c(E) substituted by Council Directive 92/111/EEC of 14 December 1992, art 1(13) with effect from 1 January 1993.

6   Art 28c originally inserted by Council Directive 91/680/EEC of 16 December 1991, art 1(22) with effect from 1 January 1993.

Cross-references

Period of application: art 28l.

[*Article 28d*
Chargeable event and chargeability of tax

1. The chargeable event shall occur when the intra-Community acquisition of goods is effected. The intra-Community acquisition of goods shall be regarded as being effected when the supply of similar goods is regarded as being effected within the territory of the country.

2. For the intra-Community acquisition of goods, tax shall become chargeable on the 15th day of the month following that during which the chargeable event occurs.

[**3.** By way of derogation from paragraph 2, tax shall become chargeable on the issue of the invoice or other document serving as invoice provided for in the first subparagraph of Article 22(3)(*a*) where that invoice or document is issued to the person acquiring the goods before the fifteenth day of the month following that during which the taxable event occurs.][1]

4. By way of derogation from Article 10(2) and (3), tax shall become chargeable for supplies of goods effected under the conditions laid down in Article 28c(A) on the 15th day of the month following that during which the chargeable event occurs.

[However, tax shall become chargeable on the issue of the invoice provided for in the first subparagraph of Article 22(3)(*a*) or other document serving as invoice where that invoice or document is issued before the fifteenth day of the month following that during which the taxable event occurs.][2]][3]

Amendments
1 Para (3) substituted by Council Directive 92/111/EEC of 14 December 1992, art 1(14) with effect from 1 January 1993.
2 Substituted by Council Directive 92/111/EEC of 14 December 1992, art 1(15) with effect from 1 January 1993.
3 Art 28d inserted by Council Directive 91/680/EEC of 16 December 1991, art 1(22) with effect from 1 January 1993.

[*Article 28e*
Taxable amount and rate applicable

1. In the case of the intra-Community acquisition of goods, the taxable amount shall be established on the basis of the same elements as those used in accordance with Article 11(A) to determine the taxable amount for supply of the same goods within the territory of the country. [In particular, in the case of the intra-Community acquisition of goods referred to in Article 28a(6), the taxable amount shall be determined in accordance with Article 11(A)(1)(*b*) and paragraphs 2 and 3.][1]

Member States shall take the measures necessary to ensure that the excise duty due or paid by the person effecting the intra-Community acquisition of a product subject to excise duty is included in the taxable amount in accordance with Article 11(A)(2)(*a*).

[When, after the moment the intra-Community acquisition of goods was effected, the acquirer obtains the refund of excise duties paid in the Member State from which the goods were dispatched or transported, the taxable amount shall be reduced accordingly in the Member State where the intra-Community acquisition took place.][2]

[**2.** For the supply of goods referred to in Article 28c(A)(*d*), the taxable amount shall be determined in accordance with Article 11(A)(1)(*b*) and paragraphs 2 and 3.][3]

[**3.**][4]The tax rate applicable to the intra-Community acquisition of goods shall be that in force when the tax becomes chargeable.

[**4.**][4] The tax rate applicable to the intra-Community acquisition of goods shall be that applied to the supply of like goods within the territory of the country.][5]

Amendments
1 Substituted by Council Directive 92/111/EEC of 14 December 1992, art 1(16) with effect from 1 January 1993.
2 Inserted by Council Directive 92/111/EEC of 14 December 1992, art 1(16) with effect from 1 January 1993.
3 Inserted by Council Directive 92/111/EEC of 14 December 1992, art 1(17) with effect from 1 January 1993.
4 Substituted by Council Directive 92/111/EEC of 14 December 1992, art 1(17) with effect from 1 January 1993.
5 Art 28e inserted by Council Directive 91/680/EEC of 16 December 1991, art 1(22) with effect from 1 January 1993.

Cross-references
Period of application: art 28l.

[*Article 28f*
Right of deduction

1. [*Substitutes art 17(2), [(2a)]*[1]*, (3), (4).*]

2. [*Substitutes art 18(1).*]

3. [*Inserts art 18(3a).*]][2]

Amendments
1 Amended by Council Directive 95/7/EC of 10 April 1995 art 1(10) with effect from 25 May 1995.
2 Art 28f inserted by Council Directive 91/680/EEC of 16 December 1991, art 22 with effect from 1 January 1993 and amended by Council Directive 92/111/EEC of 14 December 1992, art 1(18) with effect from 1 January 1993.

Cross-references
Period of application: art 28l.

[Article 28g
Persons liable for payment of the tax

[*Substitutes art 21*]¹

Amendments
1 Art 28g inserted by Council Directive 91/680/EEC of 16 December 1991, art 1(22) with effect from 1 January
   1993 and amended by Council Directive 92/111/EEC of 14 December 1992, art 1(19) with effect from 1 January
   1993. Subsequently amended by Council Directive 95/7/EC of 10 April 1995, art 1(10) with effect from 25 May
   1995.
Cross-references
Period of application: art 28l.

[Article 28h
Obligations of persons liable for payment

[*Substitutes art 22*]¹

Amendments
1 Art 28h inserted by Council Directive 91/680/EEC of 16 December 1991, art 1(22) with effect from 1 January
   1993 and amended by Council Directive 92/111/EEC of 14 December 1992, art 1(20) with effect from 1 January
   1993. Subsequently amended by Council Directive 95/7/EC of 10 April 1995 art 1(12) with effect from 25 May
   1995.
Cross-references
Period of application: art 28l.

[Article 28i
Special scheme for small undertakings

[*Amends art 24(3)*]]¹

Amendments
1 Art 28i inserted by Council Directive 91/680/EEC of 16 December 1991, art 1(22) with effect from 1 January 1993
   and amended by Council Directive 92/111/EEC of 14 December 1992, art 1(21) with effect from 1 January 1993.
Cross-references
Period of application: art 28l.

[Article 28j
Common flat-rate scheme for farmers

1. [*Amends art 25(4)*]

2. [*Substitutes art 25(5), (6)*]

3. [*Amends art 25(9)*]]¹

Amendments
1 Art 28j inserted by Council Directive 91/680/EEC of 16 December 1991, art 1(22) with effect from 1 January
   1993.

[Article 28k
Miscellaneous provisions

The following provisions shall apply until 30 June 1999:

1. Member States may exempt supplies by tax-free shops of goods to be carried
away in the personal luggage of travellers taking intra-Community flights or sea
crossings to other Member States. For the purposes of this Article:

> (*a*) **"tax-free shop"** shall mean any establishment situated within an
> airport or port which fulfils the conditions laid down by the competent
> public authorities pursuant, in particular, to paragraph 5;
>
> (*b*) **"traveller to another Member State"** shall mean any passenger
> holding a transport document for air or sea travel stating that the
> immediate destination is an airport or port situated in another Member
> State;

(*c*) **"intra-Community flight or sea crossing"** shall mean any transport, by air or sea, starting within the territory of the country as defined in Article 3, where the actual place of arrival is situated within another Member State.

Supplies of goods effected by tax-free shops shall include supplies of goods effected on board aircraft or vessels during intra-Community passenger transport.

This exemption shall also apply to supplies of goods effected by tax-free shops in either of the two Channel Tunnel terminals, for passengers holding valid tickets for the journey between those two terminals.

2. Eligibility for the exemption provided for in paragraph 1 shall apply only to supplies of goods:

(*a*) the total value of which per person per journey does not exceed the limits laid down by the Community provisions in force for the movement of travellers between third countries and the Community.

Where the total value of several items or of several supplies of goods, per person per journey exceeds those limits, the exemption shall be granted up to those amounts, on the understanding that the value of an item may not be split;

(*b*) involving quantities per person per journey not exceeding the limits laid down by the Community provisions in force for the movement of travellers between third countries and the Community.

The value of supplies of goods effected within the quantitative limits laid down in the previous subparagraph shall not be taken into account for the application of (*a*).

3. Member States shall grant every taxable person the right to a deduction or refund of the value added tax referred to in Article 17(2) insofar as the goods and services are used for the purposes of his supplies of goods exempt under this Article.

4. Member States which exercise the option provided for in Article 16(2) shall also grant eligibility under that provision to imports, intra-Community acquisitions and supplies of goods to a taxable person for the purposes of his supplies of goods exempt pursuant to this Article.

5. Member States shall take the measures necessary to ensure the correct and straightforward application of the exemptions provided for in this Article and to prevent any evasion, avoidance or abuse.][1]

Amendments
1 Art 28k inserted by Council Directive 91/680/EEC of 16 December 1991, art 1(22) with effect from 1 January 1993.
Cross-references
Period of application: art 28l.

[*Article 28l*
Period of application

The transitional arrangements provided for in this Title shall enter into force on 1 January 1993. Before 31 December 1994 the Commission shall report to the Council on the operation of the transitional arrangements and submit proposals for a definitive system.

The transitional arrangements shall be replaced by a definitive system for the taxation of trade between Member States based in principle on the taxation in the Member State of origin of the goods or services supplied. To that end, after having made a detailed examination of that report and considering that the conditions for transition to the definitive system have been fulfilled satisfactorily the Council acting unanimously on a proposal from the Commission and after consulting the European Parliament, shall decide before 31 December 1995 on the arrangements necessary for the entry into force and the operation of the definitive system.

The transitional arrangements shall enter into force for four years and shall accordingly apply until 31 December 1996. The period of application of the transitional arrangements shall be extended automatically until the date of entry into force of the definitive system and in any event until the Council has decided on the definitive system.]¹

Amendments
1 Art 28l inserted by Council Directive 91/680/EEC of 16 December 1991, art 1(2) with effect from 1 January 1993.
Cross-references
Period of application: art 28l.

[*Article 28m*
Rate of conversion

To determine the equivalents in their national currencies of amounts expressed in ICUs in this Title Member States shall use the rate of exchange applicable on 16 December 1991 (OJ C 328, 17.12.1991, p 4).]¹

Amendments
1 Art 28m inserted by Council Directive 91/680/EEC of 16 December 1991, art 1(22) with effect from 1 January 1993.
Cross-references
Period of application: art 28l.

[*Article 28n*
Transitional measures

1. When goods:

— entered the territory of the country within the meaning of Article 3 before 1 January 1993,

and

— were placed, on entry into the territory of that country, under one of the regimes referred to in Article 14(1)(*b*) or (*c*), or Article 16(1)(A),

and

— have not left that regime before 1 January 1993, the provisions in force at the moment the goods were placed under that regime shall continue to apply for the period, as determined by those provisions, the goods remain under that regime.

2. The following shall be deemed to be an import of goods within the meaning of Article 7(1):

(*a*) the removal, including irregular removal, of goods from the regime referred to in Article 14(1)(*c*) under which the goods were placed before 1 January 1993 under the conditions set out in paragraph 1;

(*b*) the removal, including irregular removal, of goods from the regime referred to in Article 16(1)(A) under which the goods were placed before 1 January 1993 under the conditions set out in paragraph 1;

(*c*) the termination of a Community internal transit operation started before 1 January 1993 in the Community for the purpose of supply of goods for consideration made before 1 January 1993 in the Community by a taxable person acting as such;

(*d*) the termination of an external transit operation started before 1 January 1993;

(*e*) any irregularity or offence committed during an external transit operation started under the conditions set out in (*c*) or any Community external transit operation referred to in (*d*);

(f) the use within the country, by a taxable or non-taxable person, of goods which have been supplied to him, before 1 January 1993, within another Member State, where the following conditions are met:

— the supply of these goods has been exempted, or was likely to be exempted, pursuant to Article 15(1) and (2),

— the goods were not imported within the country before 1 January 1993.

For the purpose of the application of (c), the expression **"Community internal transit operation"** shall mean the dispatch or transport of goods under the cover of the internal Community transit arrangement or under the cover of a T2 L document or the intra-Community movement carnet, or the sending of goods by post.

3. In the cases referred to in paragraph 2(a) to (e), the place of import, within the meaning of Article 7(2), shall be the Member State within whose territory the goods cease to be covered by the regime under which they were placed before 1 January 1993.

4. By way of derogation from Article 10(3), the import of the goods within the meaning of paragraph 2 of this Article shall terminate without the occurrence of a chargeable event when:

(a) the imported goods are dispatched or transported outside the Community within the meaning of Article 3;

or

(b) the imported goods, within the meaning of paragraph 2(a), are other than a means of transport and are dispatched or transported to the Member State from which they were exported and to the person who exported them;

or

(c) the imported goods, within the meaning of paragraph 2(a), are means of transport which were acquired or imported before 1 January 1993, in accordance with the general conditions of taxation in force on the domestic market of a Member State, within the meaning of Article 3, and/or have not been subject by reason of their exportation to any exemption from or refund of value added tax.

This condition shall be deemed to be fulfilled when the date of the first use of the means of transport was before 1 January 1985 or when the amount of tax due because of the importation is insignificant.][1]

Amendments

1 Art 28n inserted by Council Directive 92/111/EEC of 14 December 1992, art 1(22) with effect from 1 January 1993.

[TITLE XVI*b*

Transitional provisions applicable in the field of second-hand goods, works of art, collectors' items and antiques

Article 28o

1. Member States which at 31 December 1992 were applying special tax s 12B arrangements other than those provided for in Article 26a(B) to supplies of second-hand means of transport effected by taxable dealers my continue to apply those arrangements during the period referred to in Article 281 in so far as they comply with, or are adjusted to comply with, the following conditions:

(a) the special arrangements shall apply only to supplies of the means of transport referred to in Article 28a(2)(a) and regarded as second-hand goods within the meaning of Article 26a(A)(d), effected by taxable dealers within the meaning of Article 26a(A)(e), and subject to the special tax arrangements for taxing the margin pursuant to Article 26a(B)(1) and (2). Supplies of new means of transport within the meaning of Article 28a(2)(*b*) that are carried out under the conditions specified in Article 28c(A) shall be excluded from these special arrangements;

(*b*)   the tax due in respect of each supply referred to in (*a*) is equal to the amount of tax that would be due if that supply had been subject to the normal arrangements for value added tax, less the amount of value added tax regarded as being incorporated in the purchase price of the means of transport by the taxable dealer;

(*c*)   the tax regarded as being incorporated in the purchase price of the means of transport by the taxable dealer shall be calculated according to the following method:

—   the purchase price to be taken into account shall be the purchase price within the meaning of Article 26a(B)(3),

—   that purchase price paid by the taxable dealer shall be deemed to include the tax that would have been due if the taxable dealer's supplier had subjected the supply to the normal value added tax arrangements,

—   the rate to be taken into account shall be the rate applicable within the meaning of Article 12(1), in the Member State within which the place of the supply to the taxable dealer, determined in accordance with Article 8, is deemed to be situated;

(*d*)   the tax due in respect of each supply as referred to in (*a*), determined in accordance with the provisions of (*b*), may not be less than the amount of tax that would be due if that supply had been subject to the special arrangements for taxing the margin in accordance with Article 26a(B)(3).

For the application of the above provisions, the Member States have the option of providing that if the supply had been subject to the special arrangements for taxation of the margin, that margin would not have been less then 10% of the selling price, within the meaning of B(3);

(*e*)   the taxable dealer shall not be entitled to indicate separately on the invoices he issues, or on any other document in lieu, tax relating to supplies which he is subjecting to the special arrangements;

(*f*)   taxable persons shall not be entitled to deduct from the tax for which they are liable tax due or paid in respect of second-hand means of transport supplied to them by a taxable dealer, in so far as the supply of those goods by the taxable dealer is subject to the tax arrangements in accordance with (*a*);

(*g*)   by way of derogation from Article 28a(1)(*a*), intra-Community acquisition of means of transport are not subject to value added tax where the vendor is a taxable dealer acting as such and the second-hand means of transport acquired has been subject to the tax, in the Member State of departure of the dispatch or transport, in accordance with (*a*);

(*h*)   Articles 28b(B) and 28c(A)(*a*) and (*d*) shall not apply to supplies of second-hand means of transport subject to tax in accordance with (*a*).

2. By way of derogation from the first sentence of paragraph 1, the Kingdom of Denmark shall be entitled to apply the special tax arrangements laid down in paragraph 1(*a*) to (*h*) during the period referred to in Article 281.

3. Where they apply the special arrangements for sales by public auction provided for in Article 26a(C), Member States shall also apply these special arrangement to supplies of second-hand means of transport effected by an organizer of sales by public auction acting in his own name, pursuant to a contract under which commission is payable on the sale of those goods by public auction, on behalf of a taxable dealer, in so far as the supply of the second-hand means of transport, within the meaning of Article 5(4)(*c*), by that other taxable dealer, is subject to tax in accordance with paragraphs 1 and 2.

4. For supplies by a taxable dealer of works of art, collectors' items or antiques that have been supplied to him under the conditions provided for in Article 26a(B)(2), the Federal Republic of Germany shall be entitled, until 30 June 1999, to provide for the possibility for taxable dealers to apply either the special arrangements for taxable dealers, or the normal VAT arrangements according to the following rules;

(*a*)   for the application of the special arrangements for taxable dealers to these suppliers of goods, the taxable amount shall be determined in accordance with Article 11(A)(1), (2) and (3);

(*b*)   in so far as the goods are used for the needs of his operations which are taxed in accordance with (*a*), the taxable dealer shall be authorized to deduct from the tax for which he is liable:

—   the value added tax due or paid for works of art, collectors' items or antiques which are or will be supplied to him by another taxable dealer, where the supply by that other taxable dealer has been taxed in accordance with (*a*),

—   the value added tax deemed to be included in the purchase price of the works of art, collectors' items or antiques which are or will be supplied to him by another taxable dealer, where the supply by that other taxable dealer has been subject to value added tax in accordance with the special arrangements for the taxation of the margin provided for in Article 26a(B), in the Member State within whose territory the place of that supply, determined in accordance with Article 8, is deemed to be situated.

This right to deduct shall arise at the time when the tax due for the supply taxed in accordance with (*a*) becomes chargeable;

(*c*)   for the application of the provisions laid down in the second indent of (*b*), the purchase price of the works of art, collectors' items or antiques the supply of which by a taxable dealer is taxed in accordance with (*a*) shall be determined in accordance with Article 26a(B)(3) and the tax deemed to be included in this purchase price shall be calculated according to the following method:

—   the purchase price shall be deemed to include the value added tax that would have been due if the taxable margin made by the supplier had been equal to 20% of the purchase price,

—   the rate to be taken into account shall be the rate applicable, within the meaning of Article 12(1), in the Member State within whose territory the place of the supply that is subject to the special arrangements for taxation of the profit margin, determined in accordance with Article 8, is deemed to be situated;

(*d*)   where he applies the normal arrangements for value added tax to the supply of a work of art, collectors' item or antique which has been supplied to him by another taxable dealer and where the goods have been taxed in accordance with (*a*), the taxable dealer shall be authorized to deduct from his tax liability the value added tax referred to in (*b*);

(*e*)   the category of rates applicable to these supplies of goods shall be that which was applicable on 1 January 1993;

(f) for the application of the fourth indent of Article 26a(B)(2), the fourth indent of Article 26a(C)(1) and Article 26a(D)(*b*) and (*c*), the supplies of works of art, collectors' items or antiques, taxed in accordance with (*a*), shall be deemed by Member States to be supplies subject to value added tax in accordance with the special arrangements for taxation of the profit margin provided for in Article 26a(B);

(g) where the supplies of works of art, collectors' items or antiques taxed in accordance with (*a*) are effected under the conditions provided for in Article 28c(A), the invoice issued in accordance with Article 22(3) shall contain an endorsement indicating that the special taxation arrangements for taxing the margin provided for in Article 28o(4) have been applied.][1]

Amendments
1 Title XVIb and Article 28o inserted by Council Directive 94/5/EC of 14 February 1994 art 1(7) (OJ No L 60, 3.3.1994, p 21.

[TITLE XVIc
Transitional measures applicable in the context of the accession to the European Union of Austria, Finland and Sweden

Article 28p

1. For the purpose of applying this Article:

— **"Community"** shall mean the territory of the Community as defined in Article 3 before accession,

— **"new Member States"** shall means the territory of the Member States acceding to the European Union by the Treaty signed on 24 June 1994, as defined for each of those Member States in Article 3 of this Directive,

— **"enlarged Community"** shall mean the territory of the Community as defined in Article 3, after accession.

2. When goods:

— entered the territory of the Community or of one of the new Member States before the date of accession, and

— were placed, on entry into the territory of the Community or of one of the Member States, under a temporary admission procedure with full exemption from import duties, under one of the regimes referred to in Article 16(1)(B)(*a*) to (*d*) or under a similar regime in one of the new Member States, and

— have not left that regime before the date of accession,

the provision in force at the moment the goods were placed under that regime shall continue to apply until the goods leave this regime, after the date of accession.

3. When goods:

— were placed, before the date of accession, under the common transit procedure or under another customs transit procedure, and

— have not left that procedure before the date of accession,

the provisions in force at the moment the goods were placed under that procedure shall continue to apply until the goods leave this procedure, after the date of accession.

For the purposes of the first indent, **"common transit procedure"** shall mean the measures for the transport of goods in transit between the Community and the countries of the European Free Trade Association (EFTA) and between the EFTA countries themselves, as provided for in the Convention of 20 May 1987 on a common transit procedure (OJ No L 226, 13.8.1987, p 2).

4. The following shall be deemed to be an importation of goods within the meaning of Article 7(1) where it is shown that the goods were in free circulation in one of the new Member States or in the Community:

　(*a*)　the removal, including irregular removal, of goods from a temporary admission procedure under which they were placed before the date of accession under the conditions set out in paragraph 2;

　(*b*)　the removal, including irregular removal, of goods either from one of the regimes referred to in Article 16(1)(B)(*a*) to (*d*) or from a similar regime under which they were placed before the date of accession under the conditions set out in paragraph 2;

　(*c*)　the termination of one of the procedures referred to in paragraph 3 which was started before the date of accession in one of new Member States for the purposes of a supply of goods for consideration effected before that date in that Member State by a taxable person acting as such;

　(*d*)　any irregularity or offence committed during one of the procedures referred to in paragraph 3 under the conditions set out at (*c*).

5. The use after the date of accession within a Member State, by a taxable or non-taxable person, of goods supplied to him before the date of accession within the Community or one of the new Member States shall also be deemed to be an importation of goods within the meaning of Article 7(1) where the following conditions are met:

　—　the supply of those goods has been exempted, or was likely to be exempted, either under Article 15(1) and (2) or under a similar provision in the new Member States,

　—　the goods were not imported into one of the new Member States or into the Community before the date of accession.

6. In the cases referred to in paragraph 4, the place of import within the meaning of Article 7(3) shall be the Member State within whose territory the goods cease to be covered by the regime under which they were placed before the date of accession.

7. By way of derogation from Article 10(3), the importation of goods within the meaning of paragraphs 4 and 5 of this Article shall terminate without the occurrence of a chargeable event when:

　(*a*)　the imported goods are dispatched or transported outside the enlarged Community; or

　(*b*)　the imported goods within the meaning of paragraph 4(*a*) are other than means of transport and are redispatched or transported to the Member State from which they were exported and to the person who exported them; or

　(*c*)　the imported goods within the meaning of paragraph 4(*a*) are means of transport which were acquired or imported before the date of accession in accordance with the general conditions of taxation in force on the domestic market of one of the new Member States or of one of the Member States of the Community and/or have not been subject, by reason of their exportation, to any exemption from, or refund of, value added tax.

This condition shall be deemed to be fulfilled when the date of the first use of the means of transport was before 1 January 1987 or when the amount of tax due by reason of the importation is insignificant.]¹

Amendments
1　Title XVIc and Article 28p inserted by Council Directive 94/76/EC of 22 December 1994 art 1 (OJ No L 365, 31.12.94, p 53).

TITLE XVII
Value Added Tax Committee

Article 29

1. An Advisory Committee on value added tax, hereinafter called "the Committee", is hereby set up.

2. The Committee shall consist of representatives of the Member States and of the Commission.

The chairman of the Committee shall be a representative of the Commission. Secretarial services for the Committee shall be provided by the Commission.

3. The Committee shall adopt its own rules of procedure.

4. In addition to points subject to the consultation provided for under this Directive, the Committee shall examine questions raised by its chairman, on his own initiative or at the request of the representative of a Member State, which concern the application of the Community provisions on value added tax.

TITLE XVIII
Miscellaneous

Article 30
International Agreements

The Council, acting unanimously on a proposal from the Commission, may authorize any Member State to conclude with a non-member country or an international organization an agreement which may contain derogations from this Directive. A State wishing to conclude such an agreement shall bring the matter to the notice of the Commission and provide all the information necessary for it to be considered. The Commission shall inform the other Member States within one month.

The Council's decision shall be deemed to have been adopted if, within two months of the other Member States being informed as laid down in the previous paragraph, the matter has not been raised before the Council.

Article 31
Unit of account

1. The unit of account used in this Directive shall be the European unit of account (EUA) defined by Decision 75/250/EEC (OJ L 104, 24.4.1975, p 35).

2. When converting this unit of account into national currencies, Member States shall have the option of rounding the amounts resulting from this conversion either upwards or downwards by up to 10%.

Article 32
Second-hand goods

Amendments
Deleted by Council Directive 94/5/EC of 14 February 1994 art 1(9).

[*Article 33*

1. Without prejudice to other Community provisions, in particular those laid down in the Community provisions in force relating to the general arrangements for the holding, movement and monitoring of products subject to excise duty, this Directive shall not prevent a Member State from maintaining or introducing taxes on insurance contracts, taxes on betting and gambling, excise duties, stamp duties and, more generally, any taxes, duties or charges which cannot be characterized as turnover taxes, provided however that those taxes, duties or charges do not, in trade between Member States, give rise to formalities connected with the crossing of frontiers.

2. Any reference in this Directive to products subject to excise duty shall apply to the following products as defined by the current Community provisions:

— mineral oils;

— alcohol and alcoholic beverages;

— manufactured tobacco.][1]

Amendments

1 Art 33 substituted by Council Directive 91/680/EEC of 16 December 1991, art 1(23); with effect from 1 January 1993.

Case law

Danish employment (market contribution) levy payable essentially on the same basis as VAT, in breach of EC Treaty: *EC Commission v Denmark*, [1994]STI 37, ECJ 234/91.

Tax on gaming machines not a turnover tax because it was based on the placing of the machine at the disposal of the public: *Lambert v Directeur des Services Fiscaux de l'Orne* (1989) OJ C92/8, ECJ 317/86; 48, 49, 285, 363-367/87, 65, 78-80/99; *Bergandi v Directeur Général des Impôts* [1991]STC 529, [1989]2 CMLR 933, ECJ 252/86.

Tax based on business annual turnover used to finance sickness etc benefits not a turnover tax: *Rousseau-Wilmot SA v Caisse de Compensation de l'Organisation Autonome Nationale de l'Industrie et du Commerce (Organic)* [1986]3 CMLR 677, ECJ 295/84.

Italian lawyers' national provident fund supplementary contributions (based on fee paid by client which has already been subject to VAT) not in breach of art 33: *Aldo Bozzi v Cassa Naxionale di Previdenza ed Assistenza* (1992) OJ C142/8, ECJ 347/90.

25% tax on public performance in dancehalls, restaurants etc not in breach of art 33: *Giant NV v Commune d'OVerijse* (1991) OJ C96/8, ECJ 109/90.

Fiscal charge, preliminary ruling: *Dansk Denkavit ApS and P Poulsen Trading ApS v Skatteministeriet* (1992) OJ C107/p 3, ECJ 200/90.

Consumption tax ("BVB") on passenger cars not prohibited by art 33: *Wisselink en Co BV v Staatssecretaris van Financiën* ECJ 93 and 94/88.

[*Article 33a*

1. Goods referred to in Article 7(1)(*b*) entering the Community from a territory which forms part of the customs territory of the Community but which is considered as a third territory for the purposes of applying this Directive shall be subject to the following provisions:

(*a*) the formalities relating to the entry of such goods into the Community shall be the same as those laid down by the Community customs provisions in force for the import of goods into the customs territory of the Community;

(*b*) when the place of arrival of the dispatch or transport of these goods is situate outside the Member State where they enter the Community, they shall circulate in the Community under the internal Community transit procedure laid down by the Community customs provisions in force, insofar as they have been the subject of a declaration placing them under this regime when the goods entered the Community;

(*c*) when at the moment of their entry into the Community the goods are found to be in one of the situations which would qualify them, if they were imported within the meaning of Article 7(1)(*a*), to benefit from one of the arrangements referred to in Article 16(1)(B)(*a*), (*b*), (*c*) and (*d*), or under a temporary arrangement in full exemption from import duties, the Member States shall take measures ensuring that the goods may remain in the Community under the same conditions as those laid down for the application of such arrangements.

2. Goods not referred to in Article 7(1)(*a*) dispatched or transported from a Member State to a destination in a territory that forms parts of the customs territory of the Community but which is considered as a third territory for the purposes of applying this Directive shall be subject to the following provisions:

(*a*) the formalities relating to the export of those goods outside the territory of the Community shall be the same as the Community customs provisions in force in relation to export of goods outside the customs territory of the Community;

(*b*) for goods which are temporarily exported outside the Community, in order to be reimported, the Member States shall take the measures necessary to ensure that, on reimportation into the Community, such goods may benefit from the same provisions as if they had been temporarily exported outside the customs territory of the Community.][1]

Amendments
1　Art 33a substituted by Council Directive 92/111/EEC of 14 December 1992, art 1(24) with effect from 1 January 1993.

TITLE XIX
Final provisions

Article 34

For the first time on 1 January 1982 and thereafter every two years, the Commission shall, after consulting the Member States, send the Council a report on the application of the common system of value added tax in the Member States. This report shall be transmitted by the Council to the European Parliament.

Article 35

At the appropriate time the Council acting unanimously on a proposal from the Commission, after receiving the opinion of the European Parliament and of the Economic and Social Committee, and in accordance with the interests of the common market, shall adopt further Directives on the common system of value added tax, in particular to restrict progressively or to repeal measures taken by the Member States by way of derogation from the system, in order to achieve complete parallelism of the national value added tax systems and thus permit the attainment of the objective stated in Article 4 of the first Council Directive of 11 April 1967.

Article 36

The fourth paragraph of Article 2 and Article 5 of the first Council Directive of 11 April 1967 are repealed.

Article 37

Second Council Directive 67/228/EEC of 11 April 1967 on value added tax shall cease to have effect in each Member State as from the respective dates on which the provisions of this Directive are brought into application.

Article 38

This Directive is addressed to the Member States.

Done at Brussels, 17 May 1977.

ANNEX A
List of agricultural production activities

Sch 5

I. CROP PRODUCTION

1. General agriculture, including viticulture

2. Growing of fruit (including olives) and of vegetables, flowers and ornamental plants, both in the open and under glass

3. Production of mushrooms, spices, seeds and propagating materials; nurseries

II. STOCK FARMING TOGETHER WITH CULTIVATION

1. General stock farming

2. Poultry farming

3. Rabbit farming

4. Beekeeping

5. Silkworm farming

6. Snail farming

III. FORESTRY

IV. FISHERIES

1. Fresh-water fishing

2. Fish farming

3. Breeding of mussels, oysters and other molluscs and crustaceans

4. Frog farming

V. Where a farmer processes, using means normally employed in an agricultural, forestry or fisheries undertaking, products deriving essentially from his agricultural production, such processing shall also be regarded as agricultural production

ANNEX B
List of agricultural services

Supplies of agricultural services which normally play a part in agricultural production shall be considered the supply of agricultural services, and include the following in particular:

— field work, reaping and mowing, threshing, baling, collecting, harvesting, sowing and planting

— packing and preparation for market, for example drying, cleaning, grinding, disinfecting and ensilage of agricultural products

— storage of agricultural products

— stock minding, rearing and fattening

— hiring out, for agricultural purposes, of equipment normally used in agricultural, forestry or fisheries undertakings

— technical assistance

— destruction of weeds and pests, dusting and spraying of crops and land

— operation of irrigation and drainage equipment

— lopping, tree felling and other forestry services

ANNEX C
Common method of calculation

Note
This Annex, which deals with calculation of VAT own resources is not relevant for the purposes of this work.

ANNEX D
List of the activities referred to in the third paragraph of article 4(5)

1. Telecommunications

2. The supply of water, gas, electricity and steam

3. The transport of goods

4. Port and airport services

5. Passenger transport

6. Supply of new goods manufactured for sale

7. The transactions of agricultural intervention agencies in respect of agricultural products carried out pursuant to Regulations on the common organization of the market in these products

8. The running of trade fairs and exhibitions

9. Warehousing

10. The activities of commercial publicity bodies

11. The activities of travel agencies

12. The running of staff shops, cooperatives and industrial canteens and similar institutions

13. Transactions other than those specified in Article 13A(1)(*q*), of radio and television bodies.

ANNEX E
Transactions referred to in article 28(3)(*a*)

1. ...[1]

2. Transactions referred to in Article 13A(1)(*e*)

3. ...[1]

4. ...[1]

5. ...[1]

6. ...[1]

7. Transactions referred to in Article 13A(1)(*q*)

8. ...[1]

9. ...[1]

10. ...[1]

11. Supplies covered by Article 13B(*g*) in so far as they are made by taxable persons who were entitled to deduction of input tax on the building concerned

12. ...[1]

13. ...[1]

14. ...[1]

15. The services of travel agents referred to in Article 26, and those of travel agents acting in the name and on account of the traveller, for journeys outside the Community.

Amendments

1 Abolished by Council Directive 89/465/EEC (Eighteenth Directive) of 18 July 1989 art 1(1) with effect from 1 January 1990.

ANNEX F
Transactions referred to in article 28(3)(*b*)

Sch 1(xvii) **1.** Admission to sporting events

2. Services supplied by authors, artists, performers, lawyers and other members of the liberal professions, other than the medical and paramedical professions, in so far as these are not services specified in Annex B to the second Council Directive of 11 April 1967

3. ...[1]

4. ...[1]

5. Telecommunications services supplied by public postal services and supplies of goods incidental thereto

6. Services supplied by undertakers and cremation services, together with goods related thereto

Sch 1(xix)

7. Transactions carried out by blind persons or workshops for the blind provided these exemptions do not give rise to significant distortion of competition

8. The supply of goods and services to official bodies responsible for the construction, setting out and maintenance of cemeteries, graves and monuments commemorating war dead

9. ...[1]

10. Transactions of hospitals not covered by Article 13 A (1)(*b*)

11. ...[1]

12. The supply of water by public authorities

13. ...[1]

14. ...[1]

15. ...[1]

16. Supplies of those buildings and land described in Article 4(3)

17. Passenger transport

The transport of goods such as luggage or motor vehicles accompanying passengers and the supply of services related to the transport of passengers, shall only be exempted in so far as the transport of the passengers themselves is exempt

18. ...[1]

19. ...[1]

20. ...[1]

21. ...[1]

22. ...[1]

23. The supply, modification, repair, maintenance, chartering and hiring of aircraft, including equipment incorporated or used therein, used by State institutions

24. ...[1]

25. The supply, modification, repair, maintenance, chartering and hiring of warships

26. Transactions concerning gold other than gold for industrial use

Sch 1(ix)(*a*)

27. The services of travel agents referred to in Article 26, and those of travel agents acting in the name and on account of the traveller, for journeys within the Community

---

Amendments

1 Deleted by Council Directive 89/465/EEC (Eighteenth Directive) of 18 July 1989 art 1(2) with effect from 1 January 1990.

ANNEX G
Right of option

1. The right of option referred to in Article 28(3)(*c*) may be granted in the following circumstances:

    (*a*)   in the case of transactions specified in Annex E:

Member States which already exempt these supplies but also give right of option for taxation, may maintain this right of option

(*b*)   in the case of transactions specified in Annex F:

Member States which provisionally maintain the right to exempt such supplies may grant taxable persons the right to opt for taxation

2. Member States already granting a right of option for taxation not covered by the provisions of paragraph 1 above may allow taxpayers exercising it to maintain it until at the latest the end of three years from the date the Directive comes into force.

[ANNEX H

List of supplies of goods and services which may be subject to reduced rates of VAT

In transposing the categories below which refer to goods into national legislation, Member States may use the combined nomenclature to establish the precise coverage of the category concerned.

Category   *Description*

1   Foodstuffs (including beverages but excluding alcoholic beverages) for human and animal consumption; live animals, seeds, plants and ingredients normally intended for use in preparation of foodstuffs; products normally intended to be used to supplement or substituted foodstuffs

2   Water supplies

3   Pharmaceutical products of a kind normally used for health care, prevention of diseases and treatment for medical and veterinary purposes, including products used for contraception and sanitary protection

4   Medical equipment, aids and other appliances normally intended to alleviate or treat disability, for the exclusive personal use of the disabled, including the repair of such goods, and children's car seats

5   Transport of passengers and their accompanying luggage

6   Supply, including on loan by libraries, of books (including brochures, leaflets and similar printed matter, children's picture, drawing or colouring books, music printed or in manuscript, maps and hydrographic or similar charts), newspapers and periodicals, other than material wholly or substantially devoted to advertising matter

7   Admissions to shows, theatres, circuses, fairs, amusement parks, concerts, museums, zoos, cinemas, exhibitions and similar cultural events and facilities

Reception of broadcasting services

8   Services supplied by or royalties due to writers, composers and performing artists

9   Supply, construction, renovation and alteration of housing provided as part of a social policy

10   Supplies of goods and services of a kind normally intended for use in agricultural production but excluding capital goods such as machinery or buildings

11   Accommodation provided by hotels and similar establishments including the provision of holiday accommodation and the letting of camping sites and caravan parks

12   Admission to sporting events

13   Use of sporting facilities

14   Supply of goods and services by organisations recognised as charities by

Member States and engaged in welfare or social security work, insofar as these supplies are not exempt under Article 13

15 Services supplied by undertakers and cremation services, together with the supply of goods related thereto

16 Provision of medical and dental care as well as thermal treatment in so far as these services are not exempt under Article 13

17 Services supplied in connection with street cleaning, refuse collection and waste treatment, other than the supply of such services by bodies referred to in Article 4(5)]¹

Amendments
1   Annex H inserted by Council Directive 92/77/EEC of 19 October 1992 art 1(5) with effect from 1 January 1993.

[ANNEX I
Works of art, collectors' items and antiques

For the purposes of this Directive:

(*a*)   **"works of art"** shall mean:

— pictures, collages and similar decorative plaques, paintings and drawings, executed entirely by hand by the artist, other than plans and drawings for architectural, engineering, industrial, commercial, topographical or similar purposes, hand-decorated manufactured articles, theatrical scenery, studio back cloths or the like of painted canvas (CN code 9701),

— original engravings, prints and lithographs, being impressions produced in limited numbers directly in black and white or in colour of one or of several plates executed entirely by hand by the artist, irrespective of the process or of the material employed by him, but not including any mechanical or photomechanical process (CN code 9702 00 00),

— original sculptures and statuary, in any material, provided that they are executed entirely by the artist; sculpture casts the product of which is limited to eight copies and supervised by the artist or his successors in title (CN code 9703 00 00); on an exceptional basis, in cases determined by the Member States, the limit of eight copies may be exceeded for statuary casts produced before 1 January 1989,

— tapestries (CN code 5805 00 00) and wall textiles (CN code 6304 00 00) made by hand from original designs provided by artists, provided that there are not more than eight copies of each,

— individual pieces of ceramics executed entirely by the artist and signed by him,

— enamels on copper, executed entirely by hand, limited to eight numbered copies bearing the signature of the artist or the studio, excluding articles of jewellery and goldsmiths' and silversmiths' wares,

— photographs taken by the artist, printed by him or under his supervision, signed and numbered and limited to 30 copies, all sizes and mounts included;

(*b*)   **"collectors' items"** shall mean:

— postage or revenue stamps, postmarks, first-day covers, pre-stamped stationery and the like, franked, or if unfranked not being of legal tender and not being intended for use as legal tender (CN code 9704 00 00),

— collections and collectors' pieces of zoological, botanical, mineralogical, anatomical, historical, archaeological, palaetological, ethnographic or numismatic interest (CN code 9705 00 00);

(*c*) **"antiques"** shall mean objects other than works of art or collectors' items, which are more than 100 years old (CN code 9706 00 00).][1]

Amendments

1 Annex I inserted by Council Directive 94/5/EC of 14 February 1994 art 1(10).

[ANNEX J

Description of goods	CN code
Tin	8001
Copper	7402
	7403
	7405
	7408
Zinc	7901
Nickel	7502
Aluminium	7601
Lead	7801
Indium	ex 8112 91
	ex 8112 99
Cereals	1001 to 1005
	1006:
	unprocessed rice only
	1007 to 1008
Oil seeds and oleaginous fruit	1201 to 1207
Coconuts, Brazil nuts and cashew nuts	0801
Other nuts	0802
Olives	0711 20
Grains and seeds (including soya beans)	1201 to 1207
Coffee, no roasted	0901 11 00
	0901 12 00
Tea	0902
Cocoa beans, whole or broken, raw or roasted	1801
Raw sugar	1701 11
	1701 12
Rubber, in primary forms or in plates, sheets or strip	4001
	4002
Wool	5101
Chemicals in bulk	Chapters 28 and 29
Mineral oils (including propane and butane; also including crude petroleum oils)	2709
	2710
	2711 12
	2711 13
Silver	7106
Platinum (palladium, rhodium)	7110 11 10
	7110 21 00
	7110 31 00
Potatoes	0701
Vegetable oils and fats and their fractions, whether or not refined, but not chemically modified	1507 to 1515][1]

Amendments

1 Annex J inserted by Council Directive 95/7/EC of 10 April 1995 art 1(13) with effect from 1 January 1996.

[COUNCIL DIRECTIVE

of 19 December 1977

77/799/EEC

(OJ L336, 27.12.1977, p 15)

Concerning mutual assistance by the competent authorities of the Member States in the fields of direct taxation and value added tax][1]

THE COUNCIL OF THE EUROPEAN COMMUNITIES,

Having regard to the Treaty establishing the European Economic Community, and in particular Article 100 thereof,

Having regard to the proposal from the Commission,

Having regard to the opinion of the European Parliament (OJ No C293, 12.12.1976, p 34),

Having regard to the opinion of the Economic and Social Committee (OJ No C56, 7.3.1977, 66),

Whereas practices of tax evasion and tax avoidance extending across the frontiers of Member States lead to budget losses and violations of the principle of fair taxation and are liable to bring about distortions of capital movements and of conditions of competition; whereas they therefore affect the operation of the common market;

Whereas, for these reasons the Council adopted on 10 February 1975 a resolution on the measures to be taken by the Community in order to combat international tax evasion and avoidance (OJ No C35, 14.2.1975, p 1);

Whereas the international nature of the problem means that national measures, whose effect does not extend beyond national frontiers, are insufficient; whereas collaboration between administrations on the basis of bilateral agreements is also unable to counter new forms of tax evasion and avoidance, which are increasingly assuming a multinational character;

Whereas collaboration between tax administrations within the Community should therefore be strengthened in accordance with common principles and rules;

Whereas the Member States should, on request, exchange information concerning particular cases; whereas the State so requested should make the necessary enquiries to obtain such information;

Whereas the Member States should exchange, even without any request, any information which appears relevant for the correct assessment of taxes on income and on capital, in particular where there appears to be an artificial transfer of profits between enterprises in different Member States or where such transactions are carried out between enterprises in two Member States through a third country in order to obtain tax advantages, or where tax has been or may be evaded or avoided for any reason whatever;

Whereas it is important that officials of the tax administration of one Member State be allowed to be present in the territory of another Member State if both the States concerned consider it desirable;

Whereas care must be taken to ensure that information provided in the course of such collaboration is not disclosed to unauthorised persons, so that the basic rights of citizens and enterprises are safeguarded; whereas it is therefore necessary that the Member States receiving such information should not use it, without the authorisation of the Member State supplying it, other than for the purposes of taxation or to facilitate legal proceedings for failure to observe the tax laws of the receiving State; whereas it is also necessary that the receiving States afford the information the same degree of confidentiality which it enjoyed in the State which provided it, if the latter so requires;

Whereas a Member State which is called upon to carry out enquires or to provide information shall have the right to refuse to do so where its laws or administrative practices prevent its tax administration from carrying out these enquiries or from collecting or using this information for its own purposes, or where the provision of such information would be contrary to public policy or would lead to the disclosure of a commercial, industrial or professional secret or of a commercial process, or where the Member State for which the information is intended is unable for practical or legal reasons to provide similar information.

Whereas collaboration between the Members States and the Commission is necessary for the permanent study of cooperation procedures and the pooling of experience in the fields considered, and in particular in the field of the artificial transfer of profits within groups of enterprises, with the aim of improving those procedures and of preparing appropriate Community rules,

Amendments

1   Heading substituted by Council Directive of 6 December 1979 79/1070/EEC art 1(1).

HAS ADOPTED THIS DIRECTIVE:

Article 1
General provisions

1. In accordance with the provisions of this Directive the competent authorities of the Member States shall exchange any information that may enable them to effect a correct assessment of taxes on income and capital [and also of value added tax][1].

2. There shall be regarded as taxes on income and on capital, irrespective of the manner in which they are levied, all taxes imposed on total income, on total capital, or on elements of income or of capital, including taxes on gains from the disposal of movable or immovable property, taxes on the amounts of wages or salaries paid by enterprises, as well as taxes on capital appreciation.

3. The taxes referred to in paragraph 2 are at present, in particular:

in Belgium:

Impôt des personnes physiques/Personenbelasting

Impôt des sociétés/Vennootschapsbelasting

Impôt des personnes morales/Rechtspersonenbelasting

Impôt des non-résidents/Belasting der niet-verblijfhouders

in Denmark:

Indkomstskaten til staten

Selsskabsskat

Den Kommunale indkomstskat

Den amtskommunale indkomstskat

Folkepensionsbidragene

Sømandsskatten

Den saerlige indkomstskat

Kirkeskatten

Formueskatten til staten

Bidrag til dagpengefonden

in Germany:

Einkommensteurer

Körperschaftsteuer

Vermögensteurer

Gewerbesteuer

Grundsteuer

in France:

Impôt sur le revenu

Impôt sur les sociétés

Tax professionelle

Taxe foncière sur les propriétés bâties

Taxe foncière sur les propriétés non bâties

in Ireland:

Income tax

Corporation tax

Capital gains tax

Wealth tax

in Italy:

Imposta sul reddito delle persone fisiche

Imposta sul reddito delle persone giuridiche

Imposta locale sui redditi

in Luxembourg:

Impôt sur le revenu des personnes physiques

Impôt sur le revenu de collectivés

Impôt commercial communal

Impôt sur la fortune

Impôt foncier

in the Netherlands:

Inkomstenbelasting

Vennootschapsbelasting

Vermogensbelasting

[*in Spain:*

Impuesto sobre la Renta de las Personas Fisicas

Impuesto sobre Sociedades

Impuesto Extraordinario sobre el Patrimonio de las Personas Fisicas][2] *in Portugal:*

Contribuicao predial

Imposto sobre a industria agricola

Contribuicao industrial

Imposto de capitais

Imposto profissional

Imposto complementar

Imposto de mais-valias

Imposto sobre o rendimento do petroleo

Os adicionais devidos sobre os impostos precedentes.]

in the United Kingdom:

Income tax

Corporation tax

Capital gains tax

Petroleum revenue tax

Development land tax

[*in Greece:*

Φορος :ισοδηματοζφυσικων προσωπων
Φορος :ισοδηματοζφομικων προσωπων
Φορος αεκινητου ιεεριουσιζ]³

4. Paragraph 1 shall also apply to any identical or similar taxes imposed subsequently, whether in addition to or in place of the taxes listed in paragraph 3. The competent authorities of the Member States shall inform one another and the Commission of the date of entry into force of such taxes.

5. The expression **"competent authority"** means:

in Belgium:

De minister van financiën or an authorised representative

Le ministre des finances or an authorised representative

in Demark:

Ministeren for skatter og afgifter or an authorised representative

in Germany:

Der Bundesminister der Finanzen or an authorised representative

in France:

Le ministre de l'économie or an authorised representative

in Ireland:

The Revenue Commissioners or their authorised representative

in Italy:

Il Ministro per le finanze or an authorised representative

in the Netherlands:

De minister van financiën or an authorised representative

[*in Spain:*

El Ministro de Economia y Hacienda or an authorised representative

in Portugal:

O Ministro da Financas e do Plano or an authorised representative]²

in the United Kingdom:

[— The Commissioners of Customs and Excise or an authorised representative for information required solely for the purposes of value added tax,

[— The Commissioners of Inland Revenue or an authorised representative for all other information.]³

[*in Greece:*

Υπουρεγος Οικονομικων   or an authorised representatives]⁴

Amendments
1 Inserted by Council Directive 79/1070/EEC of 6 December 1979, art 1(2)(*a*).
2 Inserted by the Act of Accession 1985, art 26, Annex I, Part V, Point 7.
3 Substituted by Council Directive 79/1070/EEC of 6 December 1979: art 1(2)(*b*).
4 Inserted by the Act of Accession 1979, art 2, Annex I, Part VI, Point 2.

Article 2
Exchange on request

1. The competent authority of a Member State may request the competent authority of another Member State to forward the information referred to in Article 1(1) in a particular case. The competent authority of the requested State need not comply with the request if it appears that the competent authority of the State making the request has not exhausted its own usual sources of information, which it could have utilised, according to the circumstances, to obtain the information requested without running the risk of endangering the attainment of the sought after result.

2. For the purpose of forwarding the information referred to in paragraph 1, the competent authority of the requested Member State shall arrange for the conduct of any enquiries necessary to obtain such information.

Article 3
Automatic exchange of information

For categories of cases which they shall determine under the consultation procedure laid down in Article 9, the competent authorities of the Member States shall regularly exchange the information referred to in Article 1(1) without prior request.

Article 4
Spontaneous exchange of information

1. The competent authority of a Member State shall without prior request forward the information referred to in Article 1(1), of which it has knowledge, to the competent authority of any other Member State concerned, in the following circumstances:

(*a*) the competent authority of the one Member State has grounds for supposing that there may be a loss of tax in the other Member State;

(*b*) a person liable to tax obtains a reduction in or an exemption from tax in the one Member State which would give rise to an increase in tax or to liability to tax in the other Member State;

(c)   business dealings between a person liable to tax in a Member State and a person liable to tax in another Member State are conducted through one or more countries in such a way that a saving in tax may result in one or the other Member States or in both;

(d)   the competent authority of a Member State has grounds for supposing that a saving of tax may result from artificial transfers of profits within groups of enterprises;

(e)   information forwarded to the one Member State by the competent authority of the other Member State has enabled information to be obtained which may be relevant in assessing liability to tax in the latter Member State.

2. The competent authorities of the Member State may, under the consultation procedure laid down in Article 9, extend the exchange of information provided for in paragraph 1 to cases other than those specified therein.

3. The competent authorities of the Member States may forward to each other in any other case, without prior request, the information referred to in Article 1(1) of which they have knowledge.

Article 5
Time limit for forwarding information

The competent authority of a Member State which, under the preceding Articles, is called upon to furnish information, shall forward it as swiftly as possible. If it encounters obstacles in furnishing the information or if it refuses to furnish the information, it shall forthwith inform the requesting authority to this effect, indicating the nature of the obstacles or the reasons for its refusal.

Article 6
Collaboration by officials of the State concerned

For the purpose of applying the preceding provisions, the competent authority of the Member State providing the information and the competent authority of the Member State for which the information is intended may agree, under the consultation procedure laid down in Article 9, to authorise the presence in the first Member State of officials of the tax administration of the other Member State. The details for applying this provision shall be determined under the same procedure.

Article 7
Provisions relating to secrecy

1. All information made known to a Member State under this Directive shall be kept secret in that State in the same manner as information received under its domestic legislation.

In any case, such information:

— may be made available only to the persons directly involved in the assessment of the tax or in the administrative control of this assessment,

— may in addition be made known only in connection with judicial proceedings or administrative proceedings involving sanctions undertaken with a view to, or relating to, the making or reviewing the tax assessment and only to persons who are directly involved in such proceedings; such information may, however, be disclosed during public hearings or in judgments if the competent authority of the Member State supplying the information raises no objection,

— shall in no circumstances be used other than for taxation purposes or in connection with judicial proceedings or administrative proceedings involving sanctions undertaken with a view to, or in relation to, the making or reviewing the tax assessment.

2. Paragraph 1 shall not oblige a Member State whose legislation or administrative practice lays down, for domestic purposes, narrower limits than those contained in the provisions of that paragraph, to provide information if the State concerned does not undertake to respect those narrower limits.

3. Notwithstanding paragraph 1, the competent authorities of the Member State providing the information may permit it to be used for other purposes in the requesting State, if, under the legislation of the informing State, the information could, in similar circumstances, be used in the informing State for similar purposes.

4. Where a competent authority of a Member State considers that information which it has received from the competent authority of another Member State is likely to be useful to the competent authority of a third Member State, it may transmit it to the latter competent authority with the agreement of the competent authority which supplied the information.

Article 8
Limits to exchange of information

1. This Directive shall impose no obligation to have enquiries carried out or to provide information if the Member State, which should furnish the information, would be prevented by its law or administrative practices from carrying out these enquiries or from collecting or using this information for its own purposes.

2. The provision of information may be refused where it would lead to the disclosure of a commercial, industrial or professional secret or of a commercial process, or of information whose disclosure would be contrary to public policy.

3. The competent authority of a Member State may refuse to provide information where the State concerned is unable, for practical or legal reasons, to provide similar information.

Article 9
Consultations

1. For the purposes of the implementation of this Directive, consultations shall be held, if necessary in a Committee, between:

— the competent authorities of the Member States concerned at the request of either, in respect of bilateral questions,

— the competent authorities of all the Member States and the Commission, at the request of one of those authorities or the Commission, in so far as the matters involved are not solely of bilateral interest.

2. The competent authorities of the Member States may communicate directly with each other. The competent authorities of the Member States may by mutual agreement permit authorities designated by them to communicate directly with each other in specified cases or in certain categories of cases.

3. Where the competent authorities make arrangements on bilateral matters covered by this Directive other than as regards individual cases, they shall as soon as possible inform the Commission thereof. The Commission shall in turn notify the competent authorities of the other Member States.

Article 10
Pooling of experience

The Member States shall, together with the Commission, constantly monitor the cooperation procedure provided for in this Directive and shall pool their experience, especially in the field of transfer pricing within groups of enterprises, with a view to improving such cooperation and, where appropriate, drawing up a body of rules in the fields concerned.

Article 11
Applicability of wider-ranging provisions of assistance

The foregoing provisions shall not impede the fulfilment of any wider obligations to exchange information which might flow from other legal acts.

Article 12
Final provisions

1. Member States shall bring into force the necessary laws, regulations and administrative provisions in order to comply with this Directive not later than 1 January 1979 and shall forthwith communicate them to the Commission.

2. Member States shall communicate to the Commission the texts of any important provisions of national law which they subsequently adopt in the field covered by this Directive.

Article 13: This Directive is addressed to the Member States.

Done at Brussels, 19 December 1977

EIGHTH COUNCIL DIRECTIVE

of 6 December 1979

79/1072/EEC

(OJ L331, 6.12.1979, p 11)

Refunds to foreign traders

THE COUNCIL OF THE EUROPEAN COMMUNITIES,

Having regard to the Treaty establishing the European Economic Community,

Having regard to Sixth Council Directive 77/388/EEC of 17 May 1977 on the harmonisation of the laws of the Member States relating to turnover taxes — Common system of value added tax (uniform basis of assessment)(OJ L 145, 13.6.77, p 1) and in particular Article 17(4) thereof,

Having regard to the proposal from the Commission (OJ C26, 1.2.1978, p 5),

Having regard to the opinion of the European Parliament (OJ C39, 12.2.1979, p 14),

Having regard to the opinion of the Economic and Social Committee (OJ C269, 13.11.1978, p 51),

Whereas, pursuant to Article 17(4) of Directive 77/388/EEC, the Council is to adopt Community rules laying down the arrangements governing refunds of value added tax, referred to in paragraph 3 of the said Article, to taxable persons not established in the territory of the country;

Whereas rules are required to ensure that a taxable person established in the territory of one member country can claim for tax which has been invoiced to him in respect of supplies of goods or services in another Member State or which has been paid in respect of imports into that other Member State, thereby avoiding double taxation;

Whereas discrepancies between the arrangements currently in force in Member States, which give rise in some cases to deflection of trade and distortion of competition, should be eliminated;

Whereas the introduction of Community rules in this field will mark progress towards the effective liberalization of the movement of persons, goods and services thereby helping complete the process of economic integration;

Whereas such rules must not lead to the treatment of taxable persons differing according to the Member State in the territory of which they are established;

Whereas certain forms of tax evasion or avoidance should be prevented;

Whereas, under Article 17(4) of Directive 77/388/EEC, Member States may refuse the refund or impose supplementary conditions in the case of taxable persons not established in the territory of the Community; whereas steps should, however, also be taken to ensure that such taxable persons are not eligible for refunds on more favourable terms than those provided for in respect of Community taxable persons;

Whereas, initially, only the Community arrangements contained in this Directive should be adopted; whereas these arrangements provide, in particular, that decisions in respect of applications for refund should be notified within six months of the date on which such applications were lodged; whereas refunds should be made within the same period; whereas, for a period of one year from the final date laid down for the implementation of these arrangements, the Italian Republic should be authorized to notify the decisions taken by its competent services with regard to applications lodged by taxable persons not established within its territory and to make the relevant refunds within nine months, in order to enable the Italian Republic to reorganize the system at present in operation, with a view to applying the Community system;

Whereas further arrangements will have to be adopted by the Council to supplement the Community system; whereas, until the latter arrangements enter into force, Member States will refund the tax on the services and the purchases of goods which are not covered by this Directive, in accordance with the arrangements which they adopt pursuant to Article 17(4) of Directive 77/388/EEC,

HAS ADOPTED THIS DIRECTIVE:

Article 1
Definition of claimant

For the purposes of this Directive, 'a taxable person not established in the territory of the country' shall means a person as referred to in Article 4(1) of Directive 77/388/EEC who, during the period referred to in the first and second sentences of the first subparagraph of Article 7(1), has had in that country neither the seat of his economic activity, nor a fixed establishment from which business transactions are effected, nor, if no such seat or fixed establishment exists, his domicile or normal place of residence, and who, during the same period, has supplied no goods or services deemed to have been supplied in that country, with the exception of:

(a) transport services and services ancillary thereto, exempted pursuant to Article 14(1)(i), Article 15 or Article 16(1), B, C and D of Directive 77/388/EEC;

(b) services provided in cases where tax is payable solely by the person to whom they are supplied, pursuant to Article 21(1)(b) of Directive 77/388/EEC.

Article 2
Right to refund

Each Member State shall refund to any taxable person who is not established in the territory of the country but who is established in another Member State, subject to the conditions laid down below, any value added tax charged in respect of services or movable property supplied to him by other taxable persons in the territory of the country or charged in respect of the importation of goods into the country, in so far as such goods and services are used for the purposes of the transactions referred to in Article 17(3)(a) and (b) of Directive 77/388/EEC and of the provision of services referred to in Article 1(b).

Article 3
Requirements— where no goods or services supplied

To qualify for refund, any taxable person as referred to in Article 2 who supplies no goods or services deemed to be supplied in the territory of the country shall:

(a) submit to the competent authority referred to in the first paragraph of Article 9 an application modelled on the specimen contained in Annex A, attaching originals of invoices or import documents. Member States shall make available to applicants an explanatory notice which shall in any event contain the minimum information set out in Annex C;

(b) produce evidence, in the form of a certificate issued by the official authority of the State in which he is established, that he is a taxable person for the purposes of value added tax in that State. However, where the competent authority referred to in the first paragraph of Article 9 already has such evidence in its possession, the taxable person shall not be bound to produce new evidence for a period of one year from the date of issue of the first certificate by the official authority of the State in which he is established. Member States shall not issue certificates to any taxable persons who benefit from tax exemption pursuant to Article 24(2) of Directive 77/388/EEC;

(c) certify by means of a written declaration that he has supplied no goods or services deemed to have been supplied in the territory of the country during the period referred to in the first and second sentences of the first subparagraph of Article 7(1);

(d) undertake to repay any sum collected in error.

Article 4
Requirements — where certain services supplied

To be eligible for the refund, any taxable person as referred to in Article 2 who has supplied in the territory of the country no goods or services deemed to have been supplied in the country other than the services referred to in Article 1(*a*) and (*b*) shall:

(*a*) satisfy the requirements laid down in Article 3(*a*), (*b*) and (*d*);

(*b*) certify by means of a written declaration that, during the period referred to in the first and second sentences of the first subparagraph of Article 7(1), he has supplied no goods or services deemed to have been supplied in the territory of the country other than services referred to in Article 1(*a*) and (*b*).

Article 5
Qualifying goods and services

For the purposes of this Directive, goods and services in respect of which tax may be refundable shall satisfy the conditions laid down in Article 17 of Directive 77/388/EEC as applicable in the Member State of refund.

This Directive shall not apply to supplies of goods which are, or may be, exempted under item 2 of Article 15 of Directive 77/388/EEC.

Article 6
Restriction on imposition of further obligations

Member States may not impose on the taxable persons referred to in Article 2 any obligation, in addition to those referred to in Articles 3 and 4, other than the obligation to provide, in specific cases, the information necessary to determine whether the application for refund is justified.

Article 7
Miscellaneous provisions

1. The application for refund provided for in Articles 3 and 4 shall relate to invoiced purchases of goods or services or to imports made during a period of not less than three months or not more than one calendar year. Applications may, however, relate to a period of less than three months where the period represents the remainder of a calendar year. Such applications may also relate to invoices or import documents not covered by previous applications and concerning transactions completed during the calendar year in question. Applications shall be submitted to the competent authority referred to in the first paragraph of Article 9 within six months of the end of the calendar year in which the tax became chargeable.

If the application relates to a period of less than one calendar year but not less than three months, the amount for which application is made may not be less than the equivalent in national currency of 200 European units of account; if the application relates to a period of a calendar year or the remainder of a calendar year, the amount may not be less than the equivalent in national currency of 25 European units of account.

2. The European unit of account shall be that defined in the Finance Regulation of 21 December 1977. (OJ L356, 31.12.1977, p 1) as determined on 1 January of the year of the period referred to in the first and second sentences of the first subparagraph of paragraph 1. Member States may round up or down, by up to 10% the figures resulting from this conversion into national currency.

3. The competent authority referred to in the first paragraph of article 9 shall stamp each invoice and/or import document to prevent their use for further application and shall return them within one month.

4. Decisions concerning applications for refund shall be announced within six months of the date when the applications, accompanied by all the necessary documents required under this Directive for examination of the application, are submitted to the competent authority referred to in paragraph 3. Refunds shall be made before the end of the above mentioned period, at the applicant's request, in either the Member State of refund or the State in which he is established. In the latter case, the bank charges for the transfer shall be payable by the applicant.

The grounds for refusal of an application shall be stated. Appeals against such refusals may be made to the competent authorities in the Member State concerned, subject to the same conditions as to form and time limits as those governing claims for refunds made by taxable persons established in the same State.

5. Where a refund has been obtained in a fraudulent or in any other irregular manner, the competent authority referred to in paragraph 3 shall proceed directly to recover the amounts wrongly paid and any penalties imposed, in accordance with the procedure applicable in the Member State concerned, without prejudice to the provisions relating to mutual assistance in the recovery of value added tax.

In the case of fraudulent applications which cannot be made the subject of an administrative penalty, in accordance with national legislation, the Member State concerned may refuse for a maximum period of two years from the date on which the fraudulent application was submitted any further refund to the taxable person concerned. Where an administrative penalty has been imposed but has not been paid, the Member State concerned may suspend any further refund to the taxable person concerned until it has been paid.

Article 8
Non-EEC traders

... [1]

Refunds may not be granted on terms more favourable than those applied in respect of taxable persons established in the territory of the Community.

Amendments

1 Deleted by Thirteenth Council Directive 86/560/EEC of 17 November 1986 art 7.

Article 9
Competent authorities

Member States shall make known, in an appropriate manner, the competent authority to which the application referred to in Article 3(*a*) and in Article 4(*a*) are to be submitted.

The certificates referred to in Article 3(*b*) and in Article 4(*a*), establishing that the person concerned is a taxable person, shall be modelled on the specimens contained in Annex B.

Article 10
Date of implementation

Member States shall bring into force the provisions necessary to comply with this Directive no later than 1 January 1981. This Directive shall apply only to applications for refunds concerning value added tax charged on invoiced purchases or services or in imports made as from that date.

Member States shall communicate to the Commission the texts of the main provisions of national law which they adopt in the field covered by this Directive. The Commission shall inform the other Member States thereof.

Article 11
Derogation

By way of derogation from Article 7(4), the Italian Republic may, until 1 January 1982, extend the period referred to in this paragraph from six to nine months.

Article 12

Operation review

Three years after the date referred to in Article 10, the Commission shall, after consulting the Member States, submit a report to the Council on the application of this Directive, and in particular Articles 3, 4 and 7 thereof.

Article 13

Scope

This Directive is addressed to the Member States.

Done at Brussels, 6 December 1979

COUNCIL DIRECTIVE

of 28 March 1983

83/181/EEC

Determining the scope of Article 14(1)(d) of Directive 77/388/EEC as regards exemption from Value Added Tax on the final importation of certain goods

---

Note

This Directive ceases to have effect on 31 December 1992 as regards relations between Member States; see Council Directive 91/680/EEC of 16 December 1991, art 2(1).

THE COUNCIL OF THE EUROPEAN COMMUNITIES

Having regard to the Treaty establishing the European Economic Community, and in particular Articles 99 and 100 thereof,

Having regard to the proposal from the Commission,

Having regard to the opinion of the European Parliament,

Having regard to the opinion of the Economic and Social Committee,

Whereas, pursuant to Article 14(1)(*d*) of Council Directive 77/388/EEC of 17 May 1977 on the harmonisation of the laws of the Member States relating to turnover taxes - Common system of value added tax: uniform basis of assessment (OJ No L145, 13.6.1977, p 1), Member States shall, without prejudice to other Community provisions and under conditions which they shall lay down for the purpose, *inter alia*, of preventing any possible evasion, avoidance or abuse, exempt final importation of goods qualifying for exemption from customs duties other than as provided for in the Common Customs Tariff or which would qualify therefor if they were imported from a third country;

Whereas, in accordance with Article 14(2) of the above mentioned Directive, the Commission is required to submit to the Council proposals designed to lay down Community tax rules clarifying the scope of the exemptions referred to in paragraph 1 of the said Article and detailed rules for their implementation;

Whereas, while it is deemed desirable to achieve the greatest possible degree of uniformity between the system for customs duties and that for value added tax, account should be taken, in applying the latter system of the differences as regards objective and structure between customs duties and value added tax;

Whereas arrangements for value added tax should be introduced that differ according to whether goods are imported from third countries or from other Member States and to the extent necessary to comply with the objectives of tax harmonisation; whereas the exemptions on importation can be granted only on condition that they are not liable to affect the conditions of competition on the home market;

Whereas certain reliefs at present applied in the Member States stem from conventions with third countries or with other Member States which, given their purpose, concern only the signatory Member States; whereas it is not expedient to define at Community level conditions for granting such reliefs, and whereas the Member States concerned need merely be authorised to retain them,

HAS ADOPTED THIS DIRECTIVE:

Article 1

1. The scope of the exemptions from value added tax referred to in Article 14(1)(*d*) of Directive 77/388/EEC and the rules for their implementation referred to in Article 14(2) of that Directive shall be defined by this Directive. In accordance with the aforesaid Article, the Member States shall apply the exemptions laid down in this Directive under the conditions fixed by them in order to ensure that such exemptions are correctly and simply applied and to prevent any evasion, avoidance or abuses.

2. For the purposes of this Directive:

> (*a*) **"imports"** means imports as defined in Article 7 of 77/388/EEC and the entry for home use after being subject to one of the systems provided for in Article 16(1)(A) of the said Directive or a system of temporary admission or transit;

> (*b*) **"personal property"** means any property intended for the personal use of the persons concerned or for meeting their household needs.
>
> The following, in particular, shall constitute "personal property":
>
> — household effects,
>
> — cycles and motor-cycles, private motor vehicles and their trailers, camping caravans, pleasure craft and private aeroplanes.
>
> Household provisions appropriate to normal family requirements, household pets and saddle animals shall also constitute "personal property".
>
> The nature or quantity of personal property shall not reflect any commercial interest, nor shall they be intended for an economic activity within the meaning of Article 4 of Directive 77/388/EEC. However, portable instruments of the applied or liberal arts, required by the person concerned for the pursuits of his trade or profession, shall also constitute personal property;

> (*c*) **"household effects"** means personal effects, household linen and furnishings and items of equipment intended for the personal use of the persons concerned or for meeting their household needs;

> (*d*) **"alcoholic products"** means products (beer, wine, aperitifs with a wine or alcohol base, brandies, liqueurs and spirituous beverages, etc) falling within heading Nos [22.03 to 22.08][1] of the Common Customs Tariff;

> (*e*) **"Community"** means the territory of the Member States where Directive 77/388/EEC applies.

Amendments
1   Substituted by Commission Directive 89/219/EEC of 7 March 1989, art 1.

TITLE I
Importation of personal property belonging to individuals coming from countries situated outside the Community

CHAPTER I
Personal property of natural persons transferring their normal place of residence from a third country to the community

Article 2

Subject to Articles 3 to 10, exemption from VAT on importation shall be granted on personal property imported by natural persons transferring their normal place of residence from outside the Community to a Member State of the Community.

Article 3

Exemption shall be limited to personal property which:

> (*a*) except in special cases justified by the circumstances, has been in the possession of and, in the case of non-consumable goods, used by the person concerned at his former normal place of residence for a minimum of six months before the date on which he ceases to have his normal place of residence outside the Community;

> (*b*) is intended to be used for the same purpose at his new normal place of residence.

The Member States may in addition make exemption conditional upon such property having borne, either in the country of origin or in the country of departure, the customs and/or fiscal charges to which it is normally liable.

Article 4

Exemption may be granted only to persons whose normal place of residence has been outside the Community for a continuous period of at least 12 months.

However, the competent authorities may grant exceptions to this rule provided that the intention of the person concerned was clearly to reside outside the Community for a continuous period of at least 12 months.

Article 5

Exemption shall not be granted in respect of:

(*a*)   alcoholic products;

(*b*)   tobacco or tobacco products;

(*c*)   commercial means of transport;

(*d*)   articles for use in the exercise of a trade or profession, other than portable instruments of the applied or liberal arts.

Vehicles intended for mixed use for commercial or professional purposes may also be excluded from exemption.

Article 6

Except in special cases, exemption shall be granted only in respect of personal property entered for permanent importation within 12 months of the date of establishment, by the person concerned, of his normal place of residence in the Member State of importation.

The personal property may be imported in several separate consignments within the period referred to in the preceding paragraph.

Article 7

1. Until 12 months have elapsed from the date of the declaration for its final importation, personal property which has been imported exempt from tax may not be lent, given as security, hired out or transferred, whether for a consideration or free of charge, without prior notification to the competent authorities.

2. Any loan, giving as security, hiring out or transfer before the expiry of the period referred to in paragraph 1 shall entail payment of the relevant value added tax on the goods concerned, at the rate applying on the date of such loan, giving as security, hiring out or transfer, on the basis of the type of goods and the customs value ascertained or accepted on that date by the competent authorities.

Article 8

1. By way of derogation from the first paragraph or Article 6, exemption may be granted in respect of personal property permanently imported before the person concerned establishes his normal place of residence in the Member State of importation, provided that he undertakes actually to establish his normal place of residence there within a period of six months. Such undertaking shall be accompanied by a security, the form and amount of which shall be determined by the competent authorities.

2. Where use is made of the provisions of paragraph 1, the period laid down in Article 3 shall be calculated from the date of importation into the Member States concerned.

Article 9

1. Where, owing to occupational commitments, the person concerned leaves the country situated outside the Community where he had his normal place of residence without simultaneously establishing his normal place of residence in the territory of a Member State, although having the intention of ultimately doing so, the competent authorities may authorise exemption in respect of the personal property which he transfers into the said territory for this purpose.

2. Exemption in respect of the personal property referred to in paragraph 1 shall be granted in accordance with the conditions laid down in Articles 2 to 7, on the understanding that:

(*a*) the periods laid down in Article 3(*a*) and the first paragraph of Article 6 shall be calculated from the date of importation;

(*b*) the period referred to in Article 7(1) shall be calculated from the date when the person concerned actually establishes his normal place of residence in the territory of a Member State.

3. Exemption shall also be subject to an undertaking from the person concerned that he will actually establish his normal place of residence in the territory of a Member State within a period laid down by the competent authorities in keeping with the circumstances. The latter may require this undertaking to be accompanied by a security, the form and amount of which they shall determine.

Article 10

The competent authorities may derogate from Articles 3(*a*) and (*b*), 5(*c*) and (*d*) and 7 when a person has to transfer his normal place of residence from a country situated outside the Community to the territory of a Member State as a result of exceptional political circumstances.

CHAPTER II
Goods imported on the occasion of a marriage

Article 11

1. Subject to Articles 12 to 15, exemption shall be granted in respect of trousseaux and household effects, whether or not new, belonging to a person transferring his or her normal place of residence from a country outside the Community to the territory of a Member State on the occasion of his or her marriage.

[**2.** Exemption shall also be granted in respect of presents customarily given on the occasion of a marriage which are received by a person fulfilling the conditions laid down in paragraph 1 from person having their normal place of residence in a country situated outside the Community. The exemption shall apply to presents of a unit value not more than 200 ECU. Member States may, however, grant exemption for more than 200 ECU provided that the value of each exempt present does not exceed 1,000 ECU.][1]

3 The Member State may make exemption of the goods referred to in paragraph 1 conditional on their having borne, either in the country of origin or in the country of departure, the customs and/or fiscal charges to which they are normally liable.

Amendments
1 Substituted by Council Directive 88/331/EEC of 13 June 1988, art 1(1).

Article 12

1. The exemption referred to in Article 11 may be granted only to persons:

(*a*) whose normal place of residence has been outside the Community for a continuous period of at least 12 months. However, derogations from this rule may be granted provided that the intention of the person concerned was clearly to reside outside the Community for a continuous period of at least 12 months;

(*b*) who produce evidence of their marriage.

Article 13

No exemption shall be granted for alcoholic products, tobacco or tobacco products.

Article 14

1. Save in exceptional circumstances, exemption shall be granted only in respect of goods permanently imported:

- not earlier than two months before the date fixed for the wedding (in this case exemption may be made subject to the lodging of appropriate security, the form and amount of which shall be determined by the competent authorities), and

- not later than four months after the date of the wedding.

2. Goods referred to in Article 11 may be imported in several separate consignments within the period referred to in paragraph 1.

Article 15

1. Until 12 months have elapsed from the date of the declaration for their final importation, goods which have been imported exempt from tax may not be lent, given as security, hired out or transferred, whether for a consideration or free of charge, without prior notification to the competent authorities.

2. Any loan, giving as security, hiring out or transfer before the expiry of the period referred to in paragraph 1 shall entail payment of the relevant value added tax on the goods concerned, at the rate applying on the date of such loan, giving as security, hiring out or transfer, on the basis of the type of goods and the value ascertained or accepted on that date by the competent authorities.

CHAPTER III
Personal property acquired by inheritance

Article 16

Subject to Articles 17 to 19, exemption shall be granted in respect of personal property acquired by inheritance by a natural person having his normal place of residence in a Member State.

Article 17

Exemption shall not be granted in respect of:

- (*a*)   alcoholic products;

- (*b*)   tobacco or tobacco products;

- (*c*)   commercial means of transport

- (*d*)   articles for use in the exercise of a trade or profession, other than portable instruments of the applied or liberal arts, which were required for the exercise of the trade or profession of the deceased;

- (*e*)   stocks of raw materials and finished or semi-finished products;

- (*f*)   livestock and stocks of agricultural products exceeding the quantities appropriate to normal family requirements.

Article 18

1. Exemption shall be granted only in respect of personal property permanently imported not later than two years from the date on which the person becomes entitled to the goods (final settlement of the inheritance).

However, this period may be extended by the competent authorities on special grounds.

2. The goods may be imported in several separate consignments within the period referred to in paragraph 1.

Article 19

Articles 16 to 18 shall apply *mutatis mutandis* to personal property acquired by inheritance by legal persons engaged in a non-profitmaking activity who are established in the territory of a Member state.

TITLE II
School outfits, scholastic materials and other scholastic household effects

Article 20

1. Exemption shall be granted in respect of outfits, scholastic materials and household effects representing the usual furnishings for a student's room and belonging to pupils or students coming to stay in a Member State for the purposes of studying there and intended for their personal use during the period of their studies.

2. For the purposes of this Article:

    (*a*)   pupil or student means any person enrolled in an educational establishment in order to attend full-time the courses offered therein;

    (*b*)   outfit means underwear and household linen as well as clothing, whether or not new;

    (*c*)   scholastic materials means articles and instruments (including calculators and type-writers) normally used by pupils or students for the purposes of their studies.

Article 21

Exemption shall be granted at least once per school year.

TITLE III
Imports of negligible value

[Article 22

Goods of a total value not exceeding 10 ECU shall be exempt on admission. Member States may grant exemption for imported goods of a total value of more than 10 ECU but not exceeding 22 ECU.

However, Member Sates may exclude goods which have been imported on mail order from the exemption provided for in the first sentence of the first subparagraph.][1]

Amendments

1   Art 22 substituted by Council Directive 88/331/EEC of 13 June 1988, art 1(2).

Article 23

Exemption shall not apply to the following:

    (*a*)   alcoholic products;

    (*b*)   perfumes and toilet waters;

    (*c*)   tobacco or tobacco products.

TITLE IV
Capital goods and other equipment imported on the transfer of activities

Article 24

1. Without prejudice to the measures in force in the Member State with regard to industrial and commercial policy, and subject to Articles 25 to 28, Member states may allow exemption, on admission, for imports of capital goods and other equipment belonging to undertakings which definitively cease their activity in the country of departure in order to carry on a similar activity in the Member State into which the goods are imported and which, in accordance with Article 22(1) of Directive 77/388/EEC, have given advance notice to the competent authorities of the Member State of importation of the commencement of such activity.

Where the undertaking transferred is an agricultural holding, its livestock shall also be exempt on admission.

2. For the purposes of paragraph 1:

— **"activity"** means an economic activity as referred to in Article 4 of Directive 77/388/EEC,

— **"undertaking"** means an independent economic unit of production or of the service industry.

Article 25

1. The exemption referred to in Article 24 shall be limited to capital goods and equipment which:

(a) except in special cases justified by the circumstances, have actually been used in the undertaking for a minimum of 12 months prior to the date on which the undertaking ceased to operate in the country of departure;

(b) are intended to be used for the same purposes after the transfer;

(c) are to be used for the purposes of an activity not exempted under Article 13 of Directive 77/388/EEC;

(d) are appropriate to the nature and size of the undertaking in question.

2. However, Member States may exempt capital goods and equipment imported from another Member State by charitable or philanthropic organisations at the time of the transfer of their principal place of business to the Member State of importation.

Such exemption shall, however, be granted only on condition that at the time when they were acquired the capital goods and equipment in question were not exempt under Article 15(12) of Directive 77/388/EEC.

3. Pending entry into force of the common rules referred to in the first subparagraph of Article 17(6) of Directive 77/388/EEC, Member States may exclude from the exemption, in whole or in part, capital goods in respect of which they have availed themselves of the second subparagraph of that paragraph.

Article 26

No exemption shall be granted to undertakings established outside the Community and the transfer of which into the territory of a Member State is consequent upon or is for the purpose of merging with, or being absorbed by, an undertaking established in the Community, without a new activity being set up.

Article 27

No exemption shall be granted for:

(a) means of transport which are not of the nature of instruments of production or of the service industry;

(b) supplies of all kinds intended for human consumption or for animal feed;

(c) fuel and stocks of raw materials or finished or semi-finished products;

(d) livestock in the possession of dealers.

Article 28

Except in special cases justified by the circumstances, the exemption referred to in Article 24 shall be granted only in respect of capital goods and other equipment imported before the expiry of a period of 12 months from the date when the undertaking ceased its activities in the country of departure.

TITLE V
Importation of certain agricultural products and products intended for agricultural use

CHAPTER I
Products obtained by community farmers on properties located in a state other than the state of importation

Article 29

1. Subject to Articles 30 and 31, agricultural, stock-farming, bee-keeping, horticultural and forestry products from properties located in a country adjoining the territory of the Member State of importation which are operated by agricultural producers having their principal undertaking in that Member State and adjacent to the country concerned shall be exempt on admission.

2. To be eligible under paragraph 1, stock-farming products must be obtained from animals reared, acquired or imported in accordance with the general tax arrangements applicable in the Member State of importation.

3. Pure-bred horses, not more than six months old and born outside the Member State of importation of an animal covered in that State and then exported temporarily to give birth, shall be exempt on admission.

Article 30

Exemption shall be limited to products which have not undergone any treatment other than that which normally follows their harvest or production.

Article 31

Exemption shall be granted only in respect of products imported by the agricultural producer or on his behalf.

Article 32

This Chapter shall apply *mutatis mutandis* to the products of fishing or fish-farming activities carried out in the lakes or waterways bordering the territory of the Member State of importation by fishermen established in that Member State and to the products of hunting activities carried out on such lakes or waterways by sportsmen established in that Member State.

CHAPTER III
Seeds, fertilizers and products for the treatment of soil and crops

Article 33

Subject to Article 34, seeds, fertilizers and products for the treatment of soil and crops, intended for use on property located in a Member State adjoining a country situated outside the Community or another Member State and operated by agricultural producers having the principal undertaking in the said country situated outside the Community or Member State adjacent to the territory of the Member State of importation shall be exempt on admission.

Article 34

1. Exemption shall be limited to the quantities of seeds, fertilizers or other products required for the purpose of operating the property.

2. It shall be granted only for seeds, fertilizers or other products introduced directly into the importing Member State by the agricultural producer or on his behalf.

3. Member States may make exemption conditional upon the granting of reciprocal treatment.

TITLE VI
Importation of therateutic substances, medicines, laboratory animals and biological or chemical substances

CHAPTER I
Laboratory animals and biological or chemical substances intended for research

Article 35

1. The following shall be exempt on admission:

   (*a*)   animals specially prepared and sent free of charge for laboratory use;

   (*b*)   biological or chemical substances:

   —   which are imported free of charge from the territory of another Member State, or

   —   which are imported from countries outside the Community subject to the limits and conditions laid down in [Article 60][1] of Council Regulation (EEC) No 918/83 of 28 March 1983 setting up a Community system of reliefs from customs duty.

2. The exemption referred to in paragraph 1 shall be limited to animals and biological or chemical substances which are intended for:

   —   either public establishments principally engaged in education or scientific research including those departments of public establishments which are principally engaged in education or scientific research,

   —   or private establishments principally engaged in education or scientific research and authorised by the competent authorities of the Member States to receive such articles exempt from tax.

Amendments
1   Substituted by Council Directive 88/331/EEC of 13 June 1988, art 1(3).

CHAPTER II
Therapeutic substances of human origin and blood-grouping and tissue-typing reagents

Article 36

1. Without prejudice to the exemption provided for in Article 14(1)(a) of Directive 77/388/EEC and subject to Article 37, the following shall be exempted:

   (*a*)   therapeutic substances of human origin;

   (*b*)   blood-grouping reagents;

   (*c*)   tissue-typing reagents.

2. For the purposes of paragraph 1:

   —   **"therapeutic substances of human origin"** means human blood and its derivatives (whole human blood, dried human plasma, human albumin and fixed solutions of human plasma protein, human immunoglobulin and human fibrinogen),

   —   **"blood grouping reagents"** means all reagents, whether of human, animal, plant or other origin used for blood-type grouping and for the detection of blood incompatibilities,

   —   **"tissue-typing reagents"** means all reagents whether of human, animal, plant or other origin used for the determination of human tissue-types.

Article 37

Exemption shall be limited to products which:

- (*a*)   are intended for institutions or laboratories approved by the competent authorities, for use exclusively for non-commercial medical or scientific purposes;

- (*b*)   are accompanied by a certificate of conformity issued by a duly authorised body in the country of departure;

- (*c*)   are in containers bearing a special label identifying them.

Article 38

Exemption shall include the special packaging essential for the transport of therapeutic substances of human origin or blood-grouping or tissue-typing reagents and also any solvents and accessories needed for their use which may be included in the consignments.

[CHAPTER II*a*
Reference substances for the quality control of medical products

Article 38(*a*)

Consignments which contain samples of reference substances approved by the World Health Organisation for the quality control of materials used in the manufacture of medicinal products and which are addressed to consignees authorised by the competent authorities of the Member States to receive such consignments free of tax shall be exempt on admission.][1]

Amendments
1   Added by Council Directive 88/331/EEC of 13 June 1988, art 1(4).

CHAPTER III
Pharmaceutical products used at international sports events

Article 39

Pharmaceutical products for human or veterinary medical use by persons or animals participating in international sports events shall, within the limits necessary to meet their requirements during their stay in the Member State of importation, be exempt on admission.

TITLE VII
Goods for charitable or philanthropic organisations

Article 40

Member States may impose a limit on the quantity or value of the goods referred to in Articles 41 to 55, in order to remedy any abuse and to combat major distortions of competition.

CHAPTER I
Goods imported for general purposes

Article 41

1. Subject to Articles 42 to 44, the following shall be exempt on admission:

- (*a*)   basic necessities obtained free of charge and imported by State organisations or other charitable or philanthropic organisations approved by the competent authorities for distribution free of charge to needy persons;

- (*b*)   goods of every description sent free of charge, by a person or organisation established in a country other than the Member State of importation, and without any commercial intent on the part of the sender, to State organisations or other charitable or philanthropic organisations approved by the competent authorities, to be used for fund raising at occasional charity events for the benefit of needy persons;

(*c*) equipment and office materials sent free of charge, by a person or organisation established in a country other than the Member State of importation, and without any commercial intent on the part of the sender, to charitable or philanthropic organisations approved by the competent authorities, to be used solely for the purpose of meeting their operating needs or carrying out their stated charitable or philanthropic aims.

2. For the purposes of paragraph 1(*a*) **"basic necessities"** means those goods required to meet the immediate needs of human beings, eg food, medicine, clothing and bed-clothes.

Article 42

Exemption shall not be granted in respect of:

(*a*) alcoholic products;

(*b*) tobacco or tobacco products;

(*c*) coffee and tea;

(*d*) motor vehicles other than ambulances.

Article 43

Exemption shall be granted only to organisations accounting procedures of which enable the competent authorities to supervise their operations and which offer all the guarantees considered necessary.

Article 44

1. Exempt goods may not be put out by the organisation entitled to exemption for loan, hiring out or transfer, whether for a consideration or free of charge, for purposes other than those laid down in Article 41(1)(*a*) and (*b*), unless the competent authorities have been informed thereof in advance.

2. Should goods and equipment be lent, hired out or transferred to an organisation entitled to benefit from exemption pursuant to Articles 41 and 43, the exemption shall continue to be granted provided that the latter uses the goods and equipment for purposes which confer the right to such exemption.

In other cases, loan, hiring out or transfer shall be subject to prior payment of value added tax at the rate applying on the date of the loan, hiring out or transfer, on the basis of the type of goods and equipment and the value ascertained or accepted on that date by the competent authorities.

Article 45

1. Organisations referred to in Article 41 which cease to fulfil the conditions giving entitlement to exemption, or which are proposing to use goods and equipment exempt on admission for purposes other than those provided for by that Article, shall so inform the competent authorities.

2. Goods remaining in the possession of organisation which cease to fulfil the conditions giving entitlement to exemption shall be liable to the relevant import value added tax at the rate applying on the date on which those conditions cease to be fulfilled, on the basis of the type of goods and equipment and the value as ascertained or accepted on that date by the competent authorities.

3. Goods used by the organisation benefiting from the exemption for purposes other than those provided for in Article 41 shall be liable to the relevant import value added tax at the rate applying on the date on which they are put to another use on the basis of the type of goods and equipment and the value as ascertained on that date by the competent authorities.

CHAPTER II
Articles imported for the benefit of handicapped persons

Article 46

1. Articles specially designed for the education, employment or social advancement of blind or other physically or mentally handicapped persons shall be exempt on admission where:

    (*a*)   they are imported by institutions or organisations that are principally engaged in the education of or the provision of assistance to handicapped persons and are authorised by the competent authorities of the Member States to receive such articles exempt from tax; and

    (*b*)   they are donated to such institutions or organisations free of charge and with no commercial intent on the part of the donor.

2. Exemption shall apply to specific spare parts, components or accessories specifically for the articles in question and to the tools to be used for maintenance, checking, calibration and repair of the said articles, provided that such spare parts, components, accessories or tools are imported at the same time as the said articles or, if imported subsequently, that they can be identified as being intended for articles previously exempt on admission or which would be eligible to be so exempt at the time when such entry is requested for the specific spare parts, components or accessories and tools in question.

3. Articles exempt on admission may not be used for purposes other than the education, employment or social advancement of blind or other handicapped persons.

Article 47

1. Goods exempt on admission may be lent, hired out or transferred, whether for a consideration or free of charge, by the beneficiary institutions or organisations on a non-profitmaking basis to the persons referred to in Article 46 with whom they are concerned, without payment of valued added tax on importation.

2. No loan, hiring out or transfer may be effected under conditions other than those provided for in paragraph 1 unless the competent authorities have first been informed.

Should an article be lent, hired out or transferred to an institution or organisation itself entitled to benefit from this exemption, the exemption shall continue to be granted, provided the latter uses the article for purposes which confer the right to such exemption.

In other cases, loan, hiring out or transfer shall be subject to prior payment of value added tax, at the rate applying on the date of the loan, hiring out or transfer, on the basis of the type of goods and the value ascertained or accepted on that date by the competent authorities.

Article 48

1. Institutions or organisations referred to in Article 46 which cease to fulfil the conditions giving entitlement to exemption, or which are proposing to use articles exempt on admission for purposes other than those provided for by that Article shall so inform the competent authorities.

2. Articles remaining in the possession of institutions or organisations which cease to fulfil the conditions giving entitlement to exemption shall be liable to the relevant import value added tax at the rate applying on the date on which those conditions cease to be fulfilled, on the basis of the type of goods and the value ascertained or accepted on that date by the competent authorities.

3. Articles used by the institution or organisation benefiting from the exemption for purposes other than those provided for in Article 46 shall be liable to the relevant import value added tax at the rate applying on the date on which they are put to another use on the basis of the type of goods and the value ascertained or accepted on that date by the competent authorities.

CHAPTER III
Goods imported for the benefit of disaster victims

Article 49

1. Subject to Articles 50 to 55, goods imported by State organisations or other charitable or philanthropic organisations approved by the competent authorities shall be exempt on admission where they are intended:

(*a*) for distribution free of charge to victims of disaster affecting the territory of one or more Member States; or

(*b*) to be made available free of charge to the victims of such disasters, while remaining the property of the organisations in question.

2. Goods imported by disaster-relief agencies in order to meet their needs during the period of their activity shall also benefit upon admission from the exemption referred to in paragraph 1 under the same conditions.

Article 50

No exemption shall be granted for materials and equipment intended for rebuilding disaster areas.

Article 51

Granting of the exemption shall be subject to a decision by the Commission, acting at the request of the Member State or States concerned in accordance with an emergency procedure entailing the consultation of the other Member States. This decision shall, where necessary, lay down the scope and the conditions of the exemption.

Pending notification of the Commission's decision, Member States affected by a disaster may authorise the suspension of any import value added tax chargeable on goods imported for the purposes described in Article 49, subject to an undertaking by the importing organisation to pay such tax if exemption is not granted.

Article 52

Exemption shall be granted only to organisations the accounting procedures of which enable the competent authorities to supervise their operations and which offer all the guarantees considered necessary.

Article 53

1. The organisations benefiting from the exemption may not lend, hire out or transfer, whether for a consideration or free of charge, the goods referred to in Article 49(1) under conditions other than those laid down in that Article without prior notification thereof to the competent authorities.

2. Should goods be lent, hired out or transferred to an organisation itself entitled to benefit from exemption pursuant to Article 49, the exemption shall continue to be granted, provided the latter uses the goods for purposes which confer the right to such exemption.

In other cases, loan, hiring out or transfer shall be subject to prior payment of value added tax, at the rate applying on the date of the loan, hiring out or transfer, on the basis of the type of goods and the value ascertained or accepted on that date by competent authorities.

Article 54

1. The goods referred to in Article 49(1)(*b*), after they cease to be used by disaster victims, may not be lent, hired out or transferred, whether for a consideration or free of charge, unless the competent authorities are notified in advance.

2. Should goods be lent, hired out or transferred to an organisation itself entitled to benefit from exemption pursuant to Article 49 or, if appropriate, to an organisation entitled to benefit from exemption pursuant to Article 41(1)(*a*), the exemption shall continue to be granted, provided such organisations use them for purposes which confer the right to such exemption.

In other cases, loan, hiring out or transfer shall be subject to prior payment of value added tax, at the rate applying on the date of the loan, hiring out or transfer, on the basis of the type of goods and the value ascertained or accepted on that date by competent authorities.

Article 55

1. Organisations referred to in Article 49 which cease to fulfil the conditions giving entitlement to exemption, or which are proposing to use the goods exempt on admission for purposes other than those provided for by that Article shall so inform the competent authorities.

2. In the case of goods remaining in the possession of organisations which cease to fulfil the conditions giving entitlement to exemption, when these are transferred to an organisation itself entitled to benefit from exemption pursuant to this chapter or, if appropriate, to an organisation entitled to benefit from exemption pursuant to Article 41, the exemption shall continue to be granted, provided the organisation uses the goods in question for purposes which confer the right to such exemptions. In other cases, the goods shall be liable to the relevant import value added tax at the rate applying on the date on which those conditions cease to be fulfilled, on the basis of the type of goods and the value ascertained or accepted on that date by the competent authorities.

3. Goods used by the organisations benefiting from the exemption for purposes other than those provided for in this chapter shall be liable to the relevant import value added tax at the rate applying on the date on which they are put to another use, on the basis of the type of goods and the value ascertained or accepted on that date by the competent authorities.

TITLE VII
Importation in the context of certain aspects of international relations

CHAPTER I
Honorary decorations or awards

Article 56

On production of satisfactory evidence to the competent authorities by the person concerned, and provided the operations involved are not in any way of a commercial character exemption shall be granted in respect of:

(*a*) decorations conferred by the government of a country other than the Member State of importation on persons whose normal place of residence is in the latter State;

(*b*) cups, medals and similar articles of an essentially symbolic nature which, having been awarded in a country other than the Member State of importation to persons having their normal place of residence in the latter State as a tribute to their activities in fields such as the arts, the sciences, sport or the public service or in recognition of merit at a particular event, are imported by such persons themselves;

(*c*) cups, medals and similar articles of an essentially symbolic nature which are given free of charge by authorities or persons established in a country other than the Member State of importation, to be presented in the territory of the latter State for the same purposes as those referred to in (*b*).

[(*d*) Awards, trophies and souvenirs of a symbolic nature and of limited value intended for distribution free of charge to persons normally resident in a country other than that of import, at business conferences or similar international events; their nature, unitary value or other features, must not be such as might indicate that they are intended for commercial purposes.][1]

Amendments

1 Art 56(*d*) inserted by Council Directive 88/331/EEC of 13 June 1988, art 1(5).

CHAPTER II
Presents received in the context of international relations

Article 57

Without prejudice, where relevant, to the provisions applicable to the international movement of travellers, and subject to Articles 58 and 59, exemption shall be granted in respect of goods:

(*a*) imported by persons who have paid an official visit in a country other than that of their normal residence and who have received such goods on that occasion as gifts from the host authorities;

(*b*) imported by persons coming to pay an official visit in the Member State of importation and who intend to offer them on that occasion as gifts to the host authorities;

(*c*) sent as gifts, in token of friendship or goodwill, by an official body, public authority or group carrying on an activity in the public interest which is located in a country other than the Member State of importation, to an official body, public authority or group carrying on an activity in the public interest which is located in the Member State of importation and approved by the competent authorities to receive such goods exempt from tax.

Article 58

No exemption shall be granted for alcoholic products, tobacco or tobacco products.

Article 59

Exemption shall be granted only:

— where the articles intended as gifts are offered on an occasional basis,

— where they do not, by their nature, value or quantity, reflect any commercial interest,

— if they are not used for commercial purposes.

CHAPTER III
Goods to be used by monarchs or heads of state

Article 60

Exemption from tax, within the limits and under the conditions laid down by the competent authorities, shall be granted in respect of:

(*a*) gifts to reigning monarchs and heads of State;

(*b*) goods to be used or consumed by reigning monarchs and heads of State of another State, or by persons officially representing them, during their official stay in the Member State of importation. However, exemption may be made subject, by the Member State of importation, to reciprocal treatment.

The provisions of the preceding subparagraph are also applicable to persons enjoying prerogatives at international level analogous to those enjoyed by the reigning monarchs or heads of State.

TITLE IX
Importation of goods for the promotion of trade

CHAPTER I
Samples of negligible value

Article 61

1. Without prejudice to Article 65(1)(*a*), samples of goods which are of negligible value and which can be used only to solicit orders for goods of the type they represent shall be exempt on admission.

2. The competent authorities may require that certain articles, to qualify for exemption on admission, be rendered permanently unusable by being torn, perforated, or clearly and indelibly marked, or by any other process, provided such operation does not destroy their character as samples.

For the purposes of paragraph 1, **"samples of goods"** means any article representing a type of goods whose manner of presentation and quantity, for goods of the same type or quality, rule out its use for any other purpose other than that of seeking orders.

CHAPTER II
Printed matter and advertising material

[*Article 62*

Subject to Article 63, printed advertising matter such as catalogues, price lists, directions for use or brochures shall be exempt on admission provided that they relate to:

    (*a*)   goods for sale or hire by a person established outside the Member State of import, or

    (*b*)   services offered by a person established in another Member State, or

    (*c*)   transport, commercial insurance or banking services offered by a person established in a third country.][1]

Amendments

1 Art 62 substituted by Council Directive 88/331/EEC of 13 June 1988, art 1(6).

[*Article 63*

The exemption referred to in Article 62 shall be limited to printed advertisements which fulfil the following conditions:

    (*a*)   printed matter must clearly display the name of the undertaking which produces, sells or hires out the goods, or which offers the services to which it refers;

    (*b*)   each consignment must contain no more than one document or a single copy of each document if it is made up of several documents. Consignments comprising several copies of the same document may nevertheless be granted exemption provided their total gross weight does not exceed one kilogram;

    (*c*)   printed matter must not be the subject of grouped consignments from the same consignor to the same consignee.

However, the conditions under (*b*) and (*c*) shall not apply to printed matter relating to either goods for sale or hire or services offered by a person established in another Member State provided that the printed matter has been imported, and will be distributed, free of charge.][1]

Amendments

1 Art 63 substituted by Council Directive 88/331/EEC of 13 June 1988, art 1(6).

Article 64

Articles for advertising purposes, of no intrinsic commercial value, sent free of charge by suppliers to their customers which, apart from their advertising function, are not capable of being used shall also be exempt on admission.

CHAPTER III
Goods used or consumed at a trade fair or similar event

Article 65

1. Subject to Articles 66 to 69, the following shall be exempt on admission:

(*a*) small representative samples of goods intended for a trade fair or similar event;

(*b*) goods imported solely in order to be demonstrated or in order to demonstrate machines and apparatus displayed at a trade fair or similar event;

(*c*) various materials of little value, such as paints, varnishes and wallpaper, which are to be used in the building, fitting-out and decoration of temporary stands at a trade fair or similar event, which are destroyed by being used;

(*d*) printed matter, catalogues, prospectuses, price lists, advertising posters, calendars, whether or not illustrated, unframed photographs and other articles supplied free of charge in order to advertise goods displayed at a trade fair or similar event.

2. For the purposes of paragraph 1, **"trade fair or similar event"** means:

(*a*) exhibitions, fairs, shows and similar events connected with trade, industry, agriculture or handicrafts;

(*b*) exhibitions and events held mainly for charitable reasons;

(*c*) exhibitions and events held mainly for scientific, technical, handicraft, artistic, educational or cultural or sporting reasons, for religious reasons or for reasons of worship, trade union activity or tourism, or in order to promote international understanding;

(*d*) meetings of representatives of international organisations or collective bodies;

(*e*) official or commemorative ceremonies and gatherings;

but no*t* exhibitions staged for private purposes in commercial stores or premises to sell goods.

Article 66

The exemption referred to in Article 65(1)(*a*) shall be limited to samples which:

(*a*) are imported free of charge as such or are obtained at the exhibition from goods imported in bulk;

(*b*) are exclusively distributed free of charge to the public at the exhibition for use or consumption by the persons to whom they have been offered;

(*c*) are identifiable as advertising samples of low unitary value;

(*d*) are not easily marketable and, where appropriate, are packaged in such a way that the quantity of the item involved is lower than the smallest quantity of the same item actually sold on the market;

(*e*) in the case of foodstuffs and beverages not packaged as mentioned in (*d*), are consumed on the spot at the exhibition;

(*f*) in their total value and quantity, are appropriate to the nature of the exhibition, the number of visitors and the extent of the exhibitor's participation.

Article 67

The exemption referred to in Article 65(1)(*b*) shall be limited to goods which are:

(*a*) consumed or destroyed at the exhibition, and

(*b*) are appropriate, in their total value and quantity, to the nature of the exhibition, the number of visitors and the extent of the exhibitor's participation.

Article 68

The exemption referred to in Article 65(1)(*d*) shall be limited to printed matter and articles for advertising purposes which:

    (*a*)   are intended exclusively to be distributed free of charge to the public at the place where the exhibition is held;

    (*b*)   in their total value and quantity, are appropriate to the nature of the exhibition, the number of visitors and the extent of the exhibitor's participation.

Article 69

The exemption referred to in Article 65(1)(*a*) and (*b*) shall not be granted for:

    (*a*)   alcoholic products;

    (*b*)   tobacco or tobacco products;

    (*c*)   fuels, whether solid, liquid or gaseous.

TITLE X
Goods imported for examination, analysis or test purposes

Article 70

Subject to Articles 71 to 76, goods which are to undergo examination, analysis or tests to determine their composition, quality or other technical characteristics for purposes of information or industrial or commercial research shall be exempt on admission.

Article 71

Without prejudice to Article 74, the exemption referred to in Article 70 shall be granted only on condition that the goods to be examined, analysed or tested are completely used up or destroyed in the course of the examination, analysing or testing.

Article 72

No exemption shall be granted in respect of goods used in examination, analysis or tests which in themselves constitute sales promotion operations.

Article 73

Exemption shall be granted only in respect of the quantities of goods which are strictly necessary for the purposes for which they are imported. These quantities shall in each case be determined by the competent authorities, taking into account the said purpose.

Article 74

1. The exemption referred to in Article 70 shall cover goods which are not completely used up or destroyed during examination, analysis or testing, provided that the products remaining are, with the agreement and under the supervision of the competent authorities:

    —   completely destroyed or rendered commercially valueless on completion of examination, analysis or testing, or

    —   surrendered to the state without causing it any expense, where this is possible under national law, or

    —   in duly justified circumstances, exported outside the territory of the Member State of importation.

2. For the purposes of paragraph 1, **"products remaining"** means products resulting from the examinations, analyses or tests or goods not actually used.

Article 75

Save where Article 74(1) is applied, products remaining at the end of the examinations, analyses or tests referred to in Article 70 shall be subject to the relevant import value added tax, at the rate applying on the date of completion of the examinations, analyses or tests, on the basis of the type of goods and the value ascertained or accepted on that date by the competent authorities.

However, the interested party may, with the agreement and under the supervision of the competent authorities, convert products remaining to waste or scrap. In this case, the import duties shall be those applying to such waste or scrap at the time of conversion.

Article 76

The period within which the examinations, analyses or tests must be carried out and the administrative formalities to be completed in order to ensure the use of the goods for the purposes intended shall be determined by the competent authorities.

TITLE XI
Miscellaneous exemptions

CHAPTER I
Consignments sent to organisations protecting copyrights or industrial and commercial patent rights

Article 77

Trademarks, patterns or designs and their supporting documents, as well as applications for patents for invention or the like, to be submitted to the bodies competent to deal with the protection of copyrights or the protection of industrial or commercial patent rights shall be exempt on admission.

CHAPTER II
Tourist information literature

Article 78

The following shall be exempt on admission:

(*a*)   documentation (leaflets, brochures, books, magazines, guidebooks, posters, whether or not framed, unframed photographs and photographic enlargements, maps, whether or not illustrated, window transparencies, and illustrated calendars) intended to be distributed free of charge and the principal purpose of which is to encourage the public to visit foreign countries, in particular in order to attend cultural, tourist, sporting, religious or trade or professional meetings or events, provided such literature contains not more than 25% of private commercial advertising and that the general nature of its promotional aims is evident;

(*b*)   foreign hotel lists and yearbooks published by official tourist agencies, or under their auspices, and timetables for foreign transport services, provided that such literature is intended for distribution free of charge and contains not more than 25% of private commercial advertising;

(*c*)   reference material supplied to accredited representatives or correspondents appointed by official national tourist agencies and not intended for distribution, i.e. yearbooks, lists of telephone or telex numbers, hotel lists, fairs catalogues, specimens of craft goods of negligible value, and literature on museums, universities, spas or other similar establishments.

CHAPTER III
Miscellaneous documents and articles

Article 79

The following shall be exempt on admission:

(*a*)   documents sent free of charge to the public services of Member States;

(*b*)   publications of foreign governments and publications of official international bodies intended for distribution without charge;

(c)   ballot papers for elections organised by bodies set up in countries other than the Member State of importation;

(d)   objects to be submitted as evidence or for like purposes to the courts or other official agencies of the Member State;

(e)   specimen signatures and printed circulars concerning signatures sent as part of customary exchange of information between public services or banking establishments;

(f)   official printed matter sent to the central banks of the Member States;

(g)   reports, statements, notes, prospectuses, application forms and other documents drawn up by companies with headquarters outside the Member States of importation and sent to the bearers or subscribers of securities issued by such companies;

(h)   recorded media (punched cards, sound recordings, microfilms, etc) used for the transmission of information sent free of charge to the addressee, in so far as exemption does not give rise to abuses or to major distortions of competition;

(i)   files, archives, printed forms and other documents to be used in international meetings, conferences or congresses, and reports on such gatherings;

(j)   plans, technical drawings, traced designs, descriptions and other similar documents imported with a view to obtaining or fulfilling orders in a country other than the Member State of importation or to participating in a competition held in that State;

(k)   documents to be used in examinations held in the Member State of importation by institutions set up in another country;

(l)   printed forms to be used as official documents in the international movement of vehicles or goods, within the framework of international conventions;

(m)   printed forms, labels, tickets and similar documents sent by transport undertakings or by undertakings of the hotel industry located in a country other than the Member State of importation to travel agencies set up in that State;

(n)   printed forms and tickets, bills of lading, way-bills and other commercial or office documents which have been used;

(o)   official printed forms from national or international authorities, and printed matter conforming to international standards sent for distribution by associations of countries other than the Member State of importation to corresponding associations located in that State;

(p)   photographs, slides and stereotype mats for photographs, whether or not captioned, sent to press agencies to newspaper or magazine publishers;

(q)   articles listed in the Annex to this Directive which are produced by the United Nations or one of its specialised agencies whatever the use for which they are intended:

(r)   collectors' pieces and works of art of an educational, scientific or cultural character which are not intended for sale and which are imported by museums, galleries and other institutions approved by the competent authorities of the Member States for the purpose of duty-free admission of these goods. The exemption is granted only on condition that the articles in question are imported free of charge or, if they are imported against payment, that they are not supplied by a taxable person.

[(s)   importations of official publications issued under the authority of the country of export, international institutions, regional or local authorities and bodies under public law established in the country of export, and printed matter distributed on the occasion of elections to the European Parliament or on the occasion of national elections in the country in which the printed matter originates by foreign political organisation officially recognised as such in the Member States, insofar as such publications and printed matter have been subject to tax in the country of export and have not benefited from remission of tax on export.][1]

Amendments
1 Art 79(*s*) inserted by Council Directive 88/331/EEC of 13 June 1988, art 1(7).

CHAPTER IV
Ancillary materials for the stowage and protection of goods during their transport

Article 80

The various materials such as rope, straw, cloth, paper and cardboard, wood and plastics which are used for the stowage and protection - including heat protection - of goods during their transport to the territory of a Member State, shall be exempt on admission, provided that:

(*a*) they are not normally re-usable; and

(*b*) the consideration paid for them forms part of the taxable amount as defined in Article 11 of Directive 77/388/EEC.

CHAPTER V
Litter, fodder, and feedingstuffs for animals during their transport

Article 81

Litter, fodder and feedingstuffs of any description put on board the means of transport used to convey animals to the territory of a Member State for the purpose of distribution to the said animals during the journey shall be exempt on admission.

CHAPTER VI
Fuel and lubricants present in land motor vehicles and special containers

[*Article 82*

1. Subject to Articles 84, 84 and 85, the following shall be exempt on admission:

(*a*) fuel contained in the standard tanks of

— private and commercial motor vehicles and motor cycles; ·

— special containers;

(*b*) fuel contained in portable tanks carried by private motor vehicles and motor cycles, up to a maximum of 10 litres per vehicle and without prejudice to national provisions on the holding and transport of fuel.

2. For the purposes of paragraph 1:

(*a*) **"commercial motor vehicle"** means any motorised road vehicle (including tractors with trailers) which, by its type of construction and equipment, is designed for, and capable of, transporting, whether for payment or not:

— more than nine persons including the drive,

— goods,

and any road vehicle for a special purpose other than transport as such;

(*b*) **"private motor vehicles"** means any motor vehicle not covered by the definition set out in (*a*);

(*c*) **"standard tanks"** means:

— the tanks permanently fixed by the manufacturer to all motor vehicles of the same type as the vehicle in question and whose permanent fitting enables fuel to be used directly, both for the purpose of propulsion and, where appropriate, for the operation, during transport, of refrigeration systems and other systems.

Gas tanks fitted to motor vehicles designed for the direct use of gas as a fuel and tanks fitted to ancillary systems with which the vehicle may be equipped shall also be considered to be standard tanks,

— tanks permanently fixed by the manufacturer to all containers of the same type as the container in question and whose permanent fitting enables fuel to be used directly for the operation, during transport, of refrigeration systems and other systems with which special containers are equipped;

(d) **"special container"** means any container fitted with specially designed apparatus for refrigeration systems, oxygenation systems, thermal insulation systems, or other systems.][1]

Amendments

1   Art 82 substituted by Council Directive 88/331/EEC of 13 June 1988, art 1(9).

[*Article 83*

Member States may limit the application of the exemption for fuel contained in the standard fuel tanks of commercial motor vehicles [and special containers][1]:

(a)   when the vehicle comes from a third country, to 200 litres per vehicle and per journey;

(b)   when the vehicle comes from another Member State:

— to 200 litres per vehicle and per journey in the case of vehicles designed for, and capable of, the transport, with or without remuneration, of goods;

— to 600 litres per vehicle and per journey in the case of vehicles designed for, and capable of, the transport, with or without remuneration, of more than nine persons, including the driver.

Acting in accordance with the procedures provided for by the Treaty on this point, the Council shall decide, on a proposal from the Commission, before 1 July 1986, on the increase of the quantity of fuel admitted duty-free and contained in the standard fuel tanks of the vehicles referred to in the first indent of (b) of the first subparagraph.

[(c)   to 200 litres per special container and per journey.][2]][3]

Amendments

1   Inserted by Council Directive 88/331/EEC of 13 June 1988, art 1(10).
2   Para (c) inserted by Council Directive 88/331/EEC of 13 June 1988, art 1(10).
2   Art 83 substituted by Council Directive 85/346/EEC of 8 July 1985.

Article 84

Member States may limit the amount of fuel exempt on admission in the case of:

[(a)   commercial motor vehicles engaged in international transport coming from third countries to their frontier zone, to a maximum depth of 25 kilometres as the crow flies, where such transport consists of journeys made by persons residing in that zone;][1]

(b)   private motor vehicles belonging to persons residing in the frontier zone, to a maximum depth of 15 km as the crow flies, contiguous with a third country.

Amendments

1   Para (a) substituted by Council Directive of 8 July 1985 (85/346/EEC).

Article 85

Fuel exempt on admission may not be used in a vehicle other than that in which it was imported nor be removed from that vehicle and stored, except during necessary repairs to that vehicle, or transferred for a consideration or free of charge by the person granted the exemption.

Non-compliance with the preceding paragraph shall give rise to application of the import value added tax relating to the products in question at the rate in force on the date of such non-compliance, on the basis of the type of goods and the value ascertained or accepted on that date by the competent authorities.

Article 86

The exemption referred to in Article 82 shall also apply to lubricants carried in motor vehicles and required for their normal operation during the journey in question.

CHAPTER VII
Goods for the construction, upkeep or ornamentation of memorials to, or cemeteries for, war victims

Article 87

Exemption from tax shall be granted in respect of goods imported by organisations authorised for that purpose by the competent authorities, for use in the construction, upkeep or ornamentation of cemeteries and tombs of, and memorials to, war victims of a country other than the Member State of importation who are buried in the latter State.

CHAPTER VIII
Coffins, funerary urns and ornamental funerary articles

Article 88

The following shall be exempt on admission:

(*a*) coffins containing bodies and urns containing the ashes of deceased persons, as well as the flowers, funeral wreaths and other ornamental objects normally accompanying them;

(*b*) flowers, wreaths and other ornamental objects brought by persons resident in a Member State other than that of importation, attending a funeral or coming to decorate graves in the territory of a Member State of importation provided these importations do not reflect, by either their nature or their quantity, any commercial intent.

TITLE XII
General and final provisions

Article 89

Where this Directive provides that the granting of an exemption shall be subject to the fulfilment of certain conditions, the person concerned shall, to the satisfaction of the competent authorities, furnish proof that these conditions have been met.

Article 90

1. The exchange value in national currency of the ECU to be taken into consideration for the purposes of this Directive shall be fixed once a year. The rates to be applied shall be those obtaining on the first working day in October and shall take effect on 1 January the following year.

2. Member States may round off the amounts in national currency arrived at by converting the amounts in ECU.

3 Member States may continue to apply the amounts of the exemptions in force at the time of the annual adjustment provided for in paragraph 1, if conversion of the amounts of the exemptions expressed ECU leads, before the rounding-off provided for in paragraph 2, to an alteration of less than 5% in the exemption expressed in national currency [or to a reduction in that exemption][1].

Amendments
1   Inserted by Council Directive 88/331/EEC of 13 June 1988, art 1(11).

Article 91

No provision of this Directive shall prevent Member States from continuing to grant:

(*a*)   the privileges and immunities granted by them under cultural, scientific or technical co-operation agreements concluded between them or with third countries;

(*b*)   the special exemptions justified by the nature of frontier traffic which are granted by them under frontier agreements concluded between them or with countries outside the Community.

[(*c*)   exemptions in the context of agreements entered into on the basis of reciprocity with third countries that are Contracting Parties to the Convention on International Civil Aviation (Chicago 1944) for the purposes of implementing Recommended Practices 4.42 and 4.44 in Annex 9 to the Convention (eighth edition, July 1980).][1]

Amendments
1   Para (*c*) inserted by Council Directive 88/331/EEC of 13 June 1988.

Article 92

Until the establishment of Community exemptions upon importation, Member States may retain the exemptions granted to:

(*a*)   merchant-navy seamen;

(*b*)   workers returning to their country after having resided for at least six months outside the importing Member State on account of their occupation.

Article 93

1. Member States shall bring into force the measures necessary to comply with this Directive with effect from 1 July 1984.

2. Member States shall inform the Commission of the measures which they adopt to give effect to this Directive, indicating, where the cases arise, those measures which they adopt by simple reference to identical provisions of Regulation (EEC) No 918/83.

Article 94

This Directive is addressed to the Member States.

Done at Brussels, 28 March 1983

ANNEX
Visual and auditory materials of an educational, scientific or cultural character

CN code	Description
3704 00	Photographic plates, film, paper, paperboard and textiles, exposed but not developed:
ex 3704 00 10	- Plates and film: - Cinematograph film, positives, of an educational, scientific or cultural character
ex 3705	Photographic plates and film, exposed and developed, other than cinematograph film: - Of an educational, scientific or cultural character
3706	Cinematograph film, exposed and developed, whether or not incorporating sound track or consisting only of sound track:

3706 10	- Of a width of 35 mm or more: — Other:
ex 3706 10 99	— Other positives: —— Newsreels (with or without sound track) depicting events of current news value at the time of importation, and imported up to a limit of two copies of each subject for copying purposes —— Archival film material (with or without soundtrack) intended for use in connection with newsreel films —— Recreational films particularly suited for children and young people —— Other films of educational, scientific or cultural character
3706 90	- Other: — Other: — Other positives:
ex 3706 90 51	—— Newsreels (with or without sound track) depicting events of current news value at the time of importation, and imported up to a limit of two copies of each subject for copying purposes
ex 3706 90 91	—— Archival film material (with or without soundtrack) intended for use in connection with newsreel films
ex 3706 90 99	—— Recreational films particularly suited for children and young people —— Other films of educational, scientific or cultural character:
4911	Other printed matter, including printed pictures and photographs: - Other:
49 11 99	— Other:
ex 4911 99 90	—- Other: —— Microcards or other information storage media required in computerised information and documentation services of an educational, scientific or cultural character —— Wall charts designed solely for demonstration and education
ex 8524	Records, tapes and other recorded media for sound or other similarly recorded phenomena including matrices and masters for the production of records, but excluding products of Chapter 37: - Of an educational, scientific or cultural character
ex 9023 00	Instruments, apparatus and models, designed for demonstration purposes (for example, in education or exhibitions), unsuitable for other uses: - Patters, models and wall charts of an educational, scientific or cultural character, designed solely for demonstration and education - Mock-ups or visualisations of abstract concepts such a molecular structures or mathematical formulae
Various	Holograms for laser projection Multimedia kits Materials for programmed instructions, including materials in kit form with the corresponding printed materials

Amendments

1 Annex replaced by Commission Directive of 7 March 1989 (89/219/EEC), art 1.

COUNCIL DIRECTIVE

of 28 March 1983

83/182/EEC

(OJ L105, 23.4.1983, p 53)

On tax exemptions within the Community for certain means of transport temporarily imported into one Member State from another

---

Note

This Directive ceases to have effect on 31 December 1992 as regards its provisions on VAT; see Council Directive 91/680/EEC of 16 December 1991, art 2(2).

COUNCIL DIRECTIVE

of 28 March 1983

83/183/EEC

(OJ L105, 23.4.1983, p 64)

Note

This Directive ceases to have effect on 31 December 1992 as regards its provisions on VAT; see Council Directive 91/680/EEC of 16 December 1991, art 2(2).

TENTH COUNCIL DIRECTIVE

of 31 July 1984

84/386/EEC

(OJ No. L208/58, 3.8.1984)

Hiring out of movable tangible property (other than means of transport)

THE COUNCIL OF THE EUROPEAN COMMUNITIES,

Having regard to the Treaty establishing the European Economic Community, and in particular Articles 99 and 100 thereof,

Having regard to the Sixth Council Directive 77/388/EEC of 17 May 1977 on the harmonisation of the laws of the Member States relating to turnover taxes Common system of value added tax: uniform basis of assessment,

Having regard to the proposal from the Commission,

Having regard to the opinion of the European Parliament,

Having regard to the opinion of the Economic and Social Committee,

Whereas, pursuant to Article 4(2) of the aforementioned Directive, the hiring out of movable tangible property may constitute an economic activity subject to value added tax;

Whereas application of Article 9(1) of the aforementioned Directive to the hiring out of movable tangible property may lead to substantial distortions of competition where the lessor and the lessee are established in different Member States and the rates of taxation in those States differ;

Whereas it is therefore necessary to establish that the place where a service is supplied is the place where the customer has established his business or has a fixed establishment for which the service has been supplied or, in the absence thereof, the place where he has his permanent address or usually resides;

Whereas, however, as regards the hiring out of forms of transport, Article 9(1) should, for reasons of control, be strictly applied, the place where the supplier has established his business being treated as the place of supply of such services,

HAS ADOPTED THIS DIRECTIVE

Article 1
Services affected

Notes

Para (1) deleted Sixth Directive art 9(2)(*d*); para (2) amended Sixth Directive art 9(2)(*e*); para (3) amended Sixth Directive art 9(3).

Article 2
Date of implementation

1. Member States shall bring into force the measures necessary to comply with this Directive by 1 July 1985.

2. Member States shall inform the Commission of the provisions which they adopt for the purpose of applying this Directive. The Commission shall inform the other Member States thereof.

Article 3
Scope

This Directive is addressed to the Member States.

Done at Brussels, 31 July 1984.

Case law
Failure to fulfil obligations under Tenth Directive: *EC Commission v Italy* (1989) OJ C66/5, ECJ 353/87.

SEVENTEENTH COUNCIL DIRECTIVE

of 16 July 1985

85/362/EEC

(OJ L192, 24.7.1985, p 20)

*On the harmonisation of the laws of the Member States relating to turnover taxes —
exemption from value added tax on the temporary importation of goods other than means
of transport*

Note
This Directive ceases to have effect on 31 December 1992 as regards relations between Member States; see Council Directive 91/680/EEC of 16 December 1991 art 2(1).

THIRTEENTH COUNCIL DIRECTIVE

of 17 November 1986

86/560/EEC

(OJ L326, 21.11.1968, p 40)

On the harmonisation of the laws of the Member States relating to turnover taxes — arrangements for the refund of value added tax to taxable persons not established in Community territory

THE COUNCIL OF THE EUROPEAN COMMUNITIES,

Having regard to the Treaty establishing the European Economic Community, and in particular Articles 99 and 100 thereof,

Having regard to Sixth Council Directive 77/388/EEC of 17 May 1977 on the harmonisation of the laws of the Member States relating to turnover taxes — Common system of value added tax: uniform basis of assessment (OJ L145, 13.6.1977, p 1), and in particular Article 17(4) thereof,

Having regard to the proposal from the Commission (OJ C223, 27.8.1982, p 5 and OJ C196, 23.7.1983, p 6),

Having regard to the opinion of the European Parliament (OJ C161, 20.6.1983, p 111),

Having regard to the opinion of the Economic and Social Committee (OJ C176, 4.7.1983, p 22),

Whereas Article 8 of Eighth Council Directive 79/1072/EEC (OJ No L331, 21.12.1979, p 11) on the arrangements for the refund of value added tax to taxable persons not established in the territory of the country provides that in the case of taxable persons not established in the territory of the Community, Member States may refuse refunds or impose special conditions;

Whereas there is a need to ensure the harmonious development of trade relations between the Community and third countries based on the provisions of Directive 79/1072/EEC, while taking account of the varying situations found in third countries;

Whereas certain forms of tax evasion or avoidance should be prevented,

HAS ADOPTED THIS DIRECTIVE:

Article 1

For the purposes of this Directive:

1. "A taxable person not established in the territory of the Community" shall mean a taxable person as referred to in Article 4(1) of Directive 77/388/EEC who, during the period referred to in Article 3(1) of this Directive, has had in that territory neither his business nor a fixed establishment from which business transactions are effected, nor, if no such business or fixed establishment exists, his permanent address or usual place of residence, and who, during the same period, has supplied no goods or services deemed to have been supplied in the Member State referred to in Article 2, with the exception of:

(*a*) transport services and services ancillary thereto, exempted pursuant to Article 14(1)(i), Article 15 or Article 16(1)B, C and D of Directive 77/388/EEC;

(*b*) services provided in cases where tax is payable solely by the person to whom they are supplied, pursuant to Article 21(1)(*b*) of Directive 77/388/EEC;

2. "Territory of the Community" shall mean the territories of the Member States in which Directive 77/388/EEC is applicable.

Article 2

1. Without prejudice to the provisions of Articles 3 and 4, each Member State shall refund to any taxable person not established in the territory of the Community, subject to the conditions set out below, any value added tax charged in respect of services or movable property supplied to him in the territory of the country by other taxable persons or charged in respect of the importation of goods into the country in so far as such goods and services are used for the purposes of the transactions referred to in Article 17(3)(*a*) and (*b*) of Directive 77/388/EEC or of the provision of the services referred to in point 1(*b*) of Article 1 of this Directive.

2. Member States may make the refund referred to in paragraph 1 conditional upon the granting by third States of comparable advantages regarding turnover taxes.

3. Member States may require the appointment of a tax representative.

Article 3

1. The refunds referred to in Article 2(1) shall be granted upon application by the taxable person. Member States shall determine the arrangements for submitting applications, including the time limits for doing so, the period which applications should cover, the authority competent to receive them and the minimum amounts in respect of which applications may be submitted. They shall also determine the arrangements for making refunds, including the time limits for doing so. They shall impose on the applicant such obligations as are necessary to determine whether the application is justified and to prevent fraud, in particular the obligation to provide proof that he is engaged in an economic activity in accordance with Article 4(1) of Directive 77/388/EEC. The applicant must certify, in a written declaration that, during the period prescribed, he has not carried out any transaction which does not fulfil the conditions laid down in point 1 of Article 1 of this Directive.

2. Refunds may not be granted under conditions more favourable than those applied to Community taxable persons.

Article 4

1. For the purposes of this Directive, eligibility for refunds shall be determined in accordance with Article 17 of Directive 77/388/EEC, as applied in the Member State where the refund is paid.

2. Member States may, however, provide for the exclusion of certain expenditure or make refunds subject to additional conditions.

3. This Directive shall not apply to supplies of goods which are or may be exempted under point 2 of Article 15 of Directive 77/388/EEC.

Article 5

1. Member States shall bring into force the laws, regulations and administrative provisions necessary to comply with this Directive by 1 January 1988 at the latest. This Directive shall apply only to applications for refunds concerning value added tax charged on purchases of goods or services invoiced or on imports effected on or after that date.

2. Member States shall communicate to the Commission the texts of the main provisions of national law which they adopt in the field covered by this Directive and shall inform the Commission of the use they make of the option afforded by Article 2(2). The Commission shall inform the other Member States thereof.

Article 6

Within three years of the date referred to in Article 5, the Commission shall, after consulting the Member States, submit a report to the Council and to the European Parliament on the application of this Directive, particularly as regards the application of Article 2(2).

Article 7

As from the date on which this Directive is implemented and at all events by the date mentioned in Article 5, the last sentence of Article 17(4) of Directive 77/388/EEC and Article 8 of Directive 79/1072/EEC shall cease to have effect in each Member State.

Article 8

This Directive is addressed to the Member States.

EIGHTEENTH COUNCIL DIRECTIVE

of 18 July 1989

89/465/EEC

(OJ L226, 3.8.1988, p 21)

on the harmonization of the laws of the Member States relating to turnover taxes —
Abolition of certain derogations provided for in Article 28(3) of the Sixth Directive, 77/
388/EEC

THE COUNCIL OF THE EUROPEAN COMMUNITIES,

Having regard to the Treaty establishing the European Economic Community, and in particular Article 99 thereof,

Having regard to the proposal from the Commission (OJ C347, 29.12.1984, p 3 and OJ C183, 11.7.1987, p 9)

Having regard to the opinion of the European Parliament (OJ C125, 11.5.1987, p 27),

Having regard to the opinion of the Economic and Social Committee. (OJ C218, 29.8.1985, p 11),

Whereas Article 28(3) of the Sixth Council Directive, 77/388/EEC, of 17 May 1977 on the harmonization of the laws of the Member States relating to turnover taxes — Common system of value added tax: uniform basis of assessment, (OJ L145, 13.6.1977, p 1), as last amended by the Act of Accession of Spain and Portugal, allows Member States to apply measures derogating from the normal rules of the common system of value added tax during a transitional period; whereas that period was originally fixed at five years; whereas the Council undertook to act, on a proposal from the Commission, before the expiry of that period, on the abolition, where appropriate, of some or all of those derogations;

Whereas many of those derogations give rise, under the Communities' own resources system, to difficulties in calculating the compensation provided for in Council Regulation (EEC, Euratom) No 1553/89 of 29 May 1989 on the definitive uniform arrangements for the collection of own resources accruing from value added tax (OJ L155, 7.6.1989, p 9) whereas, in order to ensure that that system operates more efficiently, there are grounds for abolishing those derogations;

Whereas the abolition of those derogations will also contribute to greater neutrality of the value added tax system at Community level;

Whereas some of the said derogations should be abolished respectively from 1 January 1990, 1 January 1991, 1 January 1992 and 1 January 1993;

Whereas, having regard to the provisions of the Act of Accession, the Portuguese Republic may, until 1 January 1994 at the latest, postpone the abolition of the exemption of the transactions referred to in points 3 and 9 in Annex F to Directive 77/388/EEC;

Whereas it is appropriate that, before 1 January 1991, the Council should, on the basis of a Commission report, review the situation with regard to the other derogations provided for in Article 28(3) of Directive 77/388/EEC, including the one referred to in the second subparagraph of point 1 of Article 1 of this Directive, and that it should take a decision, on a proposal from the Commission, on the abolition of these derogations, bearing in mind any distortion of competition which has resulted from their application or which may arise in connection with the future completion of the internal market,

HAS ADOPTED THIS DIRECTIVE:

Article 1

Directive 77/388/EEC is hereby amended as follows:

1. With effect from 1 January 1990 the transactions referred to in points 1, 3 to 6, 8, 9, 10, 12, 13 and 14 of Annex E shall be abolished.

Those Member States which, on 1 January 1989, subjected to value added tax the transactions listed in Annex E, points 4 and 5, are authorized to apply the conditions of Article 13A(2)(*a*), final indent, also to services rendered and goods delivered, as referred to in Article 13A(1)(*m*) and (*n*), where such activities are carried out by bodies governed by public law.

2. In Annex F:

    (*a*)   The transactions referred to in points 3, 14 and 18 to 22 shall be abolished with effect from 1 January 1990;

    (*b*)   The transactions referred to in points 4, 13, 15 and 24 shall be abolished with effect from 1 January 1991;

    (*c*)   The transaction referred to in point 9 shall be abolished with effect from 1 January 1992;

    (*d*)   The transaction referred to in point 11 shall be abolished with effect from 1 January 1993.

Article 2

The Portuguese Republic may defer until 1 January 1994 at the latest the dates referred to in Article 1, point 2(*a*), for the deletion of point 3 from Annex F and in Article 1, point 2(*c*), for the deletion of point 9 from Annex F.

Article 3

By 1 January 1991 the Council, on the basis of a report from the Commission, shall review the situation with regard to the other derogations laid down in Article 28(3) of Directive 77/388/EEC, including that referred to in the second subparagraph of point 1 of Article 1 of this Directive and, acting on a Commission proposal, shall decide whether these derogations should be abolished, having regard to any distortions of competition which have resulted from their having been applied or which might arise from measures to complete the Internal Market.

Article 4

In respect of the transactions referred to in Article 1, 2 and 3, Member States may take measures concerning deduction of value added tax in order totally or partially to prevent the taxable persons concerned from deriving unwarranted advantages or sustaining unwarranted disadvantages.

Article 5

1. Member States shall take the necessary measures to comply with this Directive not later than the dates laid down in Article 1 and 2.

2. Member States shall inform the Commission of the main provisions of national law which they adopt in the field governed by this Directive.

Article 6

This Directive is addressed to the Member States.

COUNCIL DIRECTIVE

of 16 December 1991

91/680/EEC

(OJ L376, 31.12.91, p 1)

Supplementing the common system of value added tax and amending Directive 77/388/ EEC with a view to the abolition of fiscal frontiers

THE COUNCIL OF THE EUROPEAN COMMUNITIES,

Having regard to the Treaty establishing the European Economic Community, and in particular Article 99 thereof,

Having regard to the proposal from the Commission,(OJ C252, 22.9.1987, p 2, OJ C176, 17, 17.7.1990, p 8 and OJ C131, 22.5.1991, p 3),

Having regard to the Opinion of the European Parliament,(OJ C324, 24.12.1990, p 97),

Having regard to the Opinion of the Economic and Social Committee,(OJ C237, 12.9.1988, p 19, OJ C332, 31.12.1990, p 121),

Whereas Article 8a of the Treaty defines the internal market as an area without internal frontiers in which the free movement of goods, persons, services and capital is ensured in accordance with the provisions of the treaty;

Whereas the completion of the internal market requires the elimination of fiscal frontiers between Member States and that to that end the imposition of tax on imports and the remission of tax on exports in trade between Member States be definitively abolished;

Whereas fiscal controls at internal frontiers will be definitively abolished as from 1 January 1993 for all transactions between Member States;

Whereas the imposition of tax on imports and the remission of tax on exports must therefore apply only to transactions with territories excluded from the scope of the common system of value added tax;

Whereas, however, in view of the conventions and treaties applicable to them, transactions originating in or intended for the Principality of Monaco and the Isle of Man must be treated as transactions originating in or intended for the French Republic and the United Kingdom of Great Britain and Northern Ireland respectively;

Whereas the abolition of the principle of the imposition of tax on imports in relations between the Member States will make provisions on tax exemptions and duty-free allowances superfluous in relations between the Member States; whereas, therefore, those provisions should be repealed and the relevant Directives adapted accordingly;

Whereas the achievement of the objective referred to in Article 4 of the First Council Directive of 11 April 1967 (OJ 71, 14.4.1967, p 1301/67) as last amended by the Sixth Directive 77/388/EEC (OJ L145, 13.6.1977, p 1) requires that the taxation of trade between Member States be based on the principle of the taxation in the Member State of origin of goods and services supplied without prejudice, as regards Community trade between taxable persons, to the principle that tax revenue from the imposition of tax at the final consumption stage should accrue to the benefit of the Member State in which that final consumption takes place;

Whereas, however, the determination of the definitive system that will bring about the objectives of the common system of value added tax on goods between Member States requires conditions that cannot be completely brought about by 31 December 1992;

Whereas, therefore, provision should be made for a transitional phase, beginning on 1 January 1993 and lasting for a limited period, during which provisions intended to

635

facilitate transition to the definitive system for the taxation of trade between Member States, which continues to be the medium-term objective, will be implemented;

Whereas during the transitional period intra-Community transactions carried out by taxable persons other than exempt taxable persons should be taxed in the Member States of destination, at those Member States' rates and under their conditions;

Whereas intra-Community acquisitions of a certain value by exempt persons or by non-taxable legal persons and certain intra-Community distance selling and supplies of new means of transport to individuals or exempt or non-taxable bodies should also be taxed, during the transitional period, in the Member States of destination, at those Member States' rates and under their conditions, insofar as such transactions would, in the absence of special provisions, be likely to cause significant distortions of competition between Member States;

Whereas the necessary pursuit of a reduction of administrative and statistical formalities for undertakings, particularly small and medium-sized undertakings, must be reconciled with the implementation of effective control measures and the need, on both economic and tax grounds, to maintain the quality of Community statistical instruments;

Whereas advantage must be taken of the transitional period of taxation of intra-Community trade to take measures necessary to deal with both the social repercussions in the sectors affected and the regional difficulties, in frontier regions in particular, that might follow the abolition of the imposition of tax on imports and of the remission of tax on exports in trade between Member States; whereas the Member States should therefore be authorised, for a period ending on 30 June 1999, to exempt supplies of goods carried out within specified limits by duty-free shops in the context of air and sea travel between Member States;

Whereas the transitional arrangements will enter into force for four years and will accordingly apply until 31 December 1996; whereas they will be replaced by a definitive system for the taxation of trade between Member States based on the principle of the taxation of goods and services supplied in the Member State of origin, so that the objective referred to in Article 4 of the First Council Directive of 11 April 1967 is achieved;

Whereas to that end the Commission will report to the Council before 31 December 1994 on the operation of the transitional arrangements and make proposals for the details of the definitive system for the taxation of trade between Member States; whereas the Council, considering that the conditions for transition to the definitive system have been fulfilled satisfactorily, will decide before 31 December 1995 on the arrangements necessary for the entry into force and the operation of the definitive system, the transitional arrangements being automatically continued until the entry into force of the definitive system and in event until the Council has decided on the definitive system;

Whereas, accordingly, Directive 77/388/EEC as last amended by Directive 89/465/EEC should be amended,

HAS ADOPTED THIS DIRECTIVE:

Article 1

Notes

Para (1) substituted Sixth Directive art 3; para (2) substituted of Sixth Directive art 7; para (3) amended Sixth Directive art 8(1)(*a*); para (4) added Sixth Directive art 8(1)(*c*); para (5) substituted Sixth Directive art 8(2); para (6) substituted Sixth Directive art 10(3); para (7) substituted Sixth Directive art 11B(1) and deleted art 11B(2); para (8) substituted of Sixth Directive art 11B(3); para (9) amended Sixth Directive art 11(B)(5); para (10) substituted Sixth Directive art 11C(2); para (11) deleted Sixth Directive art 14(1)(*b*), amended Sixth Directive art 14(1)(*d*), (*e*), deleted Sixth Directive art 14(1)(*f*), and amended Sixth Directive art 14(1)(*g*); para (12) substituted Sixth Directive art 15 heading; para (13) amended Sixth Directive art art 15(1)-(2); para (14) substituted Sixth Directive art 15(3); paras (15)-(16) amended Sixth Directive art 15(10); para (17) amended Sixth Directive art 15(12); para (18) substituted Sixth Directive art 15(13); para (19) amended Sixth Directive art 15(14); para (20) substituted Sixth Directive art 16(1A), substituted Sixth Directive art 16(1B), substituted Sixth Directive art 16(1C), substituted Sixth Directive art 16(1D); para (21) inserted Sixth Directive art 28(3a); para (22) inserted Sixth Directive TITLE XVIa, arts 28*a*-28*m*; para (23) substituted Sixth Directive art 33; para (24) inserted Sixth Directive art 33a.

Article 2

1. The following Directives shall cease to have effect on 31 December 1992 as regards relations between Member States:

—Directive 83/181/EEC (OJ L105, 23, 4.1983, p 38), as last amended by Directive 89/219/EEC (OJ L92, 5.4.1989, p 13)

—Directive 85/362/EEC (OJ L 192, 24.7.1985).

2. The provisions on value added tax laid down in the following Directive shall cease to have effect on 31 December 1992:

—Directive 74/651/EEC (OJ L354, 30.12.1974, p 6), as last amended by Directive 88/663/EEC (OJ L382, 31.12.1988, p 40),

—Directive 83/182/EEC (OJ L105, 23.4.1983, p 59),

—Directive 83/183/EEC (OJ L105, 23.4.1983, p 64), as amended by Directive 89/604/EEC.

3. The provisions of Directive 69/169/EEC (OJ L133, 4.6.1969, p 6), as last amended by Directive 91/191/EEC (OJ L 94 16.4.1991, p 24) relating to value added tax shall cease to have effect on 31 December 1992 as regards relations between Member States.

Article 3

1. Member States shall adapt their present value added tax systems to this Directive.

They shall bring into force such laws, regulations and administrative provisions as are necessary for their arrangements thus adapted to Article 1(1) to (20) and (22) to (24) and 2 of this Directive to enter into force on 1 January 1993.

2. Member States shall inform the Commission of the provisions which they adopt to apply this Directive.

3. Member States shall communicate to the Commission the texts of the provisions of national law which they adopt in the field governed by this Directive.

4. When Member States adopt such measures they shall include a reference to this Directive or shall accompany them by such a reference on the occasion of their official publication.

The manner in which such references shall be made shall be laid down by the Member States.

Article 4

This Directive is addressed to the Member States.

Done at Brussels, 16 December 1991.

COUNCIL DIRECTIVE

of 19 October 1992

92/77/EEC

(OJ L 316, 31.10.92, p 1)

*supplementing the common system of value added tax and amending Directive 77/388/
EEC (approximation of VAT rates)*

THE COUNCIL OF THE EUROPEAN COMMUNITIES,

Having regard to the Treaty establishing the European Economic Community, and in particular Article 99 thereof,

Having regard to the proposal from the Commission (OJ No C 176, 17.7.1990, p 8),

Having regard to the opinion of the European Parliament (OJ No C 324, 24.12.1990, p 104),

Having regard to the opinion of the Economic and Social Committee (OJ No C 332, 31.12.1990, p 1),

Whereas completing the internal market, which is one of the fundamental objectives of the Community, requires as a first step that fiscal controls at the frontiers be abolished;

Whereas, if distortions are to be avoided, such abolition implies in the case of value added tax, not only a uniform tax base but also a number of rates and rate levels which are sufficiently close as between Member States; whereas it is therefore necessary to amend Directive 77/388/EEC (OJ No L 145, 13.6.1977, p 1. Last amended by Directive 91/680/ EEC (OJ No L 376, 31.12.1991, p 1);

Whereas, during the transitional period, certain derogations concerning number and level of rates should be possible,

HAS ADOPTED THIS DIRECTIVE:

Article 1

Notes
This article amended Directive 77/388/EEC as follows:
para 1 substituted art 12(3);
para 2 deleted the 1st sentence of art 12(4);
para 3 added subparagraph to art 12(4);
para 4 substituted art 28(2);
para 5 inserted Annex H.

Article 2

1. Member States shall bring into force the laws, regulations and administrative provisions necessary to comply with this Directive not later than 31 December 1992. They shall forthwith inform the Commission thereof.

When Member States adopt these measures, they shall contain a reference to this Directive or shall be accompanied by such reference on the occasion of their official publication. The methods of making such reference shall be laid down by the Member States.

2. Member States shall communicate to the Commission the texts of the provisions of national law which they adopt in the field governed by this Directive.

Article 3

This Directive is addressed to the Member States.

Done at Luxembourg, 19 October 1992.

COUNCIL DIRECTIVE

of 14 December 1992

92/111/EEC

(OJ L384/47, 30.12.92)

Amending Directive 77/388/EEC and introducing simplification measures with regard to value added tax

THE COUNCIL OF THE EUROPEAN COMMUNITIES,

Having regard to the Treaty establishing the European Economic Community, and in particular Article 99 thereof,

Having regard to the proposal from the Commission,

Having regard to the opinion of the European Parliament (OJ C337, 21.12.1992),

Having regard to the opinion of the Economic and Social Committee (Opinion delivered on 24 November 1992 (not yet published in the Official journal)),

Whereas Article 3 of the Council Directive 91/680/EEC of 16 December 1991 supplementing the common system of value added tax and amending Directive 77/388/ EEC with a view to the abolition of fiscal frontiers (OJ L376, 31.12.1991, p 1) sets 1 January 1993 as the date for the entry into force of these provisions in all the Member States;

Whereas in order to facilitate the application of these provisions and to introduce the simplifications needed, it is necessary to supplement the common system of value added tax, as applicable on 1 January 1993, so as to clarify how the tax shall apply to certain operations carried out with third territories and certain operations carried out inside the Community, as well to define the transitional measures between the provisions in force on 31 December 1992 and those which will enter into force as from 1 January 1993;

Whereas in order to guarantee the neutrality of the common system of turnover tax in respect of the origin of goods, the concept of a third territory and the definition of an import must be supplemented;

Whereas certain territories forming part of the Community customs territory are regarded as third territories for the purposes of applying the common system of value added tax; whereas value added tax is therefore applied to trade between the Member States and those territories according to the same principles as apply to any operation between the Community and third countries; whereas it is necessary to ensure that such trade is subject to fiscal provisions equivalent to those which would be applied to operations carried out under the same conditions with territories which are not part of the Community customs territory; whereas as a result of these provisions the Seventeenth Council Directive 85/362/EEC of 16 July 1985 on the harmonisation of the laws of the Member States relating to turnover taxes — Exemption from value added tax on the temporary importation of goods other than means of transport (OJ L192, 24.7.1985, p 20. Directive as last amended by Directive 90/237/EEC (OJ L133, 24.5.1990, p 91)), becomes null and void;

Whereas it is necessary to state exactly how the exemptions relating to certain export operations or equivalent operations will be implemented; whereas it is necessary to adapt the other Directives concerned accordingly;

Whereas it is necessary to clarify the definition of the place of taxation of certain operations carried out on board ships, aircraft or trains transporting passengers inside the Community;

Whereas the transitional arrangements for taxation for trade between the Member States must be supplemented to take account both of the Community provisions relating to excise duties and the need to clarify and simplify the detailed rules for the application of the tax of certain operations which will be carried out between the Member States as from 1 January 1993;

Whereas Council Directive 92/12/EEC of 25 February 1992 on the general arrangements of products subject to excise duty and on the holding, movement and monitoring of such products (OJ L76, 23.3.1992, p 1) lays down particular procedures and obligations in relation to declarations in the case of shipments of such products to another Member State; whereas as a result the methods of applying tax to certain supplies and intra-Community acquisitions of products liable to excise duties can be simplified to the benefit both of the persons liable to pay tax and the competent administrations;

Whereas it is necessary to define the scope of the exemptions referred to in Article 28c of Directive 77/388/EEC (OJ L145, 13.6.1977, p 1. Directive as amended by Directive 92/77/EEC (OJ L316, 31.10.1992, p 1); whereas it is also necessary to supplement the provisions concerning the chargeability of the tax and the methods of determining the taxable amount of certain intra-Community operations;

Whereas, for taxable operations in the domestic market linked to intra-Community trade in goods which are carried out during the period laid down in Article 28l of Directive 77/388/EEC by taxable persons not established in the Member State referred to in Article 28b(A)(1) of the said Directive, it is necessary to take simplification measures guaranteeing equivalent treatment in all the Member States; whereas to achieve this, the provisions concerning the taxation system and the person liable to tax in respect of such operations must be harmonised;

Whereas in order to take account of the provisions relating to the person liable to pay tax in the domestic market and to avoid certain forms of tax evasion or avoidance, it is necessary to clarify the Community provisions concerning the repayment to taxable persons not established in the country of the value added tax referred to in Article 17(3) of Directive 77/388/EEC as amended by Article 28f of the said Directive;

Whereas the abolition as from 1 January 1993 of tax on imports and tax relief on exports for trade between the Member States makes it necessary to have transitional measures in order to ensure the neutrality of the common system of value added tax and to avoid situations of double-taxation or non-taxation;

Whereas it is therefore necessary to lay down special provisions for cases where a Community procedure, started before 1 January 1993 for the purposes of a supply effected before that date by a taxable person acting as such in respect of goods dispatched or transported to another Member State, is not completed until after 31 December 1992;

Whereas such provisions should also apply to taxable operations carried out before 1 January 1993 to which particular exemptions were applied which as a result delayed the taxable event;

Whereas it is also necessary to lay down special measures for means of transport which, not having been acquired or imported subject to the general domestic tax conditions of a Member State, have benefited, by the application of national measures, from an exemption from tax because of their temporary import from another Member State;

Whereas the application of these transitional measures, both in relation trade between the Member States and to operations with third territories, presupposes supplementing the definition of the operations to be made subject to taxation as from 1 January 1993 and the clarification for such cases of the concepts of the place of taxation, the taxable event and the chargeability of the tax;

Whereas, on account of the current economic situation, the Kingdom of Spain and the Italian Republic have requested that, as a transitional measure, provisions derogating from the principle of immediate deduction laid down in the first subparagraph of Article 18(2) of Directive 77/388/EEC be applied; whereas this request should be granted for a period of two years which may not be extended;

Whereas this Directive lays down common provisions for simplifying the treatment of certain intra-Community operations; whereas, in a number of cases, it is for the Member States to determine the conditions for implementing these provisions; whereas certain

Member States will not be able to complete the legislative procedure necessary to adapt their legislation on value added tax within the period laid down; whereas an additional period should therefore be allowed for the implementation of this Directive; whereas a maximum period of twelve months is sufficient for this purpose;

Whereas it is accordingly necessary to amend Directive 77/388/EEC,

1. - 25. ....

Notes
Para (1) replaced art 3(4);
para (2) replaced art 7(1)(*b*);
para (3) amended art 7(3), and added art 7(3)(2nd subpara);
para (4) replaced art 7(1)(*c*);
para (5) replaced art 11(B)(1);
para (6) replaced art 12(1)(*b*);
para (7) replaced art 12(3)(*a*);
para (8) deleted art 14(1)(*c*) and added para to art 14(1)(*d*);
para (9) extended art 15(2), amended art 15(3), replaced art 15(4)(2nd subpara), amended art 15(10), replaced art 15(1)(3rd subpara), and replaced art 15(13);
para (10) replaced art 28a(1)(*a*)(2nd subpara), added art 28a(1)(*c*), inserted art 28a(1*a*), added para to art 28a(5)(*b*), and added para to art 28a(*b*);
para (11) added art 28b(1)(*a*)(2nd subpara);
para (12) replaced art 28c(A)(*c*) and added art 28c(A)(*d*);
para (13) replaced art 28c(E);
para (14) replaced art 28d(3);
para (15) replaced art 28d(4);
para (16) amended art 28e(1);
para (17) renumbered art 28e(2)-(3) as art 28e(3)-(4) and inserted a new art 28e(2);
para (18) by amending art 28f, added para to art 17(4);
para (19) by amending art 28g, substituted art 21(1)(*a*)-(*b*);
para (20) by amending art 28h, extended art 22(1)(*c*), art 22(3)(*b*), replaced art 22(4)(*c*)(3rd indent), replaced art 22(6)(*b*)(1st subpara), amended art 22(6)(*b*)(3rd subpara, 1st indent), amended art 22(6)(*b*)(4th subpara, 1st indent), added art 22(6)(*b*)(new subpara), amended art 22(11);
para (21) replaced art 28i;
para (22) added art 28n;
para (23) replaced art 33a(1)-(2);
para (24) revoked Directive 85/362/EEC, as last amended by Directive 90/237/EEC, with effect from 31 December 1992;
para (25) revoked Directive 69/169/EEC, Directive as last amended by Directive 91/680/EEC, art 6 with effect from 1 January 1993.

Article 2

1. As from 1 January 1993 and for a period of two years, which may not be extended, the Kingdom of Spain and the Italian Republic shall be authorised to apply provisions derogating from the principle of immediate deduction provided for in the first subparagraph of Article 18(2). These provisions may not have the effect of delaying by more than one month the time when the right to deduction, having arisen, may be exercised under Article 18(1).

However, for taxable persons who file the returns provided for in Article 22(4) for quarterly tax periods, the Kingdom of Spain and the Italian Republic shall be authorised to provide that the right to deduction which has come into being which could, under Article 18(1), be exercised in a given quarter, may not be exercised until the following quarter. This provision shall only apply where the Kingdom of Spain or the Italian Republic authorises such taxable persons to opt for the filing of monthly returns.

2. By way of derogation from the third subparagraph of Article 15(10), the Portuguese Republic, the French Republic, the Kingdom of the Netherlands and the Federal Republic of Germany shall be authorised, in regard to contracts concluded after 31 December 1992, to abolish the repayment, procedure, where it is prohibited by this Directive by 1 October 1993 at the latest.

Article 3

The Council, acting unanimously on a Commission proposal, shall adopt before 30 June, 1993, detailed rules for the taxation of chain transactions between taxable persons, so that such rules may enter into force on 1 January 1994.

Article 4

1. The Member States shall adapt their present value added tax system to the provisions of this Directive.

They shall adopt the necessary laws, regulations and administrative provisions for their adapted systems to enter into force 1 January 1993.

Member States may, however, provide that information relating to transactions referred to in the last subparagraph of Article 22(6)(*b*) for which the tax becomes payable during the first three calendar months of 1993 must appear at the latest on the summary statement signed for the second calendar quarter of 1993.

2. By way of derogation from the second subparagraph of paragraph 1, Member States shall be authorised to adopt the necessary laws, regulations and administrative provisions in order to implement by 1 January 1984 at the latest the provisions laid down in the following paragraphs of Article 1:

— paragraph 11,

— paragraph 13, insofar as it relates to Article 28c(E)(3);

— paragraph 19, insofar as it relates to the third subparagraph of Article 21(1)(*a*),

— paragraph 20, insofar as it relates to obligations in respect of the transactions referred to in the preceding indents.

Member States which, on 1 January 1993, apply measures equivalent to those mentioned above shall adopt the necessary measures to ensure that the principles laid down in Article 22(6) and in current Community provisions on administrative cooperation in the area of indirect taxation are complied with as from 1 January 1993 without fail.

3. By way of derogation from the second subparagraph of paragraph 1, the Federal Republic of Germany shall be authorised to adopt the necessary laws, regulations and administrative provisions in order to implement by 1 October 1993 at the latest the provisions laid down in Article 1(10) with regard to Article 28a(1*a*)(*a*).

4. Member States shall inform the Commission of the provisions which they adopt to apply this Directive.

5. Member States shall communicate the provisions of domestic law which they adopt in the field covered by this Directive to the Commission.

6. When Member States adopt these provisions, they shall contain a reference to this Directive or shall be accompanied by such reference on the occasion of their official publication. The methods of making such a reference shall be laid down by the Member States.

Article 5

This Directive is addressed to the Member States.

Done at Brussels, 14 December 1992.

COUNCIL DIRECTIVE

of 14 February 1994

94/5/EC

(OJ No L 60, 3.3.1994, p 16)

supplementing the common system of value added tax and amending Directive 77/388/ EEC — Special arrangements applicable to second-hand goods, works of art, collectors' items and antiques

THE COUNCIL OF THE EUROPEAN UNION,

Having regard to the Treaty establishing the European Community, and in particular Article 99 thereof,

Having regard to the opinion of the European Parliament (OJ No C 323, 27.12.1989, p 120),

Having regard to the opinion of the Economic and Social Committee (OJ No C 201, 7.8.1989, p 6),

Whereas, in accordance with Article 32 of the Sixth Council Directive 77/388/EEC of 17 May 1977 on the harmonizaion of the laws of the Member States relating to turnover taxes — Common system of value added tax: uniform basis of assessment (OJ No L 145, 13.6.1977, p 1. Directive as last amended by Directive 92/11/EEC (OJ No L 384, 30.12.1992, p 47), the Council is to adopt a Community taxation system to be applied to used goods, works of art, antique and collectors' items;

Whereas the present situation, in the absence of Community legislation, continues to be marked by the application of very different systems which cause distortion of competition and deflection of trade both internally and between Members States; whereas these differences also include a lack of harmonization in the levying of the own resources of the community; whereas consequently it is necessary to bring this situation to an end as soon as possible;

Whereas the Court of Justice has, in a number of judgments, noted the need to attain a degree of harmonization which allows double taxation in intra-community trade to be avoided;

Whereas it is essential to provide, in specific areas, for transitional measures enabling legislation to be gradually adapted;

Whereas, within the internal market, the satisfactory operation of the value added tax mechanisms means that Community rules with the purpose of avoiding double taxation and distortion of competition between taxable persons must be adopted;

Whereas it is accordingly necessary to amend Directive 77/388/EEC,

Has adopted this Directive:

Article 1

Notes

This article amended Directive 77/388/EEC as follows:
Para (1)(*a*) by inserting art 11(A)(4)
Para (1)(*b*) by inserting art 11(B)(6)
Para (2)(*a*) by substituting art 12(3)(*c*)
Para (2)(*b*) by substituting art 12(5)
Para (3) by inserting art 26a
Para (4) by inserting art 28(1a)
Para (5) by inserting art 28(2)(*e*) additional provision
Para (6) by substituting art 28a(2)(*b*)
Para (7) by inserting Title XVIb and Article 28o
Para (8) by deleting from art 28(3)(*e*) "5(4)(c),"
Para (9) by deleting art 32
Para (10) by inserting Annex I

Article 2

Member States may take measures concerning the right to deduct value added tax in order to avoid the taxable dealers concerned enjoying unjustified advantages or sustaining unjustified loss.

Article 3

Acting unanimously on a proposal from the Commission, the Council may authorize any Member State to introduce particular measures for the purpose of combating fraud, by providing that the tax due in application of the arrangements for taxing the profit margin provided for in Article 26a(B) cannot be less than the amount of tax which would be due if the profit margin were equal to a certain percentage of the selling price. This percentage shall be fixed taking into account the normal profit margins realized by economic operators in the sector concerned.

Article 4

1. Member States shall adapt their present value added tax system to this Directive.

They shall bring into force such laws, regulations and administrative provisions as are necessary for their system thus adapted to enter into force on 1 January 1995 at the latest.

2. Member States shall inform the Commission of the provisions which they adopt to apply this Directive.

3. Member States shall communicate to the Commission the provisions of national law which they adopt in the field covered by this Directive.

4. When Member States adopt such provisions, they shall contain a reference to this Directive or be accompanied by such reference on the occasion of their official publication. The methods of making such a reference shall be laid down by the Member States.

Article 5

This Directive is addressed to the Member States.

COUNCIL DIRECTIVE

of 22 December 1994

94/76/EC

(OJ No L 365, 31.12.94, p 53)

amending Directive 77/388/EEC by the introduction of transitional measures applicable, in the context of the enlargement of the European Union on 1 January 1995, as regards value added tax

THE COUNCIL OF THE EUROPEAN UNION

Having regard to the 1994 Accession Treaty, and in particular Articles 2 and 3 thereof, and the 1994 act of Accession, and in particular Article 169 thereof,

Having regard to the proposal from the Commission,

Whereas, subject to the special provisions set out in Chapter IX of Annex XV to the Act of Accession, the common system of value added tax is to apply to the new Member States as from the date on which the Accession Treaty enters into force;

Whereas, as a result of the abolition on that date of the imposition of tax on importation and remission of tax on exportation in trade between the Community as constituted at present and the new Member States, and between the new Member States themselves, transitional measures are necessary to safeguard the neutrality of the common system of value added tax and prevent situations of double taxation or non-taxation;

Whereas such measures must, in this respect, meet concerns akin to those that led to the measures adopted on completion of the internal market on 1 January 1993, and in particular the provisions of Article 28n of Council Directive 77/388/EEC of 17 May 1977 on the harmonization of the laws of the Member States relating to turn-over — Common system of value added tax: uniform basis of assessment (OJ No L 145, 13.6.1977, p 1. Directive as last amended by Directive 94/5/EC (OJ No 60, 3.3.1994, p 16));

Whereas, in the customs sphere, goods will be deemed to be in free circulation in the enlarged Community where it is shown that they were in free circulation in the current Community or in one of the new Member States at the time of accession; whereas conclusions should be drawn from this, particularly for Article 7(1) and (3) and Article 10(3) of Directive 77/388/EEC;

Whereas it is necessary in particular to cover situations in which goods have been placed, prior to accession, under one of the arrangements referred to in Article 16(1)(B)(*a*) to (*d*), under a temporary admission procedure with full exemption from import duties or under a similar procedure in the new Member States;

Whereas it is also necessary to lay down specific arrangements for cases where a special procedure (export or transit), initiated prior to the entry into force of the Accession Treaty in the framework of trade between the current Community and the new Member States and between those Member States for the purposes of a supply effected prior to that date by a taxable person acting as such, is not terminated until after the date of accession,

HAS ADOPTED THIS DIRECTIVE:

Article 1

Note
Article 1 inserted Directive 77/388/EEC, Title XVIc and Article 28p.

Article 2

1. Subject to the entry into force of the 1994 Accession Treaty, Member States shall bring into force the laws, regulations and administrative provisions necessary to comply with

647

this Directive on the date of entry into force of this Directive. They shall forthwith inform the Commission thereof.

When Member States adopt those provisions, they shall contain a reference to this Directive or shall be accompanied by such reference on the occasion of their official publication. The methods of making such a reference shall be laid down by the Member States.

2. Member States shall communicate to the Commission the provisions of domestic law which they adopt in the field covered by this Directive.

Article 3

This Directive shall enter into force on the same date as the 1994 Accession Treaty.

Article 4

This Directive is addressed to the Member States.

Done at Brussels, 22 December 1994.

COUNCIL DIRECTIVE

of 10 April 1995

95/7/EC

(OJ L 102, 5.5.95, p 18)

amending Directive 77/388/EEC and introducing new simplification measures with regard to value added tax (scope of certain exemptions and practical arrangements for implementing them

THE COUNCIL OF THE EUROPEAN UNION,

Having regard to the Treaty establishing the European Community, and in particular Article 99 thereof,

Having regard to the proposal from the Commission,

Having regard to the opinion of the European Parliament,

Having regard to the opinion of the Economic and Social Committee,

Whereas the operation of the internal market can be improved by introducing common rules clarifying the scope of, and arrangements for, applying some of the exemptions provided for in Articles 14(1), 15, point 2, and 16(1) of the Sixth Council Directive 77/388/EEC of 17 May 1977 on the harmonization of the laws of the Member States relating to turnover taxes (common system of value added tax: uniform basis of assessment (OJ No L 145, 13.6.1977, p 1. Directive as last amended by Directive 94/76/EC (OJ No L 365, 31.12.1994, p 53); whereas the introduction of such common rules is provided for by the aforesaid Directive, and in particular Articles 14(2) and 16(3) thereof;

Whereas Article 3 of Council Directive 92/111/EEC of 14 December 1992 amending Directive 77/388/EEC and introducing simplification measures with regard to value added tax (OJ No 384, 30.12.1992, p 47) provides for the adoption of special rules for the taxation of chain transactions between taxable persons; whereas such rules must ensure not only compliance with the principle of neutrality of the common system of value added tax as regard the origin of goods and services but also compliance with the choices made as the principles governing value added tax and its monitoring arrangements during the transitional period;

Whereas it is appropriate to include in the taxable amount on importation all ancillary costs arising from the transport of goods to anyplace of destination in the Community since that place is known at the time the importation is carried out; whereas, as a result, the supplies of services in question enjoy the exemptions provided for in Article 14(1)(i) of Directive 77/388/EEC;

Whereas Article 15(2) of that Directive provides that the Commission shall submit to the Council proposals to establish Community tax rules specifying the scope of, and practical arrangements for implementing, the export exemptions applicable to supplies of goods carried in the personal luggage of travellers;

Whereas it is appropriate that the period serving as a basis for calculating the adjustments provided for by Article 20(2) of the said Directive should be extended up to 20 years by Member States for immovable property acquired as capital goods, bearing in mind the duration of their economic life;

Whereas Member States should be enabled to maintain the rate applicable to goods after making up work which they carried out under a contract to make up work on 1 January 1993;

Whereas the rules governing territorial application and the tax arrangements applicable in the field of intra-community goods-transport services function in a simple and satisfactory manner for both traders and the authorities in the Member States;

Whereas, by treating a transport operation with a Member State as an intra-Community goods-transport operation where it is directly linked to a transport operation between Member States, it is possible to simplify not only the principles and arrangements for taxing those domestic transport services but also the rules applicable to ancillary services and to services supplied by intermediaries involved in the supply of these various services;

Whereas the qualification of certain works on movable property as work carried out under a contract to make up work is a source of difficulty and should be eliminated;

Whereas, with a view to facilitating intra-Community trade in the field of work on movable tangible property, the tax arrangements applicable for these transactions should be modified when they are carried out for a person who is identified for value added tax purposes on a Member State other than that of their physical execution;

Whereas Article 16(1)(B) to (E) of the said Directive, taken together in particular with Article 22(9) concerning release from obligations, makes it possible to overcome the difficulties encountered by traders participating in transaction chains involving goods placed and kept under warehousing arrangements;

Whereas it is necessary in this connection to ensure that the tax treatment applied to supplies of goods and the provision of services relating to certain of the goods which may be placed under customs warehousing arrangements can also be applied to the same transactions involving goods placed under warehousing arrangements other than customs warehousing;

Whereas these transactions concern principally raw materials and other goods negotiated on international forward markets; whereas a list of the goods covered by these provisions should be drawn up;

Whereas, subject to consultation of the Committee on Value Added Tax, the Member States are responsible for defining those warehousing arrangements other than customs warehousing; whereas it is necessary nevertheless to exclude in principle from such arrangements goods that are intended to be supplied at the retail stage;

Whereas it is necessary to clarify some of the rules for applying tax when goods cease to be covered by the arrangements provided for in Article 16(1)(B) to (E) of the said Directive, particularly as regard the person liable for payment of the tax due;

Whereas it is necessary to clarify the scope of those provisions of Article 17(2)(*a*) of the said Directive that are applicable during the transitional period referred to in Article 28 1;

Whereas it is accordingly necessary to amend Directive 77/388/EEC,

HAS ADOPTED THIS DIRECTIVE:

Article 1

Notes

From 25 May 1995:

para (1) substituted Council Directive 77/388/EEC art 5(5);

para (2) substituted Council Directive 77/388/EEC art 11(B)(3)(*b*)(3rd subpara);

para (3) substituted Council Directive 77/388/EEC art 15(2)(2nd and 3rd subparas);

para (4) substituted Council Directive 77/388/EEC art 20(2)(last subpara);

para (5) inserted Council Directive 77/388/EEC art 28(2)(*h*);

para (6) substituted Council Directive 77/388/EEC art 28a(5)(introductory para), deleted art 28a(5)(*a*), deleted art 28a(5)(*b*)(2nd subpara 3rd indent);

para (7) substituted a full stop for a comma in Council Directive 77/388/EEC art 28h(C)(1)(1st indent) and inserted a subpara, inserted art 28h(F);

para (8) substituted "as defined in Article 5" for "as defined in Articles 5 and 28a(5)(*a*)";

para (9) substituted Council Directive 77/388/EEC art 16(1) and added para (1*a*) by substituting Council Directive 77/388/EEC art 28c(E)(1);

para (10) substituted Council Directive 77/388/EEC art 17(2)(*a*) by amending Council Directive 77/388/EEC art 28f(1);

para 11 substituted Council Directive 77/388/EEC art 21(1)(*b*) by amending Council Directive 77/388/EEC art 28g;

para 12 substituted Council Directive 77/388/EEC art 22(2)(*b*), art 22(3)(*b*)(2nd subpara)(1st indent), art 22(6)(*b*)(1st subpara), art 22(6)(*b*)(3rd subpara) and deleted art 22(6)(*b*)(5th subpara);

para 13 inserted Council Directive 77/388/EEC Annex J.

Article 2

1. Member States shall bring into force the laws, regulations and administrative provisions necessary to comply with this Directive on 1 January 1996. They shall forthwith inform the Commission thereof.

When Member States adopt these measures, they shall contain a reference to this Directive or shall be accompanied by such reference on the occasion of their official publication. The methods of making such reference shall be laid down by Member States.

2. By way of derogation from the first subparagraph of paragraph 1, Member States may take measures by way of law, regulation or administrative action in order to bring the provisions in Article 1(3), (4) and (9) into force not later than 1 January 1996.

However, the Federal Republic of Germany and the Grand Duchy of Luxembourg are authorized to take measures by way of law, regulation or administrative action in order to apply the provisions in Article 1(9) not later than 1 January 1997.

3. Member States shall communicate to the Commission the text of the provisions of national law which they adopt in the field governed by this Directive.

Article 3

This Directive shall enter into force on the 20th day following its publication in the Official Journal of the European Communities.

Article 4

This Directive is addressed to the Member States.

Done at Luxembourg, 10 April 1995.

COUNCIL DIRECTIVE

of 25 June 1996

96/42/EC

(OJ L170, 9.7.1996, p 34)

amending Directive 77/388/EEC on the common system of value added tax

THE COUNCIL OF THE EUROPEAN UNION,

Having regard to the Treaty establishing the European Community, and in particular Article 99 thereof,

Having regard to the proposal from the Commission,

Having regard to the opinion of the European Parliament (OJ No C17, 22.1.1996, p 26),

Having regard to the opinion of the Economic and Social Committee (OJ No C236, 11.9.1995, p 10),

Whereas Article 12(3)(*d*) of Directive 77/388/EEC (OJ L145, 13.6.1977, p 1. Directive as last amended by Directive 95/7/EC (OJ No L102, 5.5.1995, p 18)) lays down that the rules concerning the taxation of agricultural outputs other than those falling within category 1 of Annex H are to be decided unanimously by the Council before 31 December 1994 on a proposal from the Commission; whereas, until that date, those Member States which had already been applying a reduced rate might continue to do so while those appling a standard rate could not apply a reduced rate; whereas that allowed a two-year postponement in the application of the standard rate;

Whereas experience has shown that the structural imbalance in the VAT rates applicable by Member States to agricultural outputs of the floricultural and horticultural sectors has led to reported cases of fraudulent activities; whereas that structural imbalance is a direct result of the application of Article 12(3)(*d*) and should be redressed accordingly;

Whereas the most appropriate solution would be to extend to all Member States, on a transitional basis, the option of applying a reduced rate to supplies of agricultural outputs of the floricultural and horticultural sectors and of wood used as firewood,

HAS ADOPTED THIS DIRECTIVE:

Article 1

Note

This Article amended Directive 77/388/EEC as follows:
Para 1 deleted art 12(3)(*d*);
para 2 inserted art 28(2)(*i*).

Article 2

Member States shall communicate to the Commission the text of the provisions of domestic law which they adopt in the field covered by this Directive.

Article 3

This Directive shall apply from 1 January 1995.

Article 4

This Directive is addressed to the Member States.

Done at Luxembourg, 25 June 1996.

EUROPEAN UNION REGULATIONS

Goods imported into Ireland are valued for VAT purposes in the same manner as for customs purposes (VATA 1972 s 15(3) and Sixth Directive art 11B(2)). The valuation rules are contained in the Community Customs Code which effectively consolidated the European Union customs regulations into two regulations: Council Regulation 92/2913/EEC of 12 October 1992 established the Community Customs Code, and Commission Regulation 92/2454/EEC of 2 July 1993 provided detailed rules for the implementation of the Code.

With the introduction of the single market with effect from 1 January 1993, taxable persons are obliged to maintain more records and make additional statistical returns to the Revenue Commissioners. The relevant European Union regulations are reproduced in this section.

COUNCIL REGULATION

of 7 November 1991

91/3330/EEC

On the statistics relating to the trading of goods between Member States

(OJ L316, 16.11.91, p 1)

THE COUNCIL OF THE EUROPEAN COMMUNITIES,

Having regard to the Treaty establishing the European Economic Community, and in particular Article 100a thereof,

Having regard to the proposal from the Commission (OJ No C 254, 9.10.1990, p. 7 and OJ No C 47, 23.2.1991, p. 10),

In cooperation with the European Parliament (OJ No C 324, 24.12.1990, p. 268 and OJ No C 280, 28.10.1991),

Having regard to the opinion of the Economic and Social Committee (OJ No C 332, 31.12.1990, p.1),

Whereas abolishing physical barriers between Member States is necessary to complete the internal market; whereas a satisfactory level of information on the trading of goods between Member States should thus be ensured by means other than those involving checks, even indirect ones, at internal frontiers;

Whereas an analysis of the situation of the Community and the Member States after 1992 reveals that a number of specific requirements will persist as regards information on the trading of goods between Member States;

Whereas these requirements are not of a macro-economic nature, unlike those relating, for example, to national accounts or the balance of payments, and many of them cannot be met by means of highly aggregated data alone; whereas matters such as trade policy, sectoral analyses, competition rules, the management and guidance of agriculture and fisheries, regional development, energy projections and the organization of transport must on the contrary be based on statistical documentation providing the most up-to-date, accurate and detailed view of the internal market;

Whereas it is precisely information on the trading of goods between Member States which will contribute to measuring the progress of the internal market, thereby speeding up its completion and consolidating it on a sound basis; whereas this kind of information could prove to be one of the means of assessing the development of economic and social cohesion;

Whereas until the end of 1992 statistics relating to the trading goods between Member States will benefit from the formalities, documentation and controls which the customs authorities, for their own requirements or for those of other departments, prescribe for consignors and consignees of goods in circulation between Member States, but which will disappear through the elimination of physical frontiers and tax barriers;

Whereas it will consequently be necessary to collect directly from the consignors and consignees the data necessary to compile statistics relating to the trading of goods between Member States, using methods and techniques which will ensure that they are exhaustive, reliable and up to date, without giving rise for the parties concerned, in particular for small and medium-sized businesses, to a burden out of proportion to the results which users of the said statistics can reasonably expect;

Whereas the relevant legislation must henceforth apply to all statistics relating to the trading of goods between Member States, including those statistics which are not to be harmonized or made compulsory by the Community before 1993;

Whereas the statistics relating to the trading of goods between Member States are a function of the movements of goods involved; whereas they may include data on transport, which can be collected simultaneously with the data specific to each of these categories of statistics, thus lightening the overall statistical burden;

Whereas private individuals will derive obvious advantages from the internal market; whereas it is necessary to ensure that these advantages are not diminished in their eyes by requirements for statistical information; whereas the provision of such information would undoubtedly impose an obligation which private individuals would consider inconvenient at the very least and which would be impossible to check on without employing excessive measures; whereas it is therefore reasonable not to regard private individuals as responsible for providing such information, apart from suitable periodic surveys;

Whereas the new collection system to be introduced is to apply to all statistics relating to the trading of goods between Member States; whereas it must therefore be defined first in a general context involving new concepts, particularly as regards the scope, the party responsible for providing the information and the transmission of data;

Whereas the actual concept of the system resides in the use of related administrative networks, and in particular, that of the value added tax (VAT) authorities, to provide the statistical services with a minimum degree of indirect verification without thereby increasing the burden on taxpayers; whereas it is nonetheless necessary to avoid confusion arising in the minds of the parties responsible for providing information between their statistical and their tax obligations;

Whereas it is vital to use existing sources to compile basic documentation in each Member State regarding consignors and consignees of goods which are covered by statistics of trade between Member States, so as to identify, in preparation for 1992, the main parties concerned and to develop modern data transmission techniques with their assistance;

Whereas implementation alone will reveal loopholes or weaknesses in the new collection system; whereas improvements and simplifications should be introduced within a reasonable period of time in order to prevent defects from having negative repercussions on the trading of goods between Member States;

Whereas, among the statistics relating to the trading of goods between Member States, statistics of trade between Member States must receive priority, for obvious reasons of importance and continuity; whereas, however, substantial adjustments must be made to these statistics in order to take account of the new conditions on the internal market after 1992; whereas it will be necessary to review inter alia, the definition of their content, the goods classification applicable to them and the list of data to be collected to compile them; whereas it is desirable to adopt forthwith the principle on which the statistical thresholds will operate in order to avoid small and medium-sized businesses incurring expenditure which is disproportionate to overheads;

Whereas the Commission should be assisted by a committee to ensure the regular cooperation of the Member States, in particular to resolve the problems which are bound to arise in connection with information on the trading of goods between Member States following the numerous innovations introduced by the new collection system;

Whereas relevant Community legislation should be supplemented systematically by provisions adopted either by the Council or by the Commission;   ·

Whereas some of the provisions of this Regulation must enter into force without delay so that the Community and its Member States can prepare for the practical consequences· which it will entail as from 1 January 1993;

Whereas one of these consequences is that Council Regulation (EEC) No 2954/85 of 22 October 1985 laying down certain measures for the standardisation and simplification of the statistics of trade between Member States (OJ No L 285, 25.10.1985, p.1) must be repealed and that Council Regulation (EEC) No 1736/75 of 24 June 1975 on the external trade statistics of the Community and statistics of trade between Member States (OJ No L 183, 14.7.1975, p. 3), as last amended by Regulation (EEC) No 1629/88 (OJ No L 147, 14.6.1988, p. 1), will no longer be applicable to statistics relating to the trading of goods between Member States,

HAS ADOPTED THIS REGULATION

Article 1

The Community and its Member States shall compile statistics relating to the trading of goods between Member States, in accordance with the rules laid down by this Regulation, during the transitional period which shall begin on 1 January 1993 and end on the date of changeover to a unified system of taxation in the Member State of origin.

CHAPTER
General provisions

Article 2

For the purposes of this Regulation and without prejudice to any individual provisions:

(*a*) **"trading of goods between Member States"** means any movement of goods from one Member State to another;

(*b*) **"goods"** means all movable property, including electric current;

(*c*) **"Community goods"** means goods:

— entirely obtained in the customs territory of the Community, without the addition of goods from non-member countries or territories which are not part of the customs territory of the Community,

— from countries or territories not forming part of the customs territory of the Community which have been released for free circulation in a Member State,

— obtained in the customs territory of the Community either from the goods referred to exclusively in the second indent or from the goods referred to in the first and second indents;

(*d*) **"non-Community goods"** means goods other than those referred to in (*c*). Without prejudice to agreements concluded with non member countries for the implementation of the Community transit arrangements, goods which, while fulfilling the conditions laid down in (*c*), are reintroduced into the customs territory of the Community after export therefrom are also considered as non-Community goods;

(*e*) **"Member-State",** when the term is used in the geographical sense, means its statistical territory;

(*f*) **"statistical territory of a Member State"** means the territory occupied by that Member State within the statistical territory of the Community, as this latter is defined in Article 3 of Regulation (EEC) No 1736/75;

(*g*) **"goods in free movement on the internal market of the Community"** means goods authorised, pursuant to Directive 77/388/EEC, to move from one Member State to another without prior formalities or formalities linked to the crossing of internal frontiers;

(*h*) **"private individual"** means any natural person not liable to account for VAT in connection with a given movement of goods.

Article 3

1. All goods which move from one Member State to another shall be the subject of statistics relating to the trading of goods between Member States.

In addition to the goods which move within the statistical territory of the Community, goods shall be considered as moving from one Member State to another if, in so doing, they cross the external frontier of the Community, whether or not they subsequently enter the territory of a non-member State.

[**2.**] Paragraph 1 shall apply both to non-Community and Community goods, whether or not they are the subject of a commercial transaction.

Article 4

1. Of the goods referred to in Article 3:

(a) transit statistics shall be compiled on those which are transported, with or without transhipment, across a Member State without being stored there for reasons not inherent in their transport;

(b) storage statistics shall be compiled on those referred to in Article 2(2) of Regulation (EEC) No 1736/75, as well as those which enter or leave storage facilities determined by the Commission in accordance with Article 30 of this Regulation;

(c) statistics of trade between Member States shall be compiled on those which do not meet the conditions of (a) and (b) or which, while meeting either of those conditions, are expressly designated by this Regulation or by the Commission pursuant to Article 30;

(d) the Council, on a proposal from the Commission, shall determine the goods that are to be the subject of other statistics relating to the trading of goods between Member States.

2. Without prejudice to Community provisions on statistical returns in respect of carriage of goods, the data on the movement of goods subject to the statistics referred to in paragraph 1 shall be included, as necessary, in the list of data relating to each of these categories of statistics on the conditions and terms laid down by this Regulation or by the Commission pursuant to Article 30.

Article 5

Without prejudice to Article 15, private individuals shall be exempt from the obligations implied by the preparation of the statistics referred to in Article 4.

This exemption shall also apply to the party responsible for providing information who, being liable to account for VAT, qualifies, in the Member State in which he is responsible for providing information, for one of the special schemes provides for by Articles 24 and 25 of Directive 77/388/EEC. This provision shall be extended, *mutatis mutandis*, to [legal persons not liable to account for VAT][1] and to [parties liable to account who carry out only transactions not entitling them to any deductions of VAT][2], who, [pursuant to Council Directive 91/680/EEC][3] , are not required to submit a tax declaration.

Amendments
1 Substituted by Council Regulation 92/3046/EEC of 22 October 1992, art 22(2).
2 Substituted by Council Regulation 92/3046/EEC of 22 October 1992, art 22(2).
3 Substituted by Council Regulation 92/3046/EEC of 22 October 1992, art 22(1).

CHAPTER II
Statistical collection system: Intrastat

Article 6

With a view to compiling the statistics relating to the trading of goods between Member States, a statistical collection system shall be set up, hereinafter referred to as the "Intrastat system".

Article 7

1. The Intrastat system shall be applied in the Member States whenever they are deemed to be partner countries in the trading of goods between Member States by virtue of paragraph 4.

2. The Intrastat system shall be applied to the goods referred to in Article 3:

(a) which are in free movement on the internal market of the Community;

(b) which, since they may move on the internal market of the Community only after completion of the formalities prescribed by Community legislation on the circulation of goods, are expressly designated either by this Regulation or by the Commission pursuant to Article 30.

3. The collection of data on the goods referred in to Article 3 to which the Intrastat system does not apply shall be regulated by the Commission pursuant to Article 30 within the framework of the formalities referred to in paragraph 2(*b*).

4. The Intrastat system shall apply:

(*a*)   to statistics of trade between Member States, pursuant to Article 17 to 28;

(*b*)   to transit and storage statistics, in accordance with provisions laid down by the Council on a proposal from the Commission pursuant to Article 31.

5. Saving a decision to the contrary by the Council on a proposal from the Commission, in particular pursuant to Article 31, national provisions on the statistics referred to in paragraph 4 of this Article, in so far as they relate to data collection, shall cease to apply after 31 December 1992.

Article 8

Without prejudice to Article 5, the obligation to supply the information required by the Intrastat system shall be incumbent on any natural or legal person who is involved in the trading of goods between Member States.

Among those incurring this obligation, the party responsible for providing information for each category of statistics by the Intrastat system shall be designated by the relevant specific provisions.

Article 9

1. The party responsible for providing the information required by the Intrastat system may transfer the task of providing the information to a third party residing in a Member State, but such transfer shall in no way reduce the responsibility of the said party.

The party responsible for providing information shall provide such third party with all the information necessary to fulfil his obligations as party responsible.

2. The party responsible for providing information may be required, at the express request of the departments responsible for compiling statistics on the trading of goods between Member States, to notify them that for a given reference period,

— all the information which is to be the subject of the periodic declaration referred to in Article 13(1) has been provided either by himself or by a third party.

— he has transferred the task of providing the information required by the Intrastat system to that third party, whom he shall identify.

3. Paragraph 1 shall not apply:

(*a*)   in cases where Article 28(4) applies;

(*b*)   in Member States where the periodic declaration referred to in Article 13(1) is not distinct from the periodic declaration required for tax purposes and inasmuch as the tax rules in force relating to declaration obligations prevent the transfer referred to in the abovementioned paragraph 1.

4. The implementing rules for paragraphs 1, 2 and 3 shall be laid down by the Commission in accordance with Article 30.

Article 10

1. Member States shall take the measures necessary to ensure that those of their departments which are responsible for compiling statistics relating to the trading of goods between Member States, have a register of intra-Community operators at their disposal by 1 January 1993.

2. For the purposes of applying paragraph 1, a list shall be established of upon dispatch the consignors, upon arrival the consignees and where necessary the declarants, within the meaning of Commission Regulation (EEC) No 2792/86(1), who are involved from 1 January 1991 to 31 December 1992 in trade between Member States.

3. Paragraph 2 shall not apply to those Member States which take the measures necessary to ensure that their tax authorities have at their disposal, by 1 January 1993 at the latest, a register:

> (*a*)   listing the parties liable to account for VAT who, during the 12 months prior to that date, took part in the trading of goods between Member States, as consignors upon dispatch and as consignees upon arrival;

> (*b*)   intended to list [legal persons not liable to account for VAT][1] and [parties liable to account who carry out only transactions not entitling them to any deduction of VAT][2] who, from that date, carry out their acquisitions, [within the meaning of Directive 91/680/EEC.][3]

In those Member States, the abovementioned tax authorities shall, in addition to the identification number referred in paragraph 6, supply the statistical departments referred to in paragraph 1 with the information included in that register which is used to identify those intra-Community operators, under the conditions required for application of this Regulation.

4. The list of minimum data to be recorded in the register of intra-Community operators in addition to the identification number referred to in paragraph 6 shall be laid down by the Commission pursuant to Article 30.

5. From 1 January 1993, the register of intra-Community operators shall be managed and updated in the Member States by the relevant departments on the basis of the declarations referred to in Article 13(1), or the lists referred to in Article 11(1), or other administrative sources.

Where required, the Commission shall draw up, in accordance with Article 30, the other rules relating to the management and updating of the register of intra-Community operators to be applied in the Member States by the relevant departments.

6. Apart from exceptions which they shall justify to the parties responsible for providing statistical information, the relevant statistical departments shall use in their relations with those parties, and in particular with a view to application of Article 13(1), the identification number allocated to those parties by the tax authorities responsible.

Amendments
1 Substituted by Council Regulation 92/3046/EEC of 22 October 1992, art 22(2).
2 Substituted by Council Regulation 92/3046/EEC of 22 October 1992, art 22(2).
3 Substituted by Council Regulation 92/3046/EEC of 22 October 1992, art 22(1).

Article 11

1. The tax authorities responsible in each Member State shall, at least once every three months, furnish the departments in that Member State responsible for compiling statistics relating to the trading of goods between Member States with the lists of those liable to account for VAT who have declared that, during the period in question, they have made acquisitions in other Member States or deliveries to other Member States.

2. The lists referred to in paragraph 1 shall also include:

> (*a*)   parties liable to account for VAT who have declared that, during the period in question, they have conducted trading of goods between Member States which, although not resulting from acquisitions or deliveries, must be the subject of a periodic tax declaration;

> (*b*)   [legal persons not liable to account for VAT][1] and [parties liable to account who carry out only transactions not entitling them to any deduction of VAT][2] who have declared that, during the same period, they have conducted trading of goods between Member States which must be the subject of a periodic tax declaration.

3. The lists shall indicate, for each operator, on them, the value of trading of goods between Member States which the operator has mentioned in his periodic tax declaration in accordance with [Directive 91/680/EEC]³.

4. Under restrictive conditions, which the Commission shall determine pursuant to Article 30, each Member State's competent tax authorities shall in addition furnish the departments in that Member State responsible for compiling statistics relating to the trading of goods between Member States, on their own initiative or at the request of the latter, with any information capable of improving the quality of statistics which those liable to account for VAT normally submit to the competent tax authorities to comply with tax requirements.

The information communicated to them in accordance with the first subparagraph shall be treated by the statistical departments, vis-a-vis third parties, in accordance with the rules applied to it by the tax authorities.

5. Whatever the administrative structure of the Member State, the party responsible for providing statistical information may not be compelled to justify, other than within the limits laid down by paragraph 1, 2 and 3 and by the provisions provided for in paragraph 4, the information he supplies in comparison with the data he communicates to the competent tax authorities.

6. In their relations with persons liable to account for VAT regarding the periodic declaration which such persons must forward to it for tax purposes, the competent tax authorities shall draw attention to the obligations which they may incur as parties responsible for providing the information required by the Intrastat system.

7. For the purposes of applying paragraphs 4 and 6. "parties liable to account for VAT" shall also mean [legal persons not liable to account for VAT]¹ and [parties liable to account who carry out only transactions not entitling them to any deduction of VAT]² who carry out acquisitions within the meaning of Article 28(7) of [Directive 91/680/EEC]³.

8. Administrative assistance between national departments of different Member States responsible for compiling statistics relating to the trading of goods between Member States shall, as necessary, be regulated by the Commission pursuant to Article 30.

Amendments
1 Substituted by Council Regulation 92/3046/EEC of 22 October 1992, art 22(2).
2 Substituted by Council Regulation 92/3046/EEC of 22 October 1992, art 22(2).
3 Substituted by Council Regulation 92/3046/EEC of 22 October 1992, art 22(1).

Article 12

1. The statistical information media required by the Intrastat system shall be set up by the Commission pursuant to Article 30 in respect of each category of statistics relating to the trading of goods between Member States.

2. In order to take account of their particular administrative arrangements, Member States may set up media other than those referred to in paragraph 1, provided that those responsible for providing information may choose which of these media they will use.

Member States exercising this option shall inform the Commission accordingly.

3. Paragraphs 1 and 2 shall not apply:

  (*a*) in cases where Article 28(4) applies:

  (*b*) in Member States where the periodic declaration referred to in Article 13(1) is not distinct from the periodic declaration required for tax purposes and inasmuch as the tax rules in force relating to declaration obligations prevent such application.

Article 13

1. The statistical information required by the Intrastat system shall be covered in periodic declarations to be sent by the party responsible for providing the information to the competent national departments, by deadlines and under conditions which the Commission shall lay down pursuant to Article 30.

2. The Commission shall determine, pursuant to Article 30:

— where not laid down by this Regulation, the reference period applicable to each category of statistics relating to the trading of goods between Member States,

— the procedures for the transmission of the information, especially with a view to making available to the parties responsible for providing information networks of regional data collection offices.

3. The periodic declarations referred to in paragraph 1 or, in any case, the information which they contain shall be retained by the Member States for at least two years following the end of the calendar year of the reference period to which those declarations relate.

Article 14

Failure by any party responsible for providing statistical information to fulfil his obligations under this Regulation shall be liable to the penalties which the Member States shall lay down in accordance with their national provisions.

Article 15

Pursuant to Article 30, periodic surveys may be organized on the trading of goods between Member States by private individuals and on movements of goods or on intra-Community operators excluded from the returns benefiting from simplification measures under specific provisions relating to the various statistics on the trading of goods.

Article 16

The Commission shall report to the European Parliament and the Council in good time on the operation of the Intrastat system for each category of statistics relating to the trading of goods between Member States covered by the Intrastat system, with a view to possible adaptation of the system at the end of the transitional period referred to in Article 1.

CHAPTER III
Statistics on trade between Member States

Article 17

Statistics on trade between Member States shall cover, on the one hand, movements of goods leaving the Member State of dispatch and, on the other, movements of goods entering the Member State of arrival.

Article 18

1. The Member State of dispatch shall be the Member State in which the goods leaving it are the subject of a dispatch.

"Dispatch" shall mean the shipment of goods referred to in paragraph 2 to a destination in another Member State.

2. In a given Member State the following may be the subject of a dispatch:

(*a*) Community goods which, in that Member State:

— are not in direct or interrupted transit,

— are in direct or interrupted transit, but, having entered that Member State as non-Community goods, have subsequently been released for free circulation there;

(*b*) non-Community goods placed, maintained or obtained in that Member State under inward processing customs arrangements or under arrangements for processing under customs control.

Article 19

The Member State of arrival shall be the Member State in which the goods entering it:

(*a*) as Community goods:

—   are not in direct or interrupted transit in that Member State,

—   are in direct or interrupted transit in that Member State but leave it following formalities for export from the statistical territory of the Community;

(*b*)   as non-Community goods referred to in Article 18(2)(*b*), are:

     (1)   released for free circulation;

     (2)   maintained under inward processing customs arrangements or under arrangements for processing under customs control or again made subject to such arrangements.

Article 20

With a view to collecting the data required for the statistics of trade between Member States, the provisions of Chapter II shall be supplemented as follows:

(1) without prejudice to Article 34, the Intrastat system shall apply to the goods referred to in Articles 18(2)(*a*) and 19(*a*);

(2) the partner countries in trading of goods between Member States within the meaning of Article 7(1) shall be the Member State of dispatch and the Member State of arrival;

(3) within the Intrastat system, the Member State of dispatch shall be defined as that in which the goods which are dispatched from there to another Member State come under the terms of Article 18(2)(*a*) ...[1];

(4) within the Intrastat system, the Member State of arrival shall be defined as that in which the goods which enter from another Member State come under the terms of Article 19(*a*) ...[1];

(5) the party responsible for providing the information referred to in Article 8 shall be the natural or legal person who:

(*a*)   [registered for value added tax][2] in the Member State of dispatch:

—   has concluded the contract, with the exception of transport contracts, giving rise to the dispatch of goods or, failing this,

—   dispatches or provides for the dispatch of the goods or, failing this,

—   is in possession of the goods which are the subject of the dispatch;

(*b*)   [registered for value added tax][2] in the Member State of arrival:

—   has concluded the contract, with the expection [*sic*] of transport contracts, giving rise to the delivery of goods or, failing this,

—   takes possession or provides for possession to be taken of the goods or, failing this,

—   is in possession of the goods which are the subject of the delivery;

(6) the Commission shall adopt the provisions provided for in Article 7(3) in due course;

[(7) the reference period referred to in the first indent of Article 13(2) shall be:

—   for goods to which the Intrastat system applies, the calendar month during which the value-added tax becomes due on intra-Community deliveries or acquisitions of goods, the movements of which are to be recorded pursuant to this Article; when the period to which the periodic fiscal declaration of a party liable to account for VAT refers does not correspond with a calendar month, quarter, half-year or year, the Member States may adapt the periodicity of the obligations relating to the statistical declarations of that party to the periodicity of his obligations relating to fiscal declarations,

—   for goods to which the Intrastat system does not apply, according to the circumstances:

—   the calendar month during which the goods are either placed or maintained under the inward processing customs procedure (suspension system) or the procedure of processing under customs control or placed in free circulation as a result of one of these procedures,

— the calendar month during which the goods, circulating between parts of the statistical territory of the Community, at least one of which is not part of the territory of the Community pursuant to Council Directive 77/388/EEC, have been subject to dispatch or arrival procedures.][3]

Amendments
1 Deleted by Council Regulation 92/3046/EEC of 22 October 1992, art 22(1).
2 Substituted by Council Regulation 92/3046/EEC of 22 October 1992, art 22(3)(*a*).

Article 21

On the statistical data medium to be transmitted to the competent departments:

— without prejudice to Article 34, goods shall be designated in such a way as to permit easy and precise classification in the finest relevance subdivision of the version of the combined nomenclature in force at the time;

— the eight-digit code number of the corresponding subdivision of the combined nomenclature shall also be given for each type of goods.

Article 22

1. On the statistical data medium, the Member States shall be described by the alphabetical or numerical codes which the Commission shall determine pursuant to Article 30.

2. Without prejudice to the provisions adopted by the Commission pursuant to Article 30, the parties responsible for providing information shall comply, for the purposes of paragraph 1, with the instructions issued by the competent national departments regarding the compiling of statistics on trade between Member States.

Article 23

1. For each type of goods, the statistical data medium to be transmitted to the competent departments must provide the following data:

(*a*) in the Member State of arrival, the Member State of consignment of the goods, within the meaning of Article 24(1);

(*b*) in the Member State of dispatch, the Member State of destination of the goods, within the meaning of Article 24(2);

(*c*) the quantity of goods, in net mass and supplementary units;

(*d*) the value of the goods;

(*e*) the nature of the transaction;

(*f*) the delivery terms;

(*g*) the presumed mode of transport.

2. Member States may not prescribe that data other than those listed in paragraph 1 be provided on the statistical data medium, except for the following:

(*a*) in the Member State of arrival, the country of origin; however, this item may be required only as allowed by Community law;

(*b*) in the Member State of dispatch, the region of origin; in the Member State of arrival, the region of destination;

(*c*) in the Member State of dispatch, the port or airport of loading; in the Member State of arrival, the port or airport of unloading;

(*d*) in the Member State of dispatch and in the Member State of arrival, the presumed port or airport of transhipment situated in another Member State provided the latter prepares transit statistics;

(*e*)   where appropriate, statistical procedure.

3. Insofar as not laid down in this Regulation, the data referred to in paragraphs 1 and 2 and the rules governing their inclusion on the statistical data medium shall be defined by the Commission pursuant to Article 30.

Article 24

1. When, before reaching the Member State of arrival, goods have entered one or more countries in transit and have been subject in those countries to halts or legal operations not inherent in their transport, the Member State of consignment shall be taken to be the last Member State where such halts or legal operations occurred. In other cases, the Member State of consignment shall be the same as the Member State of dispatch.

2. "Member State of destination" means the last country to which it is known, at the time of dispatch, that the goods are to be dispatched.

3. Notwithstanding Article 23(1)(*a*), the party responsible for providing information in the Member State of arrival may, in the following order:

—   If he does not know the Member State of consignment, state the Member State of dispatch;

—   if he does not know the Member State of dispatch, state the Member State of purchase, within the meaning of paragraph 4.

4. "The Member State of purchase" means the Member State of residence of the contracting partner of the natural or legal person who has concluded the contract, with the exception of transport contracts, giving rise to the delivery of goods in the Member State of arrival.

Article 25

1. The Community and the Member States shall compile statistics on trade between Member States from the data referred to in Article 23(1).

2. Member States which do not compile statistics on trade between Member States from the data referred to in Article 23(2) shall refrain from ordering the collection of such data.

3. The Community and the Member States shall compile statistics on trade between Member States, having regard to such provisions as the Commission may adopt pursuant to Article 30 on general and specific exemptions and the statistical thresholds.

4. Any provision which has the effect of excluding goods referred to in Articles 18 and 19 from the compilation of the statistics of trade between Member States shall suspend the obligation to supply statistical information on the goods thus excluded.

Article 26

1. Member States shall transmit to the Commission their monthly statistics on trade between Member States. These statistics shall cover the data referred to in Article 23(1).

2. Where necessary, the procedure for such transmission shall be laid down by the Commission pursuant to Article 30.

3. Data declared confidential by the Member States under the conditions referred to in Article 32 shall be transmitted by them in accordance with Council Regulation (Euratom, EEC) No 1588/90 of 11 June 1990 on the transmission of data subject to statistical confidentiality to the Statistical Office of the European Communities (OJ No L 151, 15.6.1990, p. 1).

Article 27

Provisions regarding the simplification of statistical information shall be adopted by the Council on a proposal from the Commission.

Article 28

1. For the purposes of this Chapter, statistical thresholds shall be defined as limits expressed in terms of value, at which level the obligations incumbent on parties responsible for providing information shall be suspended or reduced.

These thresholds shall apply without prejudice to the provisions of Article 15.

2. The statistical thresholds shall be known as exclusion, assimilation or simplification thresholds.

3. Exclusion thresholds shall apply to the parties required to provide information referred to in the second subparagraph of Article 5.

They shall apply in all Member States and shall be determined, by each of the said Member States, in accordance with national tax provisions adopted pursuant to Directive 77/388/EEC.

4. Assimilation thresholds shall exempt parties required to provide information from having to supply the declarations referred to in Article 13(1); the periodic tax declaration which they make as parties liable to account for VAT, including parties within the meaning of Article 11(7), shall be considered to be the statistical declaration.

Assimilation thresholds shall apply in all Member States and shall be set, by each of the said Member States, at higher levels than the exclusion thresholds.

5. Simplification thresholds shall exempt parties required to provide information from the full provisions of Article 23; the declarations referred to in Article 13(1) need only state for each type of goods, in addition to the code number referred to in the second indent of Article 21, the Member State of consignment or destination and the value of the goods.

Without prejudice to the first subparagraph of paragraph 9, they shall be applied at the levels determined by paragraph 8 in Member States whose assimilation thresholds are lower than these levels.

In Member States whose assimilation thresholds are set at levels equal to or, pursuant to the first subparagraph of paragraph 9, higher than those determined by paragraph 8, simplification thresholds shall be optional.

6. Assimilation and simplification thresholds shall be expressed in annual values of intra-Community trade operations.

They shall be determined by dispatch or arrival flows.

They shall apply separately to intra-Community operators at the dispatch stage and to intra-Community operators at the arrival stage. Without prejudice to paragraph 10, those Member States which elect to use the option set out in the first subparagraph of paragraph 9 may, however, determine the obligations of those responsible for providing the information at both the dispatch and the arrival stages in accordance with the flow for which the annual value of their intra-Community operations is highest.

The assimilation and simplification thresholds may vary from one Member State to another, by product group and by period.

7. With a view to the application of the assimilation and simplification thresholds by the Member States, the Commission shall determine, pursuant to Article 30, the quality requirements which must be met by the statistics compiled by the Member States under Article 25(1).

8. The simplification thresholds shall be set at ECU 100,000 for dispatch and ECU 100 000 for arrival.

Provided that the quality requirements referred to in paragraph 7 above are met pursuant to Article 30, the Commission may raise the simplification threshold levels.

9. Member States may, provided that the quality requirements set out in paragraph 7 above are met, set their assimilation and simplification thresholds at levels higher than those in paragraph 8. They shall inform the Commission thereof.

Member States may, in order to comply with the requirements set out in paragraph 7, derogate to the extent necessary from the requirements of the second subparagraph of paragraph 5. They shall inform the Commission thereof.

The Commission may ask the Member States to justify the measures which they take by providing it with all appropriate information.

10. If Member States" application of the assimilation and simplification thresholds affects the quality of intra-Community trade statistics, bearing in mind the data supplied by the Member States, or increases the burden on parties required to provide information, such that the objectives of this Regulation are compromised, the Commission shall adopt, pursuant to Article 30, provisions which restore the conditions needed to ensure the required quality or to ease the burden.

CHAPTER IV
Committee on statistics relating to the trading of goods between Member States

Article 29

1. A Committee on the statistics relating to the trading of goods between Member States, hereinafter called "the Committee", is hereby established. It shall be composed of representatives of the Member States and chaired by a Commission representative.

2. The Committee shall draw up its rules of procedure.

3. The Committee may examine any question relating to the implementation of this Regulation raised by its chairman, either on his own initiative or at the request of the representative of a Member State.

Article 30

1. The provisions required for the implementation of this Regulation shall be adopted according to the procedure laid down in paragraph 2 and 3.

2. The representative of the Commission shall submit to the committee a draft of the measures to be taken. The Committee shall deliver its opinion on the draft within a time limit which the chairman may lay down according to the urgency of the matter. The opinion shall be delivered by the majority laid down in Article 148(2) of the Treaty in the case of decisions which the Council is required to adopt on a proposal from the Commission. The votes of the representatives of the Member States within the committee shall be weighted in the manner set out in that Article. The chairman shall not vote.

3. The Commission shall adopt measures which shall apply immediately. However, if these measures are not in accordance with the opinion of the committee, they shall be communicated by the Commission to the Council forthwith.

In that event, the Commission may defer application of the measures which it has decided for a period of not more than one month from the date of such communication.

The Council, acting by a qualified majority, may take a different decision within the time limit referred to in the second subparagraph.

CHAPTER V
Final provisions

Article 31

On a proposal from the Commission, the Council shall adopt the provisions necessary to enable the Community or its Member States to compile the statistics other than statistics of trade between Member States referred to in Article 4.

Article 32

1. On a proposal from the Commission, the Council shall decide on the conditions under which the Member States may declare data compiled in accordance with this Regulation, or the Regulations provided for herein, to be confidential.

2. Until the conditions referred to in paragraph 1 have been laid down, Member States' provisions on this matter shall apply.

Article 33

The Commission may, by the procedure laid down in Article 30, adapt as necessary the provisions of this Regulation:

— to the consequences of amendments to Directive 77/388/EEC;

— to specific movements of goods within the meaning of the statistical regulations of the Community.

Article 34

1. In respect both of goods subject to the Intrastat system and of other goods, the Commission may, for the purpose of facilitating the task of the parties responsible for providing information, establish in accordance with Article 30 simplified data collection procedures and in particular create the conditions for increased use of automatic data processing and electronic data transmission.

2. In order to take account of their individual administrative arrangements, Member States may establish simplified procedures other than those referred to in paragraph 1, provided that those responsible for providing information may choose the procedures they will use.

Member States exercising this option shall inform the Commission accordingly.

Article 35

This Regulation shall enter into force on the third day following that of its publication in the Official Journal of the European Communities.

Except insofar as they require the Council or the Commission to adopt provisions implementing this Regulation before that date, Article 1 to 9, 11, 13(1) and 14 to 27 shall apply as from the date of implementation of Council Regulation (EEC) No 2726/90 of 17 September 1990 on Community transit (OJ No L 262, 26.9.1990, p. 1).

As from the date referred to in the second subparagraph, Regulation (EEC) No 2954/85 shall be repealed and Regulation (EEC) No 1736/75 shall cease to apply to the statistics relating to the trading of goods between Member States to which it was applicable.

This Regulation shall be binding in its entirety and directly applicable in all Member States.

Done at Brussels, 7 November 1991

COUNCIL REGULATION

of 27 January 1992

92/218/EEC

On administrative cooperation in the field of indirect taxation (VAT)

(OJ L24, 1.2.1992, p 1)

THE COUNCIL OF THE EUROPEAN COMMUNITIES,

Having regard to the Treaty establishing the European Economic Community, and in particular Article 99 thereof,

Having regard to the proposal from the Commission,

Having regard to the opinion of the European Parliament,

Having regard to the opinion of the Economic and Social Committee,

Whereas the establishment of the internal market in accordance with Article 8a of the Treaty requires the creation of an area without internal frontiers in which the free movement of goods, persons, services and capital is ensured; whereas the internal market requires changes in the legislation on value added tax as provided in Article 99 of the Treaty;

Whereas in order to avoid tax revenue losses for Member States the tax harmonisation measures taken to complete the internal market and for the transitional period must include the establishment of a common system for the exchange of information on intra-Community transactions between the competent authorities of the Member States;

Whereas in order to permit the abolition of fiscal controls at internal frontiers in accordance with the aims set out in Article 8a of the Treaty the transitional value added tax system introduced by Directive 91/680/EEC, amending Directive 77/388/EEC, must be effectively established without the risk of fraud which might cause distortions of competition;

Whereas this Regulation provides for a common system for the exchange of information on intra-Community transactions, supplementing Directive 77/799/EEC, as last amended by Directive 79/1070/EEC, and intended to serve tax purposes;

Whereas the Member States should provide the Commission with any value added tax information which may be of interest at Community level;

Whereas the establishment of a common system of administrative cooperation may affect individuals' legal positions, in particular because of the exchange of information concerning their tax positions;

Whereas care must be taken to ensure that the provisions concerning the control of indirect taxes are in balance with administrations' needs for effective control and administrative burdens imposed on taxable persons;

Whereas the operation of such a system requires the establishment of a standing committee on administrative cooperation;

Whereas the Member States and the Commission must establish an effective system for the electronic storage and transmission of certain data for value added tax control purposes;

Whereas care must be taken to ensure that information provided in the course of such collaboration is not disclosed to unauthorised persons, so that the basic rights of citizens and undertakings are safeguarded; whereas it is therefore necessary that an authority receiving such information should not, without the authorisation of the authority supplying it, use it for purposes other than taxation or to facilitate legal proceedings for failure to comply with the tax laws of the Member States concerned; whereas the receiving authority must also accord such information the same degree of confidentiality as it enjoyed in the Member State which provided it, if the latter so requires;

Whereas the Member States and the Commission must collaborate on the continuous analysis of cooperation procedures and the pooling of the experience gained in the fields in question, with the aims of improving those procedures and drawing up appropriate Community rules,

HAS ADOPTED THIS REGULATION:

Article 1

This Regulation lays down the ways in which the administrative authorities in the Member States responsible for the application of laws on value added tax shall cooperate with each other and with the Commission to ensure compliance with those laws.

To that end it lays down procedures for the exchange of value added tax information on intra-Community transactions by electronic means and any subsequent exchange of information between Member States' competent authorities.

Article 2

1. For the purposes of this Regulation:

— **"competent authority"** shall mean the authority appointed to act as correspondent as defined in paragraph 2,

— **"applicant authority"** shall mean the competent authority of a Member State which makes a request for assistance,

— **"requested authority"** shall mean the competent authority of a Member State to which a request for assistance is made,

— **"person"** shall mean:

— a natural person,

— a legal person or,

— where the possibility is provided for under the legislation in force, an association of persons recognised as having the capacity to perform legal acts but lacking the legal status of a legal person,

— **"to grant access"** shall mean authorising access to the relevant electronic date base and providing data by electronic means,

— **"value added tax identification number"** shall mean the number provided for in with Article 22(1)(c), (d) and (e) of Directive 77/388/EEC,

— **"intra-Community transactions"** shall mean the intra-Community supply of goods and the intra-Community supply of services as defined in this paragraph,

— **"intra-Community supply of goods"** shall mean any supply of goods which must be declared in the recapitulative statement provided for in Article 22(6)(b) of Directive 77/388/EEC,

— **"intra-Community supply of services"** shall mean any supply of services covered by Article 28b(C), (D) or (E) of Directive 77/388/EEC,

— **"intra-Community acquisition of goods"** shall mean acquisition of the right to dispose as owner of movable tangible property as defined in Article 28a(3) of Directive 77/388/EEC.

2. Each Member State shall notify the other Member States and the Commission of the competent authorities appointed to act as correspondents for the purpose of applying this Regulation. In addition, each member State shall nominate a central office with principal responsibility for liaison with other Member States in the field of administrative cooperation.

3. The Commission shall publish a list of competent authorities in the *Official Journal of the European Communities* and, where necessary, update it.

TITLE I
Exchange of information — general provisions

Article 3

1. The obligation to give assistance provided for in this Regulation shall not cover the provision of information or documents obtained by the administrative authorities referred to in Article 1 at the request of a judicial authority.

However, in cases of applications for assistance, such information and documents shall be provided whenever the judicial authority, to which reference must be made, gives its consent.

2. This Regulation shall not restrict the application of provisions of other agreements or instruments relating to cooperation on tax matters.

3. This Regulation shall not affect the application in the Member States of the rules on mutual assistance in criminal matters.

TITLE II
Exchange of information relating to value added tax in connection with intra-Community transactions

Article 4

1. The competent authority of each Member State shall maintain an electronic data base in which it shall store and process the information that it collects in accordance with Article 22(6)(*b*) of Directive 77/388/EEC. To allow the use of this information in the procedures provided for in this Regulation the information shall be stored for at least five years after the end of the calendar year in which access to the information was to be granted. Member States shall ensure that their data bases are kept up to date, complete and accurate. Under the procedure laid down in Article 10 criteria shall be defined to determine what amendments that are not significant, material or useful need not be made.

2. From the data collected in accordance with paragraph 1, the competent authority of a Member State shall obtain directly and without delay from each Member State, or may have direct access to, the following information:

— the value added tax identification numbers issued by the Member State receiving the information, and

— the total value of all intra-Community supplies of goods made to the persons to whom those numbers were issued by all operators identified for the purposes of value added tax in the Member State; the value shall be expressed in the currency of the Member State providing the information and shall relate to calendar quarters.

3. From the data collected in accordance with paragraph 1 and solely in order to combat tax fraud, the competent authority of a Member State shall, wherever it considers it necessary for the control of intra-Community acquisitions of goods, obtain directly and without delay, or have direct access to, the following information:

— the value added tax identification numbers of all persons who have made the supplies referred to in the second indent of paragraph 2, and

— the total value of such supplies from each such person to each person to whom one of the value added tax identification numbers referred to in the first indent of paragraph 2 has been issued; the values shall be expressed in the currency of the Member State providing the information; the value shall be expressed in the currency of the Member State providing the information and shall relate to calendar quarters.

4. Where the competent authority of a Member State is obliged to grant access to information under this Article it shall, as regards the information referred to in paragraphs 2 and 3, do so within three months of the end of the calendar quarter to which the information relates. By way of derogation from this rule, where information is added to a data base in the circumstances provided for in paragraph 1, access to such additions shall be granted as quickly as possible and in any event no more than three months after the end of the quarter in which the additional information was collected; the conditions under which access to the corrected information may be granted shall be defined by means of the procedure laid down in Article 10.

5. Where, for purposes of the application of this Article, the competent authorities of the Member States keep information in electronic data bases and exchange such information by electronic means they shall take all measures necessary to ensure compliance with Article 9.

Article 5

1. Where the information provided under Article 4 is insufficient, the competent authority of a Member State may at any time and in specific cases request further information. The requested authority shall provide the information as quickly as possible and in any event no more than three months after receipt of the request.

2. In the circumstances described in paragraph 1 the requested authority shall at least provide the applicant authority with invoice numbers, dates and values in relation to individual transactions between persons in the Member States concerned.

Article 6

1. The competent authority of each Member State shall maintain an electronic data base which shall contain a register of persons to whom value added tax identification numbers have been issued in that Member State.

2. At any time the competent authority of a Member State may obtain directly or have communicated to it, from the data collected in accordance with Article 4(1), confirmation of the validity of the value added tax identification number under which a person effected or received an intra-Community supply of goods or of services. On specific request the requested authority shall also communicate the date of issue and, where appropriate, the date of cessation of the validity of the value added tax identification number.

3. Where it is so requested a competent authority shall also provide without delay the name and address of the person to whom a number has been issued, provided that such information is not stored by the applicant authority with a view to its possible use at some future time.

4. The competent authority of each Member State shall ensure that persons involved in the intra-Community supply of goods or of services are allowed to obtain confirmation of the validity of the value added tax identification number of any specified person.

5. Where, for purposes of the application of this Article, the competent authorities of the Member States keep information in electronic data bases and exchange such information by electronic means they shall take all measures necessary to ensure compliance with Article 9.

TITLE III
Conditions governing the exchange of information

Article 7

1. A requested authority in one Member State shall provide an applicant authority in another Member State with the information referred to in Article 5(2) provided that:

— the number and the nature of the requests for information made by the applicant authority within a specific period of time do no impose a disproportionate administrative burden on that requested authority,

— that applicant authority exhausts the usual sources of information which it can use in the circumstances to obtain the information requested, without running the risk of jeopardising the achievement of the desired end,

— that applicant authority requests assistance only if it would be able to provide similar assistance to the applicant authority of another Member State.

In accordance with the procedure laid down in Article 10 and taking into account experience of the new administrative cooperation system during its first year of operation, the Commission shall submit general criteria for the definition of the scope of these commitments before July 1994.

2. If an applicant authority is unable to comply with the general provisions of paragraph 1 it shall notify the requested authority accordingly without delay, stating its reasons. If a requested authority considers that the general provisions of paragraph 1 are not complied with and that it is therefore not obliged to provide the information, it shall notify the applicant authority accordingly without delay, stating its reasons. The applicant authority and the requested authority shall attempt to reach agreement. If they fail to reach agreement within one month of notification either authority may request that the matter be examined under Article 11.

3. This Article shall be without prejudice to the application of Directive 77/799/EEC as regards the exchange of information referred to in Article 5(1).

Article 8

In cases of exchanges of information as defined in Article 5, where the national legislation in force in a Member State provides for notification of the person concerned of the exchange of information, those provisions may continue to apply except where their application would prejudice the investigation of tax evasion in another Member State. In the latter event, at the express request of the applicant authority, the requested authority shall refrain from such notification.

Article 9

1. Any information communicated in whatever form pursuant to this Regulation shall be of a confidential nature. It shall be covered by the obligation of professional secrecy and shall enjoy the protection extended to similar information under both the national law of the Member State which received it and the corresponding provisions applicable to Community authorities.

In any case, such information:

— may be made available only to the persons directly concerned with the basis of assessment, collection or administrative control of taxes for the purposes of the assessment of taxes, or to persons employed by Community institutions whose duties require that they have access to it,

— may in addition be used in connection with judicial or administrative proceedings that may involve sanctions, initiated as a result of infringements of tax law.

2. By way of derogation from paragraph 1, the competent authority of the Member State providing the information shall permit its use for other purposes in the Member State of the applicant authority, if, under the legislation of the Member State of the requested authority, the information could be used in the Member State of the requested authority for similar purposes.

3. Where the applicant authority considers that information which it has received from the requested authority is likely to be useful to the competent authority of a third Member State, it may transmit it to the latter with the agreement of the requested authority.

TITLE IV
Consultation and coordination procedures

Article 10

1. The Commission shall be assisted by a Standing Committee on Administrative Cooperation in the field of Indirect Taxation, hereinafter referred to as "the Committee". It shall consist of representatives of the Member States and have a representative of the Commission as chairman.

2. The measures required for the application of Articles 4 and 7(1) shall be adopted in accordance with the procedure laid down in paragraphs 3 and 4 of this Article.

3. The Commission representative shall submit to the Committee a draft of the measures to be adopted. The Committee shall deliver its opinion on that draft within a time limit which the chairman may lay down according to the urgency of the matter. The Committee's opinion shall be delivered by a majority, the Member States' votes being weighted in accordance with Article 148(2) of the Treaty. The chairman shall not vote.

4. The Commission shall adopt the measures contemplated where they are in accordance with the Committee's opinion.

Where those measures are not in accordance with the Committee's opinion of if the Committee does not deliver an opinion, the Commission shall without delay submit to the Council a proposal on the measures to be adopted. The Council shall act by a qualified majority.

If within three months of the proposal's being submitted to it the Council has not acted, the proposed measures shall be adopted by the Commission, unless the Council has decided against those measures by a simple majority.

Article 11

The Member States and the Commission shall examine and evaluate the operation of the arrangements for administrative cooperation provided for in this Regulation and the Commission shall pool the Member States' experience, in particular that concerning new means of tax avoidance and evasion, with the aim of improving the operation of those arrangements. To that end the Member States shall also communicate to the Commission any value added tax information on intra-Community transactions that may be of interest at Community level.

Article 12

1. On matters of bilateral interest, the competent authorities of the Member States may communicate directly with each other. The competent authorities of the Member States may by mutual agreement permit authorities designated by them to communicate directly with each other in specified cases or categories of cases.

2. For the purpose of applying this Regulation, Member States shall take all necessary steps to:

(*a*) ensure efficient internal coordination between the competent authorities referred to in Article 1;

(*b*) establish direct cooperation between the authorities specially empowered for the purposes of such coordination;

(*c*) make suitable arrangements to ensure the smooth operation of the arrangements for the exchange of information provided for in this Regulation.

3. The Commission shall communicate to the competent authority of each Member State, as quickly as possible, any information which it receives and which it is able to supply.

TITLE V
Final provisions

Article 13

Member States shall waive all claims for the reimbursement of expenses incurred in applying this Regulation except, as appropriate, in respect of fees paid to experts.

Article 14

1. Every two years after the date of entry into force of this Regulation, the Commission shall report to the European Parliament and the Council on the conditions of application of this Regulation on the basis, in particular, of the continuous monitoring procedures provided for in Article 11.

2. Member States shall communicate to the Commission the texts of any provisions of national law which they adopt in the field governed by this Regulation.

Article 15

This Regulation shall enter force on the third day following it publication in the *Official Journal of the European Communities*.

No exchange of information under this Regulation shall take place before 1 January 1993.

Done at Brussels, 27 January 1992.

COMMISSION REGULATION

of 31 July 1992

92/2256/EEC

On statistical thresholds for the statistics on trade between Member States

(OJ L219, 4.8.1992, p 40)

THE COMMISSION OF THE EUROPEAN COMMUNITIES,

Having regard to the Treaty establishing the European Economic Community,

Having regard to Council Regulations (EEC) No 3330/91 of 7 November 1991 on the statistics relating to the trading of goods between Member States, and in particular Article 30 thereof,

Whereas the burden on intra-Community operators must be lightened as much as possible, either by exempting them from statistical obligations or by simplifying procedures;

Whereas this lightening of the burden must be limited only by the demands of statistics of a satisfactory quality, which must consequently be defined by common accord;

Whereas, once this quality has been defined, all the Member States must have their necessary instruments to ensure it, while taking account of their own economic and commercial structure; where it is for the Member States themselves to strike the most appropriate balance between lightening of the statistical burden and quality on the basis of the information available to them;

Whereas the information to be analysed by the Member States in order to fix their thresholds differs, particularly as regards coverage, depending on whether they are to be introduced in 1993 or to be adapted as from 1994; whereas a distinction should therefore be drawn between the rules to be followed on one single occasion, as in the first case, and those to be followed each year, as in the second case;

Whereas the obligations of the persons responsible for providing information should be defined in such a way as to take maximum account of their interests, particularly if their intra-Community transactions are expanding;

Whereas the measures provided for in this Regulation are in accordance with the opinion of the Committee on Statistics relating to the trading of goods between Member States.

HAS ADOPTED THIS REGULATION:

Article 1

The Member States shall set annually, in national currency, the assimilation and simplification thresholds referred to in Article 28 of Regulation (EEC) No 3330/91, hereinafter **"the Basic Regulation"**. They shall ensure when setting these thresholds that, first, they meet the quality requirements laid down in this Regulation and, secondly, they exploit to the full the ensuing opportunities to relieve the burden on intra-Community operators.

Article 2

For the purposes of this Regulation:

(*a*) **"error"** means the discrepancy between the results obtained with and without application of the thresholds referred to in Article 1; when a correction procedure is applied to the results obtained following application of the thresholds, the error is calculated in relation to the corrected results;

(*b*)   **"total value"** means:

— for the introduction of the thresholds in 1993, the value either of the outgoing goods or of the incoming goods, accounted for by intra-Community operators over a period of twelve months,

— for the adjustment of the thresholds from 1994, the value of either of the outgoing goods or of the incoming goods accounted for by intra-Community operators over a twelve-month period, other than those who are exempt under Article 5 of the Basic Regulation;

(*c*)   **"coverage"** means in relation to a given total value, the proportionate value of the outgoing goods or of the incoming goods, accounted for by the intra-Community operators who lie above the assimilation threshold.

Article 3

1. For the introduction of the assimilation thresholds in 1993, the Member States shall meet the following quality requirements:

(*a*)   Results by goods category

Each Member State shall ensure that the error in annual values does not exceed 5% for 90% of the eight-digit sub-headings of the combined Nomenclature which represent 0,005% or more of the total value of its outgoing or incoming goods.

However, each Member State may raise this quality requirement up to the point that the error in annual values does not exceed 5% for 90% of the eight-digit sub-headings of the Combined Nomenclature which represent 0,001% or more of the total value of its outgoing or incoming goods.

(*b*)   Results by partner country

Each Member State shall ensure that the error in the annual values of its results by partner country, excluding countries which represent less than 3% of the total value of its outgoing or incoming goods, does not exceed 1%.

(*c*)   Time series

Each Member State shall ensure that:

— for 90% of the eight-digit sub-headings of the combined nomenclature which represent the percentage of the total value of its outgoing or incoming goods laid down in point (*a*), and

— for 90% of its results by partner country,

The fluctuation over time of the error in annual values will not exceed the limits (L) laid down in the Annex.

If in any Member State applying the requirement leads to an increase in the number of parties responsible for providing information who are required to submit the periodic declaration laid down in Article 13 of the Basis Regulation that is excessive in proportion to the number involved under the more stringent of the other two requirements, the Member State concerned may take steps to reduce the imbalance accordingly. It shall inform the Commission of the action taken.

2. When a Member State's share of the total value of outgoing or incoming goods in the Community is less than 3%, that Member State may depart from the quality requirements laid down in the first subparagraph of paragraph 1(*a*) and the first indent of the first subparagraph of paragraph 1(*c*). In such cases, the 90% and 0,005% shares shall be replaced by 70% and 0,01% respectively.

3. To meet the quality requirements set out in paragraphs 1 and 2, the Member States shall base the calculation of their thresholds on the results of trade with the other Member States for twelve-month periods prior to the introduction of the thresholds.

For Member States unable to make this calculation because figures are incomplete, the assimilation thresholds shall be fixed at a level not lower than the lowest, nor higher than the highest, thresholds set by the other Member States. However, this provision shall not be binding for Member States which are exempt under paragraph 2.

4. If, for certain groups of goods, the application of the thresholds calculated in accordance with the provisions of this Article yields results which, *mutatis mutandis*, fail to meet the quality requirements set out in paragraphs 1 and 2 above, and if the thresholds cannot be lowered without reducing the relief which Article 1 guarantees to intra-Community operators, appropriate measures may be taken, at the initiative of the Commission or the request of a Member State, in accordance with the procedure laid down in Article 40 of the Basic Regulation.

Article 4

For the introduction of the simplification thresholds in 1993, the Member States may set these:

— at levels above ECR 100,000 pursuant to the first subparagraph of Article 28(9) of the Basic Regulation, provided that they ensure that at least 95% of the total value of their outgoing or incoming goods is covered by periodic declarations containing all the information required under Article 23 of the Basic Regulation,

— where they are exempt under Article 3(2), at levels below ECU 100,000 pursuant to the second subparagraph of Article 28(9) of the Basic Regulation, to the extent necessary to ensure that at least 95% of the total value of their outgoing or incoming goods is covered by periodic declarations containing all the information required under Article 23 of the Basic Regulation.

Article 5

The information relating to the information of the assimilation and simplification thresholds in 1993 shall be published not later than 31 August 1992.

Article 6

1. For the adjustment of the assimilation thresholds from 1994, the quality requirements specified in Article 3 shall be regarded as met if the coverage is maintained at the level which obtained when the thresholds were introduced.

2. The condition laid down in paragraph 1 shall be met if Member States:

(*a*) calculate their thresholds for the year following the current year on the basis of the latest available results for their trade with the other Member States over a twelve-month period, and

(*b*) set their thresholds at a level which allows the same coverage for the period thus defined as for the period used as a basis for calculating their thresholds for the current year.

Member States shall notify the Commission if they use a different method to meet this condition.

3. Member States may lower their coverage provided that the quality requirements laid down in Article 3 continue to be met.

4. Member States shall calculate adjustments to their assimilation thresholds each year. The thresholds shall be adjusted if the adjustment involves a charge of at least 10% in the threshold values for the current year.

Article 7

1. For the adjustment of the simplification thresholds from 1994, the Member States which set these thresholds

— at levels higher than the values laid down in by Article 28(8) of the Basic Regulation, shall ensure that the condition laid down in the first indent of Article 4 of this Regulation is met,

— at levels below these values, since they are exempt pursuant to Article 3(2) above, shall ensure that they comply with the limit laid down in the second indent of Article 4 of this Regulation.

2. To ensure that the condition referred to in the first indent of Article 4 is met or that the limit referred to in the second indent of Article 4 is complied with, it shall be sufficient for Member States to calculate the adjustment of the simplification thresholds using the method laid down in Article 6(2) for adjusting the assimilation thresholds. Member States shall notify the Commission if they use a different method.

Article 8

The information relating to the adjustment of assimilation and simplification thresholds from 1994 shall be published not later than 31 October of the preceding year.

Article 9

1. Parties responsible for providing information shall be freed from their obligations to the extent allowed by application of the assimilation and simplification thresholds set for a given year, provided they have not exceeded these thresholds during the previous year.

2. For each statistical threshold, the provisions adopted shall apply for the whole year.

However, if the value of the intra-Community transactions carried out by a party responsible for providing information at some time during the year exceeds the threshold applicable to him, he shall provide information on his intra-Community transactions from the month in which this threshold was exceeded in accordance with the provisions applying to the threshold which becomes applicable. If this provision involves the transmission of the periodic declarations referred to in Article 13 of the Basic Regulation, the Member States shall lay down the time limit for transmitting these declarations in accordance with their particular administrative arrangements.

Article 10

The Member States shall communicate to the Commission the information regarding the thresholds they have calculated at least two weeks before publication. At the Commission's request, they shall also communicate the information required for assessing these thresholds, both for the period on which their calculation is based and for a given calendar year.

Article 11

This Regulation shall enter into force on the seventh day following its publication in the *Official Journal of the European Communities*.

This Regulation shall be binding in its entirety and directly applicable in all Member States.

Done at Brussels, 31 July 1992.

ANNEX

Notes
This annex contains the relevant mathematical formulae used to compute the limits.

COUNCIL REGULATION

of 12 October 1992

92/2913/EEC

establishing the Community Customs Code

(OJ No L 302, 19.10.1992)

TITLE I
General provisions

TITLE II
Factors on the basis of which import duties or export duties and the other measures prescribed in respect of trade in goods are applied

TITLE III
Provisions applicable to goods brought into the customs territory of the Community until they are assigned a customs approved treatment or use

TITLE IV
Customs-approved treatment or use

TITLE VII
Customs debt

TITLE VIII
Appeals

TITLE IX
Final provisions

THE COUNCIL OF THE EUROPEAN COMMUNITIES,

Having regard to the Treaty establishing the European Economic Community, and in particular Articles 28, 100a and 113 thereof,

Having regard to the proposal from the Commission (OJ No C 128, 23.5.1990, p 1),

In cooperation with the European Parliament (OJ No C 72, 18.3.1991, p 176 and Decision of 16 September 1992 (not yet published in the Official Journal),

Having regard to the opinion of the Economic and Social Committee (OJ No C 60, 8.3.1991, p 5),

Whereas the Community is based upon a customs union; whereas it is advisable, in the interests both of Community traders and the customs authorities, to assemble in a code the provisions of customs legislation that are at present contained in a large number of Community regulations and directives; whereas this task is of fundamental importance from the standpoint of the internal market;

Whereas such a Community Customs Code (hereinafter called 'the Code') must incorporate current customs legislation; whereas it is, nevertheless, advisable to amend that legislation in order to make it more consistent, to simplify it and to remedy certain omissions that still exist with a view to adopting complete Community legislation in this area;

Whereas, based on the concept of an internal market, the Code must contain the general rules and procedures which ensure the implementation of the tariff and other measures introduced at Community level in connection with trade in goods between the Community and third countries; whereas it must cover, among other things, the implementation of common agricultural and commercial policy measures taking into account the requirements of these common policies;

Whereas it would appear advisable to specify that this Code is applicable without prejudice to specific provisions laid down in other fields; whereas such specific rules as may exist or be introduced in the context, *inter alia*, of legislation relating to agriculture, statistics, commercial policy or own resources;

Whereas, in order to secure a balance between the needs of the customs authorities in regard to ensuring the correct application of customs legislation, on the one hand, and the rights of traders to be treated fairly, on the other, the said authorities must be granted, *inter alia*, extensive powers of control and the said traders a right of appeal; whereas the implementation of a customs appeals system will require the United Kingdom to introduce new administrative procedures which cannot be effected before 1 January 1995;

Whereas in view of the paramount importance of external trade for the Community, customs formalities and controls should be abolished or at least kept to a minimum;

Whereas it is important to guarantee the uniform application of this Code and to provide, to that end, for a Community procedure which enables the procedures for its implementation to be adopted within a suitable time; whereas a Customs Code Committee should be set up in order to ensure close and effective cooperation between the Member States and the Commission in this field;

Whereas in adopting the measures required to implement this Code, the utmost care must be taken to prevent any fraud or irregularity liable to affect adversely the General Budget of the European Communities,

HAS ADOPTED THIS REGULATION:

TITLE I
General provisions

CHAPTER 1
Scope and basic definitions

Article 1

Customs rules shall consist of this Code and the provisions adopted at Community level or nationally to implement them. The Code shall apply, without prejudice to special rules laid down in other fields

— to trade between the Community and third countries,

— to goods covered by the Treaty establishing the European Coal and Steel Community, the Treaty establishing the European Economic Community or the Treaty establishing the European Atomic Energy Community.

Article 2

1. Save as otherwise provided, either under international conventions or customary practices of a limited geographic and economic scope or under autonomous Community measures, Community customs rules shall apply uniformly throughout the customs territory of the Community.

2. Certain provisions of customs rules may also apply outside the customs territory of the Community within the framework of either rules governing specific fields or international conventions.

Article 3

[The customs territory of the Community shall comprise:

— the territory of the Kingdom of Belgium,

— the territory of the Kingdom of Denmark, except the Faroe Islands and Greenland,

— the territory of the Federal Republic of Germany, except the Island of Heligoland and the territory of Busingen (Treaty of 23 November 1964 between the Federal Republic of Germany and the Swiss Confederation),

— the territory of the Kingdom of Spain, except Ceuta and Melilla,

— the territory of the French Republic, except the overseas territories and 'collectivites territoriales',

— the territory of the Hellenic Republic,

— the territory of Ireland,

— the territory of the Italian Republic, except the municipalities of Livigno and Campione d'Italia and the national waters of Lake Lugano which are between the bank and the political frontier of the area between Ponte Tresa and Porto Ceresio,

— the territory of the Grand Duchy of Luxembourg,

— the territory of the Kingdom of the Netherlands in Europe,

— the territory of the Republic of Austria,

— the territory of the Portuguese Republic,

— the territory of the Republic of Finland, including the Aland Islands, provided a declaration is made in accordance with Article 227 (5) of the EC Treaty,

— the territory of the Kingdom of Sweden,

— the territory of the United Kingdom of Great Britain and Northern Ireland and of the Channel Islands and the Isle of Man;][1]

2. The following territories situated outside the territory of the Member States shall, taking the conventions and treaties applicable to them into account, be considered to be part of the customs territory of the Community:

...[2]

(*b*) FRANCE

The territory of the Principality of Monaco as defined in the Customs Convention signed in Paris on 18 May 1963 (*Journal officiel* of 27 September 1963, p 8679).

(*c*) ITALY

The territory of the Republic of San Marino as defined in the Convention of 31 March 1939 (Law of 6 June 1939, no 1220).

3. The customs territory of the Community shall include the territorial waters, the inland maritime waters and the airspace of the Member States, and the territories referred to in paragraph 2, except for the territorial waters, the inland maritime waters and the airspace of those territories which are not part of the customs territory of the Community pursuant to paragraph 1.

Amendments
1 Substituted by the Fourth Act of Accession 1994.
2 Deleted by the Fourth Act of Accession 1994.

Article 4

For the purposes of this Code, the following definitions shall apply:

(1) **'Person'** means:

— a natural person,

— a legal person,

— where the possibility is provided for under the rules in force, an association of persons recognized as having the capacity to perform legal acts but lacking the legal status of a legal person.

(2) **'Persons established in the Community'** means:

— in the case of a natural person, any person who is normally resident there,

— in the case of a legal person or an association of persons, any person that has in the Community its registered office, central headquarters or a permanent business establishment.

(3) **'Customs authorities'** means the authorities responsible *inter alia* for applying customs rules.

(4) **'Customs office'** means any office at which all or some of the formalities laid down by customs rules may be completed.

(5) **'Decision'** means any official act by the customs authorities pertaining to customs rules giving a ruling on a particular case, such act having legal effects on one or more specific or identifiable persons; this term covers *inter alia* a binding tariff information within the meaning of Article 12.

(6) **'Customs status'** means the status of goods as Community or non-Community goods.

(7) **'Community goods'** means goods:

— wholly obtained or produced in the customs territory of the Community under the conditions referred to in Article 23 and not incorporating goods imported from countries or territories not forming part of the customs territory of the Community,

— imported from countries or territories not forming part of the customs territory of the Community which have been released for free circulation,

— obtained or produced in the customs territory of the Community, either from goods referred to in the second indent alone or from goods referred to in the first and second indents.

(8) **'Non-Community goods'** means goods other than those referred to in subparagraph 7. Without prejudice to Articles 163 and 164, Community goods shall lose their status as such when they are actually removed from the customs territory of the Community.

(9) **'Customs debt'** means the obligation on a person to pay the amount of the import duties (customs debt on importation) or export duties (customs debt on exportation) which apply to specific goods under the Community provisions in force.

(10) **'Import duties'** means:

— customs duties and charges having an effect equivalent to customs duties payable on the importation of goods,

— agricultural levies and other import charges introduced under the common agricultural policy or under the specific arrangements applicable to certain goods resulting from the processing of agricultural products.

(11) **'Export duties'** means:

— customs duties and charges having an effect equivalent to customs duties payable on the exportation of goods,

— agricultural levies and other export charges introduced under the common agricultural policy or under the specific arrangements applicable to certain goods resulting from the processing of agricultural products.

(12) **'Debtor'** means any person liable for payment of a customs debt.

(13) **'Supervision by the customs authorities'** means action taken in general by those authorities with a view to ensuring that customs rules and, where appropriate, other provisions applicable to goods subject to customs supervision are observed.

(14) **'Control by the customs authorities'** means the performance of specific acts such as examining goods, verifying the existence and authenticity of documents, examining the accounts of undertakings and other records, inspecting means of transport, inspecting luggage and other goods carried by or on persons and carrying out official inquiries and other similar acts with a view to ensuring that customs rules and, where appropriate, other provisions applicable to goods subject to customs supervision are observed.

(15) **'Customs-approved treatment or use of goods'** means:

(*a*) the placing of goods under a customs procedure;

(*b*) their entry into a free zone or free warehouse;

(*c*) their re-exportation from the customs territory of the Community;

(*d*) their destruction;

(*e*) their abandonment to the Exchequer.

(16) **'Customs procedure'** means:

(*a*) release for free circulation;

(*b*) transit;

(*c*) customs warehousing;

(*d*) inward processing;

(*e*) processing under customs control;

(*f*) temporary admission;

(*g*) outward processing;

(*h*) exportation.

(17) **'Customs declaration'** means the act whereby a person indicates in the prescribed form and manner the wish to place goods under a given customs procedure.

(18) **'Declarant'** means the person making the customs declaration in his own name or the person in whose name a customs declaration is made.

(19) **'Presentation of goods to customs'** means the notification to the customs authorities, in the manner laid down, of the arrival of goods at the customs office or at any other place designated or approved by the customs authorities.

(20) **'Release of goods'** means the act whereby the customs authorities make goods available for the purposes stipulated by the customs procedure under which they are placed.

(21) **'Holder of the procedure'** means the person on whose behalf the customs declaration was made or the person to whom the rights and obligations of the abovementioned person in respect of a customs procedure have been transferred.

(22) **'Holder of the authorization'** means the person to whom an authorization has been granted.

(23) **'Provisions in force'** means Community or national provisions.

(24) **'Committee procedure'** means the procedure provided for in Article 249.

CHAPTER 2

Sundry general provisions relating in particular to the rights and obligations of persons with regard to customs rules

SECTION 1
Right of representation

Article 5

1. Under the conditions set out in Article 64(2) and subject to the provisions adopted within the framework of Article 243(2)(b), any person may appoint a representative in his dealings with the customs authorities to perform the acts and formalities laid down by customs rules.

2. Such representation may be:

— direct, in which case the representative shall act in the name of and on behalf of another person, or

— indirect, in which case the representative shall act in his own name but on behalf of another person.

A Member State may restrict the right to make customs declarations:

— by direct representation, or

— by indirect representation,

so that the representative must be a customs agent carrying on his business in that country's territory.

3. Save in the cases referred to in Article 64(2)(*b*) and (3), a representative must be established within the Community.

4. A representative must state that he is acting on behalf of the person represented, specify whether the representation is direct or indirect and be empowered to act as a representative.

A person who fails to state that he is acting in the name of or on behalf of another person or who states that he is acting in the name of or on behalf of another person without being empowered to do so shall be deemed to be acting in his own name and on his own behalf.

5. The customs authorities may require any person stating that he is acting in the name of or on behalf of another person to produce evidence of his powers to act as a representative.

SECTION 2
Decisions relating to the application of customs rules

Article 6

1. Where a person requests that the customs authorities take a decision relating to the application of customs rules that person shall supply all the information and documents required by those authorities in order to take a decision.

2. Such decision shall be taken and notified to the applicant at the earliest opportunity.

Where a request for a decision is made in writing, the decision shall be made within a period laid down in accordance with the existing provisions, starting on the date on which the said request is received by the customs authorities. Such a decision must be notified in writing to the applicant.

However, that period may be exceeded where the customs authorities are unable to comply with it. In that case, those authorities shall so inform the applicant before the expiry of the abovementioned period, stating the grounds which justify exceeding it and indicating the further period of time which they consider necessary in order to give a ruling on the request.

3. Decisions adopted by the customs authorities in writing which either reject requests or are detrimental to the persons to whom they are addressed shall set out the grounds on which they are based. They shall refer to the right of appeal provided for in Article 243.

4. Provision may be made for the first sentence of paragraph 3 to apply likewise to other decisions.

Article 7

Save in the cases provided for in the second subparagraph of Article 244, decisions adopted shall be immediately enforceable by customs authorities.

Article 8

1. A decision favourable to the person concerned shall be annulled if it was issued on the basis of incorrect or incomplete information and:

— the applicant knew or should reasonably have known that the information was incorrect or incomplete, and

— such decision could not have been taken on the basis of correct or complete information;

2. The persons to whom the decision was addressed shall be notified of its annulment.

3. Annulment shall take effect from the date on which the annulled decision was taken.

Article 9

1. A decision favourable to the person concerned shall be revoked or amended where, in cases other than those referred to in Article 8, one or more of the conditions laid down for its issue were not or are no longer fulfilled.

2. A decision favourable to the person concerned may be revoked where the person to whom it is addressed fails to fulfil an obligation imposed on him under that decision.

3. The person to whom the decision is addressed shall be notified of its revocation or amendment.

4. The revocation or amendment of the decision shall take effect from the date of notification. However, in exceptional cases where the legitimate interests of the person to whom the decision is addressed so require, the customs authorities may defer the date when revocation or amendment takes effect.

Article 10
(Annulment of decisions on grounds unconnected with customs legislation)

Articles 8 and 9 shall be without prejudice to national rules which stipulate that decisions are invalid or become null and void for reasons unconnected with customs legislation.

Section 3
Information

Article 11

1. Any person may request information concerning the application of customs legislation from the customs authorities.

Such a request may be refused where it does not relate to an import or export operation actually envisaged.

2. The information shall be supplied to the applicant free of charge. However, where special costs are incurred by the customs authorities, in particular as a result of analyses or expert reports on goods, or the return of the goods to the applicant, he may be charged the relevant amount.

Article 12

Note
Articles 20-26 are outside the scope of this work.

SECTION 4
Other provisions

Article 13

The customs authorities may, in accordance with the conditions laid down by the provisions in force, carry out all the controls they deem necessary to ensure that customs legislation is correctly applied.

Article 14

For the purposes of applying customs legislation, any person directly or indirectly involved in the operations concerned for the purposes of trade in goods shall provide the customs authorities with all the requisite documents and information, irrespective of the medium used, and all the requisite assistance at their request and by any time limit prescribed.

Article 15

All information which is by nature confidential or which is provided on a confidential basis shall be covered by the obligation of professional secrecy. It shall not be disclosed by the customs authorities without the express permission of the person or authority providing it; the communication of information shall be permitted where the customs authorities may be obliged or authorized to do so pursuant to the provisions in force, particularly in respect of data protection, or in connection with legal proceedings.

Article 16

The persons concerned shall keep the documents referred to in Article 14 for the purposes of control by the customs authorities, for the period laid down in the provisions in force and for at least three calendar years, irrespective of the medium used. That period shall run from the end of the year in which:

(*a*)   in the case of goods released for free circulation in circumstances other than those referred to in (*b*) or goods declared for export, from the end of the year in which the declarations for release for free circulation or export are accepted;

(*b*)   in the case of goods released for free circulation at a reduced or zero rate of import duty on account of their end-use, from the end of the year in which they cease to be subject to customs supervision;

(*c*)   in the case of goods placed under another customs procedure, from the end of the year in which the customs procedure concerned is completed;

(*d*)   in the case of goods placed in a free zone or free warehouse, from the end of the year on which they leave the undertaking concerned.

Without prejudice to the provisions of Article 221(3), second sentence, where a check carried out by the customs authorities in respect of a customs debt shows that the relevant entry in the accounts has to be corrected, the documents shall be kept beyond the time limit provided for in the first paragraph for a period sufficient to permit the correction to be made and checked.

Article 17

Where a period, date or time limit is laid down pursuant to customs legislation for the purpose of applying legislation, such period shall not be extended and such date or time limit shall not be deferred unless specific provision is made in the legislation concerned.

Article 18

1. The value of the ecu in national currencies to be applied within the framework of customs legislation shall be fixed once a year. The rates to be applied shall be those obtaining on the first working day of October, with effect from January 1 of the following calendar year. If a rate is not available for a particular national currency, the rate to be applied for that currency shall be that obtaining on the last day for which a rate was published in the *Official Journal of the European Communities*.

2. However, where a change in the bilateral central rate of one or more national currencies occurs:

(*a*) during a calendar year, the amended rates shall be used for converting the ecu into national currencies for the purposes of determining the tariff classification of goods and customs duties and charges having equivalent effect. They shall take effect from the 10th day after the date on which those rates are available;

(*b*) after the first working day of October, the amended rates shall be used for converting the ecu into national currencies for the purposes of determining the tariff classification of goods and customs duties and charges having equivalent effect and shall be applicable, by way of derogation from paragraph 1, throughout the following calendar year, except where a change in the bilateral central rate occurs during that period, in which case subparagraph (*a*) shall apply.

'Amended rates' means the rates obtaining on the first day after a change in the bilateral central rate, where such rates are available for all Community currencies.

Article 19

The procedure of the Committee shall be used to determine in which cases and under which conditions the application of customs legislation may be simplified.

TITLE II
Factors on the basis of which import duties or export duties and the other measures prescribed in respect of trade in goods are applied

Chapter 1
Customs Tariff of the European Communities and tariff classification of goods

Articles 20-26

Note
Articles 20-26 are outside the scope of this work.

SECTION 2
Preferential origin of goods

Article 27

The rules on preferential origin shall lay down the conditions governing acquisition of origin which goods must fulfil in order to benefit from the measures referred to in Article 20(3)(*d*) or (*e*).

Those rules shall:

(*a*) in the case of goods covered by the agreements referred to in Article 20(3)(*d*), be determined in those agreements;

(*b*) in the case of goods benefiting from the preferential tariff measures referred to in Article 20(3)(*e*), be determined in accordance with the Committee procedure.

CHAPTER 3
Value of goods for customs purposes

Article 28

The provisions of this Chapter shall determine the customs value for the purposes of applying the Customs Tariff of the European Communities and non-tariff measures laid down by Community provisions governing specific fields relating to trade in goods.

Article 29

1. The customs value of imported goods shall be the transaction value, that is, the price actually paid or payable for the goods when sold for export to the customs territory of the Community, adjusted, where necessary, in accordance with Articles 32 and 33, provided:

(*a*) that there are no restrictions as to the disposal or use of the goods by the buyer, other than restrictions which:

— are imposed or required by law or by the public authorities in the Community,

— limit the geographical area in which the goods may be resold,

or

— do not substantially affect the value of the goods;

(*b*) that the sale or price is not subject to some condition or consideration for which a value cannot be determined with respect to the goods being valued;

(*c*) that no part of the proceeds of any subsequent resale, disposal or use of the goods by the buyer will accrue directly or indirectly to the seller, unless an appropriate adjustment can be made in accordance with Article 32; and

(*d*) that the buyer and seller are not related, or, where the buyer and seller are related, that the transaction value is acceptable for customs purposes under paragraph 2.

2. (*a*) In determining whether the transaction value is acceptable for the purposes of paragraph 1, the fact that the buyer and the seller are related shall not in itself be sufficient grounds for regarding the transaction value as unacceptable. Where necessary, the circumstances surrounding the sale shall be examined and the transaction value shall be accepted provided that the relationship did not influence the price. If, in the light of information provided by the declarant or otherwise, the customs authorities have grounds for considering that the relationship influenced the price, they shall communicate their grounds to the declarant and he shall be given a reasonable opportunity to respond. If the declarant so requests, the communication of the grounds shall be in writing.

(*b*) In a sale between related persons, the transaction value shall be accepted and the goods valued in accordance with paragraph 1 wherever the declarant demonstrates that such value closely approximates to one of the following occurring at or about the same time:

(i) the transaction value in sales, between buyers and sellers who are not related in any particular case, of identical or similar goods for export to the Community;

(ii) the customs value of identical or similar goods, as determined under Article 30(2)(*c*);

(iii) the customs value of identical or similar goods, as determined under Article 30(2)(*d*).

In applying the foregoing tests, due account shall be taken of demonstrated differences in commercial levels, quantity levels, the elements enumerated in Article 32 and costs incurred by the seller in sales in which he and the buyer are not related and where such costs are not incurred by the seller in sales in which he and the buyer are related.

(c)   The tests set forth in subparagraph (*b*) are to be used at the initiative of the declarant and only for comparison purposes. Substitute values may not be established under the said subparagraph.

3.   (a)   The price actually paid or payable is the total payment made or to be made by the buyer to or for the benefit of the seller for the imported goods and includes all payments made or to be made as a condition of sale of the imported goods by the buyer to the seller or by the buyer to a third party to satisfy an obligation of the seller. The payment need not necessarily take the form of a transfer of money. Payment may be made by way of letters of credit or negotiable instruments and may be made directly or indirectly.

(b)   Activities, including marketing activities, undertaken by the buyer on his own account, other than those for which an adjustment is provided in Article 32, are not considered to be an indirect payment to the seller, even though they might be regarded as of benefit to the seller or have been undertaken by agreement with the seller, and their cost shall not be added to the price actually paid or payable in determining the customs value of imported goods.

Article 30

1. Where the customs value cannot be determined under Article 29, it is to be determined by proceeding sequentially through subparagraphs (*a*), (*b*), (*c*) and (*d*) of paragraph 2 to the first subparagraph under which it can be determined, subject to the proviso that the order of application of subparagraphs (*c*) and (*d*) shall be reversed if the declarant so requests; it is only when such value cannot be determined under a particular subparagraph that the provisions of the next subparagraph in a sequence established by virtue of this paragraph can be applied.

2. The customs value as determined under this Article shall be:

(a)   the transaction value of identical goods sold for export to the Community and exported at or about the same time as the goods being valued;

(b)   the transaction value of similar goods sold for export to the Community and exported at or about the same time as the goods being valued;

(c)   the value based on the unit price at which the imported goods or identical or similar imported goods are sold within the Community in the greatest aggregate quantity to persons not related to the sellers;

(d)   the computed value, consisting of the sum of:

— the cost or value of materials and fabrication or other processing employed in producing the imported goods,

— an amount for profit and general expenses equal to that usually reflected in sales of goods of the same class or kind as the goods being valued which are made by producers in the country of exportation for export to the Community,

— the cost or value of the items referred to in Article 32(1)(*e*).

3. Any further conditions and rules for the application of paragraph 2 above shall be determined in accordance with the committee procedure.

Article 31

1. Where the customs value of imported goods cannot be determined under Articles 29 or 30, it shall be determined, on the basis of data available in the Community, using reasonable means consistent with the principles and general provisions of:

—   the agreement on implementation of Article VII of the General Agreement on Tariffs and Trade,

—   Article VII of the General Agreement on Tariffs and Trade,

—   the provisions of this Chapter.

2. No customs value shall be determined under paragraph 1 on the basis of:

    (*a*)   the selling price in the Community of goods produced in the Community;

    (*b*)   a system which provides for the acceptance for customs purposes of the higher of two alternative values;

    (*c*)   the price of goods on the domestic market of the country of exportation;

    (*d*)   the cost of production, other than computed values which have been determined for identical or similar goods in accordance with Article 30(2)(*d*);

    (*e*)   prices for export to a country not forming part of the customs territory of the Community;

    (*f*)   minimum customs values; or

    (*g*)   arbitrary or fictitious values.

Article 32

1. In determining the custom's value under Article 29, there shall be added to the price actually paid or payable for the imported goods:

    (*a*)   the following, to the extent that they are incurred by the buyer but are not included in the price actually paid or payable for the goods:

        (i)   commissions and brokerage, except buying commissions,

        (ii)   the cost of containers which are treated as being one, for customs purposes, with the goods in question,

        (iii)   the cost of packing, whether for labour or materials;

    (*b*)   the value, apportioned as appropriate, of the following goods and services where supplied directly or indirectly by the buyer free of charge or at reduced cost for use in connection with the production and sale for export of the imported goods, to the extent that such value has not been included in the price actually paid or payable:

        (i)   materials, components, parts and similar items incorporated in the imported goods,

        (ii)   tools, dies, moulds and similar items used in the production of the imported goods,

        (iii)   materials consumed in the production of the imported goods,

        (iv)   engineering, development, artwork, design work, and plans and sketches undertaken elsewhere than in the Community and necessary for the production of the imported goods;

    (*c*)   royalties and licence fees related to the goods being valued that the buyer must pay, either directly or indirectly, as a condition of sale of the goods being valued, to the extent that such royalties and fees are not included in the price actually paid or payable;

    (*d*)   the value of any part of the proceeds of any subsequent resale, disposal or use of the imported goods that accrues directly or indirectly to the seller;

    (*e*)   (i)the cost of transport and insurance of the imported goods, and

        (ii)   loading and handling charges associated with the transport of the imported goods

to the place of introduction into the customs territory of the Community.

2. Additions to the price actually paid or payable shall be made under this Article only on the basis of objective and quantifiable data.

3. No additions shall be made to the price actually paid or payable in determining the customs value except as provided in this Article.

4. In this Article, the term **'buying commissions'** means fees paid by an importer to his agent for the service of representing him in the purchase of the goods being valued.

5. Notwithstanding paragraph 1(*c*):

    (*a*)   charges for the right to reproduce the imported goods in the Community shall not be added to the price actually paid or payable for the imported goods in determining the customs value; and

    (*b*)   payments made by the buyer for the right to distribute or resell the imported goods shall not be added to the price actually paid or payable for the imported goods if such payments are not a condition of the sale for export to the Community of the goods.

Article 33

1. Provided that they are shown separately from the price actually paid or payable, the following shall not be included in the customs value:

    (*a*)   charges for the transport of goods after their arrival at the point of introduction into the customs territory of the Community;

    (*b*)   charges for construction, erection, assembly, maintenance or technical assistance, undertaken after importation on imported goods such as industrial plant, machinery or equipment;

    (*c*)   charges for interest under a financing arrangement entered into by the buyer and relating to the purchase of imported goods, irrespective of whether the finance is provided by the seller or another person, provided that the financing arrangement has been made in writing and where required, the buyer can demonstrate that:

        —   such goods are actually sold at the price declared as the price actually paid or payable, and

        —   the claimed rate of interest does not exceed the level for such transactions prevailing in the country where, and at the time when, the finance was provided;

    (*d*)   charges for the right to reproduce imported goods in the Community;

    (*e*)   buying commissions;

    (*f*)   import duties or other charges payable in the Community by reason of the importation or sale of the goods.

Article 34

Specific rules may be laid down in accordance with the procedure of the committee to determine the customs value of carrier media for use in data processing equipment and bearing data or instructions.

Article 35

Where factors used to determine the customs value of goods are expressed in a currency other than that of the Member State where the valuation is made, the rate of exchange to be used shall be that duly published by the competent authorities of the Member State concerned.

Such rate shall reflect as effectively as possible the current value of such currency in commercial transactions in terms of the currency of such Member State and shall apply during such period as may be determined in accordance with the procedure of the committee.

Where such a rate does not exist, the rate of exchange to be used shall be determined in accordance with the procedure of the committee.

Article 36

1. The provisions of this chapter shall be without prejudice to the specific provisions regarding the determination of the value for customs purposes of goods released for free circulation after being assigned a different customs-approved treatment or use.

2. By way of derogation from Articles 29, 30 and 31, the customs value of perishable goods usually delivered on consignment may, at the request of the declarant, be determined under simplified rules drawn up for the whole Community in accordance with the committee procedure.

TITLE III
Provisions applicable to goods brought into the customs territory of the Community until they are assigned a customs-approved treatment or use

CHAPTER 1
Entry of goods into the customs territory of the Community

Article 37

1. Goods brought into the customs territory of the Community shall, from the time of their entry, be subject to customs supervision. They may also be subject to control by the customs authority in accordance with the provisions in force

2. They shall remain under such supervision for as long as necessary to determine their customs status, if appropriate, and in the case of non-Community goods and without prejudice to Article 82(1), until their customs status is changed, they enter a free zone or free warehouse or they are re-exported or destroyed in accordance with Article 182.

Article 38

1. Goods brought into the customs territory of the Community shall be conveyed by the person bringing them into the Community without delay, by the route specified by the customs authorities and in accordance with their instructions, if any:

    (*a*)   to the customs office designated by the customs authorities or to any other place specified or approved by those authorities; or,

    (*b*)   to a free zone, if the goods are to be brought into that free zone direct:

        —   by sea or air, or

        —   by land without passing through another part of the customs territory of the Community, where the free zone adjoins the land frontier between a Member State and a third country.

2. Any person who assumes responsibility for the carriage of goods after they have been brought into the customs territory of the Community, *inter alia* as a result of transhipment, shall become responsible for compliance with the obligation laid down in paragraph 1.

3. Goods which, although still outside the customs territory of the Community, may be subject to the control of the customs authority of a Member State under the provisions in force, as a result of *inter alia* an agreement concluded between that Member State and a third country, shall be treated in the same way as goods brought into the customs territory of the Community.

4. Paragraph 1(*a*) shall not preclude implementation of any provisions in force with respect to tourist traffic, frontier traffic, postal traffic or traffic of negligible economic importance, on condition that customs supervision and customs control possibilities are not thereby jeopardized.

5. Paragraphs 1 to 4 and Articles 39 to 53 shall not apply to goods which have temporarily left the customs territory of the Community while moving between two points in that territory by sea or air, provided that carriage has been effected by a direct route and by regular air service or shipping line without a stop outside Community customs territory.

This provision shall not apply to goods loaded in third country ports or airports or at free ports.

6. Paragraph 1 shall not apply to goods on board vessels or aircraft crossing the territorial sea or airspace of the Member States without having as their destination a port or airport situated in those Member States.

Article 39

1. Where, by reason of unforeseeable circumstances or *force majeure*, the obligation laid down in Article 38(1) cannot be complied with, the person bound by that obligation or any other person acting in his place shall inform the customs authorities of the situation without delay. Where the unforeseeable circumstances or *force majeure* do not result in total loss of the goods, the customs authorities shall also be informed of their precise location.

2. Where, by reason of unforeseeable circumstances or *force majeure*, a vessel or aircraft covered by Article 38(6) is forced to put into port or land temporarily in the customs territory of the Community and the obligation laid down in Article 38(1) cannot be complied with, the person bringing the vessel or aircraft into the customs territory of the Community or any other person acting in his place shall inform the customs authorities of the situation without delay.

3. The customs authorities shall determine the measures to be taken in order to permit customs supervision of the goods referred to in paragraph 1 as well as those on board a vessel or aircraft in the circumstances specified in paragraph 2 and to ensure, where appropriate, that they are subsequently conveyed to a customs office or other place designated or approved by the authorities.

CHAPTER 2
Presentation of goods to customs

Article 40

Goods which, pursuant to Article 38(1)(*a*), arrive at the customs office or other place designated or approved by the customs authorities shall be presented to customs by the person who brought the goods into the customs territory of the Community or, if appropriate, by the person who assumes responsibility for carriage of the goods following such entry.

Article 41

Article 40 shall not preclude the implementation of rules in force relating to goods:

(*a*) carried by travellers;

(*b*) placed under a customs procedure but not presented to customs.

Article 42

Goods may, once they have been presented to customs, and with the permission of the customs authorities, be examined or samples may be taken, in order that they may be assigned a customs-approved treatment or use. Such permission shall be granted, on request, to the person authorized to assign the goods such treatment or use.

CHAPTER 3
Summary declaration and unloading of goods presented to customs

Article 43

Subject to Article 45, goods presented to customs within the meaning of Article 40 shall be covered by a summary declaration.

The summary declaration shall be lodged once the goods have been presented to customs. The customs authorities may, however, allow a period for lodging the declaration which shall not extend beyond the first working day following the day on which the goods are presented to customs.

Article 44

1. The summary declaration shall be made on a form corresponding to the model prescribed by the customs authorities. However, the customs authorities may permit the use, as a summary declaration, of any commercial or official document which contains the particulars necessary for identification of the goods.

2. The summary declaration shall be lodged by:

> (*a*)   the person who brought the goods into the customs territory of the Community or by any person who assumes responsibility for carriage of the goods following such entry, or
>
> (*b*)   the person in whose name the persons referred to in subparagraph (*a*) acted.

Article 45

Without prejudice to the provisions governing goods imported by travellers and consignments by letter and parcel post, the customs authorities may waive the lodging of a summary declaration on condition that this does not jeopardize customs supervision of the goods, where, prior to the expiry of the period referred to in Article 43, the formalities necessary for the goods to be assigned a customs-approved treatment or use are carried out.

Article 46

1. Goods shall be unloaded or transhipped from the means of transport carrying them solely with the permission of the customs authorities in places designated or approved by those customs authorities.

However, such permission shall not be required in the event of the imminent danger necessitating the immediate unloading of all or part of the goods. In that case, the customs authorities shall be informed accordingly forthwith.

2. For the purpose of inspecting goods and the means of transport carrying them, the customs authorities may at any time require goods to be unloaded and unpacked.

Article 47

Goods shall not be removed from their original position without the permission of the customs authorities.

CHAPTER 4
Obligation to assign goods presented to customs a customs-approved treatment or use

Articles 48-57

Note

Articles 48-57 are outside the scope of this work.

TITIE IV
Customs-approved treatment or use

CHAPTER 1
General

Article 58

1. Save as otherwise provided, goods may at any time, under the conditions laid down, be assigned any customs-approved treatment or use irrespective of their nature or quantity, or their country of origin, consignment or destination.

2. Paragraph 1 shall not preclude the imposition of prohibitions or restrictions justified on grounds of public morality, public policy or public security, the protection of health and life of humans, animals or plants, the protection of national treasures possessing artistic, historic or archaeological value or the protection of industrial and commercial property.

CHAPTER 2
Customs procedures

SECTION 1
Placing of goods under a customs procedure

Article 59

1. All goods intended to be placed under a customs procedure shall be covered by a declaration for that customs procedure.

2. Community goods declared for an export, outward processing, transit or customs warehousing procedure shall be subject to customs supervision from the time of acceptance of the customs declaration until such time as they leave the customs territory of the Community or are destroyed or the customs declaration is invalidated.

Article 60

Insofar as Community customs legislation lays down no rules on the matter, Member States shall determine the competence of the various customs offices situated in their territory, account being taken, where applicable, of the nature of the goods and the customs procedure under which they are to be placed.

Article 61

The customs declaration shall be made:

- (*a*) in writing; or
- (*b*) using a data-processing technique where provided for by provisions laid down in accordance with the committee procedure or where authorized by the customs authorities; or
- (*c*) by means of an oral declaration or any other act whereby the holder of the goods expresses his wish to place them under a customs procedure, where such a possibility is provided for by the rules adopted in accordance with the committee procedure.

A. Declarations in writing

I. Normal procedure

Article 62

1. Declarations in writing shall be made on a form corresponding to the official specimen prescribed for that purpose. They shall be signed and contain all the particulars necessary for implementation of the provisions governing the customs procedure for which the goods are declared.

2. The declaration shall be accompanied by all the documents required for implementation of the provisions governing the customs procedure for which the goods are declared.

Article 63

Declarations which comply with the conditions laid down in Article 62 shall be accepted by the customs authorities immediately, provided that the goods to which they refer are presented to customs.

Article 64

1. Subject to Article 5, a customs declaration may be made by any person who is able to present the goods in question or to have them presented to the competent customs authority, together with all the documents which are required to be produced for the application of the rules governing the customs procedure in respect of which the goods were declared.

2. However,

- (*a*) where acceptance of a customs declaration imposes particular obligations on a specific person, the declaration must be made by that person or on his behalf;

- (*b*) the declarant must be established in the Community.

    However, the condition regarding establishment in the Community shall not apply to persons who:

    — make a declaration for Community transit or temporary importation;

    — declare goods on an occasional basis, provided that the customs authorities consider this to be justified.

3. Paragraph 2(*b*) shall not preclude the application by the Member States of bilateral agreements concluded with third countries, or customary practices having similar effect, under which nationals of such countries may make customs declarations in the territory of the Member States in question, subject to reciprocity.

Article 65

The declarant shall, at his request, be authorized to amend one or more of the particulars of the declaration after it has been accepted by customs. The amendment shall not have the effect of rendering the declaration applicable to goods other than those it originally covered.

However, no amendment shall be permitted where authorization is requested after the customs authorities:

- (*a*) have informed the declarant that they intend to examine the goods; or,

- (*b*) have established that the particulars in question are incorrect; or,

- (*c*) have released the goods.

Article 66

1. The customs authorities shall, at the request of the declarant, invalidate a declaration already accepted where the declarant furnishes proof that goods were declared in error for the customs procedure covered by that declaration or that, as a result of special circumstances, the placing of the goods under the customs procedure for which they were declared is no longer justified.

Nevertheless, where the customs authorities have informed the declarant of their intention to examine the goods, a request for invalidation of the declaration shall not be accepted until after the examination has taken place.

2. The declaration shall not be invalidated after the goods have been released, except in cases defined in accordance with the committee procedure.

3. Invalidation of the declaration shall be without prejudice to the application of the penal provisions in force.

Article 67

Save as otherwise expressly provided, the date to be used for the purposes of all the provisions governing the customs procedure for which the goods are declared shall be the date of acceptance of the declaration by the customs authorities.

Article 68

For the verification of declarations which they have accepted, the customs authorities may:

(*a*) examine the documents covering the declaration and the documents accompanying it. The customs authorities may require the declarant to present other documents for the purpose of verifying the accuracy of the particulars contained in the declaration;

(*b*) examine the goods and take samples for analysis or for detailed examination.

Article 69

1. Transport of the goods to the places where they are to be examined and samples are to be taken, and all the handling necessitated by such examination or taking of samples, shall be carried out by or under the responsibility of the declarant. The costs incurred shall be borne by the declarant.

2. The declarant shall be entitled to be present when the goods are examined and when samples are taken. Where they deem it appropriate, the customs authorities shall require the declarant to be present or represented when the goods are examined or samples are taken in order to provide them with the assistance necessary to facilitate such examination or taking of samples.

3. Provided that samples are taken in accordance with the provisions in force, the customs authorities shall not be liable for payment of any compensation in respect thereof but shall bear the costs of their analysis or examination.

Article 70

1. Where only part of the goods covered by a declaration are examined, the results of the partial examination shall be taken to apply to all the goods covered by that declaration.

However, the declarant may request a further examination of the goods if he considers that the results of the partial examination are not valid as regards the remainder of the goods declared.

2. For the purposes of paragraph 1, where a declaration form covers two or more items, the particulars relating to each item shall be deemed to constitute a separate declaration.

Article 71

1. The results of verifying the declaration shall be used for the purposes of applying the provisions governing the customs procedure under which the goods are placed.

2. Where the declaration is not verified, the provisions referred to in paragraph 1 shall be applied on the basis of the particulars contained in the declaration.

Article 72

1. The customs authorities shall take the measures necessary to identify the goods where identification is required in order to ensure compliance with the conditions governing the customs procedure for which the said goods have been declared.

2. Means of identification affixed to the goods or means of transport shall be removed or destroyed only by the customs authorities or with their permission unless, as a result of unforeseeable circumstances or *force majeure*, their removal or destruction is essential to ensure the protection of the goods or means of transport.

Article 73

1. Without prejudice to Article 74, where the conditions for placing the goods under the procedure in question are fulfilled and provided the goods are not subject to any prohibitive or restrictive measures, the customs authorities shall release the goods as soon as the particulars in the declaration have been verified or accepted without verification. The same shall apply where such verification cannot be completed within a reasonable period of time and the goods are no longer required to be present for verification purposes.

2. All the goods covered by the same declaration shall be released at the same time.

For the purposes of this paragraph, where a declaration form covers two or more items, the particulars relating to each item shall be deemed to constitute a separate declaration.

Article 74

1. Where acceptance of a customs declaration gives rise to a customs debt, the goods covered by the declaration shall not be released unless the customs debt has been paid or secured. However, without prejudice to paragraph 2, this provision shall not apply to the temporary importation procedure with partial relief from import duties.

2. Where, pursuant to the provisions governing the customs procedure for which the goods are declared, the customs authorities require the provision of a security, the said goods shall not be released for the customs procedure in question until such security is provided.

Article 75

Any necessary measures, including confiscation and sale, shall be taken to deal with goods which:

(*a*) cannot be released because:

— it has not been possible to undertake or continue examination of the goods within the period prescribed by the customs authorities for reasons attributable to the declarant; or,

— the documents which must be produced before the goods can be placed under the customs procedure requested have not been produced; or,

— payments or security which should have been made or provided in respect of import duties or export duties, as the case may be, have not been made or provided within the period prescribed; or

— they are subject to bans or restrictions;

(*b*) are not removed within a reasonable period after their release.

II. Simplified procedures

Article 76

1. In order to simplify completion of formalities and procedures as far as possible while ensuring that operations are conducted in a proper manner, the customs authorities shall, under conditions laid down in accordance with the committee procedure, grant permission for:

(*a*) the declaration referred to in Article 62 to omit certain of the particulars referred to in paragraph 1 of that Article for some of the documents referred to in paragraph 2 of that Article not to be attached thereto;

(*b*) a commercial or administrative document, accompanied by a request for the goods to be placed under the customs procedure in question, to be lodged in place of the declaration referred to in Article 62;

(*c*) the goods to be entered for the procedure in question by means of an entry in the records; in this case, the customs authorities may waive the requirement that the declarant present the goods to customs.

The simplified declaration, commercial or administrative document or entry in the records must contain at least the particulars necessary for identification of the goods. Where the goods are entered in the records, the date of such entry must be included.

2. Except in cases to be determined in accordance with the committee procedure, the declarant shall furnish a supplementary declaration which may be of a general, periodic or recapitulative nature.

3. Supplementary declarations and the simplified declarations referred to in subparagraphs 1(*a*), (*b*) and (*c*), shall be deemed to constitute a single, indivisible instrument taking effect on the date of acceptance of the simplified declarations; in the cases referred to in subparagraph 1(*c*), entry in the records shall have the same legal force as acceptance of the declaration referred to in Article 62.

4. Special simplified procedures for the Community transit procedure shall be laid down in accordance with the committee procedure.

B. Other declarations

Article 77

Where the customs declaration is made by means of a data-processing technique within the meaning of Article 61(*b*), or by an oral declaration or any other act within the meaning of Article 61(*c*), Articles 62 to 76 shall apply *mutatis mutandis* without prejudice to the principles set out therein.

C. Post-clearance examination of declarations

Article 78

1. The customs authorities may, on their own initiative or at the request of the declarant, amend the declaration after release of the goods.

2. The customs authorities may, after releasing the goods and in order to satisfy themselves as to the accuracy of the particulars contained in the declaration, inspect the commercial documents and data relating to the import or export operations in respect of the goods concerned or to subsequent commercial operations involving those goods. Such inspections may be carried out at the premises of the declarant, of any other person directly or indirectly involved in the said operations in a business capacity or of any other person in possession of the said documents and data for business purposes. Those authorities may also examine the goods where it is still possible for them to be produced.

3. Where revision of the declaration or post-clearance examination indicates that the provisions governing the customs procedure concerned have been applied on the basis of incorrect or incomplete information, the customs authorities shall, in accordance with any provisions laid down, take the measures necessary to regularize the situation, taking account of the new information available to them.

SECTION 2
Release for free circulation

Article 79

Release for free circulation shall confer on non-Community goods the customs status of Community goods.

It shall entail application of commercial policy measures, completion of the other formalities laid down in respect of the importation of goods and the charging of any duties legally due.

Article 80

1. By way of derogation from Article 67, provided that the import duty chargeable on the goods is one of the duties referred to in the first indent of Article 4(10) and that the rate of duty is reduced after the date of acceptance of the declaration for release for free circulation but before the goods are released, the declarant may request application of the more favourable rate.

2. Paragraph 1 shall not apply where it has not been possible to release the goods for reasons attributable to the declarant alone.

Article 81

Where a consignment is made up of goods falling within different tariff classifications, and dealing with each of those goods in accordance with its tariff classification for the purpose of drawing up the declaration would entail a burden of work and expense disproportionate to the import duties chargeable, the customs authorities may, at the request of the declarant, agree that import duties be charged on the whole consignment on the basis of the tariff classification of the goods which are subject to the highest rate of import duty.

Article 82

1. Where goods are released for free circulation at a reduced or zero rate of duty on account of their end-use, they shall remain under customs supervision. Customs supervision shall end when the conditions laid down for granting such a reduced or zero rate of duty cease to apply, where the goods are exported or destroyed or where the use of the goods for purposes other than those laid down for the application of the reduced or zero rate of duty is permitted subject to payment of the duties due.

2. Articles 88 and 90 shall apply *mutatis mutandis* to the goods referred to in paragraph 1.

Article 83

Goods released for free circulation shall lose their customs status as Community goods where:

(a)   the declaration for release for free circulation is invalidated after release in accordance with Article 66, or

(b)   the imported duties payable on those goods are repaid or remitted:

— under the inward processing procedure in the form of the drawback system;

or

— in respect of defective goods or goods which fail to comply with the terms of the contract, pursuant to Article 238; or

— in situations of the type referred to in Article 239 where repayment or remission is conditional upon the goods being re-exported or being assigned an equivalent customs-approved treatment or use.

SECTION 3
Suspensive arrangements and customs procedures with economic impact

A. Provisions common to several procedures

Article 84

1. In Articles 85 to 90:

(a)   where the term **'procedure'** is used, it is understood as applying, in the case of non-Community goods, to the following arrangements:

— external transit;

— customs warehousing;

— inward processing in the form of a system of suspension;

— processing under customs control;

— temporary importation;

(b)   where the term **'customs procedure with economic impact'** is used, it is understood as applying to the following arrangements:

— customs warehousing;

— inward processing;

— processing under customs control;

— temporary importation;

— outward processing.

2. **'Import goods'** means goods placed under a suspensive arrangement and goods which, under the inward processing procedure in the form of the drawback system, have undergone the formalities for release for free circulation and the formalities provided for in Article 125.

3. 'Goods in the unaltered state' means import goods which, under the inward processing procedure or the procedures for processing under customs control, have undergone no form of processing.

Article 85

The use of any customs procedure with economic impact shall be conditional upon authorization being issued by the customs authorities.

Article 86

Without prejudice to the additional special conditions governing the procedure in question, the authorization referred to in Article 85 and that referred to in Article 100(1) shall be granted only:

— to persons who offer every guarantee necessary for the proper conduct of the operations;

— where the customs authorities can supervise and monitor the procedure without having to introduce administrative arrangements disproportionate to the economic needs involved.

Article 87

1. The conditions under which the procedure in question is used shall be set out in the authorization.

2. The holder of the authorization shall notify the customs authorities of all factors arising after the authorization was granted which may influence its continuation or content.

Article 88

The customs authorities may make the placing of goods under a suspensive arrangement conditional upon the provision of security in order to ensure that any customs debt which may be incurred in respect of those goods will be paid.

Special provisions concerning the provision of security may be laid down in the context of a specific suspensive arrangement.

Article 89

1. A suspensive arrangement with economic impact shall be discharged when a new customs-approved treatment or use is assigned either to the goods placed under that arrangement or to compensating or processed products placed under it.

2. The customs authorities shall take all the measures necessary to regularize the position of goods in respect of which a procedure has not been discharged under the conditions prescribed.

Article 90

The rights and obligations of the holder of a customs procedure with economic impact may, on the conditions laid down by the customs authorities, be transferred successively to other persons who fulfil any conditions laid down in order to benefit from the procedure in question.

B. External transit

I. General provisions

Articles 91-200

Note
Articles 91-200 are outside the scope of this work.

CHAPTER 2
Incurrence of a customs debt

Article 201

1. A customs debt on importation shall be incurred through:

    (*a*)   the release for free circulation of goods liable to import duties, or

    (*b*)   the placing of such goods under the temporary importation procedure with partial relief from import duties.

2. A customs debt shall be incurred at the time of acceptance of the customs declaration in question.

3. The debtor shall be the declarant. In the event of indirect representation, the person on whose behalf the customs declaration is made shall also be a debtor.

Where a customs declaration in respect of one of the procedures referred to in paragraph 1 is drawn up on the basis of information which leads to all or part of the duties legally owed not being collected, the persons who provided the information required to draw up the declaration and who knew, or who ought reasonably to have known that such information was false, may also be considered debtors in accordance with the national provisions in force.

Article 202

1. A customs debt on importation shall be incurred through:

    (*a*)   the unlawful introduction into the customs territory of the Community of goods liable to import duties, or

    (*b*)   the unlawful introduction into another part of that territory of such goods located in a free zone or free warehouse.

For the purpose of this Article, unlawful introduction means any introduction in violation of the provisions of Articles 38 to 41 and the second indent of Article 177.

2. The customs debt shall be incurred at the moment when the goods are unlawfully introduced.

3. The debtors shall be:

—   the person who introduced such goods unlawfully,

—   any persons who participated in the unlawful introduction of the goods and who were aware or should reasonably have been aware that such introduction was unlawful, and

—   any persons who acquired or held the goods in question and who were aware or should reasonably have been aware at the time of acquiring or receiving the goods that they had been introduced unlawfully.

Article 203

1. A customs debt on importation shall be incurred through:

—   the unlawful removal from customs supervision of goods liable to import duties.

2. The customs debt shall be incurred at the moment when the goods are removed from customs supervision.

3. The debtors shall be:

—   the person who removed the goods from customs supervision,

—   any persons who participated in such removal and who were aware or should reasonably have been aware that the goods were being removed from customs supervision,

— any persons who acquired or held the goods in question and who were aware or should reasonably have been aware at the time of acquiring or receiving the goods that they had been removed from customs supervision, and

— where appropriate, the person required to fulfil the obligations arising from temporary storage of the goods or from the use of the customs procedure under which those goods are placed.

Article 204

1. A customs debt on importation shall be incurred through:

(*a*) non-fulfilment of one of the obligations arising, in respect of goods liable to import duties, from their temporary storage or from the use of the customs procedure under which they are placed, or

(*b*) non-compliance with a condition governing the placing of the goods under that procedure or the granting of a reduced or zero rate of import duty by virtue of the end-use of the goods,

in cases other than those referred to in Article 203 unless it is established that those failures have no significant effect on the correct operation of the temporary storage or customs procedure in question.

2. The customs debt shall be incurred either at the moment when the obligation whose non-fulfilment gives rise to the customs debt ceases to be met or at the moment when the goods are placed under the customs procedure concerned where it is established subsequently that a condition governing the placing of the goods under the said procedure or the granting of a reduced or zero rate of import duty by virtue of the end-use of the goods was not in fact fulfilled.

3. The debtor shall be the person who is required, according to the circumstances, either to fulfil the obligations arising, in respect of goods liable to import duties, from their temporary storage or from the use of the customs procedure under which they have been placed, or to comply with the conditions governing the placing of the goods under that procedure.

Article 205

1. A customs debt on importation shall be incurred through:

— the consumption or use, in a free zone or a free warehouse, of goods liable to import duties, under conditions other than those laid down by the legislation in force.

Where goods disappear and where their disappearance cannot be explained to the satisfaction of the customs authorities, those authorities may regard the goods as having been consumed or used in the free zone or the free warehouse.

2. The debt shall be incurred at the moment when the goods are consumed or are first used under conditions other than those laid down by the legislation in force.

3. The debtor shall be the person who consumed or used the goods and any persons who participated in such consumption or use and who were aware or should reasonably have been aware that the goods were being consumed or used under conditions other than those laid down by the legislation in force.

Where customs authorities regard goods which have disappeared as having been consumed or used in the free zone or the free warehouse and it is not possible to apply the preceding paragraph, the person liable for payment of the customs debt shall be the last person known to these authorities to have been in possession of the goods.

Article 206

1. By way of derogation from Articles 202 and 204(1)(*a*), no customs debt on importation shall be deemed to be incurred in respect of specific goods where the person concerned proves that the non-fulfilment of the obligations which arise from:

— the provisions of Articles 38 to 41 and the second indent of Article 177, or

— keeping the goods in question in temporary storage, or

— the use of the customs procedure under which the goods have been placed,

results from the total destruction or irretrievable loss of the said goods as a result of the actual nature of the goods or unforeseeable circumstances or *force majeure*, or as a consequence of authorization by the customs authorities.

For the purposes of this paragraph, goods shall be irretrievably lost when they are rendered unusable by any person.

2. Nor shall a customs debt on importation be deemed to be incurred in respect of goods released for free circulation at a reduced or zero rate of import duty by virtue of their end-use, where such goods are exported or re-exported with the permission of the customs authorities.

Article 207

Where, in accordance with Article 206(1), no customs debt is deemed to be incurred in respect of goods released for free circulation at a reduced or zero rate of import duty on account of their end-use, any scrap or waste resulting from such destruction shall be deemed to be non-Community goods.

Article 208

Where in accordance with Article 203 or 204 a customs debt is incurred in respect of goods released for free circulation at a reduced rate of import duty on account of their end-use, the amount paid when the goods were released for free circulation shall be deducted from the amount of the customs debt.

This provision shall apply *mutatis mutandis* where a customs debt is incurred in respect of scrap and waste resulting from the destruction of such goods.

Article 209

1. A customs debt on exportation shall be incurred through:

— the exportation from the customs territory of the Community, under cover of a customs declaration, of goods liable to export duties.

2. The customs debt shall be incurred at the time when such customs declaration is accepted.

3. The debtor shall be the declarant. In the event of indirect representation, the person on whose behalf the declaration is made shall also be a debtor.

Article 210

1. A customs debt on exportation shall be incurred through:

— the removal from the customs territory of the Community of goods liable to export duties without a customs declaration.

2. The customs debt shall be incurred at the time when the said goods actually leave that territory.

3. The debtor shall be:

— the person who removed the goods, and

— any persons who participated in such removal and who were aware or should reasonably have been aware that a customs declaration had not been but should have been lodged.

Article 211

1. A customs debt on exportation shall be incurred through:

— failure to comply with the conditions under which the goods were allowed to leave the customs territory of the Community with total or partial relief from export duties.

2. The debt shall be incurred at the time when the goods reach a destination other than that for which they were allowed to leave the customs territory of the Community with total or partial relief from export duties or, should the customs authorities be unable to determine that time, the expiry of the time limit set for the production of evidence that the conditions entitling the goods to such relief have been fulfilled.

3. The debtor shall be the declarant. In the event of indirect representation, the person on whose behalf the declaration is made shall also be a debtor.

Article 212

The customs debt referred to in Articles 201 to 205 and 209 to 211 shall be incurred even if it relates to goods subject to measures of prohibition or restriction on importation or exportation of any kind whatsoever. However, no customs debt shall be incurred on the unlawful introduction into the customs territory of the Community of counterfeit currency or of narcotic drugs and psychotropic substances which do not enter into the economic circuit strictly supervised by the competent authorities with a view to their use for medical and scientific purposes. For the purposes of criminal law as applicable to customs offences, the customs debt shall nevertheless be deemed to have been incurred where, under a Member State's criminal law, customs duties provide the basis for determining penalties, or the existence of a customs debt is grounds for taking criminal proceedings.

Article 213

Where several persons are liable for payment of one customs debt, they shall be jointly and severally liable for such debt.

Article 214

1. Save as otherwise expressly provided by this Code and without prejudice to paragraph 2, the amount of the import duty or export duty applicable to goods shall be determined on the basis of the rules of assessment appropriate to those goods at the time when the customs debt in respect of them is incurred.

2. Where it is not possible to determine precisely when the customs debt is incurred, the time to be taken into account in determining the rules of assessment appropriate to the goods concerned shall be the time when the customs authorities conclude that the goods are in a situation in which a customs debt is incurred.

However, where the information available to the customs authorities enables them to establish that the customs debt was incurred prior to the time when they reached that conclusion, the amount of the import duty or export duty payable on the goods in question shall be determined on the basis of the rules of assessment appropriate to the goods at the earliest time when existence of the customs debt arising from the situation may be established from the information available.

3. Compensatory interest shall be applied, in the circumstances and under the conditions to be defined in the provisions adopted under the committee procedure, in order to prevent the wrongful acquisition of a financial advantage through deferment of the date on which the customs debt was incurred or entered in the accounts.

Article 215

1. A customs debt shall be incurred at the place where the events from which it arises occur.

2. Where it is not possible to determine the place referred to in paragraph 1, the customs debt shall be deemed to have been incurred at the place where the customs authorities conclude that the goods are in a situation in which a customs debt is incurred.

3. Where a customs procedure is not discharged for goods, the customs debt shall be deemed to have been incurred at the place where the goods:

—   were placed under that procedure, or

—   enter the Community under that procedure.

4. Where the information available to the customs authorities enables them to establish that the customs debt was already incurred when the goods were in another place at an earlier date, the customs debt shall be deemed to have been incurred at the place which may be established as the location of the goods at the earliest time when existence of the customs debt may be established.

Article 216

1. In so far as agreements concluded between the Community and certain third countries provide for the granting on importation into those countries of preferential tariff treatment for goods originating in the Community within the meaning of such agreements, on condition that, where they have been obtained under the inward processing procedure, non-Community goods incorporated in the said originating goods are subject to payment of the import duties payable thereon, the validation of the documents necessary to enable such preferential tariff treatment to be obtained in third countries shall cause a customs debt on importation to be incurred.

2. The moment when such customs debt is incurred shall be deemed to be the moment when the customs authorities accept the export declaration relating to the goods in question.

3. The debtor shall be the declarant. In the event of indirect representation, the person on whose behalf the declaration is made shall also be a debtor.

4. The amount of the import duties corresponding to this customs debt shall be determined under the same conditions as in the case of a customs debt resulting from the acceptance, on the same date, of the declaration for release for free circulation of the goods concerned for the purpose of terminating the inward processing procedure.

CHAPTER 3
Recovery of the amount of the customs debt

SECTION 1
Entry in the accounts and communication of the amount of duty to the debtor

Articles 217-232

Note
Articles 217-232 are outside the scope of this work.

CHAPTER 4
Extinction of customs debt

Article 233

Without prejudice to the provisions in force relating to the time-barring of a customs debt and non-recovery of such a debt in the event of the legally established insolvency of the debtor, a customs debt shall be extinguished:

(*a*)   by payment of the amount of duty;

(*b*)   by remission of the amount of duty;

(*c*)   where, in respect of goods declared for a customs procedure entailing the obligation to pay duties:

— the customs declaration is invalidated in accordance with Article 66,

— the goods, before their release, are either seized and simultaneously or subsequently confiscated, destroyed on the instructions of the customs authorities, destroyed or abandoned in accordance with Article 182 or destroyed or irretrievably lost as a result of their actual nature or of unforeseeable circumstances or *force majeure*;

(*d*)   where goods in respect of which a customs debt is incurred in accordance with Article 202 are seized upon their unlawful introduction and are simultaneously or subsequently confiscated.

In the event of seizure and confiscation, the customs debt shall, nonetheless for the purposes of the criminal law applicable to customs offences, be deemed not to have been extinguished where, under a Member State's criminal law, customs duties provide the basis for determining penalties or the existence of a customs debt is grounds for taking criminal proceedings.

Article 234

A customs debt, as referred to in Article 216, shall also be extinguished where the formalities carried out in order to enable the preferential tariff treatment referred to in Article 216 to be granted are cancelled.

CHAPTER 5
Repayment and remission of duty

Articles 235-242

Note
Articles 235-242 are outside the scope of this work.

TITLE VIII
Appeals

Article 243

1. Any person shall have the right to appeal against decisions taken by the customs authorities which relate to the application of customs legislation, and which concern him directly and individually.

Any person who has applied to the customs authorities for a decision relating to the application of customs legislation and has not obtained a ruling on that request within the period referred to in Article 6(2) shall also be entitled to exercise the right of appeal.

The appeal must be lodged in the Member State where the decision has been taken or applied for.

2 The right of appeal may be exercised:

    (*a*)   initially, before the customs authorities designated for that purpose by the Member States;

    (*b*)   subsequently, before an independent body, which may be a judicial authority or an equivalent specialized body, according to the provisions in force in the Member States.

Article 244

The lodging of an appeal shall not cause implementation of the disputed decision to be suspended.

The customs authorities shall, however, suspend implementation of such decision in whole or in part where they have good reason to believe that the disputed decision is inconsistent with customs legislation or that irreparable damage is to be feared for the person concerned.

Where the disputed decision has the effect of causing import duties or export duties to be charged, suspension of implementation of that decision shall be subject to the existence or lodging of a security. However, such security need not be required where such a requirement would be likely, owing to the debtor's circumstances, to cause serious economic or social difficulties.

Article 245

The provisions for the implementation of the appeals procedure shall be determined by the Member States.

Article 246

This title shall not apply to appeals lodged with a view to the annulment or revision of a decision taken by the customs authorities on the basis of criminal law.

TITLE IX
Final provisions

CHAPTER 1
Customs Code Committee

Article 247

1. A Customs Code committee, hereinafter called "the committee', composed of representatives of the Member States with a representative of the Commission as chairman, is hereby established.

2. The committee shall adopt its rules of procedure.

Article 248

1. The committee may examine any question concerning customs legislation which is raised by its chairman, either on his own initiative or at the request of a Member State's representative.

Article 249

1. The provisions required for the implementation of this Code, including implementation of the Regulation referred to in Article 184, except for Title VIII and subject to Articles 9 and 10 of Regulation (EEC) No 2658/87 (OJ No L 256, 7.9.1987, p 1) and to paragraph 4, shall be adopted in accordance with the procedure laid down in paragraphs 2 and 3, in compliance with the international commitments entered into by the Community.

2. The representative of the Commission shall submit to the committee a draft of the measures to be taken. The committee shall deliver its opinion on the draft within a time limit which the chairman may lay down according to the urgency of the matter. The opinion shall be delivered by the majority laid down in Article 148(2) of the Treaty in the case of decisions which the Council is required to adopt on a proposal from the Commission. The votes of the representatives of the Member States within the committee shall be weighted in the manner set out in that Article. The chairman shall not vote.

3.   (*a*)   The Commission shall adopt the measures envisaged if they are in accordance with the opinion of the committee.

      (*b*)   If the measures envisaged are not in accordance with the opinion of the committee, or if no opinion is delivered, the Commission shall, without delay, submit to the Council a proposal relating to the provisions to be adopted. The Council shall act by a qualified majority.

      (*c*)   If, on the expiry of a period of three months from the date of referral to the Council, the Council has not acted, the proposed measures shall be adopted by the Commission.

4. The provisions necessary for implementing Articles 11, 12 and 21 shall be adopted by the procedure referred to in Article 10 of Regulation (EEC) No 2658/87.

CHAPTER 2
Legal effects in a Member State of measures taken, documents issued and findings made in another Member State

Article 250

Where a customs procedure is used in several Member States,

— the decisions, identification measures taken or agreed on, and the documents issued by the customs authorities of one Member State shall have the same legal effects in other Member States as such decisions, measures taken and documents issued by the customs authorities of each of those Member States;

— the findings made at the time controls are carried out by the customs authorities of a Member State shall have the same conclusive force in the other Member State as the findings made by the customs authorities of each of those Member States;

CHAPTER 3
Other final provisions

Article 251

1. The following Regulations and Directives are hereby repealed:

— Council Regulation (EEC) No 1224/80 of 28 May 1980 on the valuation of goods for customs purposes (OJ No L 134, 31.5.1980, p 1), as last amended by Regulation (EEC) No 4046/89 (OJ No L 388, 30.12.1989, p 24);

— Council Regulation (EEC) No 2151/84 of 23 July 1984 on the customs territory of the Community (OJ No L 197, 27.7.1984, p 1), as last amended by the Act of Accession of Spain and Portugal;

Note
Repeals within the scope of this work only are mentioned: other repeals have been omitted.

Article 252

Note
Article 252 is outside the scope of this work.

Article 253

This Regulation shall enter into force on the third day following that of its publication in the *Official Journal of the European Communities.*

It shall apply from 1 January 1994.

Title VIII shall not apply to the United Kingdom until 1 January 1995.

However, Article 161 and, in so far as they concern re-exportation, Articles 182 and 183 shall apply from 1 January 1993. In so far as the said Articles make reference to provisions in this Code and until such time as such provisions enter into force, the references shall be deemed to allude to the corresponding provisions in the Regulations and Directives listed in Article 251.

Before 1 October 1993, the Council shall, on the basis of a Commission progress report on discussions regarding the consequences to be drawn from the monetary conversion rate used for the application of common agricultural policy measures, review the problem of trade in goods between the Member States in the context of the internal market. This report shall be accompanied by Commission proposals if any, on which the Council shall take a decision in accordance with the provisions of the Treaty.

Before 1 January 1998, the Council shall, on the basis of a Commission report, review this Code with a view to making such adaptations as may appear necessary taking into account in particular the achievement of the internal market. This report shall be accompanied by proposals, if any, on which the Council shall take a decision in accordance with the provisions of the Treaty.

This Regulation shall be binding in its entirety and directly applicable in all Member States.

COMMISSION REGULATION

of 22 October 1992

92/3046/EEC

Laying down provisions implementing and amending Council Regulation (EEC) No 3330/91 on the statistics relating to the trading of goods between Member States

(OJ L307, 23.10.1992, p 27)

THE COMMISSION OF THE EUROPEAN COMMUNITIES,

Having regard to the Treaty establishing the European Economic Community,

Having regard to Council Regulation (EEC) No 3330/91 of 7 November 1991 on the statistics relating to the trading of goods between Member States (OJ No L 316, 16.11.1991, p 1), and in particular Article 30 thereof,

Whereas, with a view to establishing the statistics relating to the trading of goods between Member States, the field of application of the Intrastat system should be precisely defined in relation to both the goods to be included and those to be excluded;

Whereas the date from which the intra-Community operator shall in practice comply with his obligations to supply information must be determined; whereas the extent of the obligations of the third party to whom the party responsible for providing the information may transfer that task should be defined;

Whereas certain of the rules to be complied with by the departments concerned must be specified in detail in particular with a view to efficient management of the registers of intra-Community operation; whereas it is useful to specify the provisions relating to certain fiscal aspects of statistical information;

Whereas there should be additions to the definition of the data to be reported and to the arrangements for reporting such data;

Whereas a list should be drawn up of the goods to be excluded from the statistical returns relating to the trading of goods;

Whereas account should be taken initially of existing simplified procedures and of the special requirements of certain sectors;

Whereas the amendments to Council Directive 77/388/EEC (OJ No L 145, 13.6.1977, p 1) by Directive 91/680/EEC require certain provisions of Regulation (EEC) No 3330/91 (OJ No L 376, 31.12.1977, p 1) to be adapted, pursuant to the first indent of Article 33 thereof;

Whereas the measures provided for in this Regulation are in accordance with the opinion of the Committee on the statistics relating to the trading of goods between Member States,

HAS ADOPTED THIS REGULATION:

Article 1

With a view to establishing the statistics relating to the trading of goods between Member States, the Community and its Member States shall apply Regulation (EEC) No 3330/91, hereinafter referred to as **the Basic Regulation**, in accordance with the rules laid down in this Regulation.

Article 2

1. In connection with trade between the Community as constituted on 31 December 1985 and Spain or Portugal, and between those two last-mentioned Member States, the Intrastat system shall also apply to goods still liable to certain customs duties and charges having equivalent effect or which remain subject to other measures laid down by the Act of Accession.

2. The Intrastat system shall apply to the products referred to in Article 3(1) of Council Directive 92/12/EEC OJ No L 76, 23.3.1992, p 1), regardless of the form and content of the document accompanying them, when they move between the territories of the Member States.

Article 3

1. The Intrastat system shall not apply:

- (*a*) to goods placed or obtained under the inward processing customs procedure (suspension system) or the procedure of processing under customs control;

- (*b*) to goods circulating between parts of the statistical territory of the Community, at least one of which is not part of the territory of the Community pursuant to Council Directive 88/388/EEC.

2. The Member States shall be responsible for collecting data on the goods referred to in paragraph 1 on the basis of the customs procedures applicable to such goods.

3. If the statistical copy of the Single Administrative Document containing the data listed in Article 23 of the Basic Regulation, with the exception of the information referred to in paragraph 2(*e*) of that Article, is not available, the customs departments shall at least once a month send the relevant statistical departments a periodic list of those same data by type of goods, in accordance with the arrangements agreed upon by the said departments.

4. Articles 2, 4, 8, 9, 12(1), (3), (4), (5), (6) and (7); 13, 14, 19, 21 and 22(3)(*a*) and (*b*), first indent, shall not apply to the goods referred to in paragraph 1.

The other provisions of this Regulation shall apply to these goods without prejudice to any customs regulations which otherwise apply.

Article 4

1. Any natural or legal person carrying out an intra-Community operation for the first time, whether the goods are arriving or being dispatched, shall become responsible for providing the required information within the meaning of Article 20(5) of the Basic Regulation.

2. The party referred to in paragraph 1 shall provide the data on his intra-Community operations via the periodic declarations referred to in Article 13 of the Basic Regulation as from the month during which the assimilation threshold is exceeded, in accordance with the provisions relating to the threshold which become applicable to him.

The Member States shall determine the deadline for transmission in line with their particular administrative organisation.

3. When the VAT registration number of a party responsible for providing the information is amended as a result of a change of ownership, name, address, legal status or similar change which does not affect his intra-Community operations to a significant extent, the rule defined in paragraph 1 need not be applied to the party in question at the time of the change. It shall remain subject to the statistical obligations to which it was subject before the change.

Article 5

1. The third party referred to in Article 9(1) of the Basic Regulation is hereinafter referred to as the declaring third party.

2. The declaring third party shall provide the competent national departments with the following information:

- (*a*) in accordance with Article 6(1), the information necessary:

  — to identify himself,

  — to identify each of the parties responsible for providing the information who have transferred this task to him;

(*b*) for each of the parties responsible for providing information, the data required by the Basic Regulation and in implementation thereof.

Article 6

1. The information necessary to identify an intra-Community operator within the meaning of Article 10 of the Basic Regulation shall be the following:

— full name of the person or firm,

— full address including post code,

— under the circumstances laid down in Article 10(6) of the Basic Regulation, the VAT registration number.

However, the statistical departments referred to in Article 10(1) of the Basic Regulation may dispense with one or more of the abovementioned items of information or, under circumstances to be determined by them, exempt the intra-Community operators from providing them.

In the Member States referred to in Article 10(3) of the Basic Regulation, the information which serves to identify an intra-Community operator shall be supplied to the abovementioned statistical departments by the tax authorities referred to in the said Article as and when it becomes available to the latter unless there is an agreement to the contrary between the departments concerned.

2. The minimum of list data to be recorded in the register of intra-Community operators, within the meaning of Article 10 of the Basic Regulation, shall contain, for each intra-Community operator, the following:

(*a*) the year and month of entry in the register;

(*b*) the information necessary to identify the operator as laid down in paragraph 1;

(*c*) where applicable, whether the operator is the consignor, consignee or declarant, or, as from 1 January 1993, a party responsible for providing information or declaring third party, upon either consignment or receipt; in the Member States referred to in Article 10(3) of the Basic Regulation, the information stipulated in paragraph 1 of the present Article shall show whether each operator in question is a consignor or a consignee;

(*d*) in the case of a consignor or consignee or, as from 1 January 1993, a party responsible for providing information, the total value of his intra-Community operations, by month and by flow, together with, as from that same date the value referred to in Article 11(3) of the Basic Regulation; however, this information need not be recorded:

— prior to 1993, in those Member States referred to in Article 10(3) of the Basic Regulation,

— if the checking of the information recorded as statistics using the information referred to in article 11(3) of the Basic Regulation and the functioning of the statistical thresholds referred to in Article 28 of the said Regulation are organised separately from the management of the register of intra-Community operators.

The competent national departments may record other data in the register in accordance with their requirements.

Article 7

With a view to implementing Article 10(6) of the Basic Regulation, the case where responsibility for the information, for given operations, lies not with the operator as a legal entity *per se* but with a constituent part of this entity, such as a branch office, a kind-of-activity unit or local unit, may be considered a justified exception.

Article 8

In the lists referred to in Article 11(1) of the Basic Regulation, the tax authorities responsible shall mention intra-Community operators who, as a result of a scission, merger or cessation of activity during the period under review will no longer appear on the said lists.

Article 9

1. The party responsible for providing information shall transmit the data required under the Basic Regulation and in implementation thereof:

(*a*)   in accordance with the Community provision in force;

(*b*)   direct to the competent national departments or via the collection offices which the Member States have set up for this or for other statistical or administrative purposes;

(*c*)   or a given reference period, at his discretion:

     — either by means of a single declaration, within a time limit which the competent national departments shall lay down in their instructions to the parties responsible for providing information and which shall be between the fifth and the tenth working day following the end of that period,

     — or by means of several part-declarations; in this case, the competent national departments may require agreement to be reached with them on the frequency of transmission and deadlines, but the last part-declaration must be transmitted within the time limit laid down under the first indent above.

2. By way of derogation from paragraph 1, a party responsible for providing information who benefits from exemption by virtue of application of the assimilation threshold provided for in Article 28(4) of the Basic Regulation must, when transmitting the information, conform only to the regulations of the tax authorities responsible.

3. Pursuant to Article 34 of the Basic Regulation, the provisions of this Article relating to the periodicity of the declaration shall not prevent the conclusion of an agreement providing for the supply of data in real time, when the data are transmitted electronically.

4. By way of derogation to paragraph 1 above, in those Member States where the periodic statistical declaration is the same as the periodic tax declaration, the provisions relating to the transmission of the statistical declaration shall be drawn up in line with Community or national tax regulations.

Article 10

In the medium for the information, the Member States whose statistical territory is described in the nomenclature of countries annexed to Council Regulation (EEC) No 1736/75 (OJ No L 183, 14.7.1975, p 3) shall be designated by either alphabetical or numerical codes, as follows:

France:	FR	or	001,
Belgium and Luxembourg:	BL	or	002,
Netherlands:	NI	or	003,
Germany:	DE	or	004,
Italy:	IT	or	005,
United Kingdom:	GB	or	006,
Ireland:	IE	or	007,
Denmark:	DK	or	008,
Greece:	GR	or	009,
Portugal:	PT	or	010;
Spain:	ES	or	011.

Article 11

When the quantity of goods to be mentioned on the data medium is determined:

(*a*) **"net mass"** shall mean the actual mass of the good excluding all packaging; it must be given in kilograms;

(*b*) **"supplementary units"** shall mean the units measuring quantity, other than the units measuring mass expressed in kilograms; they must be mentioned in accordance with the information set out in the current version of the combined nomenclature, opposite the subheadings concerned, the list of which is published in Part I "Preliminary provisions" of the said nomenclature.

Article 12

1. The value of the goods, as referred to in Article 23(1)(*d*) of the Basic Regulation, shall be given as follows:

— by type of goods, the statistical value,

— by statistical declaration, the amount invoiced.

2. The statistical value shall be fixed:

— upon dispatch, on the basis of the taxable amount to be determined the taxation purposes in accordance with Directive 77/388/EEC for deliveries of goods specified under Section A(1)(*a*) and, where appropriate, for the operations specified under section A(1)(*b*) of Article 11 of the same Directive, minus, however, any taxes deductible because of the dispatch; it shall, on the other hand, include transport and insurance costs relating to that part of the journey which takes place on the statistical territory of the Member State of dispatch,

— on arrival, on the basis of the taxable amount to be determined for taxation purposes, in accordance with Article 28e of the Directive referred to above, for acquisition of goods, minus, however, taxes due because of the release for consumption and transport and insurance costs relating to that part of the journey which takes place on the statistical territory of the Member State of arrival.

The statistical value must be declared in accordance with the first subparagraph, even if the taxable amount does not have to be determined for taxation purposes.

For goods resulting from processing operations, the statistical value shall be established as if those goods had been produced entirely in the Member State of processing.

3. The amount invoiced shall be the total amount (excluding VAT) of invoices or documents servings as invoices relating to all the goods included in a statistical declaration.

4. The party responsible for providing information may indicate the invoiced amount broken down by type of goods.

By way of derogation to paragraph 1, the Member States may require the invoiced amount to be broken down by type of goods. In this case, they shall calculate the statistical value and exempt the party responsible for providing the statistical information from the need to mention it. However, those responsible for providing the information may be required to supply information on ancillary costs on a sample basis.

The second subparagraph shall apply either to all parties required to transmit the periodic declaration referred to in Article 13(1) of the Basic Regulation or solely to those parties who benefit from the application of simplification thresholds.

5. The Member States may exercise the option laid down in the second subparagraph of paragraph 4, even if their particular administrative organisation prevents them from taking the simplification measure which, by virtue of this subparagraph, must accompany the exercise of this option, namely, exemption from the requirement to mention the statistical value.

In the instructions relating to the statistical declaration to the parties responsible for providing information, the technical reasons why both the statistical value and the invoiced amount must be mentioned, by type of goods, shall be indicated in advance.

The Member States shall transmit a copy of these instructions to the Commission before 1 November 1992 and, thereafter, whenever they are updated.

6. In the case of work under contract, the amount invoiced shall be the amount entered in the accounts for the work, including any ancillary costs. It shall be mentioned only in the case of the dispatch and the arrival which follow the contract work.

7. "Ancillary costs" means the costs incurred in the movement of goods between the Member State of dispatch and the Member State of arrival, such as transport and insurance costs.

Article 13

1. For the purposes of this Regulation:

(a) **"transaction"** shall mean any operation, whether commercial or not, which leads to a movement of goods covered by statistics on the trading of goods between Member States;

(b) **"nature of the transaction"** shall mean all those characteristics which distinguish one transaction from another.

2. A distinction shall be made between transactions which differ in nature, in accordance with the list in Annex I.

The nature of the transaction shall be specified, on the information medium, by the code number corresponding to the appropriate category of column A in the abovementioned list.

3. Within the limits of the list referred to in paragraph 2, the Member States may prescribe the collection of data on the nature of the transaction up to the level which they use for the collection of data on trade third countries, regardless of whether they collect them in this connection as data on the nature of the transaction or as data on customs procedures.

Article 14

1. For the purposes of this Regulation, **"delivery terms"** shall mean those provisions of the sales contract which lay down the obligations of the seller and the buyer respectively, in accordance with the Incoterms of the International Chamber of Commerce listed in Annex II.

2. Within the limits of the list referred to in paragraph 1 and without prejudice to paragraph 3:

(a) those Member States which apply the second subparagraph of Article 12(4) shall stipulate that data on delivery terms shall be collected on the information medium and shall give details of how they are to be mentioned;

(b) the other Member States may stipulate that data on delivery terms shall be collected on the information medium up to the level at which they collect data on trade with third countries.

3. The delivery terms shall be indicated, for each type of goods, by one of the abbreviations in the list referred to in paragraph 1.

Article 15

1. "Presumed mode of transport" shall indicate, upon dispatch, the mode of transport determined by the active means of transport by which the goods are presumed to be going to leave the statistical territory of the Member State of dispatch and, upon arrival, the mode of transport determined by the active means of transport by which the goods are presumed to have entered the statistical territory of the Member State on arrival.

2. The modes of transport to be mentioned on the information medium are as follows:

Code	Title
1	Transport by sea
2	Transport by rail
3	Transport by road
4	Transport by air
5	Consignments by post
7	Fixed transport installations
8	Transport by inland waterway
9	Own propulsion

The mode of transport shall be designated on the said medium by the corresponding code number.

Article 16

1. "Country of origin" shall mean the country where the goods originate.

Goods which are entirely obtained in a country originate in that country.

An item in the production of which two or more countries are involved originates in the country where the last significant processing or working, economically justified and carried out in an enterprise equipped for this purpose and leading to the manufacture of a new product or representing an important stage of manufacture, takes place.

2. The country of origin shall be designated by the code number given to it in the current version of the country nomenclature annexed to Regulation (EEC) No 1736/75, without prejudice to the last sentence of Article 47 of the said Regulation.

Article 17

1. "Region of origin" shall mean the region of the Member State of dispatch where the goods were produced or were erected, assembled, processed, repaired or maintained; failing this, the region of origin shall be replaced either by the region where the commercial process took place or by the region where the goods were dispatched.

2. "Region of destination" shall mean the region of the Member State of arrival where the goods are to be consumed or erected, assembled, processed, repaired or maintained; failing this, the region of destination shall be replaced either by the region where the commercial process is to take place or by the region to which the goods are dispatched.

3. Each Member State exercising the option provided for in Article 23(2)(*b*) of the Basic Regulation shall draw up a list of its regions and determine the code, which shall have a maximum of two characters, by which those regions shall be indicated on the information medium.

Article 18

1. "Port or airport of loading" shall means the port or airport situated on the statistical territory of the Member State of dispatch at which the goods are loaded onto the active means of transport on or in which they are presumed to be going to leave that territory.

2. "Port or airport of unloading" shall mean the port or airport situated on the statistical territory of the Member State of arrival at which the goods are unloaded from the active means of transport on or in which they are presumed to have entered that territory.

3. Each Member State exercising the option provided for in Article 23(2)(*c*) or (*d*) of the Basic Regulation shall draw up a list of ports and airports to be mentioned on the information medium and shall fix the code by which they are to be indicated on that medium.

Article 19

1. "Statistical procedure" shall mean the category of dispatch or arrival within which a given intra-Community operation takes place and which is not adequately referred to in column A or column B of the list of transactions in Annex I.

2. Any Member State wising to exercise the option provided for in Article 23(2)(*e*) of the Basic Regulation shall draw up a list of the statistical procedures to be mentioned on the information medium and fix the code by which they are to be indicated on that medium.

Article 20

Data relating to the goods listed in Annex III shall be excluded from compilation and, consequently, pursuant to Article 25(4) of the Basic Regulation, from collection.

Article 21

1. For the purposes of this Regulation, **"specific movements of goods"** shall mean movements of goods having specific features which have some significance for the interpretation of the information and stem either from the movement as such or from the nature of the goods or from the transaction which results in the movement of the goods or from the consignor or consignee of the goods.

2. In the absence of provisions drawn up under Article 33 of the Basic Regulation, the Member States may apply, as regards data to specific movements of goods, the simplified procedures which were applied, under Regulation (EEC) No 1736/75, prior to the date referred to in the second paragraph of Article 35 of the Basic Regulation.

3. Those Member States wishing to have more detailed information than that resulting from the application of Article 21 of the Basic Regulation may, by way of derogation from that Article, organise the collection of that information, for one or more specific product groups, provided that the party responsible for providing the information is allowed to elect to supply it in accordance with either the combined nomenclature or the additional subdivisions.

Those Member States exercising that option shall notify the Commission that they are doing so. At the same time, they shall state the reasons for their decision, supply the list of relevant combined nomenclature subheadings and describe the collection method they are using.

Article 22

[*Amends references to Council Directive 77/388/EEC in Council Regulation 3330/91*]

Article 23

This Regulation shall enter into force on the seventh day following its publication in the *Official Journal of the European Communities.*

Those of its provisions which relate to the Articles referred to in the second paragraph of Article 35 of the Basic Regulation shall apply from the same date as those said Articles.

This Regulation shall be binding in its entirety and directly applicable in all Member States.

Done at Brussels, 22 October 1992.

COMMISSION REGULATION

of 11 December 1992

92/3590/EEC

(OJ L364, 12.12.1992, p 32)

concerning the statistical information media for statistics on trade between Member States

THE COMMISSION OF THE EUROPEAN COMMUNITIES,

Having regard to the Treaty establishing the European Economic Community,

Having regard to Council Regulation (EEC) No 3330/91 of 7 November 1991, on the statistics relating to the trading of goods between Member States (OJ L 316, 16.11.1991, p 1), as amended by Commission Regulation (EEC) No 3046/92 (OJ 1307, 23.10.1992, p 27), and in particular Article 12 thereof,

Whereas in the context of statistics on trade between Member States, it is necessary to adopt standard statistical forms for regular use by the parties responsible for providing information in order to ensure that the declarations required of them adhere to a consistent format, irrespective of the Member State where they are made; whereas the choice accorded to the parties responsible for providing information by Article 12(2) of the abovementioned Regulation is only available if the Commission sets up the appropriate information media; whereas, moreover, certain Member States would rather use Community media than produce national forms of their own;

Whereas it is important to provide the competent authorities with all the technical details required for the printing of these forms;

Whereas it is advisable in order to ensure uniform treatment of the parties responsible for providing information, to contribute towards the cost of these forms; whereas it is necessary to estimate the amount of Community funds required for this; whereas this amount must be in line with the financial perspective set out in the Interinstitutional Agreement of 29 June 1988 on Budgetary Discipline and Improvement of the Budgetary Procedure OJ L 185, 15.7.1988, p 33); whereas, in compliance with this Agreement, the appropriations actually available must be determined in accordance with budgetary procedure;

Whereas it is necessary to take account of other modes of transmitting information, and, in particular, to promote the use of magnetic or electronic information media;

Whereas the measures provided for in this Regulation reflect the opinion of the Committee on Statistics Relating to the Trading of Goods between Member States,

HAS ADOPTED THIS REGULATION:

Article 1

1. With a view to the drawing-up by the Community and its Member States of statistics on trade between the Member States, the statistical information media provided for in Article 12, paragraph 1, of Council Regulation (EEC) No 3330/91, hereafter referred to as **"the basic Regulation"**, shall be set up in accordance with the provisions of this Regulation.

2. In Member States where no distinction is made between the periodic declaration and the periodic declaration required for tax purposes, the provisions necessary for the setting-up of information media shall, insofar as necessary, be adopted within the framework of Community or national tax regulations, and in conformity with the other implementing provisions of the basic Regulation.

Article 2

Without prejudice to provisions adopted pursuant to Article 34 of the basic Regulation, Intrastat forms *N-Dispatch, R-Dispatch* and *S-Dispatch* and *N-Arrival, R-Arrival* and *S-Arrival*, specimens of which are annexed to this Regulation, shall be used in conformity with the provisions set out below.

-   Forms N shall be used by parties responsible for providing information who are not subject to the dispensations resulting from the assimilation and simplification thresholds fixed by each Member State, nor to the exemption provided for in the following indent.

-   Forms R shall be used by parties responsible for providing information whom the competent national authorities have exempted from giving a description of the goods.

-   Forms S shall be used by parties responsible for providing information who are subject to the dispensations resulting from the simplification threshold.

Article 3

1. The forms referred to in Article 2 shall consist of a single sheet, which shall be delivered to the competent national authorities.

The Member States may, however, require parties responsible for providing information to retain a copy in accordance with the instructions of the competent national authorities.

2. The forms shall be printed on paper which is suitable for writing and weighs no less than 70 g/m^2

The colour of the paper used shall be white. The colour of the print shall be red. The paper and the print used must meet the technical requirements of optical character recognition (OCR) equipment.

The fields and subdivisions shall be measured horizontally in units of one-tenth of an inch and vertically in units of one-sixth of an inch.

The forms shall measure 210 x 297 mm, subject to maximum tolerances as to length of -5mm and +8mm.

3. The conditions under which the forms may be produced using reproduction techniques departing from the provisions of paragraph 2, first and second subparagraphs, shall be determined by the Member States, which shall inform the Commission accordingly.

Article 4

The Member States shall, without charge, supply parties responsible for providing information with the forms reproduced in specimen in the Annex hereto.

The Commission shall contribute annually, at the end of the reporting period, to the costs which the Member States have incurred in printing these forms and distributing them via official postal channels. This contribution shall be calculated in proportion to the number of forms which the parties responsible for providing information have actually transmitted to the competent national authorities during the year in question.

Article 5

Parties responsible for providing information who wish to use magnetic or electronic media shall give prior notice of this intention to the national authorities responsible for compiling statistics on trade between Member States. Parties responsible for providing information shall, in this event, comply with any relevant provisions adopted by the Commission and with any national instructions issued by the abovementioned authorities pursuant to the said provisions, bearing in mind the technical equipment available to them. These instructions shall include in their structuring rules the Cusdec message designed and updated by the United Nations Edifact Board - Message Design Group 3, and shall comply with the provisions relating to the Instat subset of that message, which the Commission shall publish in a user manual.

Article 6

1. In derogation from Article 2, parties responsible for providing information who which to use as an information medium the statistical forms of the Single Administrative Document as provided for in Council [*sic*] 717/91 (OJ L 78, 26.3.1991, p 1) shall comply with the instructions issued by the competent national authorities. The latter shall send a copy of these instructions to the Commission.

2. Member States which set up media other than those provided for in Article 2 or Article 5 above, or paragraph 1 of this Article, shall inform the Commission accordingly in advance. They shall send the Commission an example of such media and/or provide details as to their use.

Article 7

This Regulation shall enter into force on the seventh day following that of its publication in the *Official Journal of the European Communities*.

It shall apply from the date provided in Article 35, second indent, of the basic Regulation.

This Regulation shall be binding in its entirety and directly applicable in all Member States.

Done at Brussels, 11 December 1992.

COUNCIL REGULATION

of 5 April 1993

93/854/EEC

on Transit Statistics Relating to the Trading of Goods between Member States

THE COUNCIL OF THE EUROPEAN COMMUNITIES

Having regard to the Treaty establishing the European Economic Community, and in particular Article 100a thereof,

Having regard to the proposal from the Commission (OJ C107, 28.4.1992, p 16),

In cooperation with the European Parliament (OJ C337, 21.12.1992, p 210; OJ C72, 15.3.1993),

Having regard to the opinion of the Economic and Social Committee (OJ C223, 31.8.1992, p 6),

Whereas the abolition of customs formalities, controls and documentation for all movements of goods across internal frontiers is necessary for the completion of the internal market;

Whereas, in the Member States, statistics on the trading of goods between Member States resulting from transit movements and movements into and out of warehouses may nevertheless still be needed;

Whereas Council Regulation (EEC) No 3330/91 of 7 November 1991 on the statistics relating to the trading of goods between Member States (OJ L316, 16.11.1991, p 1) prohibits the Member States from introducing or maintaining compulsory formalities for the purpose of keeping statistics on transit and storage; whereas it is necessary for that purpose to provide a Community legal base;

Whereas the framework in which the Member States are authorised to organise their statistical surveys on these movements must be determined in order to prevent the burden on those responsible for providing information varying excessively from one Member State to another;

Whereas, within that framework, it is necessary to determine the purpose of transit and storage statistics and the consequences for the collection of information, to ensure that responsibility for collecting that information is directed towards existing administrative sources and to make use of the competent services of the latter to fill any gaps, without increasing the burden on those responsible for providing information;

Whereas that burden must not exceed certain limits, as regards classification, data to be declared or data media;

Whereas it is important that the burden of transit and storage statistics be alleviated, particularly for small and medium-sized enterprises; whereas this should be effected by means of statistical thresholds;

Whereas the Commission must not only adopt provisions implementing this Regulation but must also ensure that other implementing provisions adopted by the Member States do not compromise the alleviation of the burden on those responsible for providing information; whereas the Commission should be assisted in this task by the Committee on Statistics relating to the Trading of Goods between Member States,

HAS ADOPTED THIS REGULATION:

Article 1

1. With a view to compiling transit statistics and storage statistics, Member States may collect data on the trading of goods between Member States, acting in conformity with the rules laid down in this Regulation.

2. Member States which exercise this option shall accordingly inform the Commission.

Article 2

1. For the purposes of this Regulation, the definitions given in Article 2(*a*), (*b*), (*c*), (*d*), (*e*) and (*f*) of Regulation (EEC) No 3330/91 shall apply.

2. For the purpose of this Regulation:

(*a*)   transit: means the crossing of a given Member State by goods which are being transported between two places situated outside that Member State;

(*b*)   interrupted transit: means transit during which a break in transport occurs; this also includes transhipment;

(*c*)   customs warehousing procedure: means the customs warehousing procedure as defined in Articles 1 and 2 of Council Regulation (EEC) No 2503/88 of 25 July 1988 on customs warehouses (OJ L225, 15.8.1988, p 1);

(*d*)   competent statistical services: means those services in each Member State which are responsible for compiling statistics on the trading of goods between Member States.

Article 3

Of the goods referred to in Article 3 of Regulation (EEC) No 3330/91, data shall be collected for the purpose of compiling statistics on transit through a given Member State on those goods which are in interrupted transit in that Member State, with the exception of goods which having entered that Member State as non-Community goods, have subsequently been put into free circulation there.

Article 4

Of the goods referred to in Article 3 of Regulation (EEC) No 3330/91, data shall be collected for the purpose of compiling storage statistics in a given Member State on:

(*a*)   those which, though the customs warehousing procedure has not terminated, are transferred, within the meaning of Article 20 of Regulation (EEC) No 2503/88, from a customs warehouse situated in that Member State to one situated in another Member State;

(*b*)   those which, though the customs warehousing procedure has not terminated, are transferred, within the meaning of Article 20 of Regulation (EEC) No 2503/88, to a customs warehouse situated in that Member State from a customs warehouse situated in another Member State;

(*c*)   those which are subject to the customs warehousing procedure in that Member State and are sent to another Member State under the procedure for external Community transit;

(*d*)   those which are subject to the customs warehousing procedure in that Member State, having come from another Member State under the procedure for external Community transit.

Article 5

1. Under conditions which they themselves shall determine, Member States shall authorise those responsible for providing statistical information to use administrative or commercial documents already required for other purposes as the statistical data medium.

However, with a view to the standardisation of their basic documentation, Member States may establish exclusively statistical media provided that those required to provide statistical information are free to choose which of these media they use.

2. Member States shall inform the Commission of the media which they authorise or establish.

Article 6

1. In a given Member State, the person responsible for providing statistical information as referred to in Article 8 of Regulation (EEC) No 3330/91 shall be the natural or legal person who, engaged in that Member State in the trading of goods between Member States, draws up the administrative or commercial document designated as the statistical data medium pursuant to the first subparagraph of Article 5(1).

In the absence of such a person and by way of derogation from Article 8 of Regulation (EEC) No 3330/91, each Member State shall designate from among the administrative services to which the document referred to in the first subparagraph is made available, one service which shall provide the information.

2. Member States shall be entitled to proceed in accordance with the second subparagraph of paragraph 1 in order to relieve persons responsible for supplying information of their obligations, in whole or in part.

3. The person or service referred to in paragraph 1 shall conform to the provisions of this Regulation, the provisions adopted pursuant to Article 30 of Regulation (EEC) No 3330/91 and the measures taken by Member States to implement those provisions.

Article 7

1. On the statistical data medium to be sent to the competent services:

— without prejudice to Article 34 of Regulation (EEC) No 3330/91, goods shall be designated according to their usual trade description in sufficiently precise terms to permit their identification and their immediate and unequivocal classification in the most detailed relevant subdivision of the current version of either the classification of the harmonised system for transit statistics or the combined nomenclature for storage statistics, irrespective of the level at which these classifications are applied; however, this provision shall not prevent the Member States applying the standard goods classification for transport statistics—revised (NST/R) instead of the abovementioned classifications, where permissible under the rules governing the medium used,

— the code number corresponding to the abovementioned nomenclature subdivision may also be required by type of goods.

2. On the statistical data medium, countries shall be described by the alphabetical or numerical codes laid down in Council Regulation (EEC) No 1736/75 of 24 June 1975 on the external trade statistics of the Community and statistics of trade between Member States (as last amended by Council Regulation 1629/88/EEC; see respectively OJ L183, 14.7.1975, p 3 and OJ L147, 14.6.1988, p 1).

For the purposes of the first subparagraph, the parties responsible for providing information shall comply with the instructions issued by the national services competent for compiling statistics on trade between Member States.

Article 8

1. Member States which compile transit statistics shall determine which of the following data are to be included on the statistical data medium, by type of goods:

    (*a*)   the country of consignment, within the meaning of Article 9;

    (*b*)   the country of destination, within the meaning of Article 9;

    (*c*)   the quantity of goods in gross mass, within the meaning of Article 9;

    (*d*)   the mode of transport in accordance with Article 9(*f*)(1);

    (*e*)   the place where the interruption in transit took place in accordance with Article 9.

2. Member States which compile storage statistics shall determine which of the following data are to be included on the statistical data medium, by type of goods:

(*a*)   the Member State of consignment, in the Member State which the goods enter within the meaning of Article 9;

(*b*)   the Member State of destination, in the Member State which goods leave within the meaning of Article 9;

(*c*)   the country of origin, within the meaning of Article 9; however, this item may be required only as allowed by Community law;

(*d*)   the quantity of goods expressed in gross mass or net mass within the meaning of Article 9 and in supplementary units in accordance with the combined nomenclature, where it is used pursuant to Article 7(1);

(*e*)   the customs value;

(*f*)   the presumed mode of transport, in accordance with Article 9(f)(2);

(*g*)   the region of destination, in the Member State which the goods enter.

3. In so far as is not laid down in this Regulation, the data referred to in paragraphs 1 and 2 and the rules governing their inclusion on the statistical data medium shall be defined in accordance with the procedure laid down in Article 30 of Regulation (EEC) No 3330/91.

Article 9

For the purposes of applying Article 8:

(*a*)   country/Member State of consignment: means the last country/Member State in which the goods were subject to halts or legal operations not inherent in their transport:

(*b*)   country/Member State of destination: means the last country/Member State to which it is known, at the time the statistical data medium is drawn up, that the goods are to be sent;

(*c*)   country of origin: means the country in which the goods originated within the meaning of Council Regulation (EEC) No 802/68 of 27 June 1968 on the common definition of the concept of origin of goods (as last amended by Council Regulation 456/91/EEC; see respectively OJ L148, 28.6.1968, p 1 and OJ L54, 28.2.1991, p 4);

(*d*)   gross mass: means the cumulated mass of the goods and all their packaging with the exclusion of the transport equipment, and in particular containers;

(*e*)   net mass: means the mass of the goods, all packaging removed;

(*f*)   mode of transport: means that actually used

1 before or after the interruption of transit;

2 on entry to or exit from the warehouse.

Modes of transport are as follows:

Code Designation

1   Sea transport

2   Rail transport

3   Road transport

4   Air transport

5   Post

7   Fixed transport installations

8   Inland waterway transport

9   Self-propelled

If the mode of transport is given as one of those listed under codes 1, 2, 3, 4 or 8, Member States may require that it also be stated whether the goods are transported in containers within the meaning of Article 15(3) of Regulation (EEC) No 1736/75;

(g) place of interruption of transit: means the port, airport or any other place where transit is interrupted within the meaning of Article 2(2)(b).

Article 10

1. Where the data referred to in Articles 7 and 8 need not be shown on the administrative or commercial document referred to in the first subparagraph of Article 5(1) for the purposes for which such documents are required, Member States shall instruct the administrative service referred to in the second subparagraph of Article 6(1) to collect them and transmit them to the competent statistical services in accordance with procedures which they shall lay down, bearing in mind the stated requirements of these statistical services.

2. Without prejudice to the second subparagraph of Article 5(1), Member States shall establish the media to be used by the abovementioned administrative service for transmitting these data.

Article 11

1. For the purposes of this Regulation, statistical thresholds shall be defined as limits, expressed in gross mass for transit statistics and in terms of value or in mass for storage statistics, below which the obligations on those responsible for providing information are suspended.

2. The threshold for transit statistics shall be fixed per type of goods at least:

— 50 kg in the case of air transport,

— 1 000 kg for other modes of transport.

3. The threshold for storage statistics shall be fixed at least ECU 800 per type of goods, irrespective of the mass of the goods, or at least 50 kg per type of goods in the case of air transport or at least 1 000 kg per type of goods for other modes of transport, irrespective of the value of the goods.

Article 12

1. The provisions necessary for implementing this Regulation shall be adopted in accordance with the procedure laid down in Article 30 of Regulation (EEC) No 3330/91.

2. Member States may adopt the provisions required for collecting information in order to compile transit and storage statistics where such provisions are not laid down in this Regulation or adopted in accordance with paragraph 1.

However, if the effect of these national arrangements is to compromise the alleviation of the burden on those responsible for providing information, provisions to restore the conditions for alleviating that burden shall be adopted in accordance with the abovementioned Article.

Article 13

Member States shall communicate to the Commission the measures which they take to implement this Regulation.

Article 14

The Committee on Statistics relating to the Trading of Goods between Member States, set up by Article 29 of Regulation (EEC) No 3330/91, may examine any question, relating to the implementation of this Regulation raised by its chairman, either on his own initiative or at the request of the representative of a Member State.

Article 15

This Regulation shall enter into force on the third day following its publication in the Official Journal of the European Communities.

The Regulation shall remain in force until 31 December 1996. No later than three months before this date, the Commission shall present a report on the application of this Regulation and if necessary put forward a proposal.

This Regulation shall be binding in its entirety and directly applicable in all Member States.

COMMISSION REGULATION

of 2 July 1993

93/2454/EEC

Commission Regulation 2 July 1993 provisions for the implementation of Council Regulation (EEC) No 2913/92 establishing the Community Customs Code

PART I: General implementing provisions

TITLE I: General

TITLE V: Customs value

TITLE VI: Introduction of goods into the customs territory

TITLE VII: Customs declarations — normal procedure

TITLE VIII: Examination of the goods, findings of the customs office and other measures taken by the customs office

PART IV: Customs debt

TITLE I: Security

TITLE II: Incurrence of the debt

PART V: Final provisions

THE COMMISSION OF THE EUROPEAN COMMUNITIES,

Having regard to the Treaty establishing the European Economic Community,

Having regard to Council Regulation (EEC) No 2913/92 of 12 October 1992 establishing the Community Customs Code (OJ No L 302, 19.10.1992), hereinafter referred to as the 'Code', and in particular Article 249 thereof,

Whereas the Code assembled all existing customs legislation in a single legal instrument; whereas at the same time the Code made certain modifications to this legislation to make it more coherent, to simplify it and to plug certain loopholes; whereas it therefore constitutes complete Community legislation in this area;

Whereas the same reasons which led to the adoption of the Code apply equally to the customs implementing legislation; whereas it is therefore desirable to bring together in a single regulation those customs implementing provisions which are currently scattered over a large number of Community regulations and directives;

Whereas the implementing code for the Community Customs Code hereby established should set out existing customs implementing rules; whereas it is nevertheless necessary, in the light of experience:

— to make some amendments in order to adapt the said rules to the provisions of the Code;

— to extend the scope of certain provisions which currently apply only to specific customs procedures in order to take account of the Code's comprehensive application;

— to formulate certain rules more precisely in order to achieve greater legal security in their application;

Whereas the changes made relate mainly to the provisions concerning customs debt;

Whereas it is appropriate to limit the application of Article 791(2) until 1 January 1995 and to review the subject matter in the light of experience gained before that time;

Whereas the measures provided for by this Regulation are in accordance with the opinion of the Customs Code Committee,

HAS ADOPTED THIS REGULATION:

PART I
General implementing provisions

TITLE I
General

CHAPTER 1
Definitions

Article 1

For the purposes of this Regulation

1. Code means: Council Regulation (EEC) No 2913/92 of 12 October 1992 establishing a Community Customs Code;

[**2.** *ATA carnet* means: the international customs document for temporary importation established by virtue of the ATA Convention or the Istanbul Convention;][1]

3. *Committee* means: the Customs Code Committee established in Article 247 of the Code;

4. *Customs Cooperation Council* means: the organization set up by the Convention establishing a Customs Cooperation Council, done at Brussels on 15 December 1950;

5. *Particulars required for identification of the goods* means: on the one hand, the particulars used to identify the goods commercially allowing the customs authorities to determine the tariff classification and, on the other hand, the quantity of the goods;

6. *Goods of a non-commercial nature* means: goods whose entry for the customs procedure in question is on an occasional basis and whose nature and quantity indicate that they are intended for the private, personal or family use of the consignees or persons carrying them, or which are clearly intended as gifts;

7. *Commercial policy measures* means: non-tariff measures established, as part of the common commercial policy, in the form of Community provisions governing the import and export of goods, such as surveillance or safeguard measures, quantitative restrictions or limits and import or export prohibitions;

8. *Customs nomenclature* means: one of the nomenclatures referred to in Article 20(6) of the Code;

9. *Harmonised System* means: the Harmonised Commodity Description and Coding System;

10. *Treaty* means: the Treaty establishing the European Economic Community.

[**11.** Istanbul Convention means: the Convention on Temporary Admission agreed at Istanbul on 26 June 1990.][2]

Amendments
1 Substituted by Commission Regulation (EC) No 1762/95 art 2(1)(*a*). See OJ L171, 21.7.95, p 8).
2 Inserted by Commission Regulation (EC) No 1762/95 art 2(1)(*b*) See OJ L171, 21.7.95, p 8).

[*Article 1a*

For the purposes of applying Articles 16 to 34 and 291 to 308, the countries of the Benelux Economic Union shall be considered as a single Member State.][1]

Amendments
1 Inserted by Commission Regulation 3665/93 EEC; see OJ L335, 31.12.93, p 1.

CHAPTER 2
Decisions

Article 2

Where a person making a request for a decision is not in a position to provide all the documents and information necessary to give a ruling, the customs authorities shall provide the documents and information at their disposal.

Article 3

A decision concerning security favourable to a person who has signed an undertaking to pay the sums due at the first written request of the customs authorities, shall be revoked where the said undertaking is not fulfilled.

Article 4

A revocation shall not affect goods which, at the moment of its entry into effect, have already been placed under a procedure by virtue of the revoked authorization.

However, the customs authorities may require that such goods be assigned to a permitted customs-approved treatment or use within the period which they shall set.

[CHAPTER 3
Data processing techniques

Article 4a

1. Under the conditions and in the manner which they shall determine, and with due regard to the principles laid down by customs rules, the customs authorities may provide that formalities shall be carried out by a data-processing technique. For this purpose:

— **'a data-processing technique'** means:

    (*a*)   the exchange of EDI standard messages with the customs authorities;

    (*b*)   the introduction of information required for completion of the formalities concerned into customs data-processing systems;

— **'EDI'** (electronic data interchange) means, the transmission of data structured according to agreed message standards, between one computer system and another, by electronic means,

— **'standard message'** means a predefined structure recognized for the electronic transmission of data.

2. The condition laid down for carrying out formalities by a data-processing technique shall include inter alia measures for checking the source of data and for protecting data against the risk of unauthorized access, loss alteration or destruction.

Article 4b

Where formalities are carried out by a data-processing technique, the customs authorities shall determine the rules for replacement of the handwritten signature by another technique which may be based on the use of codes.]¹

Amendments
1 Inserted by EC Commission Regulation 3665/93 . See OJ L335 of 31.12.93 p 1.

Articles 5-140

Notes
Articles 5-140 are outside the scope of this work.

TITLE V
Customs value

CHAPTER 1
General provisions

Article 141

1. In applying the provisions of Articles 28 to 36 of the Code and those of this title, Member States shall comply with the provisions set out in Annex 23.

The provisions as set out in the first column of Annex 23 shall be applied in the light of the interpretative note appearing in the second column.

2. If it is necessary to make reference to generally accepted accounting principles in determining the customs value, the provisions of Annex 24 shall apply.

Article 142

1. For the purposes of this title:

    (*a*)   **'the Agreement'** means the Agreement on implementation of Article VII of the General Agreement on Tariffs and Trade concluded in the framework of the multilateral trade negotiations of 1973 to 1979 and referred to in the first indent of Article 31(1) of the Code.

    (*b*)   **'produced goods'** includes goods grown, manufactured and mined;

    (*c*)   **'identical goods'** means goods produced in the same country which are the same in all respects, including physical characteristics, quality and reputation. Minor differences in appearance shall not preclude goods otherwise conforming to the definition from being regarded as identical;

    (*d*)   **'similar goods'** means goods produced in the same country which, although not alike in all respects, have like characteristics and like component materials which enable them to perform the same functions and to be commercially interchangeable; the quality of the goods, their reputation and the existence of a trademark are among the factors to be considered in determining whether goods are similar;

    (*e*)   **'goods of the same class or kind'** means goods which fall within a group or range of goods produced by a particular industry or industry sector, and includes identical or similar goods.

2. 'Identical goods' and 'similar goods', as the case may be, do not include goods which incorporate or reflect engineering, development, artwork, design work, and plans and sketches for which no adjustment has been made under Article 32 (1)(*b*)(iv) of the Code because such elements were undertaken in the Community.

Article 143

1. For the purposes of Articles 29(1)(*d*) and 30(2)(*c*) of the Code, persons shall be deemed to be related only if:

(*a*)   they are officers or directors of one another's businesses;

(*b*)   they are legally recognized partners in business;

(*c*)   they are employer and employee;

(*d*)   any person directly or indirectly owns, controls or holds 5% or more of the outstanding voting stock or shares of both of them;

(*e*)   one of them directly or indirectly controls the other;

(*f*)   both of them are directly or indirectly controlled by a third person;

(*g*)   together they directly or indirectly control a third person; or

(*h*)   they are members of the same family. Persons shall be deemed to be members of the same family only if they stand in any of the following relationships to one another:

— husband and wife,

— parent and child,

— brother and sister (whether by whole or half blood),

— grandparent and grandchild,

— uncle or aunt and nephew or niece,

— parent-in-law and son-in-law or daughter-in-law,

— brother-in-law and sister- in-law.

2. For the purposes of this title, persons who are associated in business with one another in that one is the sole agent, sole distributor or sole concessionaire, however described, of the other shall be deemed to be related only if they fall within the criteria of paragraph 1.

Article 144

1. For the purposes of determining customs value under Article 29 of the Code of goods in regard to which the price has not actually been paid at the material time for valuation for customs purposes, the price payable for settlement at the said time shall as a general rule be taken as the basis for customs value.

2. The Commission and the Member States shall consult within the Committee concerning the application of paragraph 1.

Article 145

Where goods declared for free circulation are part of a larger quantity of the same goods purchased in one transaction, the price actually paid or payable for the purposes of Article 29(1) of the Code shall be that price represented by the proportion of the total price which the quantity so declared bears to the total quantity purchased.

Apportioning the price actually paid or payable shall also apply in the case of the loss of part of a consignment or when the goods being valued have been damaged before entry into free circulation.

Article 146

Where the price actually paid or payable for the purposes of Article 29(1) of the Code includes an amount in respect of any internal tax applicable within the country of origin or export in respect of the goods in question, the said amount shall not be incorporated in the customs value provided that it can be demonstrated to the satisfaction of the customs authorities concerned that the goods in question have been or will be relieved therefrom for the benefit of the buyer.

Article 147

1. For the purposes of Article 29 of the Code, the fact that the goods which are the subject of a sale are declared for free circulation shall be regarded as adequate indication that they were sold for export to the customs territory of the Community. [In the case of successive sales before valuation, only the last sale, which led to the introduction of the goods into the customs territory of the Community, or a sale taking place in the customs territory of the Community before entry for free circulation of the goods shall constitute such indication.

Where a price is declared which relates to a sale taking place before the last sale on the basis of which the goods were introduced into the customs territory of the Community, it must be demonstrated to the satisfaction of the customs authorities that this sale of goods took place for export to the customs territory in question.

The provisions of Articles 178 to 181a shall apply.][1]

2. ...[2], where goods are used in a third country between the time of sale and the time of entry into free circulation the customs value need not be the transaction value.

3. The buyer need satisfy no condition other than that of being a party to the contract of sale.

Amendments
1 Substituted by Commission Regulation (EC) No 1762/95 art 1(2)(*a*). See OJ L 171, 21.7.95, p 8.
2 Deleted by Commission Regulation (EC) No 1762/95 art 1(2)(*b*). See OJ L 171, 21.7.95, p 8.

Article 148

Where, in applying Article 29(1)(*b*) of the Code, it is established that the sale or price of imported goods is subject to a condition or consideration the value of which can be determined with respect to the goods being valued, such value shall be regarded as an indirect payment by the buyer to the seller and part of the price actually paid or payable provided that the condition or consideration does not relate to either:

    (*a*)   an activity to which Article 29(3)(*b*) of the Code applies, or

    (*b*)   a factor in respect of which an addition is to be made to the price actually paid or payable under the provisions of Article 32 of the Code.

Article 149

1. For the purposes of Article 29(3)(*b*) of the Code, the term 'marketing activities' means all activities relating to advertising and promoting the sale of the goods in question and all activities relating to warranties or guarantees in respect of them.

2. Such activities undertaken by the buyer shall be regarded as having been undertaken on his own account even if they are performed in pursuance of an obligation on the buyer following an agreement with the seller.

Article 150

1. In applying Article 30(2)(*a*) of the Code (the transaction value of identical goods), the customs value shall be determined by reference to the transaction value of identical goods in a sale at the same commercial level and in substantially the same quantity as the goods being valued. Where no such sale is found, the transaction value of identical goods sold at a different commercial level and/or in different quantities, adjusted to take account of differences attributable to commercial level and/or to quantity, shall be used, provided that such adjustments can be made on the basis of demonstrated evidence which clearly establishes the reasonableness and accuracy of the adjustment, whether the adjustment leads to an increase or a decrease in the value.

2. Where the costs and charges referred to in Article 32(1)(*e*) of the Code are included in the transaction value, an adjustment shall be made to take account of significant differences in such costs and charges between the imported goods and the identical goods in question arising from differences in distances and modes of transport.

3. If, in applying this Article, more than one transaction value of identical goods is found, the lowest such value shall be used to determine the customs value of the imported goods.

4. In applying this Article, a transaction value for goods produced by a different person shall be taken into account only when no transaction value can be found under paragraph 1 for identical goods produced by the same person as the goods being valued.

5. For the purposes of this Article, the transaction value of identical imported goods means a customs value previously determined under Article 29 of the Code, adjusted as provided for in paragraphs 1 and 2 of this Article.

Article 151

1. In applying Article 30(2)(*b*) of the Code (the transaction value of similar goods), the customs value shall be determined by reference to the transaction value of similar goods in a sale at the same commercial level and in substantially the same quantity as the goods being valued. Where no such sale is found, the transaction value of similar goods sold at a different commercial level and/or in different quantities, adjusted to take account of differences attributable to commercial level and/or to quantity, shall be used, provided that such adjustments can be made on the basis of demonstrated evidence which clearly establishes the reasonableness and accuracy of the adjustment, whether the adjustment leads to an increase or a decrease in the value.

2. Where the costs and charges referred to in Article 32(1)(*e*) of the Code are included in the transaction value, an adjustment shall be made to take account of significant differences in such costs and charges between the imported goods and the similar goods in question arising from differences in distances and modes of transport.

3. If, in applying this Article, more than one transaction value of similar goods is found, the lowest such value shall be used to determine the customs value for the imported goods.

4. In applying this Article, a transaction value for goods produced by a different person shall be taken into account only when no transaction value can be found under paragraph 1 for similar goods produced by the same person as the goods being valued.

5. For the purposes of this Article, the transaction value of similar imported goods means a customs value previously determined under Article 29 of the Code, adjusted as provided for in paragraphs 1 and 2 of this Article.

Article 152

1.   (*a*)   If the imported goods or identical or similar imported goods are sold in the Community in the condition as imported, the customs value of imported goods, determined in accordance with Article 30(2)(*c*) of the Code, shall be based on the unit price at which the imported goods or identical or similar imported goods are so sold in the greatest aggregate quantity, at or about the time of the importation of the goods being valued, to persons who are not related to the persons from whom they buy such goods, subject to deductions for the following:

      (i)   either the commissions usually paid or agreed to be paid or the additions usually made for profit and general expenses (including the direct and indirect costs of marketing the goods in question) in connection with sales in the Community of imported goods of the same class or kind;

      (ii)   the usual costs of transport and insurance and associated costs incurred within the Community;

      (iii)   the import duties and other charges payable in the Community by reason of the importation or sale of the goods.

  (*b*)   If neither the imported goods nor identical nor similar imported goods are sold at or about the time of importation of the goods being valued, the customs value of imported goods determined under this Article shall, subject otherwise to the provisions of paragraph 1(*a*), be based on the unit price at which the imported goods or identical or similar imported goods are sold in the Community in the condition as imported at the earliest date after the importation of the goods being valued but before the expiration of 90 days after such importation.

2. If neither the imported goods nor identical nor similar imported goods are sold in the Community in the condition as imported, then, if the importer so requests, the customs value shall be based on the unit price at which the imported goods, after further processing, are sold in the greatest aggregate quantity to persons in the Community who are not related to the persons from whom they buy such goods, due allowance being made for the value added by such processing and the deductions provided for in paragraph 1(*a*).

3. For the purposes of this Article, the unit price at which imported goods are sold in the greatest aggregate quantity is the price at which the greatest number of units is sold in sales to persons who are not related to the persons from whom they buy such goods at the first commercial level after importation at which such sales take place.

4. Any sale in the Community to a person who supplies directly or indirectly free of charge or at reduced cost for use in connection with the production and sale for export of the imported goods any of the elements specified in Article 32(1)(*b*) of the Code should not be taken into account in establishing the unit price for the purposes of this Article.

5. For the purposes of paragraph 1(*b*), the 'earliest date' shall be the date by which sales of the imported goods or of identical or similar imported goods are made in sufficient quantity to establish the unit price.

Article 153

1. In applying Article 30(2)(*d*) of the Code (computed value), the customs authorities may not require or compel any person not resident in the Community to produce for examination, or to allow access to, any account or other record for the purposes of determining this value. However, information supplied by the producer of the goods for the purposes of determining the customs value under this Article may be verified in a non-Community country by the customs authorities of a Member State with the agreement of the producer and provided that such authorities give sufficient advance notice to the authorities of the country in question and the latter do not object to the investigation.

2. The cost or value of materials and fabrication referred to in the first indent of Article 30(2)(*d*) of the Code shall include the cost of elements specified in Article 32(1)(*a*)(ii) and (iii) of the Code.

It shall also include the value, duly apportioned, of any product or service specified in Article 32(1)(*b*) of the Code which has been supplied directly or indirectly by the buyer for use in connection with the production of the imported goods. The value of the elements specified in Article 32(1)(*b*)(iv) of the Code which are undertaken in the Community shall be included only to the extent that such elements are charged to the producer.

3. Where information other than that supplied by or on behalf of the producer is used for the purposes of determining a computed value, the customs authorities shall inform the declarant, if the latter so requests, of the source of such information, the data used and the calculations based on such data, subject to Article 15 of the Code.

4. The 'general expenses' referred to in the second indent of Article 30(2)(*d*) of the Code, cover the direct and indirect costs of producing and selling the goods for export which are not included under the first indent of Article 30(2)(*d*) of the Code.

Article 154

Where containers referred to in Article 32(1)(*a*)(ii) of the Code are to be the subject of repeated importations, their cost shall, at the request of the declarant, be apportioned, as appropriate, in accordance with generally accepted accounting principles.

Article 155

For the purposes of Article 32(1)(*b*)(iv) of the Code, the cost of research and preliminary design sketches is not to be included in the customs value.

Article 156

Article 33(*c*) of the Code shall apply *mutatis mutandis* where the customs value is determined by applying a method other than the transaction value.

CHAPTER 2
Provisions concerning royalties and licence fees

Article 157

1. For the purposes of Article 32(1)(*c*) of the Code, royalties and licence fees shall be taken to mean in particular payment for the use of rights relating:

— to the manufacture of imported goods (in particular, patents, designs, models and manufacturing know-how), or

— to the sale for exportation of imported goods (in particular, trade marks, registered designs), or

— to the use or resale of imported goods (in particular, copyright, manufacturing processes inseparably embodied in the imported goods).

2. Without prejudice to Article 32(5) of the Code, when the customs value of imported goods is determined under the provisions of Article 29 of the Code, a royalty or licence fee shall be added to the price actually paid or payable only when this payment:

— is related to the goods being valued, and

— constitutes a condition of sale of those goods.

Article 158

1. When the imported goods are only an ingredient or component of goods manufactured in the Community, an adjustment to the price actually paid or payable for the imported goods shall only be made when the royalty or licence fee relates to those goods.

2. Where goods are imported in an unassembled state or only have to undergo minor processing before resale, such as diluting or packing, this shall not prevent a royalty or licence fee from being considered related to the imported goods.

3. If royalties or licence fees relate partly to the imported goods and partly to other ingredients or component parts added to the goods after their importation, or to post-importation activities or services, an appropriate apportionment shall be made only on the basis of objective and quantifiable data, in accordance with the interpretative note to Article 32(2) of the Code in Annex 23.

Article 159

A royalty or licence fee in respect of the right to use a trade mark is only to be added to the price actually paid or payable for the imported goods where:

— the royalty or licence fee refers to goods which are resold in the same state or which are subject only to minor processing after importation,

— the goods are marketed under the trade mark, affixed before or after importation, for which the royalty or licence fee is paid, and

— the buyer is not free to obtain such goods from other suppliers unrelated to the seller.

Article 160

When the buyer pays royalties or licence fees to a third party, the conditions provided for in Article 157(2) shall not be considered as met unless the seller or a person related to him requires the buyer to make that payment.

Article 161

Where the method of calculation of the amount of a royalty or licence fee derives from the price of the imported goods, it may be assumed in the absence of evidence to the contrary that the payment of that royalty or licence fee is related to the goods to be valued.

However, where the amount of a royalty or licence fee is calculated regardless of the price of the imported goods, the payment of that royalty or licence fee may nevertheless be related to the goods to be valued.

Article 162

In applying Article 32(1)(c) of the Code, the country of residence of the recipient of the payment of the royalty or licence fee shall not be a material consideration.

CHAPTER 3
Provisions concerning place of introduction into the Community

Article 163

1. For the purposes of Article 32(1)(e) and Article 33(a) of the Code, the place of introduction into the customs territory of the Community shall be:

 (a)   for goods carried by sea, the port of unloading, or the port of transhipment, subject to transhipment being certified by the customs authorities of that port;

 (b)   for goods carried by sea and then, without transhipment, by inland waterway, the first port where unloading can take place either at the mouth of the river or canal or further inland, subject to proof being furnished to the customs office that the freight to the port of unloading is higher than that to the first port;

 (c)   for goods carried by rail, inland waterway, or road, the place where the first customs office is situated;

 (d)   for goods carried by other means, the place where the land frontier of the customs territory of the Community is crossed.

[**2.** The customs value of goods introduced into the customs territory of the Community and then carried to a destination in another part of that territory through the territories of Belarus, Bulgaria, the Czech Republic, Estonia, Hungary, Latvia, Lithuania, Poland, Russia, Romania, the Slovak Republic, Switzerland, or former Yugoslavia in its borders of 1 January 1991 shall be determined by reference to the first place of introduction into the customs territory of the Community, provided that goods are carried direct through the territories of those countries by a usual route across such territory to the place of destination.][1]

3. The customs value of goods introduced into the customs territory of the Community and then carried by sea to a destination in another part of that territory shall be determined by reference to the first place of introduction into the customs territory of the Community, provided the goods are carried direct by a usual route to the place of destination.

[**4.** Paragraphs 2 and 3 of this Article shall also apply where the goods have been unloaded, transhipped or temporarily immobilized in the territories of Belarus, Bulgaria, the Czech Republic, Estonia, Hungary, Latvia, Lithuania, Poland, Russia, Romania, the Slovak Republic, Switzerland, or former Yugoslavia in its borders of 1 January 1991 for reasons related solely to their transport.][1]

5. For goods introduced into the customs territory of the Community and carried directly from one of the French overseas departments to another part of the customs territory of the Community or vice versa, the place of introduction to be taken into consideration shall be the place referred to in paragraphs 1 and 2 situated in that part of the customs territory of the Community from which the goods came, if they were unloaded or transhipped there and this was certified by the customs authorities.

6. When the conditions specified at paragraphs 2, 3 and 5 are not fulfilled, the place of introduction to be taken into consideration shall be the place specified in paragraph 1 situated in that part of the customs territory of the Community to which the goods are consigned.

Amendments

1   Substituted by the Act of Accession of Austria, Finland and Sweden. See OJ C 241 of 29.8.94, p 1.

CHAPTER 4
Provisions concerning transport costs

Article 164

In applying Article 32(1)(*e*) and 33(*a*) of the Code:

(*a*)   where goods are carried by the same mode of transport to a point beyond the place of introduction into the customs territory of the Community, transport costs shall be assessed in proportion to the distance covered outside and inside the customs territory of the Community, unless evidence is produced to the customs authorities to show the costs that would have been incurred under a general compulsory schedule of freight rates for the carriage of the goods to the place of introduction into the customs territory of the Community;

(*b*)   where goods are invoiced at a uniform free domicile price which corresponds to the price at the place of introduction, transport costs within the Community shall not be deducted from that price. However, such deduction shall be allowed if evidence is produced to the customs authorities that the free-frontier price would be lower than the uniform free domicile price;

(*c*)   where transport is free or provided by the buyer, transport costs to the place of introduction, calculated in accordance with the schedule of freight rates normally applied for the same modes of transport, shall be included in the customs value.

Article 165

1. All postal charges levied up to the place of destination in respect of goods sent by post shall be included in the customs value of these goods, with the exception of any supplementary postal charge levied in the country of importation.

2. No adjustment to the declared value shall, however, be made in respect of such charges in determining the value of consignments of a non-commercial nature.

3. Paragraphs 1 and 2 are not applicable to goods carried by the express postal services known as EMS - Datapost (in Denmark, EMS - Jetpost, in Germany, EMS Kurierpostsendungen, in Italy, CAI-Post).

Article 166

The air transport costs to be included in the customs value of goods shall be determined by applying the rules and percentages shown in Annex 25.

CHAPTER 5
Valuation of certain carrier media for use in ADP equipment

Article 167

1. Notwithstanding Articles 29 to 33 of the Code, in determining the customs value of imported carrier media bearing data or instructions for use in data processing equipment, only the cost or value of the carrier medium itself shall be taken into account. The customs value of imported carrier media bearing data or instructions shall not, therefore, include the cost or value of the data or instructions, provided that such cost or value is distinguished from the cost or value of the carrier medium in question.

2. For the purposes of this Article:

    (*a*)   the expression 'carrier medium' shall not be taken to include integrated circuits, semiconductors and similar devices or articles incorporating such circuits or devices;

    (*b*)   the expression 'data or instructions' shall not be taken to include sound, cinematographic or video recordings.

CHAPTER 6
Provisions concerning rates of exchange

Article 168

For the purposes of Articles 169 to 171 of this chapter:

    (*a*)   **'rate recorded'** shall mean:

         —   the latest selling rate of exchange recorded for commercial transactions on the most representative exchange market or markets of the Member State concerned, or

         —   some other description of a rate of exchange so recorded and designated by the Member State as the 'rate recorded' provided that it reflects as effectively as possible the current value of the currency in question in commercial transactions;

    (*b*)   **'published'** shall mean made generally known in a manner designated by the Member State concerned;

    (*c*)   **'currency'** shall mean any monetary unit used as a means of settlement between monetary authorities or on the international market.

Article 169

1. Where factors used to determine the customs value of goods are expressed at the time when that value is determined in a currency other than that of the Member State where the valuation is made, the rate of exchange to be used to determine that value in terms of the currency of the Member State concerned shall be the rate recorded on the second-last Wednesday of a month and published on that or the following day.

2. The rate recorded on the second-last Wednesday of a month shall be used during the following calendar month unless it is superseded by a rate established under Article 171.

3. Where a rate of exchange is not recorded on the second-last Wednesday indicated in paragraph 1, or, if recorded, is not published on that or the following day, the last rate recorded for the currency in question published within the preceding 14 days shall be deemed to be the rate recorded on that Wednesday.

Article 170

Where a rate of exchange cannot be established under the provisions of Article 169, the rate of exchange to be used for the application of Article 35 of the Code shall be designated by the Member State concerned and shall reflect as effectively as possible the current value of the currency in question in commercial transactions in terms of the currency of that Member State.

Article 171

1. Where a rate of exchange recorded on the last Wednesday of a month and published on that or the following day differs by 5% or more from the rate established in accordance with Article 169 for entry into use the following month, it shall replace the latter rate from the first Wednesday of that month as the rate to be applied for the application of Article 35 of the Code.

2. Where in the course of a period of application as referred to in the preceding provisions, a rate of exchange recorded on a Wednesday and published on that or the following day differs by 5% or more from the rate being used in accordance with this Chapter, it shall replace the latter rate and enter into use on the Wednesday following as the rate to be used for the application of Article 35 of the Code. The replacement rate shall remain in use for the remainder of the current month, provided that this rate is not superseded due to operation of the provisions of the first sentence of this paragraph.

3. Where, in a Member State, a rate of exchange is not recorded on a Wednesday or, if recorded, is not published on that or the following day, the rate recorded shall, for the application in that Member State of paragraphs 1 and 2, be the rate most recently recorded and published prior to that Wednesday.

Article 172

When the customs authorities of a Member State authorize a declarant to furnish or supply at a later date certain details concerning the declaration for free circulation of the goods in the form of a periodic declaration, this authorization may, at the declarant's request, provide that a single rate be used for conversion into that Member State's currency of elements forming part of the customs value as expressed in a particular currency. In this case, the rate to be used shall be the rate, established in accordance with this Chapter, which is applicable on the first day of the period covered by the declaration in question.

CHAPTER 7
Simplified procedures for certain perishable goods

Article 173

1. For the purpose of determining the customs value of products referred to in Annex 26, the Commission shall establish for each classification heading a unit value per 100 kg net expressed in the currencies of the Member States. The unit values shall apply for periods of 14 days, each period beginning on a Friday.

2. Unit values shall be established on the basis of the following elements, which are to be supplied to the Commission by Member States, in relation to each classification heading:

(*a*)   the average free-at-frontier unit price, not cleared through customs, expressed in the currency of the Member State in question per 100 kg net and calculated on the basis of prices for undamaged goods in the marketing centres referred to in Annex 27 during the reference period referred to in Article 174(1);

(*b*)   the quantities entered into free circulation over the period of a calendar year with payment of import duties.

3. The average free-at-frontier unit price, not cleared through customs, shall be calculated on the basis of the gross proceeds of sales made between importers and wholesalers. However, in the case of the London, Milan and Rungis marketing centres the gross proceeds shall be those recorded at the commercial level at which those goods are most commonly sold at those centres.

There shall be deducted from the figures so arrived at:

—   a marketing margin of 15% for the marketing centres of London, Milan and Rungis and of 8% for the other marketing centres,

—   costs of transport and insurance within the customs territory,

—   a standard amount of ECU 5 representing all the other costs which are not to be included in the customs value.

   This amount shall be converted into the currencies of the Member States on the basis of the latest rates in force established in accordance with Article 18 of the Code.

—   import duties and other charges which are not to be included in the customs value.

4. The Member States may fix standard amounts for deduction in respect of transport and insurance costs in accordance with paragraph 3. Such standard amounts and the methods for calculating them shall be made known to the Commission immediately.

Note
Annex 26 is not reproduced because it is subject to frequent changes.

Article 174

1. The reference period for calculating the average unit prices referred to in Article 173(2)(*a*) shall be the period of 14 days ending on the Thursday preceding the week during which new unit values are to be established.

2. Average unit prices shall be notified by Member States not later than 12 noon on the Monday of the week during which unit values are established pursuant to Article 173. If that day is a non-working day, notification shall be made on the working day immediately preceding that day.

3. The quantities entered into free circulation during a calendar year for each classification heading shall be notified to the Commission by all Member States before 15 June in the following year.

Article 175 ˎ

1. The unit values referred to in Article 173(1) shall be established by the Commission on alternate Tuesdays on the basis of the weighted average of the average unit prices referred to in Article 173(2)(*a*) in relation to the quantities referred to in Article 173(2)(*b*).

2. For the purpose of determining the weighted average, each average unit price as referred to in Article 173(2)(*a*) shall be converted into ecu on the basis of the last conversion rates determined by the Commission and published in the *Official Journal of the European Communities* prior to the week during which the unit values are to be established. The same conversion rates shall be applied in converting the unit values so obtained back into the currencies of the Member States.

3. The last published unit values shall remain applicable until new values are published. However, in the case of major fluctuations in price in one or more Member States, as a result, for example, of an interruption in the continuity of imports of a particular product, new unit values may be determined on the basis of actual prices at the time of fixing those values.

Article 176

1. Consignments which at the material time for valuation for customs purposes contain not less than 5% of produce unfit in its unaltered state for human consumption or the value of which has depreciated by not less than 20% in relation to average market prices for sound produce, shall be treated as damaged.

2. Consignments which are damaged may be valued:

— either, after sorting, by application of unit values to the sound portion, the damaged portion being destroyed under customs supervision, or

— by application of unit values established for the sound produce after deduction from the weight of the consignment of a percentage equal to the percentage assessed as damaged by a sworn expert and accepted by the customs authorities, or

— by application of unit values established for the sound produce reduced by the percentage assessed as damaged by a sworn expert and accepted by the customs authorities.

Article 177

1. In declaring or causing to be declared the customs value of one or more products which he imports by reference to the unit values established in accordance with this Chapter, the person concerned joins the simplified procedure system for the current calendar year in respect of the product or products in question.

2. If subsequently the person concerned requires the use of a method other than the simplified procedures for the customs valuation of one or more of the products he imports, the customs authorities of the Member State concerned shall be entitled to notify him that he will not be allowed to benefit from the simplified procedures for the remainder of the current calendar year in regard to the product or products concerned; this exclusion can be extended for the following calendar year. Such notified exclusion shall be communicated without delay to the Commission, which shall in turn immediately inform the customs authorities of the other Member States.

CHAPTER 8

Declarations of particulars and documents to be furnished

Article 178

1. Where it is necessary to establish a customs value for the purposes of Articles 28 to 36 of the Code, a declaration of particulars relating to customs value (value declaration) shall accompany the customs entry made in respect of the imported goods. The value declaration shall be drawn up on a form D.V. 1 corresponding to the specimen in Annex 28, supplemented where appropriate by one or more forms D.V. 1 *bis* corresponding to the specimen in Annex 29.

2. It shall be a particular requirement that the value declaration prescribed in paragraph 1 shall be made only by a person who has his residence or place of business in the customs territory of the Community and is in possession of the relevant facts.

3. The customs authorities may waive the requirement of a declaration on the form referred to in paragraph 1 where the customs value of the goods in question cannot be determined under the provisions of Article 29 of the Code. In such cases the person referred to in paragraph 2 shall furnish or cause to be furnished to the customs authorities such other information as may be requested for the purposes of determining the customs value under another Article of the said Code; and such other information shall be supplied in such form and manner as may be prescribed by the customs authorities.

4. The lodging with a customs office of a declaration required by paragraph 1 shall, without prejudice to the possible application of penal provisions, be equivalent to the engagement of responsibility by the person referred to in paragraph 2 in respect of:

— the accuracy and completeness of the particulars given in the declaration,

— the authenticity of the documents produced in support of these particulars, and

— the supply of any additional information or document necessary to establish the customs value of the goods.

5. This Article shall not apply in respect of goods for which the customs value is determined under the simplified procedure system established in accordance with the provisions of Articles 173 to 177.

Article 179

1. Except where it is essential for the correct application of import duties, the customs authorities shall waive the requirement of all or part of the declaration provided for in Article 178(1):

(*a*) where the customs value of the imported goods in a consignment does not exceed ECU 5 000, provided that they do not constitute split or multiple consignments from the same consignor to the same consignee; or

(*b*) where the importations involved are of a non- commercial nature; or

(*c*) where the submission of the particulars in question is not necessary for the application of the Customs Tariff of the European Communities or where the customs duties provided for in the Tariff are not chargeable pursuant to specific customs provisions.

2. The amount in ecu referred to in Paragraph 1(*a*) shall be converted in accordance with Article 18 of the Code. The customs authorities may round-off upwards or downwards the sum arrived at after conversion.

The customs authorities may maintain unamended the exchange value in national currency of the amount determined in ecu if, at the time of the annual adjustment provided for in Article 18 of the Code, the conversion of this amount, before the rounding-off provided for in this paragraph, leads to an alteration of less than 5% in the exchange value expressed in national currency or to a reduction thereof.

3. In the case of continuing traffic in goods supplied by the same seller to the same buyer under the same commercial conditions, the customs authorities may waive the requirement that all particulars under Article 178(1) be furnished in support of each customs declaration, but shall require them whenever the circumstances change and at least once every three years.

4. A waiver granted under this Article may be withdrawn and the submission of a D.V. 1 may be required where it is found that a condition necessary to qualify for that waiver was not or is no longer met.

Article 180

Where computerized systems are used, or where the goods concerned are the subject of a general, periodic or recapitulative declaration, the customs authorities may authorize variations in the form of presentation of data required for the determination of customs value.

Article 181

1. The person referred to in Article 178(2) shall furnish the customs authorities with a copy of the invoice on the basis of which the value of the imported goods is declared. Where the customs value is declared in writing this copy shall be retained by the customs authorities.

2. In the case of written declarations of the customs value, when the invoice for the imported goods is made out to a person established in a Member State other than that in which the customs value is declared, the declarant shall furnish the customs authorities with two copies of the invoice. One of these copies shall be retained by the customs authorities; the other, bearing the stamp of the office in question and the serial number of the declaration at the said customs office shall be returned to the declarant for forwarding to the person to whom the invoice is made out.

3. The customs authorities may extend the provisions of paragraph 2 to cases where the person to whom the invoice is made out is established in the Member State in which the customs value is declared.

[Article 181a

1. The customs authorities need not determine the customs valuation of imported goods on the basis of the transaction value method if, in accordance with the procedure set out in paragraph 2, they are not satisfied, on the basis of reasonable doubts, that the declared value represents the total amount paid or payable as referred to in Article 29 of the Code

2. Where the customs authorities have the doubts described in paragraph 1 they may ask for additional information in accordance with article 178(4). If those doubts continue, the customs authorities must, before reaching a final decision, notify the person concerned, in writing if requested, of the grounds for those doubts and provide him with a reasonable opportunity to respond. A final decision and the grounds therefor shall be communicated in writing to the person concerned.][1]

Amendments

1   Inserted by EC Commission Regulation 3254/94. See OJ L 346 of 31.12.94, p 1.

TITLE VI
Introduction of goods into the customs territory

CHAPTER 1
Examination of the goods and taking of samples by the person concerned

Article 182

TITLE VII
Customs declarations — normal procedure

CHAPTER 1
Customs declaration in writing

SECTION 1
General provisions

Article 198

1. Where a customs declaration covers two or more articles, the particulars relating to each article shall be regarded as constituting a separate declaration.

2. Component parts of industrial plant coming under a single Combined Nomenclature Code shall be regarded as constituting a single item of goods.

Article 199

Without prejudice to the possible application of penal provisions, the lodging with a customs office of a declaration signed by the declarant or his representative shall render him responsible under the provisions in force for:

— the accuracy of the information given in the declaration,

— the authenticity of the documents attached,

and

— compliance with all the obligations relating to the entry of the goods in question under the procedure concerned.

[**2.** Where the declarant uses data-processing systems to produce his customs declarations, the customs authorities may provide that the handwritten signature may be replaced by another identification technique which may be based on the use of codes. This facility shall be granted only if the technical and administrative conditions laid down by the customs authorities are complied with.

The customs authorities may also provide that declarations produced using customs data-processing systems may be directly authenticated by those systems, in place of the manual or mechanical application of the customs office stamp and the signature of the competent official.

3. Under the conditions and in the manner which they shall determine, the customs authorities may allow some of the particulars of the written declaration referred to in Annex 37 to be replaced by sending these particulars to the customs office designated for that purpose by electronic means, where appropriate in coded form.][1]

Amendments
1 Inserted by EC Commission Regulation 3665/93 art 1(11). See OJ L335 of 31.12.93, p 1.

Article 200

Documents accompanying a declaration shall be kept by the customs authorities unless the said authorities provide otherwise or unless the declarant requires them for other operations. In the latter case the customs authorities shall take the necessary steps to ensure that the documents in question cannot subsequently be used except in respect of the quantity or value of goods for which they remain valid.

Article 201

1. The declaration shall be lodged with the customs office where the goods were presented. It may be lodged as soon as such presentation has taken place.

2. The customs authorities may authorize the declaration to be lodged before the declarant is in a position to present the goods. In this case, the customs authorities may set a time limit, to be determined according to the circumstances, for presentation of the goods. If the goods have not been presented within this time limit, the declaration shall be considered not to have been lodged.

3. Where a declaration has been lodged before the goods to which it relates have arrived at the customs office or at another place designated by the customs authorities, it may be accepted only after the goods in question have been presented to customs.

Article 202

1. The declaration shall be lodged with the competent customs office during the days and hours appointed for opening.

However, the customs authorities may, at the request of the declarant and at his expense, authorize the declaration to be lodged outside the appointed days and hours.

2. Any declaration lodged with the officials of a customs office in any other place duly designated for that purpose by agreement between the customs authorities and the person concerned shall be considered to have been lodged in the said office.

Article 203

The date of acceptance of the declaration shall be noted thereon.

Article 204

The customs authorities may allow or require the corrections referred to in Article 65 of the Code to be made by the lodging of a new declaration intended to replace the original declaration. In that event, the relevant date for determination of any duties payable and for the application of any other provisions governing the customs procedure in question shall be the date of the acceptance of the original declaration.

SECTION 2
Forms to be used

Article 205

1. The official model for written declarations to customs by the normal procedure, for the purposes of placing goods under a customs procedure or re-exporting them in accordance with Article 182(3) of the Code, shall be the Single Administrative Document.

2. Other forms may be used for this purpose where the provisions of the customs procedure in question permit.

3. The provisions of paragraphs 1 and 2 shall not preclude:

— waiver of the written declaration prescribed in Articles 225 to 236 for release for free circulation, export or temporary importation,

— waiver by the Member States of the form referred to in paragraph 1 where the special provisions laid down in Articles 237 and 238 with regard to consignments by letter or parcel-post apply,

— use of special forms to facilitate the declaration in specific cases, where the customs authorities so permit,

— waiver by the Member States of the form referred to in paragraph 1 in the case of existing or future agreements or arrangements concluded between the administrations of two or more Member States with a view to greater simplification of formalities in all or part of the trade between those Member States,

— use by the persons concerned of loading lists for the completion of Community transit formalities in the case of consignments composed of more than one kind of goods,

— printing of export, transit or import declarations and documents certifying the Community status of goods not being moved under internal Community transit procedure by means of official or private-sector data-processing systems, if necessary on plain paper, on conditions laid down by the Member States,

— provision by the Member States to the effect that where a computerized declaration-processing system is used, the declaration, within the meaning of paragraph 1, may take the form of the Single Administrative Document printed out by that system.

4. ...[1].

5. Where in Community legislation, reference is made to an export, re-export or import declaration or a declaration placing goods under another customs procedure, Member States may not require any administrative documents other than those which are:

— expressly created by Community acts or provided for by such acts,

— required under the terms of international conventions compatible with the Treaty,

— required from operators to enable them to qualify, at their request, for an advantage or specific facility,

— required, with due regard for the provisions of the Treaty, for the implementation of specific regulations which cannot be implemented solely by the use of the document referred to in paragraph 1.

Amendments
1 Deleted by EC Commission Regulation 3665/93 art 1(12). See OJ L 335 of 31.12.93, p 1.

Article 206

The Single Administrative Document form shall, where necessary, also be used during the transitional period laid down in the Act of Accession of Spain and Portugal in connection with trade between the Community as constituted on 31 December 1985 and Spain or Portugal and between those two last-mentioned Member States in goods still liable to certain customs duties and charges having equivalent effect or which remain subject to other measures laid down by the Act of Accession.

For the purposes of the first paragraph, copy 2 or where applicable copy 7 of the forms used for trade with Spain and Portugal or trade between those Member States shall be destroyed.

It shall also be used in trade in Community goods between parts of the customs territory of the Community to which the provisions of Council Directive 77/388/EEC (OJ No L 145, 13.6.1977, p 1) apply and parts of that territory where those provisions do not apply, or in trade between parts of that territory where those provisions do not apply.

Article 207

Without prejudice to Article 205(3), the customs administrations of the Member States may in general, for the purpose of completing export or import formalities, dispense with the production of one or more copies of the Single Administrative Document intended for use by the authorities of that Member State, provided that the information in question is available on other media.

Article 208

1. The Single Administrative Document shall be presented in subsets containing the number of copies required for the completion of formalities relating to the customs procedure under which the goods are to be placed.

2. Where the Community transit procedure or the common transit procedure is preceded or followed by another customs procedure, a subset containing the number of copies required for the completion of formalities relating to the transit procedure and the preceding or following procedure may be presented.

3. The subsets referred to in paragraphs 1 and 2 shall be taken from:

— either the full set of eight copies, in accordance with the specimen contained in Annex 31,

— or, particularly in the event of production by means of a computerized system for processing declarations, two successive sets of four copies, in accordance with the specimen contained in Annex 32.

4. Without prejudice to Articles 205(3), 222 to 224 or 254 to 289, the declaration forms may be supplemented, where appropriate, by one or more continuation forms presented in subsets containing the declaration copies needed to complete the formalities relating to the customs procedure under which the goods are to be placed. Those copies needed in order to complete the formalities relating to preceding or subsequent customs procedures may be attached where appropriate.

The continuation subsets shall be taken from:

— either a set of eight copies, in accordance with the specimen contained in Annex 33,

— or two sets of four copies, in accordance with the specimen contained in Annex 34.

The continuation forms shall be an integral part of the Single Administrative Document to which they relate.

5. By way of derogation from paragraph 4, the customs authorities may provide that continuation forms shall not be used where a computerized system is used to produce such declarations.

Article 209

1. Where Article 208(2) is applied, each party involved shall be liable only as regards the particulars relating to the procedure for which he applied as declarant, principal or as the representative of one of these.

2. For the purposes of paragraph 1, where the declarant uses a Single Administrative Document issued during the preceding customs procedure, he shall be required, prior to lodging his declaration, to verify the accuracy of the existing particulars for the boxes for which he is responsible and their applicability to the goods in question and the procedure applied for, and to supplement them as necessary.

In the cases referred to in the first subparagraph, the declarant shall immediately inform the customs office where the declaration is lodged of any discrepancy found between the goods in question and the existing particulars. In this case the declarant shall then draw up his declaration on fresh copies of the Single Administrative Document.

Article 210

Where the Single Administrative Document is used to cover several successive customs procedures, the customs authorities shall satisfy themselves that the particulars given in the declarations relating to the various procedures in question all agree.

Article 211

The declaration must be drawn up in one of the official languages of the Community which is acceptable to the customs authorities of the Member State where the formalities are carried out.

If necessary, the customs authorities of the Member State of destination may require from the declarant or his representative in that Member State a translation of the declaration into the official language or one of the official languages of the latter. The translation shall replace the corresponding particulars in the declaration in question.

By way of derogation from the preceding subparagraph, the declaration shall be drawn up in an official language of the Community acceptable to the Member State of destination in all cases where the declaration in the latter Member State is made on copies other than those initially presented to the customs office of the Member State of departure.

Article 212

1. The Single Administrative Document must be completed in accordance with the explanatory note in Annex 37 and any additional rules laid down in other Community legislation.

2. The customs authorities shall ensure that users have ready access to copies of the explanatory note referred to in paragraph 1.

3. The customs administrations of each Member State may, if necessary, supplement the explanatory note.

Article 213

The codes to be used in completing the forms referred to in Article 205(1) are listed in Annex 38.

Article 214

In cases where the rules require supplementary copies of the form referred to in Article 205(1), the declarant may use additional sheets or photocopies of the said form for this purpose.

Such additional sheets or photocopies must be signed by the declarant, presented to the customs authorities and endorsed by the latter under the same conditions as the Single Administrative Document. They shall be accepted by the customs authorities as if they were original documents provided that their quality and legibility are considered satisfactory by the said authorities.

Article 215

1. The forms referred to in Article 205(1) shall be printed on self-copying paper dressed for writing purposes and weighing at least 40 g/m^2 per square metre. The paper must be sufficiently opaque for the information on one side not to affect the legibility of the information on the other side and its strength should be such that in normal use it does not easily tear or crease.

The paper shall be white for all copies. However, on the copies used for Community transit (1,4,5 and 7), box 1 (first and third subdivisions), 2, 3, 4, 5, 6, 8, 15, 17, 18, 19, 21, 25, 27, 31, 32, 33 (first subdivision on the left), 35, 38, 40, 44, 50, 51, 52, 53, 55 and 56 shall have a green background.

The forms shall be printed in green ink.

2. The boxes are based on a unit of measurement of one tenth of an inch horizontally and one sixth of an inch vertically. The subdivisions are based on a unit of measurement of one-tenth of an inch horizontally.

3. A colour marking of the different copies shall be effected in the following manner:

    (*a*)   on forms conforming to the specimens shown in Annexes 31 and 33:

        —   copies 1, 2, 3 and 5 shall have at the right hand edge a continuous margin, coloured respectively red, green, yellow and blue,

        —   copies 4, 6, 7 and 8 shall have at the right hand edge a broken margin coloured respectively blue, red, green and yellow.

    (*b*)   on forms conforming to the specimens shown in Annexes 32 and 34, copies 1/ 6, 2/7, 3/8 and 4/5 shall have at the right hand edge a continuous margin and to the right of this a broken margin coloured respectively red, green, yellow and blue.

The width of these margins shall be approximately 3 mm. The broken margin shall comprise a series of squares with a side measurement of 3 mm each one separated by 3 mm.

4. The copies on which the particulars contained in the forms shown in Annexes 31 and 33 must appear by a self-copying process are shown in Annex 35.

The copies on which the particulars contained in the forms shown in Annexes 32 and 34 must appear by a self-copying process are shown in Annex 36.

5. The forms shall measure 210 by 297 mm with a maximum tolerance as to length of 5 mm less and 8 mm more.

6. The customs administrations of the Member States may require that the forms show the name and address of the printer or a mark enabling the printer to be identified. They may also make the printing of the forms conditional on prior technical approval.

SECTION 3

Particulars required according to the customs procedure concerned

Article 216

1. The maximum list of boxes to be used for declarations of entry for a particular customs procedure using the Single Administrative Document is contained in Annex 37.

2. Annex 37 also contains the minimum list of boxes to be used of declarations of entry for a particular customs procedure.

Article 217

The particulars required when one of the forms referred to in Article 205(2) is used depend on the form in question. They shall be supplemented where appropriate by the provisions relating to the customs procedure in question.

SECTION 4

Documents to accompany the customs declaration

Article 218

1. The following documents shall accompany the customs declaration for release for free circulation:

(*a*) the invoice on the basis of which the customs value of the goods is declared, as required under Article 181;

(*b*) where it is required under Article 178, the declaration of particulars for the assessment of the customs value of the goods declared, drawn up in accordance with the conditions laid down in the said Article;

(*c*) the documents required for the application of preferential tariff arrangements or other measures derogating from the legal rules applicable to the goods declared;

(*d*) all other documents required for the application of the provisions governing the release for free circulation of the goods declared.

2. The customs authorities may require transport documents or documents relating to the previous customs procedure, as appropriate, to be produced when the declaration is lodged.

Where a single item is presented in two or more packages, they may also require the production of a packing list or equivalent document indicating the contents of each package.

3. However, where goods qualify for duties under Article 81 of the Code, the documents referred to in paragraph 1(*b*) and (*c*) need not be required.

In addition, where goods qualify for relief from import duty, the documents referred to in paragraph 1(*a*), (*b*) and (*c*) need not be required unless the customs authorities consider it necessary for the purposes of applying the provisions governing the release of the goods in question for free circulation.

Article 219

1. The transit declaration shall be accompanied by the transport document. The office of departure may dispense with the presentation of this document at the time of completion of the formalities. However, the transport document shall be presented at the request of the customs office or any other competent authority in the course of transport.

2. Without prejudice to any applicable simplification measures, the customs document of export/dispatch or re-exportation of the goods from the customs territory of the Community or any document of equivalent effect shall be presented to the office of departure with the transit declaration to which it relates.

3. The customs authorities may, where appropriate, require production of the document relating to the preceding customs procedure.

Article 220

1. The documents to accompany the declaration of entry for a customs procedure with economic impact, except for the outward processing procedure, shall be as follows:

(*a*)   the documents laid down in Article 218, except in cases of entry for the customs warehousing procedure in a warehouse other than type D;

(*b*)   the authorization for the customs procedure in question or a copy of the application for authorization where the second sub-paragraph of Article 556(1) applies, except in cases of entry for the customs warehousing procedure or where Articles 568(3), 656(3) or 695(3) apply.

2. The documents to accompany the declaration of entry for the outward processing procedure shall be as follows:

(*a*)   the documents laid down in Article 221;

(*b*)   the authorization for the procedure or a copy of the application for authorization where the second subparagraph of Article 751(1) applies, except where Article 760(2) applies.

3. Article 218(2) shall apply to declarations of entry for any customs procedure with economic impact.

4. The customs authorities may allow the documents referred to in paragraphs 1(*b*) and 2(*b*) to be kept at their disposal instead of accompanying the declaration.

Article 221

1. The export or re-export declaration shall be accompanied by all documents necessary for the correct application of export duties and of the provisions governing the export of the goods in question.

2. Article 218(2) shall apply to export or re-export declarations.

CHAPTER 2
[Customs declarations made using a data-processing technique

Article 222

1. Where the customs declaration is made by a data-processing technique, the particulars of the written declaration referred to in Annex 37 shall be replaced by sending to the customs office designated for that purpose, with a view to their processing by computer, data in codified form, or data made out in any other form specified by the customs authorities and corresponding to the particulars required for written declarations.

2. A customs declaration made by EDI shall be considered to have been lodged when the EDI message is received by the customs authorities.

Acceptance of a customs declaration made by EDI shall be communicated to the declarant by means of a response message containing at least the identification details of the message received and/or the registration number of the customs declaration and the date of acceptance.

3. Where the customs declaration is made by EDI, the customs authorities shall lay down the rules for implementing the provisions laid down in Article 247.

4. Where the customs declaration is made by EDI, the release of the goods shall be notified to the declarant, indicating at least the identification details of the declaration and the date of release.

5. Where the particulars of the customs declaration are introduced into customs data-processing systems, paragraphs 2, 3 and 4 shall apply *mutatis mutandis*.

[*Article 223*

Where a paper copy of the customs declaration is required for the completion of other formalities, this shall, at the request of the declarant, be produced and authenticated, either by the customs office concerned, or in accordance with the second subparagraph of Article 199(2).][1]

Amendments
1 Substituted by EC Commission Regulation 3665/93 art 1(13). See OJ L 335 of 31.12.93, p 1.

[*Article 224*

Under the conditions and in the manner which they shall determine, the customs authorities may authorize the documents required for the entry of goods for a customs procedure to be made out and transmitted by electronic means.][1]

Amendments
1 Substituted by EC Commission Regulation 3665/93 art 1(13). See OJ L 335 of 31.12.93, p 1.

CHAPTER 3
Customs declarations made orally or by any other act

SECTION 1
Oral declarations

Article 225

Customs declarations may be made orally for the release for free circulation of the following goods:

    (*a*)   goods of a non-commercial nature:

        —   contained in travellers' personal luggage, or

        —   sent to private individuals, or

        —   in other cases of negligible importance, where this is authorized by the customs authorities;

    (*b*)   goods of a commercial nature provided:

        —   the total value per consignment and per declarant does not exceed the statistical threshold laid down in the Community provisions in force, and

        —   the consignment is not part of a regular series of similar consignments, and

        —   the goods are not being carried by an independent carrier as part of a larger freight movement;

    (*c*)   the goods referred to in Article 229, where these qualify for relief as returned goods;

    (*d*)   the goods referred to in Article 230(*b*) and (*c*).

Article 226

Customs declarations may be made orally for the export of:

(*a*)   goods of a non-commercial nature:

— contained in travellers' personal luggage, or

— sent by private individuals;

(*b*)   the goods referred to in Article 225(*b*);

(*c*)   the goods referred to in Article 231(*b*) and (*c*);

(*d*)   other goods in cases of negligible economic importance, where this is authorized by the customs authorities.

Article 227

1. The customs authorities may provide that Articles 225 and 226 shall not apply where the person clearing the goods is acting on behalf of another person in his capacity as customs agent.

2. Where the customs authorities are not satisfied that the particulars declared are accurate or that they are complete, they may require a written declaration.

Article 228

Where goods declared to customs orally in accordance with Articles 225 and 226 are subject to import or export duty the customs authorities shall issue a receipt to the person concerned against payment of the duty owing.

Article 229

1. Customs declarations may be made orally for the temporary importation of the following goods, in accordance with the conditions laid down in Article 696:   .

[(*a*) — animals for the uses referred to in points 12 and 13 of Annex 93a and equipment satisfying the conditions laid down in point (*b*) of Article 685(2),

— packings listed in Article 679, imported filled, bearing the permanent, indelible markings of a person established outside the customs territory of the Community,][1]

— radio and television production and broadcasting equipment and vehicles specially adapted for use for the above purpose and their equipment imported by public or private organizations established outside the customs territory of the Community and approved by the customs authorities issuing the authorization for the procedure to import such equipment and vehicles,

— instruments and apparatus necessary for doctors to provide assistance for patients awaiting an organ transplant pursuant to Article 671(2)(*c*).

(*b*)   the goods referred to in Article 232;

(*c*)   other goods, where this is authorized by the customs authorities.

2. The goods referred to in paragraph 1 may also be the subject of an oral declaration for re-exportation discharging a temporary importation procedure.

Amendments

1   Substituted by EC Commission Regulation 3665/93 art 1(14). See OJ L 335 of 31.12.93, p 1.

SECTION 2
Customs declarations made by any other act

Article 230

The following, where not expressly declared to customs, shall be considered to have been declared for release for free circulation by the act referred to in Article 233:

(a) goods of a non-commercial nature contained in travellers' personal luggage entitled to relief either under Chapter I, Title XI of Council Regulation (EEC) No 918/83 (OJ No L 105, 23.4.1983, p 1), or as returned goods;

(b) goods entitled to relief under Chapter I, Titles IX and X of Council Regulation (EEC) No 918/83;

(c) means of transport entitled to relief as returned goods;

(d) goods imported in the context of traffic of negligible importance and exempted from the requirement to be conveyed to a customs office in accordance with Article 38(4) of the Code, provided they are not subject to import duty.

Article 231

The following, where not expressly declared to customs, shall be considered to have been declared for export by the act referred to in Article 233(b):

(a) goods of a non-commercial nature not liable for export duty contained in travellers' personal luggage;

(b) means of transport registered in the customs territory of the Community and intended to be re-imported;

(c) goods referred to in Chapter II of Council Regulation (EEC) No 918/83;

(d) other goods in cases of negligible economic importance, where this is authorized by the customs authorities.

Article 232

1. The following, where not declared to customs in writing or orally, shall be considered to have been declared for temporary importation by the act referred to in Article 233, in accordance with Articles 698 and 735:

(a) travellers' personal effects and goods imported for sports purposes listed in Article 684;

(b) the means of transport listed in Articles 718 to 725.

2. Where they are not declared to customs in writing or orally, the goods referred to in paragraph 1 shall be considered to have been declared for re-exportation discharging the temporary importation procedure by the act referred to in Article 233.

Article 233

[**1.**]¹ For the purposes of Articles 230 to 232, the act which is considered to be a customs declaration may take the following forms:

(a) in the case of goods conveyed to a customs office or to any other place designated or approved in accordance with Article 38(1)(a) of the Code:

— going through the green or 'nothing to declare' channel in customs offices where the two-channel system is in operation,

— going through a customs office which does not operate the two-channel system without spontaneously making a customs declaration,

— affixing a 'nothing to declare' sticker or customs declaration disc to the windscreen of passenger vehicles where this possibility is provided for in national provisions;

(*b*) in the case of exemption from the obligation to convey goods to customs in accordance with the provisions implementing Article 38(4) of the Code, in the case of export in accordance with Article 231 and in the case of re-exportation in accordance with Article 232(2):

— the sole act of crossing the frontier of the customs territory of the Community.

[**2.** Where goods covered by point (*a*) of Article 230, point (*a*) of Article 231, point (*a*) of Article 232(1) or Article 232(2) contained in a passenger's baggage are carried by rail unaccompanied by the passenger and are declared to customs without the passenger being present in person the document referred to in Annex 38a may be used within the terms and limitations set out in it.][2]

Amendments

1 Inserted by Commission Regulation (EC) No 1762/95 art 1(3)(*a*). See OJ L 171, 21.7.95, p 8.
2 Inserted by Commission Regulation (EC) No 1762/95 art 1(3)(*b*). See OJ L 171, 21.7.95, p 8.

Article 234

1. Where the conditions of Articles 230 to 232 are fulfilled, the goods shall be considered to have been presented to customs within the meaning of Article 63 of the Code, the declaration to have been accepted and release to have been granted, at the time when the act referred to in Article 233 is carried out.

2. Where a check reveals that the act referred to in Article 233 has been carried out but the goods imported or taken out do not fulfil the conditions in Articles 230 to 232, the goods concerned shall be considered to have been imported or exported unlawfully.

SECTION 3
Provisions common to Sections 1 and 2

Article 235

The provisions of Articles 225 to 232 shall not apply to goods in respect of which the payment of refunds or other amounts or the repayment of duties is sought, or which are subject to a prohibition or restriction or to any other special formality.

Article 236

For the purposes of Sections 1 and 2, '**traveller**' means:

A. on import:

1. any person temporarily entering the customs territory of the Community, not normally resident there, and

2 any person returning to the customs territory of the Community where he is normally resident, after having been temporarily in a third country.

B. on export:

1. any person temporarily leaving the customs territory of the Community where he is normally resident, and

2. any person leaving the customs territory of the Community after a temporary stay, not normally resident there.

SECTION 4
Postal traffic

Article 237

1. The following postal consignments shall be considered to have been declared to customs:

A. for release for free circulation:

(*a*)   at the time when they are introduced into the customs territory of the Community:

—   postcards and letters containing personal messages only,

—   braille letters,

—   printed matter not liable for import duties, and

—   all other consignments sent by letter or parcel post which are exempt from the obligation to be conveyed to customs in accordance with provisions pursuant to Article 38(4) of the Code;

(*b*)   at the time when they are presented to customs:

—   consignments sent by letter or parcel post other than those referred to at (*a*), provided they are accompanied by a C1 and/or C2/CP3 declaration.

B. for export:

(*a*)   at the time when they are accepted by the postal authorities, in the case of consignments by letter and parcel post which are not liable to export duties.

(*b*)   at the time of their presentation to customs, in the case of consignments sent by letter or parcel post which are liable to export duties, provided they are accompanied by a C1 and/or a C2/CP3 declaration.

2. The consignee, in the cases referred to in paragraph 1A, and the consignor, in the cases referred to in paragraph 1B, shall be considered to be the declarant and, where applicable, the debtor. The customs authorities may provide that the postal administration shall be considered as the declarant and, where applicable, as the debtor.

3. For the purposes of paragraph 1, goods not liable to duty shall be considered to have been presented to customs within the meaning of Article 63 of the Code, the customs declaration to have been accepted and release granted:

(*a*)   in the case of imports, when the goods are delivered to the consignee;

(*b*)   in the case of exports, when the goods are accepted by the postal authorities.

4. Where a consignment sent by letter or parcel post which is not exempt from the obligation to be conveyed to customs in accordance with provisions pursuant to Article 38(4) of the Code is presented without a C1 and/or C2/CP3 declaration or where such declaration is incomplete, the customs authorities shall determine the form in which the customs declaration is to be made or supplemented.

Article 238

Article 237 shall not apply:

—   to consignments containing goods for commercial purposes of an aggregate value exceeding the statistical threshold laid down by the Community provisions in force; the customs authorities may lay down higher thresholds;

—   to consignments containing goods for commercial purposes which form part of a regular series of like operations;

—   where a customs declaration is made in writing, orally or using a data-processing technique;

—   to consignments containing the goods referred to in Article 235.

TITLE VIII

Examination of the goods, findings of the customs office and other measures taken by the customs office

Articles 239-856

Note

Articles 239-856 are outside the scope of this work.

PART IV

Customs debt

TITLE I

Security

Article 857

1. The types of security other than cash deposits or guarantors, within the meaning of Articles 193, 194 and 195 of the Code, and the cash deposit or the submission of securities for which Member States may opt even if they do not comply with the conditions laid down in Article 194(1) of the Code, shall be as follows:

(*a*) the creation of a mortgage, a charge on land, an antichresis or other right deemed equivalent to a right pertaining to immovable property;

(*b*) the cession of a claim, the pledging, with or without surrendering possession, of goods, securities or claims or, in particular, a savings bank book or entry in the national debt register;

(*c*) the assumption of joint contractual liability for the full amount of the debt by a third party approved for that purpose by the customs authorities and, in particular, the lodging of a bill of exchange the payment of which is guaranteed by such third party;

(*d*) a cash deposit or security deemed equivalent thereto in a currency other than that of the Member State in which the security is given;

(*e*) participation, subject to payment of a contribution, in a general guarantee scheme administered by the customs authorities.

2. The circumstances in which and the conditions under which recourse may be had to the types of security referred to in paragraph 1 shall be determined by the customs authorities.

Article 858

Where security is given by making a cash deposit, no interest thereon shall be payable by the customs authorities.

TITLE II

Incurrence of the debt

CHAPTER 1

Failures which have no significant effect on the operation of temporary storage or of the customs procedure

Article 859

The following failures shall be considered to have no significant effect on the correct operation of the temporary storage or customs procedure in question within the meaning of Article 204(1) of the Code, provided:

— they do not constitute an attempt to remove the goods unlawfully from customs supervision,

— they do not imply obvious negligence on the part of the person concerned, and

— all the formalities necessary to regularize the situation of the goods are subsequently carried out:

1. exceeding the time limit allowed for assignment of the goods to one of the customs-approved treatments or uses provided for under the temporary storage or customs procedure in question, where the time limit would have been extended had an extension been applied for in time;

761

2.   in the case of goods placed under a transit procedure, exceeding the time limit for presentation of the goods to the office of destination, where such presentation takes place later;

3.   in the case of goods placed in temporary storage or under the customs warehousing procedure, handling not authorized in advance by the customs authorities, provided such handling would have been authorized if applied for;

4.   in the case of goods placed under the temporary importation procedure, use of the goods otherwise than as provided for in the authorization, provided such use would have been authorized under that procedure if applied for;

5.   in the case of goods in temporary storage or placed under a customs procedure, unauthorized movement of the goods, provided the goods can be presented to the customs authorities at their request;

6.   in the case of goods in temporary storage or placed under a customs procedure, removal of the goods from the customs territory of the Community or their entry into a free zone or free warehouse without completion of the necessary formalities;

7.   in the case of goods having received favourable tariff treatment by reason of their end-use, transfer of the goods without notification to the customs authorities, before they have been put to the intended use, provided that:

    (*a*)   the transfer is recorded in the transferor's stock records, and

    (*b*)   the transferee is the holder of an authorization for the goods in question.

Article 860

The customs authorities shall consider a customs debt to have been incurred under Article 204(1) of the Code unless the person who would be the debtor establishes that the conditions set out in Article 859 are fulfilled.

Article 861

The fact that the failures referred to in Article 859 do not give rise to a customs debt shall not preclude the application of provisions of criminal law in force or of provisions allowing cancellation and withdrawal of authorizations issued under the customs procedure in question.

CHAPTER 2
Natural wastage

Article 862

1. For the purposes of Article 206 of the Code, the customs authorities shall, at the request of the person concerned, take account of the quantities missing wherever it can be shown that the losses observed result solely from the nature of the goods and not from any negligence or manipulation on the part of that person.

2. In particular, negligence or manipulation shall mean any failure to observe the rules for transporting, storing, handling, working or processing the goods in question imposed by the customs authorities or by normal practice.

Article 863

The customs authorities may waive the obligation for the person concerned to show that the goods were irretrievably lost for reasons inherent in their nature where they are satisfied that there is no other explanation for the loss.

Article 864

The national provisions in force in the Member States concerning standard rates for irretrievable loss due to the nature of the goods themselves shall be applied where the person concerned fails to show that the real loss exceeds that calculated by application of the standard rate for the goods in question.

CHAPTER 3
[Goods in special situations]¹

Amendments
1 Substituted by EC Commission Regulation 3665/93 art 1(68). See OJ L335 of 31.12.93, p 1.

Article 865

The presentation of a customs declaration for the goods in question, or any other act having the same legal effects, and the production of a document for endorsement by the competent authorities, shall be considered as removal of goods from customs supervision within the meaning of Article 203(1) of the Code, where these acts have the effect of wrongly conferring on them the customs status of Community goods.

Article 866

Without prejudice to the provisions laid down concerning prohibitions or restrictions which may be applicable to the goods in question, where a customs debt on importation is incurred pursuant to Articles 202, 203, 204 or 205 of the Code and the import duties have been paid, those goods shall be deemed to be Community goods without the need for a declaration for entry into free circulation.

Article 867

The confiscation of goods pursuant to Article 233(*c*) and (*d*) of the Code shall not affect the customs status of the goods in question.

[*Article 867a*

1. Non-Community goods which have been abandoned to the Exchequer or seized or confiscated shall be considered to have been entered for the customs warehousing procedure.

2. The goods referred to in paragraph 1 may be sold by the customs authorities only on the condition that the buyer immediately carries out the formalities to assign them a customs-approved treatment or use.

Where the sale is at a price inclusive of import duties, the sale shall be considered as equivalent to release for free circulation, and the customs authorities themselves shall calculate the duties and enter them in the accounts.

In these cases, the sale shall be conducted according to the procedures in force in the Member States.

3. Where the administration decides to deal with the goods referred to in paragraph otherwise than by sale, it shall immediately carry out the formalities to assign them one of the customs-approved treatments or uses laid down in Article 4(15)(*a*),(*b*),(*c*) and (*d*) of the code.]¹

Amendments
1 Art 867*a* inserted by Commission Regulation 3665/93/EEC. See OJ L335, 31.12.93, p 1.

PART V
Final provisions

Article 913

1. The following Regulation and Directives shall be repealed:

— Commission Regulation (EEC) No 1494/80 of 11 June 1980 on interpretative notes and generally accepted accounting principles for the purposes of customs value (OJ No L 154, 21.6.1980, p 3),

— Commission Regulation (EEC) No 1495/80 of 11 June 1980 implementing certain provisions of Council Regulation (EEC) No 1224/80 on the valuation of goods for customs purposes (OJ No L 154, 21.6.1980, p 14), as last amended by Regulation (EEC) No 558/91 (OJ No L 62, 8.3.1991, p 24),

— Commission Regulation (EEC) No 1496/80 of 11 June 1980 on the declaration of particulars relating to customs value and on documents to be furnished (OJ No L 154, 21.6.1980, p 16), as last amended by Regulation (EEC) No 979/93 (OJ No L 101, 27.4.1993, p 7),

— Commission Regulation (EEC) No 3177/80 of 5 December 1980 on the place of introduction to be taken into consideration in applying Article 14 (2) of Council Regulation (EEC) No 1224/80 on the valuation of goods for customs purposes (OJ No L 335, 12.12.1980, p 1) as last amended by Regulation (EEC) No 2779/90 (OJ No L 267, 29.9.1990, p 36),

— Commission Regulation (EEC) No 3179/80 of 5 December 1980 on postal charges to be taken into consideration when determining the customs value of goods sent by post (OJ No L 335, 12.12.1980, p 62), as last amended by Regulation (EEC) No 1264/90 (OJ No L 124, 15.5.1990, p 32),

— Commission Regulation (EEC) No 1577/81 of 12 June 1981 establishing a system of simplified procedures for the determination of the customs value of certain perishable goods (OJ No L 154, 13.6.1981, p 26), as last amended by Regulation (EEC) No 3334/90 (OJ No L 321, 21.11.1990, p 6),

— Commission Regulation (EEC) No 3158/83 of 9 November 1983 on the incidence of royalties and licence fees in customs value (OJ No L 309, 10.11.1983, p 19),

— Commission Regulation (EEC) No 1766/85 of 27 June 1985 on the rates of exchange to be used in the determination of customs value(OJ No L 168, 28.6.1985, p 21), as last amended by Regulation (EEC) No 593/91 (OJ No L 66, 13.3.1991, p 14),

— Commission Regulation (EEC) No 3903/92 of 21 December 1992 on air transport costs (OJ No L 393, 31.12.1992, p 1).

Article 914

References to the provisions repealed shall be understood as referring to this Regulation.

Article 915

This Regulation shall enter into force on the third day following its publication in the *Official Journal of the European Communities*.

It shall apply from 1 January 1994.

...

This Regulation shall be binding in its entirety and directly applicable in all Member States.

Note
Words omitted are outside the scope of this work.

ANNEX 23
Interpretative Notes on Customs Value

First column	*Second column*
Reference to provisions of the Customs Code	*Notes*
Article 29(1)	The price actually paid or payable refers to the price for the imported goods. Thus the flow of dividends or other

payments from the buyer to the seller that do not relate to the imported goods are not part of the customs value.

Article 29(1)(*a*) third indent

An example of such restriction would be the case where a seller requires a buyer of automobiles not to sell or exhibit them prior to a fixed date which represents the beginning of a model year.

Article 29(1)(*b*)

Some examples of this include:

(*a*) the seller establishes the price of the imported goods on condition that the buyer will also buy other goods in specified quantities;

(*b*) the price of the imported goods is dependent upon the price or prices at which the buyer of the imported goods sells other goods to the seller of the imported goods;

(*c*) the price is established on the basis of a form of payment extraneous to the imported goods, such as where the imported goods are semi-finished goods which have been provided by the seller on condition that he will receive a specified quantity of the finished goods.

However, conditions or considerations relating to the production or marketing of the imported goods shall not result in rejection of the transaction value. For example, the fact that the buyer furnishes the seller with engineering and plans undertaken in the country of importation shall not result in rejection of the transaction value for the purposes of Article 29(1).

Article 29(2)

1 Paragraphs 2(*a*) and (*b*) provide different means of establishing the acceptability of a transaction value.

2 Paragraph 2(*a*) provides that where the buyer and the seller are related, the circumstances surrounding the sale shall be examined and the transaction value shall be accepted as the customs value provided that the relationship did not influence the price. It is not intended that there should be an examination of the circumstances in all cases where the buyer and the seller are related. Such examination will only be required where there are doubts about the acceptability of the price. Where the customs authorities have no doubts about the acceptability of the price, it should be accepted without requesting further information from the declarant. For example, the relationship, or it may already have detailed information concerning the buyer and the seller, and may already be satisfied from such examination or information that the relationship did not influence the price.

3 Where the customs authorities are unable to accept the transaction value without further inquiry, it should give the declarant an opportunity to supply such further detailed information as may be necessary to enable it to examine the circumstances surrounding the sale. In this

context, the customs authorities should be prepared to examine relevant aspects of the transaction, including the way in which the buyer and seller organise their commercial relations and the way in which the price in question was arrived at, in order to determine whether the relationship influenced the price. Where it can be shown that the buyer and seller, although related under the provisions of Article 143 of this Regulation, buy from and sell to each other as if they were not related, this would demonstrate that the price had not been influenced by the relationship. As an example of this, if the price had been settled in a manner consistent with the normal pricing practices of the industry in question or with the way the seller settles prices for sales to buyers who are not related to him, this would demonstrate that the price had not been influenced by the relationship. As a further example, where it is shown that the price is adequate to ensure recovery of all costs plus a profit which is representative of the firm's overall profit realised over a representative period of time (eg on an annual basis) in sales of goods of the same class or kind, this would demonstrate that the price had not been influenced.

4 Paragraph 2(*b*) provides an opportunity for the declarant to demonstrate that the transaction value closely approximates to a "test" value previously accepted by the customs authorities and is therefore acceptable under the provisions of Article 29. Where a test under paragraph 2(*b*) is met, it is not necessary to examine the question of influence under paragraph 2(*a*). If the customs authorities already have sufficient information to be satisfied, without further detailed inquiries, that one of the tests provided in paragraph (2)(*b*) has been met, there is no reason for them to require the declarant to demonstrate that the test can be met.

Article 29(2)(*b*)

A number of factors must be taken into consideration in determining whether one value "closely approximates" to another value. These factors include the nature of the imported goods, the nature of the industry itself, the season in which the goods are imported, and, whether the difference in values is commercially significant. Since these factors may vary from case to case, it would be impossible to apply a uniform standard such as a fixed percentage, in each case. For example, a small difference in value in a case involving one type of goods could be unacceptable while a large difference in a case involving another type of goods might be acceptable in determining whether the transaction value closely approximates to the "test" values set forth in Article 29(2)(*b*).

Article 29(3)(*a*)

An example of an indirect payment would be the settlement by the buyer, whether in whole or in part, of a debt owed by the seller.

Article 30(2)(*a*),(*b*)

1 In applying these provisions, the customs authorities shall, wherever possible, use a sale of identical or similar

goods, as appropriate, at the same commercial level and in substantially the same quantity as the goods being valued. Where no such sale is found, a sale of identical or similar goods, as appropriate, that takes place under any one of the following three conditions may be used:

(*a*) a sale at the same commercial level but in a different quantity;

(*b*) a sale at a different commercial level but in substantially the same quantity; or

(*c*) a sale at a different commercial level and in a different quantity.

2 Having found a sale under any one of these three conditions adjustments will then be made, as the case may be, for:

(*a*) quantity factors only;

(*b*) commercial level factors only; or

(*c*) both commercial level and quantity factors.

3 The expression "and/or" allows the flexibility to use the sales and make the necessary adjustments in any one of the three conditions described above.

4 A condition for adjustment because of different commercial levels or different quantities is that such adjustment, whether it leads to an increase or a decrease in value, be made only on the basis of demonstrated evidence that clearly establishes the reasonableness and accuracy of the adjustment, eg valid price lists containing prices referring to different levels or different quantities. As an example of this, if the imported goods being valued consist of a shipment of 10 units and the only identical or similar imported goods, as appropriate, for which a transaction value exists involved a sale of 500 units, and it is recognised that the seller grants quantity discounts, the required adjustment may be accomplished by resorting to the seller's price list and using that price applicable to a sale of 10 units. This does not require that a sale had to have been made in quantities of 10 as long as the price list has been established as being bona fide through sales at other quantities. In the absence of such an objective measure, however, the determination of a customs value under the provisions of Article 30(2)(*a*) and (*b*) is not appropriate.

Article 30(2)(*d*)

1 As a general rule, customs value is determined under these provisions on the basis of information readily available in the Community. In order to determine a computed value, however, it may be necessary to examine the costs of producing the goods being valued and other information which has to be obtained from outside the Community. Furthermore, in most cases the producer of the goods will be outside the jurisdiction of the authorities of the Member States. The use of the computed value method

will generally be limited to those cases where the buyer and seller are related, and the producer is prepared to supply to the authorities of the country of importation the necessary costings and to provide facilities for any subsequent verification which may be necessary.

2 The "cost or value" referred to in Article 30(2)(*d*), first indent, is to be determined on the basis of information relating to the production of the goods being valued supplied by or on behalf of the producer. It is to be based upon the commercial accounts of the producer, provided that such accounts are consistent with the generally accepted accounting principles applied in the country where the goods are produced.

3 The "amount for profit and general expenses" referred to in Article 30(2)(*d*), second indent, is to be determined on the basis of information supplied by or on behalf of the producer unless his figures are inconsistent with those usually reflected in sales of goods of the same class or kind as the goods being valued which are made by producers in the country of exportation for export to the country of importation.

4 No cost or value of the elements referred to in this Article shall be counted twice in determining the computed value.

5 It should be noted in this context that the "amount for profit and general expenses" has to be taken as a whole. It follows that if, in any particular case, the producer's profit figure is low and his general expenses are high, his profit and general expenses taken together may nevertheless be consistent with that usually reflected in sales of goods of the same class or kind. Such a situation might occur, for example of a product were being launched in the Community and the producer accepted a nil or low profit to offset high general expenses associated with the launch. Where the producer can demonstrate that he is taking a low profit on his sales of the imported goods because of particular commercial circumstances, his actual profit figures should be taken into account provided that he has valid commercial reasons to justify them and his pricing policy reflects usual pricing policies in the branch of industry concerned. Such a situation might occur, for example, where producers have been forced to lower prices temporarily because of an unforeseeable drop in demand, or where they sell goods to complement a range of goods being produced in the country of importation and accept a low profit to maintain competitivity. Where the producer's own figures for profit and general expenses are not consistent with those usually reflected in sales of goods of the same class or kind as the goods being valued which are made by producers in the country of exportation for export to the country of importation, the amount for profit and general expenses may be based upon relevant information

other than that supplied by or on behalf of the producer of the goods.

6 Whether certain goods are "of the same class or kind" as other goods must be determined on a case-by-case basis with reference to the circumstances involved. In determining the usual profits and general expenses under the provisions of Article 30(2)(*d*), sales for export to the country of importation of the narrowest group or range of goods, which includes the goods being valued, for which the necessary information can be provided, should be examined. For the purposes of Article 30(2)(*d*), "goods of the same class or kind" must be from the same country as the goods being valued.

Article 31(1)

1 Customs values determined under the provisions of Article 31(1) should, to the greatest extent possible, be based on previously determined customs values.

2 The methods of valuation to be employed under Article 31(1) should be those laid down in Articles 29 and 30(2), but a reasonable flexibility in the application of such methods would be in conformity with the aims and provisions of Article 31(1).

3 Some examples of reasonable flexibility are as follows:

(*a*) *Identical goods* — the requirement that the identical goods should be exported at or about the same time as the goods being valued could be flexibly interpreted; identical imported goods produced in a country other than the country of exportation of the goods being valued could be the basis for customs valuation; customs values of identical imported goods already determined under the provisions of Article 30(2)(*c*) and (*d*) could be used.

(*b*) *Similar goods* — the requirement that the similar goods should be exported at or about the same time as the goods being valued could be flexibly interpreted; similar imported goods produced in a country other than the country of exportation of the goods being valued could be the basis for customs valuations; customs values of similar imported goods already determined under the provisions of Article 30(2)(*c*) and (*d*) could be used.

(*c*) *Deductive method* — the requirement that the goods shall have been sold in the "condition as imported" in Article 152(1)(*a*) could be flexibly interpreted the "90 days" requirement could be administered flexibly.

Article 32(1)(*b*)(ii)

1 There are two factors involved in the apportionment of the elements specified in Article 32(1)(*b*)(ii) to the imported goods - the value of the element itself and the way in which that value is to be apportioned to the imported goods. The apportionment of these elements should be made in a reasonable manner appropriate to the circum-

stances and in accordance with generally accepted accounting principles.

2 Concerning the value of the element, if the buyer acquires the element from a seller not related to him at a given cost, the value of the element is that cost. If the element was produced by the buyer or by a person related to him, its value would be the cost of producing it. If the element had been previously used by the buyer, regardless of whether it had been acquired or produced by him, the original cost of acquisition or production would have to be adjusted downwards to reflect its use in order to arrive at the value of the element.

3 Once a value has been determined for the element, it is necessary to apportion that value to the imported goods. Various possibilities exist. For example, the value might be apportioned to the first shipment, if the buyer wishes to pay duty on the entire value at one time. As another example, he may request that the value be apportioned over the number of units produced up to the time of the first shipment. As a further example, he may request that the value be apportioned over the entire anticipated production where contracts of firm commitments exist for the production. The method of apportionment used will depend upon the documentation provided by the buyer.

4 As an illustration of the above, a buyer provides the producer with a mould to be used in the production of the imported goods and contracts with him to buy 10,000 units. By the time of arrival of the first shipment of 1,000 units, the producer has already produced 4,000 units. The buyer may request the customs authorities to apportion the value of the mould over 1,000, 4,000 or 10,000 units.

Article 32(1)(b)(iv)

1 Additions for the elements specified in Article 32(1)(b)(iv) should be based on objective and quantifiable data. In order to minimise the burden for both the declarant and customs authorities in determining the values to be added, data readily available in the buyers commercial record system should be used in so far as possible.

2 For those elements supplied by the buyer which were purchased or leased by the buyer, the addition would be the cost of the purchase or the lease. No addition shall be made for those elements available in the public domain, other than the cost of obtaining copies of them.

3 The ease with which it may be possible to calculate the values to be added will depend on a particular firm's structure and management practice, as well as its accounting methods.

4 For example, it is possible that a firm which imports a variety of products from several countries maintains the records of its design centre outside the country of importation in such as way as to show accurately the costs attributable to a given product. In such cases, a direct

adjustment may appropriately be made under the provisions of Article 32.

5 In another case, a firm may carry the cost of the design centre outside the country of importation as a general overhead expense without allocation to specific products. In this instance, an appropriate adjustment could be made under the provisions of Article 32 with respect to the imported goods by apportioning total design centre costs over total production benefiting from the design centre and adding such apportioned cost on a unit basis to imports.

6 Variations in the above circumstances will, of course, require different factors to be considered in determining the proper method of allocation.

7 In cases where the production of the element in question involves a number of countries and over a period of time, the adjustment should be limited to the value actually added to that element outside the country of importation.

Article 32(1)(*c*)

The royalties and licence fees referred to in Article 32(1)(*c*) may include, among other things, payments in respect of patents, trademarks and copyrights.

Article 32(2)

Where objective and quantifiable data do not exist with regard to the additions required to be made under the provisions of Article 32, the transaction value cannot be determined under the provisions of Article 29. As an illustration of this, a royalty is paid on the basis of the price in a sale in the importing country of a litre of a particular product that was imported by the kilogram and made up into a solution after importation. If the royalty is based partially on the imported goods and partially on other factors which have nothing to do with the imported goods (such as when the imported goods are mixed with domestic ingredients and are no longer separately identifiable, or when the royalty cannot be distinguished from special financial arrangements between the buyer and the seller), it would be inappropriate to attempt to make an addition for the royalty. However, if the amount of this royalty is based only on the imported goods and can be readily quantified, an addition to the price actually paid or payable can be made.

Article 143(1)(*e*)

One person shall be deemed to control another when the former is legally or operationally in a position to exercise restraint or direction over the latter.

Article 152(1)(*a*)(i)

1 The words "profit and general expenses" should be taken as a whole. The figure for the purposes of this deduction should be determined on the basis of information supplied by the declarant unless his figures are inconsistent with those obtaining in sales in the country of importation of imported goods of the same class or kind. Where the declarant's figures are inconsistent with such figures, the amount for profit and general expenses may be based

upon relevant information other than that supplied by the declarant.

2 In determining either the commissions or the usual profits and general expenses under this provision, the question whether certain goods are of the same class or kind as other goods must be determined on a case-by-case basis by reference to the circumstances involved. Sales in the country of importation of the narrowest group or range of imported goods of the same class or kind, which includes the goods being valued, for which the necessary information can be provided, should be examined. For the purposes of this provision, "goods of the same class or kind" includes goods imported from the same country as the goods being valued as well as goods imported from other countries.

Article 152(2)

1 Where this method of valuation is used, deductions made for the value added by further processing shall be based on objective and quantifiable data relating to the cost of such work. Accepted industry formulas, recipes, methods of construction, and other industry practices would form the basis of the calculations.

2 This method of valuation would normally not be applicable when, as a result of the further processing, the imported goods lose their identity. However, there can be instances where, although the identity of the imported goods is lost, the value added by the processing can be determined accurately without unreasonable difficulty.

On the other hand, there can also be instances where the imported goods maintain their identity but form such a minor element in the goods sold in the country of importation that the use of this valuation method would be unjustified. In view of the above, each situation of this type must be considered on a case-by-case basis.

Article 152(3)

1 As a example of this, goods are sold from a price list which grants favourable unit prices for purchases made in larger quantities.

Sale quantity	Unit price	Number of sales	Total quantity sold at each price
One to 10 units	100	10 sales of five units Five sales of three units	65
11 to 25 units	95	Five sales of 11 units	55
Over 25 units	90	One sale of 30 units	80
		One sale of 50 units	

The greatest number of units sold at a price is 80; therefore, the unit price in the greatest aggregate quantity is 90.

2 As another example of this, two sales occur. In the first sale 500 units are sold at a price of 95 currency units each. In the second sale 400 units are sold at price of 90 currency units each. In this example, the greatest number of units sold at a particular price is 500; therefore, the unit price in the greatest aggregate quantity is 95.

3 A third example would be the following situation where various quantities are sold at various prices.

(*a*) *Sales*

Sale quantity	unit price
40 units	100
30 units	90
15 units	100
50 units	95
25 units	105
35 units	90
5 units	100

(*b*) *Total*

Total quantity sold	Unit price
65	90
50	95
60	100
25	105

In this example, the greatest number of units sold at a particular price is 65; therefore, the unit price in the greatest aggregate quantity is 90.

ANNEX 24

Application of generally accepted accounting principles for the determination of Customs Value

1 "Generally accepted accounting principles" refers to the recognised consensus or substantial authoritative support within a country at a particular time as to which economic resources and obligations should be recorded as assets and liabilities, which changes in assets and liabilites should be recorded, how the assets and liabilities and changes in them should be measured, what information should be disclosed and how it should be disclosed, and which financial statements should be prepared. These standards may be broad guidelines of general application as well as detailed practices and procedures.

2 For the purposes of the application of the customs valuation provisions, the customs administration concerned shall utilise information prepared in a manner consistent with generally accepted accounting principles in the country which is appropriate for the Article in question. For example, the determination of usual profit and general expenses under the provisions of Article 152(1)(*a*)(i) of this Regulation would be carried out utilising information prepared in a manner consistent with generally accepted accounting principles of the country of importation. On the other hand, the determination of usual profit and general expenses under the provisions of Article 30(2)(*d*) of the Code would be carried out utilising information prepared in a manner consistent with generally accepted accounting principles of the country of production. As a further example, the determination of an element provided for in Article 32(1)(*b*)(ii) of the Code undertaken in the country of importation would be carried out utilising information in a manner consistent with the generally accepted accounting principles of that country.

ANNEX 25
Air transport costs to be included in the customs value

Introduction

1 The following table showed:

    (*a*)   third countries listed by continent (column 1);

    (*b*)   airports of departure in third countries (column 2);

    (*c*)   airports of arrival in the Community with the percentages which represent the part of the air transport costs to be included in the customs value (column 3 and following columns).

2 When the goods are shipped to or from airports not included in the following table, other than the airports referred to in paragraph 3, the percentage given for the airport nearest to that of departure or arrival shall be taken.

3 As regards the French overseas departments of Guadeloupe, Guyana, Martinique and Reunion, of which territories the airports are not included in the table, the following rules shall apply:-

    (*a*)   for goods shipped direct to those departments from third countries, the whole of the air transport cost is to be included in the customs value;

    (*b*)   for goods shipped to the European part of the Community from third countries and transhipped or unloaded in one of those departments, the air transport costs which would have been incurred for carrying the goods only as far as the place of transhipment or unloading are to be included in the customs value;

    (*c*)   for goods shipped to those departments from third countries and transhipped or unloaded in an airport in the European part of the Community, the air transport costs to be included in the customs value are those which result from the application of the percentages given in the following table to the costs which would have been incurred for carrying the goods from the airport of departure to the airport of transhipment or unloading.

The transhipment or unloading shall be certified by an appropriate endorsement by the customs authorities on the air waybill or other air transport document, with the official stamp of the office concerned; failing this certification the provisions of the last subparagraph of Article 14(3) of Regulation (EEC) No 1224/80 shall apply.

Percentages of air transport costs to be included in the customs value

LIST I (*Federal Republic of Germany*) (not reproduced)

LIST II (*Benelux*) (not reproduced)

LIST III (*France*) (not reproduced)

LIST IV (*Italy*) (not reproduced)

LIST V (*Ireland*) (reproduced)

LIST VI (*Greece*) (not reproduced)

LIST VII (*Spain*) (not reproduced)

LIST VIII (*Portugal*) (not reproduced)

LIST V (Ireland)

Third countries	*Airport of departure*	*Ireland all airports*
1	2	3
[I. EUROPE		
Albania	all airports	38
Armenia	all airports	58
Belarus	all airports	38
Bosnia-Herzogovina	all airports	18
Bulgaria	all airports	33
Croatia	all airports	17
Cyprus	see Asia	
Czech Republic	Ostrava	21
	Prague	9
Estonia	all airports	44
Faroe Islands	all airports	36
Georgia	all airports	64
Gibraltar	all airports	0
Hungary	all airports	8
Iceland	all airports	59
Latvia	all airports	24
Lithuania	all airports	34
Former Yugoslav		
Republic of Macedonia	all airports	37
Malta	all airports	6
Moldova	all airports	35
Montenegro	all airports	34
Norway	Ålesund, Bodø, Trondheim,	
	Alta, Kirkenes	73
	Bergen	51
	Kristiansand	51
	Oslo	59
	Stavanger	47
Poland	Bydgoszcz, Cracow, Gdansk,	
	Rzeszow, Wroclaw	33
	Poznan	13
	Szczecin (Stettin)	0
	Warsaw	25
Romania	all airports	32
Russia	Gorky, Kuibishev, Perm,	
	Rostov, Volgograd	48
	St. Petersburg	29
	Moscow, Orel, Voronej	49
	Irkutsk, Kirensk, Krasnoyarsk,	
	Novosibirsk, Khabarovsk,	
	Vladivostok	74
	Omsk, Sverdlovsk	69
Serbia	all airports	19
Slovakia	Bratislava	0
	Kosice, Presov	31
Slovenia	all airports	10
Switzerland	Basel	0
	Bern	4
	Geneva	0
	Zurich	2

Turkey (European part)	all airports	7
Turkey (Asian part)	Adana, Afyon, Antalya, Elâzig, Gasziantep, Iskenderun, Kastamonu, Konya, Malatya, Samsun, Trabzon	20
	Agri, Diyarbakir, Erzurum, Kars, Van	30
	Akhisar, Ankara, Balikezir, Bandirma, Bursa, Kütahya, Zonguldak	17
	Izmir	16
Ukraine	all airports	44][2]

II. AFRICA

Algeria	Algiers	16
	Annaba, Constantine	23
	El Golea	34
Angola	all airports	79
Benin	all airports	61
Botswana	all airports	68
Burkina Faso	all airports	42
Burundi	all airports	54
Cameroon	all airports	74
Republic of Cape Verde	all airports	27
Central African Republic	all airports	75
Chad	all airports	70
Comoros	all airports	64
Congo	all airports	78
Djibouti	all airports	48
Egypt	all airports	18
Equatorial Guinea	all airports	77
Ethiopia	all airports	44
Gabon	all airports	74
Gambia	all airports	27
Ghana	all airports	61
Guinea	all airports	39
Guinea Bissau	all airports	39
Ivory Coast	all airports	61
Kenya	all airports	55
Lesotho	all airports	68
Liberia	all airports	39
Libya	Benghazi	24
	Sebha	41
	Tripoli	28
Madagascar	all airports	64
Malawi	all airports	59
Mali	all airports	42
Mauritania	all airports	27
Mauritius	all airports	64
Morocco	Casablanca	12
	Fez, Rabat	12
	Ifni	27
	Tangiers, Tetuan	0
Mozambique	all airports	65
Namibia	all airports	68
Niger	all airports	42

Nigeria	all airports	61
Rwanda	all airports	54
Saò Tomé and Principe	all airports	77
Senegal	all airports	27
Seychelles	all airports	64
Sierra Leone	all airports	39
Somalia	all airports	55
Republic of South Africa	all airports	68
St. Helena	all airports	73
Sudan	all airports	40
Swaziland	all airports	68
Tanzania	all airports	59
Togo	all airports	61
Tunisia	Djerba	22
	Tunis	11
Uganda	all airports	54
Zaire	all airports	78
Zambia	all airports	64
Zimbabwe	all airports	64

III. AMERICA
1. *North America*

Canada	Edmonton, Vancouver, Winnipeg	85
	Gander, Moncton	76
	Halifax, Montreal, Ottawa, Quebec, Toronto	76
Greenland	all airports	75
United States of America	Akron, Albany, Atlanta, Baltimore, Boston, Buffalo, Charleston, Chicago, Cincinnati, Columbus, Detroit, Indianapolis, Jacksonville, Kansas City, New Orleans, Lexington, Louisville, Memphis, Milwaukee, Minneapolis, Nashville, New York, Philadelphia, Pittsburgh, St. Louis, Washington DC	81
	Albuquerque, Austin, Billings, Dallas, Denver, Houston, Las Vegas, Los Angeles, Oklahoma, Phoenix, Portland, Salt Lake City, San Francisco, Seattle	87
	Anchorage, Fairbanks, Juneau	82
	Honolulu	94
	Miami	85
	Puerto Rico	86

2. *Central America*

Bahamas	all airports	83
Belize	all airports	84
Bermuda	all airports	83
Costa Rica	all airports	84
Cuba	all airports	84
Curacao	all airports	71
Dominican Republic	all airports	83
El Salvador	all airports	84

Guatemala	all airports	84
Haiti	all airports	83
Honduras	all airports	84
Jamaica	all airports	84
Mexico	all airports	86
Nicaragua	all airports	84
Panama	all airports	84
Virgin Islands	see West Indies	
West Indies	all airports	71

3. *South America*

Argentina	all airports	71
Aruba	all airports	71
Bolivia	all airports	71
Brazil	all airports	71
Chile	all airports	71
Colombia	all airports	71
Ecuador	all airports	71
Guyana	all airports	71
Paraguay	all airports	71
Peru	all airports	71
Suriname	all airports	71
Trinidad and Tobago	all airports	71
Uruguay	all airports	71
Venezuela	all airports	71

IV. ASIA

Afghanistan	all airports	59
Azerbaijan	all airports	64
Bahrain	all airports	37
Bangladesh	all airports	59
Bhutan	see Nepal	
Brunei	see Malaysia	
Burma	all airports	69
China	all airports	72
Cyprus	all airports	13
Hong Kong	all airports	72
India	all airports	59
Indonesia	all airports	72
Iran	all airports	37
Iraq	all airports	30
Israel	all airports	18
Japan	all airports	78
Jordan	all airports	19
Kampuchea	all airports	69
Kazakhstan	all airports	65
North Korea	all airports	72
South Korea	all airports	72
Kuwait	all airports	38
Kyrgyzstan	all airports	65
Laos	all airports	69
Lebanon	all airports	16
Macao	all airports	72
Malaysia	all airports	72
Maldives	all airports	65

Mongolia	all airports	74
Muscat and Oman	all airports	48
Nepal	all airports	59
Oman	see Muscat and Oman	
Uzbekistan	all airports	65
Pakistan	all airports	59
Philippines	all airports	72
Qatar	all airports	37
Saudi Arabia	all airports	37
Singapore	all airports	72
Sri Lanka	all airports	72
Syria	all airports	19
Tajikistan	all airports	19
Taiwan	all airports	65
Thailand	all airports	69
Turkey	see Europe	
Turkmenistan	all airports	65
United Arab Emirates	all airports	48
Vietnam	all airports	72
Yemen Arab Republic	all airports	45

V. AUSTRALIA
and OCEANIA | all airports | 79

TABLE OF CASES

INDEX

How to use this index: There are five Parts to this book:

Part 1 contains Irish Legislation, which is in chronological order. References to this Part of the book end in **A** for Act eg VATA 1972 s 12, FA 1993 s 85. Therefore if you find a reference ending in **A**, go to Part 1 (the material before the first black edgemark on the side) of the book, and look at the running heads at the top of the page. Since the legislation is in chronological order, you will quickly find the reference by moving forwards or backwards from the page where have opened the book.

Part 2 contains Irish Regulations, which are in chronological order. References to this Part of the book end in **R** for Regulation eg VATR 1979 r 19, EC(EPICG)R 1985 r 18. Therefore if you find a reference ending in **R**, go to Part 2 (the material before the second black edgemark on the side) of the book, and look at the running heads at the top of the page. Since the regulations are in chronological order, you will quickly find the reference by moving forwards or backwards from the page where have opened the book.

Part 3 contains Irish Orders, which are in chronological order. References to this Part of the book end in **O** for Order eg VAT(RT)(No 25)**O** 1993. Therefore if you find a reference ending in **O**, go to Part 3 (the material before the third black edgemark on the side) of the book, and look at the running heads at the top of the page. Since the orders are in chronological order, you will quickly find the reference by moving forwards or backwards from the page where have opened the book.

Part 4 contains EU Legislation (Directives) which are in chronological order. References to this Part of the book end in **Dir** for Directive eg 6th **Dir** art 13B(*a*). Therefore if you find a reference ending in **Dir**, go to Part 4 (the material before the fourth black edgemark on the side) of the book, and look at the running heads at the top of the page. Since the Directives are in chronological order, you will quickly find the reference by moving forwards or backwards from the page where have opened the book.

Part 5 contains EU Regulations, which are in chronological order. References to this Part of the book end in **Reg** for Regulation and the same principle applies as discussed in the foregoing paragraphs.

Accommodation
non deductible tax, VATA 1972 s 12(3)

Accountant
service taxed where received, VATA 1972 Sch 4 para (iii)

Accounts
to be kept by taxpayers, VATR 1979 r 9

Advance payments
advance payment received, obligation to issue invoice, VATA 1972 s 17(8)

Advertising articles
VAT free importation, EC(EPICG)R 1985 r 18

Advertising services
taxed where received, VATA 1972 Sch 4 para (ii)

Advance payment
each 1 December, VATA 1972 s 19(6)

Agent
development of photos etc, rate of tax, VATA 1972 Sch 6 para (xxvi)
export, zero rating, VATA 1972 Sch 2 para (vi)
simultaneous supply to and by the agent,
  goods, VATA 1972 s 3(4)
  greyhounds, livestock, VATA 1972 s 3(3)(*b*)
  services, VATA 1972 s 5(4)
taxable amount determinable by regulation, VATA 1972 s 10(7)
foreign firms not established in State, may be held accountable, VATA 1972 s 37
Revenue may substitute for a principal, VATA 1972 s 37

Agricultural activities
See: 6th Dir Annex A
beekeeping, VATA 1972 Sch 5
crop production, VATA 1972 Sch 5
crustacean breeding, VATA 1972 Sch 5
fish farming, VATA 1972 Sch 5
flower growing, VATA 1972 Sch 5

forestry, VATA 1972 Sch 5
freshwater fishing, VATA 1972 Sch 5
fruit growing, VATA 1972 Sch 5
mollusc breeding, VATA 1972 Sch 5
mushroom growing, VATA 1972 Sch 5
mussel breeding, VATA 1972 Sch 5
nurseries, VATA 1972 Sch 5 ·
oyster breeding, VATA 1972 Sch 5
poultry farming, VATA 1972 Sch 5
product processing, VATA 1972 Sch 5
rabbit farming, VATA 1972 Sch 5
seed growing, VATA 1972 Sch 5
silkworm farming, VATA 1972 Sch 5
snail farming, VATA 1972 Sch 5
spice growing, VATA 1972 Sch 5
stock farming, VATA 1972 Sch 5
vegetable growing, VATA 1972 Sch 5
viticulture, VATA 1972 Sch 5

Agricultural produce
cleaning of, agricultural service, VATA 1972 Sch 5
collecting of, agricultural service, VATA 1972 Sch 5
defined, VATA 1972 ss 1(1), 8(9); 6th Dir art 25, Annex A
disinfecting of, agricultural service, VATA 1972 Sch 5
drying of, agricultural service, VATA 1972 Sch 5
ensilage of, agricultural service, VATA 1972 Sch 5
grinding of, agricultural service, VATA 1972 Sch 5
packing of, agricultural service, VATA 1972 Sch 5
processing of, agricultural activity, VATA 1972 Sch 5
storage of, agricultural service, VATA 1972 Sch 5

Agricultural service
See: 6th Dir Annex B
baling, VATA 1972 Sch 5
  rate of tax, VATA 1972 Sch 6 para (x)
cleaning agricultural products, VATA 1972 Sch 5
collecting, VATA 1972 Sch 5
crop dusting, VATA 1972 Sch 5.

special scheme for, VATA 1972 s 10B
tax clearance requirements, FA 1992 s 242

Authorised officer
inspection of records, defined, VATA 1972 s 18(5)

Awards
VAT free importation, EC(EPICG)R 1985 r 16(1)

Baling
agricultural service, VATA 1972 Sch 5

Banking
exempted activity, VATA 1972 Sch 1 para (i)
service taxed where received, VATA 1972 Sch 4 para (v)

Bankruptcy
assignee is liable, VATR 1979 r 36
VAT as a preferential debt, FA 1976 s 62

Barrister
legal services, deemed simultaneous supply to and by insured person, VATA 1972 s 5(4B)
service taxed where received, VATA 1972 Sch 4 para (iii)

Beekeeping
agricultural activity, VATA 1972 Sch 5

Betting
acceptance of bets, exempted activity, VATA 1972 Sch 1 para (xv)

Blood
storage etc, exempted activity, VATA 1972 Sch 1 para (xviii)

Body of persons
defined, VATA 1972 ss 1(1)

Books
zero rating, VATA 1972 Sch 2 para (xva)

Books of account
duty to keep, VATA 1972 s 16(1)

Bread
defined, zero rating, VATA 1972 Sch 2 para (xii)(d)

Builders
rate of tax, VATA 1972 Sch 6 para (xxix)
two-thirds rule, VATA 1972 s 10(8)(a)

Buildings
cleaning of, rate of tax, VATA 1972 Sch 6 para (xxx)
short term letting, exempted activity, VATA 1972 Sch 1 para (iv)
supply of, taxable, 6th Dir art 4(3)

Business
defined, VATA 1972 ss 1(1)

Cafes
food and drink provided through, a service, VATA 1972 s 5(2)

Cancellation of registration
repayment of tax paid over repaid where taxpayer elected to register, VATA 1972 s 8(5)

Candles
zero rating, VATA 1972 Sch 2 para (xx)

Canteens
food and drink provided through,
  a service, VATA 1972 s 5(2)
  rate of tax, VATA 1972 Sch 6 para (ii)
  staff, deemed a business, VATR 1979 r 24

Capital allowances
VAT-exclusive where VAT is reclaimable, FA 1975 s 29

Capital goods
VAT free importation, EC(EPICG)R 1985 r 9

Car
non deductible VAT, VATA 1972 s 12(3)(a)(iii)
second hand bought by car dealer from unregistered person, relief, VAT(SHMV)R 1988

Caravan
fixed, repayment of tax, VAT(RT)(No 12)O 1980

Cash receipts basis
administrative procedures, VAT(DTDBRMR)R 1992
entitlement, VATA 1972 s 14

Catalogues
VAT free importation, EC(EPICG)R 1985 r 21

Catering
a service, VATA 1972 s 5(2)
for hospital etc patients, exempted activity, VATA 1972 Sch 1 para (xxv)
rate of tax, VATA 1972 Sch 6 para (ii)

Cattle
defined, VATA 1972 ss 1(1)

Central Bank
gold supplied to, zero rating, VATA 1972 Sch 2 para (x)
issue of currency, exempted activity, VATA 1972 Sch 1 para (i)(d)

Central Fund
tax owed is debt due to Minister for Finance for benefit of, VATA 1972 s 24

Cessation of business
business sold as going concern, transfer of goods not a supply, VATA 1972 s 3(5)(b)(iii)

Chain of suppliers
deemed simultaneous supplies by and to each member, VATA 1972 s 3(2)

Charge to tax
charging section, VATA 1972 s 2; 6th Dir art 10

Charitable goods
VAT free importation, EC(EPICG)R 1985 r 13

Child
clothing, zero rating, VATA 1972 Sch 2 para (xvii)
shoes, zero rating, VATA 1972 Sch 2 para (xix)

Child minding
non profit making, exempted activity, VATA 1972 Sch 1 para (vi)

Cinema
admission, rate of tax, VATA 1972 Sch 6 para (iv)

Circuit Court
appeal hearing, further appeal, VATA 1972 s 25(2)(h)
defined, IA 1937 Sch

Circus
not exempted activity, VATA 1972 Sch 1 para (viii)

Citations
construction of, IA 1937 s 11(f)

Cleaning of buildings
rate of tax, VATA 1972 Sch 6 para (xxx)

Clinic
care, exempted activity, VATA 1972 Sch 1 para (v)

Interpretation
Where words defined in Interpretation Act: IA 1937 s 12

Intra-Community
acquisition of goods, defined, VATA 1972 ss 1(1), 3A(1); 6th Dir art 28a(3)
charge to tax, VATA 1972 s 2(1A)
option for Member States to exempt acquisitions, 6th Dir art 16(2)
supplies, return, VATA 1972 s 19A
taxable amount,
   defined, VATA 1972 s 10(1A)
   no double charge, VATA 1972 s 10(5A)
taxable person, VATA 1972 s 8(1A)
taxable person may deduct tax where properly documented, VATA 1972 s 12(1)
tax due, VATA 1972 s 19(1A)
transport of goods,
   defined, VATA 1972 s 5(6)(*h*)
   place of supply, VATA 1972 s 5(6)(*f*); 6th Dir art 28b
   zero rating, VATA 1972 Sch 2 para (iii*a*)

Invoices
advance payment received, obligation to issue, VATA 1972 s 17(8)
details to be shown, VAT(IOD)R 1992 r 3(*a*); 6th Dir art 22(3)(*b*)
duty to keep copies, VATA 1972 s 16(2)
electronic, VATA 1972 s 17(1A)
finance houses, VATA 1972 s 17(1)(proviso)
issued, but lower VAT rate should have applied, VATA 1972 s 17(3A)
issuer is liable on amount stated, VATA 1972 s 17(5)-(6A)
obligation to issue to other taxable persons, VATA 1972 s 17(1); 6th Dir art 22(3)
separate totals for different rates, VAT(IOD)R 1992 r 5
settlement vouchers, VATA 1972 s 17(10)
time limit for issuing, VATA 1972 s 17(7), VAT(TLICD)R 1992 r 3

Irrigation equipment
operation of, agricultural service, VATA 1972 Sch 5

Jail
criminal offences, FA 1983 s 94

Jockey
rate of tax, VATA 1972 Sch 6 para (xx)

Laboratory
refund of tax on imported medical equipment, VAT(RT)(No 14)O 1980
VAT free importation,
   research substances etc, EC(EPICG)R 1985 r 12
   test samples, EC(EPICG)R 1985 r 20

Land
rate of tax, VATA 1972 Sch 6 para (xxviii)
short term letting, exempted activity, VATA 1972 Sch 1 para (iv)
taxable amount, VATA 1972 s 10(9)

Lawyer
service taxed where received, VATA 1972 Sch 4 para (iii)

Legal services
service taxed where received, VATA 1972 Sch 4 para (iii)

Licence
assignment of, taxed where received, VATA 1972 Sch 4 para (i)
tax clearance requirements, FA 1992 s 242

Lifeboat service
refund of VAT to sea rescue groups, VAT(RT)(No 18)O 1985
zero rating, VATA 1972 Sch 2 para (xi)

Light house service
zero rating, VATA 1972 Sch 2 para (ix)

Liquidation of companies
liquidator is liable, VATR 1979 r 36
preferential status of VAT, FA 1976 s 62
VAT return, liquidator, VATA 1972 s 19(3)(*b*)

Literary manuscripts
rate of tax, VATA 1972 Sch 6 para (xvii)

Livestock
auction, simultaneous supply to and by the auctioneer, VATA 1972 s 3(3)(*a*)
defined, VATA 1972 ss 1(1)

Loading or unloading services
place of supply, VATA 1972 s 5(6)(*c*)
zero rating, VATA 1972 Sch 2 para (iv)

Local authority
defined, VATA 1972 ss 1(1)
Minister may deem to be a taxable person, VATA 1972 s 8(2A)
services supplied by, VATA 1972 s 8(3E)
taxable amount determinable by regulation, VATA 1972 s 10(7)

Lottery
exempted activity, VATA 1972 Sch 1 para (xvi)

Machinery
fixed machinery let separately, regarded as hire of movable goods, VATA 1972 s 11(6)

Maintenance service
rate of tax, VATA 1972 Sch 6 para (xviii)

Marginal notes
not part of enactment, IA 1937 s 11(*g*)

Margin scheme
defined, VATA 1972 s 1(1), 10A
goods, VATA 1972 s 10A

Marriage
transfer of residence on, VAT free importation, EC(EPICG)R 1985 r 5

Market value
open market price, defined, VATA 1972 s 10(10)
taxable amount where consideration not all money, VATA 1972 s 10(2)

Masculine
words include feminine, IA 1937 s 11(*b*)

Means of transport
new, defined, VATA 1972 ss 1(1)
supplied by taxable dealers, special scheme, VATA 1972 s 12B

Media materials
VAT free importation, EC(EPICG)R 1985 r 23(*h*), (*p*)

Medical services
provision of, exempted activity, VATA 1972 Sch 1 para (iii)

Medicine
oral, zero rating, VATA 1972 Sch 2 para (xiii)-(xiv)

Microfilm
microfilming services, rate of tax, VATA 1972 Sch 6
para (xxv)(*b*)

Midnight
defined, IA 1937 Sch

Minister of the Government
defined, IA 1937 Sch

Mobile home
See CARAVAN

Mollusc breeding
agricultural activity, VATA 1972 Sch 5

Moneys received basis
administrative procedures, VAT(DTDBRMR)R
1992
entitlement, VATA 1972 s 14

Month
defined, IA 1937 Sch

Monthly control statement
details, VAT(MCS)R 1992
defined, VATA 1972 ss 1(1)
obligation to issue, VATA 1972 s 17(1B)

Motor vehicles
disabled drivers, refund of tax, FA 1989 s 92
Intra-Community acquisition, return, VATA 1972 s
19(4)
non deductible tax, VATA 1972 s 12(3)

Movable goods
defined, VATA 1972 ss 1(1)

Mowing
agricultural service, VATA 1972 Sch 5

Mushroom growing
agricultural activity, VATA 1972 Sch 5

Musical performances
live, exempted activity, VATA 1972 Sch 1 para (viii)

Mussel breeding
agricultural activity, VATA 1972 Sch 5

National broadcasting service
exempted activity, VATA 1972 Sch 1 para (xiii)

Negligence
failure to rectify errors that come to attention, VATA
1972 s 27(3)
fraudulent etc returns, penalty, VATA 1972 s 27(1)-
(2)

Newspapers
rate of tax, VATA 1972 Sch 6 para (xii)

Non-deductible tax
accommodation, VATA 1972 s 12(3)(*a*)(i)
apportionment of deductible and non deductible tax,
VATA 1972 s 12(4)
cars, VATA 1972 s 12(3)(*a*)(iii)
food, drink, VATA 1972 s 12(3)(*a*)(i)
entertainment expenses, VATA 1972 s 12(3)(*a*)(ii)
personal services, VATA 1972 s 12(3)(*a*)(i).
petrol, VATA 1972 s 12(3)(*a*)(iv)
supply of goods, exempted activity, VATA 1972 Sch
1 para (xxiv)

Non-profit making organisations
goods and services provided to members, exempted
activity, VATA 1972 Sch 1 para (vii)

Nurseries
agricultural activity, VATA 1972 Sch 5

Nursing home
care, exempted activity, VATA 1972 Sch 1 para (v)

Oath
defined, IA 1937 Sch

Obstruction
of authorised officer, inspection or removal of
records, VATA 1972 s 18(3)

Offence
under two laws, IA 1937 s 14

Official secrecy
Revenue may disclose information to:
the Ombudsman, FA 1981 s 52
rating authority, FA 1978 s 51

Oireachtas
defined, IA 1937 Sch

Ombudsman
Revenue may disclose information to, FA 1981 s 52

Open market price
defined, VATA 1972 s 10(10)

Optician
exempted activity, VATA 1972 Sch 1 para (iii*b*)

Oyster breeding
agricultural activity, VATA 1972 Sch 5

Package of goods
at different rates, rate of tax, VATA 1972 s 11(3)

Packing materials
VAT free importation, EC(EPICG)R 1985 r 24

Patent rights
assignment of, taxed where received, VATA 1972
Sch 4 para (i)

Patterns
VAT free importation, EC(EPICG)R 1985 r 21

Payment
advance payment,
adjustment and refund, VATA 1972 s 19(3)(proviso)
each 1 December, VATA 1972 s 19(6)
annual accounting authorisation etc, VATA 1972 s
19(3)(*aa*)
generally, VATA 1972 s 19(3)

Peat
rate of tax, VATA 1972 Sch 6 para (i)

Penalty
assisting in making incorrect return etc, VATA 1972
s 28
body of persons, separate penalty, VATA 1972 s
26(3)
contravention of security requirements, VATA 1972
s 26(3B)
failure to register, VATA 1972 s 26(1)
flat rate addition, VATA 1972 s 26(1), (2A)
fraudulent return, VATA 1972 s 27(1)-(2)
goods allegedly exported liable to forfeiture, VATA
1972 s 27(9)-(9A)
keeping of records, VATA 1972 s 26(1)
High Court proceedings, VATA 1972 s 29
improper importation of goods, VATA 1972 s 27(4)
inspection of records, obstruction of officer, VATA
1972 s 26(3A)
issuing of invoices, VATA 1972 ss 26(1), 27(5)
mitigation, VATA 1972 s 31